The Busy Quilter's Survival Guide

THE BUSY QUILTER'S SURVIVAL GUIDE

"I am so proud to be a quilter! My quilts will bear evidence that I passed through this life. Hopefully, they will last many, many years. Hopefully, loving hands will caress them and wonder about the by-gone relative who created them. They are my story in stitches!

I have warned my family, "If I ever see my quilts flying in the breeze, covering an old refrigerator in the back of a pick-up truck....I will come down from heaven....and haunt you!"

About the author:

A Television Broadcaster/Producer of 18 years, Joyce gained valuable experience in marketing, advertising and merchandising. She founded The Joyce Livingston Shop, a womens retail clothing store, which she sold several years ago when she retired from television and Quilting took over her life.

An accomplished speaker and former member of the National Speakers Association, she now presents Quilting Programs and Workshops across the country. Her most popular Program, *JACKETS AND EMBELLISHMENTS*, contains 54 quilted jackets which she has personally designed and constructed. Another popular Program, *MY PERSONAL QUILTS*, is a collection of 18 bed-sized quilts and a number of wallhangings....all which she designed, made and hand-quilted, plus 3 prize-winning quilts from her TV Shows. Through these programs, she has designed a line of twelve jacket and vest patterns which she now markets along with her original tee shirts designs.

While in broadcasting she wrote and published four books: one on personal color, two cookbooks, and a devotional book for women. She co-authored two others on personal motivation. Her articles and features now appear in numerous Quilting, Craft, and Women's Magazines. Joyce is listed in Foremost Women in Communications, and Who's Who of American Women.

The Busy Quilter's Survival Guide

QUILTERS
FROM ALL OVER THE UNITED STATES
AND SEVERAL OTHER COUNTRIES
SHARE
PERSONAL TIPS ON QUILTING
QUILTING EXPERIENCES, STORIES, & ADVICE
HOUSEKEEPING TIPS & FAVORITE RECIPES
PLUS
YARDAGE CHART
FREQUENTLY-USED TEMPLATES
QUILT PATTERNS FOR COLORING
QUICK CUTTING AND PIECING TECHNIQUES
& MORE!

BY
JOYCE LIVINGSTON
GOOD LIFE TREASURES   COUNCIL GROVE, KS 66846

Acknowledgments and Special Thanks

• to Don Livingston, my supportive husband, who puts up with all my wild ideas. Who loves leftovers. Who stands over my shoulder, encouraging me when deadlines approach. Who built my wonderful playroom (no work to it...pure play!), equipping it with everything a quilter could want. Don, who not only drives me to my Presentations, but loads and unloads many quilts, dozens of jackets, racks, boxes, etc. without a word of complaint. I'm thankful for him. He's a good guy, and I love him!

• for encourgement from my wonderful children....Dawn Lee, Don, Mark, Dari Lynn, Matthew, & Luke and their spouses (our *in-law* children): Helen, Cat, Wally, Sherry, and Tammie
and our extra special grandchildren:
Cherri & Tadd, Matthew, Melissa & Ralph
Sunshine & Cameron
Willow, Autumn, Sky & Banyan
Daiquari, Brandi, Burgandi, Bronze, Blaze, Kandi, Kami, Breeze, Hozanna & Stormi
Whisper & Noah

• for the love I feel from each one of them, and for the time they spend with Grandma and Grandpa.

• to my LORD for blessing me with a such a loving, affectionate husband and family, good health, and an abundance of energy.

• A SPECIAL BIG THANKS to CAROLYN RIDDLE, CPR PRODUCTIONS IN KANSAS CITY, for willingly sharing her expertise, knowledge, and encouragement, and cheerfully answering my endless questions!

• to Johnson County Community College of Kansas City for their comprehensive course on publishing.

• to Tammie Livingston, who did the major portion of proofreading with help from Don, Matthew and Sherry Livingston

• And most of all.....to each Quilter who has contributed to The Busy Quilter's Survival Guide. Without them......there would be no book!

Publisher's Cataloging in Publication
(Prepared by Quality Books, Inc.)

Livingston, Joyce.
    The busy quilter's survival guide / by Joyce Livingston.
    p. cm.
    Includes index.
    Preassigned LCCN: 95-94267.
    ISBN 0-9646049-0-6

    1. Quilting--Miscellanea. 2. Quiltermakers. I. Title.
TT835.L58 1995   746.46
                                                                              QBI95-

---

Cover design by Joyce Livingston

All rights reserved. Printed in the United States of America. No part of this book may be reproduced in any form or by any electronic or mechanical means including information storage and retrieval systems without permission in writing from the publisher, except by a reviewer, who may quote brief passages in a review.

The Busy Quilter's Survival Guide published by Good Life Treasures, Council Grove, KS 66846
Copyright 1995 by Joyce Livingston, Council Grove, KS 66846

Contents

Introduction	6
Dedication	7
Meet the Quilting Magazine Editors, Television Hosts, and a National Quilt Show Chairman	8
Poem *Ode to a Quilter*	14
Quilters tell about their lives and their love of Quilting	15
Quilters explain "Why I am a Quilter"	85
I'm a Patchwork Person	126
Quilters share Time-saving Household Hints	127
Quilters share Hints for Better Quilting	151
Why I am a Quilter	188
Quilters share Advice on Quilting	189
Frequently-used Templates	227
A Quilter's Coloring Book	230
Main Dish and Casserole Recipes	241
Salad Recipes	275
Vegetable Recipes	293
Dessert Recipes	305
Miscellaneous Recipes	335
Index	357
Order Blanks	360

INTRODUCTION

Hello! My name is Joyce Livingston. My husband, Don, and I live in our little cabin on a lake, in the middle of Kansas, in the middle of the USA. I'm the mother of six loving (now-adult) children, who will always be my babies. I'm so proud of each one of them and their accomplishments, and we're grandparents of 21 (yes, 21!) remarkably brilliant and beautiful grandchildren and one great grandson. You'll find their names on the Acknowledgement Page at the beginning of this book, you'll be surprised when you see them! I have been quilting, passionately, since 1982, and (like many of you) quilting has taken over my life! Quilting is a combination of everything I love to do most. Sew, design, write, present programs and workshops, work with my computer, make new friends, learn new things, it's always challenging me in ways I least expected.

None of my family made quilts. If there were to be quilts in my life, it was up to me to make them. I wish you could have seen my first quilt, I did everything wrong! My family thought it was perfect! I've learned much, since that first quilt...by reading countless books, experimenting, attending many Quilt Shows, and most importantly...by joining a Quilt Guild. Quilters eagerly share their expertise with all who want to learn, fortunately for me!

The idea for this book came into being for that very reason. I have learned so much from others, I thought it would be wonderful if Quilters from all over the country could share their tips and ideas, in book form. Not only quilting tips, but homemaking tips, personal experiences, advice and their favorite recipes! And, since I am always rummaging through my papers looking for my notes on those special new techniques for quick quilting, I decided it would be a real boon to Quilters to add a few of them to this book, along with a cutting guide that will allow you to get the most possible pieces from a yard of fabric. And, those templates we use over and over again, like 2", 3", and 4" squares, circles and triangles, I've put them into this book, too. And...I've added several pages of traditional quilts diagrams, so you can experiment by filling in your personal selection of colors.

I hope you enjoy **The Busy Quilter's Survival Guide**. Try the tips and hints. Prepare the recipes. Savor the personal experience. Listen to the advice. Use the templates. Pretend each quilter is sitting there beside you as you read, a new friend you've just met!

May **The Busy Quilter's Survival Guide** be just that.....a guide that provides all you need, to survive as a Quilter.....all under one cover. I'd love to hear from you, for I consider you my new quilting friend.

Joyce Livingston

Dedication

This book is dedicated to women who weren't even aware of how much their work has meant to me. If it were not for them and the guidance I received from them, I might never have ventured into this world of quilting and missed all the wonderful joys and opportunities it has given to me. You'll find each one featured on this and the next few pages of The Busy Quilter's Survival Guide.

These talented women have added richly to my quilting education. They have not only provided an abundance of information on quilting and quilt making, but their busy lives have been an inspiration to me. Many of us live out in the *boonies*, it is not possible for us to take classes frequently or run over to a quilter friend's house for advise and direction. Quilting magazines, books, Quilt Shows, and television have become our source for all kinds of quilting knowledge. They challenge us to go above and beyond our *comfort zone* and try new things, new combinations, new techniques! They tell us, "You can do it, here's how!"

These women who write, edit and produce have become our mentors and friends. I'm so pleased to share their lives with you, take time to read every word about them, get to know them in a personal way. Encourage them with your letters of appreciation. They add so much to our lives. It is with great pleasure that I dedicate this book to them!

∞∞∞∞∞∞∞∞∞∞∞∞∞∞∞∞∞∞∞

Georgia J. Bonesteel
Author, Lecturer and Teacher
Author of Lap Quilting, More Lap Quilting, Bright Ideas for Lap Quilting, and New Ideas for Lap Quilting, all published by Oxmoor House®
Host of a series on Public TV Broadcasting taken from her books.

"When Joyce Livingston announced the title of her book, my first thought was, "Thank heavens, maybe she will have some clues for this quilting fast track."

How can I make more time? One thing I have learned over the years is that it's O.K., and even normal, to have three or four projects in progress at the same time. In fact, I practice the "Monet Method". When he painted his London Bridges, he kept a canvas in progress for different times of the day to catch the changing light. What makes all this so personal is that my ancestors are related to Claude Monet. This makes it even more legal for switching quilt projects. All kidding aside, I feel very fortunate in my lifetime to have discovered a hobby and business that consumes most working hours.

Phyllis K. Barbieri
Sussex, New Jersey
MSC Publishing, Inc.
Editor of Traditional Quilter Magazine

I have been married for 29 years and have five children, all of whom, with the exception of my youngest daughter, are married. I am the grandmother of four, two boys and two girls. I live on a nine acre, rural mini-ranch with three horses, two calves, and a dog. All this, in the state of New Jersey.

I worked for many years as an embroidery designer. I also worked as a layout and paste up artist. But mostly, I worked as a wife, mother and quilter. I have quilted for 15 years and have lost count of the number of quilts I have made. I very much enjoy designing quilts and have found the modified curve to be the technique most useful in the free-form infant and children's quilts that I design.

Almost seven years ago, I kept an appointment with the Editorial Director of All American Crafts, Camille Pomaco.

I was armed with two garbage bags full of quilts and a manuscript for a book of my designs. Although the company's business cards stated they published books, I was to find out they did not, but Camille asked me if I would like to come and work for the company as an editor for a quilt magazine.

I was dumbfounded! I could think of any number of reasons why I might not be qualified, not the least of which was that I had never even played editor as a kid.

But Camille was impressed with my ability to draft patterns and write directions. She offered me a good salary, as well as training. If the company didn't like my work or I hated editing, I could just go back to making quilts. It seemed like a win-win situation, so I accepted.

Not only did I become an editor, I also developed the entire concept for Traditional Quilter Magazine. We have enjoyed a steady growth and lovely success over these past seven years and 50 issues.

I was over 50 years old when I started this new career and I cannot begin to tell you how much I have learned. I tell this to all of you who may think it is too late to begin a new direction in your lives.

You may think you are not educated, knowledgeable, talented, or simply, too old. No way! I have never had so much fun in my life. As I look back I am reminded of the old axiom "ignorance is bliss." It may be for awhile, but learning and experiencing new things is exciting and lots of fun, too.

I never dreamed that I would have a job that sent me to quilting conventions and paid for my classes as well.

I have three hints for quilters:

1. Keep on keeping on. Finish what you have started. Anne Oliver said that the difference between her and other quilters is only that she finishes what she starts. If you finish enough quilts, you will get really good at it.

2. It's your quilt until you say otherwise. We all make quilts with the idea that we will enter it in a big contest. Perhaps we will. Or perhaps we will give it away or it will find a home on one of our own beds. But, no matter what end you visualize, start and make your quilts to please yourself.

3. Enjoy the process! Quilting is fun. Keep asking yourself, "Are we having fun yet?"

My advice to quilters is to send a picture of your work to magazines. You don't have to be a first place winner to be published!

• Read more about Phyllis Barbieri in the other sections of this book.

Sandra L. Hatch
Lincoln, Maine
House of White Birches
Editor of Quilt World and Quick & Easy Quilting Magazines

I married my high school sweetheart in 1968 with two years left of college. I earned a Bachelor of Science degree at the University of Maine in 1970. Until 1982 I worked as a middle school home economics teacher in Methuen, Mass. During that time I also had two children. My first, a son named Joseph, was born in 1974. My daughter, Sarah, came along in 1978. I took a year's leave of absence when Joe was born and two years when Sarah was born. My daughter really has no interest in quilting or sewing and I don't push her. I hope one day she will turn to quiltmaking to satisfy a need and will come to enjoy it as I do.

I made my first quilt when I was 10 years old. My grandmother and mother were both 4-H leaders and I learned to sew when I was in first grade. That quilt was a crazy patchwork quilt in which I featured every piece of the dress I had made for the style dress review the previous year. I still remember that dress and when I see that fabric in the quilt the memory is vivid. I was very proud of the blue ribbon I earned at the fair that year for my quilt. Along with a blue ribbon came a $1.75 prize--a fortune for a 10-year-old then. Of course, I entered other categories and prize money was my major source of income!

During college, I made another crazy patchwork quilt. It wasn't until I became friends with a very special teacher at the school where I taught, that I really became interested in any other kinds of quiltmaking. She loved to embroider, both crewel and cross-stitch. She made several cross-stitch embroidered quilts. She encouraged me when I took a class to improve my skills. She hand-stitched a quilt for me and I use it lovingly. She died several years ago, but she still influences me in many ways. She was a dear friend.

I met some ladies in the New Hampshire town in which we had built our house. One of them was Ruth Swasey, who remains my very good friend even though I have moved away from there now. She later became editor of *Stitch 'N Sew Quilts*. Through her I became involved with the magazines and later when I left teaching, I became the editor of all of the House of White Birches quilting titles. The company changed hands during that time and Ruth could not keep up with the demands placed on her by the changes. She became my assistant for several years. She is a talented designer and quilter and I cherish her ideas and friendship.

Sandra is editor of many booklets and books for House of White Birches. Sandra Hatch and Ann Boyce co-authored the book *Putting on the Glitz*. She is presently working on *Grandmother's Favorite Quilts*, a 160 page hardcover book of patterns for over 35 quilts from the 1930s. She lectures on judging, borders and her work. She also judges quilting events and says she learns from each quilt she examines. She has been listed in Who's Who in American Women several times.

•Read more about Sandra Hatch in the other sections of this book!

Jean Ann Eitel
Marietta, Georgia
Harris Publications, Inc
Editor of QUILT, Country Quilts, Quilt Almanac, Old Fashioned Patchwork
Big Block Quilts, and Miniature Quilt Ideas Magazines

All of the above magazines are published by Harris Publications, Inc. of New York. I have recently become involved with communicating with other quilters by cyberspace, one of the popular *online* computer services, I make quilts, write about quilts, design quilts, talk about quilts, judge quilt shows and teach quilting classes. I have judged, taught and lectured for the American International Quilt Association in Salzburg, Austria and Houston, Texas. I have also taught for the Houston Quilt Festival. I have also judged and taught in England and Canada. I hope New Zealand and Australia will be next on my travel venue. A wonderful advantage of my career is that it affords many opportunities for travel and for making friends all throughout the world.

I am author of *Creative Quiltmaking in the Mandala Tradition* published by Chilton Books in 1985 and illustrator for the *Missouri Heritage Quilt Book* by Bettina Havig and published by the American Quilters' Society in 1986.

I am a single grandmother of five darling grandchildren, all under six years of age. They are Robert, Ryan, Meredith and Madeline Gaffney and Matthew Cressionnie. I am the mother of three lovely grown daughters, Elaine Cressionnie of Arlington, Texas, Ellen Gaffney of Acworth, Georgia and Heidi Eitel of Washington, D.C. All are college graduates. Elaine and Ellen are presently full time mothers and both have made at least one quilt.

Heidi is a recent college graduate and budding artist. When I am not quilting I can be found visiting my children or entertaining and playing with my grandchildren.

I am an ordained Deacon in the Episcopal Church. My Sunday mornings are taken up assisting in the celebration of the Eurcharist and worship. I also teach classes and give volunteer time in the community working with troubled teenagers and their families. I have served on the board for the Association for Retarded Citizens and for a shelter for abused teenaged girls.

I have made quilts for over thirty years, but it was the year I turned forty that I became obsessed with quiltmaking. My friends were having "one last baby" before the change of life and I could not...so I had a quilt class instead. Now, thirteen years later, they are dealing with teenage children that they have to keep all the time (unlike the teenagers that I work with on a volunteer basis), and I am making quilts, in fact quilts have become my life and my career. This is wonderful because quilts never talk back, they don't sneak out of the bedroom at night to go down to the park to smoke a cigarette, they can't wreck the car, or break a dating curfew. I am truly blessed to have had a quilt and not a baby for my change of life crisis.

• Read more about Jean Eitel in the other sections of this book.

Kaye Wood
Kaye Wood Publishing Company
West Branch, Michigan
Teacher, Writer and PBS Television Host

I married Bill Wood in 1956. We have five children, one girl and four boys, ages 28 to 37. And, we have 13 grandchildren. I graduated with a BS degree in Business Education from Michigan State University in 1971. Over the years I have taught swimming, lifesaving and canoeing, leadership training for Girl Scout leaders, business skills for adult education, sewing and quilting. I began sewing lessons for sanity when I had 4 pre-schoolers at one time! After a few years of lessons, I took the Bishop® Method teacher's training and taught basic sewing, fitting and pattern drafting. I traveled throughout Michigan teaching and published 2 books on machine embroidery/monogramming. I travelled throughout the US and internationally teaching, and published 16 books on strip quilting. I've designed 5 tools and produced several quilting videos, and two PBS-TV series: "Strip Piecing" and "Quilting for the "90s". I'm president of my company, Kaye Wood Publishing Company, with 8 full time employees. It includes mail order (from TV series) - distributor, wholesale, and retail.

I really consider myself a teacher of people - who happens to be teaching quilting at this time. Teaching people with all their quirks and mannerisms is much more interesting than just teaching quilting. Even the *problem* students liven up a class.

I have never made a quilt that was not a teaching sample for classes. But, that was only possible because of my strong background in sewing techniques; I just transferred that knowledge to sewing strips. Mainly I try to simplify the techniques for piecing quilts and when I have solved all the problems that my students might encounter, my quilt is done; it has achieved its purpose even though it may never get finished.

<u>Tips & Hints:</u> Encourage your husband to retire; mine does all the cooking, shopping and cleaning. After all, he had to have something to do. My job is more than a full time job - but the minute it isn't fun any more, then I will be on to something else.

Since I am primarily a writer and teacher, my computer is my main love. The hardest thing I ever had to do was to hire a full time computer graphics person, because I wanted to do it myself. My computers rank right up there with my sewing machines - I want the newest and the best toys. But my most popular hint to my students has been my *Perfect Miter®* technique.

<u>My advice:</u> •Have fun with your quilting! Remember, not every quilt deserves to be finished!
•Don't get hung up on the *rules* - they don't always apply.
•The more children you have, the less you have to entertain each one (I always had time for my sewing hobby).
•It's OK to just collect fabric; you don't have to use it - just buy and enjoy!
•Take lots of different classes from lots of different teachers - then do your own thing!
•If you really goof on a quilt, learn to say proudly, "That's the way I wanted it to be" - or learn to rip. I'd rather say I planned it that way!

Sue Hausmann
Lincolnshire, Illinois
Host of the *Keep America Sewing* PBS Television Program

As I travel across the country sharing the joy of sewing with others, I say my job is to *Keep America Sewing*. My actual job title is Vice President of Education and Consumer Motivation for Viking and White Sewing and hostess of The Art of Sewing/Keep America Sewing Public Broadcasting series. I oversee all consumer education programs for the company as well as training for the retailers. This job actually began after our four children were grown as my real job for many years was that of homemaker and part time sewing teacher and sewing machine sales-person. I have always appreciated that several neighbors and 4-H taught me to sew as a youngster and that lifeskill has served me well! As a young married I made everything out of necessity and doing alterations at home allowed me to earn income while caring for our young family. As they grew, alterations became tiresome and I realized my chore was to continue to sew for others or to teach them to do it for themselves. I chose the latter and this began my career in the sewing industry.

Some years later Viking asked me how I was selling so many sewing machines and I shared our class program which included a great deal of machine quilting (quite new at the time). Viking asked if I would consider traveling to teach how to teach the classes and although it sounded really exciting, I declined saying "I have a 15 1/2 year old at home that doesn't need a mother, but deserves one. And a husband that doesn't deserve me, but needs me!" (A joke, of course.) Less than two years later our family moved to all parts of the U.S. and our nest was empty. My precious husband of 35 years, Herb, encouraged me to give the traveling job a try. That was almost 10 years ago. Today I travel 50 weeks a years, sharing my enthusiasm for sewing and although it does wear me out sometimes, I feel blessed to have this gift and opportunity to meet so many wonderful people. As a Christian, I ask daily for life direction and believe this is where God wants me to be today.

Thanks to my travel, Herb and I visit our children and 5 darling grandchildren often, and we all were able to celebrate my folk's birthdays (they were 75 and 80) last October at their home in Arizona.

I believe we are all blessed with talents and have the ability to learn daily from every life experience. In the program *How Did You Get This Job, When I Knew You, You Were A Mommy*, I share that women today can have it all - they don't necessarily have to have it all at once! And that there is life after 40 (even after 50!) so take your abilities and build on them. Look for the opportunity in every day and every happening. When a door opens at least...peek in! Life changes...each day is something new, each year a new life stage. We must look to every day for the best and be our best in the midst of it!

•Read more about Sue Hausmann in the other sections of this book!

Bonnie Kay Kirkland Browning
The American Quilter's Society
Quilt Show Chairman
AQS Show in Paducah, Kentucky

I was born in Muscatine, Iowa and graduated from Muscatine High School. I married Wayne G. Browning, and worked as an executive secretary for 15 years. In 1980, as a result of a project for a college art class, I made my first quilt. As with many quilters, it took just one quilt and I was hooked on quilting. Entering contests and winning many ribbons led to teaching, and in 1986 I received my certification as a quilt judge from the National Quilting Association. I am qualified to judge master quilts. I have served on the boards of art councils and quilt guilds, the National Quilting Association. In August 1994, I joined the staff of the American Quilter's Society as Quilt Show Chairman. My husband, Wayne, and I reside in Paducah, Kentucky.

Why do I quilt? I quilt because it allows me to fulfill many things in my life. The socializing aspect of the old-fashioned quilting bees still exists, and I especially enjoy the camaraderie of working with my quilting friends. It provided a wonderful outlet for my creativity, using fabric as my medium. I have always enjoyed crafts, needlework, painting and teaching others. Quilting encompasses all of those facets. The quilted line has always intrigued me, and quilting can add so much to the finished quilt. My favorite part of quiltmaking is the designing process, choosing fabrics, and putting the last stitch in the binding.

A quilting tip I'd like to pass on: Don't forget to quilt the borders! As I travel across the country teaching and judging, I find many quilters who put a lot of quilting in the center of the quilt and run out of steam by the time they reach the borders. Often, this causes the quilt to have rippled edges and not hang straight. The solution is to have approximately the same amount of quilting over the entire quilt.

My advice to quilters would be: "Do your own thing...and enjoy what you are doing. As we've moved to different locations, it has always been comforting to know that I could attend a quilt guild meeting and not feel like a stranger. Quilters talk the same language all over the world.

If your quilt guild has a judged quilt show, plan to enter one of your quilts. The judging process, I think, has helped us to make our quilts better so they will be around for many years to come. I always say that having a judge evaluate your quilt is the cheapest private quilting lesson you can take, with an evaluation of the parts of your work that are done well and the parts that could use some improvement. "Today we are making tomorrow's heirlooms."

• Read more about Bonnie Browning in the other sections of this book.

•After hearing the poem about getting *old* and wearing *purple,* I decided I didn't want to be remembered in that way! I got to thinking about me, my life, my quilting....and wrote this poem...my version of growing old...as a Quilter! I close all my Programs by reading it, and have found all quilters love it and identify with it! My husband says we're all alike. Do you recognize yourself in any of the lines?

(See the order blank on the back page for a copy suitable for framing.)

Ode to a Quilter!

Written by Joyce Livingston

"When I'm old, I'll wear purple!" says a poem I've heard,
    It tells of old age with nary a word
        of loving and kindness and gentleness, too
            Which I think are virtues of Quilters, don't you?
We may have a fondness for fabric we've bought
    But, basically we are a reasonable lot
        of women who see patterns where there are none,
            And colors and pictures and circles and blocks
We keep it all stored away in a box...
    And a box, and a box, and a box, and a box...
        On a shelf, and a shelf, and a shelf, and a shelf
            In this room and that room, and under a bed,
In a chest, and a drawer, it's even been said...
    In a can, in a tin, in the hamper with clothes
        We Quilters buy fabric wherever we go...
            And needles, and pins, rotary cutter or two
In fact, we buy any Quilter's tool that's new!
    Triangle, square, hexagon or quadrangle,
        A ruler that's clear...to help cut any angle
        A 40 or 60 or any degree,
You see...as a quilter, it's all up to me!
    Decisions, selections, which color, what pattern?
        Baltimore, Nine Patch, Evening Star, Chinese lantern?
            Log Cabin, Bear Paw, Flying Geese, Inner City?
Can't make them all! My oh, my! What a pity!
    I put florals with plaids, solids with prints,
        Use cotton with rayon, poly and chintz
            Have batting in my belfry, holes in my sox
Buttons off shirts, keys without locks
    Cobwebs on my ceiling, dust balls under my bed,
        Spoiled food in the fridge, books scattered-unread,
            But....I'm healthy! I'm happy! I love life, and show it!
I may be eccentric....and not even know it!
    So, when I'm old I'll wear purple or even lime green
        Or yellow, or turquoise, that way I'll be seen....
            As one who loves color and refuses to complain....
When old age comes along with an ache or a pain
    As long as tomorrow is sunny and bright,
        Or cloudy and cold, any weather's just right
           Since I am a quilter, with needle and thread
                and fabric and scissors, I'll just quilt til I'm dead!

Copyright 1993

Busy Quilters Tell About Their Lives and Their Love of Quilting!

Author's Note: In this section you will find not only the Quilter's name and city of residence, but also the names of any Quilting Guilds and Quilting Organizations to which they belong and listed.

Unfortunately, many quilters are too bashful to mention their quilting accomplishments, they don't seem to realize that we enjoy hearing about one another since we have a certain kinship. I have tried to add an author's note where I had additional information about that quilter, things I thought you would enjoy reading. Wish I could have been better informed about each and everyone of them.

Joyce Livingston
Council Grove, Kansas
Emporia Regional Quilt Guild
Kansas Quilters Organization

My husband, Don, and I live in our cozy cabin on a lake in the middle of Kansas, on a dead end road, and love every minute of it! Most of our neighbors are only here during the summer and on occasional weekends, so it's quiet and I have very few interruptions when working on quilting and quilt-related projects in my *Playroom* (that's right! I call it *playroom*, for there's no work to it....it's pure *play!*").

I'm a former television broadcaster of 18 years, wife of Don (my supportive husband who drives our van, and loads and unloads all the things for the Programs and Workshops I present, and who built my Playroom), mother and grandmother of the *bestest* family in the world!

My children all seem to appreciate my quilts. They'll get them all...eventually! But, for now, I love seeing them all snuggled up under them when they come to see us. We live 100 miles or less from five of our six families. Since we live on a lake, we enjoy having them come for the entire weekend, so we can swim and boat together, and play games, too. With a family as large as ours, it takes many quilts to bed everyone down, sometimes as many as 30 to 35 of us. That's when I pull out my quilts!

Everyone helps with the cooking, dishes and clean-up, so it's fun for everyone! I came into the kitchen once, and found four of the teenage granddaughters doing dishes with their life jackets on! We have a rule....no one, regardless how great a swimmer they are....goes into the lake without a life jacket! We are all so used to wearing them, we almost forget we have them on.

Several of the girls are quilting now, making beautiful quilts, and smaller pieces. It's one more thing we can share together! Now the grand daughters are quilting! Hooray!

As mentioned, I present Programs and Workshops (which help support my quilting habit), and am a writer. You'll find most of my writing in Quilting Magazines, Women's magazines, and this book!

Like many of you, Quilting has literally taken over my life, it seems most everything I do, is related in some way, to Quilting! So many people put off "learning to quilt" until that *someday* when they'll have more time. I only wish they knew what they were missing! It would help relieve some of that stress many people experience daily. One of the most relaxing and satisfying hobbies one can have!

Elizabeth A. Akana
Kaneohe, Hawaii
Hawaii Quilt Guild

I'd like to share with you a part of my life that started in 1963. I was an East Coast girl, born in Patterson, New Jersey and raised in Baltimore, Maryland, who married a part Hawaiian man. After our wedding, in Baltimore, Maryland, on September 28, 1963, we established our home in Hawaii.

That first year, my husband and I bought a house and I gave birth to our daughter, Jean. We were also given two Hawaiian quilts, that had been made and presented to my husband, Ronald, upon his birth. We had no place to store our beautiful treasures, because we had very little furniture, so our quilts went up on the walls as art. I seemed to be drawn to the quilts, and enjoyed just looking at them. This was the beginning of a *love* affair.

At first, I was not aware of anything more than just a warm feeling. Next thing, I was silently greeting the quilts. In my mind, they always returned the greeting with *love*, and so my days were off to a great start.

Four years zoomed by. Our son, John, was born, and we moved a mile away to a beautiful new home. We now had furniture, and the quilts took new places on the children's beds. The pink on white/U'Lei Berries was on Jean's bed, and the blue on white/Beauty of Kalihi, was on John's. I taught the children to be respectful of these *loving* treasures and once again, every morning, we were greeted with their *love*, as we made the beds.

Anita S. Henry, my neighbor, was making a queen size Hawaiian quilt. I would kid her about a project that would surely take ten years of her life to complete. It took only three. In an effort to end my kidding, Anita cut and basted a 22" Pineapple pillow, and instructed me on how to start. It worked, I became so engrossed in my endeavor to complete the pillow, that I not only stopped teasing Anita, I knew I had to learn more. The *love* I felt from the large quilts was no less from the pillow I made.

In 1969, following my quest to know more about making the quilts and pillows, I took Hawaiian quilting classes from Mealii Kalama. Mealii, who sadly left this life in 1992, was a grand lady who was a master of Hawaiian design, a beautiful quilter and a wonderful spirit. She believed that each quilt was "God in expression". Mealii told our class that *"Love is the key note of quilting"* and her quilts reflected that love. She also recognized that her remarkable talents were God's gift, and felt that *"If you share your talent, God will add to it"*. Mealii always gave thanks as we started each class session. This was a way for us to focus on our *love*, thus releasing our creativeness.

With the confidence I gained in Mealii's classes, Anita and I started a small Hawaiian quilt pillow kit business, which I ultimately took over. I named my new company EA of Hawaii, and designed 30 new pillow patterns and 10 quilt patterns for it. The *love* grew. The Hawaiian quilts and designs were a major part of our lives.

Author's Note: Elizabeth doesn't know it, but she is responsible for my decision to make a Hawaiian Quilt. I saw her on one of the PBS Television Programs several years ago. From the instructions she gave, I designed and made a king-size appliqued cornflower blue quilt with the design cut from one piece of white fabric, which I then appliqued to the background. I cut the pattern, free-hand from paper, and transferred it to the white fabric, which had been folded into sixteenths (snowflake style). It came out very well, I'm quite proud of it.

I did encounter one problem. I make my quilts in sections, quilting each section by hand, before it is joined to the next section, lap quilting method, without a frame or hoop.

I decided this would be the perfect project to try with a frame, since I had to quilt it all in one piece. So....I bought the floor Q-Snap frame and set about to quilt in a frame! After several hours of frustration caused by everything being so immovable and slow.....I took the quilt out of the frame, took the frame apart and put it back into it's box, where it has remained! I quilted the entire king-size quilt by-hand without a frame or hoop....and continue to do all my quilting that way....with tiny even stitches, and speedily.

I had heard all Hawaiian Quilts had Hawaiian names, so (not knowing Hawaiian) I named my quilt *Meeny Meeny Weeky Tu Du*, which freely translated means.."Many, many weeks to do!" Thank you, Elizabeth!

Betty Lou Cassidy
Linwood, New Jersey
South Shore Stitches
Wind Rose Quilters
Tri-State Quilters

I was born in Hazleton, Pennsylvania and grew to school age on a small dairy farm in Drums, Pennsylvania. Here, I was close to both my grandmothers, who were hard-working, resourceful, and self-sufficient. My father's mother quilted, but only to make practical warm blankets -- nothing fancy. My mother's mother was crafty and loved making things of left-overs or cast-aways. From these women, I learned to appreciate hard work, creativity, and *using up, making do, or doing without*.

After my grandfather died, and Highway 81 cut through the farm, my parents kept the remaining land, but moved our family to New Jersey. For a time, my father tried farming in Ringoes, New Jersey, and this is where I joined a 4-H sewing club offered by the public school. I stayed with 4-H, even after we moved to a house in South Bound Brook. I learned tailoring, cooking, and *childcare* and won several awards for these efforts. I still use the Singer® shears I received as an award, when I was twelve.

I was graduated from Newark State College (now Kean College) Union, New Jersey, in 1970. In 1971 my husband, Charles, and I were married and moved to Atlantic City, eventually settling in Linwood. I was hired by the Margate City School system and have taught special education, Resource Room, and various regular grades there for twenty-nine years.

Teaching young children has always been a great source of pleasure and accomplishment in my life. I have been honored with several awards over the years - - Teacher of the Year Award 1974, Atlantic County Adults and Children with Learning Disabilities Award 1989, and ACLD New Jersey State Award 1986.

My husband, Charles, is an accountant with a degree in Business and Economics from Monmouth College in New Jersey. We have no children, just two spoiled West Highland White Terriers - - Tullulah Terrier and Vanna (West Highland) White. Vanna is 3 years younger than Tullulah, and usually stays by me while I quilt or sew in the spare bedroom. When she feels I'm spending too much time with my "quilting toys", she will steal spools of thread or climb on top of the pile of fabrics I'm using. When I go to school, Vanna acts out her frustration by pulling white beaded quilting pins out of my arm rest, and strewing them over my seat cushion or floor. Sometimes she chews and bends the pins. Now I barricade my chair, but when I forget, Vanna gets even.

Vanna and Tullulah are often "show stoppers" wherever we go. We dress them in children's tee shirts to keep them clean, and to keep them warm in the winter. They travel with us and love to go on *vacation* to a hotel. While I am in classes or viewing quilts, my husband drives around the area *antiquing*, the dogs ride in the back seat.

Eileen, a friend and Guild member, once went to the Lancaster Show and didn't see anyone she knew, even though a bus load of our members were attending the show that day. She did, however, recognize Tullulah and Vanna sitting in the back seat of the car!

Ruth Rhoades
Toccoa, Georgia
Currabee Quilters
Mt. Laurel Quilt Guild

Retired now, but formerly a high school business and math teacher for 13 years. One of my *I never would have believed I'd be doing that* adventures, was starting a quilter's retreat at a local conference center. In 3 years, it went from 33 to 137. One of those immediate success stories, evidently there was a need for it. My interest in old fabrics and quilts has grown to 28 old quilts and 19 tops, displayed in a beautiful walnut display cabinet my husband made last year. And, I can't leave out feed sacks!

Louise Murphy
Mammouth Lakes, California

I live in a ski resort at approximately 8,000 feet. The closest small town being 45 miles, and closest large city (Reno, Nevada) 180 miles. I have been married 30 years to my high school sweetie, Kevin. My husband has been in law enforcement 27 years. I have two grown daughters and a 5 1/2 year old granddaughter, Katie, who lives with us. One family pet, a Lab mix, Emma, a real mountain dog! I was born in New England, therefore the cold harsh winters we experience in the Eastern Sierras seem second nature to me. My sister Judy (2 years younger) and I, both inherited our love of the cloth and needle from our maternal grandmother.

My sister and I are both avid quilters, and both have a love of gardening.

My husband is a model train collector. We try to plan weekend trips for train shows, and incorporate quilt shop stops, as well as visa versa. I have had the pleasure of visiting quilt shops from Seattle to San Diego, and a few into the eastern states. It helps to find a hobby store, both store and ice cream shop within close proximity for Kevin and Katie. Sometimes, even a park will do. Some of the nicest people I have encountered, have been in quilt shows or at quilt shops, and we truly are kindred spirits!

Meet the Quilters, page 19

Jean S. Branham
Halifax, North Carolina
Roanoke Valley Quilters Guild

I work 3rd shift, so it is hard for me to find time to quilt. But, believe me, I find time. I love to quilt, everything I make I give to my family. I have three children, Esther Beal, Tracy Butts and John Branham, when I start something new, they will ask me "Whose is that?" They don't like it, if I make something for someone else. I also have 2 beautiful granddaughters, Hannah Beal and Taylor Branham.

Karen Crollick
St. George, Australia

I am married to David, who is a plumber, and we have three children, two girls: Jodi, who is 17 years old, and Peita who is 14. And, Matthew is 9. I work on a casual basis for Australia Post. My hobbies include: quilting, collecting teddy bears, dolls, post cards and genealogy.

I am in a partnership with my husband with our Plumbing business. I'm also secretary of our local Craft Shop, and work volunteer at the Shop once a month. Being a non-sewer, before my Patchwork Days, I did not have any fabrics until the tutor arrived for the Quilting Seminar. St. George is remote, being two hours drive from the nearest larger towns. I have to rely on mail orders. The fabrics are starting to grow though, and I have five U.F.O.s waiting for me to finish them.

Beverly J. Relph
Leavenworth, Kansas
Kaw Valley Quilters Guild
Northeast Kansas Quilters Guild
Greater Kansas City Quilters Guild

I live with my retired husband (Bill), two "kids" (Yorkshire terriers, Fred and Mildred), two sewing machines, and a *big pot* I also have one son, Brock J. Brown, Ph.S., Geography, who teaches several Geography courses at Southwest Texas State University, San Marcos, Texas, during the regular school year, and directs geography institutes for the National Geographic Society, during the summer months.

About twenty-five years ago, I designed and made some clothes for Magnolia Blossom (my little Chihuahua), which somehow eventually led to one-of-a-kind wearable art. My label, "Prairie Strings by Bev", is recognized on all my clothing. The Kenny G. coat lives in London, England, and another piece belongs to a New Zealand quilter.

Credits: I've been involved in sewing and selling wearable art for some time. I have my latest creations completed by the end of October, and offer them for sale at that time. My pattern, "Prairie Strings by Bev", was a national contest winner through Needle Craft Magazine, June 1989. My clothes were featured in the Kansas City Quilt Guild's annual fashion shows held at Crown Center, at the same time as their annual Quilt Shows in 1993 and 1994. A cut work vest took Best of Show at the Kansas State Fair, Hutchinson, Kansas 1994. Also, I have won several Grand Champion awards at the Leavenworth County Fair during the past five years, as well as numerous "Special" awards and first place blue ribbons.

Thelma Tiefel
Clay City, Indiana
Clay City Calico Quilters

I have been a farm wife for 45 years. Raised three children: Karen, Vic and Bonnie.

We also had a large garden and raised cattle, hogs and chickens, which provided a lot of our food. I also had a small egg route which furnished enough money to pay the phone bill and buy the rest of the groceries we needed. For seven years my mother spent equal time with me and my two brothers. My mother and grandmothers were influential in my early years to learn to sew.

These three children have given us five grandchildren and four great-grandchildren, soon to be one more addition. And we love them all! We moved from the farm 15 years ago. This is when I became interested in quilting. I had lots of scraps stashed away, left from having quilted all the years. My first quilt to make was the Flower Garden, which used up a lot of different prints. The second one was the double wedding ring.

When I was looking for someone to quilt the Flower Garden, the lady I asked wanted to know what kind I wanted quilted, and when I told her the Flower Garden, her reply was "well, if you pieced that one, you can quilt it!" What she didn't know was that I hadn't quilted before. Since I couldn't find anyone to do the quilting, I gave it a try. And, have been quilting all my own ever since.

It has been quite a challenge. Since these first two, I have made quilts for our three children, grandchildren, and great-grandchildren.

Author's Note: Thelma sent along snapshots of her beautiful quilts with notations on the back, of the ribbons they had won. She should be very proud, they are beautiful!

Glenda Phipps
Whitman, Nebraska

My name is Glenda Phipps and I live on a ranch at Whitman, Nebraska. I have 3 children, ages 12, 6, and 4. We live 23 miles from the nearest town, population 40. It is 100 miles in any direction to the nearest town with a population of over 1000. We raise Quarter Horses and feed out steers on our ranch. I enjoy helping with the work here whenever possible, and in addition, am home schooling all three of my kids. Life really interferes with my quilting, maybe that is why I am getting slower. Surely it's not because I'm getting older.

I started quilting five years ago, due to necessity. My best friend was getting married and I needed a really wonderful gift for her. I knew she liked quilts and I had always wanted to learn how to make them, so this seemed like the perfect time. All I knew about quilting was that the stitches were supposed to be small, but women have been making quilts for generations, how hard could it be! I was unable to take classes, due to distance problems and the ages of my kids, so I read everything I could find about quilting and started my trial and error education (mostly error at first). Much to my surprise, my first quilt turned out rather well and I was hooked from that point on.

My trial and error continued, as I tried to learn new methods and techniques. Recently, one of my boys sat down to "sew with Mommy". The first thing he did was pick up a seam ripper and start tearing out stitches, after all, that is how Mommy spends most of her time. Oh well, it's the finished product that counts.

I was fortunate to have an excellent teacher, Jean Younkin, living reasonably close that I could call whenever I was totally confused. She even showed me the right way to baste quilts, after I basted one to my living room carpet.
I have learned to make use of whatever resources are available, including TV programs about quilting. Imagine my excitement to spend weeks sewing 512 diamonds into a lone star quilt one at a time, only to turn on TV to discover how I could have "Quilted it in a Day!" In spite of these major blunders, I have continued with my hobby, believe it or not, it is a great stress reducer when you are snowed in with 3 kids, a husband, and a small zoo, for weeks at a time each winter.

I have just finished two heirloom quilts for two of my kids and am gathering strength to start a third. I have recently discovered the joys of quilt shows and have won a couple of Best of Shows, a Viewers Choice, and second place at the State Fair. I guess I am continuing to improve as my husband no longer refers to my quilts as "that thing you are working on", and our feed dealer no longer calls them my "pretty blankets"!

I machine piece all my quilts and hand quilt them. My next goal is to master applique and Celtic quilting.

Jill Marie Tanking
Liberal, Kansas
Needles & Friends
Quilt Guild

I am a native Southwestern Kansan. Grew up in the restaurant/motel business. In school, when the girls were sewing and cooking, the teachers had me in the Art Department. Probably had one year of sewing in junior high. When I sewed, if it wasn't right, forget it. I was not going to take it out. Isn't it amazing how much taking out I do now to get some quilt item to look just right? When I got married in 1970, we traveled with Western Electric, a division of AT&T. Five years of that (was based in Dodge City) husband, Jerry, took early retirement and

Meet the Quilters, page 21

bought my folk's motel, which had Yellow Freight stationed there. About 7 years of that, and was presented the opportunity to sell it. In the meantime, I had a farmer farming my farm in Oklahoma die, so we took over the farming. Land that had been in my family for four generations. It is amazing how we go through life seeing all kinds of experiences and really don't see it until you get into some craft that these experiences could be expressed. Now that I quilt more seriously, I see more things that could be expressed by a quilt. I have a part time job with the Ambassador, a division of Hallmark. It is fun to look at the new cards coming in, do get some great ideas from those cards.

Nadine Dozier
North Augusta, South Carolina
Pieceful Hearts Quilt Guild
South Carolina State Guild

I'm a 39 year old homemaker, married for 18 years to a piping engineer. We have three teenage sons. Besides quilting, my other main hobby is my family. I also love to cross-stitch, work with house plants, and I have two doll houses I'm always working on. I am a charter member of our local guild and am currently Vice-President, and Quilt Show Committee Chairman. I'm also a member of the Quilters of South Carolina State Guild.

Elaine Helen (Revier) Baker
Watertown, Minnesota

I'm 26 years old with a pitiful typewriter. I've been married for 8 years and have two daughters. Tabitha, 7 years old, is learning to quilt and is aspiring to be a karate champ. She's also learning to piece on my sewing machine (a rather frightening experience). Jazmin is 4 years old, and is into finger paint and play dough. I do day care for two pre-schoolers for up to 14 hours per day. But I still have time to quilt!

We live in a very rural area within 10 miles of my parents and in-laws. My mother is a seamstress, so I get all her scraps. She makes most of my daughters' clothing, so when I make a quilt, they recognize a little bit of themselves in each of my quilts. I come from a blended family, so am the youngest of nine (all my siblings are halves, steps, or fosters).

I am closer to my mom than any of my friends. I guess it's because I live very close to her and we have many things in common, i.e. sewing, art work and my girls, also gardening and the great out-doors. My other hobbies, other than quilting, include gardening, as I mentioned (perennials, bulbs and some veggies) I have seven gardens, and enjoy soft sculpture (mostly little people), reading mysteries (and horror), drawing (I draw almost every quilt before making it), fabric painting (yes, on some quilts, too) and quilting pen pals, charm and fabric trades, and block trades. I drink lots of coffee to keep busy, busy, busy (I love cappaccino). I still find time each day to walk at least 2 miles.

I've had many a down day due to assorted illnesses. It started when I was 12. Then on to seizures, and nasty medication when I was 16 (the seizures were from an unintentional overdose from asthma medication). Yes, there's more. After the birth of my third (and last) child, I was diagnosed with systemic lupus. But I refuse to let any of it take my enjoyment away from me.

I collect cows, kewpies and angels, and of course, fabric, and fun notions. This is basically me, frightening, isn't it?

Jane New house
Wedderburn, Oregon
Gold Beach Quilters Guild

I have retired from raising a family (we have 5 adult children) and being a public library librarian and from a lot of the volunteer work that accompanies those occupations. Now I garden, spin, pot, quilt and work part time in a gift and card shop.

I've gardened most of my life, it is very rewarding and a great way to relieve frustrations and to think through snags in life and projects! Spinning has been a favorite past time for years. Dyeing wool with both chemical and natural dyes is leading me into experiments in dyeing cotton fabrics for quilt projects. I recently moved into my new potting studio. Throwing pots on a wheel is also challenging, fun, and rewarding.

Suzanne K. Roy
Newkirk, Oklahoma
Pioneer Area Quilters Guild

I have a husband, Don; two boys, Jacob (age 16) and David (age 7); two dogs, Lic (short for Licorice) a labrador and Nic (short for Nichole), and two cats, Hunter and Angel. We live in an old house that was probably one of the first built in our town. I substitute teach and am teaching a college class in Interpersonal Communication.

Colleen Taylor
Indialantic, Florida
Seaside Piecemakers, Inc.

In addition to quilting, I enjoy gardening, and Bonsai. Sew most of my clothing. After marrying my wonderful husband of 34 years, Hank, we moved to Puerto Rico, lived there for a while, as well as the Bahamas and Antiqua and New Mexico. A native of Florida, we always ended up back in Florida. Quilting has taken over my life. I was president of Seaside Piecemakers, Inc. Quilt Group in 1994. We make quite a few charity quilts each year.

Barbara S. Moss
Locust Grove, Georgia

When my employer *early* retired me, I needed something to fill my life, so I chose quilting. My husband, Grady, supports me with my quilts and always answers my questions, even if he doesn't know what he is talking about. I have two horses that you can sit and talk to in the pasture, and decide what colors to use next.

Lynn Lewis Young
Houston, Texas
Quilt Guild of Greater Houston
American International Quilt Association
Studio Art Quilt Association

I use quilt making techniques to expand a full range of creative endeavors and artistic expressions, to produce both art quilts and art to wear. Two techniques have predominated my work, strip piecing and that of collage construction.

In addition to teaching in the Houston area and distant symposia and quilt associations, I also write for quilt publications. In the past, I have worked for the International Quilt Festival and Quilt Market, and have served on the board of many quilt organizations, including being president of AIQZ and the Quilt Guild of Greater Houston. I currently edit the newsletter for the Studio Art Quilt Associates.

Academically trained in the Biological Sciences, I pursued graduate studies in bio-medical research and earned a Masters of Science degree from the University of Texas Health Science Center, where I also worked on my PhD. candidacy. My B.A. from the University of Texas at Austin was in Biology and Chemistry.

I received my art training at the Glassell School of Art, Museum of Fine Art, Houston where I am completing a certificate with a concentration on jewelry. I have studied quilt making through workshops with many well known artists, including Nancy Crow, Michael James, Ruth McDowell, Nancy Halpern, Jan Myers-Newberry, Yvonne Porcella and Virginia Avery.

I have been included in the invitational Fairfield Fashion Show for 3 years. My quilts have been in many judged and juried shows throughout the United States, Europe and Japan, and my work is exhibited in galleries.

In 1994, I began publishing *Art Quilt Magazine*, a new magazine devoted to the art quilt. It is a quarterly publication in a full, color quality printed magazine to showcase art quilts, and to support the art quilt movement. My main interest in doing this magazine is to give art quilts the publicity and recognition, which print can give. and to facilitate communication between artists and all others interested in art quilts. And of course, to generate interest in art quilts in wider audiences. And to encourage writers to think and write in depth and intelligently, about quilts and art.

Meet the Quilters, page 23

Josephine Hannah Jirva Burgwyn (Jo Jo) Jackson,
North Carolina
Roanoke Valley Quilter's Guild

I am the Director of the Day Program called EVCO, which is for Developmentally Disabled Adults, and have been in this field for 15 years. This is a very rewarding job and these 44 adults are actually quilting a quilt - squares they painted! We do sub-contract work for local industry and businesses.

I love to snow ski and dream one day I'll become permanently airborn after jumping a mogul. (I dream in my sleep that I can fly, about once a month!) My other dream is to have a yellow bedroom with a quilt of yellow flowers - I've been saving yellow fabrics for years, and when my 3 year old allows me, I will begin working on it!!

Mary Anne Keppler
St. Olaf, Iowa
Northeast Iowa Quilt Guild

I own and operate Country Calico Fabrics out of our home. We farm approximately 1,000 acres and milk 140 cows. The store is in it's 11th year. We, husband Dennis and I, have 6 children and 5 1/2 grandchildren. All of our children are out of school except one - she's a freshman in high school. One grandchild will start kindergarten in the fall.

Kelly Lum Newgarde
Phillipsburg,
New Jersey
Courthouse Quilters

I am a third grade teacher. I enjoy cooking, counted cross-stitch, and quilting. Each year my mother and I create a Christmas ornament to give to our friends (we've been doing this for the past 12 years). My husband, Jamie, and I enjoy camping and canoeing.

Deb Meneely
Seattle, Washington
Quilter's Anonymous
City Stitchers

I am a married homemaker with two children. I began taking quilting classes in 1981, while pregnant with my first child, daughter Alison. In fact, I missed the final introductory class because she was born 3 weeks early!

One facet of my quilting life revolves around my computer. As a member of Compuserve's Crafts Forum, I have made dozens of new quilting friends from around the world, via my computer. One highlight last summer was meeting "in person", seven other Pacific Northwest Quilters with whom I'd been conversing via the computer previously. What a thrill!

Chloe Rhodes
Clay City, Indiana
Calico Quilters

I am a 64 year old grandmother of seven. I have a twin brother and I have 2 sets of twins, plus 1 single. Twin girls, a single boy, and a girl and boy twins..total of 5 children. My husband was killed seven years ago in a grain truck and train accident, hauling grain to the elevator. That is the reason I started making quilt tops. It fills a lot of lonely hours.

Kathryn Rippeteau
Greenwold
Niskayuna, New York
QUILTS (Quilters
United In
Learning
Together
Schenectady)

I am a quilter and also repair and appraise antique quilts. I make quilts and quilted clothing, and teach a variety of workshops and classes. In addition, I have two beautiful girls - Erica (7) and Signe (6), who are active in school, ballet and Tae Kwon Do. My husband, Larry, is a true saint! He takes me to all the quilt shows, and nods approvingly as I explain each new project. I also love to cook *and* eat, and we are all active at church.

I am now teaching quilting and quilt repair in several area shops, provide repair and restoration services for heirloom quilts, do appraisals of quilts for insurance purposes, make quilts both for exhibition and for my own enjoyment, and occasionally make quilts on commission. In addition, I offer individual instruction in a student's home or in my own home studio, teach quilting in the Niskayuna school systems After-School Education Program, and teach beginning and advanced quilting courses in the Niskayuna Adult Education Program.

Rebecca Kelly
Kingsburg, California

I am a 30 year old quilter, who has 2 small boys (pre-school), a husband and 2 small dogs. I work part-time at the local hospital, but hope to be home with my boys full-time soon. I am also an avid collector. I collect doll quilts, sock monkeys, Precious Moments, figurines, feed sack material, and thimbles. I started quilting at about 25, and see no end in sight. I feel that I'll be quilting the rest of my life.

My only honor so far, was a 1st place in the Tulare County Fair, in the category of beginning miniature quilts.

Patricia (Pat) Jones
Oroville, California
Oroville Piecemakers

I am a wife of 38 years, the mother of two married children, 4 grandchildren and 1 very spoiled ShiTzu pup. My daughter Becky, has two boys, Rusty 13, and Zach 10 years old. My son, Tim, has 2 daughters, Tara 8, and Lindsay 4 years. These children and grandchildren are the greatest joy of my life.

After raising our children and putting them through school and college, my husband, Roy, and I moved to this small town of Oroville. This move put us closer to both sets of parents!

I became a country wife very quickly, but felt that I must *learn to quilt* to make my country life perfect. I've always loved quilts, but never had time for this hobby while raising my children.

Florence _Edith_ Goggin
Eureka, California
Redwood Empire
Quilt Guild

I am a housewife and quilting teacher. I started quilting in 1970, and then teaching in 1975 for Eureka Adult Education.

In 1976, I went to work in our local Fabric Shop, teaching knitting, crochet, and helping customers with quilting problems. The job was part-time, and lasted 13 years. Quilting classes then became my main job, and I now have 20 great years behind me. Teaching is fulfilling, and it is wonderful to see the students excel and enjoy their completed projects.

With the help of my friend, Mary Ann Spencer (my mentor), I have met many wonderful Quilting Teachers. These teachers were very generous and gave me permission to teach my students what I learned from them. The students in turn, bought their books and completed many projects. Some of these students have been with me for 15 years, and others have formed small quilting groups. I keep in touch with the groups.

Mary Andrews
Grand Blanc,
Michigan
Genesee Star Quilters

My name is Mary Andrews. I am a widow, and I have 4 grown children, Tony, Theresa, Maria, and Paul, and one grandchild, Stephanie, who belongs to Maria. Stephanie and Maria live with me. I work full-time as a Dental Hygienist.

I grew up in Saginaw, Michigan, but now live in Grand Blanc. My mother taught me to sew when I was a child on a treadle sewing machine, she later got it converted to an electric. I used to make doll clothes and make my own clothes, when I was in junior high and high school. My mother would make Barbie clothes, bazaar items for the church, did Italian hemstitching, and made beautiful things with sequins and beads on them and I remember thinking, how could anyone ever have the patience to sew all those little things.

No one made quilts, but there was a beautiful crazy quilt that my great grandmother made in the family, that I would have my aunt take out and show me. I now have that beautiful quilt.

My mother died in 1976, and when I was going through some things in the attic, I found some Sunbonnet Sue squares, all made. I held on to them for awhile, and then found a patient who was a quilter, and had her show me how to put them together to make a quilt top, and then how to quilt it. It took more than 5 years to make this quilt and I said never again, until I went out to buy one, and found out how expensive they were. So I tried again. I made a scrap quilt for each of my children, which I now call their crumby quilts because they are falling apart. I took classes and went to my first quilt show about 8 years ago, and was hooked.

Another hobby I have is genealogy, that I started after my mom died. My mother and her family were all pack rats and there were boxes of pictures, newspaper articles and letters. Her sister, Elinor, and I made albums for our children, family cook books, and spent many hours researching. My genealogy finds its way into most of my quilting.

I have bought fabric depicting things my family like, and I used bits of their clothing in my quilts. Usually, I get the clothing because they are short, and I have to cut some off the bottom and hem everything they buy. But for a scarecrow quilt that I made, I dressed the scarecrows in pieces of my children's clothing, and I snipped the shirt tails off my son's shirts, hemmed them back up, and put them back into their closets, and they didn't know until they saw the quilt, what I had done.

I met Ami Simms a few years ago at a Michigan Quilt Network meeting, and she was working on her Classic Quilts book, and she had all these patterns, and needed people to help her make the quilts. I picked out two, that I thought would be easy and said I would make them. I learned a lot from Ami on this project, because she monitored every step and gave suggestions. Both of my quilts are in her book. One is circles that I made crazy quilt style, and used pieces of lace of my grandmothers, little cross stitch pieces of my daughters, parts of their old jewelry, a music note from my grand daughter's sock, a girl scout pin, a piece of fabric from my son's army fatigues, and various other things.

By this time, my children had figured out what I am doing, so they started bringing me things. Friends are so helpful, too, when they see you working on a project, they reach into their stash and give you something to put on your quilt.

After Classic Quilts was finished, Ami said she was going to do a book on scrapbook quilts. When I saw this, with my genealogy background, I had to try it. This was my first original quilt. I gathered up my pictures and sent them off to Indiana to be put on fabric, and put together my Dandy Brandi Family Album quilt that is in her scrapbook quilt book. There are lots of family embellishments on this one. I decided to try to enter this one into Paducah. Ami had photographed it about the time it could be entered. It got in, and what a thrill it was to see my quilt with all the other beautiful quilts from around the world.

My bedroom is my *studio*. I am lucky that it is very big. There are boxes of genealogy stuff everywhere. My sewing machine and ironing board are up all the time. I gave my granddaughter my old Singer® machine, and she has hers up on a little table by mine. I leave things out all the time, so I can work on them, whenever I get even a few minutes. Ruth doesn't clean my room because she wouldn't know where to begin, sometimes she runs the vacuum a few feet inside the door. One day Paul came into my room, and asked me if I slept there, or if I slept in Stefi's bed with her. I told him I slept in my own bed, if it was completely full, I would move a few things to the floor for the night.

Patti Centeno
San Antonio, Texas
Alamo Heritage
   Quilt Guild

I am married to a football/track coach and we have two children. Our life centers around sports, and on any given night of the week, we can be found at some stadium in the city of San Antonio. We do not limit ourselves to just his high school sport, but anything athletic in the city. It has been a wonderful way to spend quality time with our children, and they learned to appreciate their father's job and his hours away, by attending many sporting events together, as a family.

Now, because I have such a high energy level and require little sleep, I can be found at these events with a quilt project in progress. I will be able to relate some key moments or plays, if asked, and very seldom not know what the score is, or who got the last hit. My husband is amazed at this true, womanly feat of being able to quilt, talk, and watch all at the same time. (I don't tell him that I often have to ask someone what just happened.)

I have found quilting to be a very relaxing and rewarding craft for me. It has allowed my creative juices to flow and I receive great joy from seeing a pattern develop from a thought, or dress, into reality. Quilting has been a great source of therapy for me, as I teach 8th grade American History in a large middle school. Most people offer their condolences when I tell them that I teach for a living. I love the middle school child, but like grandchildren, I'm glad to send them home at the end of the day.

Minabess P. Randolph
Toms River,
New Jersey
Beach Plum Quilters
of the Jersey
Shore

I started quilting 25 years ago. Quilters were coming together to share and grow, and many of the groups were just beginning to form. I went to some workshops and guild meetings, during the next few years, but mostly I just experimented with all types of quilting techniques. Around 1984, I began searching out other quilters in Ocean County, and from that, the Beach Plum quilters of the Jersey Shore was founded. I also began teaching at 3 local quilt shops. I received my N.Q.A. teacher certification in 1992.

Martha G. Wilson
Roanoke Rapids,
North Carolina
Roanoke Valley
Quilters Guild

I retired recently, and I have found out you don't catch up with your quilting, you just keep working on it. Since childhood, I have loved quilting. It was such fun, watching my mother and aunts quilt. My husband helps me with the cutting. When he sees me with a piece of fabric, he goes and gets the rotary cutter and board. It is a pleasure to see the joy others receive when you give them something hand-made.

Mary Jane Cemer
Trenton, Nebraska

I do not work out of my home. My husband is not in the best of health, and I need to be around home. I'm married to William W. Cemer (Bud), a former Sheriff of this county. He was in law enforcement 28 years. We have a combined family. My children are a son, Rocky Stone, who is married to Carolyn. They have kids, Jason 11, Kyle 9, Mindy 15 and James 14. Daughter Rebecca, is married to Jesse Dutcher. Their children are: Jeremy 19, Joshua 16, Bethany 9, Kasey 17 and 10 month old Jordan (whom I baby sit full time). What a love!

My son, Buck Stone, is married to Sandi, and their kids are Josey 11, Elizabeth 9, Seth 7.

Bud's daughter is Donna, who is married to John Corliss. Their children are Dean 24, Ursula 16, and Angie 23.

We don't have pets, but the animals that live here that I feed, to list a few are: Red Heeler dogs, Rudy and Red Dog, Tiana, a huge cat that actually belongs to a neighbor, a stray Tom cat who got caught in a raccoon trap...twice, named Lucifer. Rotten Cat, a kitten Jeremy rescued. Plus calves, chicks, hens, roosters, ducks and a drake.

We live 1/2 mile from town, and did some cattle raising until hubby couldn't anymore, now the ground is rented out. Hubby does wood-turning on a lathe, did a lot of woodworking until his back got so bad. Dabbled in several things, including antiques and craft stuff. No profit in it, you use all your income laying it out. Ha! I got back into quilts, and that's about all I do now.

Richard F.
Zimmerman
New Milford,
New Jersey
Tri-State Quilt making
Teachers

I was born in Patterson, New Jersey on a hot August Day, so they tell me, in 1939. I grew up in an extended household with my parents, my younger brother, Alan, and my maternal grandmother. Both of my grandmothers had worked in the textile industry before their marriages, my father managed a textile factory, and everyone in

Meet the Quilters, page 27

the family was familiar with fabric, sewing machines and how to use them.

I hold a B.F.A. degree from the Art School of Pratt Institute, Brooklyn, New York, and M.A. from Teachers' College, Columbia University, N.Y., N.Y. I am certified as a public school teacher in the areas of fine arts and crafts. I have been a teacher in the New Jersey Public Schools for 32 years.

I began serious sewing in 1964, first for myself, then for my wife, Andrea, and then for our children, Stephen, Victoria and Margaret.

In 1971, I began working with a fifth grade teacher, to develop a _Colonial Crafts_ unit to correlate with that grades social studies curriculum. As part of that project, we did a very simple _Patchwork Quilt_. Victoria was 2 1/2 years old at this point, as I worked on an example for the class. As I cut up and sewed scraps left over from clothing projects, she watched intently. Finally she said, "I want a quilt - JUST LIKE THAT ONE - and I want all the pieces to have flowers in them." Well, what should a father do? Of course, I pieced a quilt top using my paternal grandparents' old _Wheeler and Wilson_ treadle machine. We purchased a length of pre-quilted fabric at a local surplus store, tacked the top to it with yarn knots, slapped on a blanket binding and there we were with a _quilt_.

Well, Stephen could not be outdone, so I had to make one for him, too. This one was a pinwheel quilt of bright scraps and muslin - same flawless construction.

Well, after these _successes_, I was HOOKED. I did a baby quilt with a new fifth grade class, appliquing their designs with the help of some fusing web, then taught the children some basic embroidery stitches, so that they could add details. After assembling the 10" blocks into a double sized quilt, I machine quilted the piece together using transparent thread. This was to be a gift to their classroom teacher. She was thrilled; the children were thrilled; and I was delighted that we had been so successful.

I finally taught myself to really quilt, by assembling a wall hanging top, purchasing a cheap quilting frame from a catalogue store, and setting lining, batting and top together in said frame. Then with the help of a little book of instructions resting on the frame, I began to work needle and thread up and down, up and down through the layers. The book said "five to seven stitches to the inch?", but did not explain how to count them. I assumed one counted only what one could see on the quilt top, so I kept a ruler handy, so I could check on myself.

Every few inches, I would stop, lay a ruler against my line of stitches, and count. If five, six, or seven stitches fell within the inch, they stayed. If there were less than five, I pulled out the offending stitches, and redid them to the specifications. Needless to say, this procedure really slowed me down. It took me two months, working at least 2 hours, and sometimes as many as 4 hours each day, to quilt the 38x68" top, but by the time I was finished, I knew how to quilt. (I still work for 5-7 stitches per inch, counting only those showing on the quilt top.)

I began to share my knowledge in 1979, by offering adult education classes in basic patchwork and quilting. At the present time I not only teach beginners, but also hold intermediate and advanced classes. I do lecture/slide programs, and run workshops on various techniques for guilds and at quilt shows.

Throughout this evolution, my wife, Andrea, has been very supportive. When we moved into our former home where we lived for 17 years, it was she who worked to pay for the addition to the house that provided me with studio space on the top floor, so that I would have a light, airy space in which to work.

Before I was a Quilter, there were many other creative activities that I enjoyed. I mentioned earlier about my involvement with clothing construction. At the same time that I was working in clothing and a little costume design, I was also working in ceramic clay, building by hand and wheel throwing all kinds of pottery. When I wasn't working in clay or cloth, I would be doing print making, via the silk screen. There were times especially around Christmas, when every flat surface in our home would have a printed sheet of paper lying there to dry.

All that is gone now, since I contracted the QUILT VIRUS!

Author's Note: Richard appeared on the HOME SHOW television program, _Real Men Do Quilt_, with John Flynn and David Eartly.

Joanna Bessey
Rhinelander, Wisconsin
Rhinelander Northwoods Quilters

My husband, Bill, and I live in Northern Wisconsin on our 52 acre pine and hardwood plantation, and year 'round enjoy the changing seasons of our "backwoods". I am retired from the salaried work-force after 20 years, being a former highschool teacher and the marketing/training coordinator at our local community credit union. Our sons, Judd and Todd, are now grown with families of their own, including three much-loved grandsons ages 9, 12, & 13. Bill and I actively share many interests - gardening, previous down-hill skiing and the National Ski Patrol, now cross-country skiing, collecting antiques and depression glass, traveling, and Civil War reenacting and competitive skirmish events with our two live-firing cannons. Other personal interests of mine are sewing, handcrafts - especially crocheting and cross-stitch, playing bridge, and of course, first and foremost - quilting.

Tonya St. Berg
Woodinville, Washington
Block Party Quilters

I am on leave of absence, attending college, working toward a doctorate in psychology. I have an art background, but have found the sciences will serve me better where I work or if I decide to have my own business. I am very fortunate my husband, Roger Berg, cross stitches and understands the need for tools and supplies. When we travel, we pull out our quilting and cross stitch atlas, and stop at as many stores as possible. If I need a certain color of fabric for my project, Roger will show or bring me several bolts of fabric from which to pick. If he is out of the country on business and I decide not to go along, he'll bring back fabric native to that area.

Jan Jacobson
Tripoli, Wisconsin
Rhinelander Northwoods Quilters
Crazy Hearts Quilters
Wisconsin Quilters, Inc.
Rock Valley Quilters, Inc.

I have sold May Kay Cosmetics for 16 years, and I work part time in a small town grocery store. My husband, Carlyn, and I, along with our German Shepherd, Laska, moved to northern Wisconsin five years ago. We're almost done building a hand crafted log home, situated on 40 acres with a river running through within sight of our house. Working in a grocery store was a nice way to get acquainted with people. We have three children and four grandchildren.

Susan Hanna
Brownlee, Nebraska

My husband, Don, and I were married 36 years ago, and have lived on the family ranch at Brownlee the entire time. We have 3 children, Jim and his wife Shirley, and daughter Megan are in partnership with us on the ranch. Anne, and husband, Graeme, and daughter, Sara, live in Omaha. Anne does research and development work for Con Agra, and Graeme is with Mutual of Omaha. David lives in Lincoln, and works at a bank there.

I am an avid gardener, love to bake and gather dry flowers for arrangements and potpourris. I find that making a wonderful fragrant loaf of bread, a bottle or two of herb vinegar, or a batch of potpourri helps stir up the creative juices that spill over into my quilt making.

Barbara MacDonald
Oscoda, Michigan
Michigan Quilt Network

My husband, Bryan, and I have been married for 27 years and have 2 grown children, Mike and Michelle. We spent 23 years in the Air Force and have lived many places. The most interesting place was England, we lived there for 6 years and did a lot of sightseeing. I didn't start quilting until about 12 years ago, and I knew I was hooked immediately. We were living here in Oscoda, Michigan at the time, and there was a small quilt shop in town. I spent hours there, taking as many classes as I could. In fact, I was there so much, I was offered a job! It was a dream come true! I've worked at Loose Threads Quilt Shop for 8 years now. The Shop is much larger now, a Quilter's Heaven, with over 1500 bolts of fabric.

Peggy Gunwall
Perham, Minnesota

I am semi-retired. I do bookwork for a shop here in Perham, and I also work when needed, at Bay Window Crafts, where I took my first quilting classes under a very excellent teacher, Linda Boedigheimer. I have 21 grandchildren and four great grandchildren. Two of my daughters, Cheryl Wieglenda of Jamestown, North Dakota, and Reyne Johnson of Mandan, North Dakota, have been caught by the quilting bug and are doing as much of it as their busy lives will allow.

Bonnie Swecker
Roanoke Rapids,
North Carolina
Roanoke Valley
Quilters Guild

My background is in business education. But, because my husband, Mark, was in the Air Force right out of college, I found secretarial jobs easier to find, while stationed in Louisiana and California. When Mark went back to graduate school in Virginia, I was a secretary again at the university where he attended. One of the few things we had to move during those early years, was the sewing machine he'd given me as a wedding gift. I'd learned to sew in junior high school, and took Mom's machine to college with me - even made a gown for a formal dance. I was not yet into quilting, but loved the quilts both my grandmothers made.

After graduate school, Mark began his career as a forester, and I began mine as a mother. We have three sons - Matt, Kent and Adam. I sewed a lot for them when they were small. I got into all kinds of handcrafts, but focused on, and taught basketry for quite awhile.

I started quilting just a few years ago, when our local guild advertised a wall-hanging class they were starting. I joined up, the wall hangings were displayed in Williamsburg, Virginia, and mine and two others were chosen by *Quilting Today* to be in their April, 1992 issue (page 41). As a beginner, I was thrilled and encouraged. Guess my sewing background paid off!

Lassie Wittman
Rochester, Washington
Quilters Anonymous
of Seattle

I have demonstrated and sold OMNIGRID PRODUCTS, working with Peg Schafer (Mrs. Omnigrid) for six years, traveling to Quilt Shows throughout the U.S. It has given me the opportunity to sell my shirt pattern, two seminole patchwork books, other patterns, gift items and patchwork shirts. I was a textile and clothing major in college. I worked for 7 years as a demonstrator for Bucilla Yarn Company in the needle arts. My husband of 40 years, is a retired school teacher, we have 3 grown children (my daughter-in-law, Nancy, created several items for *THE COMPLETE BOOK OF SEMINOLE PATCHWORK*, one of my books). And, we have 2 grand children. We square dance, bike ride and do low impact Aerobics.

Jean Eng Underhill
Flemington,
New Jersey
Courthouse Quilters
Hunterdon County
Quilters

Before settling down with a family, my work in maternal and child nutrition in Laos and Papua New Guinea, expanded into Nutrition policy in Education, Agriculture and Health. Then came an innovative and challenging job of establishing an Information Center at Cenderwasih University, Indonesia, with an initial focus of health and nutrition, dealing with both missionary and government agencies.

I left an active career overseas, to establish a quiet home life in the U.S., and found a void, as there was nothing to keep my mind active away from my family responsibilities. I had not sewn since I left high school, and didn't know that quilting existed. Then a friend, Babette, from my children's play group,

Page 30, Meet the Quilters

introduced me and it wasn't until several years later, that I began my first hand stitched, hand quilted quilt while pregnant with my 3rd child. 5 years later I am still hooked on quilting, and everyone, especially the girls, Ngaire 8 years old, and Kara 5 years, are into making quilts. My 10 year old son, Alan, will be trying his hand in it this year, and Geoff, my husband, will be our faithful critic. The family cat, Tiki, always checks out every quilt, to make sure it feels just right.

Joyce Nichols
Bethany, Missouri

My getting into quilting is one of those sad stories. My father died in 1979, leaving my 54 year old Mother alone. She needed an income and tried working out, but her nerves wouldn't take that. In 1982, she answered an ad in a magazine, asking for hand-quilters. It worked out great! I was a stay-at-home wife and mother, and needed something to do, but I was afraid to try quilting. She was getting all kinds of things to do (she even quilted a design on a satin wedding dress skirt). Finally, I tried making a kit quilt. It came out pretty good, so I contacted mom's employer, and starting making quilts. It was great. I had lots of work, and everything was going fine.

We were at the edge of fame several times. One of Mom's quilts went to Sophia Loren, and one I made was purchased by Mr. Rand of the 'map' people. We had quilts (with our pictures) in the Smithsonian museum one year when their theme was *made in America*. A few years later, the market was flooded with foreign quilts, our employer retired, and we had nothing to do.

My Amish friends helped me get in touch with a buyer, and since 1992, I've made hundreds of small quilts and wall hangings. This buyer supplies mom with as many tops as she wants to quilt.

When I started quilting, my youngest child started to school, I worked the same hours. After the 2 daughters moved on, my carpenter sons built shelves in their bedroom, and I finally had a work space of my own. No more putting my work-table and stuff away each night, so we could go to bed. My husband had his own business in our garage, so I've lived by the clock for years. Now that my husband is unable to work, I can't get away from my time-table. Our 21 year old son is still here, and comes home from work for lunch, so I may always be stuck to a schedule.

I discovered that my brother makes beautiful quilts. He retired early from the Postal Service and needed something to do. He tried to keep it quiet, but when he asked me if I knew anyone who needed quilting done, the secret was out! A friend who is a quilt collector, has been wanting tops quilted for a long time, so I helped get them together, and they're both happy. She has had pictures and write-ups in several magazines, and now....who knows....maybe one he quilts for her will be in one some day. I think my brother, Jim Campbell, and his wife, Judy, have started a new career.

Jean Van Dusen
Kingsford, Michigan
Spinning Spools
Quilt Guild

I am a retired nurses aide from a local nursing home. I worked there 23 years, on the 11-7 shift, so I could be at home days with my family, and later it became a way of life. I have three sons. The oldest, Gary, after 4 years in the navy, followed in his Dad's footsteps as a logger. The other two are career navy. Carl, with 20 years, is Command Master Chief on the Normandy, and Gene is in Guam.

Eugenia A. Barnes
(Genie)
Marcellus, New York
Thumbstall
Quilt Guild
PAAQT
A.Q.S. AND A.Q.S. 6

I am a quilt maker, National Level Circuit Teacher, Lecturer. I am an Appraiser, Certified by AQS. I teach at 2 Community Colleges and a local Quilt Shop, when not on the road. I have had several opportunities to contribute to quilt-related books and magazines. I am married (34 years) and have 3 children, 7 grand children, and I raise and show Irish Wolfhounds. My work is based on variations of traditional patterns/techniques, and I love to laugh.

Meet the Quilters, page 31

Ann Littleton
Fairfax, Virginia
Quilters Limited
(Burke Chapter)

I've been quilting for about ten years. I'm married to Joe, a U.S. Navy pilot, who by the time this book is published will have transitioned to the _civilian world_, whatever that is. Joe and I have two children: a daughter, Courtney, who is a senior in high school. She's a gifted vocalist, who wants to pursue a career in music. A son, Jay, who is a freshman in high school. He's our artist, and has a unique way of bringing humor into our family, especially when the atmosphere gets tense, as it does in any family.

We have a family pet, a cat named Samantha. Last year we tried to adopt a five-year-old dog, named Toby. Unfortunately, or fortunately (depending on who is telling the story), he had to return to his previous owner. Toby and Samantha just couldn't come to a peaceful co-existence. Jimmy Carter was not available for negotiations at that time.

After Toby's departure, Samatha spent two weeks doing back flips around the house, and has been much friendlier to everyone, strangers included. I guess Toby must have represented a near-death experience for her, because it certainly has changed her personality (for the better). She still loves to dive under the quilt blocks, so neatly laid out, causing them to become completely disarrayed. At other times, she places herself majestically in the middle of a finished project, as if it was created just for her pleasure.

Back to me. I have a BS in Elementary Education and Speech Pathology. Because of the ever-mobile lifestyle of Joe's military career and my full-time commitment to raising two _well-adjusted_ children, I've held lots of interesting part-time jobs: substitute teaching, decorating Christmas trees in a little shop in Freeport, Maine, assisting in the acquisition department of the library at Bowdoin College, selling crafts, volunteering, etc.

Currently, I'm teaching music at Knollwood Community Preschool in Burke, Virginia. This is my third year at the school, and I love working with the children and teachers. This job has been a challenge since I was led to an area of teaching that was definitely "out of my comfort zone" of expertise. I've been able to use my quilts in my classes, and the children seem to enjoy them. They especially like the three-dimensional ones with embellishment.

Helen Blankenship
Flint, Michigan
Genesee Star Quilters

I am a retired RN, mother of seven. Four girls and three boys, all married and living in 6 different states, 13 grandchildren. Am working on the last 4 quilts, one for each of the above. I turned to quilting after I retired, it was something I always wanted to do, but time did not permit. It gives me great pleasure, to leave each one with a quilt to remember me by, also helps to fill my days with pleasure and the fun of new and interesting techniques.

Edna R. Harbison
Ontonagon, Michigan
Ontonagon
Quilters Guild

My husband and I, and 2 small dogs, live in a 22x24' log cabin we built 18 years ago in a remote area of the Upper Peninsula of Michigan. We have a small flock of free-ranging bantam chickens we call our lawn ornaments, and we raise orphaned and injured animals and birds for the Department of Natural Resources. We've made our living from quilted wall hangings, and my husband's woodworking for over 10 years, selling it through Arts & Craft shows in Michigan and Wisconsin, as well as from home. I come from a rich quilting heritage, my parents were horse and buggy Mennonites. I've received 42 awards at juried art shows, and national quilt shows for my work.

Eleanor K. Hunnel
Johnston, Nebraska
Nebraska State
Quilter's Guild

I grew up in Idaho during the depression years, learning all the usual hand crafts, such as knitting, crocheting, tatting, embroidery, etc. My Mother, her sisters, and their mother were all quilt makers, but I don't remember seeing Mom working on a quilt - no doubt she kept her projects stashed away, until we children were off at school. All of these ladies did fine handwork, but when they acquired sewing machines, (all Singer® treadles) they used them for almost all of their sewing. We all oohed and aahed over fine hand stitching, but it was usually done years ago, of necessity - surely not so we latter day quilt afficionados would usually be impressed. However, we all just love to note: "It's all hand stitched...'"

I am the proud possessor of quilts made by Mom, and her mother and her sister. Some of them are filled with raw wool, which was plucked by them from the barbed wire fences, where bands of sheep passed through their cattle ranch. As a child, I helped with some of the carding of little pluffs of hand-washed wool - the airy little pieces arranged on a cheesecloth to be used, when of sufficient amount.

In my teens, my Mother gave me small blocks she had appliqued - A for Apple, B for Bird, etc. I thought them not particularly appealing, and buried them in a corner of my hope chest. Not until I was expecting one of my last babies did I sew them together by machine, with a juvenile print. Corners didn't match well, all was a bit lumpy as I used a piece of blanket for batting. It served as a crib quilt for two babies, and was again folded and tucked away in the chest. Then several years later, I was invited to give a quilting class. I was no quilter, but was giving classes in crocheting and knitting so there was no doubt I thought, to be able to quilt, too. A class was set up, several ladies came - I was hooked at first stitch. Ah! quilts and quilt making, the story of my life since.

I now have a collection of quilts made by the other women in my life, which I enjoy showing with those of my own making. *Each quilt has a personality of its own and a tale to tell.*

I have given show-and-tell programs around the state at various quilt guilds and clubs, and have been a speaker and presenter at NSQG conventions.

I'm included in *Nebraska Quilts and Quiltmakers* published by the Lincoln University Press, 1991. As a member of the Nebraska Quilters Guild, I am a recipient of the Golden Threads award in 1992 at Lincoln.

∞∞∞∞∞∞∞∞∞∞∞∞∞∞∞∞∞∞∞

Carole P. Kenny
Providence,
Rhode Island
Quilters by the Sea
Narragansett Bay
Quilters
Association

A retired TV traffic manager, I have been a serious quilter since 1989. This was preceeded by a veritable "craft of the month" existence, sewing, knitting, crochet, stain glass, leather crafting, etc. backed up with an Industrial Design Degree. I also sing and act.

My first quilt was started in 1957 when a friend gave me a kit to cross-stitch. I saw one like it recently in an antique magazine. Maybe I should finish mine.

Strip piecing is now my forte', and I enjoy getting others *hooked* on quilting using this method. I teach a wonderful group of *active seniors*, a few classes at the local quilt shop, plus occasional workshops and lectures.

I am affiliated with Quilters by the Sea, (V.P./Prog coordinator), Narragansett Bay Quilters Association, New England Quilters Guild and American Quilters Society.

Currently the house is being shared with one husband (Robert), 1 son (Gunner), our daughter, Erin, is in Minnesota, two doctoral students from Brown University, two adult Queensland Blueheelers (Australian cattle dogs), and nine puppies.

∞∞∞∞∞∞∞∞∞∞∞∞∞∞∞∞∞∞∞

Dotti Greto
Ocean City,
New Jersey
South Shore Stitchers
Wild Rose Quilt Guild

You know what *they* say, "Life begins when the dog dies and the kids move away". Fortunately, I waited till all that happened, before I discovered quilting, so I was never torn between...I live with my retired husband, Vic, in Sanibel, Florida during the winter, and Ocean City, New Jersey in the summer. We have a son, Andrew, a photographer in New York City, and a daughter and son-in-law, Ginger and Dick in Monroe, Connecticut, and triplet grandsons, who will be three in April. Adam, David and Joseph. Last, but not least, I'm 60 years old, and most of my quilting

Meet the Quilters, page 33

friends are almost half my age - but when we're quilting - who counts!

Michelle Hazelhoff
Mt. Evelyn,
Vic Australia

My name is Michelle Hazelhoff, I'm in my late twenties, happily married to a great guy named Steve, with three children, Timothy, Skye and Zack. I live in the Dandenong Ranges, about an hours drive east of Melbourne. I'm currently not employed, however I do sell my craft, which helped me to finance a quilting tour of the USA in April 1995.

I grew up the eldest of four children, in a country suburb on the outskirts of Melbourne. We were a sporting family, and my mother was always involved in knitting and dressmaking, and I was doing both, before I went to school.

Besides being an avid quilter, I also do cross stitch, tapestry, dressmaking, and knitting. We have half an acre of land which we've been slowly making into a garden of our own. My husband and I both play competition badminton, I've played since I could hold a racquet, in fact that's how we met, he was on one side of the net and I was on the other. I am also a compulsive bookworm. I love fiction historical reference books, and have been known to read a book from cover to cover in an evening.

Judy Allen
Nevada, Iowa
Iowa Quilters Guild

I am a cartographer for the Department of Transportation. I started quilting about 12 years ago, and am now doing a copy of the quilt my great-grandmother made for me - when she was 75. I am using her quilting patterns and colors. I love the hand quilting, but because there are so many quilts and so little time, I am learning to machine quilt.

Jeanne K. Ferg
Asheville,
North Carolina
Asheville Quilt Guild
East Asheville
Quilters

My age is undecided, sometimes 100, then again, still 39. I am co-parent of four wonderful children with Nelson Ferg, my husband. Since my youth, I have nursed, until several years ago, when I decided I should spend most of my time doing more pleasurable things. At that time, I became involved in sewn crafts, such as clothing, quilted wall hangings, stuffed toys and animals. This became highly profitable after several years, so at this time I sell my quilted note papers, sock monkeys, and quilts through a shop.

In Asheville, we have several wonderful quilt groups. I belong to the Asheville Quilt Guild and East Asheville Quilters, and stay active in each.

Back to the first of this, our children are all grown and in other parts of our beautiful country. Our only grandchild *loves my quilts*, so has been the recipient of a number of them.

Susan D. Fellin
Flemington,
New Jersey
Courthouse Quilters

I am a receptionist for a medical doctor in Belle Mead, New Jersey, who practices nutritional medicine. My husband, Bart, of 8 years, is very supportive of my quilting, cross-stitch, crafts and sewing. We have 1 son (a cat), and will be adopting another son (a dog), in a few weeks. I pretty much learned my sewing skills through 4-H clubs and my mother. I truly enjoy going to quilt shows, and taking new quilting classes. You could say that I am a pattern collector, someday maybe, when I retire, I will get to them.

Lori Hauswirth
Iron River, Michigan
Rhinelander
Northwoods
Quilters

I'm 31 years old, a wife of nine years, and a mother of two very active, rambunctious boys - Jake 7, and Alex 4. I have worked as a dental assistant for the last three years (almost full time). Before that, I worked in a beauty salon as a licensed hairdresser. (Just a jack of all trades!)

After working hours, my family devotes a lot of free time to sports related activities. My husband, Bill, is a high school football and track coach. We also like to cross-country ski in the winter; golf in the summer. We live in the Upper Peninsula of Michigan - above Wisconsin. Cold and snow are a way of life, where quilts keep us warm in the cold days of January.

Susan Nicholson
Muskegon, Michigan
West Michigan Quilt Guild

I have been teaching elementary school for 30 years, and am retiring in June. I have a husband, Bill, and a grown son, Doug. Willie is our Siamese cat, who has no idea he's supposed to act regal. I was brought up to believe that a hobby is essential, not just nice to have. It's okay to become a fanatic in some constructive way. I have been quilting for 30 years, and in earnest for 15. I've been teaching classes for several local Community Schools for 12 years. This is the fun part beyond actual construction. I'm looking forward to retirement, and more time for quilts!

Paula Kay Garrison
& Duncan Garrison
New Braunfels, Texas
New Braunfels Area Quilt Guild

I commute every week 200 miles one way to work. On weekends it is a Quilt-a-thon! I always take along quilting to do on my lunch hour at work. My husband designs...& builds houses.

Doris Holland
Winterset, Iowa
Honey Bee Quilters

I am retired, and enjoying being a housewife. I worked part time for several years, as a Homemaker Home Health Aide, going into peoples homes to help them. It was very rewarding. My husband's health is very poor. Frank finally came home from the hospital on December 16th, after being there 9 weeks, following a stroke. We have four children, one grandson, 9 step grandchildren, and 2 step great-grandchildren.

Paula Gore
Osmond, Nebraska
Country Piecemakers

I am a medical technologist, I supervised a busy hospital blood bank for 12 years. I am extremely active with my husband, Tom, and my children, Katie Jo and Ian. Tom is a veterinarian, who swore he was going through mid life crisis, and so he sold his private practice that he had owned for 18 years, and went to work for the USDA in meat inspection. Moving us from western Colorado to northeast Nebraska, I went from being a career person to a domestic engineer.

We live on an acreage, and have many horses. My husband's passion, besides me of course, is hunting. So we all hunt. The children have been taken along - elk, deer, pheasant hunting, since they were born. First, in a snugli, then backpack, and now on horseback, alone. We take great pleasure in being together as a family, and have many adventures. I truly believed that when I quit working outside the home, I would have more time to quilt, but I am so incredibly busy that I'm sure I have less.

Janet Kugler
Holdrege, Nebraska
Prairie Quilt Guild of Holdrege
Nebraska State Quilt Guild
Colorado Quilt Council

Husband, Dennis, has been self-employed in a machine shop for nearly 22 years. He's very supportive. Has gotten so he will fix supper on nights I get home at 8 p.m. Also fixes his own lunch each day. Does his own grocery shopping. Only pet we have now is Mollie, a 14 year old Dalmatian that is the machine shop dog. On October 28, 1991, I opened Quilter's Delight. In April, of the year the building had become available, my husband said "Go for it." Little did he know, that was the end of home cooked meals and a clean house!! The store, Quilter's Delight, has really been fun. It has grown from approximately 50 bolts of fabric to over 2,000 bolts of 100% cotton fabric.

Have been quilting since mid-70's, but seriously since 86', when Nebraska State Quilt Guild was started. Started local

Guild in October 86', to keep quilting friendships going. Served on NSQG board in 88', and was Meeting Coordinator for annual convention in 89'. Have learned a lot of organizing skills from both of these jobs. I'm interested in any type of needlework.

Sherry Cook
Council Grove, Kansas
Emporia Regional Quilters Guild

I am a graduate of Emporia State University. I married my college sweetheart, Rick, we've been married for 23 years, and have a 14 year old kitty, "Tiff". I retired as accountant from Emporia State University Endowment Association. I enjoy quilt related crafts and quilting. I teach quilting classes at the Fabric Corner in Emporia, teach and lecture statewide, and have a quilt block in an Elly Sienkiewicz upcoming book. I am listed as honored teacher in Baltimore Album Revival.

Audrey Derscha
Flint, Michigan
Evening Star Quilters

I began quilting 15 years ago. I have experience in both piecing and applique. But my real love of quilting has settled on applique.

About 5 years ago, a group of 5 began a work/study group, who selected Elly Sienkiewicz's Baltimore Beauties and Beyond, Volume 1. We met, and read, and then divided the lessons, and went home and did our portion of the lesson. Then met, and discussed what we had read and produced. We each made our own decisions about what worked better, and what worked not at all. This continued for about two years.

But, after two years, the interest waned for everyone but me, of the group, and I just couldn't get enough of it. It had become an addiction!!! And, just like all addicts, I would do anything (almost) to continue spreading the word about the *Wonderful World of Applique.*

I received so many requests from people who wanted to learn applique, that I got busy and prepared a class in basic applique. Then, they wanted even more. So, I finally made a decision to teach Baltimore Album style quilts.

I feel wonderful about all the students that I have taught, that have gone on to do award winning quilts.

I now teach all over the state of Michigan, and am proud to say, I even have students that commuted 110 miles one way from Ontario, Canada for 8 weeks. They had seen my work and wanted to learn the methods. I was thrilled. I have a lot of repeat students. (I say that they must come again, until they do it the right way. Ha! Ha!) But, in all honesty, they feel the need for motivation to complete enough of the blocks to complete a quilt.

My teaching has expanded to Beginning Baltimore's, Intermediate Baltimore's, Dimensional Baltimore's, and Baltimore Center Medallions. This summer I begin a class in assembling the top and borders.

I am nearing completion of a Baltimore, done in Jewel Tones. (Teal, purple, fuchia, black and various shades of all the colors listed).

I am going to take a class from Elly in May, in Petoskey, Michigan, and this will be the first time I have met her. I am looking forward to that.

Marilyn Guy
Delhi, New York
Delaware County Town & Country Quilters

I was born Marilyn Thomas in Norwich, NY in 1932. My early childhood was spent in Garrison, NY. Since I was an only child, I always enjoyed handwork. I learned to knit when I was nine, and later loved embroidery and needlepoint. I hated sewing!

In 1955, I married Marc Guy, a pharmacist, in Norwich, NY. We moved to Delhi, where we operated a drug store until 1984. We adopted three children, a daughter and two sons. We have three grandchildren. After we sold the drug store, we opened a Hallmark Card and Gift Shop in the same building. I ran that until we sold it in 1993, and my husband continued his profession.

In the 70's, my mother, Alzada, started bringing quilting patterns to me. She was sure I would love quilting. I reminded her that I did not like to sew. She was persistent, but I shrugged it off. My mother and I were very close and when she died suddenly at the age of 63 in 1977, I was devastated. As you know, quilting began a huge comeback in 1976. I was starting to see quilts everywhere. One day out of the blue, I wondered if I could do patchwork. I bought three fabrics, light, medium and dark, and started. I didn't know how to draft a pattern, so I was at the mercy of the magazines. When I saw a pattern I liked that was 12 inches, I tried it. I ended up with a sampler. I experimented with color placement, and did some patterns over with the lights and darks in different positions, and learned a lot that way. I saw someone making a cathedral window block once, and wanted to try that. I got scraps from everyone, and bought fat quarters. I had no stash at that time. I made a quilt of that, and from then on, I was hooked.

Then there was a notice in the paper about quilt classes being held at the historical building. I went, and the teacher was an elderly lady named Madeline Sanford, who loved quilting. I told her I wanted to make a Lone Star Quilt, and I hated to sew. She thought she had her work cut out for her. I learned so much from her, and she could tell me how to piece a block over the phone, when I got stuck on the complicated blocks.

Quilting took over my life and was really my salvation. I can't tell you how much it helped me to survive the grief I was feeling. I felt as if my mother was with me, and I knew she was pleased. Since then, quilting is the most important thing in my life, next to my family.

I belong to the Delaware County Town and Country Quilters, and often join another Friday group here in town. My greatest joy is getting other people interested in quilting. I taught a group of ladies from scratch in my home, and they still come.

My husband has been very supportive, and encouraged me to build a library. I have about 200 books, and loan them to all who come. They sign out what they need, and return later. I am convinced that anyone who wants to, can piece and quilt.

Kathy Palmiter
Williams, Indiana

My family moved from northern Indiana, to rural southern Indiana in 1986, to escape big city life and harsh winters. We live in an earth banked home (three sides are built into a bank of earth) on 6.5 acres. Our early years here were spent "taming" our acreage. Now we have much more time for our hobbies, me with quilting, and my husband, Mike, for his model railroads.

In 1987, I joined a quilt group that meets every Thursday, and quickly made some dear friends. Shortly thereafter, I was interviewing for a part time job. My future employer explained my duties, pay rate, etc., and that I would be working Tuesdays and Thursdays. After a moments hesitation, I blurted out "Thursdays are bad for me, would Friday be OK?" I've since changed jobs, but still have my Thursdays free for quilting.

I started entering quilt contests in 1991, just to see if my quilts would be accepted. Much to my amazement, I've won some honors:

1991-QUILT AMERICA-Special Miniature Award sponsored by Little Quilts

1993-QUILT AMERICA-1st place Miniature category

1993-MINIATURES FROM THE HEART contest-Best of Show

1994-QUILTFEST, Jacksonville, Florida, 1st place-small Wall Quilt category. 2nd place-Miniature category

Contests keep me focused on a project, and give me a deadline. I'm great at starting projects, but sometimes have trouble finishing. I've also had several articles published:

AMERICAN QUILTER-
                Winter 1993
MINIATURE QUILTS-
                Winter 1994

My award winning "Little Bit of Baltimore" was included in an article by Tina Gravatt, in the November 1994 issue of Country Living, indeed an honor.

Mary Lou Sayers
Clarkson, Nebraska
Calico Quilt Club
of Columbus,
Nebraska

I'm a 58 year old quilter living with my husband, Alvin, on a 200 acre farm near Clarkson, Nebraska. We've lived in this area for 42 years, and raised 3 daughters, Deb Karel of Clarkson, Janet O'berg of Richland, and Gayle Sayers of Milford, Nebraska. My husband,

Alvin, is retired from farming. I say I'm semi-retired. Meaning, I still have my housework, my gardening, and we have a large yard that takes an awful lot of time in summer. I quilt year 'round, and consider it both hobby and profession, as I teach quilt classes every fall for 8-10 weeks. I have many quilting projects in various stages of production. I'm very laid back about quilting, as I feel if it's not fun, I don't want to be doing it. I teach quick piecing methods and can piece a reasonable quilt, but really prefer applique.

We have 5 grandchildren, all of whom have already received their first full-size quilts. I was just recently reminded that it's time to make new ones, by a couple of grandkids. The granddaughters all want to learn to quilt, but are at present too busy with school, etc.

I wish I had started to quilt, when I was much younger. I started in 1979. I have so many quilts I want to make, I'll never get them all done.

The biggest thrill I ever got, was when a Lone Star Quilt I made was chosen to go with The Omaha Playhouse troop to Russia, when they took the production "The Quilters" there on tour. Second thrill was in 1991, when an antique quilt I entered in the NQA show in Lincoln, Nebraska, received a second prize ribbon in the Capitol Hill division.

The most gratifying thing I get from quilting, is to see rank beginners, regardless of age, finish their first quilt. My students range from early 20's to their 80's, so we never lack for variety. This year in my 5 classes, the students produced 65 quilts in all sizes, from baby quilts to King-size. That's a lot of yards of fabric.

My husband and I have been married 42 years, and we enjoy yard and garden and occasional trips to the Casino's in the area for a whirl at the slots. Grandkids and our daughters and sons-in-law also keep us busy. Hope I haven't gotten carried away. Just to let you know, that I do love quilting and I can blame Joan Waldman for my addition!

Edna E. Holdsworth Johnston,
Rhode Island Narragansett Bay Quilters

After working many years as a professional seamstress, I am now retired and able to quilt to my hearts' desire. My sister, Dorothy Eramian, and I combined our households a few years back. As she is a quilter also, we find it a great help to have an instant critic in the same house. My son, Mark Holdsworth, is a Doctor of Pharmacology at the University of New Mexico, and lives in the Sandia Mountains, which I visit annually, usually when there is a quilt show in that area. Since my retirement, I have been able to indulge my love of travel, touring Europe twice, once on a lovely cruise via riverboat down the Rhine River. This past summer north to Alaska.

I've been an avid reader all my life. I am also an amateur author. I've written short stories, poems, plays and last year completed a 3-generation family history. The plays were both about quilting, and were performed by members of our local Guild, with hilarious results. Also, I write two columns for the Guild Newsletter, one on the *Quilter of the Month* and the other titled *Traveling Edna*, which features my travels to quilting events. I'm currently at work on a short story about an alien from another planet that lands in a small New England town, and the reaction of the natives to him and vice-versa. It's called *Oom*. Don't know if it will ever be published, but I must write it.

Florence L. Tyler
DeLancey, New York
Delaware County
Town and
Country Quilters
of Delhi, NY
Calico Geese of
Sullivan County
Friday G.A.L.S

I grew up on a small farm near Goshen, New York, along with a brother and sister. We had a vegetable garden for fresh vegetables, and canning the surplus for winter meals. I still garden, canning some, but also freeze for winter use. Mother also made dresses, etc. for my sister and I. She taught me to sew. I made most of my clothes from 8th grade on. I also learned thru 4-H and Home Extension, graduated from Delhi Tech - the Food Service division.

I'm married to Robert. He took over his home farm, where we

Page 38, Meet the Quilters

had a Brown Swiss dairy. We have 3 sons, I sewed for them - shirts, etc. and lots of patching. Made some utility quilts along the way. Our sons married and moved away.

We sold the dairy in 1978, then I had some more time to devote to quilting. I had done macrame', dress making, some food catering, etc, for added income, but found the most satisfaction in quilting.

In 1981, I made a vest with mariners compass on the back, 5 rows of shells around the bottom, and quilted in the shells. The next year, a vest pattern was in a magazine for an 8-point Star Block, and strip pieced. I made one - a neighbor wanted one like it. That was the beginning.

In 1985, five ladies wanted to make the Star and Strip pieced vest. We met each Friday. That was the start of our Friday G.A.L.S. Quilt Group. We still meet each Friday, and it has grown to 18 members.

I have made 80+ vests, ordered just by sight. Have vests from Maine to California, Canada to Florida. As an example; we were at a Fly-in Breakfast at a small airport near Hancock, NY. A lady approached me, asked about my vest. She bought it right off my back! She was from Stuart, Florida. I taught a vest lesson in Liberty, NY to the Calico Geese Quilt Group (a neighboring county). Later, I joined the group. Each quilt group is different, but great groups for learning and friendships. I was inducted into the Catskill Mountain Quilters Hall of Fame in 1988.

*****By the way, G.A.L.S. stands for "Gab and Laugh Sewers". Tho' all have done quilting, some members also knit, crochet, counted cross stitch, make adorable Teddy Bears, by recycling old fake fur coats. It is a friendly, sociable group, each learning from the others. As with each of the quilt groups, *Show-and-tell* is first on the program at each meeting or gathering. We all ask for *help*, ideas, arrangement of blocks, color choices, etc, how-to-do! Enjoyable days!

I help, whenever I can. I also do some teaching pertaining to quilting. Besides vest lessons, have taught log cabin, applique- using freezing paper, Pineapple using rotary cutter.

I demonstrate quilting each year at Fryeburg, ME Fair, first week of October in AG Exhibit Building. You meet the nicest people, while quilting.

I am much more at ease quilting, than trying to write.

Jennifer J. Danly
Arlington, Massachusetts
Rising Star Quilters

I have lived in New England all my life and love it here, but I enjoy traveling whenever I get the opportunity. I have a BA from Wellesley College (in Studio Art) and an M.L.S. from Simmons College (in Library Science). Formerly a librarian, I am currently *employed* as the mother of 2 young children (Chris, age 7; Sarah, age 4). My husband, Bruce, is a physicist at M.I.T. I enjoy hiking, camping, cross-country skiing, reading classic literature, and of course - quilt making, although I never find time to do it all.

Melissa Armstrong
Oshkosh, Nebraska
Nebraska State Quilt Guild

I am one of those people who took a long time to decide what they want to be, when they grow up. I went to college for 5 years, and came out with a double major in Psychology and English Education. I taught High School, then got married, and became a housewife and mother. I enjoyed that, but as my marriage started to dissolve, I needed an income. I started quilting for others, and teaching classes. Now I own my own Shop, and this is what I want to be when I grow up! I live happily with my 2 daughters, Jessica and Rebecca, and 2 cats, and quilt when I can.

PIONEER QUILTERS (ALL 50 OF THEM!)
Eugene, Oregon

Author's Note: This is the way the questionaire came back! The return postmark just said *Duncan*, no first name. Sounds like a great group!

Pioneer Quilters started meeting once weekly in September 1974, and we still meet weekly on Wednesdays, 10 a.m. to 2 p.m. We have about 50 members and until January 1994, we met in each others homes every week. We now meet in 2 classrooms at a local church. We are single, married, widowed, divorced, mothers, grandmothers, and great-grandmothers, and our ages range from 30 to 88. Our pets and hobbies vary wildly, but we are passionate about quilting.

Darlene Brazil
Escalon, California
Country Crossroads Quilters

Do I work??? Yes! and what a fun, privileged job it is! I am a quilter. I own a quilting machine, which is set up in my "work room". I mainly do innovative quilting - that is unique and individual custom work, according to each quilt top. My goal is to enhance the quilt - not just quilt it. I've been in the business now for close to 3 years. Once the word got around to the kind of quilting I do, my business soared. (Which is the reason this is so late getting to you! I am just snowed under in late fall for the Christmas season!)

Actually, my background education is in nursing. I am a Registered Nurse, however, after juggling work outside the home, kids, sitters, orthodontists, baseball, etc.....I gave it up for my first love...quilting! What a wonderful move! I now am working out of my home, at something I love! An added bonus is all the really great quilts I see, and the interested people I have met and made friends with.

Teresa A. Walton
New Braunfels, Texas

I retired from the US Air Force in 1989 after 20 years of service, with a major in Nuclear Medicine, and minor in quilting. I am currently working at McKenna Memorial Hospital, as the only Nuclear Medicine Technician, which leaves me little time for my love of quilting. However, my two greatest loves are my babies: Charles William and Mary Ann. Two beautiful Yorkies requiring,.......no, *demanding*...lots of love and attention.

Roberta Schroeder
Deer Park, Washington
Fat Quarters Quilters
Pine Needles Quilt Guild

I am a professional volunteer. I enjoy being active as President of Eastern Washington/Idaho Synodical Women's Organization of the Evangelical Luthern Church in America. This position consumes much of my time and organizational skills. I live with my husband, Bob, 2 dogs on 10 acres near Deer Park, Washington.

My sewing room has big south and west windows, which I love. I enjoy bird watching, gardening, children of all ages, including my own 4 grandchilden, cooking, walking, making crafts with my friends, and sharing time with my friends. I belong to Chapter AW-P.E.O. I love creating quilts and wall hangings, and giving them away. I give them as bridge prizes, door prizes, birthday presents, wedding gifts. I personalize items and give them away.

My sister-in-law, Barbara, is my most supportive fan and I make lots of things especially for her.

I am the mother of four grown children, and I also enjoy making them seasonal wall decorations and table runners. Each one has a quilt I have made. I took my first class in February of 1992. It was the Log Cabin class. I was hooked and promptly made about 8 quilts - all log cabin. Then I began to explore other options and make other *quilt in a day* patterns.

I enjoyed making dolls in a class I took. I made eight of them - all pretty much the same. I make something, and if someone likes it, I keep making more of them to give away.

I have a small collection of Hummel figurines, I love angels, dolls, and fresh flowers.

Dawn Golden
Milford, New Jersey
Courthouse Quilters of Hunterdon County

My name is Dawn Golden, and I am a 32 year old mother of two boys: Kyle who is just over 4 years, and Mathew who is 20 months. My husband, Jim, travels for his job and so I am alone with the children a few nights each week. Along with my full time *Mommy job*, I also

Page 40, Meet the Quilters

work part time for our Borough, and very-part-time for Bristol-Myers Squibb.

Merrilyn Muir-Rennau
Vienna, Austria, Europe
- *Patchwork Gruppe Wien von der Oesterreiche Quilter's Guild*
- *Country Patchwork Quilters Guild of Marshall, Missouri*
- *Patchwork and Quilter's Gruppe, Gaaden bei Wien*

I teach in my home in Vienna, Austria. There are classes every Thursday morning of the month, from September to June. On Tuesdays and Fridays every week of the month, there is open house for handicrafts from 10 a.m. to 4 p.m. We have sack lunches, and I serve the beverage. Fortunately, there is enough space, so women are sometimes sewing in 3 different rooms, while their children are playing in the Nursery. There are all age groups, so it is not boring. The groups are very international. (English-French-German are spoken.)

My son is 31 years old, and is employed in the Political Science Department of the Vienna University, while working toward his Masters in Philosophy.

My daughter, at 27 years, is the proud mother of two daughters. Natalie will be 3 years old in June, Stephanie will become 1 in April. My daughter and family live in Guenselsdorf, near Vienna.

I enjoy classical music. I have always been interested in other countries and customs. As the wife of an Austrian Ambassador, it was possible for me to live in many countries on 3 continents. I started a quilting class in Lagos, Nigeria.

While studying voice at the Mozarteum in Salsburg, Austria, I had the opportunity of meeting many students from all over the world.

Born in Hutchinson, Kansas, as a teenager went to Austria to study voice. When I was 21, returned to New York to give a concert in four languages at Carnegie Recital Hall. Spent 1 year traveling the "states" before returning to live permanently in Austria.

Pamela Thompson
Clinton Twp, Michigan
Metro Detroit Quilt Guild

Married to William Thompson 27 years, daughter Amy, is a first grade teacher, and son, Michael, is a junior at University of Michigan, in Ann Arbor. Boots is our Cat. I am attending Central Michigan University Extension classes, for a BS in Industrial Management. I work full-time at Anderson-Cook, Inc., as a clerk in the engineering department, and I quilt to keep my sanity. I'm fairly good at it, love it, though I'm not terribly creative. My Mom, Dora Lyda, also enjoys it and we took it up in 1987.

I have a quilt that my Grandma Myra Pence pieced, and a friend quilted for her. I'd like to give the lady credit, if I knew who she was. I'm sure she's dead and buried by now, but it would be nice information to have for my genealogy.

Mary A Sovran
Phoenix, Arizona
Arizona Quilters Guild

I started quilting around 1980. We were living in the Colorado mountains at that time, in a summer resort area. My husband, Victor., and myself, both had retail businesses catering primarily to tourists. My shop was open only during the summer months, so I had the long cold winter at home to pursue my needlework. I had done a lot of embroidery and needlework prior to 1980, and then I discovered a book entitled *Make a Quilt in 7 days*. I was intrigued, and my life has not been the same since. Each quilt led to another, and I still have so many more to look forward to.

We have since retired, and moved to warm, sunny Arizona, which we love. We are originally from Michigan.

Meet the Quilters, page 41

Carol Thelen
Pearland, Texas
Bay Area Quilt Guild

As toddlers and preschoolers, my children, Diane and Louis, watched me go through studying and graduating, with an engineering degree. My husband and I were both working in the engineering field for a few years, when my children were watching Sesame Street one day. For each letter of the alphabet, Big Bird was naming an occupation. Big Bird said, "E...Engineer". No response from the children. Big Bird says, "P....painter".. Q....Quilt maker". Both the kids jumped up and said "Mom, they said your job!!!"
I have since quit that _other thing_ to stay home full time. Now this quilt maker has more time for her _job!_

Susan Southworth
Gulf Shores, Alabama
Island Quilters Guild

I have been married for 25 years to my husband, Gary. Our oldest son, Marc, is 23 and is a tanker in the Marine Corps. at Twentynine Palms, California. Our youngest son, Michael, age 21, is in school at the University of southern Queensland, in Brisbane, Australia. We have two Yorkies, Spike and Gizmo, who are both spoiled. I refer to my husband, as You-Know-Who, in my quilting column and short stories that I write. He rides his Harley Hog a lot, which keeps him out of my way, when I am quilting.
Author's note: Susan is a very entertaining and prolific writer, you'll find her articles in many publications. She is listed on the masthead as a Contributing Editor to several Quilting Magazines including QUILT and Big Blocks.

Connie Sager
Nashville, Kansas
Pratt Area Quilt Guild

My husband, Travis, and I have been married 32 years. We have 4 great kids. Debbie is the oldest at 31, Geoff is 29, Trevor is 27, Jarrod is 19. Our family also includes daughter-in-law Patty, son-in-law Ralph, and 5 grandchildren. We love very much, a little toy poodle _Dominique_, now the only child left at home (or so she thinks). I work for a Home Health Agency, caring for those in their homes. A year ago I started taking college courses.

Cynthia England
Houston, Texas
Lakeview
Quilters Guild

In addition to teaching quilt making, I have a pattern company that is doing very well. My background in commercial art, has been very helpful in that respect. My husband, Warren, and I have 3 children, Stephen 8, Travis 6, and Monica 3.

Author's Note:
Cynthia's England's Quilts have won _many_ awards including:
• Best of Show and Award of Excellence, AIQA, Houston, Texas, 1993
• 1st Place, and Viewer's Choice Wall Quilt, AQS, Paducah 1994
• Selected for 1995 American Quilter's Society wall calendar
• You may remember seeing her beautiful pictorial quilt of trees in a forest, called _Piece and Quiet_, in some of the quilting magazines, it has taken a number of awards.

Lesley Ann Hill
Grandville, Ohio
Heart of Ohio
Quilt Guild

I am a _retired_ drug and alcohol rehab counselor. My skills have been used at the prevention, in-patient, halfway house, and aftercare level. When I got to the point that I was very frustrated with working with unhealthy people, both clients and staff, I decided to put my efforts to quilting. I had quilted before I left counseling, but obviously had not had much time.

Currently, I work very part-time at an antique store. My employer is a former co-worker in the counseling field, and one of my favorite people. Spending time amongst beautiful and such unique items, is a delight to me.

My family consists of a husband, Garrie, a 14 year old daughter, Breeanna (freshman in high school), Theron (5th grader), an English Springer Spaniel, Smudge (my shadow and a bit crazy), a miniature horse, Crimson, a micro miniature rabbit, Figgaro, and 11 fish of different types.

Besides quilting, I collect miniature (1/12 scale) furniture and houses, and I am a stamper.

My family enjoys traveling, so summers are often spent on the road. Last year we drove to Washington, D.C. and then two months later, drove to northern California, a trip of 7,000 miles.

Margo J. Clabo
Cleveland, Tennessee
Cherokee Blossom Guild of Cleveland, TN
Crazy Quilters of Chattanooga, Tennessee

I have a back ground in architecture, and discovered the World of Quilting about 3 1/2 years ago. The rest, as they say, is history! My husband, Alvin, and our two college age sons, Jason and Joshua, are my greatest fans and supporters, but I cannot imagine life without my quilting friends.

My mother, Mary Jenkins, taught me to love sewing when I was a young girl. When she died several years ago I inherited her sewing supplies, including a large drawer full of wonderful heavy duty cotton threads, she used to sew slipcovers. Although she never made a quilt, all of her grandchildren now own a quilt that has been sewn with their grandmother's thread, as I try to maintain a link between past and present generations.

John Flynn
Billings, Montana
Quilt by Association
Yellowstone Valley Quilters Guild

It all started innocently enough. A few stitches in the wife's quilt, when she wasn't looking. Then a whole block when I sat down, with every intention of watching the evening news. Before too long, Brooke, my wife (who has been quilting since 1977), could not keep up with the piecing.

I was hooked on the quilting, but in order to continue, I had to learn to piece. I began by hand piecing a baby quilt from Brooke's fabric collection. My piecing technique was a little unusual, but I completed the top and I had something to quilt.

To me, the next logical step was the queen-sized bed quilt. No problem. All I had to do was go to the fabric store, get the fabric and piece it together just like the baby quilt, right? Wrong! I'm a bearded 6'2" and the reception I got when I entered the fabric store was less than cordial. A lady with rhinestone encrusted cat-eyes hanging around her neck on a logging chain, followed me everywhere to make sure I didn't break any of the fabric. If I paused for even a moment, she whipped the glasses on, looked over them and asked if she could help me find anything in particular. I said I wasn't sure what I was looking for, and she said, "Didn't she give you a list?" At this point, I lost interest and went home.

I got Brooke to buy for me. I felt like a teenager hanging around the convenience store, trying to get someone to buy beer for me. Anyway, I finally gathered up the fabric and started hand-piecing a 1000 Pyramid quilt.

This was a big piecing job, somewhere around 1700 pieces, and I soon realized that in order to finish in this lifetime, I would have to venture away from our home with my piecing -- I build bridges and spent many of my weeks on the job site. At first I kept it in a brown paper bag in my suitcase until I was safely locked in a motel room. Next, I blacked out the windows in my trailer at the Colstrip power plant construction site, and pieced most of it right there in the midst of 5000 iron workers.

Shortly after this, I had a real setback. In fact, I was nearly cured of quilting altogether. I had taken my piecing along on a trip and ended up in the Toronto airport waiting out a long flight delay. I found a well-lit corner in the terminal and went about my piecing, I tend to lose track of time when I'm quilting, so I can't tell you how long it was until I became aware of the murmuring of a crowd. When I looked up, I was surrounded by people - nobody really looking straight at me or getting close enough to catch whatever it was that I had. Sort of like they eye the tattooed lady at the circus. I packed up my quilting and slipped out of Canada - and back to the safety of home.

Right after I completed that 1000 Pyramid, an event occurred that contributed more than any other to the total consumption of my life by this quilting habit. I was ready to buy the fabric for the back, and Brooke suggested I go to "The Patchwork Parlor", a

Meet the Quilters, page 43

quilt shop. When I went into the store, not only was I treated like a real customer, the shop was owned by my old backpacking friend, Pat Larmoyeux. What a place! I could go there and hang out after work. Talk to other quilters, touch the fabric and sort through the notions without interference. I soon discovered that all quilt shops are about the same. I traveled around the state from quilt shop to quilt shop and even managed to get one or two bridges built! I quickly amassed a sizeable fabric collection and, like most people just getting started, I was pretty guilty about this stack of unused fabric.

To conquer my mountain of fabric, I took up machine piecing. During this first machine piecing project, I learned that they don't print all fabric patterns forever. So much for any guilt about too much fabric. Anyway, I learned to piece by machine and now do most of my tops on the machine. I can get started quilting sooner that way.

Author's Note:
John Flynn has published several step-by-step work books. His works appears in a number of quilt magazines and he teaches nationally and internationally.

Jane Clark Stapel
Pittsburgh, Pennsylvania
(no bio included, but you'll find her wonderful answers in the other sections)

Marilyn Thomas
Harpster, Ohio
Wyandot Piecemakers

Bob and I have been married 42 years. We have 7 children, 12 grandchildren and 2 great grandchildren. I try to do special things for them. I'm making quilts for my grandchildren for graduations. John Thomas was first to graduate, made him a log cabin. Jenny Shields was given a Baltimore Album quilt and this year Clinton Thomas was given an applique quilt. I designed and drew the pictures. Fits a full size bed. The applique center is 45" square, Indian teepees, covered wagons, and embroidered buffalo are the main things. The buffalo took eight hours each to do. One year to do whole center.

My father (Paul Myers) ancestors came to Ohio in 1846 by covered wagon and settled in Wyandot County. My mother's (Majel Childs Myers) ancestors left Ohio to homestead in Nebraska in 1903, and before.

In 1976, my sister, Saralynn Gier, got me started in quilting. She taught classes. Loved it ever since. I used to paint, so applique is like painting, only with fabrics.

Author's Note: I wish you could all see Marilyn's quilt with the buffalos. She sent pictures along with her questionaire, and the detailing is magnificent! I can see why it took 8 hours to do one buffalo. And the center, well, you would just have to see it to appreciate it. Hope that grandson appreciates it! I'll bet he does!

Candra J. Sowder
Williamsburg, Iowa
Iowa County
Heartland Quilters

Married to Craig, an intensive care nurse. Home-school mother of 4 children (Catherine, 8, 4th grade. Curtis, 6, 1st grade. Caryn, 3. Courtney, 1). Have a Master's Degree in Library Science. Involved in church, politics, and crafting - like to cross stitch large pieces, smock, sew, and do hardanger, as well as quilt. Currently, vice-president of quilt club, which is program chairman. Love the job!

Merrilee Tieche
Ozark, Missouri
Ozark Piecemakers Quilt Guild

I am a retired travel agent with four children and eight grandchildren. We moved to this lovely little community in the Ozarks in 1988, from Los Angeles. Leaving the *Big City* behind has allowed me to indulge in the pastimes I treasure - quilting, cooking, gardening, fishing and enjoying natural beauty of this area. I am committed to a lovely man who, while a bit bewildered by my passion for quilting, helps at Quilt Shows, critiques my work, and gives me time and space to be creative in my own way.

Meet the Quilters

Diana Alfuth
Hudson, Wisconsin
Hudson Heritage Quilters

Married with 2 cats, 1 English Springer Spaniel, and another on the way. Just quit work as legal secretary/paralegal, and went to University of Minnesota pursuing a degree in horticulture. Besides quilting, I make baskets and other crafts. I also teach dog obedience classes and show my dog in obedience ring.

Juanita Gibson Yeager
Louisville, Kentucky
Louisville Nimble Thimbles

I am a Registered Nurse, and although I no longer practice my profession, for over twenty years I worked in an occupational health care office, providing first aid to ill and injured workers. I have been married to my husband, Phillip, for 33 years. We have four children (Andre', Lyn, Rene' & Mike), all adults who live away from home (thank goodness) and four grandchildren. Three boys, (Joshua, Justin & Johnathan) children of our eldest daughter Lyn, and a girl (Joslyn), the daughter of our youngest son, Mike. You will notice all of their names begin with J, in honor of me, I am told.

I am an avid reader, I start the day with the daily paper, which I read from front to back with my morning two cups of coffee. I love fiction, prefer mysteries, but will read most any thing that's published in the English language. On a rainy day there's nothing better than a pot of spiced tea and a good *who done it!*

Needlework and crafts have been a part of my life, since I was 10 years old. My paternal grandmother, Helen Gibson, was an excellent needle-woman. I loved to watch her as she tatted, or embroidered, or made crocheted doilies. Over the years I have tried my hand at most everything imaginable, from doll making to needlepoint. My home, with it's eclectic decor, is peppered with my endeavors. Ceramic vases, porcelain figurines, pottery, baskets and now, quilts, and a growing collection of elephants. I have won several awards for my quilts. Pictures of them have appeared in books by noted quiltmakers, and in magazines. The honor that I am most proud of to date, is the inclusion of one of my quilts in the permanent collection of the AQS Museum.

Donna Olson
Rogersville, Missouri
Ozark Piecemakers

Throughout the years, I have had a great love and appreciation for art. My husband and I bought our first painting, the second year we were married. Now, after 35 years, we have a wonderful collection of art. Many hours of Art History at our local university, and being a docent at the Springfield Art Museum, have kept me involved with the art world. From time to time, I would try my hand at a drawing or painting class, but realized I had very little artistic talent. I vented my desire for artistic expression through the needle arts-needlepoint, cross stitch, etc.

Jane Aruns
Franklin, Tennessee
Cumberland Valley Quilters Guild

I have a M.A. in Visual Arts, and have been a quilt maker and artist for 23 years. My quilts appear regularly in national shows, and I've won numerous awards. My work is included in collections at the Museum of American Folk Art and MSC Publishing (via Purchase Awards), and numerous private collections. I run a small Bed & Breakfast at my home in middle Tennessee. This establishment, SUGAR CREEK FARM, at 5420 Waddell Hollow Road in Franklin, allows me to stay at home, and quilt.

Shirley Gardner
Evergreen, Colorado
Colorado Quilt Council

I have studied art for years, and have a degree in textiles. After making several fabric art quilts, a shop asked for patterns and I now have a pattern company, Shirley Gardner Designs. I can't begin to tell you how delightful it is to work with quilters, designing and teaching.

Recently, I have been designing special projects for various organizations. I have appeared

Meet the Quilters, page 45

on television, and I have been in many magazines. I never dreamed a love for quilting would challenge me in so many ways. My favorite part of this fascinating business is meeting other quilters.

Carol Younce
Fairfax, Virginia
Quilters Unlimited of Northern Virginia

I am a fabric collector, who also likes to quilt. I have been drawn to working with fabrics ever since childhood, and now enjoy finding unusual pieces wherever they may be hiding, in clothing at flea markets, in baskets of scraps, remnants, anywhere!

I have been quilting for about 15 years. I am currently the Associate Editor for Lady's Circle Patchwork Quilts Magazine.

Author's Note: I hope you're all enjoying Carol's many articles and features, as much as I am.

Joyce Benitez
Omaha, Nebraska
Cottonwood Quilters
Omaha Quilt Guild

I ramble around my ranch-style home, cluttered with antiques, and any space left is then filled with Quilting *Stuff*. My Singer® Featherweight sits in a place of honor, in just the right position to watch TV and sew till all hours of the night. (I do my best sewing 7 p.m. to 3 a.m.) If I pin a quilt to the floor for pin-basting, my three cats; Wendell, Agnes and Tobias, claim it for their territory, and see who can make a tunnel under it first! I even got a comment from a Quilt Judge that there were "undetermined animal hair" on my quilt. They weren't undetermined, they were *cat hairs*. I knew it. Anyone who visits me, knew it. The judge didn't.

I have two daughters: Jana, 33, who works at First Data, and Julie, 25, who teaches at Arizona State.

I started *REAL* Quilting in 1978, with the taking of a class to learn Cathedral Window. After making 6 squares, I decided it wasn't worth it so, I took a Sampler Class taught by Lois Gotlch and Paulette Peters. That was the BEST thing I ever did. I've been involved in every aspect of Quilting. Since, I've helped be the founding father of both the Omaha Quilt Guild, and then Cottonwood Quilters, and finally Nebraska State Guild, and am now *hooked*. I often joke, "Quilting is as addictive as crack cocaine, and sometimes I think it costs more!"

I am, and have been a day care provider for more than 27 years, foster parent, Girl Scout Leader 22 years, and 4H leader for 15 years. Daily, I watch 9 or more children, infant to 6 years. I pray for 1 p.m. (That is nap time.) All to myself...2 hours to quilt, or whatever. My Featherweight® is poised, all threaded for any amount of time I can squeeze out to sew - this allows me to sit down, sew a few patches together or cut the next project.

Virginia L. Brown
Ogallala, Nebraska

My husband, Dale, and I have been married 40 years, and we have a married daughter, Vicki, and 2 grandchildren, Zachary and Casie Jo. We moved back to Nebraska in 1988. Hubby complained some what about all those boxes of fabric, but I couldn't leave it behind! I'm a self-taught quilter and have tried all types, with scrap quilts at the top of the list. I worked in a craft village in Minnesota for 2 summers, where I was demonstrating techniques and answered questions from visitors from all over the world. The ladies from India (spoke through an interpreter) were so fascinated with the battings. All they had ever done was put top and back together, and even though they didn't need the batting for warmth, they wanted that look in their quilts and were determined to take as much of it back as they could pack into 2 large packing crates to ship.

My first hand quilted quilt was a trapunto pattern I designed in 1978. Talk about *toe nail* stitches! Those will qualify without a doubt!!

Pets have been part of our lives, but one, a very mild tempered siamese cat name, Tom, stands out. He figured what was mine was his, quilts especially! I didn't get one quilt of any size made at home, that didn't get cat hairs on it! He always managed a nap sometime or other, on whatever I was working on. I even tried putting it under other pieces of fabric to

Page 46, Meet the Quilters

hide it, and guess what? Yep, I'd find Tom curled up between the pieces on top of that quilt. Another time, I had a quilt in a big frame for basting, went to answer the phone, you guessed it! Tom was in the middle of it, as if he had found the neatest hammock ever made. What a persistent cat!!

Many of my quilted pieces have been bought by people throughout the United States, Canada, and 2 countries in Europe. Most of my work has been photographed and documented. I have made over 200 pieces to date. Entering contests made me aware of the little details that make an average quilt stand out among others.

2 pieces entered in the Hoffman Challenge placed 1st and 2nd and were part of traveling exhibitions. Quilter's Newsletter has published a quilt that was entered in the Big 200 contest, and placed in the top 20 quilts that were entered.

I teach quilting classes to all levels of experienced seamstresses, in a wide variety of traditional patterns and techniques. My students add scraps to my *stash*, and I tend to add more. I enjoy the scrap quilts, and even the scraps left from those projects are sometimes used to make small gifts, pot holders, crazy quilt type place mats, etc.

Barb Bennett
Washington, D.C.

If it weren't for quilting, my life would be very dull.

Debbie Ruisard
Whitehouse Station, New Jersey
Courthouse Quilters of Hunterden County

I am a full-time mom to three beautiful little girls - Kersten age 5, Rachel age 3, and Marie age 7 months. My husband, David, and I have lived in New Jersey for 9 years, where he is the pastor of a small Reformed Church. I was born and raised in Canada, and am a *resident alien* in this country. My heritage is Dutch, my father was born in Holland and immigrated when he was 12. Because my mother is Canadian, we did not speak Dutch in the home, however she did manage to learn to cook a few Dutch dishes. I have three younger brothers, all of whom have been the recipients of my quilts.

Fran Soika
Novelty, Ohio

I am a self-taught quilt maker, making quilts for about forty years. I have been teaching throughout the country for about fifteen years. Most of my quilts are one of a kind designs, many of which are inspired by our travels.

I have done commission work for Malcolm Forbes, a quilt depicting his hot air balloons, also for the Cleveland Ballet, The American Red Cross, The Visiting Nurses Association, and many private collectors.

I have enjoyed rewarding collaborations with other artists. For eight years, I worked with Southwest Native American designs and collaborated with Drew Lewis, an Acoma potter, making the "Acoma Quilt" using traditional Acoma pottery designs.

I also worked with Ed Larson of Santa Fe, New Mexico, doing a commission piece for Household Finance and several Presidential Quilts, the latest being "The Clinton Quilt". I also did a tree ornament for the White House. I am now working with Henri Matisse Cut-out Designs.

I've done magazine work, and had my work published in books and calendars. I have won many awards, and my work is recognized throughout the country.

I have had the privilege of teaching numerous places including: North Carolina Quilt Symposium 84 & 92, Francaise du Patchwork in Paris, Wilmington College, Big Tree Quilt Conference in NY, First Quilting Cruise in the Caribbean, Arts and Ohio Humanities Council, College of Wooster, AQS in Paducah, Northeast Ohio Regional Quilt Council Get-Away-Weekend 91-93, NQA Bowling Green, Ohio, The Great American Quilt Festival in NY, "Quilting by the Lake" in NY, NQA Symposium, Bowling Green College and many other Quilting Guilds throughout the USA.

Anne-Donia B. Hafskjold
Tiller, Norway
Trondheim quiltelag

Ever since kindergarten I have enjoyed handicrafts; knitting, embroidery, sewing, weaving and so on. I used to make most of the clothes for my children, Sigierd and Liv Kristin. I have also knitted several sweaters for my husband, Bjorn, and I have made him a few vests from neckties. He is always teasing me that I should make him a quilted suit. Maybe one day! I have made big garments, though; I have embroidered two Norwegian national costumes, one with many different flowers from the fields, one with apple blossoms all over the skirt. There were many hot hours under the woolen skirt, but the result was quite worth it. And my daughter looks great in it! I am a professional teacher, but although I love handicrafts so much, I have never taught one lesson of handicrafts in school!!

Bonnie Swannack
Lamont, Washington
Cheney Country Quilters
Washington State Quilters, Spokane Chapter

I was raised on a farm near the small community of Hooper, WA. Graduated from LaCrosse High School, Whitworth College, and Deaconess Hospital School of Nursing in Spokane. I met my future husband when he was my patient at Deaconess. We were married in 1964, and I moved to his wheat and cattle ranch near Lamont, WA. We have a son, Tom, who is farming with his father and his wife, Holly, who is a teacher in Sprague. Our daughter, Janet Bowman, works in the Auditor's office for Adams County and her husband, Mark, drives a truck.

I first became interested in quilts after joining the Lamont Women's Club. Some of the winter meetings were devoted to tying quilts that different members had pieced. I had sewed clothing for many years, and thought this would be something different to try. My first attempts were two small quilts for the kids, made out of denim and corduroy scraps-just squares tied with red yarn, but I was so proud of them.

Then I discovered what was then Mary's Quilting Bee in the Spokane Valley. This was in the late 70's. After taking a class in machine quilting, and then one on hand quilting, I thought I knew all there was to know about quilting.

Many more classes followed, and I joined the Washington State Quilters, Spokane Chapter, so I could find out what was happening in the area from their newsletter. Quilting really took over my life when I joined the Cheney Country Quilters. These fellow quilters have been my motivation and inspiration for the past 10 years.

I have taught beginning quilt classes, and judged quilts at local fairs. And have enjoyed entering my quilts in fairs and local quilt shows. Winning some ribbons has been exciting, but the very best part of quilting has been the wonderful people I have met, and lasting friendships made. Quilters are the greatest!

Kathy Munkelwitz
Isle, Maine

I am a full-time quilt maker. I also have a Shop that sells all handmade items that is open in the summer, named Kathy's Quilts and Crafts. We live on a 160 acre farm and run a flock of 120 ewes, that have their lambs in April. I also have horses, three wonderful grown-up daughters (one is also a full-time quilt maker) and 10 grandkids. We lead a pretty active life, snow mobile a lot in the winter. Put up lots of hay in the summer.

Judith Clonan
Fitchburg, Massachusetts

For the past 27 years, I've worked at the local hospital, as an R.N. Joe, my husband of 33 years, and I, have 6 children and 2 grandchildren. I completed my B.S. degree in 1991, while daughters Colleen worked for Massachusetts, in Special Education, & Dierdre worked for B. Business Management. Kathleen, currently a sophomore in college, and Kevin a High School senior. Joe III lives in Washington. Sean, married and living in Florida. My former hobbies were knitting, sewing, and reading. Now....I quilt!

Page 48, Meet the Quilters

Zelda Lynch
San Augustine, Texas

I am a widow, lost my husband August 1977, after his bout with cancer for 21 years. I have just celebrated my 79th birthday. My family carried me out for dinner, I had fun. My family consists of one son, one granddaughter, and one grandson, 3 great-grands...2 boys and one girl. I love them all, including all my in-laws, they are all wonderful to me. I couldn't have a better family.

Sandra A. Anderson
Lincoln, Nebraska
Lincoln Quilters Guild
Nebraska State Quilt Guild

Born Columbus, NE, raised in Norfolk, NE. I received a Bachelor of Science/Home Economics degree at NE. I married Ivan Anderson in 1970. We have three children; Nikki Kay born October 13, 1972, Eric Scott, born July 16, 1975, and Heidi Beth born December 24, 1978. I belong to the Lincoln Quilters Guild and the Nebraska State Quilt Guild. I've held various offices in the LQG including president, vice-president and secretary. I've taught classes and lectured on Quilting. I'm also involved in my church. I was a Girl Scout and 4-H leader. I have a quilt featured in the book NEBRASKA QUILT MAKERS. I work with my husband for Speedway Motors, in the fiberglass department.

Carole Collins
Norfolk, Nebraska
Country Piecemakers Quilt Guild of Norfolk
Nebraska State Quilt Guild
Keweenaw Heritage Quilters of Calumet, Michigan

I am a registered nurse, and have not worked in many years. My husband, Hank, and I have two grown children; a daughter Pam, and a son Jeff, who recently married, and his wife's name is Penny. Several years ago, Hank and I moved to Nebraska with his job, and we bought a turn of the century home, that we are restoring. We are doing most of the work ourselves, and enjoy both the inside work of stripping the woodwork, as much as the outside work in our large vegetable and flower gardens. I do a lot of canning of the vegetables, and drying the flowers to make potpourri and arrangements. We also have grape vines, so make jelly and wreaths. We have a beagle who loves to follow us, and chase the rabbits and squirrels.

Besides quilting and gardening, I enjoy making antique-looking counted cross stitch samplers, and going to antique shops and shows. I have also started to teach quilting, and do some lectures.

Nancy Smith
Denver, Colorado
Arapahoe County Quilters

I am co-owner and founder of the retail store *Great American Quilt Factory*, pattern company *DreamSpinners*, book publishing *Possibilities*, and the children's sewing series, *I'll Teach Myself*.

Betty E. Ives
Windsor Ontario, Canada
Windsor Quilter's Guild
Greater Ann Arbor Quilters Guild in Michigan

By the time my children were teenagers, I had seen many traditional quilts completed by my mother-in-law. By 1970, I had become very enthusiastic about the craft, and wanted to learn everything I could about methods, techniques, and patterns. I enrolled in any workshop that was available (which were few at that time).

After repeated requests to share my knowledge, I taught classes at home for 2 years. Needing a classroom atmosphere, St. Clair College of Windsor, Ontario offered to run my courses through the Adult Education/Cont. Ed Dept. of their school. My courses have run at the main campus and throughout Essex County, since 1978.

Meet the Quilters, page 49

By the mid 1980's, traditional quilting was not enough to satisfy my need for creativity. With a desire to seek out a new form of expression, I was exposed to the teachings of Virginia Avery and Terrie Mangot. Their philosophy toward freedom of expression gave me the confidence to move away from the traditional, and create new pieces on my own based on my intuitive feelings, experiences, use of unusual fabrics, and new methods of expression.

Since then, I have exhibited and competed both internationally and abroad, and have been published in various books, magazines, catalogues and calendars throughout Canada, the US and Japan. My work has been taken from the bed, to the wall, to become true Art Quilts, being both juried and exhibited many places, among them: Quilt National 91, The First and Second Canadian Contemporary Shows, American Quilter's Society in Paducah, Quilt Celebration in Pennsylvania, Silver Dollar City, American International Quilt Assoc. in Houston, Visions Show in San Diego, National Quilters Assoc, Washington, and many entries in Quilt Canada Shows.

In 1990, I was the Canadian Invitational artist for the Fabric Gardens Exhibition in Osaka, Japan, where my work was featured on Japanese TV and the shows posters. This quilt then toured Japan and the USA for four years.

My most exciting achievement is my four time acceptance into Quilt Expo Europa. Other of my works have been juried into exhibits held in Salzburg, Austria, in Odense, Denmark, The Hague in the Netherlands, and are currently in route to Karlsruhe, Germany.

For visualizing my idea, inspiration or expression (much the same as a painter would) I use the textured and contemporary fabrics I collect from worldwide travels, to finalize my ideas into beautiful pieces of quilted art. For me, this is a form of relaxation and ultimate outlet of expression.

Constance T. Hall
Manington,
West Virginia
West Augusta Historical Society

I was born in a little town called Wadestown, West Virginia, 1909, the only child of Jeff and Lillie Yost Thomas. Living in the country, I had no children close to play with me. Therefore, I became very close to my Mother, wanting to do what she was doing. She was very patient with me, for many times I was in the way. She had learned to piece quilts and quilt when she was twelve years of age. Being the oldest child in her family of nine children, when the Grandfather had to go to war, my Mother had to go stay with her Grandmother. Her Grandmother being an avid Quilter, insisted that my Mother learn to piece a quilt, and then they quilted it.

I am fortunate enough to have that quilt today, and it is in good condition at 102 years old. It has won many ribbons in the Antique Class at Shows. That is the beginning of the quilting bug biting my family.

Joan Biasucci
Cedar Creek,
Nebraska
Lincoln Quilters Guild

Four years ago, my husband and I opened ANNA'S RESTAURANT. We are not *out-front* restaurant people and are the first to acknowledge that; however, we are fortunate to have on staff an excellent manager, and a highly talented chef, who along with the people reporting to them, are responsible for the day-to-day restaurant activities.

I am in charge of special events for ANNA'S, which includes coordinating many large functions throughout the year. In addition, I have incorporated my love of quilts and quilting into my job responsibilities. Each year, during the month of June, we hold our annual Quilt Show entitled *Quiltin' at the Creek*. The next Show will be our fifth annual quilt exhibit. This has become a regional show, featuring wall quilts in which we stress quality workmanship, and quilts which have not been viewed publicly in the past. We also encourage individuals who are fairly new to quilting, and often times one of our veteran exhibitors will *adopt* a newcomer and help them get off to a good start with their project.

The next show will be our fifth annual quilt exhibit and includes a three-person, round-robin project entitled *The Purple Connection*. As of this writing, we have commitments from 126 quilters who are participating in this project, including individuals from throughout Nebraska and surrounding states, as well as California, Colorado, Minnesota, Texas and Wisconsin.

Not long ago I read an article which stated, in part, that it takes a chairperson and perhaps six committees, with a total of at least thirty members, to put together a quilt exhibit the size and scope of *Quiltin' at the Creek*. Not necessarily so. My husband helps me hang the quilts, a couple of friends are excellent *sounding boards* for my ideas, and the husband of one friend is my *proof-reader*. If it doesn't read well to Wallace, I re-write. Other than that, total responsibility is mine.

Admittedly, my job takes a lot of year-round *think-time*, planning, organization, and downright physical labor. But I still find time to quilt, and I'm delighted to share some of my experiences, thoughts, and ideas with you.

Lynda Milligan
Denver, Colorado
Colorado Quilt Council
Front Range Quilters
Arapahoe County Quilters

I am co-owner and founder of a retail store *Great American Quilt Factory* (opened 1981), *DreamSpinner* Patterns, *Possibilities* Books, and the kids sewing series, *I'll Teach Myself*.

Sharon J. Mason
Coos Bay, Oregon
Coos Sand n' Sea Quilters

I am 39 years old. I was born and raised in Wakefield, Rhode Island. I have loved Quilts since I can remember, although there were none in my home growing up. It was a visit to Shelburn Museum in Vermont, that I separated from my parents to examine the quilts. I particularly loved the Crazy Quilts. I thought many times that I would someday make a quilt. Finally, I began to save pieces of fabric that I loved, and after marrying and having 3 children, while carrying my fourth child, I began my Crazy Quilt.

I forgot to mention that by this time, I've moved from New England to Lake Tahoe, CA, to Alaska. Anchorage was my home from 1976-87. It was Judith Montano's book, *The Crazy Quilt Handbook*, that gave me the knowledge to begin. Then I started going to Quilt Guild *Anchorage Log Cabin Quilters*, where some of the gals were able to show me the embroidery stitches. It was Fall, Oct. 87', when I started, it was Aug. 93', when I finished and took it straight that day to the Coos County Fair. I won, or it won Best of Division, and I still continue to add dates, holidays, etc.

Crazy quilt is the most enjoyable and relaxing pass time for me. In a couple of hours, I can get a great feeling of accomplishment and joy. Crazy Quilts are my favorite, but I do all other forms of quilting, too.

My husband's name is Tom, my 12 year old son is named Troy (my maiden name). My 10 year old son is Lee, my 8 year old daughter is Natalie Jean, and my son that I carried through most of the construction of the Crazy Quilt, is 6 years old now, and his name is Matthew.

I will try to explain what I do feel would be a nice piece to put in your book. When we moved here to Coos Bay, Oregon, it was a dream come true. We had bought 3 1/2 acres of rural property 1/2 mile from the ocean. My children were 6-4-2 and 8 months old, and after getting our house all settled, I was ready to finish my quilt. I laid it out on a table, and did some now and then, but just didn't go after it the way I used to. Finally, I boxed it up again, and felt really sad that I had lost my desire to finish it. If only there was a Quilt Guild here, if I just had a girl friend that quilted, too. Some one, any one who had the same interest in cutting up pieces of fabric and sewing them back together, like I did.

Two and 1/2 years passed, before I met a lady who said she quilted. We talked and we put an ad in our local newspaper. It read: *Anyone interested in an organizational meeting for Quilters, please attend a meeting at the Coos Bay Library, 1 p.m. Thursday.* That afternoon 13 ladies showed up, and we planned for an evening meeting. 23 ladies attended, and we were on our way. By the first Thursday in October, we had a name, a committee, and a Great Show n' Tell. Before long

Meet the Quilters, page 51

we had Quilt Block of the Month, and a newsletter, Bylaws, etc.

Now our group has an average attendance of 70-80, and paid membership of 108. We have a structured meeting each first Thursday of the month, and a workday meeting the 3rd Thursday of the month. We have a program at our structured meeting, and we are planning a Quilt Show in Sept. We just finished a Museum exhibit, and we have had 3 years of Challenge Quilts, with prizes given by the House of Fabrics.

I am no longer lonely, and have soooo much desire to make a new Quilt from the general excitement I get from our *Show n' Tell*.

If there is *no* Quilt Guild in your area, then start one. Don't be afraid. Put an ad in the Newspaper. Your public library is a great place to meet to get started. Remember, the people who come to the meeting want to get together with others like yourself. I did not have a lot of ideas, but the room was filled with ladies who did. Together you can make a group that will produce many wonderful quilts!

Author's Note: Sharon sent along a *take-off* of the Night before Christmas poem, designed for quilters, written by Sharon and several other Guild members. If you want a cute poem to use for your Guild, contact Sharon at Coos Sand N' Sea Quilters, PO Box 1234, Coos Bay, Oregon 97420. She also sent a picture of her crazy quilt. Once you see it, you know why it won Best of Division, and was exhibited at Branson, Missouri, and Sisters Outdoor Quilt Show. So much hand work!

Doris Lott Aultman
Hattiesburg, Mississippi
Pine Belt Quilters

My husband is Felton Aultman, he works for the Railroad, as an Engineer. I work full time as a Veterans Service Officer in my home county. I also collect Dept. 56 Show Villages as a Hobby, other than my Quilting. I have been quilting for 17 years, and find that I have very little time to spare, so your book does appeal to me. I am a Founding member of the Pine Belt Quilters, and the first president of this group, 1984-85. I have had work hung in Houston, and in Paducah, Kentucky. I like traditional quilts, and have copied patterns made by my Great-great Grandmother. I bring them back to life for myself and my family.

Wilma Dooley Muse
Fayetteville, Tennessee
Lincoln County Piecemakers

After twenty-eight years of working with teenagers, any hearty soul needs diversion. As a high school assistant principal (previously algebra teacher and guidance counselor) handling discipline problems daily, quilting has been my solace. In addition to this pastime, I also enjoy reading and all other types of needlework, especially stitches used on antique linen samplers. My husband, Sam, and daughter, Lynn, have been very supportive of my career, as well as my stitching activities, which include being president of the Lincoln County Piecemakers, who hosted the Tennessee Valley Quilt Association White Glove Show that had over 630 entries of quilted items, which were mostly quilts.

Suzanne Perry Schutt
Clinton, Mississippi
Mississippi Quilt Association

I am a native Mississippian, educated in my state with a major in English and Art. I am a free-lance co-ordinator, working for the Jackson Metro Convention & Visitors Bureau, and doing publicity for several organizations. I am married, have 3 children and 4 granddaughters I love to keep in smocked dresses and quilts. My cat, Fritz, loves to make a hammock out of my quilting frame!

Ellen Vollmer
Nickerson, Nebraska
Cottonwood Prairie Piecemakers

I have 2 sons, David and Frank, husband Ron, and am a stay-at-home Mom. We live on an acreage in a small village. We have a German/Collie mix dog, and 9 cats. It's like a small farm, and my home is over 90 years old. I decorate it, and make wall hangings for myself and for gifts. Have always enjoyed any kind of crafts. At Bible School, I organized the crafts for 14 years. My interest changed to doll making, wall hangings and quilts.

Pauline Hess 'Ping' White
Seaboard, North Carolina
Roanoke Valley Quilters of Roanoke Rapids, North Carolina
Colonial Piecemakers Guild of Williamsburg, Virginia

I'm a retired church secretary, married 42 years to Winston Albert White, have five children and six grandchildren. My children are:
- Carol W. Labadie, married to Robert Lee Labadie, with one son, Robert Eli, they live in Colorado.
- Mary W. Barron, married to Bob Barron, Jr., they live in Spruce Pines, N.C.
- William R. White, married to Vicky Banks, with two sons, Thomas Jason and Joshua Earl, they live near Jackson, NC.
- Sharon W. Treble, married to Charles Galen Treble, one daughter Brittany Mae, they live in Kingston, NC.

I was born near Peabody, Kansas, grew up in Ft. Collins, Colorado, and when Winston and I married, we moved to his home state of North Carolina. We lived in New Bern, NC for 37 years before retiring, then we moved to Winston's home town of Seaboard, NC.

I became interested in quilting, when I found a pattern for a cross stitched quilt in 1980. Although I come from quilters in my family (both my grandmothers), I was not around them when they were quilting. My grandmother, Elizabeth Stevenson Hess of Peabody, KS, was a Blue Ribbon winner with her quilts. She finally stopped entering her quilts in competitions, and just showed them. She did quilting for hire and was kept very busy. My Grandma, Emma Mefford, of Fort Collins, Colorado, only liked to do the piecing and would hire someone else to finish her quilts.

Since I was away from my family when I became interested in quilting, I took classes through the local community college, and have been hooked ever since.

After moving to Seaboard, I learned that the Senior Citizens Organization was looking for someone to teach quilting. So, I have been instructing classes since 1991 with the community college near by.

I have been very fortunate to enter several quilting items, quilts, wall hanging, seasonal items, etc. and have received 10 ribbons in various shows. It is a thrill for me to be able to finish a quilted item, and I love being associated with quilters. They are always an inspiration to me.

After moving to Seaboard, I have quilted and appliqued valances for my windows in the hall, living room, and dining room. I love the quilted look, any and everywhere. My children are all waiting for their first quilt. I have made them wall hangings, and quillows, but they have not received a quilt, yet. Maybe some day!

Pat Milne Hitchcock
Sequim, Washington
Sun Bonnet Sue Quilt Club

I am a retired preschool teacher, presently volunteering as an aide at the local Head Start. I am a self-taught quilter, carrying on a quilt tradition of my maternal grandmothers, Martha Cooper Chatham, who learned white women's ways from her Crow mother, Kills-Those-Who-Hurt-the-Horses, a Native American who was a guide and interpreter for the U.S. Army in the mid-nineteenth century. I lived the first six years of my life in a three room log house in St. Regis, Montana, and received all of my schooling in that state.

Jack and I were married in 1957 and moved to Seattle, Washington, where we lived until four years ago; upon retiring we moved to the small town of Sequim on the Olympic peninsula. We have two children. A daughter, Laura, who is an independent consultant in international environmental law. She does NOT have time to quilt, loves fabric, and provides me with interesting pieces from her travels. Her younger brother, Dean, has made a recent career change from the scenic art world of TV, opera, ballet, theater, and the like, to attend college to pursue journalism studies. His artistic eye gives him a special appreciation for antiques, and he has given me some really lovely antique gifts.

My hobby besides quilting is traveling - we have been

Meet the Quilters, page 53

members of a home exchange club for 20 years, and have enjoyed lengthy stays (you can do that, if you are teachers) around the U.S. and Europe. It has been great fun to take on the identity of someone else, and discover how interesting your new neighbors are.

My fond memories of quilts go back to visiting my grandmother in Lodge Grass, Montana and sleeping in a big brass bed under a most elegant velvet and silk, with embroidery crazy quilt. THAT was the company quilt; the every day quilts were patchwork made from scraps, rags, flour, sugar and animal feed sacks, some of the pieces had holes from the original stitching to close the bags, as well as some of the lettering. We cousins would unscrew the big brass ball on the bed leg, and drop our chewing gum inside before settling down for the night. I get a chuckle wondering where that bed went eventually, and how much ossified bubble gum ended up inside its legs.

I own two of Grandma's quilts, and think of the maker often when I am buying new fabrics in a specialty shop. I remember the Trading Post (it's still there!), and how I remember the kerosene lamps (you would put a basin of water by the lamp, with the hope that the moths and millers would knock themselves out while bombarding the light, and drown in the water). Grandmother used a kerosene iron, too. Inaccuracies and bobbles on her quilt tops were simply laid low, with top-stitching on the treadle Singer®! To this day, I have such admiration for really old, and even inaccurately pieced quilts - **a deep appreciation for a**

woman's desire, the NEED to create something both useful, and to her, beautiful, out of nothing - the true and original meaning of the American Patchwork tradition.

As a long time yard and garage sales enthusiast and flea-market addict, I have collected lots of things made by hand - wooden toys and kitchen ware, embroidery, crocheted items, rag rugs, woodwork, hand painted china, cut glass, jewelry, engraved silver, and the like. It was a long time before I realized that my attraction to handwork, was having been raised by parents, Rose and Cecil Milne, who were both master lapidarists; mother did not quilt, but sewed all our clothing, from majorette uniforms to formals (and when we were small, clothing from *other* clothing...). She also paints with oils, dad worked with wood and made a lot of nice furniture. As a lapidarist, he was asked many years ago, to donate a cabochon of Montana agate to the Smithsonian Museum of Natural History in Washington, DC.

My quilt "American as Mom and Apple Pie" is being published in Joen Wolfrom's next book, *The Visual Dance-Creating Spectacular Quilts!* I dedicated my quilt to my daughter, who served 2 years in the Peace Corps in Tanzania, and to her grandmother, and great-grandmother who became American citizens in 1924 (at ages 11 & 48), when Congress passed The American Indian Citizenship Act.

<u>Author's Note:</u> Pat's quilt "American as Mom and Apple Pie" is exquisite! She sent a picture and I was really impressed! No wonder Joen Wolfrom wanted it in her book!

Alice Furrey
Carter, South Dakota
Centennia Quilt Guild
of Winner,
South Dakota

My husband, Harley, and I live on a ranch, 30 miles from any town. We have 3 grown children, Lisa, Vincent, and Paul. I have always been interested in sewing and crafts, and spent 14 years decorating cakes for the neighborhood. After making my first quilt, all my crafting took second place, and now quilting is my job. I own an outlining quilting machine, and make quilts, and do quilting for others, as full time work in my home. Most of the work is done long distance, using the US Mail and UPS.

Ilene L. Burdick
Coudersport,
Pennsylvania
Allegheny Mountain
Quilters

I am currently still living in my Mother's home. The selling of Needlecraft items is my business for the past several years. The main requests are for quilts of all kinds, and baby items. I am extremely interested the field of Genealogy, and have been a member of the DAR for about 5 years. I am also involved in several community groups, and am especially concerned with activities that benefit libraries.

Sarah Bruso
Rhinelander, Wisconsin
Rhinelander Northwoods Quilter's Guild

Currently, I am a retired grandmother who babysits for her 2 grandsons, Ben and Sebastian. For several years my husband, Bob, and I ran our own business, a sports shop. He went into politics and was elected County Clerk, and I retired for the first time. I then returned to work as an accounts receivable clerk, and am retired again, as grandma. I have a daughter Andrea, and two sons, Daniel and Kevin. I am an active member of the Rhinelander Northwoods Quilters, having served as President, club historian, and twice as co-chair for our Quilt Show.

I consider myself an appliquer rather than a piecer, because I like the freedom of applique and I love flowers and what I call true curves.

I am not much of a contest enterer, but when the Fairfield company had a block contest for Baltimore Beauty Blacks, I did enter and my block won an honorable mention. The first class I ever took was one of Elly Sienkiewicz. I fell in love with "Baltimore", and to have Elly judge my block in the Fairfield contest was a real honor. I have only made one full size Baltimore Quilt, and that one won Viewers Choice at our local Quilt Show this year.

My whole family supports my quilting habits, my husband, Bob, has wall hangings in his office at the Court House. My daughter, Andrea, has hangings in her office at the local newspaper and the boys are my critics. Kevin is my color critic, and Dan, my technique critic.

I have not had any formal training or education in art, but I do have a good math background, and I feel that is a great help in quilting.

I have been sewing since I was a young girl, but now that I've found quilting, I find it hard to make clothing.

Doris Callaway,
Greensburg, Kansas
Kansas Quilters Organization
Pratt Area Quilt Guild
Central Kansas Thread Benders of Great Bend

I'm a 4th generation quilter, my mom, grandmother and great grandmother were quilters, and my father crocheted and helped my mom quilt. I've a part of a quilt he and my mother were quilting on the day he was killed...a blue & white snowball.

Marilyn A. Lewis
Glendale, Oregon

I moved to the country 18 years ago, and as I wasn't working and my children were grown, I had lots of time. I had sewn for 30 years, but had never quilted. I decided to take up the hobby, and taught myself how to make quilts. A nice lady showed me how to quilt and I was off and running. My sister's grandchildren got my first ones, but now I quilt for others. Quilt magazines really are helpful.

Laura Estes
Odessa, Washington
Fronen Steppdecker Odessa QG

I'm a professional volunteer, do tutoring, reading, coordinating the local food bank, chairing the Community Christmas Fest, and the Annual quilt Show. I teach quilting occasionally. I worked for 5 1/2 years in a fabric and yarn shop in Marysville, WA. My husband, Patrick, is a great supporter of all my activities and projects, always interested in how the current quilt is progressing. We have 2 cats, El Gato age 13, and Buddie, age 9. Besides quilting, I enjoy gardening, especially flowers.

Dean Valentine
New Braunfels, Texas
New Braunfels Area Quilt Guild
Austin Area Quilt Guild

I am a retired kindergarten teacher and very active quilter. I was the New Braunfels Quilt Show Chairman, and look forward to being their next years Vice-President/Program Chairman. My friend, Teresa, says this is pay back for winning

Meet the Quilters, page 55

the Quilt Show Raffle Quilt, and First Place Winner in the Hand Pieced/King Size Category "Double Wedding Ring".

Christine Miller
Medway, Ohio

Employed by the State of Ohio, as a habilitation specialist. I have two children, Keith age 23, and Tammi, age 21. Three grandchildren: Korey 4 years, Brian 2 years, Kristena 18 months. I'm married to John J. Miller, and have one pet female cat named "Baby". I collect stamps, thimbles, and charms (for quilt making). My interests are World-wide pen-paling and trading charms, cooking, baking, sewing, quilt making, and crafts.

Lois K. Ide
Bucyrus, Ohio

I was born June 3, 1920, on a small farm just outside Swanton, Ohio, which is about 20 miles west of Toledo. My father was a school teacher and taught me the wonderful world of books and nature. My mother was a professional dressmaker, and taught me to use a treadle sewing machine when I was four, and so little that it was necessary for me to stand on one foot, and treadle with the other. By the age of 10, I was making many of my own clothes.

At the time I was not aware of it, but she taught me many of the techniques used by the Baltimore Album Quiltmakers of the 1850's, which she used as decorations on hats and dresses she made for the wealthier ladies of Ohio. Applique, embroidery, ruching and trapunto, took many forms through Mama's skilled and creative fingers. It was not until many years later, that I recalled these wonderful techniques and began teaching them.

Mama also taught me to see designs and colors all around me. She taught me that there was a great difference between looking at something, and really seeing it. Those lessons have been most helpful in many areas in my life.

I graduated from Swanton High School and from the Toledo Hospital School of Nursing, as an R.N. Married a family practice physician, raised three children, and am now the proud grandmother of three, and great-grandmother of three, and most live close enough that my now retired husband, Carl, and I can enjoy them.

I am Life Member of Garden Club of Ohio, Inc. and past board member; am an Accredited Amateur Flower Show Judge; a member of The National Guild of Decoupeurs and past board member; belong to several National Quilt Organizations, and am an honorary member of the Square Tomato Quilter's Guild of The Netherlands.

It was not until 1976, that quilting became really important to me. It was during that bicentennial year, that I was asked by the President of the Garden Club of Ohio, Inc. to represent the State of Ohio, via a quilt block for a quilt to be presented to the National Council of State Garden Clubs President, at the National Council Meeting in Pennsylvania.

In 1978, I entered my first quilting competition with a block entitled *MARY* and was one of the 30 winners in the Stearn-Foster Famous Women and their Accomplishments Contest. I chose *Mary*, simply because of all the famous women of the past, her name is still on the lips of many throughout the world.

In 1983, at the insistence of a friend, I entered my first quilt show. It won Best of Show, and also at the next three quilt competitions. It was THIMBLE ANTHOLOGY, a white on white quilt featuring designs enlarged from antique thimble bands, that really opened wide the doors of the quilting world to me.

In 1988, my WORLD PEACE quilt was one of the 41 finalists, in the first international competition sponsored by Quilter's Newsletter Magazine, and was displayed in Salzburg, Austria at Quilt Expo Europa I. In 1989, it was "discovered" by UNICEF, and was printed as a UNICEF greeting card in Geneva, Switzerland for their European collection.

In 1988, I was awarded an Ohio Arts Council Grant, and taught quilting in the Traditional Arts division. My students work was shown at our local newly renovated library and well over 1000 visitors signed in.

In 1993, I was again asked to represent the state of Ohio, via a segment for a Christmas tree for the Blue Room of the White House. At 7:30 a.m., I received a call from the White House, asking if I would be willing to do this. I really thought this was a prank call, until the piece of green velvet and instructions for the tree skirt segment, was delivered by priority mail, two days later from the White House. Also in 1993, I was asked to do some writing for McCall's 1996 Quilt Engagement Calendar, edited by Cyril I. Nelson of Penquin Books.

Once again, I am asked to represent the state of Ohio. My quilts and I have been included in over 35 books, calendars and magazines, and it is always a thrill to be asked to contribute, and in most cases being paid for most, making quilts, and sharing and writing about them.

Author's Note: Look for her beautiful WORLD PEACE QUILT on the back of Quilt Magazines in the Fairfield ad.

Grace Moone
High Falls, New York
Little Apple Quilters

I have "alter-ego's". I work with my husband in a Country Grocery Store. I also substitute teach in the elementary school, and mornings I'm not subbing - I am the Volunteer Computer Coordinator for my daughter's elementary school...and between..I quilt for myself, and for 3 craft shows I participate in.

Merry May
Tuckahoe, New Jersey
South Shore Stitchers
Tri-State
Quilt making
Teachers

I have been making quilts since 1978, and began collecting antique quilts in 1985. This led to an interest in quilt history, and ultimately led to becoming a teacher of Basic Quilt making in 1988. I taught Basic classes for the next five years, while expanding my knowledge of quilt making, fine-tuning my techniques, and exploring many of the opportunities which quilt making can offer.

In addition, I now offer a number of lectures and workshops. I also do small-scale commission work, design my own patterns, and have won many awards for my quilt making. In 1994, I invented and developed a new product called "Gridded Geese", which (at last) allows one to mass-produce Flying Geese units using a unique paper foundation.

Pauline A. Cook
Idaho Falls, Idaho
Sanke River Valley
Quilt Guild

I've been married 31 years to my husband, Terry. We have 2 children, Christi and T.L., a son-in-law-Gregg, granddaughter-Brianne and a future daughter-in-law, Wendy. I've lived in 6 states.

I work part time in the Circulation Dept. at Idaho Falls Public Library. My husband and I trapshoot. My hobbies include: Quilting, Counted Cross Stitch, Crafting, Reading and Sewing. I have been quilting for 7 years. I have entered several challenges through our local quilt shop and the Quilt Guild.

Jacque' J. Holmes
Big Bear Lake,
California
Busy Bear Quilt Guild

I am a Mom, Grammy and Quilter.....Bona Fide and Obsessive Quilter. Not only that, Quilting has become a source of solace and refuge through some tough times. This past year has been very difficult. I lost my husband, and three weeks later, my brother died. With my wonderful family and very loving and supportive friends, I've been able to survive.

I've been quilting *seriously*, since the latter part of '85' when I opened a quilt shop in Big Bear Lake, after my husband and I retired to our mountain dream home. But after a couple of years, I realized that it is much more fun to just teach, lecture, and to reproduce my own designs into patterns. One of my favorite students is my 14 year old granddaughter, Jessica. This year she made a large *Trip around Boston Commons* Quilt for her four poster bed.

I frequently hear people turning down a class on some new quilt or method, because they haven't finished some one, four or ten other projects. Personally, I never let that stand in my way. Because I feel I have so much yet to learn. And that class I turned down could furnish me with that one trick that could open a whole new world. Those P.I.P.'S (Projects in progress) will wait. Sometimes you don't finish a project, because you are stumped over a portion of the design or method. One of those classes might produce the answer. Sometimes all you need, is to talk it out with a friend. Who knows where that answer will pop up!

Penny Hand
Woodbridge, Virginia

I was born and raised in Kansas City, Kansas and lived in Manhattan/Ft. Riley for 6 years. Have an Art Education Degree from Kansas State University, I teach High School Art, full time in Manassas, Virginia. I began quilting in '85' (seriously). My husband, Bill, is a Colonel in the US Army, retiring in May. We have 2 sons. Jeff is 25 and a KSU graduate. Jon is a VA Tech student on a baseball scholarship. We have 2 Boston Terrier dogs, KC and Cody.

Arla Schaap
Holland, Michigan
Tulip Patchers

I am retired, after working 30 years as a medical secretary. My husband, Les, is semi-retired. Together, we enjoy golfing, bowling, travel. We have one son Rick, one daughter Virginia, one grandson, Tanner Lee, who is loved very much by his grandma and grandpa.

Over the years I have enjoyed doing counted cross stitch, knitting, crochet, crafts, and sewing. My affection for sewing comes from my mother. Her gentleness and patience instilled in me, an appreciation and satisfaction for making both useful and wearable things. During the depression she sewed all the clothes for my 3 brothers and me. I remember wearing snow-pants (leggings), and mittens made from car upholstery my dad ripped out of old cars. Every winter I would be raw, where that rough upholstery rubbed between my legs.

I sewed many clothes for my children, when they were small. I still sew for myself today, but other projects and activities have somewhat limited my time for this. I occupy a chair in our church choir, because I like to sing, and they like the chairs filled. There are several activities under Women's Ministries at our church, and I seem to be involved in most of them.

Three years ago, I organized a group to sew full-size quilts for International Aid and also baby quilts for ABC Quilts. We call ourselves the Sew-Few Quilters (we're hoping to change that someday to Sew-Many!! Quilters).

Eleanor Burenheide
Emporia, Kansas
Emporia Regional
Quilters Guild
Kansas Quilter's
Organization

I was raised in a family with three brothers in Lincoln, NE. My husband, Leo, was a Kansas farmer and hog producer. I was Home Ec. Department Head at Emporia High School. We have a son, Keith, and a daughter, Nancy. Each was extremely active in 4-H and High School activities. They had horses and were competitive at showmanship, roping and rodeo events. We all enjoyed boating, swimming and water skiing. Keith enjoys hunting and fishing, while Nancy has become an avid bicyclist. We now see our four grandchildren following in their parents steps. Leo and I still boat, and in the winter, we swim daily. We are now retired, and have moved to town. My husband became the chief chef, we share the housekeeping details and then we each have our hobbies.

Author's Note: I have to say a few words about Eleanor. She was one of the first persons I met at The Emporia Regional Quilter's Guild. She was extremely friendly, and made me feel very welcome. She mentioned the Bag Ladies Team. She and Colleen Greider present Programs, dressed as two *bag ladies*, occasionally even using a shopping cart to carry their bags full of goodies! They show 60 or 70 bags and totes, and explain how they were made and their uses. It's a very popular program. Eleanor and her husband, Leo, are two of those rare persons who are willing to help with whatever is needed.

Martha A. De Turk
Kutztown,
Pennsylvania

Lucky enough to be a full time homemaker, 35 years. Enjoyed being a stay-at-home Mom of 4, and now grandmother of 8. Provide day care for my grandchildren on part-time basis, and spend many hours doing patchwork, quilting and other calico crafts. Do lots of volunteer work for Women in Crisis (Shelter for Abused Women), my Church, and am Chairman of our local Historical Society Quilt Show and Sale. My husband is an elementary school teacher and avid golfer. My hobbies are, of course quilting, walking and enjoying the outdoors.

Kathleen Nyman
Oswego, New York
Lake County Quilt Guild

I am a stay-at-home Mom with 4 children-3, 6, 10 and 15. I belong to Lake County Quilt Guild, which meets once a month. With the schedule I keep, I have more ideas than time. And lots of unfinished projects.

I started out only doing *cheater* panels - it took two years before I pieced, and then only by hand. Now I machine piece, but still hand quilt. I've been a quilter for about 8 years.

I have long, cold winters, so that's a good incentive to finish things.

Virginia H. Flowers
Flushing, Michigan
Genesee Star Quilters

Yes, I work. I'm a domestic engineer, my husband says. My husband, Bob, and I have been married for 39 years. We have 4 daughters; Kimberly, Kathy, Kristi, and Karyn. 2 sons-in-law, and 1 soon-to-be son in law, and 4 3/4 grandchildren. My hobbies are quilting, camping and traveling. I was in 4-H from the 6th grade thru high school, in the sewing and leadership programs, and have taken numerous sewing classes in knit wear, lingerie and crafts.

As our girls grew up, the need for clothing declined, so I started quilting. My idea was to make a quilt for each bed. We live in an older home, and have a lot of collectables. I enjoyed using my clothing scraps to make my first quilt. No one told me that I shouldn't use my double knit polyesters. After a number of tries, I decided I should take some quilting classes. My first teacher was Hilda Hoag. She was a student and friend of Mary Schafer. Between the two of them, I learned a lot. My sister and I have quilted a number of tops for Mary since. We hired ourselves out quilting tops for others and paid our way to a Marston and Cunningham Quilt Retreat on Beaver Island.

I started quilting about 1972. I joined the Genesee Star Quilters in 1985. Over the years, I have completed over 80 quilts in various styles and sizes. I enjoy piecing by hand, and machine and hand quilting. Most of my quilts go to family members and special friends. A few have been donated to various community organizations, for fund raisers.

As a member of Genesee Star Quilters I have held the office of Secretary for 2 terms, as President for 1 term, and Co-coordinator of our 2 Quilt Shows. I have been fortunate enough to have received a few Viewer's Choice awards at 3 different Shows.

Bernice Tessibel Inman Cashman (Tessie)
Coal City, Indiana
Clay City
Calico Quilters

I was a Home Economics and Physical Education teacher, before my marriage to John Cashman in 1970. A career change was made to full time homemaker and mother. Our children, Michael and Kimberly, are both college students now. We moved five years ago, from the western suburbs of Chicago back to the rural Indiana area, where we grew up. A life long dream of living in a home in the woods, became a reality. My pet cat is named Patchwork. In addition to my interest in sewing and all things quilted, I am a beginning oil painter. Retirement gives me time to pursue lifetime interests.

Mary R. Canning
Lincoln, Rhode Island
Narraggansett Bay Quilter's Association

16 years ago when I was 65, a group at the Church decided to continue meeting weekly following a year of doing crafts for a fair. Someone suggested learning to quilt, beginning with pillows. I am not a pillow-person, so I took sewing along. When I saw the lovely Ohio Star patterns taking shape, I became envious, and then hooked, and made three pillows, while the others were making one.

My first quilt was a quilt-as-you-go sampler, using twelve 18 inch squares. It was bright red, bright green, a dark blue print, and a white print! I sandwiched each square with thick batting, and bright red was on the back. I was really proud of that quilt, big stitches and all. I began to go to quilt shows, subscribe to quilting magazines, and saw a lot of things wrong with that quilt. My daughter loved it, and I have expressed a desire to re-quilt it, but she won't bring it back. My other daughter, my son, my sister-in-law who cared for Mother, my dentist who wanted a quilt instead of money for a denture, have all gotten quilts. 10 years ago, on our 50th Wedding Anniversary, I gave three married granddaughters, quilts. As each grandchild establishes a home, he or she gets a quilt. An attachment to my will states that the children are to divide the big quilts, and the grandchildren and great-grandchildren will receive wall hangings, after I have given some to friends.

16 years later, I am just as enthusiastic about quilting, and wonder how I'm going to use all the fabric I have. I've lost track of how many items I've made. One of these days, I must work on the scrap book I intend to make.

I subscribe to 7 quilt magazines, and am a fabricholic. I tell myself I will just look, but fabric speaks to me! I always had a consuming hobby - oil painting, afgans, genealogy (when stamps were 6 cents), but quilting has taken over. There's hardly enough time to read anymore!

I have a large quilt ready to sandwich, a wall hanging ready to quilt, a wall hanging I designed using fabric with musical instruments on it for my son, a Christmas Tree wall hanging ready for the embellishments, and 30 2-inch squares, using Christmas fabric, to be used as Christmas decorations for relatives and friends, a tradition I started about 5 years ago.

Several years ago, I saw an old red and white Ohio Star quilt hanging on the porch railing at an antique store. I stopped, but it was barely hanging together-- too much to repair. However, inside the shop was a box of squares, half muslin and half feed sack material. I took my treasures home, washed them, and spread them on any flat place on my back porch. The colors were bright and beautiful. There were several different sizes of squares, and several different kinds of muslin, but I arranged them and rearranged them, until I had enough to make a crib quilt. Later, the antique dealer found 13 Dresden Plate squares made from old fabric, which I bought. The background fabric was very stiff, but there was not doubt in my mind that I could wash the stiffness out. Not only did it not wash out, it shrank, and the two reds ran! I took them apart and appliqued them onto new muslin. I used three plain muslin squares, and quilted the Dresden Plate pattern on them. It is my husband's favorite lap quilt.

I attended the Vermont Quilt Festival and bought a packet of 20 old 9-patch squares. I could use all but two of them. They sat in a box, waiting for an inspiration about putting them together. I made new red and blue 9-patches, using them as part of the sashing. They were made of scraps, because several squares had different scraps, but I think that is part of it's charm.

I became interested in feed sack fabric, or as someone said, "Chicken Linen", after seeing an article in a quilt magazine about Jane Clark Staple, who has organized a "Feed Sack Club", which is made up of people who want to buy, sell or trade squares, or whole sacks. I accumulated enough fabric to make a quilt using a variation of the Job's Tears pattern. It is the *quilt-in-progress* at the present time.

I belong to the Narragansett Bay Quilter's Association, an all-state group which meets once a month to hear a speaker, or to show-and-tell. A quilter, chosen by the members, shows off her work at each meeting. Our church continues to meet once a week, and we hold a quilt show each April. Not many are quiltaholics like I am, so we have to ask friends who contribute each year. We have had 13 very successful shows. A very small group, the QB's, meet at my house once a month, we sit and chat and quilt and show!!

<u>Author's Note:</u> Mary mentioned Jane Clark Staple and the *Feed Sack Club*. You will find Jane's answers in the other sections of this book. Jane did not submit any information for the Bio section, but check out her great answers in the other sections.

Meet the Quilters

Ruth E. O'Connor
Burlington, Massachusetts
Burlington Quilter's Guild

Lady at Leisure! I belong to The Garden Club and Historical Society. I press flowers and teach making pressed flower pictures, etc. I love to hand piece and hand quilt. I made a king-sized Sampler Wedding Quilt in 3 months, with loads of hand quilting for my son and daughter-in-law. I am a Volunteer Guide at the New England Quilt Museum in Lowell, Mass. I'm Publicity Person for the Burlington QG. And I was just flabbergasted to have my quilt *Tom's Amish Cabin* selected from over 1,000 quilts, to be exhibited at the New England Images 4 Quilt Show.

Anna Eelman
North Plainfield, New Jersey
Harvest Quilters

I work out of my home part-time, and have a home office to do free lance work. I am also publisher of a bi-monthly Fabric Club Newsletter, and co-columnist for a Quarterly Quilting Magazine.

I am a Mother to four grown children (Dawn, Less, Bret, and Luke), and am married for 2nd time to Anton, for 18 years. I grew up in urban New Jersey and came late to quilting after years of doing other kinds of needlework. It was a natural progression, other interests include reading, writing, the study of women's history, and spectator sports like ice hockey and auto racing. In general, I am interested in the world around me.

In 1972, I was a single parent with 3 kids, and found no wholesome forum for meeting adult singles, so I started a singles ministry in my church, and continued to help run it many years after I remarried. Likewise, when I became interested in quilting and there was no local quilt guild, I started one, and that Guild will hold it's 12th annual Quilt Show in April.

Betty M. Abel
Sheboygan, Wisconsin

I've taught Quilting for our local Tech. College for ten years, also travel to Guilds and Clubs to teach. Taught in England, and made a tape on *Smashing Attic Windows* for Cable TV. After fifty years, I've recently become a widow. My sewing machine and quilting has helped me through lots of lonely nights. Have a spoiled cat named Lucy, who naps on my ironing board when I sew.

Mary J. Ruda
Elida, Ohio
West Central Ohio Quilt Guild

I was born and raised in Kansas, have been in Ohio for 28 years. We have 3 children, 1 boxer dog, and live in the country, which we love. I have a studio in my home. My husband and I have a printing business. My husband's name is Richard. I do work full time, so my quilting time is limited.

Georgina Doss
Milton, West Virginia
Creative Quilters of Huntington, West Virginia

I baby sit in my home for my friend's 2-year old tornado, named Zachary. My daughter, Rebecca, is in the first grade. I have done volunteer work at the local library for the past 5 1/2 years. Every Wednesday morning, I have a story time for children from birth to age three, called Lap Sit. I have had the children make their own crazy quilt squares for one of the summer craft projects. I have also taught quilting classes for children and have done demonstrations in the local elementary school.

Barbara G. Pietila
Baltimore, Maryland
The African American Quilters of Baltimore
The American Quilter's Society

All of my children (I have three) are adults and not longer living at home. I have six grandchildren.

For many years I worked in the medical field. I retired from dental hygiene in 1984, to move to Moscow with my husband, and lived there for four years. It

Meet the Quilters, page 61

was there, because of the shortage of quality cotton fabric, that I began to do applique. I found this was what I had been looking for all my life. Now I do pictorials, almost exclusively.

I draw inspiration for my work from my everyday life and my childhood, which is rich with conversations, memories of relatives, places, and special occasions. I believe that all African American quilts tell stories, either in the history of the fabric, the pattern, or in the making of the quilt. I try to carry on that tradition by creating scenes, which give the viewer some idea of who we are. In addition to founding the National African American Quilters, which is headquartered in Baltimore, I am also a member of Fiber Artist Network of Maryland, and The Women of Color Quilter's Network.

As a Fiber Artist/arts and Crafts Teacher, I have taught many classes, one of which was for the Howard County Center of African American Culture, Inc. In this class we gained insight into the use of design, and the step-by-step quilting process to create a design called the North Star, which appeared on quilts during the running of the Underground Railroad. The quilts were hung and used as directional maps, to assist freeing slaves in finding the route north to freedom.

I teach quilting to senior citizens, through a city program now and enjoy working with this group tremendously. In addition to teaching, I exhibit and sell my work.

My Quilt Exhibits have been shown at The Houston International Quilt Festival, and numerous galleries, colleges, and museums, including:

The Mansion Art Gallery of
   Rockville, MD
The National Civil Rights
   Museum, Memphis, TN
The National Afro-American
   Museum and Cultural
   Center, Wilberforce, Ohio
American Museum of Quilts and
   Textiles, San Jose, CA
Junior Black Academy, Dallas
Quiltfest, Louisville, KY
Morgan State University
Kimball Art Center,
   Park City, Utah
City Hall, Baltimore, MD
Fiber Artist Network,
   Silverspring, MD
Montplier Plantation,
   Laurel, MD
The Baltimore Life Gallery
   Owings Mills, MD
Hampton University Museum
Beadworks, Baltimore, MD
The Breast Cancer Center,
   Washington, DC
The Enoch Library, Baltimore
Artscape, Baltimore
Gypsy's Cafe, Baltimore
George Washington University.
   Hospital, Washington, DC
Eubie Blake National Museum
   and Cultural Center

Quilting is the most satisfying thing I have ever tried. Certainly more fun than health care, by a long shot. Quilting everyday keeps the doctor away!

<u>Author's Note:</u> In an article written by Lynn Honeywell, he says, "Barbara Pietila's Quilts are actually pictures made of fabric and they abound with double meanings. One message is slyly laid over another, much like her cloth artwork is made up of one layer of fabric appliqued over another. Life, like a quilt, consists of many layers of meaning, and so it is with Pietila's works."

Linda Boedigheimer
Perham, Minnesota
East Ottertail
   Unfinished
   Objects Quilters

I am an elementary/geography teacher, and an interior designer, by education. However, as time passed, I discovered that I much preferred quilting and picture framing. So today, I enjoy framing within my sister Sarah's shop, Bay Window Crafts in Perham, and it is in that shop I have taught hand piecing, applique, and quilting. My family members have become my critics and inspiration. Quilting decorates my husband Dan's dental office. Our daughter, Melissa, received graduation and wedding quilts. Our daughter, Angela, received a graduation *picture* quilt. Our grandson, Scott, just received a Noah's Ark quilt. Our cat, Mittens, just sits on quilts. My Christian background has also led me to design a Biblical Sampler.

Sheryl Mielke
McGregor, Iowa
Northeast Iowa
   Quilter's Guild
Mississippi Valley Q G

I am one of those homemakers that also works in the home. My husband, Wayne, and I have a family business, Meilke's Quarry, which we operate with the help of our son, Lance. We own a quarry and sell and deliver rock products and limestone to farmers and contractors. My duties include secretary, bookkeeper, receptionist, dispatcher and loader operator. My son is married, and has given us one grandchild and are expecting a second. I also have a daughter employed at a local bank. We live in the beautiful hills of N.E. Iowa, adjacent to a trout stream and Spook Cave, a tourist attraction. There are frequent sightings of deer and wild turkeys.

Susan J. Spencer
Felton, California

Born and raised in California, I am married and have 2 sons, William and Daniel. I took six months leave of absence from my job when William was born 12 1/2 years ago, and still haven't gone back. My husband, Michael, is a graphic artist and illustrator, now doing publications art. He is my *color consultant*, when I need advice for a quilt, and very helpful and supportive. In addition to quilting, I enjoy gardening and reading, and I collect and make teddy bears. I also volunteer several hours per week at my son's school.

Doris J. Haggard
Topeka, Kansas
Topeka Rose Guild
Indiana State
Quilt Guild

I have been an Elementary School Custodian for nearly 20 years, I'll retire March 31 of next year. Maybe more time for quilting!

I had my first pieced quilt in the floor frame at the time of the blizzard of 1978. I was very lucky to have two very good neighbors, who were quilters. It was great to have help getting that first one in the frame.

I had grown up with quilts in the family, so I had a general knowledge of the project. I never had a class till I attended the State Quilt Guild meeting in Elkart, the fall of 1993.

Two of my quilting sisters, Sue Christner and Gen Lehman, and I were magazine cover girls for the fall/winter 1991 issue of Heritage Country Magazine, published in Middlebury, IN. It was a quilt related issue, so we and our quilts were featured on the cover. This is one issue of that magazine that sold completely out.

In 1993 at the Topeka Quilt Show and Sale, we three were interviewed by a local man, Art Oswald for a video. They also videoed our show and this video is supposed to be for sale. At this time we have not seen it.

Sue Christner started a quilt show in 1974, at the Honeyville Store. Later, she moved it to the Shipshewana Bank in Topeka. Gen and I started to help her. After 10 years, she turned it over to us and the Topeka United Methodist Church, as they had built a Fellowship Hall, so Gen and I have co-chaired this event, and will have the 21st Annual Topeka Quilt Show and Sale the week of July 12-15. We use the Topeka Rose as our logo.

I have been the quilt lady at a couple of local pioneer fall festivals, and it is a very rewarding time to visit with the people.

We were lucky enough to get to help with the Indiana State Quilt Registry project. Sue, Gen and I went to South Bend. We were so excited to be there, Gen locked her keys in the car. It was a very exciting time to check out all those old quilts for their history.

Sue had an Amish Quilt published in the book, *Quilts of Indiana: Crossroads of Memories*. This was the book that was published after the State registry was completed. We went to Indianapolis, to the Indiana State Museum for the quilt showing and reception.

We were overnight guests of Gen's daughter and her son. The son said, "Grandmother and her quilting posse are coming for the night." So, as a posse, we have been out chasing fabric and quilt shows for a long time.

We take many photos, get the second set of prints, and exchange them. I have many albums of happy, colorful quilts from many places.

Marcia Knopp
Bay City, Michigan
Bay Heritage Quilters

I am a dentist. I work about 4 days a week. I'm single - with a cat, and try to use a lot of my free time quilting. I've been quilting for about seven years and still consider myself to have a lot to learn. Living in

Michigan, I've always kind of dreaded the arrival of winter, but I find that's when most of my quilting gets done. Summer is spent in the yard and garden.

Linda Ballard
Palo Cedro, California
Quilters Sew-ciety
of Redding

I'm married with two grown children. I had a quilt/cross stitch store for six years with a partner. We closed it three years ago, so now my job (if you want to call it that) is teaching quilting at 6 different quilt shops, plus occasionally doing a workshop with guilds.

My icing on the *cake* is my *Mystery Quilting Retreats* that I sponsor six times a year. Those are truly wonderful!!! Thirty-eight ladies at each session will escape from their homes, families, jobs and responsibilities for 3 days to do what we all love---quilt!

The retreats are a great getaway even for myself---I'm always learning something new from someone. I love showing the ladies all the little tricks and techniques that make their quilt tops go together faster and easier. My retreats, and having owned a shop, are 2 of my 4 goals I've set for myself. Someday, maybe 3 and 4 will happen!

Author's Note: I have asked the next two quilters, Judi and Nancy, to write of their unusual partnership. They appeared at our Guild, and I loved their story. I think you will, too! You'll find it after Nancy's bio.

Judi Robb
Manhattan, Kansas
Konza Prairie
       Quilters Guild
Kaw Valley
       Quilters Guild
Kansas Quilters
       Organization

I have a supportive husband, Mark, and 1 teenage daughter, Kelly. Our dog, Frosty, keeps me company during the day when I sew and quilt, and generally keeps her opinions to herself. I've sewn since I was a little girl. Majoring in clothing & textiles at KSU. I worked for about 20 years, and then retired and took up quilting. I like to read, go to auctions, and quilt.

Nancy Wagner Graves
Manhattan, Kansas
Konza Prairie
       Quilter's Guild

I've sewn since I was a teenager, and enjoyed doing all kinds of crafts. Once I tried quilting, I was hooked. I still sew some of my clothes, but quilting takes up most of my time. I have one husband (Steve), and two sons (Chris & Jonathan). My family is very supportive of my quilting, and know that sometimes the laundry and housework aren't done, until I've finished my quilt.

THE STORY OF TWO QUILTERS NAMED NANCY & JUDI!

We both joined our local Quilt Guild the same month. And, we both took our first workshop, together, the following month. Seems like it was fate, that we became best friends.

We found we had a lot in common - school age children, 1 husband each, loved baskets and bears, and we both enjoyed learning every new quilting technique offered. We have taken over 80 workshops together over the last 7 years.

Our tastes in fabric are almost amazingly identical. We have gone to quilt stores separately, and discovered later, we bought the same fabrics. It's a great benefit for us, because if one of us runs short of a fabric, the other usually has some and will, under threat, share!

We also find that we encourage each other to do things we might not do, alone. One of us will see a contest and talk the other into entering with her. Also, if we get stuck on a quilt and need advice, the other can usually come up with a solution.

Recently, a guild member talked us into giving a program at her guild. So now we're on the road together, giving a trunk show of some of the quilts we've made.

I think finding each other was one of the best things that has happened to us. Every time there's a quilt show or a fabric sale, we always know we have a partner to take along, who will enjoy it just as much.

Fanny Naught
Quincy, Illinois

Except for the first one and half years of my married life, my *job* has been home and family exclusively. With five children, school, basketball, scouts, little league baseball, and the never ending shopping trips with my girls, has been a full time job.

My husband is a building contractor, and it was my "job" to keep the books in reasonable order. All this kept me from having any time for hobbies, such as quilting at that time.

My mother did some quilting, when I was home. She made a quilt for me and my sister out of the scraps from dresses we wore. This inspired me to do the same. So, while my girls were growing up, I kept scraps, too, and for each of the four girls I made a quilt from the first 21 years of their life. They really appreciate them, and I am glad that I did. These were four-patch type, and required very little imagination. Since then, I like to think I have *come a long way, Baby*.

I am now more interested in applique. When our first grandson was born, I was inspired to make the *Transportation* quilt for him. That really started a trend. Now, we have ten grandchildren, and I find myself in a real hole. It takes me about two years to complete one quilt. Of course, there are other things going on during that time. I am currently ready to quilt a Dogwood pattern, which is the fifth quilt in line. I do all hand-quilting, and hand applique. I do use my machine to sew blocks, etc. together.

I have a sister that lives a few blocks away, and she is into the quilting mode, too, so it is fun to compare and talk quilting any day of the week.

Betty A. Lenz
Marshall, Missouri
Country Patchers QG

I have been quilting for many years (over 20). My first two quilts have all the knots on the back - I learned the hard way. I am a confirmed Purist, have cleaned out all the poly blends, love the cotton & wool battings, and only hand quilt my finished pieces. My husband, Jack, and our three grown sons and their families are very supportive & encouraging in my quilting life. I have been entering national competitions since 1990.

Dort Lee
Leicester,
North Carolina
Asheville Quilt Guild

I have a college degree in art and film-making. After teaching several years, I r*etired* to raise 2 children and some cows & goats & chickens & a large garden. (All of whom provide me with ideas for my applique quilts.) My husband, Charly, brings home the *bacon*, I bring home the beef. He cuts the firewood to keep us warm, and I make the quilts to keep us warm. We're a great partnership!

Bettie Rushin
Boulder Creek, California
Pajaro Valley Quilt Ass'n.

I am a full-time Quilt-Artist. This in essence, means that I am compulsively making quilts, or trying to devote forty hours a week to quilting. I have taught quilting classes for a number of years, and have had a One Woman Show, curated two local quilt shows for our county, been a featured artist at our local guild, and have been included in a show at the Santa Cruz Art League. However, I also am a full-time mother of five children: Steven 13, Michelle 12, Jennifer 12 (yes, they are twins), Samantha 8, and Maxwel 5. In my motherhood role, I drive at least two hours a day, wipe noses twenty minutes a day, help with homework one hour a day, help coach on a soccer team, work in the kindergarten classroom, dilemmas on a minute to minute basis. In my spare time I read, listen to Rock and Roll music, talk on the phone and sleep.

Beth Donaldson
Lansing, Michigan
Capitol City Quilt Guild

I can finally say with authority, that I am a professional quilter! I began quilting in 1983, when my daughter Katy was a toddler. To get out of the house and talk to grown women again, I took a class at Pepper Cory's Shop, Culpepper's Quilts. (See Author's Note at end of Beth's bio.) That led to dabbling in craft shows and wearable art, and then teaching for community education. A small town quilt shop opened a branch in our "big city", and I taught there for three hectic years. It was the perfect way to make extra money, work around my kid's schedule (by this time I had my daughter, Colleen), be a brownie leader, school volunteer, neighborhood activist, fabulous cook, wonderful housekeeper, devoted wife to Tom, quilt show chair, quilt retreat sponsor and totally ruined my health! This led to a period of withdrawal from many activities, except for sponsoring my quilt retreat, and feeding my dog, Mickey. I slowly emerged from the fog, and began setting my priorities in order. Currently I am editing my first book. It is titled *Block by Block* and is being published by That Patchwork Place, and will be released next summer.

Author's Note: Congratulations, Beth! We'll be looking for your book. Also, I'd like give a note of thanks to Pepper Cory for a column she wrote in QNM about her Singer® Featherweight sewing machine, and how great it was for sewing quilts, and for carrying to workshops. Because of that column, I decided I wanted a Featherweight. Not knowing the value of such machines, I ran an ad in our local paper asking for a used one. A nice lady answered my ad, invited me to her home to see her machine, and offered to sell it to me for $25. It looked to be in mint condition, with all of the original accessories and case, plus buttonholer and zig zag attachments, and it was the special Anniversary Edition. Remember, I didn't know the value, so I paid her the $25 and carried it home.

When I got to thinking about it, I told my husband, Don, "I think I *stole* that machine!" I checked with others, and was astounded at what Featherweights® were selling for. I felt guilty! I phoned to lady and told her I felt I had paid too little for it. She assured me that if I was going to use it myself, had no intentions of selling it, and planned to keep it and care for it.....she was happy with the $25! I felt much better....and wouldn't part with my little Featherweight for anything! If you want one....try advertising in your local paper...you just might get a call!

∞∞∞∞∞∞∞∞∞∞∞∞∞∞∞∞∞∞∞∞

M. Jeanne Poore
Overland Park,
Kansas
Starlight QG, Nitetime Needlers
Kansas Quilters Guild
Missouri State Quilters Guild

I was born in my grandparent's home, outside of Morrowville, Ks. My great grandmother, Elsie Ann Robinson Enfield, was born in January 1858, in Indiana and moved to Kansas in 1879. She lived to 97. She had started a quilt for my brother Gary Keith Enfield (a bow tie), which I finished--the first quilt I remember making. My paternal grandmother, Mildred Bell Wolf Enfield, born 1898 in Washington, Ks, and my maternal grandmother, Addah Vera Strayer Menzies, were both quilters. I remember them quilting when I was young, quilted with them when I got older, and have quilts made by both of them, a wonderful remembrance and heritage to be passed on to my children.

I am married to Larry L. Poore, and have two grown children, a daughter, Natalie, and a son, Darryl. Darryl is married and has three children; Daniel 8, Krista 20 months, and Kayla, born Oct. 2, 1994. Both children, all grandchildren, my parents, my father-in-law, my brother, his children and grandchildren, all have quilts that I have made. My husband and I have Brittany dogs. From the female, Taffy, we have the fifth generation, there is even a quilt with dog bones appliqued on it with all their names!

I think I was always a quilter, from making doll quilts, as a child to the current time. I took sewing in school, but could sew before that. I remember making skirts on my Grandmother Menzie's treadle machine, and making doll clothes. My cousins and I played, while Grandma quilted. My Grandma Enfield also made quilts. I quilted with family and on my own, during the years of raising the children, working part-time, then full-time. When I changed jobs in 1986, I told my husband I wanted to find a Guild that met at night (I had taken some classes at the local shops). I started with the Starlight Guild, and that led to others in quick order.

I've held various offices, and have served on the board of directors for the Missouri State QG, served as a liaison with volunteers for the Quilts Unlimited Kansas City Show. I've taught classes for Johnson County Parks and Rec for four years, taught workshops for my Guilds and others, do programs for guilds, schools and other organizations.

Helen M. Ericson
Emporia, Kansas
Emporia Regional
Quilter Guild
Northeast Kansas QG

I am a native Kansan, married 45 years, and have 2 sons, and 3 grandchildren. I took Home Ec. in school and participated in 4-H Club. In 1970, I purchased the Mrs. Danner's Pattern business, which I continue to operate. I was named a Master Folk Artist for Quilt making in 1985, and have had several Apprentices study under me. I do talks and workshops, display at Folklife Festivals and at the Kansas Museum of History. I am more interested in Traditional Quilt making and preserving it's history, and have an extensive collection of patterns, clippings, books and old blocks.

I write for the Baldwin Ledger, and have had quilts and articles in several magazines. I have made over 200 quilts, which I hope my descendants will cherish for many generations. I judge at County and State Fairs, and have been invited to show at several locations over the country. My husband and I enjoy traveling to quilt shows, historic sites, and along the Oregon and Santa Fe Trails.

Author's Note: Helen is so knowledgeable about quilts and quilting. Whenever questions arise, Helen has the answer. She is a prolific quilter and quite a historian. She is a charter member of The Emporia Regional Quilters Guild, and has won many awards.

Pat Reep
Bakersfield, California
Cotton Patch
Quilt Guild

I grew up in Monterey, California and met and married by husband, Ed, during World War II. He was a combat artist for the army at that time and was stationed in Monterey. He is a prominent artist, author and teacher of national recognition. We have four children, Susan, Cris, Janine, and Mitchell, seven grandchildren, and one very new great-grand-daughter, with another on the way. We have two very spoiled but appreciative cats, Jezebel and Joaquin. We raised our family in Los Angeles and moved to North Carolina in early 1970. My husband took a position as professor of painting, and artist-in-residence at East Carolina University, and it was at this time, that I became interested in stitchery and subsequently quilt making.

I taught needlework, and then quilting, for ten years at a community college. I also taught two workshops for the National Quilting Association--one in Bethesda, Maryland, and the other in Baltimore, Maryland. I was co-chairman of an annual quilt symposium in N.C. in 1983, which featured prominent quilt teachers and judges. I am a past president of the Greensville, N.C. Quilter's Guild.

We returned to California in 1985 and now live in Bakersfield, where I continue to quilt and teach. I am a member and past V.P. and President of Cotton Patch Quilters, which is a very active and productive guild.

I have received teaching certification by Valentine Textile Museum Certification Program in Richmond, Virginia. I have been published in a number of publications, including the National Quilters Assoc. Quarterly May 1983 and August 1984, the Quilt Art Engagement Calendar 1994, and have had a number of exhibitions, one being a Solo exhibition at Tubac Center of the Arts at Tubac, Arizona 1988.

My husband has been a wonderful influence in my work, and has taught me much about color and design. His appreciation of my quilts has been of great satisfaction to me, as we sometimes critique one another's work. I also like to garden and read, but quilting is at the top of the list.

Catherine Litwinow
Davenport, Iowa
Mississippi Valley
Quilters Guild
Iowa Quilter's Guild

My love of quilting began in 1980. I am a fourth generation Iowa quilter. I see quilting as a connection thread to the past, and a record of the present for the future. I hold memberships in the American Quilter's Society, National Quilting Association, American Quilt Study Group, Iowa Quilter's Guild, and Mississippi Valley QG. I taught Home Economics for 18 years, and currently teach quilting for Scott Community College. My work has been displayed at a number of Galleries and my quilts have won numerous awards, both locally and on the State level. My quilts were featured in the October 1994 issue of Quilting Today Magazine.

I helped with the documentation for both the Iowa and Illinois Quilt Research Projects. I've been active with the *Quilt Ladies* from the Mississippi Valley Quilter's Guild, we demonstrate at many local events. I am serving the Iowa Guild, as Pres-elect and will be President next year. My husband, Bill (who is an engineer), and I have one son, Mark, who is a freshman at Iowa State, and we have a cocker spaniel, Sandy. My day job is Career Alternatives Specialist, encouraging women to explace non-traditional career options. Good thing I'm Rosie the Riveter by Day, Becky Home Ecky at night.

Author's Note: I didn't know Catherine when I telephoned her while in the Davenport area, to see about setting up my Program for her Guild. She was not at home, but returned my call later. She had spent the afternoon at the City Library, presenting Quilting workshops for small children. Her enthusiasm for this program was contagious, as she explained it to me. If you are interested in doing such a program, you might contact Catherine through the Mississippi Valley Quilt Guild in Davenport.

Carol L. Robbins
Overland Park, Kansas
Blue Valley Quilter's Guild

This past year has been extremely busy as Vice Pres/Prog Chairman of the BVQG, Pres. of the local Society of Decorative Painters Chapter and Treasurer of the local Gold Wing Road Riders Ass'n. There are wonderful quilters in every group, and it's wonderful comparing notes. My husband, Zane, and our 12 year old son, Michael, have been very supportive and active right along with me. In fact, Michael likes piecing blocks. Our grown son and daughter, along with their families, enjoy the fruits of our labor.

Shannon Royer
Otis, Kansas
Central Kansas Thread Benders

I am a full-time wife and mother, plus work part-time for my husband's family John Deere dealership. My job in the most part, is taking care of the advertising and recording radio commercials.

After several years of prayer and searching, my husband, Eric, and I adopted our daughter Elizabeth. Having a busy three year old around the house has definitely changed my quilting habits. We also have a long-haired dachshund, Dixie, who thinks her place is as close as possible to my foot pedal, while I'm sewing. I like to collect antique sewing machines and unusual shaped trivets.

Netta Ranney
Overland Park, Kansas
Quilter's Guild of Greater Kansas City
Kaw Valley Quilt Guild
Starlight Quilt Guild

I was born and reared in England, married an American sailor in 1950. I made my first two quilts in early 50's, and came back to quilting when our first grandchild was born in 1978. We have four children and eleven grandchildren, my goal is to give each one a quilt upon their high school graduation, so I have been accumulating tops in many colors and styles.

My daughter made me a wall-hanging that says, "I quilt for a contented heart", and that is the truth. I love to make things for others, to give pleasure.

I donate small quilts to various charities, and get a thrill when I visit a home where my work is displayed. Since 1982, I have both taught and taken classes in the Art Ministry Program at Village Presbyterian Church in Prairie Village, KS. It is rewarding to have a small part keeping up the womanly arts.

I cherish the friendships I have made through quilting, and feel my life so much richer for quilting.

++++++++++++++++++++++++++++

Tedi Lambert
Los Banos, California
Gateway Quilt Guild
Los Banos
*   Piecemakers*
*   and Friends*
Turlock Quilters Guild

I am currently unemployed, and loving every moment of it! My most recent job was working for our local fabric store. There, I was a sales clerk and Quilt instructor. When the store closed, my job ended. I am married (17 years), and have three children. Two of the children are biologically mine, and one is *borrowed* for a year. My husband's name is Ralph, 16-going-on-45 year old daughter's name is Leah, 11 year old son's name is Andrew, and the one which I've *borrowed* for a year, is our Cultural Exchange daughter--17 year old, Shoko Yamanouchi, from Sakaurajima, Japan.

An amusing story: This is something, which some may identify with. Shortly after my son was born, I starting taking him to the fabric store with me. Consequently, he was most comfortable in this type of store. When he was five, we moved and had a house built. While the house was being built, I began working in the local quilt shop (where I was bitten by the quilting bug). I had been working there for about five months, when we were finally able to move into our new home. We had been in the house for less than a month, when my son asked me to take him to the fabric store. When I asked him why, he replied that he had to go to the bathroom, and that he couldn't remember where the one was in the new house, but he knew just where it was at the fabric store! My son is now 11, and has forgotten all about this story, and has lost his familiarity with fabric stores. I will never forget this event as long as I live!

++++++++++++++++++++++++++++

Julie L. Kimberlin
Anchorage, Alaska
Anchorage Log
*   Cabin Quilters*
Association of Pacific
*   Northwest*
*   Quilters*
NQA and AQS

Born and raised in Washington state. Have been sewing on the *same* Singer® sewing machine for 35 years. It has been everywhere with me. BA in Textiles, Clothing & Art, 1971 University of Washington. Worked as a purchasing agent for the US Forest Service. Met my husband, Richard, when we were both on a Forest Service Overhead Team that fights wild fires in 1979. Married in 1980. We have 1 daughter, Elysse, born in Libby, MT in 1984. I began quilting when she was 2 months old.

When we moved to Anchorage in 1991, we were going into temporary quarters. I did not want to be without my machine for a couple of months with stuff in storage. The heavy machine took up too large a percentage of our 300 pound allowance for air freight. So, I shipped my clothes, and took my machine on our flight, as my luggage! Unfortunately, the airlines dropped it, so my first order of business in Alaska was to find a repairman. It's still going strong, and clocking up the miles and hours.

Our ensemble currently includes a 125 pound German Shepherd named Chinook, two Siamese cats named Jocko Bear & Missy Bear, and Elysse's hamster, Sampson Houdini Hamster.

I'm a stay-at-home Mom, who is serving on the PTA Board at my daughter's school, and active in the Anchorage Log Cabin Quilter's Guild. I'm in my 4th year of chairing our annual Great Alaska Quilt Show. I'm also one of a very small number in the city that does quilting for hire.

P.S. My clothes showed up the next day after our arrival.

∞∞∞∞∞∞∞∞∞∞∞∞∞∞∞∞∞∞∞∞∞∞∞∞

Karen Crosby
Ocala, Florida
Country Road Quilters

I have been married for 34 years to Buddy, have 3 children; Jeff, David, and Carrie...and 3 grandchildren; Brandy, Cody and Dylan. We have one soon-to-be 10 year old german shepherd. I have been quilting for about ten years but have gotten more involved when we moved to Ocala from Central Florida 6 years ago, and wanted to meet people...so I joined a quilt group, it was the best thing I ever did. My husband and I are great Florida Gator football fans, and like to fish.

Phyllis Hansen Gierach
Madera, California
Heart of California Quilter's Guild

It's hard to condense 60 years in a paragraph, and I tend to get carried away when talking about my family, but be assured that I will try!

I have wonderful memories of growing up in Salina, KS with a wonderful Swedish mother and Danish father, and one brother, and lots of relatives. My aunt, Kay, did all sorts of handwork, and made wonderful dolls. My aunt, DeeDee, could do almost any kind of needlework. She and my mother made many quilts together, as "Grandmother Gibson" lived with my aunt and uncle for many years. They taught me how to do huck weaving, counted cross stitch and applique, as a young girl.

My mother also did lots of sewing and made several quilt tops, but never found the time to get them quilted.

Soon after graduating from Salina High School, I began dating a boy I had gone to high school with. My future husband, Gary, decided to join the Air Force just seven months after graduation. We were engaged in 1951, and married on Valentine's Day 1952, and 2 months later he shipped off to Okinawa for 18 months. I had planned to continue college, but the Lord had other plans...Michael. Michael was almost one year old before Gary got to see him. Later, we had a daughter, Janet Marie. Gary attended college in Wichita on the GI Bill, but had to move to Fresno, California to finish his classes. We fell in love with the San Joaquin Valley in California and have been there ever since. Barry was born in 1963. Later I took a two unit class from Jean Ray Laury at Fresno State College, and my life was changed forever!

I worked as a library clerk in the elementary schools and was allowed to order books, etc. We had the best selection of art and craft books in the whole district! My husband opened his own civil engineering office in Madera, and I resigned to help my husband, as bookkeeper. The office prospered and five years later, I was able to stay home and pursue quilting classes.

Helen King
Horton, Kansas
Emporia Regional Quilt Guild
Northeast Kansas Quilt Guild
Kansas Quilter's Organization

I was raised on a northeastern Kansas farm by my father, a single parent. My mother died just before I was 3 years old. The 4-H program taught me to sew. The summer I was 11, a neighbor shared her feed sack scraps and taught me to piece a Bow-Tie quilt. It was laid out on the floor, backing of feed sacks, filler of an old blanket, then the top, then tied with string salvaged from the stitching of the feed sacks. My next quilt was a *Kite*, the pattern clipped from the Weekly Kansas City Star. This bedding was desperately needed to replace the quilts my mother had made. There was no money to buy bedding in those days of the Great Depression.

My church circle gave me an embroidered Friendship quilt top and backing as a wedding/going away present when I married Carl King, July 3, 1938. Friends of my mother-in-law taught me to hand quilt that winter on the remote Atyeo Lease, in the oil fields SW of Emporia, Kansas.

Quilt making became an obsession those years before our son was born. The much published "Colonial Lady" was my finest. Our little son slept well under the crib quilt that matched the Lady. His two little sisters wore out the crib quilt. they also used the double bed "Lady" when they slept in a double bed. Now they want that quilt!

I sewed everybody's clothing and was active in church and community, so little quilt making took place in those busy years. I was grateful for the pile of quilts I had made B.J. (Before John).

When our youngest left home, I plunged into quilt making again. I lost track but have records of 250 quilts, all sizes and types. Thirty of these were hand-quilted.

Meantime, I had taken some training in creative writing and was writing a column published in the Lebanon (Illinois) Advertiser. HOMEMAKING WITH HELEN now also appears bi-weekly in the Horton (KS) Headlight and the Madison (KS) News. I have been writing the column for more than 34 years!

I had various small bits published through the years in various publications. My first acceptance in an internationally distributed magazine, *Coping with the Empty Nest* appeared in the July/August Quilt World in 1979. Since then, as much time has gone into writing and lectures, as in quilt making. My retired husband took our photographs. We published more than 200 articles before he died August 2, 1991. After I recovered emotionally, I have been back to writing and have many more published and accepted. (Total published 223, accepted 25)

My best quilts in recent years have been made as samplers, from blocks used to proof quilt patterns. We sought rarely published or new designs, and had to draft patterns. Sadly, my hands no longer permit me to hand-quilt, but I can still draw around, cut and stitch blocks on the sewing machine.

Author's Note: Helen is my mentor. It was she who encouraged me to submit my articles to Quilt Magazines, gave me the addresses and the general information necessary to write a good query. Last month I felt like I had arrived, when I received the March issue of Traditional Quilter and found that Helen and I each had an article in that issue. I'd had a number of other articles published since that first meeting with Helen, but this was the first time we had one in the same magazine. One week later, Quick & Easy Quilting arrived, and....yes! Helen and I each had an article in it, too! I highly respect Helen and her dedication to the field of quilting. She has done years of research....if Helen doesn't have the answers...*there ain't none!*

Gladys E. Shook
Hutchinson, Kansas
Heart of
Kansas Quilters

"Always sewing, always learning--Quilts are forever!"

Born the youngest of seven Olson children, I learned very early the rewards of mending and sewing buttons on shirts and blouses, while my mother ironed the family's laundry.

As a child, I learned how to create fabric yo-yos, and my mother taught me to embroider. I was always very patient and careful to make the stitches look as neat on the back side, as the front. When learning to sew garments, I used a treadle machine. By the time I went to high school in Inman, Kansas, I helped my teacher instruct the other students.

During my years of nurse's training at Trinity Lutheran Hospital in Kansas City, dirndl skirts were in vogue, and I made them for my wardrobe. Soon, I discovered the rewards of sewing for my friends, too.

After marrying John Shook, I became very good friends with his mother. She introduced me to the joys and intricacies of piecing quilts. Quilting soon became a common bond that stitched our friendship together.

My interest in sewing kept our three daughters well dressed from the first day of elementary school to prom dresses, and wedding gowns. I have continued to sew for my son-in-law, two grandsons and two granddaughters. All these years, I was interested in quilting, but didn't have the time to pursue the art, until after my daughters were married.

Then, by combining my daughters' talents and their children's creativity and ambition, the family held a Holiday House Bazaar in November for nine years.

Through the years, by joining, and soon instructing quilting groups, my projects have expanded from tote bags and wall hangings, to garments and full size quilts. I cannot imagine a more rewarding hobby than creating my quilting projects and inspiring others to enjoy the same.

Author's Note: Gladys shares her quilting expertise freely, as do so many quilters. She is available Thursdays at her local Bernina® dealer's shop to those that need help.

Teresa Binder
Olpe, Kansas
Emporia Regional
Quilt Guild

I am 36 years old. I have lived all my life in Kansas, and within

Meet the Quilters, page 71

30 minutes of Emporia. I am a physical therapist assistant, and work for a Special Education Cooperative that serves seven school districts. The children I work with are ages birth to 21, who have physical disabilities. My husband, Bob, is an assistant fire chief, and does beautiful counted cross stitch. Our son, Eric, is eight years old and in the second grade. He has taken two sewing classes and is learning to use the rotary cutter. Anna, our daughter, is 5 years old, in kindergarten and loves to *help*. We live on seven acres in the country with a pond stocked with bass, a garden, and plans for orchards and many other improvements. We share our land with Buck, a year old border collie/huskie mix, and Joey, a rabbit.

Charlotte Fry
Saint Charles,
Missouri
Little Hills Quilt Club

My job is as a domestic engineer, better known as a housewife. I have plenty to do, since we live in an historic home built in 1836. (We have 11 rooms). I do a lot of gardening, so from about May to Sept, I'm out in the yard growing the flowers I like to applique. I worked and taught the Children's quilting and piecing classes for about 5 years at a local quilt shop. I also volunteer for our local Humane Society, whenever they have fund raisers. We have one fat cat, named Tom. I've been teaching my daughter, Nada, how to make quilts. She, however, is more a purest than I am, and does *all* her work by hand. I also plan to start teaching my granddaughter, Emily, the trade.

I have a very interesting pen pal, who lives in The Netherlands. We've been corresponding since Jan. 1992. Her name is Betteke Boele-Vogelsang and the quilt she made for her Parents-in-law's 50th Anniversary is in the book of *Patchwork from the Netherlands*.

My mother and grand-mother both were quilters. My mother died when I was 15. She had taught me how to sew but we hadn't gotten to do any quilting. Sadly, I never knew my grandmother. I'm a Charter member of Little Hills Quilt Club.

I love Carol Armstrong's work and patterns. I've also been the Chairman of 3 shows our local Quilt Shop (Patches, Etc.) has sponsored of Carol's work. Every 3 years we bring her here from the U.P. of Michigan.

Barbara K. Clukey
Carriere, Mississippi
Picayune Piecemakers
Quilt Guild

I am delighted and proud to be included in THE BUSY QUILTER'S SURVIVAL GUIDE. It has taken the support of my indulgent and long suffering husband, Rod, for me to have realized many of my goals. There are times when I rise in the middle of the night to write down my ideas, so that I do not forget them. Rod will usually roll over with a tolerant grunt. I think he realizes that inspiration always shines brightest for me by the light of the midnight oil.

My daughter, Sidney Noel, lives next door. She is a talented Needle Woman. Besides the occasional stick of butter or cup of flour, we also share our thoughts, ideas, and excitement about quilting - we both enjoy hand sewing. My daughter enjoys piecework, but I love applique the best.

Although my background is in business and management, my bent has always been to include color and creativity in what I do. I have been a florist, and an illustrator of children's coloring story books. As I grew older, I adopted for my life's motto the slogan, "The Older-the Bolder!", and went back to school at the age of 53 for my degree. I loved it!

I sew under the pseudonym of *Rudy Whistler*, because my own name does not have the same artistic zing. This name is taken from a toe counting rhyme I learned as a child from my mother. She quilted well into her eighties. I hope to be creative every bit as long, it would be a bonus to be as well loved.

Helen P. Johnston
Bowie, Maryland
Southern Comforters
of Bowie
& Annapolis QG

I am a former Special Education Teacher, who is currently a licensed childcare provider. My husband, George, has a passion for books and history, so he understands and indulges my addiction to quilting. My son, George Henry Johnston V, 8 years old, is focused on the Civil War. As a family, we've spent many weekends traipsing across Civil War battlefields.

Recently I had to take a brief hiatus from quilting to sew him a second Union uniform. It was educational, I learned what a gusset is.

Edith O. McGhee
Mercer, Pennsylvania
I.Q. Quilters

My husband, Bob, and I met and married thirteen years ago. This is a second marriage for both of us. I had five children, Bob had four, and put them all together for one big family. The family has now grown to include seven children-in-law and fourteen grandchildren. Keeps life interesting!

I left teaching in the public schools of western Pennsylvania eight years ago to become a secretary. I now have a job that I like, that is close to home, and have very little contact with children. My fourteen grandchildren are enough in my old age (60).

Marcene Gunter
Hillsboro, Kansas
Country Stitchers Quilt Guild

I am married, we have two daughters and four grandchildren. I am retired now, in my past life I was head of the computer department for a group of doctors. Later, I worked as a secretary at the County Health Department. We have one cat and two dogs.

My hobbies are quilting, knitting, sewing, reading, and raising sheltie dogs. I also love to swim, water ski, camping and just plain having fun out of doors.

I have quilted for fourteen years. I teach quilting classes in my home, and have taught at a quilt store. I give lectures and workshops, wherever they will have me. I also am a Quilting and Knitting judge. I have judged both county and state fairs. I enjoy one thing, as much as the other.

Like many of you, I watched my grandmother quilt. But my first experience with quilting was when my oldest daughter (then in high school) came home one day and said she wanted to design a quilt, and would I help her sew? She took scraps, and got on the floor and designed a star quilt (of all things). We sewed it on the sewing machine. No one knew how to quilt, so we watched an older lady for awhile. She told us what needles to get. My husband made a quilting frame on two chairs. The two girls and I quilted it, wasn't toooo bad. However, I had no desire to try it again until much later.

My husband and I were building our new home. Everything was packed and stored away. I got so tired of hanging sheet rock, painting, etc. I decided to take a quilting class since I couldn't sew. It was made of scraps, because I was not going to waste money on this new thing. I was hooked. I have taken many classes since then, from many teachers, and I love my quilting.

Beulah T. Gilbert
Bellevue, Ohio
Huron Valley Quilt Guild

I am a retired factory worker, who worked for 35 years with raising a family of 5 children. We have five children and 14 great grandchildren. I enjoy them all.

Joan Waldman
Platte Center, Nebraska
Columbus Quilt Club
Norfolk Country Piecemakers
Nebraska State Quilt Guild

I am a quilter! My name is Joan Sjuts Waldman and I live in a very small Nebraska town. My husband, Harold, and I were farmers until about 15 years ago. Now we lead a more leisurely life. I work at the Columbus Wal-Mart craft department. I do in-store demonstrations one day a week (Thursdays) on sewing, quilting and crafts. I also do demonstrations for the Tulip Paint Company. I teach quilting classes in area quilt shops, fabric stores, and for the adult education dept. at the local college. I am in the process of doing my first book - Animas Press has contracted for it - will be a series of strip quilts, and is due to be released in Spring, next year.

Author's Note: Congratulations, Joan! We know you are excited about your book. I'm sure there are others in this book, that have either been published or are about to be....or are working on a book they hope to have published. You, and the others who have succeeded, are indeed an inspiration....and an encouragement!

DeEtta Beebe
Waters, Michigan
Ausable Quilt Guild

I'm sitting at the dining room table as I write this, looking at the lake, frozen over, the pine trees hanging with snow from the last snow fall, and quilting sitting next to me. I should get busy and finish my challenge from our applique group.

I'm DeEtta Beebe, married to my high school sweetheart of 28 years. I have three sons, who are on their own. Life is in a transit for us at this time, semi-retired, enjoy living in the woods, and enjoying nature at its best. Many activities and hobbies keep my life full and rewarding. A lot of volunteer work, traveling, grandchildren, and quilting. I enjoy applique, and teaching others who are interested.

Raising three boys was the most wonderful time of our lives. Sharing our interests with them, and theirs with us as a family, has been a real joy.

The boys never complained much, when they would go antiquing or to a fabric store. Everyone learned to give and share, and we always had the time for their special interests, and continue today with two daughters-in-law and two granddaughters. Quilting has captured their hearts. We, in turn, share what the *boys* enjoy also. Hunting and fishing, braving the cold, it's share with one another.

Life is a special gift to be shared with those we love . . . change what we can, except what we can't, and always give thanks for life's simple pleasures.

Quilting has never taken time away from anything or anyone in my life. I guess that's why I love it so much. It is an expression of myself. Even the unfinished projects, which adorn my sewing room shelves and boxes. Through my quilting, I have learned a lot about myself. I'm not great at quilting, but I enjoy the creating part. If finishing all my projects is one thing I can't change, that's okay, too! Until then, I will continue what I enjoy best, being me and enjoying others, because they are themselves, also. We were created to be individuals, but each one an important part to the whole picture of life.

Rebecca Dutcher
Culbertson, Nebraska

I am a social worker and with work and family, it's hard to find time to quilt. Recently, I quit smoking and since I work in a smoke-free environment, I had to go outside on breaks and at lunch to get my *fix*. Now I use that time to quilt and work on other projects. The things I work on are; lap projects, small quilts, baby quilts, and such. It is amazing how much you can get accomplished in about an hour a day. The bonus is, that I get to show off what I'm working on and get valuable input from co-workers.

LaRue Nuest
South Hutchinson,
Kansas
Kansas Quilters
Organization

I am a former teacher. When my first husband was killed in a work-related accident in 1969, I found it necessary to get a college education so I could support my four children: David 18, Daryl 15, Diana 13, and Dixie 8. So, I attended Hutchinson Community College, graduating in May, 1973, then transferred to Wichita State University, and graduated with a bachelor's degree in education, August, 1975. The same month, I started teaching accounting, typewriting, office procedures, and shorthand at Nickerson High School, Nickerson, Kansas. Later, in 1980, I completed my master's degree in secondary education. After teaching at Nickerson for 19 years, I took early retirement in May, 1994.

In early 1982, after crocheting for a hobby, I discovered quilting. I took some classes at the local quilt shop, and was soon off and running and HOOKED on quilting. (Crocheting has been set aside.) With all the stress of dealing with students and parents during my teaching years, I found quilting to be very therapeutic. To be able to come home after a stressful day at school, and spend a few minutes or hours with my quilting was a

Page 74, Meet the Quilters

lifesaver for me. I always tell my husband (I remarried in 1978), that all the money I spend on quilting, is money HE doesn't have to spend on a psychiatrist!

Alta M. Edwards
Clay City, Indiana
Clay City
Calico Quilters

I've been a school bus driver since 1967, and a farm wife. Needless to say, most of my married life, I've worked outside. My husband, John, and I have 3 children; Richard, Donna, and Joe, and 9 grandchildren, plus 1 great grandchild (almost 2, as we're expecting the call any day!)

Carole Flasch
Weslaco, Texas
Rio Grande Valley
Quilt Guild
Minnesota
Quilters, Inc.

I've been married to my wonderful husband, Ed, since I was 18 years old. We have four children, now married, and have sixteen grandchildren. All the quilts I make, are gifts for someone in the family - seems like I'm never caught up, or wonder who will get the next quilt. They are usually spoken for, and greatly appreciated.

Nancy H. Ehinger
West Branch,
Michigan
O.T.L.B. Quilters
Rifle River Quilters
Michigan Quilt
Network
National Quilt
Association

I am a retired first-grade teacher. I am married to Delbert, and have six children: Donald, Linda, Robert, Peggy, Stephen and Jeanne. All of them are married except Jeanne, who is a Junior at Eastern Michigan University, majoring in Public Relations. We have 14 grandchildren, and one great-grandchild. I have been teaching quilting since 1978. I founded the O.T.L.B. Quilters, and co-founded the Rifle River Quilt Guild. I am on the board of Michigan Quilt Network, and am Membership Chairman. I enjoy most arts and crafts and needlework, and am treasurer of West Branch Creative Arts Association, and belong to Trailing Arbutus Chapter of EGA.

Betty J. Knack
Essexville, Michigan
Bay Heritage
Quilt Guild

When I was 4 or 5 years old, I can remember my mother and grandmother (Mrs. John Harmon from Wisconsin), visiting us in Unionville, Michigan, the quilting frame was setting on the back of our dining room chairs.

Janet P. Wyckoff
Hopewell, New Jersey
Courthouse Quilters
Hopewell
Valley Quilters

My husband, Jon, and our yellow lab, Jessie, sleep under a quilt and are generally supportive, except at dinner time. I have 2 grown children, Phillip and Sara. Sara is a quilter, too, and lives in Ithaca, New York. Working 45-plus hours/week, as Manager of Pyramid Books at Pennington, has reduced my time and energy I have for quilting, but I won't give up either. I also have a PhD in Developmental Psychology which somehow, works in perfectly with quilting and book selling.

Judy Wolfrom
Southampton,
New Jersey
Berry Basket Quilters

I am a devoted quilt maker, teaching as much as doing. I squeeze in some substitute teaching, for which I was trained. Quilting is *much* more fun. My family consists of a teaching husband, and diligently learning son and daughter in high school. They have both tried sewing. Dave enjoys sewing, as long as he can run the sewing machine, forget the handwork. Becky can sew anything, and admits making quilts in much more fun than making clothing.

The best compliment I have ever received, was when my sister-in-law recently said she had never walked into a home which reflected someone's interests so completely. I think for needle women, our homes are our showcases of our work.

Diane Johnson
Rhinebeck, New York

I live in rural upstate New York with my husband, Eric, two cats, and a bird. I teach quilt making and design, and make collectible teddy bears and scale doll house miniatures, under the name Willowcreek Country Crafts. What could be better - my hobbies have become my work!

Maria Lage
Cumberland, Rhode Island
Narragansett Bay Quilters' Association

I work full-time for a department store. I'm single with no kids, 2 cats, and living with my best friend, who happens to be my brother, Alex. He and I have a lot in common, so we travel quite often together. Although he works in computers, his ambition is to someday be able to make a living as an artist. When we travel to different cities so I can go see a quilt show or take a workshop, he enjoys going to the local art museums and galleries, or just photographing the local country side, and getting ideas for his paintings. We talk quite often about collaborating on a quilt, so maybe one of these days it will come true. Although there's no quilt making tradition in my family, my mother taught me at an early age, how to sew and knit. During my teenage years, I taught myself to crochet, embroider, and sew clothes. From the age of five, when I started making clothes for my doll, I've always been proud to do things with my hands.

For several years, I taught arts and crafts at adult education classes. Quilting began for me as a continuation of all the other crafts I was involved in. Unfortunately, there's not enough time to do everything I like. During spring and summer, my garden tends to keep me pretty busy, till the sun goes down. I like growing my own fruits and vegetables, along with herbs and flowers. I tend to quilt late at night, or whenever I have free time. If I have to meet a deadline, everything else just has to wait.

Patricia L. Carl
Rhinebeck, New York

I am retired as of December 1994, from the Country Shop, my quilt shop in upstate New York, in the lovely town of Rhinebeck, where I still live with my husband. Our four children and six grandchildren also live in the area, so life is good! My shop area is now my studio, and I have been very busy re-arranging, creating, re-inventing, and playing *what-if* with all my unfinished projects, new ideas and my growing fabric collection - SUCH FUN!

Lynn G. Kough
Middletown, New Jersey
Rebecca's Reel Quilters of Poricy Park

I live in Middletown, New Jersey, with my husband, two daughters, many dogs, an inordinate amount of fabric and thread, and a vacuum cleaner on the verge of cardiac arrest!

My training in theater design and my public school teaching experience help bring a unique perspective to my programs. My work in color and design, and my quilts (which have won many awards) have been seen in Guild and Gallery Shows. I've taught and lectured for many Guilds and Shops throughout the Mid-Atlantic Region.

I'm currently at work on a book, *New Images for Traditional Quilts* being published by Quilt House Books. It will be introduced this Fall at the Quilt Market in Houston.

Lynn Graves
Albuguerque, New Mexico
New Mexico Quilter's Association

My job has been directing traffic from *my office*, which is my sewing machine. The family, my husband, Jim, and daughter,

Sarah, cats Baron and RC, with Jim's dog, Rambo, all revolve around the quilt business. This business started with me about 8 or 9 years ago, when I first began to quilt and found no one made a 1/4" foot. So, I designed Little Foot, marketed it myself, and the business, *LITTLE FOOT, LTD.* was born. No one told me you couldn't do it!

Since *LITTLE FOOT*, I have invented *BIG FOOT, JAWS*, other quilting notions, clothing patterns, and a line of foundation sheet patterns for piecing quilts.

My book, *THE FRAME GAME*, is an innovative look at the Pineapple Block.

My motto is, "Make it Easy, Make it Accurate, Make it Fun!"

Alba Lee Elliott
Asheville,
North Carolina
Asheville Quilt Club

As a child growing up in Central America, fabric of all colors and texture was available to us. Going downtown with my mother was a big event, selecting six different fabrics to have dresses made by a local seamstress, was exciting, just as exciting as it was to pick up the pieces (mine and others), which would later be dresses for my doll.

Roxanne H. McElroy
Mililani, Hawaii
Hawaii Quilt Guild

My husband, Jeff, is an executive with Chevron/USA, and that is why we have been transferred 14 times in 23 years. My daughter, DiDi, works for me as my Operations Manager, and manages our office in Martinez, California. I have the most beautiful, most intelligent grandchild in the known universe, Victoria Renee, age 3. General Sherman is our 70 pound Standard Poodle. We named him that, because I drove from Atlanta to Savannah, Georgia to buy him, a retracing of Sherman's march to the sea - and he is about that destructive!

Ruth Powers
Carbondale, Kansas
Kansas Capitol
Quilters Guild

I work at the Osage County Quilt Factory. When notice was given that the retail store would close in early 1994, thinking I would be out of a job, I started my own pattern company, "INNOVATIONS".

As it turned out, I was asked to stay on as a designer-quilt maker. Mostly now at work, I design and make samples for Fabric-Quilt in Kansas, to show their new coordinated lines of fabrics at markets and shows, or I sew Virginia Robertson designs to test patterns or make samples. My work is very enjoyable, as well as educational. I often get to travel to major markets and shows. The only problem is that after sewing all day, I usually have to come home and sew some more. I couldn't do all this without the help of my husband, Charlie, who is always supportive, and willing to cook.

I have had the honor of winning many awards for my work, including:
Discovery-500 years, Great
    American Quilt Festival,
    NY, 1990.
Several from
    Ben Franklin Stores.
The Kansas State Fair,
The Shawnee County Fair.
Silver Dollar City
The Hoffman Challenge
Labor of Love OCQF

Julie Fox
Blackwell, Oklahoma
P.M. Patches
and Pieces

I am a speech-language pathologist, working for the State of Oklahoma, in the Kay County Health Department. I have one daughter, Laura Hannah, 2 step-sons, Robbie and Steve, and a husband, Mike. We have *no* pets (3 kids are enough). Our family enjoys camping, gardening, and biking.

Lenore Scott
Pittstown, New Jersey
Courthouse Quilters

My family consists of myself, my husband Jeff, and my Zelda. Before migrating to this country in 1989, I had no concept of what *Quilting* was.

Meet the Quilters, page 77

My interest in *Quilting* is purely by accident. It came about through my need to make some fabric coasters to use on my living room tables. A friend, who's a quilter, showed me how to make the coasters (which was a heart appliqued on a circle). The same day, she showed me all her quilts and proceeded to persuade me to start quilting. I thought it would be very difficult, since I had no access to a sewing machine. This was in 1992. I got a sewing machine a couple of months later, and subsequently joined The "Courthouse Quilters" of New Jersey, and have become addicted to quilting since then.

Norma Jean Rector
Center Point, Indiana

I am a housewife, mother of four children. Two daughters (Carol and Marilyn), and two sons (Kenny and Jerry). We have fourteen grandchildren, ranging in age from 5 to 24 years old. My husband, Ray, and I were married the day the atom bomb was dropped on Hiroshima. How's that for a day in history! We will be celebrating our golden wedding anniversary this coming August. Our home is in a rural area, 22 miles from Terre Haute, Indiana. We spent the first year of married life together at Tyndall Air Force Base, Panama City, Florida. Thus, getting the proverbial *sand in our shoes*. Since Ray has retired, we spend our winter months in Bradenton, Florida. Throughout our married years, we've had a lot of interesting experiences, some with tears and some with laughter. Many have had connections with Ray's twin brother, Roy, whose wife was also, Norma. Ray and Roy were identical twins and we lived close to each other, until Roy's death. Once, my husband and I visited Roy's church. The minister reluctantly shook hands with us, as we entered the church. Never having met us before, he was quite relieved when Roy and Norma arrived and sat beside us. He said, afterwards, that he thought Roy had some nerve, bringing another woman to church.

Emily Laubaugh
Gladstone, Oregon
Gladstone
Chautauqua Quilters

I've lived in Gladstone, Oregon for 12 years now, and have been involved with the Gladstone Chautauqua Festival for 11 years. I felt that the Festival needed some kind of extra attraction, so I thought of adding a Quilt Show. I had no idea of how to get started, so I put a little notice in the city's residential newsletter requesting help.

Before I even received my own mail that day, I got a phone call from Geri Fuson who told me that she lives, eats and breathes quilts, and how can she help? What a dream come true! She was a member of the Northwest Quilters Society, and was able to show me all the necessary steps to take to put on a respectable quilt show. We put out the word throughout the city of Gladstone and some of the major Portland area, and we were able to display 50 quilts! Since then, we have been able to put on eight successful quilt shows, purchase our own equipment to display them properly, and have organized a quilt guild with a list of 20 active members who volunteer their time to make a raffle quilt each year to help with the Festival's expenses.

Many of us have become lifelong friends who would do just about anything for each other. But, have you ever met a quilter who wouldn't?

Carolyn Koopman
Carnavillo, Iowa
Northeast Iowa
Quilt Guild

I'm a quilt maker, teacher, lecturer, designer and fanatic. My sisters and I have a quilt pattern business called "All Kainz" (pronounced *kinds*), because of the variety of designs we produce and it's our maiden name. My husband, Jerry, and I and one son, Rafe, farm. We raise hogs, cows, and corn. I also have 24 laying hens, 7 guinneas, a pair of peacocks, and one angora goat named Abby. I use her hair for Santa beards. It took a while for me to figure out how to get it off her, and onto the Santa, but I think I have figured it out now.

Ella May Reussser
Blackwell, Oklahoma

I am a transplanted widow. Transplanted from home and garden to an apartment and flower bed. But I find the flower bed can also grow nice tomatoes and sweet potatoes.

When my health permits, I quilt with 3 different Church groups. Two here in Blackwell, and the one at home in Deer Creek. They say work is a blessing and I've found out quilting is a blessing for me.

Betty Verhoeven
East Jewett, New York
Patchworkers
of East Jewett
Wiltwych Quilt Guild,
Kingston, NY
Prattsville Patchers,
Prattsville
Catskill Mountain
Quilter's Hall of Fame
(President and
Co-Chairperson)

I was born in Holland, one of nine children. It was not always easy for my parents to keep us fed and clothed, especially when World War II broke out. My mother would trade eggs, butter and milk from our small farm for fabrics to make clothing for all of us. Mostly, we wore hand-me-downs that the older children had out grown, but, oh, what a treat, when we would get something new! I will always fondly remember one particular black and red calico dress my Mother made just for me!

I attended an all girls school, where we were very strictly taught by the nuns, and we worked hard to please them. As soon as you were old enough to hold a needle, you were taught to sew, knit, crochet and embroider. I remember in the first grade, we had to make a blouse. Fabric was scarce and of poor quality, and I had a thin piece of gingham to work with. Well, I had such a hard time of it, and was a terrible student. The nuns had me take out my poor stitches, over and over again, until the fabric was so frayed and ravelled, that they allowed me to make a rounded collar, instead of the required pointed one. Needless to say, I did not get a passing grade! I hated sewing!

Knitting was no better. Each day after school, my mother would insist that I knit five rows on a scarf I was working on, before I could go out with my friends to play. She would mark the starting point with a thread, so that she could see my progress. My girlfriend snuck me a needle and I moved the thread, so that it looked as though I had done the five rows, instead of the two I had actually managed to finish. I was in deep trouble when my mother finally realized that the scarf wasn't getting any longer. I had to knit double time for weeks!

As a teenager, I became more interested in sewing, since it was the only way to get new clothes. I loved to do embroidery, but that was considered *fancy work*, and was reserved for Sundays. Weekday evenings were spent doing the mending and darning. I still have one of the table cloths I embroidered as a teenager. At one time, I also made an appliqued and embroidered wall hanging I had seen in a craft magazine, but that has long been gone, although I wish I still had it.

In my early twenties, I fell in love with Jack. We married, and decided to emigrate to the United States. Since that was difficult, we went to Canada first, with the hopes of getting to the U.S. someday. We had three children, and were very happy in our new life. Jack worked hard to learn about farming in this new country, while I cared for the children, which of course, included making their clothing. There was a local ladies group that would meet at the church and tie very pretty quilts, but I had no interest in quilts at that time at all.

We soon bought a farm of our own, and were so proud to have our own place. Times were hard, but we looked forward to our first Christmas on the farm. I put my sewing skills to use once again, by tearing apart my old winter coat to make Teddy Bears for the children. We hardly had money for groceries, but it was a wonderful Christmas!

After ten years in Canada, we finally got our chance and moved to the United States. We sold the farm and moved to the Catskill Mountains of New York State, beautiful mountains and friendly people. We had an elderly woman as a neighbor, and the children loved to visit with her. They called her "Grandma Florence". She lived alone and was always working on her quilts. When I met her, she was working on a cathedral window patchwork quilt. I loved the way the folded fabric made a beautiful background for the bright patches of color. Something sparked in me, and I decided to try to make one. Grandma Florence taught me to make the patch, and I was off. Yards of muslin and bags of outgrown clothing later, I had a beautiful quilt. And it only had taken me three years!

In 1977, I met a small group of quilters right here in East Jewett. The Patchworkers had been formed just before the BiCentennial. I went to their third quilt show at the local fire house. I joined the group and became a serious quilter. As a group we make a quilt to raffle for the fire department each year, and in exchange, we get the use of the fire house for our yearly quilt show. We meet every week and work on group or individual projects. There is always a lot of sharing and advice. And because we meet in member's homes, we get to sample the hostess' *best* cakes and cookies when we end our meetings with tea.'

I have made many quilts for family members, including thirteen in Holland, made for our siblings. I think I've made about eighty quilts all told, large and small. My children each have at least one of my quilts, and grandchildren, too. I also made a special quilt for Jack and myself, which celebrates the path we took together, in our lives. It is made of 1" squares in red, white, and blue, representing the Dutch, Canadian, and American flags. the tiny pieces float across the quilt and create the respective flags along our path.

I also, just finished a quilt made with traditional Dutch Folkloric fabrics. I saw an old quilt in Holland on a visit, and adapted it to make a design, using two connecting star blocks. However, I ran out of the Dutch fabric, and had to use American fabric to complete the borders. It seems appropriate to bring the two countries I love, together.

Lately, I also seem to be very interested in clothing again. I love to design and make clothes and bring them to the fashion shows that are often connected with quilt shows. Right now, I'm knee deep in men's neck ties. The beautiful silks make terrific vests, hats, jackets and coats.

One of my daughters shares my love of quilting, and often helps me with designs. We've worked on many ideas together. So, the tradition will go on, quilting is forever!

FUNNY THINGS:

Quilting is such a big part of my life. I even dream about it! One weekend, a few friends and I were sewing together, working on crazy quilt blocks for one of the guild members. We were all excited to begin embroidering and embellishing the blocks, and had lots of ideas to share. That evening, my husband and I went to the movies and saw a Paul Newman film. That night, I had an unusual dream. In the dream, my quilting friends and I were working on the crazy quilt blocks, but now our group was being led by Paul Newman, whom we called "Dr. Newman"! He directed us to embellish the blocks with mandarin orange slices and walnuts that he handed out. I, of course, complained that these were too soggy to sew onto blocks as they were, so we arranged them on the rungs of a stepladder, placed over the woodstove to dry. But this presented another problem, because my sewing machine was at the top of the ladder, and I couldn't get to it now. I was so upset, that I woke up, very annoyed with "Dr. Newman", he should have chosen better embellishments!

One summer, my quilting friend, Hanna, read an article in a craft magazine on how to dye fabrics with mold. Not many instructions were given, but we figured we'd give it a try. Hanna had a nice old damp basement, where we could experiment. So, we all brought our fabrics and "Stuff". I stretched a nice piece of silk on the plastic covered floor, wet it down and then loaded on the goodies; tomatoes, blackberries, beets, peppers, carrots, zuchinni, strawberries, red cabbage, roots, and anything else we could think of. For good measure, we sprinkled on some spices and then some more water. It would have been difficult to explain what we were doing if someone had seen us, what a mess, but oh, it was fun! Weeks later after great anticipation, we returned to the scene to check on the progress. Mice had nibbled on some of our goodies, and the air was a bit ripe. But, after scraping and rinsing, we indeed had some beautiful fabrics! Mine resembled the heavens with all the stars and planets, all it needed was to be quilted and hung on the wall. Only my fellow quilters will understand our excitement over our garbage-dyed fabric....Crazy?

<u>Author's Note:</u> Betty sent along several pictures of her quilts. The red, white and blue one with the 1" squares was one of them. Beautiful! And, how symbolic of their lives!

She also sent along her beautiful connecting blocks quilt picture. And...a picture of her doing her garbage-dyeing! What a mess, but what fun! And what a way to re-cycle our garbage!

Margaret Kooda
Idaho Falls, Idaho
Snake River Valley Quilt Guild

I am a temporarily retired Veterinarian with four children, Evan, Thor, Kirstin and Ingrid. I grew up in Minnesota and have lived and worked in Connecticut and now reside in Idaho. Quilting has become an obsession since moving to Idaho. One of my toddlers first intelligible words were *quilt shop* and even my four cats have learned to walk around the edges of the quilt spread on the family room floor. After making a quilt for each of my children, I was planning my next project when my husband, Kevin, asked me "Just how many quilts are you planning to make?" As all the traditional and contemporary patterns flashed through my mind, I realized how fulfilling quilting had become. My answer was, "As many as I can make in my lifetime!"

Betty J. Pribil
Portland, Oregon
Chautauqua Quilters of Gladstone, Oregon
Northwest Quilters, Inc. of Portland
Valley Oak Quilters of Tulare, California

In 1979, at the age of 55, I retired from a school district in California after working for them for 21 years. That very week I enrolled in a quilt class, and have been hooked ever since. I had learned to sew at the age of 10 through 4-H and made most of my clothes until I learned about quilt making. In 1988, after my husband retired, we moved to Portland, Oregon to be near our only son and our three grandsons.

While still living in California, I had started teaching quilt making and with 12 other friends started a quilt guild, The Valley Oak Quilters. We were searching for a community service project when our vice-president suggested we make quilts to be carried in police and sheriff cars to be used when they were involved with a child. I'm happy to say this program has spread to almost every state in the union. Valley Oak Quilters alone have made over 4,000 quilts. In 1989, I joined the Northwest Quilters, Inc., Portland, Oregon, and began making quilts for Clackamas County Sheriff's Department. Later I switched to Clackamas County District Attorney's Program for Sexually and Physically Abused Children, and to date have made 587 youth size quilts. In addition, through the Retired Senior Citizens Program, I have made 373 baby quilts which are distributed by the Public Health Nurse to needy newborns. These two programs are most enjoyable to me and fill a great need.

In late 1992, I became Philanthropic chairman for Northwest Quilters. This program makes twin size quilts for children in Shriner's Hospital, Waverly Children's Home, Salvation Army, a recovery home for drug and alcoholic women and sent quilts to the flood victims in the midwest.

Each Wednesday morning, I meet with 6 other members of the Gladstone Chautauqua Quilters, and we quilt for each other. Also in August, the whole membership sponsors a quilt show.

Alyce C. Kauffman
Gridley, California
Valley Quilt Guild

I am retired, have three grown children, eight grandchildren, and a great granddaughter. My pets consist now of just a cat, seven finches, two cockateils, a parakeet, and tropical fish. Lost my sixteen year old dog last month. My cat, Cleo, loves to be a *quilting helper*. She can be asleep, but the minute I start any aspect of quilting, she must be included and is constantly awake, whether I am using the rotary cutter, sewing machine, or hand quilting. She was lying on my cutting board, and flipped her tail just as I reached the area with the rotary cutter. Safe by a hair! Now I am very alert to her movements as I pin fabric together. I must also be careful as she pulls pins out as I place them into the fabric.

Pamela T. Young
Minot Air Force Base, North Dakota

I have been quilting for eleven years. My husband, Scott, is a B-52 pilot in the Air Force, so we have lived in many different places and I have visited many different quilt shops. We have three children, ages 3 to 8, Hannah, Rebecca, and

Meet the Quilters, page 81

Benjamin. We share our home with a German Shepherd named Gretchen, Baskins Robins (the bunny), and Chester (the hamster). When I am not busy with the role of Air Force wife and mother, I sell Longaberger baskets, another love of mine. I have been the president, vice-president, newsletter editor, and state fair liaison for the Minot Prairie Quilters over the past five years. Two years ago, I convinced the Minot Prairie Quilters that we should hold a weekend quilt show and conference for quilts around the Dakota area. As the creator and director of the Prairie Quilt Festival, I am very busy. People assume because I am very active in the area quilt events, that I am a great quilter. I tell them "No, I am not a great quilter, I am a great quilt administrator." My administrative responsibilities tend to leave me with little time to actually quilt.

Sandra L. Hatch
Lincoln, Maine
Schoolhouse Quilters
Pine Tree Quilters

I became involved with a local quilting group in Newton, N.H. in addition to the Merrimack Valley Quilters in Haverhill, Mass. This was a group of 150 quilters. I was the president for one year and enjoyed that time very much. I had very special friends in that group and they encouraged me in my work. At the same time I was a member of the New England Quilter's Guild and was the chairman one year of their spring meeting which was a 3-day affair with classes and lectures. I learned then that I need to learn to say *no* when I have too much to do. I enjoyed that event, but I would not do it again unless I had more time. I don't feel I did my best work.

When I moved back to Maine where both my husband and I grew up, I already knew people from back in the old days, but mostly family. I have four sisters in the area as well as my mother and grandmother (who is 91). My husband has family here as well. We have a camp on a pond where we spend our summers. We had been doing this even when we lived in New Hampshire. My husband came for weekends and vacations. It was a wonderful life.

We still go to our camp in the summer, even though it is less than a mile from our home. There is something wonderful about the peaceful sound of water lapping on the shore at night when all is quiet and waking to the call of the loons and the sun shining off the lake. Even though I leave to go home for work, I know I will get back there and things will be the same. We love it there. Life is simple and uncluttered.

Janice A. Miller
Jaffrey,
New Hampshire
Monadnock
Quilters Guild

I am the owner/operator of The Benjamin PreScott Inn in Jaffrey, New Hampshire. The Inn was built in 1853 by the sons of Colonel Benjamin PreScott of Revolutionary War fame. I have been married to Barry for 30 years, have a son, Martin, age 25, and a daughter, Nancy, age 23. Quilting fills my free time after cooking, cleaning, the wash, ironing, and offering hospitality. If I had a choice, I would do nothing but quilt and cook.

Barbara Shook Davis
Williams, Arizona
Eclectic Quilters

I am a teacher at extremes of the spectrum, first grade Reading Specialist and College English. This involves 50 hours a week. In addition, I have a husband and a very busy thirteen year old daughter, 2 dogs, 1 cat, 3 chickens, 1 rabbit, and 2 hampsters. My one hobby and vice is quilting, quilting, quilting!!!

Pat Campbell
Rigby, Idaho
Snake River Valley
Quilt Guild

Owner of *Campbell Creations*, original applique and patchwork patterns, I sell (wholesale only) to shops in seven western states. I'm a free-lance writer, with many publications across the U.S. Just sold my twenty-first original patterns and articles to the *House of White Birches* for publication in their magazines and booklets. I have well over 200 patterns copyrighted. I've held such varied jobs as school lunch cook, assistant sexton at a cemetery, and technical librarian. I am married to George, we have two children (Nancy and Evam), and four grandchildren. I call myself a designer and fiber artist, and all my hobbies have to do with some part of quilt making. I've taught classes, including two at "Quilting in the Tetons" at Jackson Hole, Wyoming in 1992, and have taught locally.

Jean Ann Eitel
Marietta, Georgia
East Cobb Quilt Guild

Author's Note: Jean Eitel is Editor of a number of Quilt Magazines published by Harris Publications. You'll find the biographical information about her in the very front of this book. You'll find her answers in other sections.

Etta Grace Edwards
Council Grove, Kansas
Emporia Regional Quilters Guild

I was raised on country sunshine!! All my life on a farm or in the country. Right now near a lake in the country.

When I was ten I joined 4-H so my mother bought a new sewing machine and that began my sewing career. I even became a sewing leader in 4-H. The mother of one of the girls I taught to sew told me I had taught her daughter well, because she was a beautiful seamstress and makes many beautiful things.

We raised three daughters (Janet, Joyce and Julie), and two sons, (Jack and Jerry). My daughters, too, are beautiful sew-ers.

Life wasn't easy, it seemed we were accident prone. In the whole family of seven, we suffered many a broken bone, legs, arms, collar bones, ribs, breast bone, backs, and cracked skull. We even tried polio and rheumatic fever, if you thought of something, we tried it. Both boys, Jack and Jerry, were badly burned in grass fires and went thru many skin grafts, but you know that God brought us through all these with miracles.

Celeste Lipp
Idaho Falls, Idaho
Snake River Valley Quilters Guild

I work full-time as a health physicist, a specialist in worker radiation safety. I'm married to David, since 1992. We have 2 gray tabby cats, Boots and Sasha. It's no surprise that I love cat fabric and patterns! Quilting is my outlet for creativity and my favorite way to enjoy solitude. Quilting has brought me some of my best friends. I have moved around the country a lot due to work and quilting has been a constant in my life. I'm from Indiana and have finally lived in all the states that begin with an "I".

Christine Klinger
Fayetteville, Arkansas
Q.U.I.L.T. Guild of Northwest Arkansas

I have been quilting for the past 12 years. I have always admired quilts and have several family quilts that my grandmother passed on to me. Since I am one of the only people who sews in my family, I guess I was destined to become the family quilter. My early quilts were made for my home; quilts for walls and quilts for beds. Now, I just make them because I want to, and I enjoy their creation.

Mary Lou Kantz Evans
Flagstaff, Arizona

My job is as far as quilting as you can get. I work in a scientific institution that does astronomical research. You see a question about our organization in the game Trivial Pursuit. Right question, Who discovered the planet Pluto? Wrong answer, Percival Lowell.

I have a husband, Michael, whose passion is fly fishing, and dogs and cats. Numbers vary, dogs live long happy lives with us, the cats sometimes appear and disappear, except for a manx, named Ralph.

Zelda Ziegler Garner
Blackfoot, Idaho
Snake River Valley Quilt Guild
Blackfoot Piecemakers Quilt Club

I am an identical twin. Our names are Zelma and Zelda Ziegler. Zelma prefers to be called ZZ. I go by Zelda Z. or Auntie "Z" (when appropriate). Many of our quilting friends just call us the "Z's" since quite often we are together attending quilting functions. Our names have been fun, although it is

Meet the Quilters, page 83

difficult for people to comprehend one would have two "Z's" in one's name.

We were born October 24, 1923 in May, Idaho. We were premies. The doctor was having trouble getting Zelma to breathe. When that was accomplished, he went back to take care of Mother and discovered there was another baby. My problem was that I was a white baby, not the usual pink baby color. The Doctor could not decide if I was going to live. He found a vein near one ear, finally. Zelma and I have been close all our lives. I can't imagine life without her.

In 1954, I had a malignant thyroid removed and a month of X-ray Therapy. I had a recurrence in 1964, that time I was treated with a radio-active cocktail and that killed the thyroid and cancer. The problem was living four months without thyroid. Every function of one's body is affected by the thyroid or the lack thereof.

My prayer for all those years was that I could live to see my daughter reach adulthood. My prayers were granted. I also tried to teach her to be independent and give her confidence. I would tell her that she could do anything she wanted to do. My daughter is a dear, sweet, loving daughter, very accomplished and independent. She lives with her husband, Jack C. Datisman, in Forks, Washington.

My husband, and I were living in Perth, Australia. My husband, Professor Jay G. Garner, had been invited by the Western Australia Department of Agriculture to do a study on their potato industry.

I was admitted to the hospital in Perth where the doctors concluded I had a recurrence of Rheumatic Fever. I was not expected to live. The treatment is rest and penicillin. That's when I decided to take up quilting. My husband had prostate cancer and died February 11, 1993. I was able to care for him at home those last 9 days through the Hospice program. What a sweet loving man he was! I miss him so much! We lacked just 3 days of reaching our 44th wedding anniversary, February 14th.

I have won many awards for my quilts and projects. I was chosen to be the quilter in the Idaho Potato Commission National TV Commercial, in 1994. It has been a lark and such an unlikely thing to happen to a 70 year old quilter. I am happy to help sell our famous Idaho Potatoes. This commercial was aired October thru April, into 1995. Because of the commercial, the Idaho State Journal did a feature on my story. The local TV station did a special interview, too.

I am a dedicated and obsessed quilter. I plan to keep quilting as long as I can physically. It has been a most enjoyable hobby. I hope to keep learning and trying to do better each time. I've been very fortunate in being recognized for my accomplishments and will never understand my good fortune in being chosen for the commercial. I suspect they wanted to perpetuate the myth of *Little Old Gray-haired Lady Quilters.* We all know quilters are any age! It has been a challenge and I've enjoyed the journey.

Zelma Ziegler (ZZ)
Gilmore
Pocatello, Idaho
Snake River
Quilters Guild

Seventy years ago in a very small one-horse town, as we say in the West, in May, Idaho at the foot of Mount Borah (the highest mountain in Idaho) Zelma Ziegler was born October 24, 1923. That is only half of the story, however, for thirty minutes later my identical twin sister, Zelda Ziegler was born. I weighed 4 pounds, 4 ounces, while my sister weighed only 3 pounds, 14 ounces. Since we were premature and required so much care, our parents "Dutch" and Opal Ziegler took every other night's shift taking care of us. Fortunately, our parents pulled us through, which was no small feat in those days.

My twin, Zelda, has been the most influential female in my life, as one might expect. She had rheumatic fever at fourteen and it re-occured fifty-two years later when she and her husband, Jay Garner were living in Australia. When she returned to the United States, she was unable to do physical things because of the heart damage the rheumatic fever caused, so she took some quilting lessons and began quilting in 1975. She sparked my interest in quilting, but I was unable to devote much time to it since I was teaching English at Pocatello High. Zelda and I graduated from Challis High School in 1941. I waited twenty years and then attended Idaho State University part time, finally earning a degree in English education with a minor in business in 1968. In 1978, I received a masters degree in American Studies from the University of Wyoming, where I matriculated six summers.

In 1946, I married my beloved Michael J. Gilmore. We had three children, (Michael Shephen, Patricia, and Kerry Brent) of whom we are very proud.

My husband, Mike and I loved to travel so I have been in every state, except Alaska and Florida. My husband was going to take me to Europe for our fortieth wedding anniversary, but he dropped dead with a massive heart attack in 1986. I still miss him terribly. After my husband's death, my twin interested me in quilting and I started taking lessons and quickly became hooked on quilting. I feel quilting has kept me sane since my husband died. I usually take lessons every year in Idaho, Wyoming and Houston.

Some of my first lessons were from Elly Sienkiewicz in Jackson Hole, Wyoming where I learned ruching and other Baltimore Album techniques.
I have won a number of awards and honors. My first national recognition came when my twin sister, Zelda Z. Garner and I were among the quilters whose essays were published in part in the November 1991 issue of McCall's Magazine. The contestant had to write an essay and make a block honoring a woman who had made a difference in one's life. My twin and I honored each other, since an identical twin is extremely influential in the others life.

<u>Author's Note:</u> Zelma sent along a long list of honors she has received. I wish time and space permitted them all to be listed here, as well as Zelda's.

Sally Smith
Kodak, Tennessee
Sevier Valley Quilters

Being a wife and mother of two are the *main* jobs I hold, which I supplement by working out of my home as a graphic artist and calligrapher. Add to that PTO and a few other things, and it makes for a busy life! Quilting is my hobby, which I use to *zone out!* Of all the mediums I use as an artist, cloth seems to be the most satisfying, with people and things in my life as the subjects used for my quilts. Dear to my heart also are my cats. Our home is the *home for strays* in the neighborhood, so much so that our four cats occasionally have to vie for food with the oppossums and skunks.

Sue Hausmann
Lincolnshire, Illinois

I have been an avid sew-er all my life and although my mother and grandmother did not sew when I was young, Grandma had been a quilter in her younger days. For 8th grade graduation she gave me a precious quilt and my folks gave me the two that were always on the beds in her house next to ours. As a machine sew-er, I didn't think too much about quilting until suddenly several machine quilting pioneers like Nancy Martin and Eleanor Burns developed strip piecing and speed piecing methods. Then I was hooked and quilted constantly! I do remember trying a log cabin for Family Circle magazine - cutting all the pieces and then sewing through very puffy batting for total discouragement. Then buying a kit at the little schoolhouse where That Patchwork Place started and making strip vest after strip vest.

Once, while teaching this class the local newspaper came and took a picture, then ran it the next week with a caption, "Sue Hausmann strips in class!"

We have made each of our nieces and nephews quilts as wedding gifts, the *we* being Herb and me. He sits behind the machine and clips the speed pieced sections apart and stacks them next to me for the next sewing or serger step! And speed quilts are how we started our daughters-in-law sewing. One day our daughter and two daughters-in-law-to-be sat around the table speed-piecing queen-size log cabin quilts. It's such a miracle they all ended up with the right pieces! All love to sew, and Janet does wonderful quilts, piecing by machine and quilting by hand.

My only regret today is that I have less and less time to sew, so I do mainly clothing for myself, quick projects for the show and our grandchildren. However, I did about 16 speed quilts my last year of teaching in the store and we actually ran out of beds and walls. A number of people have encouraged me to say that I have moved on to the next stage which is enabling others to do this wonderful sewing experience, quilting, through the series and teaching outlines for others. I hope so!

Quilters Tell Why They Quilt!

Joyce Livingston

"Doctor, all I know is.....if I don't quilt....I wilt!"

Joyce Livingston
Council Grove, Kansas

Why do I quilt? I'd like to tell you it's because I have fond memories of playing under the quilt frame, giggling with cousins as we pretended we were elegant ladies in our make-believe house. I'd like to tell you that I have dozens of beautifully pieced and appliqued quilts made by my grandmothers and aunts as they sipped tea, quilted and chatted at weekly quilting bees.

But, alas!....I can't tell you such a wonderful story of my heritage. For you see....no one in my family made quilts. No one in my husband's family made quilts. I have no idea where my love of quilts and desire for them originated. I saw pictures of quilts in magazines, even ordered a pattern and a roll of cotton batting for an Ohio Rose Quilt from Mountain Mist when we were first married, with the hopes that someday I could create a quilt. But, when it arrived with it's myriad of instructions written in quilter's language, it went into the back of a closet.

A year or two later, I dug it out with renewed enthusiasm, but soon found that appliquing little pieces with tiny stitches was quite impossible with my four pre-schoolers romping across my lap each time I sat down to sew. Rarely did they all take naps at exactly the same time, so it seemed impossible to complete a quilt, (although I did complete the applique on 11 squares before I ran out of fabric, by not taking beautiful tiny applique stitches, but by doing an X-blanket stitch to secure them).

Many years later on my Television Show, three quilts made by EHU units to commemorate the retiring of the Extension Agent, were presented to her. That old love of quilts stirred within me, I had to have a quilt! If those ladies could make one, surely I could, after all I had been sewing most of my clothing, as well as my children's, for many years. Could it be that hard? So, why not make one? The time required! As a Television Broadcaster, I was busy, busy, busy! And, I still had four children at home, a home to take care of, and a husband I wanted to spend time with. So, once again, it was delayed, temporarily!

I had a mastectomy in 1980, so we decided to take early retirement and move to our cozy cabin on the lake. Ah! At last, time to make that quilt, a simple sampler from Georgia Bonesteel's book, but I did it! Now, I have completed 18 bed-size quilts, numerous wall hangings.....and, 54 quilted jackets (which I designed and constructed for *The Jackets & Embellishments Program* I present).

Did I ever finish that first quilt? Yes! For my husband, Don, for our 40th Wedding Anniversary! I had to scrounge up fabric to finish that 12th block, and added 12 nine-patch blocks to go with them to create the finished quilt.

No longer do I wish I had ancestors to provide my quilts (although it would have been nice to have them). If I see a quilt I like.....I make it! There is always a quilt of some sort in the works. And, I quilt everything without a frame or hoop!

The love of quilts and quiltmaking has led to so many new avenues in my life, opened so many doors of opportunity in ways I least expected.

My *playroom* seems to beckon to me....saying, "Come on in...I hold so many joys for you...put off the mundane, routine things of life. Come into this enchanting room, create, design, express your individuality, ride on your magic carpet into a world free of stress and problems. Let time stand still. Indulge! Enjoy!" I take a few steps away from it...toward the dirty dishes, the washer and dryer. I try to reach for the vacuum. But, that room calls to me. And.....I succumb, running into it with open arms....and mind, for a few hours of pure pleasure. For....I am a Quilter.

∞∞∞∞∞∞∞∞∞∞∞∞∞∞∞∞∞∞∞∞

Beverly J. Relph
Leavenworth, Kansas

I like to be creative regardless of whether I am sewing, cooking, or stripping furniture. Every ten days, at least, I need my fix, and it is off to the fabric store.

∞∞∞∞∞∞∞∞∞∞∞∞∞∞∞∞∞∞∞∞

Betty Lou Cassidy
Linwood, New Jersey

I became interested in quilting in 1976, the Bicentennial year. My husband and I opened the Wooden Nickel Card & Gift Shop in the barn on the farm in Drums, Pennsylvania, where my father still lives. We felt it was very "American" to be small business owners. We ran the shop for seven years, commuting every Friday the four hours to Drums from Linwood, then back on Sunday night. We still worked full-time jobs Monday thru Friday. When school was out for the summer, I would stay up on the farm until September. Charles would drive up and back on weekends. I bought a "Tree of Life" applique quilt kit from Lee Wards mail order. It had over 600 printed calico pieces to sew onto a marked white background. I attached about 320 pieces before giving up.

I would also watch the PBS station during dinner and learned a lot about quilters and quilting from the first Penny McMorris series.

I began attending the Elsa Williams School of NeedleArts in West Townsend, Massachusetts for a week each summer over the five year period as part of my "store education". (We had begun to add cross stitch and needlework to our inventory).

The school was unique in that up to twenty students would study under two nationally known needlewomen for a week's time. Housekeepers and kitchen staff cleaned your room, made the beds and provided snacks, afternoon tea, breakfast, lunch, and dinner. All the students had to do was stitch. It was my idea of heaven.

So I began a love affair with fibers- - crewel wool, perle cottons, rayons, and silks. I also took up painting needlepoint canvases.

In 1983, just as the school closed, I was certified in canvaswork by the Elsa Williams School. I am one of twenty-two people in the world to have this distinction and am very proud of the accomplishment. I feel it is the equivalent of a Master's Degree in Needlework. This experience taught me I could finish large projects within a deadline, just by arranging my "free time".

About this same time we sold the gift shop in Drums and vowed never to work two jobs again. In less time than six months however, a well-known needlework store came on the market and we couldn't resist the temptation to by it. So began another five years of retail, this time with Simply Elegant NeedleArts in Somers Point, New Jersey, four *minutes* from home, instead of four *hours*. We sold knitting yarns, needlepoint canvases, cross stitch and eventually 100% cotton fabrics for quilting. I have always felt that a well-rounded needlework knowledge is essential to doing quilting, which I feel can use every type of stitching. It captures our attention and keeps artists interested because it can be embroidered, hand or machine stitched, and even painted, but still within the framework of fiber.

My husband, Charles, is probably more tolerant of my quilting excesses than most husbands, but he's also had a lot more "quilt encounters", too.

Once he came home from work to a stove full of bubbling pots. "What are you making - soup?" he asked hopefully, as he dipped a spoon into one of the pots. It was just boiling water in which different fabrics bobbed up and down. I had taken a basic quilting course where the instructor insisted that we boil the fabric to be sure it was colorfast and preshrunk. I was just doing my homework. "Well, I guess we have pizza tonight." my husband said. "After all you used all the cooking pots."

I teach third grade in Margate, New Jersey and usually introduce a stitchery project each year. All the children in the school know I quilt. On my classroom door is the Celebrations Bear Banner which has removable flags for each month and stays up all year.

On the first day of school one of my new boys was so impressed with the banner that he called his aunt, who happens to be a secretary in our Junior High Building, and insisted that she come to our school after work to see it. He convinced her by saying, "Auntie, it's beautiful. It looks just like she bought it in a store!"

Ruth Rhoades
Toccoa, Georgia

My interest just grew like "Topsy"!

Thelma Tiefel
Clay City, Indiana

We moved from the farm 15 years ago. This is when I became interested in quilting. I had lots of scrap material stashed away, left from sewing all those years. My first quilt was a Flower Garden, the second Double Wedding Ring, these both used a lot of different prints and small pieces. These got me hooked, therefore I have made several since. Ten Log Cabins - one for each child and grandchild, each in their favorite color and also set together differently. One original design - which still doesn't have a name. Two Broken Dishes. One Royal Aster. One old-fashioned Dahlia - it has gathered petals. One Irish Chain. One twin-size School House Pattern.

I am really pleased with the School House. I found a material that looks like little red school houses, then in the plain blocks I appliqued things pertaining to my early school days. Such as (1-2-3) (A-B-C) (3 R-R-Rs) (CAT), a hand school bell which was used at my school to alert the children that recess was over, and the bottom middle block I made a Cap with a tassel. Now I am working on two Sunbonnet Appliques for twin beds.

Elizabeth A. Akana
Kaneohe, Hawaii

When our son, John, was five years old, he informed me that he was getting married. I said, "Great, that is the way life should proceed". He said, "No, I mean now. I want the quilt you are going to make me when I get married." The *love*. There it was again.

Now over the years since we received those first quilts, much has happened. Many things have changed and life has moved along. But the quilts have remained steadfast. They represented a given *Love*.

The children are married now and have their quilts. Now it is time to concentrate on the next generation. The quilts will be the tangible *love* that I give to my grandchildren. It is a way for my *love* to be with them, even though I'm not physically present.

History tells us that allowing your *love* to flow is the beautiful tradition of the unique Hawaiian quilts and each one of us should express our *love* through our own uniqueness.

Karen Crollick
St. George,
Australia, QLD

I have been quilting two years, my closest friend, Lee, introduced me to patchwork after finding out that my Father had cancer. (He passed away January '95) and having problems within my marriage, I became quite depressed. Quilting saved my sanity, even though I was going quite mad at times as I was having anxiety attacks regularly. Two years down the track, I'm happy to say my marriage is still going from strength to strength. The anxiety attacks are becoming far and few between and so thank you to a good friend for bringing to me the love for quilting.

Glenda Phipps
Whitman, Nebraska

Quilting has been a lifesaver for me. I can pick up my needle after a hard day and I miraculously become almost human. I have met many terrific fellow quilters and have hopefully created something of beauty that will live on long after I am gone. What more could anyone want?

Jill Marie Tanking
Liberal, Kansas

About 12 years ago a quilt shop opened in Liberal and I decided to take the Sampler Class. Would you believe the sampler is still not done? The owner's husband was transferred out-of-state. Another shop eventually opened. Another start! About that time, a quilt guild started but it took about two years before I joined. In the mean time my family had moved to the country. What an experience for the city girl of 40 some years.

My family had not been very supportive of my quilting. They thought another one of her hair-brain projects. Boy, have they changed their mind. They are very willing to give their advise and ask for some of my wall hangings for gifts. The youngest son, Tod, had the opportunity to go to Belgium for Christmas in 1994. He knew I had done an Eleanor Burns pineapple wall hanging with sunflower material. The family he was staying with collects sunflowers, so he asked for it as a Thank-You gift.

One thing I have learned from quilting, do not start with a King-size sampler. Maybe some day I will get it done. I have made a Trip-around-the-world. It started from a picture of a drape curtain and I decided if I was going to all that work then make the quilt and drape it over the rod for a curtain. At that time we did not have a basement, so everytime I got out my quilt strips, they were always in everyone's way. In 1990, we moved the house, had a basement built, put the boys in the basement. I GOT ONE OF THE UPSTAIRS BEDROOMS FOR A SEWING ROOM!! IT IS SEVENTH HEAVEN!! I have set-up my computer and CD player in my sewing room. I can almost hibernate in that room.

As for why I am a quilter, at first, it was something to do and prove myself that I could do it. I started with BIG projects like the sampler and the Trip-around-the-world. Got the top completed on the Trip Quilt and felt like the challenge was over. Quilting did not excite me. But, when I did a maple leaf wall hanging and knew that it would be hanging at the college for National Quilt Week, decided I had better learn to quilt quick and correct.

Having joined the local Quilt Guild has been a lot of help and boast to the morale. They are quick to compliment and very willing to help you figure out a problem.

Now quilting is a challenge for every project I take on. I have learned to look at a picture and figure how to make a quilt from it. Just like now, I was playing with "Triangle Paper for Quilters". Had no idea what I would do with all those triangles, so made them into pinwheels. Then found out Ragi Marino (guild president) was moving to Texas. Her little daughter likes coming out to our farm to see the baby pigs. I found some farm scene material and some pig material. So am making her a doll quilt with the farm scene for the middle and the pinwheels to represent the wind in southwest Kansas. The pig material is the backing.

Elaine Helen (Revier) Baker
Watertown, Minnesota

I started quilting as a way to cope with the death of my second daughter, Natalie. She died a little over six years ago of a heart defect. Quilting has healed me through many difficult times. I was on bed rest for six months with my last child. We had to wait through the first five months of that pregnancy before we could find out if she had the same heart defect as Nat' or not. She didn't. My oldest has ADHD. Ugh.

Tabitha was diagnosed with Attention Deficit Hyperactivity Disorder about nine months after Jazmin was born. It was tough but she's doing well (with out medication). Jazmin was a crabby and not too healthy baby (no offense, Jaz'). I find that my quilting keeps me from dwelling on all the hardships that moms go through these days.

Nadine Dozier
North Augusta, South Carolina

I made my first quilt about 11 years ago, but got more involved in quilting when a close friend formed what is our quilting guild, 6 1/2 years ago. I mainly make quilts now because my family loves to use them so much in the winter months, and it is something I can make for gifts for family and friends.

Barbara S. Moss
Locust Grove, Georgia

I quilt because: You get to talk about new quilting ideas with people. Quilters are happy people. Talking to a quilt sometimes is better than a person. Making something that will last forever for your loved ones.

Jean Van Dusen
Kingsford, Michigan

First of all, I am a quilter because I love fabric and sewing. About in 1967, I joined a Community School Quilting class. We had a wonderful teacher that made it a lot of fun. I made a Log Cabin Quilt and an appliqued Butterfly Quilt. I was hooked.

Louise Murphy
Mammoth Lakes, California

I started quilting in 1976-77 with the majority of new quilters, as did my sister and friend and neighbor. The fabrics, literature and tools were scarce, compared to today's market. Classes almost non-existent. We learned by trial and error, i.e. 16" blocks for a twin size quilt using poly-blends. Ouch!

We now have the good fortune to enjoy classes and teachers from not only our country, but overseas as well. So much talent and creativity out there. It is constantly a motivating force to strive for better quality from within ourselves. I am always feeling a challenge to try new techniques and design ideas. My maternal grandmother was a seamstress and made quilts. Mostly utility quilts.

Josephine Hannan Jirva Burgwyn (Jo Jo)
Jackson, North Carolina

I have loved quilts and wanted to know how to make them all my life and it wasn't until I graduated from college, came home, got a job, that I was able to find someone to teach me. It was *so* exciting, learning step-by-step and then making a whole quilt of my own - to keep! Of course, my first was for my husband. I did it in earth tones because he is a farmer, it's a sampler.

Colleen Taylor
Indialantic, Florida

I have always loved fabrics, began sewing in high school, but didn't begin quilting until 1979. Quilting is very relaxing, but can be very challenging as well.

Lynn Lewis Young
Houston, Texas

I find quiltmaking satisfying on all levels from simple projects just for the joy of sewing, to more artistically involved and meaningful quilts where the medium is used as another fine art medium.

Mary Ann Keppler
St. Olaf, Iowa

I am a quilter because it's part of my business, but it's a part of my business, because it's a peaceful release. When I'm quilting I can block out a lot of commotion.

Kelly Lum Newgarde
Phillipsburg, New Jersey

I have always admired the quilts I have seen. The first quilt I made has traveled to the Northeast Whole Language Conference in Vermont, the National Art Convention in Baltimore, Maryland, and now it is on display at an art gallery in New York City by Binney and Smith (the Crayola Company). My first quilt was a culminating activity for an author study about Patricia Reilly Giff. Each child illustrated a scene from one of the stories they read, on a 10" square and colored it with fabric crayons. The pictures were ironed onto muslin squares. Next, my mother, Carol Lum, and I assembled the quilt. The storybook quilt has been admired by many people. I am very proud of this first quilt.

Deb Meneely
Seattle, Washington

Besides being a person who loves fabric and working with it, I also treasure the wonderful sense of being a part of the community of quilters - both those in generations before me, (whose work I can admire) and those who share the love of quilts today with me. I have found quilters to be some of the most generous, caring and creative people I have ever met. Quilting fills my need to be creative and gives me a way to keep from getting stagnant.

Kathryn Ripeteau Greenwold
Niskayuna, New York

My grandmothers both were expert quilters and I grew up loving their beautiful bed covers. A friend got me to do my first quilting on a Bicentennial Project and I've been at it ever since. I enjoy both traditional quilting and playing with my machine for some terrific modern results.

Florence Edith Goggin
Eureka, California

My Grandmother, Edith Todd Groshong, left several tops and quilt blocks of which the Bible Blocks were my first to assemble and I was hooked on quilting. My Mother-in-law taught me to quilt and we spent many hours at the quilt frame.

I love to quilt and the wonderful feeling I have in seeing the results of 20 years of teaching students, words cannot describe it.

Chloe Rhodes
Clay City, Indiana

I only make the tops. I haven't mastered the quilting part. I started this to fill in a lot of lonely hours after I lost my husband. I really enjoy it.

Rebecca Kelly
Kingsburg, California

I believe that quilting is the perfect creative outlet for me. I am limited only by my imagination. I also feel a connection with those women of the past, because I'm a little "old-fashioned" myself.

Mary Andrews
Grand Blanc, Michigan

I love to sew. When I went to that first quilt show and class, I knew that quilting was for me. I was so inspired by the beautiful quilts, that I took rolls of pictures, so I could study them at home. One in particular was a hockey quilt. My sons have played hockey since they were little and I wanted to make one like it. I studied how it was made and took lots of pictures of it, and made a small one for my son with the jersey of the team he had been playing for the last few years. At this same quilt show, I met Marty Lawrence, who was selling her beautiful tie dyed fabric and I found a piece of blue that looked like ice for the hockey quilt. She told me about our local quilt guild and I went to the next meeting. I have met so many wonderful friends and have been so inspired by the show and tell and of course, have learned so much from everyone. Most of my best friends now are quilters.

Patricia (Pat) Jones
Oroville, California

I signed up for quilting lessons at the local Fabric Store, completely unaware of the "disease" I was about to catch! The class was taught by an elderly lady and was not a structured class, but really just informative. It definitely was not not a "Hands on" class. Oh well, I was hooked anyway and never missed a class. She briefly showed us the hand quilting stitch, gave us some magazines and books and told us to choose our own pattern. We were taught nothing about fabric, color or design. I jumped right in and began my "quilting career". At the end of 6 weeks, I had pieced and hand quilted one 15" block. The corners didn't match and the rows were crooked, but who cared? "I was a quilter".

I joined a local quilting guild and soon discovered that I really hadn't learned anything in that 6 week class. I still had a lot to learn! The Guild had many workshops and after sharing ideas and knowledge with the many other members, I began to become a true quilter.

Fifteen years later, I find myself the maker of many quilts and I have been teaching quilt classes for 7 years for our local Parks & Recreation Department. I made each of my children and their spouses a quilt, and a "fishing quilt" for my hubby. Each of the grandchildren received a baby quilt at birth, and in the past 3 years, each one has received a twin size for Christmas. They are already asking for bigger ones to cuddle up in. As a toddler, my youngest grandson, Zach, attended many guild meetings and classes with me. Often he would fall asleep on the cutting table, always under someone's quilt.

I love to take classes and attend out of town retreats. My favorite retreats are given by Linda Ballard, another California Quilt Teacher. I first met Linda during a telephone conversation. She asked me if I was the Pat Jones that had entertained a bus load of quilting ladies on the way to the "Sisters Oregon Show"? I didn't realize that I was entertaining anyone except myself! I make friends easily and can carry on a conversation with almost anyone. If they know anything about quilting, I never stop talking.

I love to collect old quilts and quilt tops. They just seem to tell their own stories. I like to touch and caress them and imagine what they would tell me, if they could talk! I wonder how far they might have traveled or whom they might have covered. Was it a gift for a newlywed, a housewarming, or maybe it covered a precious child. Did their maker love them as much as I do now?

I never miss a day of quilting or sewing in my 9x12' sewing room. My little dog is always under my sewing table, usually with her tail on the foot pedal. Wherever in my home there is a quilt, you will find me and Maggie. She loves them, too!

Page 92, Reasons why I'm a Quilter

Minabess P. Randolph
Toms River, New Jersey

I have been sewing since I took Home Ec. in 8th grade. My very first job was running errands for a lady who owned a Millinery Shop. I would go into Philadelphia to all the wholesale millinery stores to buy felts, ribbons and flowers to match swatches of fabrics, from which hats were to be made for customers. I also learned to make hats and had a hat to match each of my Sunday outfits.

The reason I am a quilter is because I had a friend who was a quilter. Every time I went to her home, she was making a quilt and I would say "one of these days I'm going to do that". One Sunday we were chatting and she was cutting little pieces of fabric. When I got up to leave she handed me all the pieces for a Dresden Plate block, and said "Now go home and do it". I did and I've never stopped quilting since that day.

Mary Jane Cemer
Trenton, Nebraska

I have no idea why I'm a quilter. Mama did. I do. It's my artist canvas. It's easy and quick and uncomplicated. It soothes my Scorpio creativity. I love it. I am sloppy, hurry too much, don't follow directions, do what I please...and have a ball!

Jan Jacobson
Tripoli, Wisconsin

I am a quilter because it is the most satisfying thing I have ever done. I could *not* quilt. I get *antsy* if I don't have a project to pick up when I sit down. My hands are not happy when idle. I came to quilting on my own. No one else in my family was a quilter. I am the "oddball". I am sure some of them think that.

Patti Centeno
San Antonio, Texas

Quilting not only allows me to express to others who I am as an artisan, but also as a person. I quilt for the pure enjoyment of it. I am very tied to the notion that we need to leave a little of ourselves for the next generation, so that they will know what things were of importance to us. Our heritage is such an important piece of evidence that we should not let the knowledge of who we are die with us. Each family member should have something that they have accomplished that they can leave for future generations to connect to.

Each year I quilt at the Hyatt Hill Country Resort in San Antonio, Texas for their Pioneer Christmas display. I get great joy watching people's faces and hearing their childhood stories of the quilt frames that hung from the ceilings, and how they recall that special quilt that was on their bed at grandma's house. It is comforting to have them touch the antique tops I'm working on and reminisce of days gone by. This is a part of history that should always be retold in families.

Tonya St. Berg
Woodinville, Washington

I started sewing by hand when I was five years old and was hooked on sewing. I learned to use a sewing machine as a teenager. Over twenty years ago, I was asked to draw the local church group, quilting, for a quilter who felt my drawing abilities could provide her with the memory of still being in the room. As I drew, she explained how to make a pocket puff quilt, the latest innovation, to another quilter. I went home and made the quilt and I have been quilting ever since.

I am a fourth generation quilter, teaching quilting, my satellite group is called Personal Touch Quilters, I have held two quilt shows, and I recently started a monthly quilt display at the Woodinville Library. I am particularly interested in history and am president of the Woodinville Historical Society. I try to incorporate fabric sacks (flour, rice, etc.) into all of my quilts because of the historical nature.

Susan Hanna
Brownlee, Nebraska

I think we all have different reasons for quilting. Some enjoy the competition of quilt contests, some quilt to provide an income, some for recognition, some to ease a sorrow. For me quilting speaks of something deep within and is part of the country lifestyle I have adopted and love. Those of you who enjoy the smell of laundry dried on the line in the fresh air, unobstructed winter sunsets, or solitude interrupted only by the sounds of birds can probably appreciate this.

My interest in fabric and sewing began very early when I would sit on the floor and play with the treadle on my grandmother's machine. Later, I accompanied her to work, where she made custom draperies and slipcovers, and I would spend hours with the many bolts of fabric. To this day, a print with cabbage roses practically reaches off the shelf and grabs me. Life with her was filled with comfort and love, and quilts say the same thing to me.

Barbara MacDonald
Oscoda, Michigan

I think you're either a quilter or you're not. It's a passion, like a thirst that's hard to quench. I believe in the saying "When the top is done, the quilt is finished." I now have 50 quilt tops to quilt. I only do hand quilting, so I will keep busy for many years to come.

I teach quilt classes all year, but my favorites are the Lock-Ins. We spend all day just sewing (and eating, of course) and when the day is over, everyone leaves with a finished top.

I also teach mystery classes. It's amazing how many quilters will come and sew all day, not really caring what they are making.

I attend the Quilt Markets every year with the owner of Loose Threads, Corrie Barber. There are so many classes offered. I take as many as I can, so I'm always learning and I try to pass on whatever I learn to my students.

Carole P. Kenny
Providence,
Rhode Island

In 1976, I made a quilt - no one told me about quilt thread, findings, etc. I designed another block, when I realized I would have to cut 3,200 pieces by scissors, I put the whole thing away. In 1989, I learned about roller cutters and strip piecing and have been hooked ever since. I now do lectures as: "The Happy Stripper".

Bonnie Swecker
Roanoke Rapids,
North Carolina

Can the love of quilting be inherited? As I mentioned in my bio, both my grandmothers made quilts. Theirs were mostly the old-time patchwork kind, quilted on a rack that was hung from the ceiling, and often quilted with the help of several lady friends. Both grandmas are gone now, but the hooks are still in the old homeplace ceilings - and the rack of one is in my attic. When I was a little girl, one of these grandmothers, Betty Mason, pieced a quilt top that I thought was so pretty. Unfortunately, her thumb was cut off in a mowing accident; so she was unable to quilt it. Would you believe that years later when I got married, I received that quilt as a wedding gift? It was quilted by my other grandmother, Martha Carawan. They both lived in the same small community. I call it my "Two-grannies" quilt - what else? Maybe the interest in quilting is inherited.

Judy Wolfrom
Southampton,
New Jersey

I went to the Kutztown, Pennsylvania Fair wanting to bring home a quilt. As reasonable as they were (now I know), I still could not afford one. So what does every seamstress say when she wants something made of fabric and thread? "I can make that!" So I took lessons and learned from an excellent teacher who is still a great friend.

Jean Eng Underhill
Flemington,
New Jersey

I quilt because it's a challenge and I can be innovative. I can produce something for my family and friends, that they can use now and pass on. It's a product of the times dated by the fabric. The quilts will pass on our memories for our children and their children. I enjoy it and my girls like it, and will be quilters themselves. Ngaire and Kara have a fabric stash they can play with now.

Page 94, Reasons why I'm a Quilter

Eugenia A. Barnes (Genie)
Marcellus, New York

Quilting satisfies all my needs, it gives me an opportunity to touch/feel fabrics, meet the challenge of colors and patterns and calms me in the eye of the storm. Quiltmaking has given me new friends and opportunities and gives my soul flight.

Quilting puts me at peace, makes me crazy when I have deadlines for class samples or up-coming shows. I rarely enter competitions but have had several gallery shows to prepare for this winter and this spring. I find that the time alone...when ever that comes, is welcome and energizing and then the fellowship of my small design group...the interplay, the discussions and the playing off each other makes the whole worthwhile. Marty Ban, editor of American Quilter is my dear friend and although she lives across the country, our frequent conversations and sharing of ideas and feelings is a most special gift...one of the many that quiltmaking has brought to me. Meeting someone like Lois has been one of those special gifts...Anita Shackelford and others from your area are just among the wonderful people my job brings to me.

"Wish I could be a mouse at your house when the mail arrives...I am sure you'll find so many different ideas!"

Ann Littleton
Fairfax, Virginia

Quilting allows me to create with fabric, colors, and designs like no other art form. It helps bring me closer to the "olden days", at least visually in my thoughts. The reproduction fabrics have made it possible to recreate some of the "cozier-looking" quilts of the past.

My quilts are a record of my life experiences.

Of fortunate times: like the time of a group gift exchange when one girl across the room opened a beautiful little quilted wallhanging (she wasn't the quilt type) and I received a casserole cover that she admired. Afterward, we "discretely traded". It now hangs above my couch over another one that was my first hand-quilted project. I used too thick of a batting and the hand-quilting was so primitive that I embroidered, HANNA, AGE 6, 1891, in the lower right-hand corner.

Of times of sickness: During one of my bouts with pneumonia, being stuck in bed for two months, I was determined to learn to hand-piece. The result: a red, white, and navy small churn dash.

Of happy times: On family camping trips, a hand-pieced project always goes along. One trip to a quilt show with a group of friends led to several of us purchasing kits for a shoo-fly miniature, which we finished. We were so proud when our little quilts appeared in an issue of *Ladies Circle Patchwork Quilts Magazine*, Jan. 1994.

Of sad times: During times of sadness, my creative juices stopped. They were times of reflection, and introspection, loneliness, despair, questioning, causing character development, increased sensitivity and compassion for others, and a renewed faith in God. I learned that I was not self-sufficient. It was during one of these times that my quilts comforted me as I wrapped up in them, cozy and warm, with memories of more joyful times.

Of thankful times: At one end-of-the-year-quilt dinner, (when I was feeling better), at each place setting was a roll of six-inch neon-colored fabric squares. These fabrics depicted how I felt inside. (Like the sunshine has come back into my life). Thus, another mini-quilt was born. It looks real strange in my country blue and rust family room, but is one of my favorites because of what it represents. (A rainbow at the end of a storm).

Of sharing times: Last summer, while Joe and Jay were backpacking in the Rockies, I hosted a July 4th weekend "Quilt Camp" for my friends. Seventeen different ladies were here at various times, as their schedules allowed. Not knowing how many would be here for meals, I chose a menu that would accommodate as few or as many as could join me. We usually had seven or eight. I have included some of the recipes. The weekend of sewing was of sharing, strengthening old friendships, and building new ones. The only hand-sewing I got done was mending my son Jay's gym shorts, which he had masking-taped together to get him through until school got out for the summer.

<u>The main reason I'm a quilter is because of the strong relationships.</u> Quilters are some of the most interesting, creative, fun loving, insightful people I know. Since this is a survival guide for quilters, I must say the relationships I share with my quilting friends are what help me survive the storms of life, as well as to provide "the icing on the cake" of life's joys.

<u>Author's note:</u> Ann was kind enough to send along her Quilt Camp itinerary and the menu for the weekend. What fun! There was even a bed time story listed each night, I wonder what that was? This retreat for quilting friends is a great idea, especially if each one helps with the cooking and work.

∞∞∞∞∞∞∞∞∞∞∞∞∞∞∞∞∞∞

Eleanor K. Hunnel
Johnstown, Nebraska

At that first quilt class, a lady brought a catalog of quilts hanging in a Lincoln, Nebraska museum and there was a child's quilt of some of the same ABC blocks as mine. With awakened feelings of appreciation I lifted that little quilt from its resting place and carefully picked it all apart, setting it together anew and quilting it all by hand. I later learned from an aunt that she and my Mother had each made a set of these blocks, when each was expecting a baby in 1937. On the block for N is an appliqued number 37. I had wondered why *that* number. The little background blocks were tobacco sacks from which Mom had picked the stitching (The tobacco used by the men of the family). The quilt hangs in a special spot - honored.

In 1992, my worst fears were realized when the doctor said "The lump is surely cancerous and we'll do the surgery one week from today". In dismay I said I just couldn't make that date, as I had a quilt class scheduled, as well as two trunk shows that next week - dates set months earlier. When he called later confirming the biopsy findings, he said "About your quilt dates? - go for it and we'll do the surgery the next week." I told no one of my problem, I didn't think I could handle their pity and concern. One of the trunk shows was at the Governor's mansion in Lincoln, where I gave a presentation at a luncheon for the wives of the Nebraska undertakers.

When my good quilting friends learned of my surgery, they sent out a block pattern and an invitation to send me a block with their name on it...Friendship Star. These blocks started arriving while I was still in the hospital and since it was unbeknownst to me - what a surprise!! Can you imagine the thrill, the great therapy it was to get all these blocks in mail - 162 in all - each usually with a written note of care, concern and hope. Altogether I pieced them into 4 quilts which are now a part of my presentations, when I tell my concern story.

Just an added note of caution and concern: I'd had yearly examinations for 20 years and numerous mammograms. My 2 sisters died with breast cancer so I was concerned, but was always assured that the lump was 'only a cyst'. I should have been more aggressive in getting a second opinion. Modern technology does not always prove reliable in finding breast cancer.

<u>Author's note:</u> I share Eleanor's story, and appreciate her telling it. I found a lump in my breast in 1980, went into surgery for a biopsy the next day, and had a mastectomy 2 days later. Six months later I had reconstructive surgery, not because of vanity, but because I'm a swimmer and I didn't want to see some *foam thing shaped like a breast* floating out of my swimming suit when I was in the water! I'm not the same size on both sides, but close enough to make me feel better about myself. It took several months of physical therapy to get my arm back into full use, but I made it! I had asked the Lord, that day I found the lump, to please let me live until my son Luke (who was in the 8th grade at the time and our youngest child) graduated from high school. The Lord has been very good to me, I not only saw him graduate high school, but college, married Tammie and became the father of two precious children, he's now 28. And, I'm still going strong, with NO recurrences. Didn't even have to have chemotherapy!

I guess what I'm saying is....get your check-ups regularly, have a mammography when your doctor tells you....and live life to it's fullest, appreciate your blessings. You never know what may be ahead. And, if something like this happens to you....it's not the end of the world.....it only seems like it at the time!

Dotti Greto
Ocean City, New Jersey

I have been sewing since I was 12 years old and have quilted several small things along the way, but really became addicted to it after seeing my sister, Debbi Fair, do several projects.

My first twin size quilt (before I knew what I was doing) had a Navy blanket for batting - can you imagine quilting through that? It's a wonder I ever went any farther. Then I made a patchwork for my daughter years later. I found out you are supposed to quilt in the plain blocks, too. I only quilted the pieced blocks.

I knew I needed some quilter friends to talk with, after I decided to make myself a Churn Dash Friendship quilt for my bed, and asked all my friends and family for an old shirt or blouse to make their block with. Several months later, one of my blouse donor friends asked me where her quilt was...she thought I was going to make everyone a quilt...with one blouse? I went right out and joined 2 quilt guilds...two of the best things I ever did.

Peggy Gunwall
Perham, Minnesota

I live alone and needed something to keep me busy and got interested in quilting through some of the models at the store, and now I eat, sleep, and drink quilting. I started out by learning to make quilted placemats and then on to quilts and wallhangings.

Martha G. Wilson
Roanoke Rapids, North Carolina

I am a quilter because of my mother. She is a good example of the saying "If you want anything done right, do it yourself." Jane, my sister, told me before I am buried, the undertaker has to bring me home to clean up my quilting mess.

Jean S. Branham
Halifax, North Carolina

Quilting is the best therapy for me. When I get frustrated, I quilt. It is probably the only vice I have.

Edna R. Harbison
Ontonagon, Michigan

I became a quilter out of necessity. It was the only skill I thought I had, when my husband and I moved to our remote cabin in the Upper Peninsula of Michigan. When I started designing wall hangings, I started liking it, and it became a major source of income. But when I started entering quilt contests and won awards, I was hooked forever.

Helen Blankenship
Flint, Michigan

In addition to GSQ, I also belong to NQA, AQS and Michigan Network, and a small group of 6 we call "Group Therapy". We learn so much by being involved with other quilters. I served for 2 1/2 years as Guild Historian and it helped me to know quilts and quilters.

Melissa Armstrong
Oshkosh, Nebraska

My Grandmother was a quiet quilter. She made quilts for all her children, grandchildren, and quilts for a few of her great-grandchildren. We took it all for granted. I started quilting when I was pregnant with Jessica, as something to do for the long wait. When she was born with congenital heart disease, quilting gave me something to do with my hands for the long surgery waits. It makes me wonder what Grandma worried about while she quilted.

Doris Holland
Winterset, Iowa

I attended a quilt class in January and February, 1987 and that is what really got me interested. I find it to be very relaxing. I started out hand piecing and hand quilting. Now I do mostly machine piecing and am thinking of trying machine quilting. One of my daughters, Marla Allsap, is a beginning quilter.

Jeanne K. Ferg
Asheville, North Carolina

Many years ago, I sewed clothing for myself and two boys, out of necessity. On occasion, I would piece quilts and tie them, out of necessity again. As time went on I discovered actual quilting, and taught myself as well as one can. This has always been a great love for me.

Susan D. Fellin
Flemington, New Jersey

I am a quilter because of my love of fabric. I love to combine colors and create new projects from patterns. I am a fabraholic, and I love to buy new quilting books and patterns.

Lori Hauswirth
Iron River, Michigan

My first quilting experience was when my mother's home extension group sponsored me as a county fair queen candidate. My "talent" was to demonstrate making some quilted pillows. I had never done this before, what was I doing? I must have done okay, as I was runner-up. I've been hooked ever since. I do mostly small quilts and wall hangings, as I like the satisfaction of getting things done quickly. I have learned a lot from Mom and am grateful we are able to share our love of quilting. We spend many hours working on projects together.

Paula Kay Garrison & Duncan Garrison
New Braunfels, Texas

Dean Valentine sparked my interest and my grandmother had always quilted. My husband has been sewing since he was a small boy. He does patterns and quilt design with Autocard on his computer. He does most of the cutting & piecing. I do quilting & applique.

Paula Gore
Osmond, Nebraska

I have always loved quilts but I never wanted to make one - I wanted to inherit. I figured I didn't have the time or talent. After all, I had a husband I was very involved with and two small children.

A friend of mine, Bonnie Noland, that worked in the lab I did, was a quilt-a-holic. And she was desperately trying to spark some interest among those of us at work, who at least knew what fabric was. Try as she might, it was going to take a minor miracle to get us quilting, we all had those standard excuses that ended with "well, maybe someday, when I'm not so busy". A small miracle later, she had 12 of us unsuspecting 'friends' recruited. The bait? A challenge quilt. A wall hanging size. The rules: we got 9 fabrics, could discard 1, add 2, it had to be done by county fair time. I figured this was a project I could finish, with proper inspiration. Little did I know how hooked I would become!!

My first attempt at machine piecing blocks was so dismal that Bonnie told me later she wouldn't have even used them as potholders! I was discouraged, but I continued to try. When I would encounter a problem we would talk about it at coffee breaks, lunch breaks, as often as we could. "Here, let me show you on a napkin" was what she would tell us. I learned more about quilt making from the back of a napkin than all the quilt books combined.

As I struggled to get my top together, my daughter, then 3, was just learning how to put puzzles together. I would sew (and rip) and sew (and rip), while baby Ian slept, and Katie Jo worked on her puzzles. One extremely frustrating day, as I was beginning to think I should give up, she said to me, "Mama, you need to do it one piece at a time." Well, out of the mouths of babes....Every time I got discouraged, I just remembered her words and the pieces went much better!!! So much better in fact, that I was cutting out my first full size quilt before I had finished the wall hanging Challenge quilt. Not only did my little quilt get done in time for the fair, but my big quilt was done in time for Christmas. I gave it to my mother, as a symbol of how important she is to me. Any way, I was addicted and now I don't have to wait to inherit a quilt (after all, there was no one for me to inherit from), I can make my own.

Sherry Cook
Council Grove, Kansas

My grandmother started me in quilting at age 5, because due to disability of Cerebral Palsy, the doctor said I was getting bored, so this was a challenging past time. Quilting has always been a satisfying hobby that gives me a feeling of accomplishment.

Janet Kugler
Holdrege, Nebraska

I'm a third generation quilter. both of my grandmothers quilted and I remember my paternal grandmother always having a quilt frame up. My mother did some quilting when I was small. I enjoy putting fabrics together and snuggling in the quilt, even during the quilting process.

Audrey Derscha
Flint, Michigan

I started by wanting to finish two tops that were made by an Aunt in Indiana. But my teacher soon shifted the gears in my head. She provoked so many ideas that those two tops are still not done 15 years later. And the ideas just keep coming!

Marilyn T. Guy
Delhi, New York

I am not machine friendly and usually do everything by hand. It is so relaxing and it can be done while with others, or watching TV or riding in the car. I take my piecing everywhere. Lately, I have tried to learn machine piecing and realize that is another whole craft that can also be satisfying.

My grandsons are very fond of quilts. One day, when Karl was about 6, he asked if he could use one of my cool blankets. I said, "What do you mean?" He said, "You know, when you first wrap up in it, it feels real cool and then after awhile, it gets real warm."

I was voted into the Catskill Mountain Quilters Hall of Fame in 1985. I have always been embarrassed about that. I am very enthusiastic and want to be sure the craft is handed down and kept alive, but I have always felt like a beginner.

Diane Johnson
Rhinebeck, New York

I learned to quilt at two wonderful shops in West Palm Beach, Florida, where it is too hot most of the year to even use quilts! It was love at first stitch! I love fabric and color and in quilt making, the possibilities are limitless. My specialities are miniature quilts and color and fabric selection!

Lynn G. Kough
Middletown,
New Jersey

•I have had a life-long love affair with fabric.

Susan Nicholson
Muskegon, Michigan

I'm a quilter because hands itch if they aren't doing some sort of needlework. In high school and college, I did A LOT of knitting and became allergic to the yarn...so...I tried cross-stitch and crewel embroidery, but thought there must be something more challenging. I knew making a quilt would be a challenge because I had always thought making a quilt was a lot like building a house. Now that's a challenge!

Kathy Palmiter
Williams, Indiana

I quilt because I love fabric and color. I was always busy with my hands as a youngster, but became serious about sewing when I took a junior high school home-ec class. From then on, I sewed clothes for myself and later my son, Paul. Over the years, I bounced from one craft to another until I found quilting. It's more than a pastime, it's a passion. My friends say I'm driven. . .and it's true. I can't quilt enough, and fast enough to ever accomplish all I want to do.

Mary Lou Sayers
Clarkson, Nebraska

I quilt for the sheer joy of it. I love color, I love handwork, I enjoy seeing other peoples work and I hoard old fabric, especially the old 1880 blues. I find quilting very relaxing, very good for easing troubles. I often tell friends that I put my troubles down on my quilt top and stitch them down. Makes problems much easier to bear. To me quilting is a continuing thread that seems to connect one generation to another. I greatly admire antique quilts, considering the conditions under which many of them were produced.

Often, I tell my students that there is no excuse for not making a lovely quilt now days, as our choices are endless. God bless our fabric designers and our pattern designers. The possibilities are endless, too.

I don't feel I do anything that profound in the quilt world. I just try to instill in my students that it should be enjoyable and not to get all tied up in the minute details. I often tell them if it's not fun to quilt, they should take up bowling!!!

Edna E. Holdsworth
Johnston, Rhode Island

I became interested in quilting just prior to the Bicentennial year when many of the old crafts were being activated again. My first quilt, Lafayette Orange Peel, was made for a wedding present. It took me three years to complete and the couple finally got it when they had been married over two years. (I told them I wanted to be sure the marriage lasted!) I find quilting a marvelous creative experience and after 20 years, I am still evolving in this art.

Teresa A. Walton
New Braunfels, Texas

Why am I a quilter? Three credit hours! I was enrolled in a life science program in 1986. I needed an art course. Since basket weaving was not offered and I owned a sewing machine, I decided quilting would be a lot easier than 16 weeks of "The Works of the Masters". I signed up for quilting! EASY....RIGHT! Reading with my husband, Steven, I was tracing, cutting, pinning, piecing, sewing, ripping, sewing, ironing, and occasionally patting myself on the back when the points on the stars met; the curves laid flat; a block was finished. After 16 weeks, the wall hanging that established the grade was completed and hanging and a 12 block sampler "quilting in progress". Every stitch by hand.

Dawn Golden
Milford, New Jersey

My passion for quilting was started about 5 years ago by a 30 minute TV Show. It was a "How To" series on one of those off beat cable stations that originally caught my eye. Material was cheap, so this would be a good hobby...or so I thought!! I became obsessed and had to try it, so I bought some material. Then my machine wasn't working right, so I had it fixed and I bought some material. Next, I got a friend interested, so we both bought new machines and some more material.

We started matching Fan Quilt Wall Hangings in 1990, they are still not finished. Soon we found the beautiful fabrics in Quilt Shops, but it wasn't so cheap anymore. That doesn't really matter because I rarely have time to actually quilt. I mainly enjoy talking about quilting, admiring my fellow Guild Members' work and waiting for a time when my children are in school so that I can make something larger than a wall hanging!

Florence L. Tyler
DeLancey, New York

I quilt because I enjoy sewing, it's so relaxing. I usually make quilted articles to give for showers, and weddings, Anniversaries, Graduations, etc., etc.

Darlene Brazil
Escalon, California

Why do I quilt?? It's second nature! or maybe first! It definitely comes before cooking! Actually, I remember my grandmother, Gustie Law, quilting when I was a child. She had a frame that raised up over the bed at night and lowered during the day. I was fascinated by the patterns and calicoes.

She would let me sit under the sewing machine and rock the treadle, as she sewed. This was probably to keep an eye on me, however, what fun I had! Also, my mother, Faye Gossett, loved to sew clothing. As I grew older, my mother and I would sew together. We would go down to JC Penneys and find a really cute dress, then buy the fabrics to make it. We would then go home and cut the pattern, freehand, out of newspapers.

I attribute my love for color, design, fabric and quilting to both of these women.

Marilyn Thomas
Harpster, Ohio

My sister taught classes so I went, got "hooked" and enjoyed it ever since. I think it is relaxful. I think it's great when a person can put her thoughts together in fabric. Thru the years I've won 2 quilt tops and many quilt block contests. Many from Fairfield Batting. Those blocks are sewn into a quilt of 20 blocks. I have been runner up many times. I hope this year to be to top block.

Pamela Thompson
Clinton Twp,
Michigan

I quilt because it's relaxing and I can create something beautiful. I also enjoy puzzles, and fabric puzzles sewn together don't seem to be such a waste of time. My quilts are usually special gifts.

PIONEER QUILTERS
Eugene, Oregon

- For my sanity.
- I love to make quilts for family.
- To have the expertise and camaraderie of the group.
- So I'll have something to do in my old age.
- To complete a top left me by my mother.

- I just enjoy it, I guess.
- I love fabric.
- I feel good doing it!
- Good therapy!

Roberta Schroeder
Deer Park,
Washington

My Mother was a fantastic seamstress and I always felt like a total klutz at the sewing machine. I always wanted to make a quilt, so I signed up for a class, 4 years after she died. I loved it and I could even sew a straight line. I love sharing my handiwork and being creative with color and designs. I wonder what my Mother is thinking, as I have far and away surpassed my notions of sewing, I ever thought I had. I am still only interested in fabric creations other than apparel. I do not sew clothes at all.

Merrilyn Muir-Rennau
Vienna, Austria,
Europe

There are several reasons I am a Quilter.
- I need to be creative.
- It's a good way to meet people.
- For me, it is very therapeutic.
- It's rewarding, that I can bring joy to my fellowman.
- While living in Lagos, Nigeria there was not enough to keep me busy as I am accustomed to being. Diplomatic life started about dinner time every night, so the days were for me to plan. The children were in school.

So I started a Patchwork and Quilters Group. It was great sharing ideas and problems with planning a quilt, also getting ideas from other countries.

I made a Christmas Quilt for a friend of mine from Marshall, Missouri. Last August, I came to the States to deliver the quilt, and ended up staying until March. The Country Patchwork Quilters Guild of Marshall accepted me so nicely. I wish all groups could be filled with so much friendship, sharing ideas and showing an interest in other member's work. Thank you all in Marshall for a very enjoyable stay in the "States". This all would not have been possible if B.J. Bryant-Day had not opened her home to me. Thank you, B.J. for being such a good friend.

Susan Southworth
Gulf Shores, Alabama

Why do I quilt? Let me count the ways...........! The idea of making something with my own hands that will last for another 100 years is one reason I enjoy quilting. When you are quietly quilting and the aroma of fresh bread is baking in the oven, it gives you a sense of completeness. I feel like I am sewing my love directly into the pieces I am working with.

Cynthia England
Houston, Texas

Besides the creative outlet, I quilt to mark the passage of time. As a young mother at home I was frustrated at not having anything to show for a day's work. Quilting offered a hobby in which small amounts of time can be put to use. It also provides relaxing, repetitive, "no-brainer" work.

Margo J. Clabo
Cleveland, Tennessee

It's not immoral, illegal or fattening, and it's cheaper than a shrink (unless there is a really good sale!)

Lesley Ann Hill
Granville, Ohio

Quilting brings enjoyment to me because it is a process in which I can see progress. Unlike laundry or dusting, etc. this process often has an end. It is creative and also good therapy. I find quilting a good way to deal with my frustrations and it certainly is healthier than taking out my stress on my husband and children.

After my mother died in a car accident on her way to see me and attend my first quilt exhibit, I was deeply in pain. I knew the pain would eventually go away, but the pain still hurt clear through emotionally, physically, and spiritually. From being a counselor, I knew the grieving process, so I decided to make a series of small grieving quilts. These quilts were so healing. The strangest part of making this series was that I was unable to design the next quilt until I had gone through that step of grieving. The five little quilts in this series are the best I have ever done, they lay flat and the sides are perfectly straight!

Mary A. Sovran
Phoenix, Arizona

Quilting is a wonderful pastime. You can create a practical warm bed cover. You can make a beautiful gift for many different occasions, with your love showing plainly in every stitch. Or, you can paint an exquisite picture to hang on the wall. I love applique the most, as it offers me the most versatility as an artist. Not many pastimes offer you this much creative expression or variety in the finished product.

John Flynn
Billings, Montana

When asked why I quilt, my reply is that I quilt for the same reason the pioneer women who settled the plains - and, probably, a lot more men than you have been led to believe - quilted. When you've spent a long day battling who-knows-what, it's a real pleasure to sit down to your quilting. Before long, the intricate coordination of hand and eye frees the mind to travel to the marketplace in St. Louis or up to a mountaintop lake on a warm August afternoon - all free of charge and without hassle.

Somehow, I have never managed to separate the quilter from the engineer and this has led to many innovations in my equipment and methods. I established the FLYNN QUILT FRAME COMPANY as a way of sharing them with fellow quilters.

I realized I had a problem sitting center court in the mall on a sunny spring day when all the cotton dresses were out and I found myself mentally undressing all the women, cutting their dresses into little pieces and sewing them into bed coverings. I developed a passion for larger women, queen size. They have more fabric in their clothes.

Candra J. Sowder
Williamsburg, Iowa

Took a quilt class with my mother in high school and made a quilt for a high school history class. Mom sent it out to get it finished when I went to college and they did a horrible job on it. Decided to learn all I could about doing it all myself. Joined the quilt club as charter member.

Maria Lage
Cumberland, Rhode Island

Everything about quilting excites me. I enjoy beginning with an idea and then watching how it grows and changes as the quilt progresses. I like all the different styles from traditional to contemporary. I quilt for my own enjoyment and relaxation. I make quilts primarily to please myself and explore my own creativity and get great personal satisfaction out of the process.

Diana Alfuth
Hudson, Wisconsin

I don't know why I'm a quilter. Back in high school, I started playing around with my mom's scrap box and ended up making my first quilt. I'm totally self-taught, and after 17 years I'm still addicted.

Shirley Gardner
Evergreen, Colorado

In 1993, I taught quilting in a piggery, a 400 year old barn on the isle of Arron in Scotland. We each had our own stall with a built-in bench and a table. Our troughs were full of flowers and a pot-bellied coal stove kept us toasty against slashing rain and wind. One evening I decided to take a romantic walk to the sea and became hopelessly tangled in rough terrain and reeds higher than my head. I returned muddy, torn, and scratched and more than a little embarrassed to find a search party forming. The search for Heathcliff will have to wait.

Juanita Gibson Yeager
Louisville, Kentucky

I love colors, nothing depresses me faster than the color brown, and I love fabric and the look and feel of a quilt. I love teaching others the technical skills needed to make them, but there is only one reason I quilt and that is, *there would be no living with myself if I didn't!*

In 1986, when our first child was still at home and driving me crazy as only a 13 year old, adventuresome boy can do, I decided to escape on Thursday evenings to a quilting class, to save my sanity and his developing self esteem. We won't mention his hide, which he was coming dangerously close to losing.

At that time I had made one quilt which was on my bed. To this day I still do not know the name of the pattern. Although I enjoyed the year it took me to make that king size quilt. I'll never make another. But I am glad that I did before anyone told me that your first quilt can not be a king size one. That first quilt was made with three fabrics; an unbleached muslin, a navy cotton/poly blend and a rose calico print, by reading the instruction book found in a book at the library. Everyone who saw it (non-quilters) told me it was great and I wanted to make another one, but before I did I needed to know if I had made the first quilt correctly. **I had not..** My first quilt had 5/8" seam allowances, instead of 1/4" seams, and tucks and darts to take up the slack in the borders. My quilting stitches weren't bad, even though I did not know how to use a frame or hoop to quilt, and didn't. During the eight week class, as I learned the steps for drafting patterns and making templates, my love of quilting began to grow, and when the class ended, I had a new best friend and I was in love with quilts and quilting.

Donna Olson
Rogersville, Missouri

About ten years ago, an organization I belonged to decided to make a quilt as a fund raiser. Even though I had never quilted, they convinced me I should help with this "Log Cabin Quilt". I completed three 18" squares in the lap quilting or block-by-block method---I was hooked! I wanted to do nothing but quilt all day. Three years later I joined the Ozark Piecemakers Quilt Guild and quickly learned how to do all the things I had been struggling with to teach myself. This membership brought me more help, encouragement and friendship, than I ever thought possible.

Jane Aruns
Franklin, Tennessee

I am a quilter because I was born creative, but have always been a craftsman at heart.

Joyce Benitez
Omaha, Nebraska

When I first went to Quilting Weekend taught by Mary Ann Fonz, I chose to sit next to Paulette Peters, teasing her I knew just the right person to sit by, because she took me under her wing to help with color choices. She has recently published her second book. I announced at Quilt Guild "See I knew the right person to sit next to...". She is a good and talented friend.

Also, one time at State Quilt Convention, Crystal Carter was teaching, she mentioned she had to get her ice cream fix. We loaded up my 12 passenger van with 20+ classmates and all headed out to find the nearest Dairy Queen. Then the best find was the General Store just down the street, which was open 24 hours a day and guess what? It had a fabric section with terrific prices....my van made runs ALL night long!

Virginia L. Brown
Ogallala, Nebraska

Nineteen years of long, cold winters in northern Minnesota and a love of creating with fabric just naturally went together for me. When the weatherman said it was going to be a "3 dog night", that meant 40 degrees below! We just snuggled under an extra quilt.

"Fabric is my art medium, and designing is my reward!"

Debra J. Ruisard
Whitehouse Station, New Jersey

Until I got married, a quilt, to me, was a bedspread you purchased from a department store. As a wedding gift, my Aunt made me a quilt. I couldn't believe people actually made them. None of my ancestors, as far as I knew, ever made a quilt. (Of course, I've since discovered some quilters in my family tree, but can't seem to find any of their quilts.) In 1987, I was asked to help my aunts and cousins make a quilt-in-a-day quilt for my parents 25th anniversary. I was shocked to see how easy it was. I immediately went down to my local quilting store and signed up for a class. What I found myself in was a hand piecing, hand quilting class. Not quite what I bargained for, but I'm adventurous so I dove in.

I spent 6 weeks making pillow tops (I actually completed 3 of them) and another 6 weeks making sampler blocks (they still sit, unattached, in my attic). I was so overwhelmed with how long it took, I actually burned out on quilting. I decided it was not for me.

Then in 1990, my brother decided to get married, so I signed up for a machine piecing, double wedding ring class. All those curves!!! I finished the top in time for the wedding and took two more years to hand quilt the thing. Again, I swore that I was not cut out to be a quilter.

After the birth of my second child, I discovered the world in quilting guilds. What an inspiration, and what a great way to learn all those short cuts. I was finally hooked. I found I despised calicos, and was eager to design my own quilts. I now have 5 baby quilts, four bedsize, and many wall hangings under my belt. I have taught a few classes, and have entered a quilt or two in shows.

I'm a quilter because it is about me, for me and re-energizes me. Having three young children does not leave much time for quilting, but I manage to fit it in at the oddest of times. I make quilts to give them away; any quilts I make for myself or just for the fun, usually get put aside when another wedding, birth or Christmas comes along. I don't make quilts to sell outright, but if someone I know asks me to make something for them and wishes to pay me, I have no objections (it supports my hobby somewhat).

Fran Soika
Novelty, Ohio

I liked the hand work in sewing. All of my quilts are done by hand and totally my own work.

Anne-Donia B. Hafskjold
Tiller, Norway

I was introduced to quilting while living in the USA. The first quilt I saw was a Sun Bonnet Sue and Farmer's Boy quilt that was tied. The quiltmaker said she had so many projects going on, she had not the time to quilt it. I fell in love with the quilt, but didn't like the tying-part so much, so I had to take a quilt class to learn to make quilts. This was in 1977, and I have been making quilts ever since.

I find quilting an important link between people who do not speak the same language. I have made many friends through quilts, the latest in Japan where I'm living for the moment. I don't speak much Japanese, but can communicate with my quilting friends there through what we have in common; love for quilts. And all quilters are such nice people.

Nancy Smith
Denver, Colorado

My life revolves around quilting and sewing. I earn my living by being in a sewing business and then, I go home and spend my evenings and weekends-sewing and quilting. Even after 20 years, I love it as much as ever.

Lynda Milligan
Denver, Colorado

My reason for being a quilter is because of the wonderful people and friends I have made. I guess quilting truly is "The Tie That Binds."

Connie Sager
Nashville, Kansas

I have had my hands in just about every type craft. Quilting seemed to be the need to create something beautiful that I had not accomplished as of yet. I have only quilted a few years. After seeing one my sister-in-law made in a class, I was totally hooked.

Carole Collins
Norfolk, Nebraska

I do not come from a family of quilters. My mother made pieced tops but then tied them, and it wasn't until we were married that I saw my first quilt. It was one that my mother-in-law made for us as a wedding gift. When I saw it, I immediately knew that someday I would learn how to quilt, but it was many years later that I had my mother-in-law show me some basics on her vacation one summer. She lived many miles away so after she went home, a lot of what I learned was by trial and error. It was 1975 and there wasn't all the information available that is today. After a few years I found a quilt club and promptly joined. Since then I have taken many classes.

Constance T. Hall
Mannington, West Virginia

I am a quilter because at the age of fourteen years I came down with what the country doctor called Neuritis. I could not attend school that year, but I could use my hands part of the time. We had moved closer to my Grandmother by this time and my Mother and Grandmother both pieced quilts (out of necessity for warm bedding) and kept a quilt in the frame all of the time. So in order to have something to do, they decided I should piece my first quilt. Of course, it was a Nine Patch. Then when it was finished my Mother said we were going to quilt it. I learned to quilt. I still have my Nine Patch and it is in fair condition for it's age of 71 years.

I did not do any while attending High School and Business College. I married Byron Hall in 1930 and had my three daughters: Mary Roselyn, Reita, and Virginia. It kept me busy sewing for them and living on the farm, doing my share of the chores.

I made most of the children's clothes from feed sacks and kept all the scraps for quilt tops.

I loved to take a bag of scraps and make a work of art from it, for that is what piecing quilts is: Works of Art.

After our daughters graduated from college and some married, I started working for H&R Block during the tax season. I worked for them for 8 years and during the Bi-Centennial year I decided I would piece a red, white and blue Quilt while working for them. We would have time between clients, so I would be sitting there piecing with my fingers as someone would come in and I'd get remarks like this: "My Grandmother used to piece quilts and wonder where they are now" or "I remember my Mother doing that" or "I wish I could do that."

I used to keep a quilt in the frames most of the time. But since one of our Grandsons, Dwight Talbot moved in with us at his graduation from New Orleans Baptist Seminary, I don't have room to keep one in the frames. I am too old fashioned to like Lap Quilting.

This grandson collects quilts. Buying them at auctions mostly. He teaches at a Christian School and decorates his bulletin board with a different quilt each month.

One of my daughters, Reita, teaches school and quilts for me. She usually quilts three a year. The other two daughters are now becoming interested in piecing and quilting quilts. So, also two granddaughters are becoming interested in piecing and quilting quilts. They all love my quilts, I have at least fifty now.

Kathy Munkelwitz
Isle, Maine

I just love fabric. I think that's the beginning of a lot of quilters. The endless colors and new fabrics are wonderful. You can do whatever you want, it's the freedom of it. I have too many stories to write down!

Zelda Lynch
San Augustine, Texas

The main reason is now I'm not able to do anything but make quilts, and I keep busy as I love putting scraps together. I have been making quilts (seems like all my life). I had 12 quilts when I married and that was 1934.

Back in '34, we used quilts to cover, our homes were not too tight so we needed quilts. I still have a quilt that was given me before I married (at 18), a friendship quilt. Everyone embroidered their name in black and today 3/4 of them have gone on, so I thank the Lord for my 79 years, and able to make quilts...all are handmade, all 90 of them.

I take a lot of quilt magazines, but I love the old time patterns best, like Grandmother's Fan, Double Wedding Ring, Grandmother's Flower Garden. I have a quilt made from Bull Durm tobacco sacks. I made and gave my son one, and need to sell the other one (I can be reached at 409-275-2349). There won't be any more Bull Durm sacks. I used to work and have sold Bull Durm for 10 cents a sack, or 3 for 25 cents. That was back in the 40's.

Sandra A. Anderson
Lincoln, Nebraska

I love mysteries and puzzles (jigsaw type). I love to put pieces and clues together to complete a picture. So quilting was a natural for me, putting small pieces together to make a design. My specialty (if that is possible for a quilter) is picture quilts. I love to design pictures and make up stories with my quilts.

I have made a quilt called *Sunbonnet Sue done it*, a mystery quilt which received an award at the 1991 NQA Show in Lincoln. Also, a *Sunbonnet Guild Meeting*. I get to let my imagination and creative side of me go wild in my quilting.

Joan Biasucci
Cedar Creek,
Nebraska

I quilt because it enables me to hang on to what is left of my sanity.

Through my part-time job with ANNA'S RESTAURANT, part during the day, part at night, and part on weekends - and truly, I have had to set my alarm for 2 a.m., get up, make a telephone call to a lady to discuss party plans, as that was the time she was available. I have learned a lot more about dealing with the public and the unpredictability of human nature, than any one probably needs to know - which has certainly provided me with a new meaning to the overused word "stress". For example...

When finalizing details for a holiday party of 34 guests to be held in a dining room which seats a maximum of 44, my contact off-handedly stated they plan to bring their own music. "CD's?" I ask. "No..the St. John's Grade School Choir. They have 44 members, I think." "But," says I, "we can't seat that many people in that room." "But," says she, "they don't need chairs....they will be standing."

Now then, fabric is much more predictable, and can be relied upon to do what we think it will do. O.K., so occasionally it's not exactly colorfast, and it may shrink a bit, but that's a little problem as compared to, say...

The administration of a well-known private college located in our state. I coordinated a dinner for them at Anna's recently, for 40 guests, in which the menu was to be pre-planned. They decided to arbitrarily order 20 beef entrees and 20 chicken entrees, rather than polling their guests to obtain individual choices. Their theory was that "the decision could be made while guests were being seated." As in, I suppose, hollering "who wants chicken?" Several participants called us that Friday evening, asking for directions, as they were enroute to ANNA'S, wandering throughout the countryside and were hopelessly lost, as the flyer sent out by the college administration did not give clear directions. A good thing they were lost....as their reservations at ANNA'S were for Saturday evening.....not Friday. And, with a little luck, they wouldn't be found until Saturday.

Fortunately, my office is in our home and is combined with my sewing room. My steno chair rolls very easily between the computer and the sewing machine!

Sharon J. Mason
Coos Bay, Oregon

Eleven years of winter in Alaska. I was going crazy after I had my first child staying home all day. TV was the worst and I needed a creative outlet. Log Cabin - Nine Patch, whatever I could figure out from a book myself. Then Quilt Guild, my true enjoyment! A stolen afternoon once a month. Thank you, Anchorage Log Cabin Quilters!

Doris Lott Aultman
Hattiesburg, Mississippi

I quilt because I can do no less for myself, my children, and for the Grandmothers who let me be a part of their quilts and quilting during my childhood. I started quilting when I was 34 years old. When all the other mothers were going to a little league, painting their nails while they waited, I quilted. I was soon left out of their conversations, and had to find my own set of friends. Thus, the Pine Belt Quilters!

Wilma Dooley Muse
Fayetteville, Tennessee

All of my life I have been under quilts - either sleeping under them or playing under them as my mother Evelyn Dooley and my aunt, Mary Kelley, quilted, or living under them as they hung from the ceiling, waiting to be stitched on again the next day.

As a child in Columbia, Tennessee, I gave quilting a try, but was not successful with "little stitches" as my mother still has the evidence to prove. I am not sure today that my "little stitches" are a whole lot smaller, but I do enjoy trying and practicing on wallhangings and pillows.

Today I give credit to my dear friend, Marie Cummins, owner of the Flower House Needle Shoppe, as being instrumental in renewing my interest in quilting. In 1987 she encouraged me to attend a "quilt as you go" sampler class. I left the first class meeting all set, but before the second class, I had a full-leg cast. You know what that meant - my quilting days were over. All my quilt was packed away and I thought "forget this".

Lo, and behold - in 1991, Marie got me excited again about finishing my quilt. On the first night we met, the first block I had started was not finished, much less quilted. Together we decided, if I made the blocks and had someone else do the quilting, then maybe I would like quilting. Well, before the night was over I was on my way to finishing the fourth block, and within a month I had all twelve blocks made and my Aunt Mary was quilting. I was hooked! I now have made several quilts and numerous pillows and wallhangings.

Jennifer J. Danly
Arlington, Massachusetts

I learned to sew as a child, and for years made clothing; in college, I studied Studio Art. Quiltmaking has become, for me, the perfect artistic medium.

I began making traditional quilts about 13 years ago, focusing mostly on quiltmaking as a craft. Now I focus mostly on artistic aspects, making pictorial applique quilts of my own design, celebrating nature - animals, landscapes.

Suzanne Peery Schutt
Clinton, Mississippi

Quilting is a wonderful form of self-expression. I love traditional patterns but incorporate personal stories in my quilts - including one about my childhood and one celebrating the 35th anniversary reunion of my class at Mississippi University for Women.

Ellen Vollmer
Nickerson, Nebraska

My grandmother was a quilter and by the time I was interested in quilting, she couldn't help so I found a class in Fremont to take.

I have gotten a quilt from my Grandmother and one from an Aunt. I have worked on raffle quilts, and my sister-in-law and sister made one for our nephew's wedding.

Pauline Hess 'Ping' White
Seaboard, North Carolina

I have always admired quilts. In 1980, I found a cross-stitch quilt I wanted to make. Since everyone I knew (Grandmas) were deceased and my mother was in Colorado, I took quilting lessons from the Community College, and I have been fascinated and in love with quilting, ever since.

Pat Milne Hitchcock
Sequim, Washington

The real reason I am writing this as a defined quilter, is a most serendipitous "find" about 17 years ago at a yard sale. While looking to buy a mattress pad, I literally picked up off the ground a folded inside-out museum quality blue and white quilt - for which I paid $1.50!! It is dated February 16, 1934. My daughter was born on Feb. 16, 1964, but I quickly realized she should not use this on her bed, and started to search for the block pattern at the library - you remember, I'm sure, when there were only a handful of quilt books? I didn't find out the name of it until 1992, when it was in a show with a request for identity. A British woman visiting our show came to me and explained that while she was studying with a needlework guild at the Victoria and Albert Museum in London, she had to research four American Patchwork blocks to qualify for membership. One of the blocks was mine, and it is called IOWA. What a thrill! Mystery solved, at last!

Meanwhile, yard sales were turning up many unfinished tops which I used to teach myself the quilting stitch and how to correct boo-boos. Prices ranged from $1 for a 1934 "Tile Flowers" (all the pieces in a box) to $50 for a velvet "Log Cabin" which only needed borders. The velvet "logs" are sewn onto parts of old dresses, feed sacks and the like.

One of my favorites is a gorgeously colored dark green, light green, peach EXTREMELY complicated tiny diamond (and obviously template-free) inaccurately pieced quilt. It is all done by hand, and the truly amazing thing is that the maker actually kept going! Parts of the blocks on the edges are missing altogether, and it has a wildly rippled border, and seems to be quilted without a hoop, so there are folds here and there. Not only that - it, in its former life had the indignity of having been used as a paint drop cloth, so has speckles and blobs of paint on it. The people I bought it from had it covering cans in their garage, and it wasn't even for sale - they had purchased it somewhere for 50 cents. I was happy to rescue it and today it is an interesting cover for our hot water tank - so much nicer than that fiber glass and plastic sheeting. I sew in my laundry room, and I also use it as a bulletin board.

Another "story" quilt is a "Trip around the world" which I received free (I spotted it under the money table) from a sorority fund raiser. It had been washed for the occasion and had lost a border. I donated $2 for it, and had no idea how wonderful it was until I got home and really saw all those pastel "trips".

My most hilarious experience (and when my husband finally DID question my sanity...) was when I bought HALF a quilt which was actually sewn onto a folding cot for a mattress pad. I HAD TO BUY THE COT FOR $10 in order to get the half quilt! It is "Goose in the Pond" made with pale peach, pink, red, and soft yellows, just an absolutely beautiful scrap quilt. Yes, I later sold the cot at MY yard sale for $10 - I knew you were wondering!

Another free quilt I acquired was the day we moved to Sequim. The moving men were walking on a hand-quilted wool, all rectangles quilt, and gave it to me when I expressed admiration for it, after extracting a promise I wouldn't tell their boss. I picked the slivers out of it, repaired a couple of blocks and sent it off to the cleaners!

Alice Furrey
Carter, South Dakota

I'm a quilter because it was meant to be. I have always loved fabric and sewing and have always been interested in color, block geometry and quilting designs. With a love of math, it all comes together with the designing and making of quilts. My mother made about a hundred quilts in her lifetime, although I didn't become interested in it till she could no longer do it and my children were grown. It satisfies a need in me to create.

Page 108, Reasons why I'm a Quilter

Ilene L. Burdick
Coudersport, Pennsylvania

The main reason I began quiltmaking was because no one in the area where I grew up, seemed to be doing any of the things that I had been told about all my growing years. (My Maternal Grandmother did everything and did it well, she died 8 years before I was born). So I decided that I should be able to do all the same crafts that she always did, and started teaching myself all of them.

Sarah Bruso
Rhinelander, Wisconsin

I guess the reason I am a quilter is because I have always wanted to be a painter (artist), but I was never to get the visions from my head to my hand, and onto the canvas. Through fabric I can accomplish this. Also, my grandmother on my fathers side was a great seamstress, and I think the love of sewing was passed on down to me. I also credit a friend, who talked me into visiting her quilt guild, after that visit I knew I wanted to make quilts as beautiful as the ones the other women had. I joined and haven't stopped since.

Merrilee Tieche
Ozark, Missouri

When we moved to Missouri, I took a basic quilt-making class to learn to quilt, but mostly meet new people. When I became involved in our Guild, I had no idea how important those people would be. My husband passed away in 1991, the ladies in the Guild gave me so much support and caring during that bleak time in my life, and now share my joys as the door to another part of my life opens up.

Dean Valentine
New Braunfels, Texas

In 1980, my heart sent me a warning to change my lifestyle. Being a kindergarten teacher, raising an "active" ten year old son, Dale, I decided I needed time for myself. Having always used my hands at creative stitchery, I became a quilter.

My first quilt was a Drunkard's Path, completely pieced by hand while carpooling to baseball, soccer, band, bowling, practices and games. In ONLY eight years, a hand pieced/hand quilted treasure! Of course, I was hooked. Not only has my quilt collection grown, but you should see my material!

My husband, Dirk, retired in 1991 and we began to build our retirement home on the banks of the Guadalupe River. My special room "The Studio" was designed by Dirk. It contains all my goodies (no guest bed), material, quilts, UFO, 5 sewing machines, and lots of books in the bookcase. I organized simply by shelves in the closet and antique chest for supplies.

Marilyn A. Lewis
Glendale, Oregon

It started for something to do on rainy, snowy winters, but now it's definitely something I love to do. I really enjoy putting someone's old quilt together and quilt it for them, they are so happy they can use that old quilt.

Christine Miller
Medway, Ohio

I have been quiltmaking for 25 years, self-taught. I have made all kinds and sizes for family and friends. Recently I've become interested in charm quilts.

Laura Estes
Odessa, Washington

In the early 80's, quilting was making a comeback. I always sewed, but those 5 1/2 years at Sew & Tell rubbed off on me. Now I hardly ever sew anything but quilts, occasionally I mend my husbands jeans. I did sew an 18 foot long snake for our community parade float this year. Jungle Book was the theme. The first "real" quilt I made was done around 70 or 80. Shades of brown in a diagonal stripe, sunshine and shadows pattern. I tried so hard to quilt "normally". What a frustration. I could never get stitches small enough, you could drive log trucks under them. The instructor gave up on me, so I just poked up with the right and down with the left. It got done and its still doing fine after 14 or 15 years of continual use.

On several other occasions I've tried to learn to do it the <u>right</u> way. I purchased dozens of thimbles and gadgets, none helped. Now we just consider it my way of quilting. I must be doing okay. I received Best of Show in the small quilt division and a special award on the two wall hangings I entered at the Lincoln County fair in Davenport this past summer.

Lois K. Ide
Bucyrus, Ohio

I am a quilter simply because I've always loved sewing, and when asked to make a quilt block to represent Ohio (which was successful) and entered a quilt block contest and was one of 30 winners, I decided that maybe I could make a quilt!

Grace Moone
High Falls, New York

I am a quilter since 1980 when I was laid up with a knee injury, and I looked back over a book I had since I was 13, about quilting, and now had the chance to get "into" it. A friend who was 90 (I was 23), a quilter, loved to go to quilt shows but her family didn't want her to go alone, I couldn't drive, but I could ride and walk...so off we'd go.

Merry May
Tuckahoe, New Jersey

Quiltmaking provides me with endless challenges - not in a negative sense, but in a way which encourages me to constantly learn more. If I live to be 106 (which I have to do in order to finish all of my projects), I'll still be learning something new about quiltmaking.

I frequently tell people that being a quilter keeps me out of trouble (for the most part). After all, who has time to stir up trouble when you're too busy?

Quiltmakers as a rule seem to be very compassionate and caring. It's rare to find a quilter with a "me first" attitude. This world could use more quilters!

Penny Hand
Woodbridge, Virginia

I quilted as a hobby, something new. However, it became a passion while at Ft. Riley, during "Desert Storm". I worked as an Art Teacher at Chapman Middle School in Chapman, KS during the day and quilted in front of the Desert Storm updates on TV in the evening.

Judith Clonan
Fitchburg, Massachusetts

My grandmother died in 1970 and Mom gave me one of her quilts. That started it all. Couldn't wait to finish college to start quilting. After a frustrating start in a class in a primarily cross stitch shop, I found Amelia's in Winchendon, Massachusetts with day time classes (I work 3-11) and teacher/owner Fay Wheeler is *always* there for us.

Arla Schaap
Holland, Michigan

In 1982, I went to a new little fabric shop in our town where women met one afternoon a week for quilting. Two of the women were cousins of my husband, and knew I was a sewer. They invited me to join and I've been hooked on quilting every since that day. Some of the ladies have retired from the group and moved away. Neither heat nor snow keeps us from meeting each Thursday in each others homes. We not only share a love of quilting, but also our personal joys & recipes, crafts, and on and on. Our group (8 women), the Tulip Patchers, has sponsored many bus trips to the AQS in Paducah, and also to Lancaster, PA. In addition, we put on an annual Tulip Time Quilt Show, which included showing the Expressions of Liberty Bi-Centennial Quilts in 1987.

When I became a "Quilter", I joined a unique group of women from all walks of life and from all over the world! I would like to share an experience I had with my quilt.

Let me begin with the inscription sewn on the back of the quilt which reads:

In the Summer of '81.
It was started and stopped
    time and again,
Because there was so many other
    things to do.
Over the years as I stitched and I sewed,
I counted the time that it took -
Over 600 hours of LOVE
    was written in my book.
Gifted by God, the quilt you now see,
Was finally finished, in April, 1993!

Yes, it took 11 years working off

and on to complete this quilt. Throughout this time, Les kept saying "I'll be long gone before you finish it. We'll never sleep under it". Well, he is still here, but we almost didn't sleep under it. Last summer I entered it into the Ottawa County Fair and it received a 1st Place Blue Ribbon & Best of Show. This qualified it for entry into the Michigan State Fair. I felt it was sort of special to be accepted, so I entered it and made plans to drive down to the fair grounds in Detroit. Les wasn't too enthused about taking it there, leaving it there for a week, and then having to go back and pick it up. If I'd listened to him, we would have been spared the events that followed.

The fair ended Sept. 7. Two days later we went to pick it up. We walked down the rows of tables, my tickets in my hand, and picked up a wall hanging and my grandsons' baby quilt that were also entered. We got to the end of the row but couldn't find my quilt. I said to one of the ladies, "Where is my quilt, I don't see it." At this point she said to me, "Are you sure?" - - and then she called the supervisor. We were told this was the second quilt that was missing.

With my heart racing and my knees shaking, I said, "I think I'm going to cry". I turned around - - and I did cry! It was a l-o-n-g, silent ride home that day. Even Les felt bad, remembering all the nights and hours I'd spent quilting. Who and why did someone take an heirloom quilt which meant nothing to them, but was irreplaceable to me? It was my prayer that the person or persons who stole my quilt would have an inner turmoil and unrest until they confessed to the crime. In all, seven prize-winning quilts were stolen.

The Detroit Free Press ran a story and a picture of Laura, a woman from Port Huron whose quilt was among those taken. Laura, too, was heartsick, having started hers in college, stopped when she was married, had children, and finally completed last year after 20 years in the making. The Michigan State Police were put on the case which they called the "Quilt Caper" and the detective in charge was nicknamed "Columbo". His comment on the case was, "It's been amazing to me, the public response to this investigation. I've worked with homicide cases in the past, but - - people didn't care about murders or anything else. They wanted to know about those quilts!"

Seventeen days after the theft, a suspect was questioned and was given the newspaper article to read. Reading Laura's story moved him to confess to the crime and he told them where he had sold the quilts. My quilt was sold to a dealer for $50, who sold it to another dealer for $85, who was negotiating another sale when police convinced him it was stolen property. One quilt had to be returned from Mexico.

By the 24th day Detective Couturier called and said he had my quilt on his desk. I could not say a word. He said to me, "half of you ladies have responded the same way - - crying on the telephone." These were tears of joy! We did not expect to see our quilts, again!

Don't misunderstand, I place a higher value on human loss than on material possessions. But - I <u>almost</u> lost a treasured chapter in my life.

This quilt was created and lovingly sewed; it has won awards and ribbons; it was stolen by a Pinkerton guard; recovered by a State Police detective; it's mug shot is in file #29-10171-93 of the Michigan State Police; events are carefully recorded in it's own scrap book and will go with it when it is handed down to the next generation. It now is back in it's rightful place of honor - - on our king size bed!

Martha A. De Turk
Kutztown,
Pennsylvania

I started quilting in 1972 because I love antiques, have several antique quilts and wanted to try my hand at creating traditional quilts to compliment my antiques in my old stone farmhouse. Quilting is very relaxing and seems like my connection to the past-simple life. My maternal great-grandmother was a quite a quilter. I never knew her, but feel close to her because of this common hobby.

Anna Eelman
North Plainfield,
New Jersey

I became a Quilter after studying the history of 19th century women. I began to see quilting as Art. Our theme for a recent Quilt Show and later Parade Float was "Quilts -

Homespun Art of Women's History".

I have finished many old quilt tops, as well as made many of my own. I have also been intrigued by the use of feedsacks in Quilts and their history.

Kathleen Nyman
Oswego, New York

I'm a quilter because it keeps my mind and hands busy - something besides carpools and dirty dishes. It gives me a sense of accomplishment when I finish something. I like being able to give something of myself to friends and relatives as gifts.

Betty M. Abel
Sheboygan, Wisconsin

My husband said to me one day, "You're really getting hooked on quilting." I answered "It's like drugs, you really become addicted." As he walked away, I heard him say, "Yes, but with drugs, you can send them away for a cure." Think he said it all, don't you?

Virginia H. Flowers
Flushing, Michigan

I really enjoy people, talking and writing about quilting. As a result, I have demonstrated quilting at the Flint Public Library, Sloan Museum, Cross Roads Village, and Flint Whaley House. I have a number of quilting pen pals around the USA, England, Australia, Canada and New Zealand.

Mary R. Canning
Lincoln, Rhode Island

When I'm piecing (almost always by hand), I like that part best, but when I'm quilting, it's quilting! I take pride in my stitches and have been known to take a few out and redo them occasionally.

At this time in my life, quilting is not only a wonderful hobby, but it is therapy. My husband is not well, and will not get well, so as his care-giver, I quilt. Thank God, (literally) that I learned to Quilt!

Mary J. Ruda
Elida, Ohio

10 years ago, I bought a New Singer Electronic Machine and was making a blouse till 3 in the morning. It didn't fit, so I said no more sewing for myself! What am I going to do with this new machine? So, I thought I'll make quilts...that's what I did!

Ruth E. O'Connor
Burlington, Massachusetts

I was asked to submit a block for a Friendship Quilt for a group of 15. All I could do was Crazy Quilt, as this quilt was for me I needed larger, so I learned very fast to hand piece 10 more blocks and sashing, and started my first quilting with Navy thread - and I must admit, I am very proud of it. (Finished my quilt a year before the other 14 girls!) I have now made approximately 20 quilts.

Geogina Doss
Milton, West Virginia

I find quilting to be very relaxing. I once fell asleep under my quilting frame while checking my stitches on the underside. (You'd be amazed at how much it resembles a stained glass window from there.)

Barbara G. Pietila
Baltimore, Maryland

I have been quilting for twenty years now. I started doing traditional quilts but, because of a shortage of good quality fabrics while living in Moscow, I began doing applique and discovered that that was what I really loved.

I now make story or narrative quilts, because I love creating pictures with fabric. For me, pictorial quilts are documents which record our lives and times. I consider them to be as important as those old photographs, Bibles, and keepsakes we value and preserve. I hope my work will be seen years down the road and provide some insights into my life, our customs, and my community.

Linda Boedigheimer
Perham, Minnesota

I just love it - it relaxes me, stimulates my creativity, allows me to produce usable items and gives me an opportunity to meet new people.

Page 112, Reasons why I'm a Quilter

A good friend, Benda Davis, convinced me to attend a quilting class in 1992. She said I needed something else to do, besides being consumed with building a new lake cabin. I reluctantly consented, and was hooked. Now I can easily be consumed with quilting. By the way, Benda didn't really like quilting, but on rare occasions she now can be seen taking classes from me!

Bernice Tessibel Inman Cashman (Tessie) Coal City, Indiana

I quilt for pure joy of quilting. My most cherished memory of my Grandmother Inman is of her and Great-Grandmother Van Horn, sitting on the porch swing on a summer day. They had a large box filled with fabric scraps and were sewing tiny little pieces of yellow fabric together. A Grandmothers Flower Garden quilt was in the making. I am happy to continue the quilting tradition of my grandmothers.

Dort Lee Leicester, North Carolina

I took a class so I could make a quilt for my first baby who was a year old at the time. When he was 8 years old, I finally got around to making him one..for a twin bed. (I made lots in between).

Sheryl Mielke McGregor, Iowa

I became an avid quilter after I retired from working outside the home, in 1988. Quilting can be easily picked up or dropped between business duties.

My earliest memories of quilts date back to my maternal grandmother. She always had a quilt in the frame. Her quilts were all made from scraps given her by family members after making their own clothes. Each of her 13 grandchildren received a quilt upon graduation. My paternal grandmother did a lot of sewing and was a crafter ahead of her time. Everything was saved to be created into a wall hanging or center piece. So my bloodline instilled in me my love for those traditional scrap quilts, but I also have learned simple applique.

By joining a guild and through teachers and quilting friends, I have learned all the hints, methods and tools. I am a sucker for any book about quilting. Each book begs to join my library.

Doris Callaway, Greensburg, Kansas

I worked over 40 years, and am retired. Now I sew, knit, crochet, do crafts, but mostly quilt. I collect thimbles and mini-quilts. Quilting is a part of my life-a very important part. After losing my husband, quilting was my salvation.

I'm a grandmother, 4 girls and 2 boys ages 22 to 6. I have 3 children..2 girls, 1 son and 2 lovely sons-in-law! Love to give talks on quilting and show my quilts, give workshops and lectures and love to buy fabric for what else? Quilting!

Nancy Wagner Graves Manhattan, Kansas

Quilting gives me a sense of accomplishment. At the end of the day or week, I can look at what or how far I got. My quilting stays done, unlike housework or laundry.

Susan J. Spencer Felton, California

My paternal grandmother, who died when I was a baby, was a quilter, and I used to love to look at the Grandmother's Flower Garden Quilt she had made. I've always been a *crafty* sort of person, and have done almost all types of needlework, but once I discovered quilting, almost seven years ago, I knew I had found my calling. I was going to make *one* quilt, but now have so many, both completed and in progress, that I've lost count.

Judi Robb Manhattan, Kansas

I love to quilt & working with my hands.

Fanny Naught Quincy, Illinois

Now that my husband is retired, (somewhat) we do a little more traveling. It is a nice arrangement for our son to take over the construction business, now Dad works for him. That means Dad can have a day off most any time.

On a trip to Hawaii, it was my experience to take a class from Aunti Mali at the Hyatt Regency Hotel. I loved it!!! A few years later we went back again, and I stopped in to see her and find out what she had been up to. There was a beautiful blue and white hawaiian quilt in the frame in the process of being hand-quilted. The fabric was very nice and of course, I wanted to buy some of it. She told me she had bought it at the Ala Moana Shopping Center. So, I hopped on the city bus and went searching for it. The ladies in the fabric shop were very helpful, but did not remember any fabric like I had described. I went back to the hotel to talk to Aunti Mali again, and THEN she told me, "Oh, that was 8 years ago". One afternoon and a learning lesson. That is okay, it made a wonderful memory.

On this same trip, my husband and I spent a rainy day on the bus traveling around the Oahu Island. I found three wonderful quilt shops. We always talk to everyone that will talk to us, so while on the bus, I talked to a local lady and she told me to get off the bus at the Old Sugar Mill. In the back was a manufacturing fabric area. It was a very primitive operation. The electricity had failed to work that day. I ended up buying a piece of Lava Lava fabric. The primary purpose of this material is to make Paureau, the tie the Island ladies tie around their bodies as a garment. The process was so interesting. They start with a white plain cloth. First it is dipped into dye, mine is lavender, then they lay it out on a wire screen. Leaves from the island are placed on top of the cloth. Bright lights are focused on for several hours. Then the leaves are removed making the whole cloth and it is beautiful. My friends think it is very nice and I am waiting to display it at our next quilt show. I am sure it will be an unusual topic of conversation.

One of my favorite memories is last summer when my granddaughter, Shay, discovered the sewing machine. She was then 12. One day she was bored with nothing to do. She came to me and said, "Grandma, if I knew how to quilt, I would help you". That was exactly what I had been waiting to hear. I had some 4" squares cut and waiting for the time this might happen. She had never used the sewing machine before, so it took some practice to follow a line and get the hang of things. A few weeks later she had made her very first nap-size quilt. She was so proud of herself, and I was once again convinced she is a super kid. That was a summer vacation the both of us will long remember.

∞∞∞∞∞∞∞∞∞∞∞∞∞∞∞∞∞∞∞∞∞∞

M. Jeanne Poore
Overland Park, Kansas

I like the fabric--just to feel it sometimes is comforting. I like the textures of it. I enjoy creating the tops--to see the design take shape. I like the quilting itself, but don't always have the time to hand-quilt everything. And I have really enjoyed the teaching--to see others develop their talents and skills. It is so wonderful to have a student show me their finished work.

This year one of my students won an award at the Wyandotte County Fair, and another student won a viewers choice award at a local show. It gives me such a warm feeling, I'm just so thrilled for them.

∞∞∞∞∞∞∞∞∞∞∞∞∞∞∞∞∞∞∞∞∞∞

Helen M. Ericson
Emporia, Kansas

I have seriously been making quilts since 1965, when the ones my grandmother had made, began to wear out and I had lots of sewing scraps to use as she did. I received Best of Show at the Kansas State Fair in 1973, and several times at county and other fairs. The oldest quilt in my collection was signed and dated by one of my great-great-grandmothers in 1831. I just finished making 4 wall hangings from blocks left unfinished by my grandmother in 1937.

I enjoy showing my quilts, speaking to groups and displaying at Folklife Festivals. When I started I was told I was 'too young' to make quilts: now it seems natural. A recent gift from a friend was a box of blocks that will make 10 quilts, dating from 1900 to 1940. They will keep me busy for quite a while; an activity I prefer to cutting up new fabric.

Beth Donaldson
Lansing, Michigan

I was watching TV one day (I am a TV-aholic!) when one of the guests on a morning show was talking about how to make a career change late in life. They said if you were unhappy, look at what you did in childhood to give you clues for what type of work might fulfill you as an adult. Now by this time I had already decided on quilting and was well on my way to being fairly successful at it, but what they said really rang true.

As a little girl I loved to color and I always stayed in the lines, now I love precision piecing. Sewing was something I enjoyed as a teenager and managed to produce a full line of unfinished garments. As an adult I also have a large display of unfinished quilt projects. I think artistically I work in a series, Unfinished I, Unfinished II, etc.

I was a great Math student and loved graph paper and numbers, now I love to draft patterns and figure out great ways to rotary cut and piece them. I also love tricky blocks and patterns like Mariner's Compasses and Isometric designs. I used to doodle all the time and when I remember back, the doodling looked suspiciously like machine quilted stippling! I was also a very good and fast writer in high school and I thank my senior English teacher, Mr. Rowan, for making us write everyday. It has certainly come in handy.

I have been very lucky. My husband, Tom, is a wonderful man and very supportive. Although our family income is not great, I have been able to stay at home while raising my daughters. The quilt teaching was scheduled around their school times or done in the evening when Tom was home. It was very important to me, and it still is, to be a part of our daughters lives. I hate to miss out on band concerts and school plays, etc. Pursuing quilting as a career has not always been easy or lucrative, but it has allowed me to be with my family and do something that I love.

Marcia Knopp
Bay City, Michigan

My grandmother used to quilt and I always loved quilts, even going so far as to make comforter-bedcovers when I was in college for the dorm, and later my apartment. I even had an amish lady make me a quilt, but I never thought I would hand quilt. I got started hand quilting when the "god-mother" of our quilt guild, who is also a patient of mine, conned me into quilting, by talking the ladies who were meeting at our local museum to quilt, into quilting two days a week. One of those days being my afternoon off. I had to go - I didn't have an excuse not to anymore, since I couldn't say "I have to work." Anyway, I've been quilting ever since.

Eleanor Burenheide
Emporia, Kansas

I am a quilter because of my husband. I took a years leave of absence from teaching. We had returned home from a vacation in California in January. Leo was reading the newspaper. He said, "They are listing a quilting class for beginners. Perhaps you would like to go see about this." Needless to say...if Leo had known then what he knows now. he might never had told me about that class!

I enjoyed that class and became HOOKED. Funny thing, I developed a new vocabulary. Words like, STASH, CALLOUS, AND NUMBER 12-SIZED NEEDLES. Found new equipment like: T-square, Olfa cutter, walking-foot, and 3/4" thick styrofoam sheet 4x8'. My library now had new books and magazines. I discovered quilts had history and even more...there were these wonderful new friends and new teachers (quilt).

As I look back, there were some very key people, who have directed my wonderful quilt experiences and knowledge. Helen Ericson taught me how to set the mind, determine the direction you wanted to go and to go for it. Barbara Brackman engrained the clues for the ages of old quilts. Her help in the Kansas Quilt Project made the project live for me.

Elly Sienkiewicz told me, as she looked, "This is not a sewing room, it is your studio!" She also taught me that grave markers tell more about genealogy. Helen Storbeck set me up as the "BAG LADY". And then there was Harriet Hargrave, whom I have to thank for the use of the electric needle, both in piecing and quilting.

I am a quilter because...I have enjoyed being involved with:
Our Church quilters, Emporia Regional Quilters Organization

(Charter member and past Pres.) Kansas Quilter's Organization, (Bd. member and 2nd VP) National Quilters Org. (My first quilt was on the cover of their magazine) Kansas Folk/Art Apprentice 1985, Kansas Quilt Project Reg. Coord., Kansas Quilt Judge, KS Quilt instructor, and 1/2 of the BAG LADIES TEAM.

Doris Haggard
Topeka, Kansas

I get much personal satisfaction and contentment from my quilting. I enjoy hand piecing, more than machine piecing. I think marking a quilt is very hard work. I think it is where one can use your creative talent to choose your designs.

Bettie Rushin
Boulder Creek, California

The biggest reason I am a quilter is I LOVE TO TOUCH ART, and the way I feel happiest is feeling color and texture under my fingers.

The other reason is that when I was a little girl we moved all the time, my dad was in the Army. I had two great friends, one was Sugar our family dog, and the other was my BLANKY; as a baby my Blanky was fuzzy with satin edging, at three it was just fuzzy, and at five it was a rag. For my fifth birthday my Grandmother turned Blanky into a quilt, my first quilt, the top had a tiny hole in it so that I could still feel Blanky's texture, it was great.

The same year I turned five, we moved to Hawaii and Sugar couldn't come. Blanky became my only best friend. Blanky and I had great times in Hawaii, we learned to hula, we went on picnics, we camped under the stars and by the sea, we were inseparable.

When it came time to move, yet again, my mother told me to put my blanket in a safe place because the movers were coming and she didn't want it lost. I was still just five, so I put Blanky in the bottom drawer of my dresser, thinking that it couldn't find a safer haven. Well, Blanky was packed, shipped, and lost for six months, and when he was returned I was the happiest little six year old on earth, and since that time I have always had some kind of stitchery in my hands, probably for the comfortable feel of an old friend and fond memories.

Catherine Litwinow
Davenport, Iowa

One of the speakers at the MVQG had said quilts are "Color creativity and comfort." Quilts are the threads that link us to the past and the legacies for the future. There have been quilts in my family for generations.

My mother made an embroidered bird quilt, while I was growing up. The 4 of us girls "sat" the embroidery off. (She later redid the quilt) The rule has been since I now make the quilts, *No sitting on the stitches!* If I quilt in the living room the dog seems to think she must sit on the quilt. She's the only one permitted to do so.

Linda Ballard
Palo Cedro, California

I love working and playing with fabrics. I've sewn all my life and quilting seems to be a natural for me.

Carol L. Robbins
Overland Park, Kansas

My sister, Betty McBride, got both of us started in a class in Loveland, Colorado six days after my family moved there in March 1991. Our mother quilted most of her life and was a real inspiration to us. As a decorative painter, I wanted to combine the two skills into unique painting and quilting experiences. Quilting is a way for me to relax and keep my hands busy, while watching TV or visiting with family members.

Shannon Royer
Otis, Kansas

I became a quilter quite by accident. My mother-in-law had signed up for a quilting class and asked me if I would be interested in joining her. I had no idea there were such tools as a rotary cutter, self-healing mats and acrylic rulers. Needless to say, I was very surprised and became totally absorbed in this new avenue of home sewing. That class was in 1987 and I have given up knitting, ceramics, needlepoint, and cross-stitch!

Page 116, Reasons why I'm a Quilter

Netta Ranney
Overland Park, Kansas

My first two quilts were appliqued, a Dutch Doll and a Sailboat made from the scraps of the children's clothing. I had no time to hand quilt, so "invented" stitch in the ditch and did the quilting by machine. Now hand quilting is my relaxation.

Karen Crosby
Ocala, Florida

I am a quilter because my sister, Jan, was so excited about it. We were always crafters and had learned to sew very young. Our grandmother and Great Aunts made some beautiful quilts that my sister and I share.

Tedi Lambert
Los Banos, California

I began quiltmaking after many years of professional dressmaking. One can only wear just so many dresses, I suppose. My children were beginning to rebel and not wear the clothing which I made for them--they wanted "store-bought" clothes. At this time we also relocated from San Jose, California to Los Banos, a city which is only about 100th the size of San Jose.

While our home was being built, I went to work for our local quilt store (a different one from my latest employment). It was while working there, that I was "bitten" by the quilting bug, that was in October of 1988. That was a number years and over 80 quilts ago! Over 75% of those 80 quilts were done for customers or donated to charity.

Julie L. Kimberlin
Anchorage, Alaska

I am a quilter, because I enjoy it. I have been a seamstress in some capacity, since I was a teenager. I love working with color which quilting allows, and I don't have to worry about how it is going to fit! I have other things I would like to do (& many projects stored away), but I can never get past all the quilting projects I want to do.

Pat Reep
Bakersfield, California

I've had a love affair with fabric all my life. I sewed clothing, embroidered and taught needlework for a number of years. One day my husband gave me a copy of the Standard Book of Quiltmaking by Marguerite Ickis. I then read The Perfect Patchwork Primer by Beth Gutcheon and from that day on, I was hooked.

If you ask why do I quilt, the answer is because I can't not quilt. It's like breathing, a necessity for my health and happiness. Quilting is totally absorbing to me and has enriched my life with creativity, excitement and friendship. It has opened doors for me and continues to do so to this day.

Phyllis Hansen Gierach
Madera, California

My early memories of my Aunt DeeDee and "Grandmother Gibson" include many happy hours of time spent with them in the evenings, while they listened to their favorite radio programs, as they did handwork that included hand sewing pieces of fabric together for a new quilt top. They usually strung each color on a long piece of quilt thread and assembled them into a beautiful pattern. I now own most of their quilts, even those that had been given to my cousin, Evelyn, who left them to me when she passed away. I recognize many of the fabrics as dresses that my mother, aunt or myself wore many years ago. They let me try a few stitches, but I'm sure they took them out when I was not around. That gave me an appreciation of quilting.

During my first college class with Jean Ray Laury, I learned to appreciate the importance of color and scale in quilt design and to be more creative with my ideas for quilts and wallhangings. In 1980, when we moved to Madera, my husband financed my venture into opening a needlework and quilting store that we called "Patchwork Pansy", which I owned until 1991. I had many wonderful experiences, but I never had time to get a quilt completed! I still have at least 25 tops in various stages of completion, and have completed many other projects.

Recently, I entered a wallhanging I titled "Harvest time in our Valley" in a county sponsored "Art Festival". It went on to the statewide sponsored "Countryside Festivals". The judges chose it as the overall theme prize, I was a very happy quilter!

Gladys Shook
Hutchinson, Kansas

I love to quilt, because I love to see things being created. I can remember when I made my first stuffed doll. As I diligently worked to create the facial features, fingers and toes, it was wonderful to see my doll come to life.

Quilting for me is definitely not limited to quilt tops. I have extended my piecing and quilting into garments, wall hangings and many other fabric and craft items.

Teresa Binder
Emporia, Kansas

My maternal grandmother and great grandmother quilted. I remember sitting on catalogs at the kitchen table cutting quilt pieces. I don't know if my contributions actually made it into quilts but I have inherited several of the quilts those dear ladies made. Some 20 years later, I stumbled across quilting again and it seems to have chosen me as a lifetime project. I'm not sure what I would be, if I weren't a quilter. Most "crafts" drive me crazy. I can't draw or paint, but I love fabric. I sew many gifts for friends and family. Small quilts, sweat shirts, T-shirts and other garments. If I can use fabric, needle and thread I am happy. A quilter is simply what I am.

Betty A. Lenz
Marshall, Missouri

I have always been *a little art-y*, but have had very little actual instruction--several Adult Education Classes in drawing, & watercolor, playing with stained glass for several years and sewing clothing since Home Ec in high school. Quilting now seems to pull all these earlier experiences together.

Charlotte Fry
St. Charles, Missouri

My one time neighbor and very dear friend, Jana Zagurski, was really the person responsible for getting me started. We had a little club of 6 women, who met really more as an excuse to get away from the children, that met every Wednesday at Jana's mother's home. Bernadette Graham is her name. We first started working on anything, then in 1976, Jana suggested we start making friendship quilts. One of the ladies in our group, Linda Morgan had been quilting since she was 5 and said she would teach us. We drew names, I got the first one. My quilt is a sampler, now very worn simply because I didn't know how to wash it properly.

Barbara Clukey
Carriere, Mississippi

My Grandmother was a quilter and, as a child, I loved her Sunbonnet Sue Quilt. I yearned to hug Sunbonnet Sue and to play with her. This desire gave me the inspiration in later years to design and make Children's Story Book Quilts. I planned that each quilt would have a moving part and a removable character, and each quilt would have its own handmade story book. Since that time, it has been my real pleasure to make many handcrafted story book quilts. "Goldilocks and the Three Bears" appeared on the cover and was featured in Stitch and Sew Quilts Magazine. I have designed and made quilts from the stories of "Jonah and the Whale", "The Princess and the Pea", "Master of all Masters," and the delightful poem, "Eletelephony" among others. Whatever excites my imagination and creativity could appear on a child's quilt. I never take orders for quilts, nor do I design with someone else's ideas in mind.

Helen P. Johnston
Bowie, Maryland

My exposure to quilts while growing up were the simple tied quilts my grandmother made, using an old blanket and squares of old or outgrown clothing. I have memories of my Nebraska grandmother's visits to our home in Massachusetts. She taught me to crochet. My mother taught me to sew clothes. As a high school student, I became attracted to needlework.

I taught myself needlepoint, knitting, macrame, and crewel embroidery.

During college in the 70's my needlework magazines began featuring quilts. They appealed to me and I decided I would make one as a wedding gift for my college roommate and best friend, Marla. I had no idea what I was getting into, but I knew I could sew clothes and embroider, so it couldn't be that hard. The quilt was an appliqued wreath of leaves with hearts in the corners of the blocks. All the quilting designs were freehand drawn (after I completed the quilt top the instructions simply said, "quilt as desired.) Each tulip I quilted was different (I now know about templates!) The quilting stitch was explained as a simple running stitch. As a result I am a STAB quilter.

I joined my first quilt group after my son was born. Watching the other accomplished quilters in the group, I realized I was quilting 'Wrong'! It was several months before I felt secure enough to do any quilting during the meeting. I've since learned my technique is not wrong, just a different style.

It was fortunate I joined them, because during that year my husband was hospitalized with a serious illness, and the women in my group were very supportive. As he recovered, I won an applique quilt top that all of us had participated in making. This activity has since become an annual tradition with the Southern Comforters.

Quilting for me has been cheaper than counseling. It's allowed me to develop friendships, challenge myself with new skills, and opens a line of communication with many new people. The offices I've held with both of my groups, have benefited me enormously. I've developed confidence in public speaking and organizing people to complete a task, and also picked up some practical skills in conflict resolution.

I arise early in the morning and rush through shower and breakfast, so I can spend 30-45 minutes each morning devoted to my quilting. The day starts off so well, when you've spent some time nurturing your own needs. It gives me a real boost and allows me to give to others through the rest of the day. My day usually ends the same way, with some quiet devotion to my quilting.

My quilts provide me with many things. The satisfaction of meeting and overcoming challenges. The enjoyment I see on other's faces as they open a quilted gift. A connection with generations of women gone by, and the common threads in our daily concerns. The pleasure of caressing a newly completed quilt. Ultimately my quilts hold my memories. As I use them, the thoughts and concerns I experienced during the making of the quilt return to me. My quilts are my memories at different times in my life.

Edith O. McGhee
Mercer, Pennsylvania

My little brother's babysitter taught me to quilt, when I was a teenager, I pieced and quilted two complete quilts before graduating from high school. Now, in my old age, I do more reading about quilts than actual quilting, but love quilts as much as ever.

Beulah T. Gilbert
Bellevue, Ohio

I have always loved quilts but I hated to sew clothing. I always knitted because I like to do things with my hands. But, when I decided I would make one quilt, I was hooked. Now I can sit and sew patches all day at the sewing machine.

Marcene Gunter
Hillsboro, Kansas

I am a quilter first of all because I enjoy it, I can sit with my husband and quilt, or spend the day at the sewing machine. I love the challenge of starting a new quilt. I have met so many nice people, and made many friendships. I enjoy working with people through my classes, etc.

When my granddaughter was eight years old, we made a quilt together. She picked out the fabrics and I designed it. She called it *MY LIFE*, her family, pets, and education. I was so proud to help her with this.

I introduced a deaf child to quilting. We worked with hand piecing, touch of fabric, needle, etc. He ironed a kitten on to a block to take home. He loved the feel of quilts, I even got a hug and kiss when he left. This is why I quilt, the gratification of helping others.

Joan Waldman
Platte Center, Nebraska

Quilting has been my life line for the last 28 years. It all started when my husband brought home an old quilt and asked me to wash it, so he could cover an engine he was working on in his shop. I washed it, but he never got it back. I began searching for the name of the quilt and found out it was called Sawtooth. During my search I became totally hooked on quilts and quilting.

I've always been interested in handwork. I learned to embroider before I started school. All during my growing up years I tried different kinds of needlework. Quilting, however, is the one thing that holds never ending fascination. The challenge of using fabrics and the tactical feel of the fabric keeps me interested. Seeing a piece take shape on my design wall is very satisfying.

DeEtta Beebe
Waters, Michigan

Quilting is a combination of many things I love in life - sewing, color, creativity, mixing pleasure with necessity and of course, sharing the gift of friends over a cup of tea with others who find the same. When I was 4 years old, I remember sitting with my mother, and having tea in my very own tea cup. As we shared this rare time of being alone together, she made me feel like the only other person in the whole wide world. Mother loved doing what she was doing at the time. The mother of four young children keeping house, doing her own baking, sewing, keeping a garden, not to mention all the demands on a Mother and Wife.

She shared that joy with me by mixing pleasure with necessity, as she still does this day. She taught me to thread my own needle and to organize my little shoe box of treasures, my own little sewing stash. As I watched her make me a new dress, I would create clothes for my own doll with scraps from my own.

I always felt special and pretty when I put on the new creation my mother had fashioned for me.

Many times the clothes I made my doll didn't fit, but pleasure still remains. It was fun to give to my dolls what had been given to me - the gift of love and the pleasure that went into each stitch will always remain close to my heart.

The same goes into my quilting today. The joy of creating and sharing and being happy where I am, rather than somewhere else.

Rebecca Dutcher
Culbertson, Nebraska

I learned to sew on an old White treadle machine at my Grandma's house at about age 8. I sewed on that machine until I was about 13 or 14, and sewed everything from doll clothes to pep skirts, to quilts. My daughter, Bethany, age 9, is now learning to sew on the old treadle. She's sewing a 9-Patch quilt and doing a wonderful job! The old treadle still runs beautifully. I'm now on my 3rd electric machine and probably when I wear this new one out, that old White treadle machine will still be sewing beautifully.

Richard F. Zimmerman
New Milford, New Jersey

There are so many advantages to quilting as a creative outlet. For one thing the raw materials are so readily available. One can find fabric, thread, needles and scissors almost anywhere. The activity is CLEAN and relatively mess free. Quilting is extremely portable (unless one quilts in a floor frame). Quilting allows the artist to work with color, texture, pattern and value in both a two dimensional and three dimensional way. It is an activity which can be picked up and put down as time allows without having to worry about it. (I have just gone back to work on a wall quilt which was complete except for the borders when I put it away in a box, when I began packing for our move to our new house). I happen to enjoy all phases of quilt construction - piecing, applique, setting the blocks or planning borders, preparing the top for quilting and the actual process of quilting the three layers - 5 to 7 stitches to the inch.

While I do use the machine once in a while, especially for setting blocks and adding borders to the quilt top and occasionally even for piecing, I prefer to work by hand. There is something very relaxing about the rhythm of needle moving up and down through fabric, almost like ocean waves washing up on the beach.

Once when I was out at a Guild Meeting on Eastern Long Island, where I was to be the guest speaker, I was questioned as to why I was piecing *Lemoine Star* blocks by hand when they could be assembled much more quickly by machine.

I thought for a moment, then made this reply: "When I sit down at the sewing machine, it is like walking into a fast food restaurant. One hurries in, orders as fast as possible, rushes to find a seat, gobbles down the order (because someone else is inevitably eyeing your table) discard the packaging, and hurry on to your next task - usually with indigestion. The sewing machine says *hurry*.

Hand sewing is relaxing. So we have to decide why it is then that we quilt. If we are into production and economy, then the machine is the tool of choice. However, if we quilt as a means of escaping the problems of the day and as a means of putting our mental house in order then, at least for me, handwork seems to be the best."

Michelle Hazelhoff
Mt. Evelyn,
Vic Australia

Quilting is something I've always been interested in. I was in Girl Guides when I was ten and we made a hexagon raffle quilt and for years I wondered how our guide leader got the papers out, you see we just constructed the flowers, and she assembled it, but she never showed us the in-between stages. At ten, I was hooked but I didn't know how to do it, and as quilting was hardly known in Australia in the seventies, it would be a decade before I did anything about it.

I was expecting my first child, and a friend's father owned a T-shirt/Windcheater printing company. He would bag the scraps up and sell them to mechanics and such, and my husband who worked on cars and around the house at the time, bought a bag for a dollar. At the time we were flat broke and I wanted to prepare for the baby coming. I got that bag before he did, it was full of pink, blue and white scraps which I cut up and stitched into a baby quilt. It was backed with an old sheet and edged with an leftover length of lace. I didn't have a sewing machine at the time and my baby's layette was all hand stitched by me, with leftover fabrics and old sheets and such, and that's the God's honest truth. It's amazing what you can achieve when you have to. I know how those pioneers felt. It wasn't until the nineties that I got into quilting in a big way. I now have my own studio, I make many of my own designs to sell, keep, and give away as gifts. I love the freedom quilting affords me and the connection with many great quilt makers in the past. I find there's nothing better than to make a new rendition of an old favorite. Besides my husband, of course, quilting is my first passion!

Alta M. Edwards
Clay City, Indiana

My sister-in-law, Estel Hyatt, took an interest in teaching me to quilt. She was a good seamstress and I never picked up a needle, so it was quite a challenge for both of us. I started in about 1978 by embroidering, then in 3 or 4 years, started to piece quilts. I quilted all of them, but one.

LaRue Nuest
South Hutchinson,
Kansas

I have always loved to sew since taking Home Economics classes in high school, and looking back, I had been interested in quilting several years before I actually started. When I was a child my mother always had a quilt in the frame during the winter months. She set it up in our large dining room, and the family just lived around the quilt frame. My favorite aunt also quilted, and gave my first husband and me a quilt as a wedding gift. I have since found some Aunt Martha quilting pamphlets that I had purchased many years before I actually started quilting. Probably the reason I didn't start earlier was because my children were young and with all the things going on at church and school with them, there was very little time for my hobbies.

When I was teaching those 19 years, there was very little time for my hobbies, but by that time I had realized the health benefits of taking time to do things I wanted to do. I LOVE fabric; selecting it, buying it, washing it, pressing it, folding it, touching it, working with it, and looking at it neatly stacked on my shelves. Is it any wonder that I love quilting?

Reasons why I'm a Quilter, Page 121

Carole Flasch
Weslaco, Texas

My mother and grandmother were excellent seamstresses. They worked with fabric, yarn, crochet thread, and oil paint. As a child, my sister and I used to love to pick out our dress fabric from the patchwork quilts on our beds. It made us feel like we were part of the quilt.

Betty J. Knack
Essexville, Michigan

Us little children used to crawl underneath the quilt and bob our heads up and down. Grandma warned us. We were having such fun though. Soon grandma was using her thimble finger and tapping our heads. It stopped being fun. My mother, Leona Harmon Strietre, taught us to make quilts when we were quite young. My first one, a butterfly quilt, was started at age 11 and finished at age 14. Second one started, age 14, finished the Rose of Sharon at the age of 16. I was born January 30, 1924, so have been quilting a long time. I prefer quilting instead of making the tops.

Nancy H. Ehinger
West Branch, Michigan

I am a quilter because of the enjoyment that it gives me, both in the executing of my quilts and in the relationships with other quilters who share my excitement. Quilting is never boring. There is always another technique, another way of doing something, another quilt to try.

Janet P. Wyckoff
Hopewell, New Jersey

My mother taught me to sew when I was 10 or so, and we talked over everything while we worked together. My first quilting experience was working on the Hopewell Bicentennial Quilt in 1976 with 50 women. I quilt because, in addition to my love of math, design, color and texture, I treasure the community of women working together.

Lynn Graves
Albuquerque, New Mexico

As a teen, I was thoroughly turned off by "sewing". Hated homemade clothes, and my Mother was a GREAT seamstress. In my 30's, domesticity set in, and I began to sew and sew and sew - mostly clothing. When quilting came along, it was love at first sight - a natural for me. Quilting suits my addictive personality!

Alba Lee Elliott
Asheville, North Carolina

I enjoy being creative, getting together with other quilters is so rewarding, a wonderful group. We talk about our family, our work, always a lot of show-and-tell in our meeting, as much love as stitches, in a quilt!

Roxanne H. McElroy
Mililani, Hawaii

I quilt because I have to. If I didn't quilt, all of these ideas I have, would pile up in my head, and it would explode. I also quilt to relax all the stress of the world, which goes on hold, and it is just me and my quilt, relaxed, happy and calm.

Ruth Powers
Carbondale, Kansas

Quilting is an art I have always admired, but assumed it took years to do, considering all of those tiny stitches, so although I had probably done every other art or crafts fad that has been in vogue, quilting was one I never aspired to. Then one day in 1989, I decided a certain wall in my home needed a special wall hanging, and that I could probably stand to do that much. Much to my surprise, I found it to be the most satisfying work I had ever done, and I haven't stopped since.

Carolyn Koopman
Carnavillo, Iowa

I quilt to satisfy creativity. One time, while making a scrap quilt, I needed a different dark from what I had been using. My husband, Jerry's robe was laying in the sewing room waiting to be repaired. It was just the fabric I needed, a nice brown paisley. so I cut out a couple of squares!

Norma Jean Rector
Center Point, Indiana

As a little girl, I used to go with my mother (Ora Fretz) to Ladie's Aid. The ladies would go early, take a covered dish, and quilt all day. Most often, they would meet in each other's homes. This was the ladies way of making money for their church, and they enjoyed their day of good food and fellowship together. I'll never forget those good times, the beautiful quilts, and those beautiful ladies. My mother and my mother-in-law made quilts and comforts for the practical purpose of covers for their beds. When I married, Mother said I needed to make my own quilts, and she started me on the basic quilting. I have learned so much more, since a group of ladies organized our quilt club in 1987. I am proud to be a charter member of the Clay City Calico Quilters.

My favorite quilt is Grandmother's Flower Garden Basket. Mother had started a flower garden quilt, but it was too tedious handwork for her arthritic fingers. Before she died in 1952, she gave me what she had started, along with many tiny patches, cut and threaded into stacks, according to colors. Many times, I'd get out that sack of little "flower" blocks and the patches, admire them, put them back in the closet, saying, "One day....". In 1992, I made up my mind that I was going to make a quilt from what Mother had started. At our quilt club's annual quilt show in June 94', my Grandmother's Flower Garden Basket won *Viewers' Choice*. It has 2,812 little hexagon patches in it.

Betty Verhoeven
East Jewett, New York

I suppose the main reason I quilt, is my love of fabrics. I just love the way they work together. It is something that always gave me pleasure. I could enjoy working with fabrics, while raising my children and caring for the family at home. I always had a stash I could go to for projects. It started out innocently, I'd buy old housedress for a dime or quarter at the local rummage sales to cut apart. And, of course, there were the outfits that the children had outgrown. But, I soon graduated to the fabric stores, where I'd spend my mad money at the remnant tables on beautiful *new* fabrics. That started a whole new era, I couldn't stop! A yard here, a yard there, and oohh, you never know when you'll need that gorgeous color! And then the sales!! Who can stop with just a yard or two?

Then, the problem comes. How do I sneak these goodies into the house without dear Hubby noticing the extra bags?

Tip: Fabric stores will put your purchases in plain brown bags!

I remember one time, I was going grocery shopping, but a funny thing happened on the way to the market, my car just automatically pulled into the parking lot of the fabric store. Since I was there anyway, I thought I might as well take a quick peek at the sale table. I came out with a good sized bag full of supplies, and continued on to the grocery store. Needless to say, I bypassed the nice juicy steaks and opted for the chopped meat. The roast beef on my list was replaced with bologna, and so on through the store, until at the checkout, I managed to save what I had already spent at the fabric store!

As I pulled into the garage at home, there was my dear husband to help me unload the car. I quickly threw some groceries into the fabric bag and took it in, with the rest, then later smuggled it into my sewing room. A week or so later, when I went to sort out the fabrics and put them away, I noticed a peculiar smell coming from the bag. I found a foul smelling cheese tucked in between the cottons and calicos! It's not easy being a FABRI-HOLIC!

Along with fabric, I think another reason I enjoy quilting is the fact that you can express yourself in a quilt. It can tell a personal story (like my "Flag" quilt), or it can just be an excuse to work with a favorite color combination or pattern. But by far, one of the best reasons for quilting is the people! Quilt people are imaginative, creative, and fun! At every quilt show or exhibit, you meet new and interesting people, and of course, the friendships I've found in my guilds are so important to me. Quilter friends are real treasures!

Pauline A. Cook
Idaho Falls, Idaho

I am a quilter because I wanted a quilt and couldn't afford an antique Quilt. After making my first Quilt project, I found I wanted to make more. Now, I have enough projects I want to do that would take 5 lifetimes to complete!

Barbara Shook Davis
Williams, Arizona

Originally, because I was a starving graduate student and wanted to decorate my house beautifully and inexpensively (with scrap fabric). Now, because I've learned you can never have too many quilts!

Pat Campbell
Rigby, Idaho

I've always been an artist, studied commercial art for two years at college, worked, got married, and needed an outlet for my creativity. I've tried all the crafts, from ceramics to tole' painting, and beyond. Nothing seemed to satisfy me until I began Japanese and Swedish paper cutting. Then, I found Hawaiian whole cloth applique, and knew I'd found my niche'. Something about cutting the fabric and creating a whole new look with color/texture/pattern lit the spark about fifteen years ago. I've been designing and creating ever since.

Etta Grace Edwards
Council Grove, Kansas

My first quilt was a large star which was lost in a box while moving. I made all my baby blankets and clothes. Most of my time to sew was after everyone was in bed. Now that Willis, my husband, is gone, and all the children are married, time is not a thing to search for.

I like to paint, crochet and make quilts, but I never keep them, they are gifts to my children and grandchildren. You know if you give them now, there can't be any fight when you're gone. Ha!

Joyce Livingston, my neighbor, friend and author of this book, got me started again in quilting after my husband died. I'm now in the process of making a queen size quilt for my daughter, Julie. I will quilt it by hand, I hope! Ha!

Celeste Lipp
Idaho Falls, Idaho

I come from a long line of embroiderers. I had done every kind of stitchery, and quilting looked like a real challenge. I took it up in 1988 and have been a devoted quilter ever since.

By 1989, I had only completed one baby quilt and had no other projects. I was newly relocated in Sycracuse, NY and was telling my can-do friend, Richard, now I had no friends and nothing to do. He said I always talked about quilting and should join a guild; START one if need be, and get busy quilting. So I did! I joined the Candle Light Quilt Guild in Baldwinsville, NY. Out of gratitude, I began a quilt for Richard and his wife, a king-sized, hand-pieced, hand-appliqued peony quilt. I had no tools but pencil, scissors, needle and thread. I'm finally quilting, a block at a time. Let's just say, if that quilt was alive, it would be in school! Richard has graciously offered me a plane ticket to Seattle to deliver this beauty - all I have to do is finish it!

In 1991, while taking a trip to a different water fountain at work, I saw someone with a quilt poster in her office. I stopped to say *hi* and see if she knew about the local quilt guild. Debbie and I became the greatest friends from that little encounter, we spent the happiest times quilting, shopping for fabric, and traveling to quilt shows and outings. I broke our hearts by moving to Idaho. Within two years we were both married to a *David*.

She and I took our dream trip last year and went to the AQS show in Paducah! We had a great, great time. At first, we marveled at the cable channel "Quilt TV", but once we had seen all of the segments 3 or 4 times, we joked that punishment for misbehaving was watching it some more. Deb had Baby #1 on the way, but we still managed to shop at Hancock's Fabrics 5 times in 4 days!

Since, she had her daughter, and I am making her a Rose of Sharon baby quilt for a first birthday present. One of the highlights of our trip was a display of Marie Webster quilts from the early 1900's. Rose of Sharon was my favorite. Debbie and I still joke about how lucky we are that she took her quilt poster to work!

Our Paducah sanity-saver: only go to view quilts after 3:30 P.M. All of the hungry quilters will be stampeding to supper and you can look at the quilts in peace.

In 1994, I made a Jacob's Ladder baby quilt for our friend Amy's little boy. She and her family admired it so much that Amy, her mother, and her grandmother plan to take quilting classes together soon.

I recently answered an ad for a quilting pen pal. I highly recommend this to anyone who likes to get mail. I was able to meet Tana, who is a delightful correspondent and my new friend. We have the same affection for cats and we are planning to do a round robin project through the mail! Suddenly 32 cents for a stamp seems like a bargain.

Mary Lou Kantz Evans
Flagstaff, Arizona

Handwork is a necessity to me, and I've been settled on quilting for the last 10 years, or so. I favor old-fashioned quilts and this recent boom in primitive patterns that combine stitching and patchwork are just my thing. I think the folks from Kindred Spirits, Red Wagon, Taylor Made Designs, and Pieces from the Heart (to name a few) remind us thru their designs what things are important in life: love, sharing, friendships and fun.

Our busy modern world often doesn't give positive feedback, so you have to find your own ways to add positive energy and enthusiasm to your life. Quilting does that for me, whether taking a class, teaching a class or getting together to visit and quilt.

Is there a better way to introduce yourself to a new community and make new friends than quilting?

Z.Z. Gilmore
Pocatello, Idaho

It kept me sane after my beloved husband, Michael Gilmore, died suddenly.

It gives me such a feeling of accomplishment. It is a great excuse for sitting down.

How else can one fondle fabrics?

Since I stay up until 3:00 a.m. quilting, it gives my neighbors an excuse for teasing me about having a secret lover who comes in the dark of the night.

Sandra L. Hatch
Lincoln Maine

I learned to sew at a young age and was encouraged by my mother and grandmother. When I met my friend Blanche, she encouraged me to try new things and I just kept going. I don't quilt as much as I should or as much as I wish I did because my work, all day every day, revolves around quilting. I can't spend every minute of every day immersed in quilts, although I know there are those who do.

Christine Klinger
Fayetteville, Arkansas

I joined my local quilt guild in 1987, after winning the raffle quilt at their first show. I attended a monthly meeting so I could pick up the quilt, and have been attending ever since.

Sue Hausmann
Lincolnshire, Illinois

I have been an avid sew-er all my life and although my mother and grandmother did not sew when I was young, Grandma had been a quilter in her younger days. For 8th grade graduation she gave me a precious quilt and my folks gave me the two that were always on the beds in her house, next to ours. As a machine sew-er, I didn't think too much about quilting until suddenly several machine quilting pioneers like Nancy Martin and Eleanor Burns developed strip piecing and speed piecing methods. Then I was hooked and quilted constantly! I do remember trying a log cabin for Family Circle magazine - cutting all the pieces and then sewing through very puffy batting for total discouragement. Then buying a kit at the little schoolhouse where That Patchwork Place started and making strip vest after strip vest.

Once, while teaching this class the local newspaper came and took a picture, then ran it the next week with a caption, "Sue Hausmann strips in class!"

We have made each of our nieces and nephews quilts as wedding gifts, the *we* being Herb and me. He sits behind the machine and clips the speed pieced sections apart and stacks them next to me for the next sewing or serger step! And speed quilts are how we started our daughters-in-law sewing. One day our daughter and two daughters-in-law-to-be sat around the table speed-piecing queen-size log cabin quilts. It's such a miracle they all ended up with the right pieces! All love to sew, and Janet does wonderful quilts, piecing by machine and quilting by hand.

My only regret today is that I have less and less time to sew, so I do mainly clothing for myself, quick projects for the show and our grandchildren. However, I did about 16 speed quilts my last year of teaching in the store and we actually ran out of beds and walls. A number of people have encouraged me to say that I have moved on to the next stage which is enabling others to do this wonderful sewing experience, quilting, through the series and teaching outlines for others. I hope so!

Jane Newhouse
Wedderburn, Oregon

I've sewn for years - clothing, doll clothes, curtains, and such, but no more!! Now, it's quilt! Selecting a pattern, picking the fabric, the planning, the piecing, the applique, each is a challenge, each is an opportunity to share the process with a quilting buddy. Taking classes, meeting new people, sharing with old friends, all of which results in a lovely quilt, wall hanging, garment, or such - what a marvelous way to spend our days.

When each of our children married, the other four and I worked together making a wedding quilt. There were some years when the U.S. Postal Service profited from this project. This tradition has been a lot of fun and means a lot to each of the children.

Sally Smith
Kodak, Tennessee

The only quilting done in my family was strictly for utilitarian reasons and long before I was ever thought of. I have a love for history and good craftsmanship and these two things are what led me to quilting. I have been fortunate to win several awards with my quilts and share my knowledge when I can. Probably the oddest thing I do is talk to my quilts (especially the *people* ones) and, of course, they talk to me. When I see fabric, it speaks of a design and vice-versa and more often than not, the name of the quilt is chosen before I've even made the first cut into the cloth.

Joanna Bessey
Rhinlander, Wisconsin

My grandmother is *the* reason for my quilting today. Although I never knew her because she died before I was born, my mom gave me her unfinished Grandmother's Flower Garden fabric pieces of the 1930's. This led me to my first quilting class and soon thereafter to our local Quilt Guild and all their enthusiasm (of which I became the treasurer before I was even an official member! - talk about avid interest!)

I was, and continue to be - *Hooked on quilting!* Plus, quilting ties in with so many of Bill's and my interests - traveling, for sure, as there's always a different shop to explore on our vacations.

I like the old and traditional, so vintage quilts and especially tops, can be wonderful finds at antique shops, while Bill continues to search for Civil War memorabilia.

I'm a patchwork person, Lord! Any calico scraps worked into a patchwork design really attract me. Quilts, pillows, wall hangings, sheets, jackets, skirts... it makes no difference, just so long as it's patchwork!

But, best of all, I guess it's the patchwork quilts I like best! All those tiny pieces of fabric worked into a pattern... well, it's simply a work of art! I especially like the ones made from dozens of different colors, all fabrics rescued from the scrapbag!

I confess, Lord, my life is a little like those patchwork quilts. Bits and pieces of this and that. Not much that really counts for anything, just a scrap of this and a remnant of that. All virtually worthless until the seamstress gathers them together and works out a plan, a design to re-fashion them into something beautiful.

You do that, God. You take my confused life and after much leading, guiding, chastening and forgiveness... you make something beautiful of my life. But, like that lovely PATCHWORK QUILT, from time to time I have to be re-worked, mended and touched up to maintain my usefulness.

Keep my life beautiful... a work of art... as only you... can do!

From PRAY GIRL, a devotional book for women written by Joyce Livingston

"Give her of the fruit of her hands, and let her own works praise her in the gates." Proverbs 31, verse 31

Quilters Share Their Best Time-Saving Household Hints!

"I have an idea! I'll quilt... and YOU do the cooking!"

Joyce Livingston

Page 128, Time-saving household tips

Author's Note:
"Get a maid!" That was the household hint that I received most, as I read through the questionaires as they were returned for this book. I found that most quilters would prefer to ignore housework, or delegate it to others! My favorite solution was the one that said, "Dust is a protective coating for fine furniture!"

≈≈≈≈≈≈≈≈≈≈≈≈≈≈≈≈≈≈≈≈≈≈≈

Joyce Livingston, Council Grove, Kansas

• Use straight vinegar to remove water spots and mineral build-up from your shower wall, faucets, etc. If you have mineral build-up in your shower head, put 1/2 cup of vinegar in a small plastic bag and fasten it over the shower head with a rubber band, making sure the head is submerged in the vinegar. Soak for an hour or so. Rinse with water and dry with a towel.
• We go through many jars of ice tea, they're tall with straight sides and have either blue, green or yellow plastic lids. Use 4, 5 or more of them, side by side, on your kitchen counter top to store items you use in your salads. They look pretty, and everything is right at your finger tips at salad time.
• Just before retiring, several times a week, pour about a 1/2 cup of pure liquid bleach into the toilet stools in the bathrooms and let stand overnight. Keeps the bowls sparkling clean and no brushing! (Don't use bleach, if you are on a septic tank system).
• Keep a clean, folded dish towel on the kitchen counter right next to the sink for hand drying. Keeps husbands and children from dribbling water across the floor while looking for a towel.
• Run soapy, hot water in the sink when you start a cooking project. Drop items in, as you finish using them. By the time you've finished preparing casseroles, cookies, etc., all they need is a quick swish, and they're clean.
• Use the same creative ideas for storing items throughout your home, as you do your quilting supplies. I wanted a workroom so I could shut the door and leave my mess-in-process, without anyone seeing it. The opposite happened! The rest of the house gets less attention. That room is my pride and joy!

≈≈≈≈≈≈≈≈≈≈≈≈≈≈≈≈≈≈≈≈≈≈≈

Jane Newhouse Wedderburn, Oregon

• I watch my *organized* friends and try to follow their examples.
• Every once in a while, I get the urge to once again do some cooking, so I take advantage of this and spend a day cooking and loading the freezer with meal size packages. I always feel so smart when I can grab something, heat or cook it, and with the addition of salad or veggies have a good meal for the two of us.

≈≈≈≈≈≈≈≈≈≈≈≈≈≈≈≈≈≈≈≈≈≈≈

Nadine Dozier North Augusta, South Carolina

• I use my crock pot a lot for planning meals. (That way my dinner is cooking, while I'm quilting).
• I'm also a firm believer in ordering out. Ha!
• Also my husband likes to cook, so he helps out a great deal.
• I plan my shopping and running errands on the same days, so I can have those things done at one time.

≈≈≈≈≈≈≈≈≈≈≈≈≈≈≈≈≈≈≈≈≈≈≈

Bonnie Kay Browning Paducah, Kentucky

• I can't do without my crockpot, my rice cooker, and my husband who can cook as well as I do. We like casseroles and stir fry dishes that are easy and quick to prepare. There are never leftovers at our house, we call them *planned overs* since we plan to have them leftover for another meal.

≈≈≈≈≈≈≈≈≈≈≈≈≈≈≈≈≈≈≈≈≈≈≈

Betty Lou Cassidy Linwood, New Jersey

• The biggest time saver is to train a husband to help you do the household chores. Since women have become "liberated" and work outside of the home more, I believe many men have found a creative outlet in cooking. My husband fancies himself a gourmet - - I'm not about to tell him he's not. If you manage to get your husband to cook, remember Rule #1 - - Don't criticize the meal. If you must, make suggestions on improvement, but eat whatever he makes. This builds up his confidence and eventually you'll gain more time to quilt. You'll be busy and he needs something to do.

≈≈≈≈≈≈≈≈≈≈≈≈≈≈≈≈≈≈≈≈≈≈≈

Thelma Tiefel Clay City, Indiana

• I prepare larger quantities of food when I cook. Therefore, the microwave comes in very handy.
• I bake two or three batches of

cookies at one time and freeze them.
• I don't quilt in the summer, so it is the time I prepare vegetables and fruit for the freezer and still raise a garden.

Ruth Rhoades
Toccoa, Georgia

• If 'things' are picked up, and the bathroom is clean, you can let the rest go (for awhile).
• Make the bed as you get out of it.

Beverly J. Relph
Leavenworth, Kansas

• I don't do windows, and the "Big Pot" saves my marriage.

Elizabeth A. Akana
Kaneohe, Hawaii

• I allow my husband to cook, vacuum, and do the laundry. The laundry was the hardest to give up. He makes all my whites...tattle tale grey!!!

Elaine Helen
(Revier) Baker
Watertown, Minnesota

• I do all of my household chores while my kids are awake so while they are asleep, I can do my cutting. This is safer, as I use a rotary cutter.
• I save all of my scraps, no matter how small, because they keep the kids busy (sorting them). When I'm sewing a lot of pieces at a time, I let my oldest trim all of the threads. My youngest does well at stacking squares and blocks. We all do something for each quilt.

Glenda Phipps
Whitman, Nebraska

• In addition to cooking for the five of us, I frequently have to cook for our hired men so I take advantage of easy to fix recipes.
• I make a lot of casseroles in the winter, and grill everything in the summer.
• I cook in large quantities so there are always plenty of leftovers (my favorite meal).
• I highly recommend having at least one daughter. With luck, you may get one that enjoys cooking which frees you to do OTHER things.
• Children can also be a boon when cleaning. While they are young and impressionable is the time to teach them the joys of vacuuming and dusting. With luck, it will last a lifetime or at least till they become teenagers, which will seem like a lifetime.
• Our children are great at spotting fabric stores when you visit a strange city. Unfortunately, mine usually try to get me to drive the other way!

Karen Crollick
St. George,
Australia, QLD

• My clothes are folded straight off the line, which cuts out half of the ironing.
• I ask my teenage daughters to help with the housework!
• I cook very quick and simple meals which don't take a lot of preparation.

Janet Kugler
Holdrege, Nebraska

• Get rid of clutter, so that dusting is easier. Or put clutter behind glass.
• Hire a housekeeper to dust and vacuum.

Jill Marie Tanking
Liberal, Kansas

• Really don't have any hints. My house has hardwood floors. The only thing I have noticed, my house doesn't get as dirty, since I've spent more time quilting. I have never liked cleaning house. Like a friend said, "Why clean when you're having company, when you will have to clean after they leave?"
• I just sweep all the rooms first thing in the morning, pick-up the junk mail and the papers, and put them in a paper bag for recycling. And start the dishwasher some time during the day. Put something in the crock-pot or put some hamburger meat out to thaw for the evening meal. And put everyone on a diet.

Barbara S. Moss
Locust Grove, Georgia

• I work out while cleaning house using very loud music to drown out working.
• Make ahead casseroles.
• Cooking meals in the oven, while you sleep.
• Try to plan doctors, dentist, etc. on the same day.
• Quilt for 2 hours, then chill out 1 hour, then quilt again, this way you don't burn out.

Page 130, Time-saving household tips

Helen M. Ericson
Emporia, Kansas

My household hint to have time for quilting is: try to schedule family activities in the middle of the day, so to have early morning and evenings to quilt and watch TV at the same time.
• Sunday morning is a great time for doing laundry, then the beginning of the week is for quilting projects.
• Put a pot of beans in the crockpot overnight on low to make Chili the next day. A quick meal is more appreciated than ones that take hours to do. I often wished I had a headset for the phone or an exercycle with a quilting hoop on the handlebars!

Chloe Rhodes
Clay City, Indiana

• My favorite hint is to let everything else go and work on quilts, hoping no one comes to see your messy house.

Louise Murphy
Mammoth Lakes, California

• Almost 20 years later, I am still trying to figure this one out. I have learned priorities. The daily or weekly chores I used to do mechanically are no longer as important as spending a few moments or hours with the needle. I am a better person for it, thus more harmony in the home.
• I do find however, to leave my current project to shovel show from the decks or a bit of time in the garden, is a necessary break to clear my head and be able to re-focus, especially on something that I am troubled with. Sometimes you walk back into the room and know exactly what you need to adjust or change for the correct result.

Josephine Hannah Jirva Burgwgn (Jo Jo)
Jackson, North Carolina

• Vacuuming twice a month instead of 4 times - someone once told me to ponder this: "Why chase dirt all your life when they're just gonna throw it on your coffin when you die?
• Cook in large quantities and freeze half for later.

Mary Anne Keppler
St. Olaf, Iowa

• I haven't found any real good hints to get out of work. At some point you still have to take care of it.

Colleen Taylor
Indialantic, Florida

• Clean only when necessary, do laundry only when you have nothing to wear.

Lynn Lewis Young
Houston, Texas

• Do as little as possible, and set a time limit when doing it - since there's no end to the amount of housework that could be done, just decide how long you can "afford" to be away from your quilting, and just work that long - you'll be more efficient, if you set a time limit.

Deb Meneely
Seattle, Washington

• I use my quilting as a "reward" for getting work done in my home. That is, if I get all my chores done by 2:00 p.m., then I can quilt for an hour before the kids come home.

Kathryn Rippeteau Greenwold
Niskayuna, New York

• Is "ignore it" a valid tip? Actually, I focus on one room each day. That way I don't feel overwhelmed and manage to keep up most of the time.

Florence <u>Edith</u> Goggin
Eureka, California

• Really don't have helpful hints. Get my housework done early and quickly so that I can quilt, plan classes, or work in the yard.

Rebecca Kelly
Kingsburg, California

• My favorite household hint is to "relax your standards"! Doing household chores is not a life or death matter. Chores can wait - children and quilting can't. Of course, keep things clean - but

Time-saving household tips, Page 131

nobody cares if they can "eat off" your floor!

Mary Andrews
Grand Blanc, Michigan

• Once I became a "serious quilter", I sure didn't have time for housework. Working full-time, having my family around and trying to sew were getting hard to juggle. I resented having to spend my day off cleaning, shopping and cooking and having no time for my sewing. So I hired a cleaning lady. Ruth comes every other week while I am at work, and I come home and the house is clean. My mother and my aunts always had housecleaning help, so it was easy to let someone else do it. I wouldn't want Ruth to know, but sometimes when I am picking things up and putting them away before she gets here, I realize that I haven't swept my kitchen floor or vacuumed between her visits.

• One day at work, one of my co-workers mentioned her milkman. My ears perked up at that word and I asked her about it. Somehow I thought the milkman disappeared like dinosaurs. Yes, her milkman came once a week with milk, eggs, juice, and yogurt. I couldn't get to the phone fast enough to get on his route. It is a little more expensive, but I figure it is actually cheaper because I am not going to the store to get the milk.

• I bought a used freezer a few years ago and wondered why I didn't do that long ago. I shop at Sam's Club and buy in bulk to cut down on trips to the store. Now if I could figure out a way to get fresh fruit and vegetables delivered, I would only have to shop about every other month.

• I'm not sure if this falls under household hints, but when I get a day to sew, I don't want to be interrupted by frivolous phone calls. So, I put my answering machine on and screen the calls. I have, on occasion when using the cordless phone, reached outside the front door and rang the doorbell to get off the phone.

Patricia (Pat) Jones
Oroville, California

• Many ladies ask how I'm able to quilt so much and still keep up my house. Well, this is what I tell them: Make a priority list with Quilting at the top and everything else to follow. My motto is: "If it ain't broke, don't fix it!" In other words, if you're not having company, don't worry about the house. One thing to remember about housework, it never goes away! When you are ready, it will still be there!

Minabess P. Randolph
Toms River, New Jersey

• I don't have any good household hints, because I'm not a good housekeeper. One suggestion I do have though, is to always repair and alter and sew your husband's and children's clothes immediately, when they ask. This makes them happy and usually only takes a few minutes and then they don't resent the hours you spend quilting.

• Our house was known as the "House of the Charcoal Chips". So when the boys were young my husband, Nelson, took over the making of the Christmas Cookies with them. Today Nelson makes the worlds best Oatmeal Raisin Cookie and I have even had ladies come into Crafty Fabrics in Toms River, NJ and asked who made the cookies we serve on special occasions.

Eleanor Burenheide
Emporia, Kansas

• Be organized. Have a place for everything and return it there after usage. Do not spend time hunting for an item.

• Spend a day preparing several recipes (doubled) and divide them down into servings for your family. Freeze them. Teach your husband, children and grandchildren how to make salads, desserts, etc. to go with them. Presto!--You have two weeks to sew and go!

• An answering machine on your phone can save you countless hours in one weeks time. Pickup on the important calls (quilters) and let the machine weed out the others (sales people).

• The crockpot is a simple, easy way to fix, and the meals are yummie. Most important, it may be eaten when *you are ready*.

• Hide your car...so the neighbors don't know you're home.

Mary Jane Cemer
Trenton, Nebraska

• Don't do anything but quilt....make blocks, read quilting magazines, sew, patchwork.

• Grocery shop, or shop for other purchases once a week, if you have to.

Page 132, Time-saving household tips

- Feed twice a day and keep the coffee pot full.
- Wash clothes when naked.
- Blow at dust.
- Wave away cobwebs.

≈≈≈≈≈≈≈≈≈≈≈≈≈≈≈≈≈≈≈≈≈≈≈≈≈

Melissa Armstrong
Oshkosh, Nebraska

- Keep it simple. Do a little as you go, all the time.
- Use the dishwasher, microwave, and the kids.
- If it gets to be too much, or for the big jobs like windows, hire it done, and *don't* feel guilty about it.
- During time of added stress, such as Christmas, find an audio or tactile reminder to keep it light. I wear bells on my shoes December 1-January 1, as a reminder to not let the little things get me down. Have fun!

≈≈≈≈≈≈≈≈≈≈≈≈≈≈≈≈≈≈≈≈≈≈≈≈≈

Paula Gore
Osmond, Nebraska

- Don't do it! The housework, that is! In view of that (in case you like a neater, cleaner house), delegate! Do it in the name of teaching responsibility. Your children won't thank you for it. We also share the work, it creates an appreciation for a clean house or clothes or food.

≈≈≈≈≈≈≈≈≈≈≈≈≈≈≈≈≈≈≈≈≈≈≈≈≈

Patti Centeno
San Antonio, Texas

Who doesn't need more time to quilt??? I am great at finding the short cut to getting more time in my day.

- I am great at crock-pot dinners. I usually plan a menu list for the entire week, since I know in advance which nights we will be gone, or who's at home to eat.
- After grocery shopping, I will slice up vegetables in advance, and store them in chilled water in the refrigerator. Then, they are ready for cooking or putting in casseroles.
- I cook a lot in my Wok. It's fast, healthy, and easy to clean up.
- I only wash clothes two nights a week. If you don't bring it to the laundry room, it doesn't get done. I also allow my children to do their own wash, if they really need something before the designated day of washing. I only wash and dry, then I put each child's clothes in their own basket for them to fold and put away. Responsibility!!

≈≈≈≈≈≈≈≈≈≈≈≈≈≈≈≈≈≈≈≈≈≈≈≈≈

Susan Hanna
Brownlee, Nebraska

- Overlapping of jobs - in the time it takes to heat water for a pot of tea, a bed can be made, bird feeders filled. Make your time do double duty.

≈≈≈≈≈≈≈≈≈≈≈≈≈≈≈≈≈≈≈≈≈≈≈≈≈

Barbara MacDonald
Oscoda, Michigan

- My favorite household hint to make more time for quilting is to be lucky enough to be married to someone who loves to clean house! I work weekends, he doesn't, and when I come home, the house is clean! When I've been in my sewing room for hours and dinner time rolls around he says, "let's just eat out!". I could never accomplish the things I do without my husband's help.

≈≈≈≈≈≈≈≈≈≈≈≈≈≈≈≈≈≈≈≈≈≈≈≈≈

Carole P. Kenny
Providence,
Rhode Island

- A cleaning lady, 4 hours every week takes the guilt out of not doing housework. If this isn't possible, find a friend and join to help each other clean both your houses the same day and forget it the rest of the week.
- Place coffee, filters and spoon in one canister and place in freezer. Keeps coffee fresher and you can think of your quilting, instead of which cupboard you put those things in.

≈≈≈≈≈≈≈≈≈≈≈≈≈≈≈≈≈≈≈≈≈≈≈≈≈

Sherry Cook
Council Grove, Kansas

- When baking cookies, always double the batch and freeze half for later use. You can always quilt while cookies are baking. It takes no more time to mix up two batches, instead of one.

≈≈≈≈≈≈≈≈≈≈≈≈≈≈≈≈≈≈≈≈≈≈≈≈≈

Jeanne K. Ferg
Asheville,
North Carolina

- I cook enormous amounts of every food, so that we "enjoy" several days of leftover foods.
- My husband tells friends I just never learned to cook for two. I am blessed with a neat and tidy spouse, so have little problem with housekeeping when it is done.

Time-saving household tips, Page 133

Bonnie Swecker
Roanoke Rapids, North Carolina

- You can always make time for what you want to do, but you also have to be responsible to do what's necessary for taking care of a family.
- I like to combine a necessity with a want, for example, sew or cut pieces while the washing machine is running. When it stops, you have to also.
- I also use the reward system. List what needs doing for the day. When you've crossed off three (or whatever seems reasonable - be honest), reward yourself with a free hour to quilt.

Jean Van Dusen
Kingsford, Michigan

- After breakfast, I allow myself an allotted amount of time for housework, and then I quilt.
- I try to do all my errands in one trip.
- If I have handwork I call a friend to come and bring her handwork and we combine a visit and quilting.

Gladys Shook
Hutchinson, Kansas

- When cleaning windows, it is easy to see which side the streaks are on, if you remember to always wash the inside of the window with a vertical motion, and the outside with a horizontal motion.

Jean Eng Underhill
Flemington, New Jersey

- I don't have a quilting/sewing room, but I do have a dining room. So for many months throughout the year, the projects I am working on are laid neatly on my dining room table where I cut and sew, every chance I have.
- I use a rice cooker so that I can't burn my rice, and I do a lot of Chinese stir-frying, healthy good and quick.

Eugenia A. Barnes (Genie)
Marcellus, New York

- Daily/weekly chores are scheduled for a.m. and then lunch on...is *my* time.
- Keep meals simple, lots of soups/stews/casseroles.
- (I also have my 80+ year old Mother and 4 grandchildren in the home). Late nights mean quiet time and no interruptions.

Ann Littleton
Fairfax, Virginia

- Plan menus in advance.
- Have ingredients on hand.
- Double recipes, and freeze one for use after an all day sewing adventure or quilter's field trip.
- Schedule one day a week for laundry and cleaning house.
- Plan one morning a week to sew with a group.
- Train the kids to help with household chores or to make simple meals.
- Plan errands all on one day.
- EAT OUT!

Eleanor K. Hunnel
Johnstown, Nebraska

- Having lost my husband to cancer several years ago, I do have somewhat unlimited time to spend working at my quilts - not that this would be mine or anyone's choice. However, I am so thankful I have this hobby, which is so very rewarding. I meet and associate with the finest of ladies, and have had a changed attitude as to buying fabric - time is short for all of us and when I see fabric I fancy - I buy it!

Dotti Greto
Ocean City, New Jersey

- Keep your house straightened up. It looks cleaner than it really is. Of course, this excludes the sewing room.

Lassie Wittman
Rochester, Washington

- As they say "Housework whenever, quilting forever!"
- No real hints here, I just don't coffee with the neighbors.

Page 134, Time-saving household tips

Edna R. Harbison
Ontonagon, Michigan

• I'm lucky. I have a natural ability to ignore cobwebs, dust, and dirty dishes, when I'm working on my wall hangings. Saturday mornings, or when guests drop in, I am amazed at how the house suddenly got so messy.

Mary Lou Sayers
Clarkson, Nebraska

• Keep a quilt project handy. A few stitches can be taken between batches of cookies, or canners of tomatoes.
• I keep projects in large clear plastic boxes, which can be put away quickly.
• I don't have carpeting in my home. Throw rugs on smooth floor coverings make for easy care.
• I firmly believe enjoying one's home is much more important than a super neat house. We call my housekeeping, creative clutter.

Helen Blankenship
Flint, Michigan

• Keep things organized.
• Plan your meals and duties early a.m. so as to avoid last minute rush.
• Usually make soup once a week - good for lunches and days I spend with quilt groups - eliminates guilt when I leave hubby to fend for himself.

Lori Hauswirth
Iron River, Michigan

• Number one hint...find a husband (or teach on old one) who does laundry. But remember not to complain, if a red shirt gets bleached!!
• Number two....Housework? What's housework, when there's quilting to be done? Especially when a quilt show draws near. Dusting will wait!!

Audrey Derscha
Flint, Michigan

• Marry a good man, so he can do it all! Ha! Ha!

Martha G. Wilson
Roanoke Rapids, North Carolina

• Jane, my sister, told me before I am buried, the undertaker has to bring me home to clean up my quilting mess.

Doris Holland
Winterset, Iowa

• I don't have any special hints, but find that I take shortcuts in doing housework to make more time for quilting.

Susan D. Fellin
Flemington, New Jersey

• When I make my list of things to do around the house, I always add to my list quilting, sewing or crafts. Then I make sure I quit at a certain time, say 9 or 10 p.m. and devote an hour or two to the craft I love the most.

Paula Kay Garrison & Duncan Garrison
New Braunfels, Texas

• Make soups & stews. They last a long time and can be heated in the microwave.

Kathy Palmiter
Williams, Indiana

• When I cook, I like to have left overs. As long as the ingredients and utensils are out, why not make a double batch-one for now, one for later, or the freezer. I like casseroles, and so does my husband, Mike.

Doris Callaway, Greensburg, Kansas

• I cook less & clean less - and no one cares much - but my quilting comes before all household jobs - ha, ha!

Edna E. Holdsworth
Johnston, Rhode Island

• It helps if you are able to keep all your quilt supplies in one place.
• Try to organize your fabrics by color.
• Keep a basket for small scraps.

- Have a rack for your thread so you can see, at a glance, which colors you have.
- If possible, don't have a rug on the floor where you cut, piece and sew - it makes a lot easier to clean the threads and cutting scraps up.
- A small bulletin board, for notices, pictures of patterns, etc. keeps them from getting lost.

Susan Nicholson
Muskegon, Michigan

- Hire a cleaning lady!

Florence Tyler
DeLancey, New York

- Store things out-of-sight, as much as possible.

Susan Southworth
Gulf Shores, Alabama

- Never do today, what you can put off till tomorrow. If you follow this advice, you will always have time to quilt. Let nothing or no one stand in your way. Quilting comes before everything else.

Dawn Golden
Milford, New Jersey

- I have no household hints that make more time for quilting, I just make more time! When I do manage to get up the nerve to start something, it is usually late at night after the kids have had their last, last glass of water and are tucked in.
- There is talk between my friend, Mary, and I of a weekend when we will travel to Lancaster County, Pennsylvania together. There we will visit the fabric stores by day, and lock ourselves in a hotel at night with our sewing machines. Maybe we will even finish those Fan Quilts! But, to date, it hasn't happened!

PIONEER QUILTERS
Eugene, Oregon

- Don't do housework! Let your husband cook, do vacuuming, clean, shop, etc., etc.
- Make large recipes and freeze them.
- Forget to eat occasionally, and lose weight!

Darlene Brazil
Escalon, California

- Don't cook - call for Pizza!
- Assemble all of the fastest, but easiest known recipes you know - then double the recipe! With this handy dandy hint, you can go for days with only making an occasional mad dash to the kitchen!!
- Also, hire a housekeeper. Using these two hints will really enable you to stay in your sewing room, without a family meeting.

Doris Haggard
Topeka, Kansas

- My thought on cleaning house is, quilting first and cleaning whenever! I like to put a big quilt in the floor frame as soon as the Christmas holidays are over.
- I try to clean good first and do chunky cleaning till the quilt is out of the frame, hopefully by Easter.

Roberta Schroeder
Deer Park, Washington

- To appear to keep a tidy house, I spend 20 minutes every day vacuuming - if the floor looks clean, so does the rest of the house. Then I treat myself to time at the sewing machine.

Merrilyn Muir-Rennau
Vienna, Austria, Europe

- Shopping early in the morning.
- Using the vacuum cleaner before going to bed at night.
- Using Saturday to cook and bake for the week. What would we do without freezers and microwave ovens?

Pamela Thompson
Clinton Twp, Michigan

- Let someone else do the housework and cooking. My dear husband is a wonderful helper. This past year we put together our daughter's wedding. I did all the flowers, made a wedding gown, and most of a wedding quilt and shower memory quilt. He doesn't cook much, but is getting much better at cleaning.

Cynthia England
Houston, Texas

• I am extremely fortunate to have a husband who likes to cook and is good at it. I'm the clean-up-crew (less time, more quilting).
• I used to reward myself for cleaning the house. For instance, if I clean the bathroom, I get to quilt for an hour. I must admit that the deeper I got into my quilting addition, this didn't work. Now the only thing that gets me really moving is, the threat of company.

Diana Alfuth
Hudson, Wisconsin

• Learn to live with things in less perfect order.

Lesley Ann Hill
Granville, Ohio

• I quilt while my children are in school and after my youngest has gone to bed. Consequently, I want to make the best use of my limited time as possible. Before I go to bed, I tidy the house. The laundry is started before the kids go to school, they help by making sure all their clothes are in the hamper and then placing their hamper in the hall.
• I take breaks about every 2 hours, at that time I put a load into the dryer and another load into the washer. The laundry is sorted as it comes out of the dryer, each child can put away their own basket full. My children do the vacuuming, sweeping, clear the table, fill the dishwasher, empty the dishwasher, clean parts of the bathroom, clean their rooms which includes making their beds daily, and stripping and remaking their beds weekly. They've been doing these tasks for 4 years, which means those things don't cut into my quilting time.

Margo J. Clabo
Cleveland, Tennessee

• Never clean a bathroom until you are ready to take a shower. First, clean the floor and place a towel on the floor in front of the shower. (A "used" towel is fine.) Then you need to get naked. (Avoid the mirror!) Get into the shower and spray everything that has turned black, pink, or green with X-14 Brand Mildew Remover. Being naked will prevent bleached spots on your clothes.
• Step out of the shower onto the towel, because you will want to wipe the X-14 off of your feet. While the mildew remover is doing it's magic, swish out the toilet, and clean the sink and countertop. (Avoid the mirror!)
• Get back into the shower with an old toothbrush and wipe any black, pink, or green spots that may remain. Take your shower and rinse the X-14 off the walls with a washcloth. (This is a good time to shampoo and shave.) After you have dried your body, spray X-14 Brand Soap Scum Remover where it is needed, usually just the tub area. While the soap scum remover is doing its magic, put on your underwear and dry your hair. Wipe out the soap scum and rinse the tub before you put your clothes on, to avoid getting your clothes wet. Clean the mirror!

Margaret Kooda
Idaho Falls, Idaho

• If I have a particularly odious chore to get done, I work on it for an hour, then take time for cutting out or piecing one section of a project. With small children, you rarely have extended time to work on a project (household, or quilting!). This way I get a lot done in both areas.

Mary A. Sovran
Phoenix, Arizona

• A cooperative husband is the number 1 priority.
• I think you must have a place to work that is your very own place. Your own sanctuary to escape to where you can create without interruption, for at least a few hours every week. You need this time to do what you love.

John Flynn
Billings, Montana

• Get your spouse interested in quilting - then neither of you will have time to notice the clutter.

Juanita Gibson Yeager
Louisville, Kentucky

• My only hint for making more time to quilt is to decide what's more important, quilts or dust

bunnies, quilts or squeaky clean windows, quilts or home baked apple pie (you get my drift).
• Treat yourself to one day a month of housecleaning services. Save all the chores you hate to do, cleaning the stove, the refrigerator, flipping the mattress, dusting the what-knots and shelf for the cleaning service to do. Use the time you would have spent doing the chores or stewing over the fact they needed to be done, and quilt, quilt, quilt.

Candra J. Sowder
Williamsburg, Iowa

• Read and follow Don Aslett's books on de-cluttering and cleaning your home.

Sandra A. Anderson
Lincoln, Nebraska

• With three kids, 1 husband, 2 cats, 1 dog and 2 turtles and a job, I can't do everything. I try to schedule large jobs like; cleaning the refrigerator, cleaning oven on a rotating basis so they don't get too out of hand.
• Also I try to clean one room really good each week, instead of the whole house at one bite.
• I also use laundry baskets, different ones, assigned to different rooms or people, so I put everything going to a specific room or person, and make one trip rather than a lot of trips.

Donna Olson
Rogersville, Missouri

• A wonderful time saver is to be sure to take your clothes from the dryer the minute they are dry, and hang shirts, pants, etc. on hangers. This leaves them without wrinkles and only requires touch-up ironing, if any.

Jane Aruns
Franklin, Tennessee

• Dustballs never killed anyone!
• Make two loaves of bread, eat one, freeze one.
• Own a good vacuum cleaner.
• Spend money on closed shelving.
• Keep your priorities straight, a finished quilt is always more satisfying than homemade spaghetti sauce.

Shirley Gardner
Evergreen, Colorado

• Favorite household hints? Eat out, dust in the spring, plan color schemes in the bathtub and upon walking, make sure the kids love the library as much as you do, carry a sketch pad everywhere you go!

Carol Younce
Fairfax, Virginia

• Don't dust. Vacuum only infrequently - only when having a bee meeting at your house.
• Set the table for dinner in the morning - then go shopping for fabric!

Jane Clark Stapel
Pittsburgh, Pennsylvania

• I travel extensively, lecturing, so household hints don't quite apply to my lifestyle, But for traveling, everything I buy such as shampoo/make-up/curling iron/hair dryer, panties, stockings, and snacks (in case I'm stranded and a restaurant is not available) goes into my case. I subscribe to a magazine that goes into my suitcase immediately and then I have reading material at all times.
• I pack a large size tote with a pair of slacks/top/underwear and MY PROGRAM. I will check my suitcase, but my PROGRAM never leaves my hands! The extra clothing is in case I go one way and my luggage goes another....as long as I have case and credit card...everything can be replaced, plus I have the extra clothes for a quick change. All of this is more important to me because of extensive traveling.
• Another travel tip...anything over two hours in flying I ask for the exit aisle seat. MORE LEG ROOM and I have easy exit to move around/use the facilities, rather than have to climb over people. If you carry a quilt/lap project you have more room to spread that out also, especially if no one has the middle seat.

Debra J. Ruisard
Whitehouse Station, New Jersey

• My first household hint is that general housework can wait. If I find myself with a half hour of free time, forget the vacuuming. I have long given up the idea that my house will ever be as clean as my mother's, and so has she. I don't dust, clean windows or iron clothing. If it gets too bad, my husband usually comes

Page 138, Time-saving household tips

through. It helps immensely to have a spouse that understands my creative impulses and overlooks the fact that I'm not a perfect housekeeper. I like to think of myself as a "homekeeper".

• My dining room has been transformed into my studio. I no longer have to entertain any more people than can sit around my kitchen table. This also eliminates the need for major housework that occurs when entertaining guests. Those who don't mind sitting in my kitchen, overlook the mess. Mind you, I don't live in a pig sty. I do the necessities regularly (bathrooms, laundry, dishes, etc.), but it does not consume my every waking moment.

Kathy Munkelwitz
Isle, Maine

• All my floors are linoleum (helps in cleanings).
• I hate to cook, so do as little of that as possible.
• I get up very early and work, no one calls or comes over at 6 a.m. in the morning.

Shannon Royer
Otis, Kansas

My household hint is more of a philosophy from my mother, and much as I hate to admit, holds pretty true.....It takes less time to keep up than catch up! Another favorite saying of mine regarding housework is "My home is clean enough to be healthy and dirty enough to be happy!", proof that spotless isn't always necessary (just on special occasions).

Fran Soika
Novelty, Ohio

• The household hint I find has served me well, is to have a place for things and keep them there. You save a lot of "looking for something" time.
• If things are kept reasonably orderly, the dust isn't nearly as obvious. If someone should notice some dust, it is their problem, not yours. One of the advantages in getting old is that even with corrective glasses, dust isn't nearly as visible.

Lynda Milligan
Denver, Colorado

• Making double amounts of main dishes, so that it lasts for more than one meal.

Suzanne Peery Schutt
Clinton, Mississippi

• Keep quilting confined to one room, but use quilts all over the house. Keep projects organized.
• Clean quickly on Saturday mornings.
• Answer mail once a week.
• Work fast.
• Walk for exercise.
• Let quilting be the relaxing, enjoyable part of your day.

Anne-Donia B. Hafskjold
Tiller, Norway

• Since I work as a full-time teacher, I have to plan my work at home. I usually make a list of all the chores that have to be done, and I tell my self--that everytime I check off one job, I get to sew for 15 minutes.

Carole Flasch
Weslaco, Texas

• Always praise and compliment your husband for the lunch or dinner he has made for you, because you lost tract of time.
• Ask his opinion on color selection or other things, so he feels that he's part of the quilt making. This will give him bragging rights, when the quilt is given as a gift.

Lois K. Ide
Bucyrus, Ohio

• My husband has always been the cook, when he and his buddies go on fishing trips. So I enlist his help often, which frees up time for quilting.
• And when I prepare meals I nearly always make extra to put in the freezer for the next tight time schedule.
• My husband cleans up the kitchen after meals, since he has been retired and what a help it is!
• Whenever I make cookies or pies I always make several, and freeze.

Bonnie Swannack
Lamont, Washington

• On my refrigerator is a magnet that says, "My idea of housework is to sweep the room with a glance". That has become my housework philosophy.

Carole Collins
Norfolk, Nebraska

• I don't have any special hints to make more time for quilting, I do try to have certain days to do certain chores, but with the restoration of our home, that is not always possible. I am very lucky to have a husband who is very supportive of me and my quilting.

IIene L. Burdick
Coudersport, Pennsylvania

• Live with someone else (like my Mother), who prefers to do all the inside work herself!!!

Zelda Lynch
San Augustine, Texas

• Being a widow, I eat when I'm hungry, and sleep when I'm sleepy. I get up at 8 or 9 a.m. and go to bed about 10:30 or after. I also take a nap after noon for about an hour. I really get started sewing about 5 and watch all the TV News.

Betty E. Ives
Windsor Ontario, Canada

• Cook enough for at least 2 days. The microwave is wonderful.
• Do housework, when the grandchildren complain their socks are getting dirty.
• I took my husband, Albert, on a quilting cruise down the Amazon. He learned to make the Ocean Waves with tropical prints, how to use the seam ripper and quilt with ordinary needle without a thimble, as his fingers are so large. We quilted together and his knowledge of time elements and planning made for a better understanding of the subject of quilting!!

Norma Jean Rector
Center Point, Indiana

• I don't really have any other than just "pretending everything is all done, and I've got all the time to myself. It helps to have a crockpot of ham and beans, or a casserole ready for dinner.

Betty Verhoeven
East Jewett, New York

• Buy multi-colored rugs for every room! They don't show dirt as much, so you can sneak a few more minutes quilting, instead of vacuuming. Plus, they hide a lot of those threads that you're always dragging around.
• Host a quilting bee in your home, and have the gall to ask everyone to bring a covered dish for the luncheon. Usually, they'll leave the left-overs, and you'll be all set, you won't have to cook for a week, giving you more time to ...quilt!

Joan Biasucci
Cedar Creek, Nebraska

• It has been said that houses should have a kitchen and that a kitchen should have a stove. This, I assume, is for resale purposes. Never, under any circumstances, turn on that kitchen stove. That way, it'll never need cleaning. I have found that a simple "wiping off the top" with one of my husbands undershirts works very well to remove any accumulated dust.
• Keep nothing in the refrigerator, except Diet Pepsi and ice cubes. If there is nothing perishable inside, it won't have to be thrown out.

Sharon J. Mason
Coos Bay, Oregon

• Make your bed as soon as you get up. Do the dishes as soon as the kids leave for school. Vacuum, shower, take something out for dinner. Call your best quilting friend, see if she can come over and sew till just before school lets out. Have fun! "Let scissors fly!"
• Keep your house work up all the time. Do one thing you really don't want to everyday. Change the sheets, clean out that closet, etc.
• Just do it quickly. Good, but quick!

Alba Lee Elliott
Asheville, North Carolina

• Organization is a must. I do my housework, when I'm home and have nothing better to do and no where to go.

Nancy Smith
Denver, Colorado

• Sending children to camp, ordering pizza, and never putting sewing projects away or cleaning up, while you're in the middle of sewing something.

Doris Lott Aultman
Hattiesburg, Mississippi

• Well, this one was tough. The only thing that I really do that makes my life easier is that I iron all my clothes at the same time, but I iron my new fabrics in between each suit of clothes. This does insure that the clothes get ironed, and gives me some pleasure, as well.

Wilma Dooley Muse
Fayetteville, Tennessee

• Just don't do housework - until you can no longer find your quilt! Take only brief breaks to straighten up, locate the necessities and continue stitching.

Jennifer J. Danly
Arlington, Massachusetts

• My housekeeping strategy is to tackle the areas that bother me the *most*. My pet peeve is clutter. Dust and dirt don't bother me as much. As long as I can keep the living room free of clutter, I can ignore the mountains of stuff on the floor of the kid's room.
• Another strategy I have, is to use time alone without the kids (while they're in school) to do my *own* projects -i.e. quilting - and save the housework for times when they are home to help out.

Ellen Vollmer
Nickerson, Nebraska

• Since I live in a large home, it is hard to do everything, so each day I do some cleaning for an hour or two. I put dishes in the sink so each time the water is running, the food doesn't stick to them.
• I do most of my sewing after kids are in bed, and no one calls after 10:00. I try to make some food dishes and freeze them so when in a hurry, they go in the microwave.

Connie Sager
Nashville, Kansas

• "Conceal it!" (the mess that needs cleaning). Since I'm home alone all week, a good going over on weekends keeps it pretty stable through the week. Since Jerrod went to college this past fall, I acquired a sewing room to keep it all contained, and can just close the "door".

Pauline Hess 'Ping' White
Seaboard, North Carolina

• If you keep newspapers, books, coats, sweaters, etc. picked up daily, and especially before bedtime, the house will not be so cluttered, and you will feel better.

Pat Milne Hitchcock
Sequim, Washington

• I don't have any real household hints to give you so that you have more time to quilt, because if you don't have an equalitarian marriage, I can't help you! Where does it say meal-making is gender specific? Neither Jack nor I like cooking - I guess you might say we "fix", and we take turns "fixing" every other day. However, if you have children, I would advise you to teach them cooking skills as soon as they can read, and put them in charge of at least one meal a week. I feel very strongly that children should see someone besides their "mother" in the kitchen. Besides, when they get better at it, it frees you up to do more sewing and their dad to pursue his interests.
• Ditto goes for laundry. "Off", "On", "Push", and "Pull" aren't such hard words for grown-up men or children to deal with!

Alice Furrey
Carter, South Dakota

• One of the drawbacks to working at home doing something you love to do, is overdoing it. It is easy to become obsessed with your work and put in a little extra time now and then, until it interferes with your life. Without setting some limits for yourself, you can reach burnout, or disregard relationships that also need a share of your time. Another drawback to working at home is

that you may not be taken seriously by those around you, and there will be additional demands on your time. You may end up working harder than if you went to another place to work.
• Cooking and cleaning are squeezed in where-ever. I unload the dishwasher as I start a meal or while something is cooking. I straighten up and clean counters, as I talk on the phone. The bathroom gets cleaned as I get ready to take a shower. Dusting and vacuuming get done only once a week, unless special company is coming.

Sarah Bruso
Rhinelander, Wisconsin

• Because I have arthritis I have to keep moving, so I quilt for 1/2 hour, then I go do something else for 1/2 hour, then back to quilting.
• When I was a waitress years ago, I learned you never move from one spot to the next, without taking something with you, or in other words, make every step count. It's amazing how much you can accomplish by following this simple rule.

Christine Miller
Medway, Ohio

• Peroxide removes blood stains.
• Laundry hints: Miracle stain remover "Fels Naptha Bar" soap removes all kinds of stains from blood to grass stain - try it - it really works (can be found with the regular bar soap, white, red and green wrapper).

Merrilee Tieche
Ozark, Missouri

• Don't do housework! The dust will still be circulating long after you're dead and gone, only your quilts and the time you've spent making memories with your loved ones will live on.

Joan Waldman
Platte Center, Nebraska

• Grocery shop only once every month or so. Pick up perishables weekly. You will be surprised how much time this will save.
• Invest in a freezer.
• Always make a double or triple batch of anything that freezes. Then all you have to do is take it out, pop it in the microwave and toss a salad and it looks like you cooked all day. We all know what really happened was that you quilted all day!!

Dean Valentine
New Braunfels, Texas

• Clean your house ONE day a week and quilt the other days. I have found that a vacuum cleaner's handle fits a spouse's hands.

Marilyn A. Lewis
Glendale, Oregon

• I keep the dishes washed up and things picked up and after that, I'm afraid, it doesn't get done often enough!

Laura Estes
Odessa, Washington

• It seems hard for creative people to get organized, but its worth the effort and takes practice.
• A routine that includes time for quilting is the only way to consistently get projects done. You have to put it on the schedule or other things will push it to the back burner.
• Keeping handwork near the phone, so your hands can be busy while you talk is a time saver. 10 minutes on the phone is 10 minutes of quilting.
• Quilt while you ride in the car. Quilt while you wait to pick up kids or husband. Quilt in waiting rooms.
• Set goals, what projects do you want done, and when?
• Be willing to learn new ways of managing your household. We all jump at new methods and gadgets to improve and speed up our quilting. Do the same with household chores. Check out every time saver hints book you can find in your library (don't waste dollars on the books when you can use them for quilt supplies). Learn, practice and improve speed cleaning and organization methods.
• Cook in batches, freeze to thaw and heat on quilting days. Use your microwave and your crockpot.
• Learn how long it takes stuff to get dirty, then don't clean it until it is.
• Say no to *junk* you don't want to do. Just because you loved doing the craft show for your church doesn't mean you have to do the one for the animal shelter, and the summer recreation program, and the community day care, etc., etc.

Page 142, Time-saving household tips

- Train your family to respect your quilting time. Unless the house is on fire, or the plug is in the drain with the water running, it can wait. "I will do that for you when I am done here."
- Now nothing works for everyone, but the point is, you have to actively seek ways to clear the clutter from your space and make room for quilting.

≈≈≈≈≈≈≈≈≈≈≈≈≈≈≈≈≈≈≈≈≈

Merry May
Tuckahoe, New Jersey

- Whenever possible, do your machine work during the day while the rest of the family is occupied elsewhere. Save the handwork for the evenings when you can spend time with your loved ones and get something accomplished at the same time.

≈≈≈≈≈≈≈≈≈≈≈≈≈≈≈≈≈≈≈≈≈

Jacque' J. Holmes
Big Bear Lake, California

- As to Household Hints....I subscribe to the theory that dust is a protective covering for fine furniture!

≈≈≈≈≈≈≈≈≈≈≈≈≈≈≈≈≈≈≈≈≈

Penny Hand
Woodbridge, Virginia

- Get a maid!

≈≈≈≈≈≈≈≈≈≈≈≈≈≈≈≈≈≈≈≈≈

Judith Clonan
Fitchburg, Massachusetts

- If I can put off housework "one more day", I have more time for quilting. Quilting, family and eating and sleeping are priorities, sometimes in that order. I work, so I can afford to quilt!

≈≈≈≈≈≈≈≈≈≈≈≈≈≈≈≈≈≈≈≈≈

Betty Rushin
Boulder Creek, California

- The best household tip I have is hire a cleaning lady!!! You can have your bathrooms, kitchen, and kid's fingerprints removed for ten dollars an hour, and you don't have to lose your quilt finger calluses.

≈≈≈≈≈≈≈≈≈≈≈≈≈≈≈≈≈≈≈≈≈

Martha A. Deturk
Kutztown, Pennsylvania

- Be an early riser! I rarely sit still, and when I sit, I'm usually busy doing hand stitching and reading to grandchildren. I've learned to make good use of time, go-go-go. By 11 p.m. I'm exhausted, but ready to start all over by 6 a.m.

≈≈≈≈≈≈≈≈≈≈≈≈≈≈≈≈≈≈≈≈≈

Carol L. Robbins
Overland Park, Kansas

- KISS..Keep it simple, sweetie! Since becoming a vegetarian (not by choice) and not serving meat to my family as often as before, a LOT of time has been saved.
- Staying organized and uncluttered helps immensely. A lot of junk mail gets thrown out - DITTO for anything we don't use over a year.

≈≈≈≈≈≈≈≈≈≈≈≈≈≈≈≈≈≈≈≈≈

Kathleen Nyman
Oswego, New York

- Don't dust or clean - ever. Once you start, you can't stop! Seriously, I use baskets to put things in. Things are out of the way, but I don't have to spend time sorting. Eventually, things get put away. I reward myself - 15 minutes of cleaning or the downstairs vacuumed, equals 10 minutes of sewing!

≈≈≈≈≈≈≈≈≈≈≈≈≈≈≈≈≈≈≈≈≈

Betty M. Abel
Sheboygan, Wisconsin

- Moved from a four bedroom home to a mobile home, master bedroom became my sewing room. Much less housework, more quilting time.
- Do everything possible on one shopping trip. Take time for quilting each day. It makes me happy and I'm worth it!

≈≈≈≈≈≈≈≈≈≈≈≈≈≈≈≈≈≈≈≈≈

Arla Schaap
Holland, Michigan

- One quick household hint - - Stack 4 or 5 paper towels. Wet sufficiently, but not dripping. Use these for a quicker-picker-upper on your kitchen floor. Does a great job of picking up crumbs, dust, fuzzies!

≈≈≈≈≈≈≈≈≈≈≈≈≈≈≈≈≈≈≈≈≈

Virginia H. Flowers
Flushing, Michigan

- My theory is family first, quilting second and other things last. I am a cookbook collector, as well. I search for recipes I

can make in my Nesco roaster, the oven, a microwave, pressure cooker cooker, anything that I don't have to keep my hands on. My husband purchased a bread machine to go along with my other appliances. I used to bake 9 loaves of bread from scratch every 2 weeks prior to quilting, and he missed it. The joke was, I did a lot of things BG (Before quilting!). Think about this, getting up, shower, make a bed, put a load of washing in the automatic washer, put coffee in the automatic coffee maker, put ingredients in for bread in the bread machine, a roast with veggies in the slow cooker, some jello in the refrigerator for dessert, unload the washer into an automatic dryer, another load in the washer.....now quilting till all the timers go off.
• Audio books while quilting is also great.

Anna Eelman
North Plainfield,
New Jersey

• Get your family to all pitch in for a quick 15 minutes, before sitting down. It is amazing how much (at least in a "once over lightly way") can be done with all those hands working. Try this once a day.

Mary J. Ruda
Elida, Ohio

• I have a cleaning woman come in every two weeks.
• After 9 p.m., I *just* sit down and work on projects.

Ruth E. O'Connor
Burlington,
Massachusetts

• Make salads in individual bowls for family in morning, for quick lunch.
• Cook squash in season in pressure cooker and freeze in microwave dishes. All set to defrost, and eat!

Georgina Doss
Milton, West Virginia

There are actually people who do household chores BEFORE they quilt? Seriously, nap time is reserved for quilting or anything else I wish to do for myself. This comes out to approximately two hours of uninterrupted time on school days.

Barbara G. Pietila
Baltimore, Maryland

My most effective ways of providing more time for quilting are:

• Cook as sporadically as possible. This takes the cooperation of those you live with, of course, but my husband eats anything and I have no small children in the house. Am I lucky, or what?
• Dust only when you can write your name on the furniture. Dust is your friend. If you don't bother it, it won't bother you. Dust bunnies make good pets. You don't have to feed, walk, or train them.
• Buy lots of panties. I only wash when I run out of clean panties. Buy a few extra pairs of shorts for your husband, too. When I'm really busy, I have been known to borrow a pair of his. I like boxers best. They're more comfortable, and unless you get hit by a car, no one will ever know!

Linda Boedigheimer
Perham, Minnesota

• Hire a cleaning person.
• Quilt with morning coffee (6-7 a.m.).
• Leave plenty of quilting books in the bathroom, and on your nightstand.
• Have dinner ready in the morning.

Bernice Tessibel
Inman Cashman
(Tessie)
Coal City, Indiana

• Make lists of what needs to be done. Organize your home. Get rid of all the excess clutter (except for quilting supplies).
• Set aside a day every so often for a cooking marathon, and freeze up casseroles, etc. for use when you just have to finish a quilting project.

Nancy Wagner Graves
Manhattan, Kansas

• Use your crockpot for meals that cook all day but seem like *you've* been busy cooking all day.
• Clean your house once a week, then just keep it picked up between cleanings.
• Try to run all errands one or two days a week.

Page 144, Time-saving household tips

Dort Lee
Leicester, North Carolina

•Ignore the housework! Or make or hire the children to do the vacuuming, dishes, etc. Or save it all for one day and race around madly doing it, so you can calmly quilt on the other days.

Susan J. Spencer
Felton, California

#1. I *delegate!* We've divided household chores so that each one of us is responsible for one room (kitchen, dining room, living room, bath) each week. The house may not always be as clean as I'd like it, but I turn a blind eye now to what isn't my responsibility.
#2. Prioritize! Don't try to do everything. Decide on the three most important tasks for the day, and complete them. The rest of the day is yours!
#3. Mail order. I make use of mail order whenever possible, since I really hate shopping. (If I could order groceries over the phone, I would!)

Judi Robb
Manhattan, Kansas

•Be organized. Plan ahead. I plan each weeks menu ahead and go to the grocery store once a week. Every household chore has a specific time of the week it gets done. I don't do anything more often than I have to.

Fanny Naught
Quincy, Illinois

•My most profitable hint for making more time for quilting, is spending it! I go for an early morning exercise class two days a week, I walk 15 minutes to get to the class, exercise for an hour and walk back home again. This undoubtedly gets your heart started and it makes me feel so good, that when I get home I am ready to tear into getting things done real quick, so I can go back to my needle and thread. There is no doubt about it, exercise is a great motivator and really works for me.
•Another hint is: I keep a small note in an envelope addressed to each family and friend that I write letters to. On this I jot down happenings I want to talk about, and a few news clips. When the time comes to write my letters, I bring out my note and typewriter and my letters are done in a jiffy.
•While my husband and I travel, I collect business cards and quilt show photos and other related information. I keep all this on file, and when I need to refer to where I bought fabric or whatever, I have the name and address right there. The photos are great memories, as well as color combinations and hints for friends. I always write on the back of photos.

M. Jeanne Poore
Overland Park, Kansas

•One of the tips, not an original, to make more time for quilting is not making the bed every morning; of course also do not cook-eat out or order in! But quilters do love to eat and are wonderful cooks, so simple meals...home-made soup, chili, navy beans, pot pies or jambalaya--that are made in large quantity and warmed up for additional meals. Besides, these are better the second and third time they are heated up.

Catherine Litwinow
Davenport, Iowa

•Divide the labor - Have all the family members help! Keep lights low, so no one sees the dust!

Linda Ballard
Palo Cedro, California

•My hint? Try and keep things caught up, so cleaning is not such an item. I knew a quilter that kept her vacuum out to make it look like she was cleaning when, she wasn't---- sounds good to me!

Beth Donaldson
Lansing, Michigan

•My household hint is to lower your standards of cleanliness and neatness. I used to think I wasn't a success if my house was a mess. I finally gave myself permission to sew or write before the house was cleaned each day. My children are now 11 and 13 and they still can mess faster than I can clean. The difference now is that I can stand the mess, almost as long as they can. Usually my husband has about had it by Saturday morning, so he corrals the troops and we all

Time-saving household tips, Page 145

clean together. I am also teaching my daughters how to cook so that occasionally they will prepare an evening meal. Hopefully in a few years they will each cook once a week. My husband is a good cook and able housekeeper, however he works long hours. He comes home every night at about 6:30 and that is really too late to start cooking.

• When quilting is your job you earn money at it, but it usually comes in clumps, so having a hardworking, employed spouse is really handy when bills need to be paid!

• The most important change, was to change my attitude. When Tom says the house is messy, my old response would have been to clean it, because it was obviously my fault! My new response is "yes", this acknowledges the fact that I am aware of the mess, but I no longer feel it is my sole responsibility to clean it. I now judge myself by how much writing or sewing I have done during the day, not how clean my house is or how fabulous the evening meal was. I treat quilting as my 9 to 5 job.

≈≈≈≈≈≈≈≈≈≈≈≈≈≈≈≈≈≈≈≈≈≈≈≈

Marcia Knopp
Bay City, Michigan

Ignore your housework!

≈≈≈≈≈≈≈≈≈≈≈≈≈≈≈≈≈≈≈≈≈≈≈≈

Netta Ranney
Overland Park, Kansas

Make large batches of soups, casseroles, etc. and freeze meal-size portions.

• Put a load of laundry in at night, put in the dryer the next morning.

• If you carpool, take along bills to pay, letters to write while waiting, also small hand-sew projects. I made 200 finger pin cushions at track meets one spring!

≈≈≈≈≈≈≈≈≈≈≈≈≈≈≈≈≈≈≈≈≈≈≈≈

Betty A Lenz
Marshall, Missouri

• I live my life by a list! I usually make a weekly list - things that *must* be completed, meetings & appointments I *must* make, household things that *must* be done within that week, then start doing and crossing off. This way, too, I can discipline myself to do these things that aren't my favorite things to do.

≈≈≈≈≈≈≈≈≈≈≈≈≈≈≈≈≈≈≈≈≈≈≈≈

Beulah T. Gilbert
Bellevue, Ohio

• I just try and work real fast when it comes to doing housework, so I can get back to doing quilting. I can even sit and see the dirt, and it doesn't bother me.

≈≈≈≈≈≈≈≈≈≈≈≈≈≈≈≈≈≈≈≈≈≈≈≈

Helen P. Johnston
Bowie, Maryland

• Lower your standards. My sanity returned once I realized the folks from Good Housekeeping didn't make surprise home inspections!

• Make logical choices. You have 30 minutes. You can:

    A. Wash the kitchen floor
    B. Quilt

"B" is the logical choice, because two minutes after you finish the floor, your eight year son will spill a full pitcher of juice on it. However, the stitches you put in your quilt will be there for a long time, won't have to be redone, and if juice is spilled on the quilt, it can easily be washed.

≈≈≈≈≈≈≈≈≈≈≈≈≈≈≈≈≈≈≈≈≈≈≈≈

Karen Crosby
Ocala, Florida

• Our group meets every Wednesday morning for a quilting bee - I just volunteer my house about once a month, so I *have* to clean and just keep surface stuff in between.

≈≈≈≈≈≈≈≈≈≈≈≈≈≈≈≈≈≈≈≈≈≈≈≈

Tedi Lambert
Los Banos, California

• Hire a housekeeper!
• If you cannot afford the housekeeper (I'm among the housekeeperless), hire the kids (if you can!).

≈≈≈≈≈≈≈≈≈≈≈≈≈≈≈≈≈≈≈≈≈≈≈≈

Edith O. McGhee
Mercer, Pennsylvania

• I cook by sound! I put supper on to cook and run to the sewing machine for a few minutes. When I hear something boil over, I know it's time to go back to the kitchen.

≈≈≈≈≈≈≈≈≈≈≈≈≈≈≈≈≈≈≈≈≈≈≈≈

Julie L. Kimberlin
Anchorage, Alaska

• My favorite "household hint" is my husband who does most of the cooking, and is very tolerant of the often-cluttered house.

Page 146, Time-saving household tips

Four levels is a lot of house to maintain and we're all accumulators. Housework is not a high-priority, because it never gets caught up. The clothes are often unfolded and the carpet usually needs vacuuming.

Pat Reep
Bakersfield, California

• My first household hint to allow room for more quilting is simply "do less housework". I do some household chores at odd times, for instance, I sometimes clean the bathroom at bath time. I do not have an outside job, so I can structure my time more easily. I can rearrange and allot my quilting time and try not to let distractions and interruptions interfere. When there is a deadline for a certain project to be finished, I block out days at a time on my calendar, and treat that time as if I were working.

• I generally allot a specific time to chores each day and stay within that time period even if I have not completed all the tasks. My emphasis is on quilting.

Phyllis Hansen Gierach
Madera, California

• I am a list maker! I use my organizer everyday and list all the important stuff first! I keep all of the cleaning supplies in a plastic tote with a handle, and I now have a cordless phone that goes with me when I'm doing serious cleaning. The one household chore that I don't like is ironing, so I sometimes take my husbands shirts to a young girl in our quilt guild, who is happy to earn a little extra money by ironing. When I was operating the quilt store I had a housekeeper once a week, because my time was better spent on teaching classes and running the store.

Teresa Binder
Olpe, Kansas

• Are there really people who iron blue jeans and underwear? I buy easy care clothes for the entire family, so ironing is not a major problem. But alas, there are many things that need the attention of the iron. Everytime I turn on the iron to press some fabric, a block or something quilt related, I iron one piece of clothing, more if I can tolerate it. This keeps my ironing under control and doesn't make the job too unbearable. If this method doesn't work, I am buying too many clothes that need ironing, or I'm not sewing enough!

Charlotte Fry
St. Charles, Missouri

• Since there are only three people living in our home, I really don't have much trouble keeping up. I try to clean one day and just pick up the rest of the week. I do heavy cleaning in the spring and fall. Also laundry once a week, that way I've only used up one day.

Barbara Clukey
Carriere, Mississippi

• One household hint that will make more time for quilting is this (and I hope it will not be to my shame). Pretend the Pastor is coming to call by 9:00 a.m. Quickly stack the dishes in the dishwasher, then gather all the extraneous debris left from the previous night and put it in a specific place in the closet to be sorted later. Make a pass over the coffee table with a duster, and you will be set for company or sewing with a clear conscience. It will help you have a room where you can make a tremendous mess and then be able to close the door and lock it.

Marcene Gunter
Hillsboro, Kansas

• Wax appliances, counter tops, etc. with kitchen wax. They do not get as dusty. Much easier to wipe off, and you don't have to do it as often.
• Also wax varnished woodwork for the same reason.
• Use lighter fluid to clean black marks off of the floors and tile. don't clean just to be cleaning, do it as needed.

Richard F. Zimmerman
New Milford, New Jersey

• If I were to suggest a household hint which would allow more time for quilting, it would be to find a wife/husband who will handle a lot of the household chores, so that you can be free to work.
• Get over the idea that your house has to be perfect. So it gets a little dirty, vacuum before the company comes.

Time-saving household tips, Page 147

DeEtta Beebe
Waters, Michigan

• I've learned to simplify other household needs or pleasures without eliminating them. Make batter breads which require little time, but give the same results - Homemade bread! Casseroles!
• Wake up one hour earlier for a few stitches.
• Be organized.

Michelle Hazelhoff
Mr. Evelyn,
Vic Australia

• I plan my weeks ahead, and set aside times for quilting. I like a clean tidy house the same as the next person, but it wasn't my first priority. We have a system that works well, whatever doesn't get done during the week we all pitch in on a Saturday morning and do it together. I clean as I go, clean the shower as you shower, fold clean washing carefully when it's dry, it requires much less ironing.
• Make double meals when you're cooking, eat one and freeze the other.

Jane P. Wyckoff
Hopewell, New Jersey

• Set priorities, and do as little housework as possible.

Alta M. Edwards
Clay City, Indiana

• Mine seems to be to let things go, as with driving the bus, extra trips and just the daily jobs....not much time. I'm getting ready to retire, then may have more time.

LaRue Nuest
South Hutchinson

• I probably don't do anything unusual in keeping house. I do try to always keep things picked up and put away, so that if someone comes unexpectedly, the house doesn't look too bad.
• I can stand a little dust on the furniture better than I can stand clutter. Besides, it is much easier to find things.

Betty J. Knack
Essexville, Michigan

• No hints - at my age, I quilt when I want to!

Barb Bennett
Washington, D.C.

• Use a dishdrainer and unload as you're preparing your next meal. Clean dishes look pretty in the drainer (or so I've convinced myself!)
• I use the telephone time for folding laundry, wiping the dust off of the leaves on my plants, flipping through quilting magazines, etc. It's amazing how much you can get done while talking...or listening.

• Keep cleaning supplies where they are needed to save steps. (like toilet bowl cleaner, glass cleaner, spray wax, etc.) in each bathroom instead of causing yourself extra steps moving them from one room to the next.

Nancy H. Ehinger
West Branch,
Michigan

• My favorite household hint is a poem by Elinor Rose entitled:

MANANA MORALE
Of all the household hints around
The greatest one I've ever found,
When work stacks up and life looks bleak,
Is let it go another week.

Diane Johnson
Rhinebeck, New York

• My best hint is to plan dinner the night before or first thing in the morning. It will mean less stress and time, with no last minute decisions to make (more time for quilting!), and less money spent on take-out (more money for fabric!) and you'll probably eat healthier food.

Judy Wolfrom
Southampton,
New Jersey

• Take over the dining room as a studio and then entertaining is out of the question.
• Enough wall-hangings around the house and the need for painting the walls won't be noticed.

Page 148, Time-saving household tips

Maria Lage
Cumberland, Rhode Island

- I couldn't really think of any. I can't wait to read what other quilters do.

Lynn G. Kough
Middletown, New Jersey

- Don't obsess about the mess!
- Teach your family to cook, dust, vacuum, and do laundry!
- Know the phone numbers of your local take-out places.
- Master the fine art of the soup-can-sauce casserole!

Lynn Graves
Albuquerque, New Mexico

- Hire ALL housework done and QUIT COOKING!
- The reason I got into this business was to have a little money of my own to support "my habit". Little did I realize! (Lynn designed the *Little Foot*.)

Roxanne H. McElroy
Mililani, Hawaii

- Take all your dishes and pans out of the cabinets in the kitchen, and move them upstairs to your sewing room and put all your quilting stuff downstairs in the kitchen. You will find that you actually make less trips up and down the stairs that way!!

Carolyn Koopman
Carnavillo, Iowa

- Loosen up with your housework. All your friends are quilters. The dust and the cobwebs will make them feel right at home!

Ella May Reusser
Blackwell, Oklahoma

- When I have a quilt in the frame, household chores seem to get done more quickly.

Suzanne K. Roy
Newkirk, Oklahoma

- My family helps with chores. that seems to be a big help. Making food in large batches also helps. Freezing things in portions helps cut down on meal preparation time.

Betty J. Pribil
Portland, Oregon

- I have a helpful husband, who helps with household chores and also I am an early riser.

Alyce C. Kauffman
Gridley, California

- Make bed(s), do dishes and pick up anything out of place daily.
- Dust as needed, only visible surfaces once a week.
- Do a thorough cleaning of one room at a time, once every 6 months.

- Enlist help from family members.
- Keep fabric and quilting supplies in order so time won't be wasted, looking for a magazine, book, pattern, fabrics, etc. Have a place for everything, and everything in it's place, when not in use.

Emily Laubaugh
Gladstone, Oregon

- One hint I learned from my dear quilt friend Anita Vanek, was to try to put aside one hour a day for quilting. You'd be surprised at how much you can get accomplished.

Ruth Powers
Carbondale, Kansas

- Get someone else to do it!

Julie Fox
Blackwell, Oklahoma

- I have a day for each household chore:
Monday..bathroom, laundry
Tuesday..living room, laundry
Wednesday..kitchen, laundry
Etc.

Pamela T. Young
Minot Air Force Base, North Dakota

- My two daughters are at home with me all day. I find that wherever I am, is where they want to be. The smartest thing I ever did was move my sewing machine and supplies into the toy room down in the basement. We also have a TV/VCR down there so the girls are quite content to let me do my thing, with minimal interruptions, while they do their thing. With my sewing room in the basement, I am able to leave whatever I am working on just where it is because no one sees my mess.

Jean Ann Eitel
Marietta, Georgia

- To make more time for quilting, I have learned to pick up my mess in other areas of the house (not the sewing room) as I make it. I wash one plate when I finish eating. I make the bed as soon as I get out of it. I fold the clothes as they come out of the dryer, etc. That way I never have to go back, do something over, and waste time by duplicating my efforts. I can walk away from a task knowing it is done and I can get on with my quilting (of which I have many unfinished projects).

Janice A. Miller
Jaffrey,
New Hampshire

- I take time for quilting while my breads are baking, or my homemade candies are setting. Also, while the washer and dryer are doing the wash.

Pauline A. Cook
Idaho Falls, Idaho

- My favorite household hint is a pair of blinders! When creativity hits, put them on and head straight for your sewing room. Remember, dull women have immaculate houses!
- Keep an extra casserole in the freezer. And use it when you don't have enough time to cook, while meeting a quilting deadline.

Barbara Shook Davis
Williams, Arizona

- A helpful husband and daughter, a bi-monthly housekeeper, lots of buildings for storage space which eliminates clutter in the house, a messy quilt room/studio as the quilt mess is not scattered.

Pat Campbell
Rigby, Idaho

- I treat my designing and quiltmaking like a job, so household chores usually have to be done before 9 a.m. or after 3 p.m. (Banker's hours). If the job requires it (or if I plan on going somewhere), I work longer, but I've found 5 to 6 hours to be my most productive time - then I start making bone-head mistakes.

Celeste Lipp
Idaho Falls, Idaho

- I look for all kinds of ways to be a *tightwad* with household expenses, so I can afford the latest fabrics. I have let my housekeeping standards slip (a lot!), so I can work on my projects. When I do housework, I take off my glasses so all that dust won't be visible, then I can quilt without guilt! Also, I know Pizza Hut's delivery menu by heart!

Christine Klinger
Fayetteville, Arkansas

- My favorite household hint is to lower my housekeeping expectations! Housework whenever, and quilting forever!
- I work on my quilts in the center of my house which is the kitchen-dining area. My quilting life has expanded over the years and I have fabric stored in a china hutch and in plastic storage containers. Friends tell me they enjoy coming to my home because they like to see all the fabrics and my works in progress.
- My favorite story is of the time I sent my son to the *dining room* to find something and he returned looking quite lost and puzzled. Nick was about ten at the time, so I was concerned that he could not follow my simple verbal directions. I repeated once more, "Nick, go to the dining room, past the table that has all that fabric on it...." "Oh," he said, "that's not the dining room, that's your quilting room!" My children didn't even know we had a dining room.

Mary Lou Kantz
Evans
Flagstaff, Arizona

- Try to be as neat as possible, so you have to do as little housework as necessary. Teach the dogs to pick up their toys and put them back in the toy basket, this idea works for children also, marry someone who believes you are in this together.

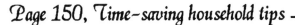

Sandra L. Hatch
Lincoln, Maine

• I don't have any favorite hints except that I do what I want, when I want. I think probably the best asset I have is my husband who never tells me what he thinks I should or should not be doing. He is patient and supports my every whim. I try to do the same for him. My children learned early that I love them, but my life does not begin and end with them and their every need. They know their mother has a life of her own and they are part of it. They have developed independence and I think they are proud of me and what I do.

Joanna Bessey
Rhinelander, Wisconsin

• Make meals and ignore the rest, until it's *crash-clean* for the next *social event*. This is a direct quote from Bill (bless him!), his advice to help make more time for my quilting. I do make the special effort for well-balanced nutritious meals, but always prepare at least double of everything. That way, I only have to start-from-scratch half as often! Also, he loves one-dish meals, like stew, chili, lasagna and most any kind of casserole, along with an easy salad, clean-up is easier and faster. Do love that man, and his love of left-overs.

• My foremost household hint for more quilting time is to Get Your Husband Involved! I don't mean necessarily the house *work*, but rather his interest and support. Bill wanted a wallhanging for his office and so he decided on the pattern - Amish, the size 6'x6'(!), and the colors, which he helped select. Of course, we both wanted it completed ASAP. Therefore, he helped with the housework, and at other times we could ignore the rest while we happily shared in the wallhanging's progress. This same principle works for quilted items made for gift-giving occasions throughout the year. I truly appreciated my husband's interest and support of my artwork. Eventually, he may even become a quilter! Except, he says there's no more room in our home *for Another Stash!*

Z.Z. Gilmore
Pocatello, Idaho

• Becoming a widow so that one only has to take care of herself.
• Learn to make stews and other one dish meals that can be frozen and zapped in the microwave oven.

Sue Hausmann
Lincolnshire, Illinois

• My one household hint is from experience. Don't be too fussy! In the first 5 years of marriage I cleaned (and buffed the floor!) every day. Everything had to be in its place at all times. I realized I could not stay married and have children with these standards, so we went the other extreme for a year or so (we never made the bed). I couldn't stand that so we came to a happy medium, the last one out of the bed makes it! Extra kitchen mess is cleaned up by the hands that made it.

• When the children were at home, everyone had chores (they were not paid for this), it was a part of belonging to our family. And a crockpot was a great help in meals the last few years.
• More recently, the hardest thing was to realize I can't do it all myself. Upon return from a trip I was cleaning the bathroom before doing anything else. So we have some help and my husband helps a lot. It helps that there are just the two of us, much less mess than a family and kid's friends! I still do the laundry and iron my husband's shirts, it's his one hold out. So I have to get home every two weeks or so, or he goes to the store and buys more underwear and socks!

Sally Smith
Kodak, Tennessee

• Breaking housework up into little pieces seems to help me have more time and not feel guilty about everything not being done.
• I enjoy a clean house, but don't enjoy the housework. So, my quilting is my *reward*, and that way I don't get nutty.
• I also keep my quilting *cornered*, so that I don't have little fingers and kitty paws making toys out of needles and my very favorite thimble - a 79¢ special bought in 1982.

Jean S. Branham
Halifax, North Carolina

• I don't do much housework. I quilt!

QUILTERS SHARE THEIR QUILTING HINTS AND TIPS!

Joyce Livingston
Council Grove, Kansas

• Hang the little lint brush that came with your sewing machine on a clear plastic suction cup, mounted on the side of your machine so it will be at your fingertips. Use it to give your machine a quick cleaning each time you change your bobbin.

• Do you have a wooden TV tray on legs? Place your little ironing board on top of it, letting the legs hang over the edge to stabilize it. It's just the right height to place next to you when you're working at your machine. Saves trips to the ironing board when pressing seams.

• A quilting friend of mine said she was cautioned by her sewing machine dealer about using the clear or smoke plastic thread on her machine. He said it would very quickly *cut* a channel into the threading areas by wearing grooves. You might want to check with your dealer about this.

• For most of my quilt machine sewing, I use serger thread in both the top and the bobbin. It's finer and only 2 ply, but it's quite strong and comes in many colors! I especially like it in the bobbin, since it's finer your bobbin will hold MUCH more thread, allowing you to sew more on one bobbin-fill.

• Save those plastic liners from the inside of your bacon packages (most brands have them). Slip them into hot soapy water, swish them around and rinse. They are wonderful for making templates or patterns. You can cut them with your scissors or rotary cutter. You can write names and dimensions on them with a permanent pen. You can also trace around them for quilting patterns.

• Try the lap quilting method! I learned to hand quilt without a frame or hoop and love it. Lap quilting allows me to quilt anywhere, anytime...even tilted back in my recliner! I teach a workshop I call UNSHACKLED QUILTING to those who want to learn to quilt without a frame or hoop, and they find it allows them to quilt faster, and with smaller stitches. Try it, but be patient, it takes a little while to get used to it.....but, it's worth it!

• When hand stitching the binding onto your quilts, use the scraps of batting to stuff the binding softly, it gives nice body to the edge of the quilt, as well as a nice finished look.

>>>>>>>>>>>>>>>>>>>>>>>>>>>>

Betty Lou Cassidy
Linwood, New Jersey

• With middle age came a difficulty in seeing well enough to stitch during the evening winter months, so now I use that time to write, plan, and make patterns so I can spend weekends and daylight hours stitching.

• I usually work on several projects at a time and have ideas for several more. From time to time, I must go fabric shopping, but easily lose track of what I came for. Just as it is smart to make a list for grocery shopping, I now make a Quilting Projects or Fabrics-I-Need-List. Then, when my mind goes blank in a crowded store, I can look at my list to re-focus and buy wisely with the money I have and not waste it on things I may not need right away.

• I often use Pigma Pens to "color out" small background sections that cannot be appliqued under. This works best when the applique' is outlined in black as many theme fabrics are.

• Take a class at a local quilt shop or evening school. It forces you to set time aside to do something you've wanted, but probably won't make time for, and it stimulates the quilting economy.

>>>>>>>>>>>>>>>>>>>>>>>>>>>>

Elizabeth A. Akana
Kaneohe, Hawaii

• I loved myself enough not to judge my work as anything more than wonderful expressions of my *love*, therefore I never create a bad piece, some just talk louder than others.

>>>>>>>>>>>>>>>>>>>>>>>>>>>>

Karen Crollick
St. George,
Australia, QLD

• As a new quilter, I haven't any hints or tips as I am still learning from more experienced quilters.

>>>>>>>>>>>>>>>>>>>>>>>>>>>>

Thelma Tiefel
Clay City, Indiana

• I still quilt in the large frames, once they are in the frames all you have to do is roll them. My frames are in the basement, so they don't take up room upstairs.

• I mark the quilts, before I put them in the frames.

• I have items I need in easy reach on the quilt; extra needles, scissors, erasers and ruler.

• Sometimes I miss a dark thread that shows through, I

Hints for better quilting, Page 153

have a very fine crochet needle, I can reach the thread and pull it out.

>>>>>>>>>>>>>>>>>>>>>>>>>>>>

Ruth Rhoades
Toccoa, Georgia

• I basted my last quilt on top of a 4" thick foam mattress that I put on top of our bed. It worked well and a good height.
• I made a sleeve with an extension piece for my Q-Snap frame, allowing me to pin the edge of the quilt to the muslin and quilt all the way to the edge.

>>>>>>>>>>>>>>>>>>>>>>>>>>>>

Louise Murphy
Mammoth Lakes, California

• I would have to say the first and foremost important time saver would have to be the rotary cutter. I remember the first class I ever took using the rotary cutter (only the small size available at the time). The teacher had instilled such a safety lesson in us, I was sure I would not keep all ten fingers. A lesson well heeded to this day.
• One of my favorite tips or hints is to use a fabric lip just inside a border or the binding, depending on where it is most effective, some quilts just cry out for one while others stand on their own without it.

Author's Note: I wrote to Louise and asked about her *fabric lip* she'd mentioned in one of her hints. She was kind enough to send a sample. It's hard to describe without seeing it, but basically it's a 1" strip of contrasting fabric folded in half lengthwise and inserted between the quilt top and the border, with the folded edge being loose and the cut edges into the seam. I hope that makes sense. As Louise said, "It makes a nice accent for a select quilt."

>>>>>>>>>>>>>>>>>>>>>>>>>>>>

Colleen Taylor
Indialantic, Florida

• Keep sewing room organized and have many different projects going at once, so you always have something you want to work on.
• Keep all items for individual projects together in one basket or box, so you don't have to look for items.

>>>>>>>>>>>>>>>>>>>>>>>>>>>>

Nadine Dozier
North Augusta, South Carolina

• I use my rotary cutter a lot when quilting my fabric.
• I love the patterns that do not require templates.
• Being organized makes my quilting more enjoyable for me. Know where your things are, and it really makes a difference in any project you want to start or finish.

>>>>>>>>>>>>>>>>>>>>>>>>>>>>

Lynn Lewis Young
Houston, Texas

• Use a dry iron - no steam, as steam lets the fabric expand and warp, especially for piecing.
• Store fabric in transparent plastic buckets (like Rubbermaid blanket storage boxes) - it keeps the dust out of the fabric - and keeps you from *sneezing* if you're allergic to dust, so you can enjoy your fabric.

>>>>>>>>>>>>>>>>>>>>>>>>>>>>

Elaine Helen (Revier) Baker
Watertown, Minnesota

• I plan every thing before even starting. I usually have a few projects going at the same time, so I don't get bored.
• I always cut many extra squares of different sizes, and baggie them up to save for trades or the occasional doll or Barbie quilt.
• Shoe boxes work great for storing smaller squares (3 inch and smaller) and the box sits nicely in your lap, when pinning sawtoothed edges into place. The lid keeps them dust free until ready to be used!

>>>>>>>>>>>>>>>>>>>>>>>>>>>>

Josephine Hannah Jirva Burgwyn (Jo Jo)
Jackson, North Carolina

• Plastic tubular frames that assemble and disassemble so quickly are my hint.

>>>>>>>>>>>>>>>>>>>>>>>>>>>>

Mary Ann Keppler
St. Olaf, Iowa

• Take your time - be precise. It saves a lot of time as far as ripping things out.
• Don't try to do everything. I pick the things I really want to do. This makes things more enjoyable and it's a good feeling to know things are finished.

Kelly Lum Newgarde
Phillipsburg, New Jersey

The best two tips I can offer are:
- Take classes - the time is set for you to quilt and to be with other quilters.
- Join a Guild! It is *very* exciting to be around so many people that share your interests. It is an opportunity to learn all about quilting.

Deb Meneely
Seattle, Washington

- Since I primarily handquilt my quilts, one item that is indispensible to me, is my "half-hoop" quilt frame. It allows me to do an accurate job of quilting outside borders near to the edge, without a fuss.
- One new item that is helping me *keep organized* is called a *worm bag*. Designed for fly fisherman by Gander Mountain Outdoorsman Catalog to hold fish bait - it is ideal to hold quilt supplies while traveling. It is essentially a book-sized zippered pouch, that has a 3 ring binder inside, with about a dozen compartments similar to zip lock bags. It's great to take to classes/workshops/quilt meetings to hold needle, thread, marking pencils, rubber needle puller, thimbles, template plastic, snapshots of finished quilts, ruby beholder, ruler, etc.

Author's note: Bonnie Browning gave a workshop for our Emporia Regional Quilters Guild last year and she had a "worm bag". She was so enthused about it, that she was going to try to get it produced for quilters, with some minor changes to make it more *quilt-oriented*. One can be found in the fishing department of most discount stores. Thanks for the idea, Deb.

Beverly J. Relph
Leavenworth, Kansas

- A boom box and Kenny G. make my day! When the music starts, the "kids" (Yorkshire Terriers, Fred and Mildred) head for their baskets because they know Mom is into serious sewing, 'til dawn.

Rebecca Kelly
Kingsburg, California

- Some of my favorite quilt making tips are to be organized.
- Make sure all fabric is pressed and ready, when inspiration strikes.
- Have several projects going at once to keep from getting bored. I usually have one in the cutting stage, one in the piecing stage, and one in the quilting stage.
- Rotary cutters are fantastic, couldn't be without one.

Chloe Rhodes
Clay City, Indiana

- I like strip quilting. The rotary cutter can't be beat!

Florence Edith Goggin
Eureka, California

- In order to organize my fabric, I first place a 2x2" gummed label to the wrong side of the fabric, and cut it out.

Information recorded on label is as follows:

Date in upper right corner
Mfg, or Designer (JRJ-J Beyer)
Amount of yardage
Where purchased
Price of yardage
Title of Fabric, if listed

These squares are then placed in a Plastic Sheet that has small pockets (slide keepers). The Sheet is then placed in a 3 hole binder according to Mfg. or designer. This makes it easy to see what I have without having to look in my cupboards.
- Special fabric like Christmas & etc. I keep in a separate place. Plaids also have their own place.
- Years of working in a fabric shop make me a good source of old fabric. Sharing with students and they with me, gives me a good variety to work with.
- After rinsing, drying and pressing, I arrange by color.

Bonnie Swecker
Roanoke Rapids, North Carolina

- Boy, if my grandmas had had a rotary cutter, think what they could have done! And they never even considered machine piecing, let alone machine quilting. Those have come into acceptance now (by some, anyway), and are such time savers. I still prefer hand quilting, but for some projects like placemats, pillows, clothing, etc., machine quilting is great.

Kathryn Rippeteau
Greenwold
Niskayuna, New York

• I love my rotary cutter and mat. I don't know what I did before I had them.
• I always try to iron seams in opposite directions when piecing, so the two sides fit snugly and make a strong, accurate seam. I can remember the first time someone showed me that trick and it was a real revelation.
• Here are two money saving tips:
1. Use the heavy rubber bands that come off of broccoli bunches for needle pullers. They are free, you are recycling and they're more convenient than the commercial rubber disks. The disks get laid down and lost easily (or eaten by the dog, as mine was). The rubber band loops around my finger easily, and is always there when I need it.
2. Instead of those expensive and small red and green value viewers, here's an idea. Use a see-thru plastic report cover. Red for cool colors, and green for warm. They give you a large viewing area, are cheap and easier to find when you need them. I keep mine in a folder in my file cabinet and always can find them.
• Here's an organizational tip: I use a peg board on one wall of my studio and hang all rulers, scissors, templates, etc. on it. Even my quilting stencils hang. I have developed a cataloging system, and then hang them in numerical order on "O" rings. This way they are right at hand, always in the same place, don't get stuck on each other and are easy to remove, use and replace.

Barbara MacDonald
Oscoda, Michigan

• I think anyone who does machine piecing will agree - the rotary cutter is heaven! I can't imagine making a log cabin without it, like our great-grandmothers did. We have so many choices now with all our quilting needs.
• A friend of mine went on one of those trips - so many countries and so many days, you know those package deals. Anyway, I suggested she purchase fabric from every country and make a Trip Around The World Quilt. She bought some fabric, some linen napkins, or scarf, or whatever she could find in the short time she was there. Then she made her Trip Around The World Quilt. It's really beautiful!
• My Mom received a handkerchief from my Dad during World War II. She gave it to me, and I gathered more old hankies and made a beautiful quilt. I made a label from an old hanky and sewed it to the back.

Mary Andrews
Grand Blanc,
Michigan

• I use a lot of freezer paper. When making a pictorial, like the hockey player, I find a picture that I want to use, and take it to work and blow it up to the size I want on the copy machine, and then trace it on to freezer paper, holding it up to the window during the day. Then I cut out the pieces from the freezer paper and stick it to the fabric, and cut about 1/8 of an inch bigger. I match it to the original pattern to keep it fairly accurate.
• When I make mistakes, I try to think up some embellishment or something to put over it. On my scrapbook quilt, the bias strip in the border was all wrinkled because I couldn't put in on straight, so I put sequins and beads all over it to cover it up.
• I use speedy triangles a lot, the ones where you sew on the dotted line and cut on the solid line and end up with lots of squares that look like 2 triangles sewn together. They are called Triangles on a Roll and put out by Quilter's Ranch, Inc. What a wonderful invention!
• I also use a lot of invisible thread. It takes a bit of getting used to, but you can't see it. I've even used it for some applique. I always use it to attach embellishments, and I've used it to machine quilt.
• I also like to use DMC machine embroidery thread to applique, because it is thinner and easier to use. It comes on a spool. I've also used one strand of embroider floss to applique when I have a hard time matching colors.
• One of my favorite things that I discovered about a year ago is Books on Tape. I love to read, too, but who has time for that except when going to bed, and then I fall asleep after a few paragraphs. One of my friends had one and I asked if I could listen to it, one book and I was hooked. I have a tape player in my bedroom and kitchen, and a Walkman to use when having it on bothers others in the room. There are four of us who share the books, all quilters. It takes about a week or less to listen to them, and we put a sticky note in the box and cross off our name as we listen to them, so we don't

get mixed up and the last one sends it back. You get to keep the book for a month, so it works out perfect. Last year I listened to 50 books. We take turns ordering, so you listen to lots of different types of books. The number for Books on Tape is 1-800-626-3333. Tell them that Mary Andrews told you about it and I will get a free book. My absolute favorite this year was The Shellseekers by Rosamond Pilcher.

Author's Note: I had been wanting to find some place to rent books on tape, so as soon as I read Mary's questionaire, I phoned the Books-on-tape 1-800 number and requested the info. Yesterday, I received my first book in the mail from them and listened to the first two tapes. And, yes, I told them Mary Andrews told me about them, so she was to get a free book. So, if you call them, now either give them Mary's name.....or mine!

>>>>>>>>>>>>>>>>>>>>>>>>>>>>>>

Patricia (Pat) Jones
Oroville, California

• One of the things that helps me to make my quilting easier, is to always keep an open mind. I never know so much that I can't learn more. I am a *book and gadget freak* so I'm always trying something new. I use many of the new tools or gadgets on the market today, because many of these are very helpful in obtaining accuracy! I'm always looking for an easier way.
• I find it very helpful to take classes with a variety of teachers. Everyone seems to do things just a little differently. This gives you many options to choose from, and you will surely find one that works for you.

• The best hint I can give you to make this hobby easier, is to have an understanding husband. He must *understand* that occasionally he will have to do his own laundry or fix his own meal!

>>>>>>>>>>>>>>>>>>>>>>>>>>>>>>

Jan Jacobson
Tripoli, Wisconsin

• I try to chain sew as many pieces as I can - saving time and thread.
• Quilters should take as many classes as possible - if you learn one new tip or idea, it's worth it.
• Have your sewing room in a spot where it's accessible - you can go in whenever you have a few free minutes.

>>>>>>>>>>>>>>>>>>>>>>>>>>>>>>

Minabess P. Randolph
Toms River,
New Jersey

• A good tool to have is a piece of foam board. I inherited a piece from one of my son's Science projects. It is great for pinning small pieces of your block while you sew them, to keep them in order. When the block is finished, you can pin it to the foam board and block it. It is also good as a display board for teaching aids.

>>>>>>>>>>>>>>>>>>>>>>>>>>>>>>

Carole P. Kenny
Providence,
Rhode Island

• Keep your tools in good shape, sharp blades, clean iron, pins handy, etc.
• Iron seams of alternate block rows...opposite directions, makes seams easy to *lock* together for good intersections.
• A small bamboo rake is great for raking up scraps and threads, especially if you work on carpeted areas, before vacuuming.

>>>>>>>>>>>>>>>>>>>>>>>>>>>>>>

Mary Jane Cemer
Trenton, Nebraska

• Use the sewing machine.
• Do not sew by hand.
• Make 48x48" lap quilts. You can see your design/idea quicker and donate them to rest homes.
• Quilt by hand only if life-threatened. Machine quilt or tie.

>>>>>>>>>>>>>>>>>>>>>>>>>>>>>>

Tonya St. Berg
Woodinville,
Washington

• I have found by using a thinner batting, it helps to decrease the resistance of the three layers, speed up the quilting stitches, and smaller stitches are easily obtained.
• Also, dedicating at least one hour per night will ensure projects to be completed in a timely manor.

>>>>>>>>>>>>>>>>>>>>>>>>>>>>>>

Paula Kay Garrison
& Duncan Garrison
New Braunfels,
Texas

• Start a lot of projects so when you are tired of one, you can immediately switch to another.

Hints for better quilting, Page 157

>>>>>>>>>>>>>>>>>>>>>>>>>>>>>
Patti Centeno
San Antonio, Texas

- I only begin quilting in the evening after everyone has gone to bed. It's my *down* time and I don't have to worry about the phone, or other interruptions.
- I keep some project in the car with me at all times. You never know when you will be stuck in the traffic or in a long line, or in the doctor's waiting room.
- I use a piece of heavy felt to pin my fabric pieces on. This helps me to keep the block in order and I make fewer mistakes. I roll this up with a pretty ribbon and carry this easily. The felt is usually cut into a 15" square.

>>>>>>>>>>>>>>>>>>>>>>>>>>>>>
Helen Blankenship
Flint, Michigan

- Love rotary cutting and easy piecing I have learned since I started in 1989, especially easy half and quarter-squares by adding 1 1/4" and 7/8" to finished size and cutting square in half, so much easier and more accurate than the old template method.

>>>>>>>>>>>>>>>>>>>>>>>>>>>>>
Author's Note: The rotary cutter seems to be the number one favorite tool of quilters. I have found that it is not only good for those straight cuts, it's marvelous for cutting out clothing patterns. It's much more accurate than a pair of scissors, but I have found the *smaller* cutter works best when cutting curves and close corners.

>>>>>>>>>>>>>>>>>>>>>>>>>>>>>
Susan Hanna
Brownlee, Nebraska

- Give yourself a break. Stop every so often and take a walk. Do a bit of housework, stir up a batch of cookies, or whatever. When I first began to sew and would get frustrated or make a mistake, my grandmother would always tell me to leave for awhile and rest my mind, advice that's served me well.

>>>>>>>>>>>>>>>>>>>>>>>>>>>>>
Jill Marie Tanking
Liberal, Kansas

- My biggest hint would be being a member of a quilting guild, if at all possible. The networking with all the different levels of quilters is one of the biggest helps. When I first started I felt like I was always getting help and advice, but as time has gone on, I am able to pass on help and hints to newer quilters, which makes me feel even better as a quilter.

Several hints that I use at home are:
- Those plastic bags you always get are a big help when I am sewing. I have a swivel chair on wheels and have set the ironing board at a working level where I do not have to get up from the chair. I have taped one of those plastic bags at the end of the ironing board for my cut threads. I could never get them in the wastebasket. I also have a large plastic bag close by for scraps of material too small for me. They go to a lady who does miniatures.
- When I am doing a project that is in units, I use the sandwich zip-lock bags for each unit.
- When traveling or waiting for an appointment, I can do moments of work on the project. Like, I am working on a YoYo vest in 9 colors, so each color is in a separate baggie. I have learned to break down each of my projects into units or blocks and not to look at an overall project.
- Another hint I got from another quilter is to staple some felt or flannel to a good size wall. I have notes up on it, or latest project on it to see how it looks. When I make a draft of a quilt that I am working on, it gets pinned up there for reference.
- Also, take a pair of binoculars and look at your quilt project from the wrong end of the glasses. It will distance your quilt from you so you can see how the colors are doing and the coming together is what you are wanting.

>>>>>>>>>>>>>>>>>>>>>>>>>>>>>
Joyce Nichols
Bethany, Missouri

- I have one of John Flynn's quilting frames (the 42" one). My sons put legs on it and it's just right for almost everything I make.
- My favorite quilting tip is waxed thread. I have an old pan full of paraffin, and wax 30 spools of Coats and Clark sewing thread at a time. I use it for all my quilting and since I baste the edges when I applique, I use lots of it.

>>>>>>>>>>>>>>>>>>>>>>>>>>>>>
Peggy Gunwall
Perham, Minnesota

- There are a lot of different ways to do it, but I think lap

quilting is the best. I make all my quilts by hand. I mark each and every piece by home-made templates and cut with scissors.
• I do all my piecing by hand and all of the quilting also. This makes a very pretty quilt, as all the points are just right and everything fits perfectly.

>>>>>>>>>>>>>>>>>>>>>>>>>>>>>
Lassie Wittman
Rochester, Washington

• Make sure the cutting table is the correct height. We use PVC pipe, 12" long, it makes the table perfect for me.
• Learn to use the left side of presser foot as a guide when sewing narrow strips (3/8" or less). Instead of taking time to mark new seam line (only way to be sure of perfect space between stitching line) when space is 1/2" or wider, use a C-thru ruler.

Author's note: Lassie sent along diagrams, which unfortunately were impossible to include in this section, about using the left side of your needle instead of the right to line up your stitching. Also, she mentioned using the needle position to make correct size seams, which most quilters have found is a real help. Try both of these techniques.

• Using all the wonderful Omnigrid rulers and the cutting equipment, and learning to cut with left hand.
• Foundation paper patterns have really helped to produce accurate piecing of miniatures - wish I had thought of it!

(Continued on page 183)

>>>>>>>>>>>>>>>>>>>>>>>>>>>>>
Jean Van Dusen
Kingsford, Michigan

• Along with belonging to the Spinning Spools Quilters Guild which meets monthly, we have a smaller group that meets on Thursday afternoon. There, we stretch and baste our quilts for quilting in a hoop. We meet at the Senior Center, so can move together as many tables as necessary, so do not have to get down on the floor. We work together.

>>>>>>>>>>>>>>>>>>>>>>>>>>>>>
Jean Eng Underhill
Flemington,
New Jersey

• When I am ironing my fabric, I always let my kids use the water spray bottle on my fabric to help me out. One time when I was working on my backing fabric of white-on-white, I turned to help my son get on his jacket to go out, that short time Tiki got into the action too, and left a trail of brown footprints across the wet fabric that was waiting to be ironed!
• When working out the color arrangement of my quilt, I like to have everything displayed on a white flannel wall sheet, so that I can see the total effect and adjust accordingly. I leave it there for a few days, continuously checking it until I am happy with the final project, and then I finish my sewing.
• Because I sew in my dining room, I have a basket of all the quilting supplies I need to use when working on the quilt. If I **have to clean up for an** emergency dinner, I can pack everything into my basket, and the table is all clean.

>>>>>>>>>>>>>>>>>>>>>>>>>>>>>
Eugenia A. Barnes
(Genie)
Marcellus, New York

• A quiet work space with all fabric and tools at the ready.
• I always have one project on the wall and one for travel.
• Good tapes and a small TV, as I am an old movie fan!
• I have a small studio space in my home, and in it I have 2 large chests, one is an antique cupboard in which I keep the majority of my fabric...large pieces, and they are sorted (sort of) by scale of print and darks, mediums and lights. In the second chest, an antique apothecary chest with a variety of drawers, I have all my small pieces of fabrics and tools. I bought a large folding table which I keep as a sewing surface, and keep my rotary mat on it and tools in a small jug on it. On the floor, I keep a large jug with rulers, T-square, etc. I also have a computer table, etc. in this space. Not much floor space, but all at the ready. I use an office chair to move over the floor from place to place and this helps, as I have a leg brace and this facilitates my moving and working.
• When I purchase new fabrics I wash then immediately, and fold them and put them in their proper place, so that they are ready when I am. Any excess materials, etc. get put in a big basket on the floor, just because there are always things that have no special home.
• I try to buy from my local quilt

shop and even though we all love bargains, I feel that it is imperative to support these shops that we as individual quilters, and then as guild members, ask for their support for shows, raffle quilts, etc.

• I have a great basket for all my scraps and it always looks so neat to see all the colors in a jumble. I also keep another basket for children's scraps so they can play.

• I have a flannel wall that is quite large, the flannel is stapled to a 45" long stick and is 2 yards long. I have two nails on the wall and hang it when I need it...when not needed, I roll it around the stick and stand it in a corner/closet/basket...wherever it lands.

• I also took a small piece of cardboard and covered it with flannel so the children will have their own "work board" to use with their scraps.

>>>>>>>>>>>>>>>>>>>>>>>>>>

Ann Littleton
Fairfax, Virginia

• The rotary cutter and strip quilting methods help speed up production.

• I tape a small paper lunch bag near the sewing machine to put loose threads in.

• I try to always have a take-along-project ready to go with me to do, while I wait for appointments or carpool pickups.

• On quilting retreats, my friend Roberta, takes along a travel iron to set up next to her machine. Use a small covered lapboard to iron on. (I try to sit next to Roberta!!!)

>>>>>>>>>>>>>>>>>>>>>>>>>>

Eleanor K. Hunnel
Johnstown, Nebraska

• What do I do with scraps? I thought you'd never ask. They are my favorite medium - using my Olfa Cutter, I turn scraps into squares of whatever size I can get or into narrow strips, placing all in separate plastic baggies. I have pieced 3 quilts and several articles using these small leftovers.

• I use a frame of cloth-wrapped 1x4's and C-clamps to stretch quilts for basting - using dozens of small safety pins. My hand quilting is done over my round table under a good light, without use of a frame or hoop of any kind.

• Machine quilting is particularly tedious, so when my machine is set up for quilting, I have other quilts I'm working on hand to give me a break-space, when I can sit in a comfortable position in another part of the house for a while, before returning to the machine.

• Finishing a project after it's started is a good habit - IF I did that I would be so self-righteous as to be unbearable - so I don't....I have several things in the making in all stages of *undone*. Once in a while I finish one which gives me great pleasure. I set my timer and when it dings, I give the next time-setting to another project.

>>>>>>>>>>>>>>>>>>>>>>>>>>

Dotti Greto
Ocean City,
New Jersey

• I keep all my magazines in order on a bookshelf. When I first look at them, if there is a pattern or idea or helpful hint I think I'll want someday, I put a white label on the front of the magazine. Example: "Baby Quilt, page 20, Pattern page 45." If I *know* I'll want it, I label the magazine, plus fill out a file card, example: "Baby Quilt, page 20, QNM #256 (Quilter's Newsletter Magazine #256)". I know right where to get it. It only takes a couple of minutes to do that every time a magazine arrives.

• I also take 2 pictures of all projects. One to include with the pattern, and one in a record book, stating who I made the item for, when and where the pattern is in my sewing room - (QNM #256). I put the pattern pieces in a clear heavyweight vinyl sheet protector from the office supply store, and put that right in the magazine! This seems like a lot of work, but it takes such a few minutes and saves hours of searching for a pattern you "know you saw somewhere". To start this system you don't have to go back and start from your first project or magazine article - just start now.

>>>>>>>>>>>>>>>>>>>>>>>>>>

Jeanne K. Ferg
Asheville,
North Carolina

• Rotary cutter, cutting mat, wonderful cutting rulers.

• The magazines and books are so filled with near-perfect patterns.

• Last, but not least, we have quilt classes out of one local college, and several shops feature various new classes. Our Guild hires teachers from

Edna R. Harbison
Ontonagon, Michigan

•My rotary cutter is something I'll never give up, now that I discovered it. Other than a 10 year old Singer sewing machine, all my tools are simple and non-electric. I've never used a store-bought pattern, but make my own.
•My favorite techniques are hand-applique, hand-quilting, and trapunto, and I've always felt that short cuts result in a wall hanging that looks like it. I think going the whole route by hand, with all its intricacies is what has kept me in business for 10 years. That, and originality.

Doris Holland
Winterset, Iowa

•The rotary cutter and strip cutting and piecing really are time savers for me.

Teresa A. Walton
New Braunfels, Texas

•In Nuclear Medicine, you must be extremely organized and careful when handling radioactive material. This organization has carried over in my fabric. I organize by color and size. I use pinking shears on the ends of new material, prior to washing, to identify as being washed and to help eliminate raveling.

•Any scraps that are close to two inches wide, I cut 2" strips for a log cabin quilt of the future and store in an old cheese box.

Florence L. Tyler
DeLancey, New York

•When piecing blocks, I pin the pieces in the correct placement to a square of muslin. Easier to sew them correctly.
•When quilting designs, hearts, flowers, leaves, etc., I cut out the design from plastic shelf paper, pin it in place and quilt around it. For a vine, I pin bias tape to quilt, quilt along one edge, remove the tape and quilt a quarter inch from first line. No pencil lines to show.
•When fingers on my left hand are sore from needlepricks, I wrap some black plastic electrical tape on my finger and continue quilting.
•I carry a ziplock bag with handwork in my pocket book. While sitting when others might be knitting, I piece. Ideal for starting conversations, sometimes an order.
•Carry a fine crochet hook with your supplies. You can often remove a dark thread from under a light fabric, when quilting.
•Use freezer paper for accurate applique.

Susan D. Fellin
Flemington, New Jersey

•I find taking classes is good discipline to do the project and finish it (providing that the class allows the time to finish it). I have done four Quilt-in-a-Day classes and three wall hangings in a day, plus a Christmas tree skirt and table runner.

Lori Hauswirth
Iron River, Michigan

•One of my quilting tips is to learn as much as you can. Attend local classes on quilting, join a club, share with friends. Even experienced quilters learn new things.
•I always have some appliqued pieces ready to be basted. (I use freezer paper). They are always easy to take on trips.

Melissa Armstrong
Oshkosh, Nebraska

•Use the best quality fabric, thread and tools that you can afford. You will never regret it.
•Some days, nothing goes right; don't fight it, just put that project aside for an hour, a day, or a year, there will come a time that it's right again. There are too many quilts to be made to struggle on one that isn't working and you aren't enjoying.

Paula Gore
Osmond, Nebraska

•I use a finger cot - those little rubber things (you can get them at an office supply store), when I am quilting. I place it on my right hand-index finger, it allows me to get a good grip on the needle to pull it through. I have carpal tunnel syndrome and this has been a big help.
•My other tip is template material - I like to use exposed X-ray film. It works

wonderfully. Most X-ray departments have some that they just throw away. The price is right.

The same basic hint came from Deb about the X-Ray film.

Deb Meneely
Seattle, Washington

• One of the best template materials around is X-Ray film. It is stiff but allows you to see through it. Ask a nurse or doctor friend for discarded films.

>>>>>>>>>>>>>>>>>>>>>>>>>>>>

Sherry Cook
Council Grove, Kansas

• When wanting to make a charm quilt, choose template, and when cutting fabrics for other projects, get out your charm template and cut one from each fabric you are using. After a few weeks you will be surprised at how many charm pieces you have collected, and without much effort. I keep my charm squares in a tin on my sewing table.

>>>>>>>>>>>>>>>>>>>>>>>>>>>>

Audrey Derscha
Flint, Michigan

• Freezer paper - I use it in a multitude of ways, both for piecing and applique.

>>>>>>>>>>>>>>>>>>>>>>>>>>>>

Janet Kugler
Holdrege, Nebraska

• When matching diagonal seams (like a lone star) use 1/4" masking tape on right side of bottom piece on seam, and on wrong side of top piece at seam, even with raw edge. Use silk pins, and pin straight thru at seam and masking tape. Remove masking tape from right side only. Sew, and when crossing seam, sew right next to tape. Remove before pressing.
• Use small plastic basket to keep pieces from separate blocks organized.
• Use silk pins from Collins #104. They're fine, and don't distort fabric so you can sew right over them.
• Invest in a decent sewing machine. Nothing can be more frustrating than a machine that doesn't work right. I had a machine before which ate fabric, didn't do satin stitches evenly, and now have a Bernina and quilting is so much easier.

>>>>>>>>>>>>>>>>>>>>>>>>>>>>

Marilyn T. Guy
Delhi, New York

• One of the best things about quilting with a group, is the sharing. I have never met a quilter who wouldn't share. We all help each other and the show-and-tell makes me want to try everything.
• I have never sold anything. I just give them away as gifts to family and very close friends. When my youngest son, Eric was 15, he had a friend, Denis, who was at our house all the time. I told them that when they each got married, I would make them a quilt. Denis spoke up very quickly and said, "I want a blue log cabin with flying geese border!" He had learned a lot by just being at the house. He was married two years ago and he got his quilt, but without the border.
• When it comes to ideas for storing my stash, I would love some new ideas. I use dresser drawers at the moment. I tried sorting colors into plastic crates that stack, but I didn't buy large enough crates. I seem to be buying larger pieces now.
• I bought a large fishing tackle box that I keep all my supplies in. I hang all my rulers and everything that will hang, on the wall in my sewing area.
• At first I didn't think I could ever do applique well enough to suit me. Then I learned about the freezer paper method and now I really enjoy that, too.
• The most fun is putting the colors and fabrics together. I can spend hours just playing with fabrics. Many people say they can always tell if it is mine, because of the colors. I usually use pastels, and prefer them.

>>>>>>>>>>>>>>>>>>>>>>>>>>>>

Kathy Palmiter
Williams, Indiana

• Since I'm plagued with dry lips, I always wear a lip balm. Not only does it keep my lips kissably soft, but it's a wonderful aid in threading tiny quilting needles. Snip the end of the thread at an angle, a quick pass or two between the lips, and the thread slips effortlessly through the needles eye - works every time.
• I like to have several projects going at once. I keep a box of piecing at work to stitch over the lunch hours. At home, I have an applique or pieced project in the works and another top or two in hoops to quilt. This way no matter what mood I'm in, there's always something ready to do.

Susan Nicholson
Muskegon, Michigan

- When I'm cutting out pieces for a quilt, I label everything right then and there! That's the only way I know that will allow me to end up with the quilt I started out to make.
- Most of my work is applique and quilting by-hand and is not quick, but so relaxing and satisfying.

Mary Lou Sayers
Clarkson, Nebraska

- Use good tools. Sharp blades in the rotary cutter, good lighting, comfortable seating.
- I don't like deadlines, as it makes for too much pressure.
- When cooking, make extra meat, potatoes, or pasta. Leftovers make quick sandwiches, or combine into quick casseroles.
- I have projects in bags that I take to doctors appointments, it's surprising how much basting and applique can be done waiting.

Edna E. Holdsworth
Johnston, Rhode Island

- In good quality cotton fabric, it saves time to tear long borders and keeps them more even.
- In selecting colors, I like to combine them on a table, stand at a distance, squinting my eyes to see if they all blend in together. If one stands out, I eliminate it and start again.
- I quilt using a 14" hoop or the Q-snap frame which allows the quilt to be portable, so I can watch TV, while I quilt. The Frame is good for borders, as you can catch the very edge of the quilt in it.
- The size 12 needles make small stitches easier.

Dawn Golden
Milford, New Jersey

- I use all the rotary cutters and rulers and gadgets that make cutting faster and more accurate. With the limited time that I have right now, templates and patterns are not for me. "Assembly line" sewing and traditional patterns interest me most. Machine quilting has also been my finish of choice so far, but I do prefer the quality and character of hand quilting.
- Classes offered by local shops and workshops at our Guild meetings offer a new quilter like me, some great hands-on experience. The Charity Blocks of the Month that our Guild has presented in the past, have given me the opportunity to try something small and new.
- I also find my fellow Guild members to be a wonderful source of information and inspiration.

Darlene Brazil
Escalon, California

- Organization is my key to quilting and I have all the tools, books, fabric, rulers, squares, rotary cutters, mats, etc, but they must be organized in a somewhat neat array.
- My Dad built me a cutting table which is the perfect height. All of my *cutting* tools are within handy reach of my table.
- Fabric, books and all other accessories are well categorized and easy to find.

Roberta Schroeder
Deer Park, Washington

- My favorite quilting style is the stipple look. I stipple quilt most of my wall hangings, I love it!
- One of the smarter investments I made, was in a walking foot for my machine.
- I have learned in pinning my quilts, that the closer I pin, the better my project looks, as I have no gathers then. I do not baste anymore with thread, I do all safety pins - as many as 600 per quilt.
- I know how to piece quilts, but I much prefer the strip method of quilt making. It seems far more accurate to me.

Merrilyn Muir-Rennau
Vienna, Austria, Europe

Drafting your blocks for planned quilt project:
- Use 16" and 10" cork squares to tack the unpieced block on.
- Cut several block varieties, because sometimes reality looks different than the planned arrangement of fabric for the blocks.
- I use clear plastic boxes for the ziplock bags of the templates.
- When sewing by machine, the height of the table and chair are important. When sitting in front of the machine, be sure your

Hints for better quilting, Page 163

arms are in a comfortable position.
- For storing large yardage of fabric, I use cylinder bolts so the fabric is not creased.
- I am fortunate to have enough space, so I made one bedroom into a nursery. Painted the walls with scrubable paint, height 4 feet. The children can draw pictures. I cut windows in large cardboard cartons and the children may glue fabric scraps on the walls or floors as a carpet. They can then use it as a doll play house.
- Also, playing the fairy tale cassettes that have the books to go with them.
- Also, Disney videos.
- Children enjoy playing with carpet and fabric scraps.

Gifts:
- Using scraps; cosmetic bags, patchwork stuffed animals.
- Patches: Quilted patchwork blocks for jeans, back of vests. Top of sewing box or laundry baskets. Boxes for stationary. I made quilted covers for cook books, small framed pictures, tote bags with side pocket, coasters, wastebasket covers, a quilted strip to edge cupboard shelves.
- Templates made of hard cardboard with sandpaper glued on backside. This way fabric and templates do not move while cutting out.
- How to sell: Make a photo portfolio of your projects, and carry it with you when going to activity meetings. Invite friends to tea and display projects. Advertise gifts and quilts in bulletins at church, school. Wear your clothing articles. Try bazaars.
- Scraps: Cut scraps into different sizes of triangles, squares, rectangles and circles. Put the different shapes into marked ziplock bags or marked boxes, also cut log cabin strips and store in a clear plastic container. From these scraps you can make miniature quilts. Cut circles and cover buttons. Make scarves or collars from scraps. Make fabric mache' bowls, animals, picture frames.
- Storing: clear plastic boxes marked with name of quilt. Cut borders and sashes, mark and put in ziplock bag. Cut pattern pieces, etc. Each in its bag in plastic box.
- If I am quilting with a hoop, it is stored on a wall hook. Large quilt frame is pushed to wall under hoop hooks.

>>>>>>>>>>>>>>>>>>>>>>>>>>>>>
Susan Southworth
Gulf Shores, Alabama

- *How to add new fabric to your stash without getting caught!*

Save several old TIDE boxes after you have used all the soap, as well as large cereal boxes. Keep them in good condition, out of sight from You-Know-Who. When you feel a fabric binge coming on, put those boxes in the trunk of your car. After you have satisfied your fabric appetite with large purchases, fold the cuts of fabric and put inside the boxes in the trunk. Then, carry them in brown bags like they are groceries, into your house. To insure success, top each bag with a box of You-Know-Who's favorite cookies and that will keep him too busy to pay attention to anything else in the bag. This works!

>>>>>>>>>>>>>>>>>>>>>>>>>>>>>
Pamela Thompson
Clinton Twp,
Michigan

- When hand quilting I use a rubber finger on my thumb. It helps pull needle through.
- When machine quilting, I use about 6 rubber fingers, 3 on each hand, it helps to grip fabric and makes guiding it easier.

>>>>>>>>>>>>>>>>>>>>>>>>>>>>>
PIONEER QUILTERS
Eugene, Oregon

- Lick your needle and the thread for ease in threading.
- Set the seam stitches before pressing open.
- Rotary cutter and precision machine piecing.
- Quilt on a frame, it's faster.

>>>>>>>>>>>>>>>>>>>>>>>>>>>>>
Cynthia England
Houston, Texas

- Hang Celotex (building insulator, porous) on the wall so you can pin projects up. You will get a different perspective, and it's easier to spot mistakes. If you can't afford Celotex (about $32 for 2 4x6' sheets), just get a $5 summer blanket at Walmart and staple it directly to the wall. Blocks will stick to the blanket and can be repositioned.
- I have many projects going at once. When I began quilting, I used to feel guilty (a woman thing) if I didn't finish one at a time. I prefer to think of the project now as "half-finished", when I come back to it.

Hints for better quilting

Lesley Ann Hill
Granville, Ohio

- Careful measuring is helpful for me in every step of quilting. By doing this, I often don't have to redo a step.
- Also, I have a journal in which I store pictures and sketches of ideas I'd like to try, so when I get stuck I have a quick source of ideas.

Mary A. Sovran
Phoenix, Arizona

- A wet toothpick kept in your mouth and used to turn the edges as you applique, is a great tool.
- After a couple of disasters, I now use a small blunt children's scissors when I quilt, so I won't clip into my quilt surface.
- Remember to photograph your quilts and blocks, and keep a record of everything you make.
- If you enter contests, keep a record of all your wins. It is a great pick-me-up on a blue day to look through your accomplishments.
- Remember to clip off the corners before washing your fabrics, this really works for less fraying.
- It's also a good idea to wash small pieces, like fat quarters, in a mesh bag to keep them from fraying too much.

Diana Alfuth
Hudson, Wisconsin

- When marking fabric or tracing templates, sand paper makes a world of difference.

Judy Allen
Nevada, Iowa

- One of the best buys I ever made, was a folding table that has 36" legs. It is great for cutting and pinning quilts - and has an advantage over counters, in that it can be moved so a person can move around all four sides.

Marilyn Thomas
Harpster, Ohio

- If you stick your finger and bleed on fabric, use your own saliva to rub blood off. Works every time!
- On my table I try to have everything I might need to applique with. I don't have room to have my ironing board up all the time. So, I put a soft towel down on counter to iron small pieces on. Spray starch helps keep fabric smooth.
- I use only 100% cotton.

Margo J. Clabo
Cleveland, Tennessee

- I love to sew the binding on my quilts, because it means that I am almost finished with this project, and can start a new one.
- When I cut continuous bias binding, I use a small rotary cutting mat on the small, pointed end of my ironing board, so that I can skip the tedious marking and scissor cutting. I let the bias tube loop over the end of the ironing board, and simply cut the strips the necessary width with a rotary cutter and ruler.
- The *Strip Ticket* is the perfect reference to know how large your square of fabric needs to be, and it also has wonderful diagrams, in case you forget exactly how to make the bias tube.

John Flynn
Billings, Montana

- Learn to sew an *accurate* 1/4" seam first time, every time; then every pattern you pick up works without adjusting.
- Don't quilt to make quilts. Quilt to enjoy the process!
- If you need a quilt in a hurry to keep warm, you are better off to go buy something.

Candra J. Sowder
Williamsburg, Iowa

- Learn all the strip quilting tricks you can, to eliminate templates and sewing together lots of pieces. Sew first - cut later!
- Learn of all the tools available, and consult people who have actually used them, to decide if they are worth the money or really make the job easier.
- Iron seams in opposite directions whenever possible, to get exact corners and seam matches.
- Take as many classes as you can.

Juanita Gibson Yeager
Louisville, Kentucky

- Use a copier to enlarge or reduce a drawing or to make multiple copies of a block design

that you can cut up or arrange endlessly, until you have the configuration you want.
• When marking around templates to keep them from slipping, I mark an X on the back of the template with repositional glue stick (Post it note brand is my favorite). The template can be used several times without re-applying the glue and it will not harm the fabric.

>>>>>>>>>>>>>>>>>>>>>>>>>>>>>>>
Donna Olson
Rogersville, Missouri

• I cut the fingers off surgical rubber gloves and place one on my right index finger. It is comfortable and saves picking up and putting down a needle gripper.
• I realize it is probably not the recommended procedure, but, the only way I can successfully quilt to my right and up and away from myself, is to push the needle with the underside of my thumbnail. Of course, if I am on a large project, the needle eventually wears a hole through my thumbnail. I discovered this past year that I can glue on an artificial thumbnail. I file it down to almost the same length as my natural nail, and few people even notice it is not my own. I have not had a needle go through my nail since.

>>>>>>>>>>>>>>>>>>>>>>>>>>>>>>>
Carol Thelen
Pearland, Texas

• When I'm hand quilting borders, I find it difficult to keep the layers in the hoop since the quilt top is shorter than the others. Before I quilt the borders, I trim all the layers and baste around the edge by machine. This enables me to keep the layers tighter in the center of the hoop. If the layers are not smooth in some places, just remove some of the basting and adjust the layers. This basting also makes it easier to attach the binding when the quilting is finished.

>>>>>>>>>>>>>>>>>>>>>>>>>>>>>>>
Jane Aruns
Franklin, Tennessee

• New fabric goes to the laundry before it goes into storage. It does not get ironed until it gets used.
• Colors have their own shelves.
• My work table is a 36" door laminated with formica and sits on 2 tall saw horses. This can be moved easily, if I need the floor space and is high enough for me to work comfortably. Important, since I do all cutting and drawing standing up.

>>>>>>>>>>>>>>>>>>>>>>>>>>>>>>>
Shirley Gardner
Evergreen, Colorado

• When drawing your own design, use a mirror as a third eye. Be loose and easy with your lines and simplify your work. The busier the pattern, the simpler the color scheme. With quilts you have total freedom and you can make anything.
• Create with colors you love and patterns you love, so you are peaceful when you work.
• Create for others, but hang on to your favorites. Just like a wonderful painting, hang it for show and be pleased you made it.

>>>>>>>>>>>>>>>>>>>>>>>>>>>>>>>
Jane Clark Stapel
Pittsburg, Pennsylvania

• When I am looking for matching fabric, I have the salesclerk snip me a small piece when purchasing (hard for them to say NO when you are standing there purchasing)....I put these snips in the plastic envelopes you use for family pictures in your wallet...then you always have your sample swatch.
• I also prefer to store my fabrics according to AMOUNT rather than color..I can see that it is red/green/blue/etc. but DO I KNOW IF IT IS A YARD, HALF YARD, OR QUARTER?
• I buy LOTS of raffle quilt tickets from guilds where I am lecturing as they make wonderful gifts...including sending one to OTHER guilds tucked in with my THANK YOU for the invitation to speak to their guild.
• I have also added a class, APPLIQUIT, SEW E-Z A CHILD CAN DO IT. An easy one step-method of appliquing and quilting the shapes already sandwiched batting and background. You'll find your child/grandchild working right along beside you.

>>>>>>>>>>>>>>>>>>>>>>>>>>>>>>>
Carol Younce
Fairfax, Virginia

I make almost all my quilt bindings on the straight grain or cross grain...not the bias. They are usually 1 1/2" strips in a big drawer and I have a ready supply of interesting log cabin strips.

Joyce Benitez
Omaha, Nebraska

• I have my cutting board, iron and machine in a U-shape, so all I have to do is swivel my chair - no having to get up, no wasted time - my portable phone close by, so I can sew and yak at the same time.

• I keep my fabric *washed* and color coordinated on shelves, and recently had to add milk crates to expand my storage area. The amish fabrics are in their own space, and then if I have small pieces of leftovers, I roll them, wrap them in a piece of paper, kind of like they do fat quarters. I have them in boxes on shelves, color coordinated, so that you can see at a glance if there is anything you need or can use...especially if you are doing charm quilting.

• I store my quilt rulers behind the couch. They are out of sight of people. But, makes it easy to store and keep from breaking, all in one place, the space seems to be just the right size. Also, the extra cutting boards, or if you are having company and have to do straightening up, they slide between the wall and dry sink and stay flat.

• As for scraps: besides all the ones I make from my own projects, I am *known* that I will dig through trash at workshops to bring home anything larger than 1", (you would be surprised what people throw away). I have made some *beautiful* things with such variety of fabric that I didn't have, this way. I made a scrap basket quilt (Mary Ann Fonz) from these for a Challenge, calling for at least 25 different fabrics. I used different whites for piecing the background also.

• When I have a few minutes to sit with children, I have a flat box with these pieces ironed. I have a ziplock bag of templates of various sizes, from postage stamp up to spokes for a fan quilt, or stacked bricks or 2 1/4" squares, and I trace and cut these, placing them in ziplock bags. Even logs for log cabin.

• Recently I used 2 1/2" squares to edge sweat shirts that I split up the center and around the bottom. The 3 1/2" squares were made into a Quilted jacket and they went together so fast, since they were all cut when I needed them. All of these were cut and traced in tiny pieces of time, snatched 5 to 10 minutes at a time over the course of a year, this all adds up to pretty things made for self and others.

• I have found that by using the several layers of paper tape (that doctors use) on the finger under quilting project, it doesn't make the needle sticky and you can feel what you are doing, at it fits like skin.

• I started several 4 year-olds sewing patches to make small blankets, kids love to sew. Anne sewed 5 quilts by age 6. They use the sewing machine.

Sharon J. Mason
Coos Bay, Oregon

• Quilt Guild! If you need to see how to do something, odds are that you'll find a gal at Guild who can show you.

• When you want to sew 2 small pieces together, instead of pinning, just use your iron. Press them together then go straight to your machine. Press gently...no stretching.

Virginia L. Brown
Ogallala, Nebraska

• I use binder clips to hold a quilt sandwich tightly together on 2 large tables. Then I pin it together with safety pins. The clips are as good as 2 or 3 extra pair of hands, and one person can handle even a king-sized quilt.

• Wrecked fingernails or sore fingers are not a problem when I hand quilt. I use a plastic thimble with a plastic fingernail taped to it on the hand under the quilt, using the nail to push up, small stitches can be made without dulling the needle. It takes a little practice, but so easy!

Anne-Donia B. Hafskjold
Tiller, Norway

• I always work with a small board in my lap. Under it is attached a bag filled with styrofoam balls, so the *table* is very stable. When I put away my work, I just carry the table over to the closet or elsewhere, where I store my projects.

• I try to finish one project before I start the next.

• When I trace around templates, I put the fabric on top of very fine sandpaper to keep the fabric from slipping, and always make the templates from sandpaper for the same reason. A sharp pencil is also important.

• I always keep a small trash bag with me. Thus, I don't have too many threads and tiny scraps sprawling all over the place.

• I always sew while listening to

Hints for better quilting, Page 167

the TV. It is a smart way to practice different languages, 'cause we don't have dubbed movies here. So, I listen to French, German and English movies and get to sew a lot. It is not so easy when it is a film in Chinese or Russian!!

>>>>>>>>>>>>>>>>>>>>>>>>>>>>>>>
Debra J. Ruisard
Whitehouse Station, New Jersey

• Two new techniques that I have learned lately have made my quilting quicker and easier. The first improves rotary cutting time some what. Let's say you want to cut 2" strips. You take your 6" wide ruler and place the whole thing on the fabric. Then you cut a six inch strip. Carefully move the ruler 2" to the left (if right handed) and cut again. Then move it once more to the left and cut again. Lift up the ruler and you have three strips cut. Repeat as many times as needed. If you need 1 1/2 inch strips you can do four at a time. I find this method faster than cutting one strip, removing the ruler, moving the strips and lining up the ruler again.

• The second technique involves a new gadget called the "Corner Mark-it". This neat tool enables you to make perfect mitered corners on your bindings. And it really works. It is marketed by The Quilted Ribbon, PO Box 811, Derby, KS 67037.

• I have the good fortune to be able to leave most of my stuff out on the table (except for the sharp stuff) all the time, so when I have a few minutes I just can sit down and work on my latest project.

>>>>>>>>>>>>>>>>>>>>>>>>>>>>>>>
Betty E. Ives
Windsor Ontario, Canada

• The Omnigrid ruler with the 45, 60 & 30 degree markings. I love the Salem folded 24" squaring up ruler, and I have a 16" clear triangle that is wonderful, also. I have a 60" metal ruler with readings on both sides, so no matter at which end you are standing, it is still readable. It also lays flat in the back of my station wagon. Purchased at an Art Supply Store for $20 many years ago. These are my favorite tools, along with the Olfa Cutter.

>>>>>>>>>>>>>>>>>>>>>>>>>>>>>>>
Bonnie Swannack
Lamont, Washington

• The rotary cutter is my best quilting friend. I rarely make templates or use scissors for cutting out.
• Also, I use a Q-snap frame and do all my hand quilting in my lap with this frame.

>>>>>>>>>>>>>>>>>>>>>>>>>>>>>>>
Lynda Milligan
Denver, Colorado

• Nancy (my partner) and I have been satisfying our need to sew by making "Partner" quilts. We choose a pattern we both like and each day each of us make 2 identical blocks. One of each pair goes to Nancy and one to me. After the blocks are made, we take them home and piece them into a quilt, choosing our own borders, etc. This is an especially busy season for us and yet we each completed two quilt tops.

>>>>>>>>>>>>>>>>>>>>>>>>>>>>>>>
Nancy Smith
Denver, Colorado

• A new tool called the *Angler*. You tape it to your sewing machine bed and it enables you to sew *snowball corners* perfectly. It's wonderful, and I wish I would have thought of it.

>>>>>>>>>>>>>>>>>>>>>>>>>>>>>>>
Connie Sager
Nashville, Kansas

• I really like using the no triangle method for making nice triangles. Chain piece and rotary cut anything I can. Applique is my favorite and I want to do a lot more some day.

>>>>>>>>>>>>>>>>>>>>>>>>>>>>>>>
Carole Collins
Norfolk, Nebraska

• For many years, all that I ever did was hand-piecing. Then about four years ago I wanted to make a *quick* quilt, and decided to piece it on the machine and my life was changed forever! The rotary cutter and all of the rulers available now, are just wonderful. I still do hand quilting, but keep learning new ways to do template-free quilting. I have always read everything I saw on quilting and tried other's methods. I have taken many workshops and there were times I didn't fully agree with a new way, but I would combine a little of it with what I already knew, trying to make my own distinctive way of quilting.

Constance T. Hall
Mannington, West Virginia

• Since I am not able to quilt at home at this time, I cannot think of many hints for getting chores done. But when I was quilting at home, I aimed to pick up everything before going to bed the night before. I also planned my meals with left-overs in mind and only had to plan a meal every other day.

• One of my time saving tips for quilting is to have some one of your family do this for you: thread a package of needles on the spool of thread. Then, as you need one slide them all but one, back beyond where you take your thread off and keep doing that, and you do not have to take time to thread your needle.

• Also, a long handled magnet on the quilt is a handy gadget to help pick up dropped pins and needles. Saves getting down on your knees, sometimes hunting.

• Another quickie is to mark the middle of your quilting frame, so that you can place the middle of your backing with it when you start to put the quilt in the frames.

Barb Bennett
Washington, D.C.

• Sorry, I'm just a beginner!

Kathy Munkelwitz
Isle, Maine

• The rotary cutter is the best thing, ever.
• The thing I use most is freezer paper. I use it for tracing, for making templates (Iron several layers together), for applique, for everything. It's a great stabilizer. Iron on back of applique blocks (machine applique), tear off when done. Try it!

Zelda Lynch
San Augustine, Texas

• I like to pick my colors, I try to match or blend colors that look best together. Then I cut out the entire quilt before I start piecing. Sometimes I have as many as 3 or 4 quilts cut, ready to piece.

• I buy all or most of my material wholesale, so I can sell quilts cheaper. I make most of my quilts about 92 inches wide and longer.

Sandra A. Anderson
Lincoln, Nebraska

• I use a lot of baggies. Cut out pieces and put individual blocks or sections of a quilt in baggies.

• I also carry (in my purse) a small snip-it scissors, thimble and needles, and a couple of colors of thread (white, black, grey) in another baggie. Whenever I go to pick up kids from school, doctor's appointment, or the dentist, school conferences, or any where I know I'll have to wait, I pull out the baggies and get a few stitches done. It is surprising how much a person can get done a little at a time.

• When I have a large quilt that I am quilting, I don't keep putting it away, I leave it out and whenever I have a few minutes, I put in a needle full of stitches, like waiting for everyone to get ready to leave in the morning, any free minutes....these add up. I am talking about non-scheduled sewing times, which to me is during my favorite TV shows.

Joan Biasucci
Cedar Creek, Nebraska

• I've never been very good at *doing as I'm told,* and so most of my quilting projects are original wall quilts. I don't care to use a pattern designed by someone else, but would rather plan as I go. Because of this, I find there is no quick way or easy way.

• As mentioned earlier, my office and my sewing room are combined. I have a flannel board hanging on the wall; and even if I'm up to my eyebrows in stuff for the restaurant, I occasionally take a moment to move something around on the flannel board, try another fabric, or whatever comes to mind. Sometimes just sitting there and looking at the project, in anticipation of ACTUALLY STITCHING, is truly wonderful.

• Exercise is important to me, especially since I spend most of my day sitting, and I find that exercise "keeps my body from rusting" as a friend once said. During the winter months, the first thing I do each morning is spend the better part of an hour on a treadmill. This is not wasted time, but is my time for planning, getting organized, and mentally trying a lot of "what if's" pertaining to my current quilt project. During the summer months, a friend and I spend about the same length of time each day walking around the lakes where we live. I refer to her as my *silent partner*, as sometimes we don't talk at all. And sometimes we talk a lot about quilts.

•My cocktail hour is also very important to me. Each day at about 3:45 p.m. I take the mail to the post office to go out that day. If I leave any later than that, I'm liable to have to wait at the railroad crossing for the train to pass by, and that is invariably when the mail truck comes, loads up, and leaves town. Timing is crucial. After successfully completing this task, I travel a bit further (about 2 blocks) uptown to the gas station run by a friend, and have my daily Diet Pepsi with ice, and four bite-sized Tootsie Rolls with 25 calories from fat. Each. We also discuss quilts.

>>>>>>>>>>>>>>>>>>>>>>>>>>>>>>

Doris Lott Aultman
Hattiesburg,
*   Mississippi*

•I always keep a bag or basket in the car that I work on while my husband drives.
•I also have so many projects started that I find myself frustrated, and figured out a way to un-complicate my life. I list all of my projects on strips of paper and put them in a basket. On the first of each month, I pull a project slip out of the basket. This is what I work on for that month. If I should complete the project, then I can pull out a second project slip. At the end of the month, I hold out the things I have been doing until I have drawn a new slip, then I return them to the basket. This may not make sense to you, but seems to help me get a grip on life and quilting.

.>>>>>>>>>>>>>>>>>>>>>>>>>>>
Wilma Dooley Muse
Fayetteville, Tennessee

•Attend classes and lectures from experienced quilters to pick-up on hints and short-cuts.
•Use a .5 mechanical pencil with a sandpaper board to draw templates.

>>>>>>>>>>>>>>>>>>>>>>>>>>>>>>
Jennifer J. Danly
Arlington,
*   Massachusetts*

•I would suggest that everyone keep a notebook of their ideas, pictures of things they like, sketches, etc. We all have more ideas for quilts than time to make them. If we keep a record, a forgotten idea may be rediscovered years from now.
•Also, join a Guild if you can find one; and don't just attend meetings - become involved. Meeting other quilters is inspirational.

>>>>>>>>>>>>>>>>>>>>>>>>>>>>
Merry May
Tuckahoe, New Jersey

•Remember that fabric has *two* sides - the *right* side and the *other* side. Don't be afraid to use the *other* side. It can give your work a whole new dimension. I promise that the *quilt police* are *not* going to come and take you away! Besides, when you think about it a little, it will occur to you that you've just doubled your fabric stash!
•If you plan to hand quilt a project and want to use safety pins to baste it, fasten the safety pins to the *back* of the quilt. That way your quilting thread won't catch on the safety pins.

>>>>>>>>>>>>>>>>>>>>>>>>>>>>>>
Suzanne Peery Schutt
Clinton, Mississippi

•I keep take-a-long projects in one tote bag.
•I quilt on a frame and listen to classical music for relaxation every day - even if it's only 15 minutes.
•Arrange fabrics in colors: this makes designing so much easier.
•Take six months off and finish *all* projects!

>>>>>>>>>>>>>>>>>>>>>>>>>>>>>>
Ellen Vollmer
Nickerson, Nebraska

•I have my fabric separated by color, and is all pre-washed before putting in a drawer. That way fabric stays clean and neat, and any color can be found quickly.
•I have an ironing board by the sewing machine and same height, so after sewing, seams can be pressed.
•I have quilt thread in a holder, so the spool isn't rolling on floor.
•If sewing many small pieces together, sew many at same time and clip thread between them.

>>>>>>>>>>>>>>>>>>>>>>>>>>>>>>
Pauline Hess 'Ping'
*   White*
Seaboard,
*   North Carolina*

•The Olfa board and cutter is a fantastic invention! My advice to any quilter, is to buy a set...along with a good ruler, and practice using them. You will

soon discover how to master this technique.
• Try any *new* ideas that you find in quilting magazines, or from another quilter. You will be amazed at how fast some things go.
• Try to continuously sew several pieces together, without breaking the thread....it is a fun and easy way to piece squares.

>>>>>>>>>>>>>>>>>>>>>>>>>>>>>

Pat Milne Hitchcock
Sequim, Washington

• I don't now, and never have had a lot of space to spread out quilting projects, so I prefer hand applique (especially the portability of it), although I do have a nice sewing machine which I use for piecing, and am doing some machine quilting.
• I figured out a way to tame the monofilament is to put the spool inside a Tupperware gravy maker, thread out through the spout, then through the eye of a small safety pin taped eye-side-up on the top right hand side of your machine.
• My mantra is "Foot pedal fast, hands slow." I practice by making dolly quilts. Wonder-under a simple shape made from that polyester stuff your neighbor gave you, onto some more "dog" fabric (you know, the stuff that followed you home) and have some fun. Little kids don't care about quality, they just love opening presents!
• My personal philosophy about fabric must be genetic (remember my grandmothers?) I buy new and specialty fabric per project, any decent *find* at garage sales, and I NEVER TURN DOWN ANYTHING ANYBODY GIVES ME. A lot of donated fabric finds its way into charity quilts, dolly quilts, ABC quilts, or gets recycled to groups who make costumes, etc.
• You can tell the difference between poly fabric and cotton, (if you are unsure), by lighting a match to the edge. The poly will leave a melted ridge, while the cotton will leave a fine grey ash.
• I keep my fabric in four under-bed boxes, categorized by color from white and light to black, with a separate category for "speciality prints" (the items with no specified color).
• Another small box is "Projects", and still another contains vintage fabrics which I use to repair quilts for people.
• I display quilts in my home all over the place, even in the bathrooms! We have all antique beds, and when a box spring and mattress are placed on them, they are very high. Many antique quilts are merely coverlet-sized on these tall beds, but by using a king-sized solid colored sheet as a spread and by placing it sideways, it goes clear to the floor and you can put your quilt over the top.

>>>>>>>>>>>>>>>>>>>>>>>>>>>>>

Alice Furrey
Carter, South Dakota

• My favorite time of day to do my own quilting projects is early in the morning. I am a *morning* person and often wake up early and go to another part of the house to sew where I will not disturb my husband who may still be sleeping. Some people are *night* persons and could work better by staying up at night to work. Either time of day is great, because there will not be the usual interruptions of phone calls, meal planning, cleaning, etc. I feel I can get twice as much done at these times rather than trying to do them at another time of day. Of course, getting up or staying up every night would not be the best idea.
• Another way I get extra projects done is to always have a hand project ready to work, on-hand to take in a travel bag. I take this with me on any trip we take when I am not the driver, or when there are overnight stays in a motel. These are projects I am not in a hurry to finish, but simply love the process of doing them. I have many unfinished projects in boxes and plastic zip-lock bags, that now and then get picked up and finished for a gift, or for that empty spot I wanted to decorate. I no longer feel guilty for having unfinished projects around, for they have come in very handy when I would not have had the time to start a whole project.

>>>>>>>>>>>>>>>>>>>>>>>>>>>>>

Betty M. Abel
Sheboygan, Wisconsin

• Keep an *Easy Angle* in my sewing drawer and often sew up a bunch of half square triangles, using lights and darks. When I want a quick scrap quilt, it's half way there.
• Use plastic storage boxes and label each box with contents. When I need an item, it's easy to find.
• Use loose leaf notebooks with plastic pages to store hints, ideas, etc.

Merrilee Tieche
Ozark, Missouri

•Speed piecing on the machine has revolutionized my quilt making, but I've had trouble maintaining accuracy. At our last Quilt Retreat a friend offered a hint that has saved my sanity. Determine a precise quarter inch from your machine needle using graph paper, and place a strip of moleskin to mark that place. It is thick enough to guide your fabric easily and the adhesive back sticks firmly to the plate. My machine is computerized, so I couldn't use the magnetic devices sold to serve the same purpose.

Beulah T. Gilbert
Bellevue, Ohio

•My favorite hint is to use a seam ripper at the sewing machine to help with the fabrics when I'm sewing. It was a great tool for holding on to while guiding the fabric.

Dean Valentine
New Braunfels, Texas

•My favorite time for quilting is early morning, sitting in my den, watching the wildlife eat our garden, a peaceful time.
•To protect my fingers from the needling, I use Johnson Waterproof 1/4" tape, although it tears easily.
•When my sister-in-law, Gail, visits from Houston, we go in my studio to quilt. Gail's very tall and I'm short. To solve the ironing board height problem, we take my old, unadjustable ironing board and put my traveling workshop ironing board on top. One end is high for Gail, and the other is just right for me.

Marilyn A. Lewis
Glendale, Oregon

•I don't baste any more. I use safety pins, and not those big ones, but medium size.
•I also like to sew my squares and triangles on one continuous thread. I press them, and in the evenings I pin the next step, and also do that on one continuous thread.
•I make lots of oven dishes, you can put them in the oven and forget them!

Sarah M. Bruso
Rhinelander, Wisconsin

•I'm not one for doing things the quick and easy way, but I do love the scrap saver tool put out by That Patchwork Place. I'd be lost without it.
•The only other hint I have is when sewing 1/4" or 1/2" strips, I always cut my strips 1/4" larger than needed. I sew the first seam, then press, then trim my excess 1/4" off. This leaves me with a straight edge again in case I didn't sew a perfectly straight seam the first time.

Christine Miller
Medway, Ohio

•Small amount of peroxide on a Q-tip will remove small amounts of blood on quilts in progress (I stick my fingers a lot!)
•Charm trading is a good way to collect loads of different fabrics.
•Check the remnant tables or choose bolts with small amounts left on them, can get them for *bolt* price usually.
•Carry small piecework to Dr's visits or to work.

Laura Estes
Odessa, Washington

•Buy a small rotary cutter, and learn to use it on curves. Cut in multiples whenever possible.
•Think like a carpenter, measure twice, cut once.
•Keep your sewing machine in tip top shape. Clean and oil it regularly and have it serviced yearly. Sewing machines are dumber than posts, so you will be wasting your time trying to teach it off-color language when it won't sew right.
•Change your sewing machine needle after each quilt top. They don't look dull, but they are, and can cause fabric to wad up or pull threads that show on the finished product. You spend money on good fabric and precious time, don't ruin it with a dull needle.
•Toss that quilting needle after each 1/4 of a quilt. I use 4 needles on a full size quilt and 1 or 2 on wall hangings. A dull needle is a slow needle.
•Learn to speed piece and chain pieces through your machine. Learn to use a bridge, a small scrap of fabric to lead off and follow the last piece through the machine. This cuts down on threads to snip and keeps your seam lines straight.
•Find and mark the exact 1/4" on your machine and follow it. Precision means speed. Time is wasted if you have to sew it twice.

Page 172, Hints for better quilting

- Collect a couple of balloons, they are the best grippers for getting needles through thick fabric.
- My Best Hint....I quilt in a hoop (was always struggling with it). I'm tall so all the floor stands were too low, causing a back ache. Solution: 2 large paper clips and an old shoe lace! Open up the clips to form an "S" shape. Tie shoe lace ends to each clip to fit comfortably around your neck. Hook the other end of the S on to hoop before tightening all the way. Result: 2 free hands and you can sit anyway you like and you can quilt faster with 2 free hands.

>>>>>>>>>>>>>>>>>>>>>>>>>>>>
Penny Hand
Woodbridge, Virginia

- I work on a ping pong table, when pinning or basting layers together. Weight of quilt helps keep fabric taut.

>>>>>>>>>>>>>>>>>>>>>>>>>>>>
Lois K. Ide
Bucyrus, Ohio

- Attach scissors to sewing machine by a long cord so that I am not forever hunting them.
- Use a small paper punch to make holes in my long, narrow permanent templates for placing pins in strategic spots to prevent template movement.
- Use two magnetic pin holders....one at sewing machine and one on ironing board. When one is empty, simply switch.
- Have a small basket or tin filled with small projects and all necessary basic sewing supplies to work on while riding in car, waiting in doctor's office, etc.
- Keep all patterns and templates in large, three-ringed notebook sheet protectors for reference.
- Mark plastic templates with Sharpie pen with size and name of quilt pattern and number to cut for each block.
- When cutting pieces for many blocks, cut however many you need for each block and thread onto a double threaded needle for entire quilt. Take off thread as blocks are sewn. Stitching goes much faster, by both hand and machine, as each block can be completely sewn before going on to the next one, and without need for cutting interruptions, etc.

>>>>>>>>>>>>>>>>>>>>>>>>>>>>
Grace Moone
High Falls, New York

- I have a miniature cathedral windows *in progress*, so I use a 3/4" scrap for it, and keep it as a kit ready to pick up at a moments notice.
- I take a 2" strip off any new fabric I get (as soon as it is washed) for my "someday" water color project and keep that in a box, as well.
- I buy a supply of 16" pizza boxes and 12" pizza boxes. I get a box *ready* for a project - some I even iron on fleece to make a small flannel board. I get everything ready together for a project on a box, then as I have time *short segments*, I grab a box (labeled on the front) work, then close it up easily.

>>>>>>>>>>>>>>>>>>>>>>>>>>>>
Jacque' J. Holmes
Big Bear Lake, California

- A useful tip I employ has to do with keeping my work neat as I go. I fold back a piece of masking tape on itself halfway around the roll and secure it by tucking it under. I place this beside my sewing machine, or next to my hand sewing area. As I trim the loose threads they adhere easily to the tape.
- Another tip always gets strange looks. I have trouble keeping a thimble on, due to the time of day and the temperature. I dab my thimble finger with a glue stick. Works like a charm!

>>>>>>>>>>>>>>>>>>>>>>>>>>>>
Judith Clonan
Fitchburg, Massachusetts

- Machine piecing and chain stitching get quilt tops completed quicker. Of course, I always have handwork, either piecing or quilting...ready to pick up.

>>>>>>>>>>>>>>>>>>>>>>>>>>>>
Martha A. De Turk
Kutztown, Pennsylvania

- My rotary cutter, mat & plastic rulers have made cutting a breeze, saves time. I'd give up my dishwasher, and clothes dryer before my rotary cutter!
- Also love my *even-feed foot* when strip piecing directly on *fluff* or sewing several layers (with batting) for baby comforters.

Hints for better quilting, Page 173

Kathleen Nyman
Oswego, New York

- When I discovered strip piecing, I thought I'd died and gone to heaven. I couldn't believe how much time it saves.
- When I quilt a large section, if I can use more than one needle, I do - on borders, or grid work.

Virginia H. Flowers
Flushing, Michigan

- The rotary cutter and mat have speeded my piecing a lot. As has chaining at the sewing machine.
- I talk with other quilters for tips, read some, and watch TV Quilt Shows.

Anna Eelman
North Plainfield, New Jersey

- I keep my work handy so I can pick it up and put it down quickly. Even when only a couple of minutes can be spared.
- Keeping quilting books, materials and notions in one room helps a lot, when I'm looking for something.

Mary J. Ruda
Elida, Ohio

- I am learning to machine quilt.
- Use a rotary cutter.
- I take many different kinds of classes, anything that is offered in this part of Ohio-Indiana.

Barbara G. Pietila
Baltimore, Maryland

- I often use fusible thread for basting my shapes in place while I applique. I like this better than using fusible webs, because I use the needle turn method and I do not want the shapes fastened down out to the edges.
- I also like silk pins rather than any other, because they are fine and sharp. They do not pucker my work and are easy to handle, if they are left in the piece while I work.
- I have tried every type of thimble ever made and never found one which fits comfortably. I now use the metal thimble with the little well in the top but I take pliers and bend the thimble to fit my finger. I finally realized that thimbles are round and fingers are oval. There's no way to get a good fit. So now I custom fit them, and my finger suffers a lot less.
- I also use those little rubber finger stalls they use in banks and offices to count money and separate sheets of paper. You buy them in office supply stores. They are thicker than the finger cots they are now selling in quilt shops to protect your fingers, they come in different sizes, and they are a lot cheaper than the others.

Marcia Knopp
Bay City, Michigan

- I think our guild may have originated the fingercot used to grasp your needle. I used them in the office before gloves were universally worn and many of us, me included, wear one on the thumb and first finger of your *quilting* hand. It really allows you to pile the stitches on your needle, because the latex is "sticky", and you can grasp the needle easily to pull it through the fabric.

Susan J. Spencer
Felton, California

- Use your rotary cutter and bias square to square up your pieces at each stage of construction. It only takes a couple of minutes, but can save hours of frustration, when assembling the block into a quilt, since your blocks will be the same size.
- I do all my piecing on the machine, it really pays to keep your machine cleaned and oiled, and change the needle *often*. Since I *chain piece* a lot, I now keep a pile of pre-cut squares or triangles next to my machine to sew together in pairs, as *bridges* between the sewn squares of my project, 9-patch blocks, stars using half-square triangles, etc. (Most books suggest using scrap fabric for the *bridges*, but I kept losing my scraps, and decided it was a waste of time, this way, I'm ahead of the game, working on two projects at once!)
- Use a grapefruit spoon (with a serrated bowl) to help fasten safety pins when pin basting quilts - and unfasten them. It really saves your fingers.

Linda Boedigheimer
Perham, Minnesota

- I always carry zip lock baggies full of piecing projects in my purse or suitcase, for times I have to wait.
- I also organize my supplies in

various sized tackle boxes (my husband is a fisherman).

Bernice Tessibel Inman Cashman (Tessie)
Coal City, Indiana

• When threading a needle, knot the thread on the end where it is cut from the spool, this helps avoid knots when stitching.
• Use a tiny quilting needle when appliquing.
• I quilt without a hoop or frame by pinning the three layers together. I loosely baste the three layers together, then place the area I want to quilt in a hoop, straighten the fabric on the top and bottom of the quilt, and then closely pin. I then remove the hoop, and quilt. Baste around the outside edges of the quilt to prevent fraying of the batt.

Nancy Wagner Graves
Manhattan, Kansas

• Always have a sewing tin or baggie filled with a hand sewing project ready to grab as you go out the door. Make sure it contains thread, scissors, thimble, etc. You'd be amazed at how much you can get done while waiting at the doctor's, baseball games, music lessons, etc.
• I find that using a design wall is a great help. I pinned a flannel sheet up on one wall. When I'm trying to decide where to place the blocks, I rearrange them until I'm satisfied with it. I usually live with the arrangements 2 or 3 days before sewing together.

• I try to always have a quilt to quilt on. Every evening I try to quilt 2 hours. That way my fingers stay toughened up!
• I write down or sketch future quilt patterns I would like to do. Every time I go to a quilt show or guild meeting, I take my camera and take pictures of the quilts I like. When I need inspirations or an idea for a border or quilting pattern, I look through my pictures. It helps to see how other quilters have handled their design problems.
• I keep records of all the quilts I make. When I get finished with the quilt, I take a photo of it. I keep a notebook with the photo, size, date made, techniques used and why I made it. Also, name and if it won any awards.
• I usually have 3 or 4 projects going at a time (one quilt to piece, one to applique and one quilt to be quilted). That way when I run into a snag on one quilt, I just switch to another one.
• Storing Quilts: I have an extra bed and I lay the quilts out, face down on it. That way they don't fade or get creases.

Judi Robb
Manhattan, Kansas

• I always am working on 5 to 7 projects at the same time. (Some in the cutting stage, some in the piecing stage, some I work on in the car while traveling, etc.)
• Take as many workshops as come your way. You will always learn something that will make you a better quilter.

Eleanor Burenheide
Emporia, Kansas

• Keep your eyes and ears open to new and different ways that are faster and easier.
• Piece and Quilt with the electric needle (The Sewing Machine).
• When finished with a project, pile the leftover fabric. Children are fantastic sorters. They also fold neatly and can put it in the correct container. Besides, it's fun!
• Always have a lap project...READY TO GO...Even bagged with it's own scissors, thimble, etc.

Fanny Naught
Quincy, Illinois

• My quilt tips are not anything out of the ordinary. I do try to keep my sewing room in some reasonable order, with rulers where they can be found again, and other things in the proper place. I have a lawyer's oak stacked bookcase to put all my books and magazines in. I am looking for another one, as this one will soon be to capacity. It holds a lot of information, for no more floor space than it takes.

Catherine Litwinow
Davenport, Iowa

• All quilting is easy! I do *my quilting the* old-fashioned way, cutting out each piece individually, hand piecing and hand quilting, this way each quilt has a history. A lot can happen in my life, or the world during the year(s) it takes me to make a quilt. Much of this happening goes on the label on the back. I feel there is too much hurry, hurry in the world. The joy of touching each piece of fabric many times is a wonderful part of the quilt. There's too much hurry up in my work life. Quilting and piecing is *my* time to think, plan, wish, pray and relax. On days I wish to escape a book on tape is in the stereo - I at least get up and change tapes every 30 minutes. I've make enough quilts already to leave a little of me to the next 100 years and future generations.

Since I work so slowly and there are so many quilts to make, I am passionate about purchasing antiques. Most of the purchases have occurred when shopping with dear quilting friends.

>>>>>>>>>>>>>>>>>>>>>>>>>>>>>>

Betty Rushin
Boulder Creek,
California

- My favorite tip for quick quiltmaking is use your favorite color, if you use your favorite color you won't become bored with your project and you will finish. You can also carry small applique projects around with you and work on them while you wait.
- Try cutting your applique shapes out of freezer paper, freezer paper gives you a hard edge to needle turn your applique seam allowances against.
- When I give advice to new quilt makers, I always tell them to use the best quality tools, get a good rotary cutter, good rulers, and learn to draft their own patterns, because if you have good tools, you cut out the frustration factor and it saves you time and angst.

>>>>>>>>>>>>>>>>>>>>>>>>>>>>>>

M. Jeanne Poore
Overland Park,
Kansas

- Use THE RIGHT TOOLS. If you are going to hand quilt, use the right batting, needles, thread. It makes your work go faster, you get more done and are much happier with the results. If the needle bends, get a new one. If it gets dull or drags through the quilt, get a new one.
- Always cut the quilting thread at an angle to make threading the needle easier. Wet the eye of the needle to make for easier threading--this is also true of your sewing machine needles (lick your finger and rub it over the eye of the sewing machine needle, and it is easier to thread).
- Men know the importance of good tools, keeping them in good working order. That is true of quilting--use good tools, keep your machine cleaned and oiled. Keep scissors and cutters sharp.
- Use good fabric.
- Go to shows and take classes, workshops. The shows will inspire you and the classes/workshops teach you techniques. I've never gone to a class/workshop that I haven't learned something that will make the quiltmaking process either easier or more enjoyable.
- When the children are very young, you have to make time for quiltmaking that is separate. But when they get older, they enjoy helping select fabrics, using the scraps for play--a glue stick and scraps can be turned into fun pictures--and girls making doll quilts.
- I have given my sorority secret sister a wall hanging each year depicting either their family members (gloves with children's' names), to pets or something of particular interest to them.
- I also like to make gift bags of fabric--it is reusable or they can use it for storage. I have given pin cushions, thumb cushions, label pins, spool holders and thimble pins as gifts. Because quilters are creative and have all those wonderful scraps, small gifts such as those mentioned are economical to give and personal--I believe more appreciated than purchased items.
- I organize my stash (incidentally, my husband calls my fabric my RAGS) by color in large boxes--that is my quilting fabric--such as big totes, see-thru plastic preferably. I also have clothing fabric and that is usually by type--denim, blouse, pre-quilted. That is stored on shelves. I also have some project boxes which contain fabrics and patterns for the project (sometimes a UFO) so it is all together till finished. I clearly label the boxes on all sides.
- My small scraps are kept in plastic bags by color. I use my small scraps for gift items, blocks for exchanges and give a piece of everything to a friend who is collecting to do a postage stamp quilt of 1" squares.
- A group I quilt with, called the Legler Barn Quilters, made Quilter's Jam this last year as part of the Spinach Festival activities (cut-up scraps, put in a jelly jar, put a fabric cap on it) so I used up some of my scraps for that.
- I keep my threads on a large peg board in the sewing corner of the wall above a counter my husband built, where my sewing

machines are set. My books I keep on shelves, my magazines organized in large loose leaf notebooks that are labeled. My rulers are kept in a decorated popcorn tin (the 7 to 10 gallon size) that has been lined with fabric, that I can either set on the floor or on the table where I do my cutting.

•By the way, my cutting table is a regulation size pocket billiard table that I have put the cardboard cutting board on with the cutting mat on top of it. It is a better height for me which makes it easier on my back. My sister-in-law, Peggy Poore, used a card table with Crisco cans under each of the legs for a while, until her brother made her a cutting table with the right height.

•As far as what I do to protect my fingers--I have to feel the needle underneath and so far nothing I have tried works any better than just building up a callus. I've tried tape (which is what my grandmothers would do occasionally), on a plastic thimble. If my one finger gets sore, I switch to another. The liquid bandage products give some protection.

•I try to have a carry along project--small quilting items or parts of large quilts. I have a yo-yo quilt that I finished in 1989 that has 3,989 yo-yo's in it. I started it in the 70's--parts were done on trips, in doctors and dentist offices, ball games and waiting for kids in car pools. I also have a cathedral window. Parts of it have been in California, Hawaii, Kansas, Missouri, Arkansas, Iowa and Nevada. I have met some interesting people while traveling because of these projects. They come up to you, tell you about their families and their lives. Quilting has opened doors for me, given me the opportunity to meet people from all over the country as well as other countries. I can't think of a nicer way to have made the friendships I have than through quilting.

•*Not new tip*, but tried and true - keep a scrap of fabric under foot with needle in, use it to begin sewing project, especially great for strip piecing and chaining - and - use at end of stitching - keeps thread from knotting up under the machine and keeps machine from "eating" the material. It always saves on thread - uses less.

•One of the things I do, that I haven't seen or read about anywhere else, is to wrap any binding I have left from a project around an empty thread spool. I place a small note in hole of spool that gives the yardage - usually in inches, the size and whether it is bias or not, like "63", 3" wide bias binding. It is easier to do at the time and then when I need bindings, or smaller projects - wall quilts or gift items - I know exactly what I have already.

>>>>>>>>>>>>>>>>>>>>>>>>>>>>>>>

Phyllis Hansen Gierach
Madera, California

•I keep my fabrics sorted by color and then by value, or intensity. When possible, I cut left over fabrics into strips and store them in plastic containers by size. I use 1 1/2", 2", 2 1/2", and 3" wide strips that are cut as long as possible. My favorite tool, of course, is the rotary cutter and acrylic rulers, and I have several sizes of them, as well as triangles and squares. I use an engineer's triangle for finding the cross grain of the fabric.

•My other suggestion may be difficult to accomplish, but marrying an engineer is a great help for quilters! I loved geometry in high school and use it a lot, but some of the formulas, such as finding a square root of two had become pretty fuzzy.

•When finding the size of a triangle needed when turning quilt blocks on point, I measure one side of the square and then divide that number by 1.414 and that will give you the size of the square you need to cut, and then you cut the square once diagonally. This will give you the 45 degree triangle needed to sew on each side of your square, to frame your quilt square with triangles. When I still operated the quilt store and was attending trade shows, my husband would occasionally accompany me, and it was really amazing to see how many other engineer husbands were there. I haven't figured out why quilters are attracted to engineers, but there has to be a compatibility factor in there somewhere.

•Presently, I am learning to use my computer for designing quilts. In the past I always used large graph papers.

•I also like to use freezer paper when doing applique projects, but also just do needle turn applique, if the project calls for it.

≈≈≈≈≈≈≈≈≈≈≈≈≈≈≈≈≈≈≈≈≈≈≈≈≈

Doris Callaway,
Greensburg, Kansas

•I usually buy 3 yards of a given material - so I'll be sure and have enough to complete a project. I store my fabrics in a cabinet - with all the same colors together.

Julie L. Kimberlin
Anchorage, Alaska

• I don't look for quilting to be *quicker & easier*. Part of my enjoyment of the art is the process of getting from beginning to end. I'm an advocate of hand-quilting. I thoroughly enjoy it.

Doris Haggard
Topeka, Kansas

• I have a busy box next to my chair in front of the TV, so my hands are very busy. I'm ready to cut and piece the green paths around my second hand pieced flower garden. I rotary cut the strips, draw on the octagons and then using a small ruler, cut off the corners. The prints I used for these 2 quilts are from the 1940's. I bought a box at an auction several years ago. It took me several years to collect enough solid colors to go with them. I really enjoy the older fabric and look forward to finding an estate sale with fabric listed.
• I keep my stash of fabric in cardboard boxes that reams of copy paper has come in. I write on the ends of the boxes, what is the contents.
• I believe quilting is about friendship, as well as fabric.
• For baby comforters, I look for printed fabric with repeat pattern that has a design that can be knotted every 4 to 6 inches, in the same design and doesn't have to be marked. One can be done in an afternoon. I use the 2 1/2" bias binding folded, machine-stitched on top and hand stitched on the bottom. Our quilt club made some of these for the local police cars.

Sheryl Mielke
McGregor, Iowa

• I like to use freezer paper in my applique to acquire a smooth edge. An inch before I finish a piece, I stop and pull the freezer paper out from the front with tweezers. I feel cutting a slit and removing the paper from the back weakens the quilt.
• Another hint I would like to pass along is the use of spray sizing. All my material is 100% cotton and washed before any use for color fastness. When you want sharp points, like on a Mariner's Compass, iron spray sizing back on your material and those points are easier to do.

Charlotte Fry
St. Charles, Missouri

• Of course the rotary cutter and mat have been a God-send. Just think how many unfinished tops there would be out there, if our mothers and grandmothers would have the tools we have today. I still use an old Singer from 1950. I find I don't need a fancy machine for what I do.
• I do a lot of applique and find using freezer paper makes it easier, but I iron it on the front, that way I don't have to cut the back to remove the paper and I don't have to reverse my design.

Helen M. Ericson
Emporia, Kansas

• People say they don't have the time or patience to make a quilt: I tell them that it is the desire to do so that counts.
• Any quiet time can be used to sketch layouts to make a quilt more *yours* than the pattern indicated.
• Learn to draft patterns to test ones printed, or ones from magazine patterns: do not be discouraged if it does not go together exactly as the paper plan, as often the quilt is more *rememberable* for the problem solved.
• I used to machine piece, but now do it, and all quilting, by-hand.
• I use a cutter for border pieces, but still draw a pencil line for stitching.
• Quilting designs that can be done from a few dots and masking tape, or cut-out paper design pinned on, will make a cleaner quilt, and you will have saved the time of marking it on.

Linda Ballard
Palo Cedro, California

• I like to pre-wash fabrics right away, so I can sew when I'm ready and not wait for the laundry.
• When I store my fabric, I have the piece folded into 4 layers (selvage to selvage, then one more fold), then *fan fold* or "accordion fold" the piece. When you start to cut, the piece just *peels* off, making it more manageable.

Carol L. Robbins
Overland Park, Kansas

• The rotary cutter is my favorite tool! My scissors are ALMOST obsolete!
• Having a small balloon (deflated) close by helps immensely in pulling the needle thru difficult areas.
• I always use beeswax on my thread to make it stronger and easier to handle (less tangles).

Beth Donaldson
Lansing, Michigan

• My favorite time saving tip is to slow down. When I am patient and relaxed, I make fewer errors and produce better quilts. It is like the tortoise and the hare. The time I lose by cutting and sewing accurately, I make up for when it is time to put the top together. I spend no time trimming blocks or fudging things together. I am less frustrated and more relaxed. Even the parts of quilting I hate (like basting), I just take a deep breath and work through. After all, I am choosing to make quilts, no one is forcing me and so I have decided I am no longer going to race myself. I savor the time I have to make my quilts.

Shannon Royer
Otis, Kansas

• There are a few little things that I have come across that combine recycling and quilting: Used dryer sheets make great stabilizer for machine applique, (and) trace your block design with permanent pen for foundation piecing.
• Old toothbrushes usually get delegated for cleaning. I turn mine into a multi-purpose quilter's tool, by cutting off the head with wire cutters and sanding the cut end at an angle. I've used this for holding seam allowances as I sew, turning sharp corners, and stuffing small pieces - it works great and the bright colors are easy to find!

Betty A. Lenz
Marshall, Missouri

• I try all things others tell me. I was very slow to go to rotary cutting, now it's the *only* way.
• I have been working for some time with foundation piecing, mainly paper, and intend to use it much more in what I'm doing in the future. I feel good about the finished product when it's foundation construction.

Tedi Lambert
Los Banos, California

• For teaching quilting, my computer has proven invaluable. I have a place which is hard to lose, in which I store my *lessons*, patterns, etc.
• For storage of stencils, I use a clothing rack and pants hangers, which have clips on them to "hang" them up in my sewing room. The larger ones won't warp and the smaller ones don't get lost.
• I keep a small set of shelves next to my sewing table, to hold such things as buttons, fabric paints, current project, etc.
• I store the majority of my sewing miscellaneous in a chest of drawers. They are kept neat and out of sight.
• Fabric is stored on a large shelving unit.
• I use a large cork bulletin board for a table top to which I pin my blocks which are all laid out in their proper sequence. This way when I'm interrupted, I'm less likely to lose my place or my pieces!

Michelle Hazelhoff
Mt. Evelyn, Vic Australia

• I use my time productively. I find there are many shortcuts available in the form of tools and methods. The rotary cutter I think, is the best thing since sliced bread, and I use the strip piecing method wherever possible and leave templates for my masterpiece projects.
• Accuracy and precision are probably the most important things. For instance, binding and quilting before you applique gives the quilt a much better look, and seems to make placement of applique pieces easier.
• A walking foot is another great tool of the quilter, it can make such a difference in piecing. Chain sewing, which is feeding through one piece after another, is a great thread and time saver also.

Netta Ranney
Overland Park, Kansas

• Strip piecing, chain stitching, and an ironing board at right angles to the sewing machine.
• Rotary cutters are next best thing to sliced bread for speed

and accuracy.

• I always use a small double strip of fabric to start sewing on the machine when chain piecing, then snip it off and use it to end off. This saves time and thread and you don't have to keep re-threading the needle.

>>>>>>>>>>>>>>>>>>>>>>>>>>>>>>
Karen Crosby
Ocala, Florida

• When you have finished cutting out a project, cut the remaining fabric into strips. (I cut 2 1/2") or square (6 1/2"). This way you are all ready for most scrap quilts, and these are much easier to store.

>>>>>>>>>>>>>>>>>>>>>>>>>>>>>>
Pat Reep
Bakersfield, California

• I keep quilt blocks or whatever I am sewing, in readiness at the sewing machine, hence if I have only a spare 10 minutes or so, I am ready to accomplish something. It is at these spare minutes that I rewind bobbins, cut a few strips of cloth needed for a project, or take care of general busy work.

• I have found the self-stick pages in photo albums to be very useful. I keep a record of fabric used in each quilt by putting small amounts of fabric on a page. When I am lacking particular colors for a future project, I insert pieces of fabric that I am contemplating on one of these pages, and take it with me to the fabric store to aid in my selection. The pieces remain in place and are easy to handle. In searching for new and different color schemes and when I have a block of time, I play with fabric, compiling color combinations I like and put them on photo pages for future reference.

• I have made several lap boards in various sizes, which I use constantly. I use a small 11x13" lap board for hand-piecing while I am watching TV. Other sizes include a 16x16" board to hold the fabric pieces in place while machine-sewing, and larger boards (i.e., 24x24" and 36x36") for objective viewing of quilts in progress. This procedure is employed for smaller works when my larger wall surface is not necessary. In constructing my lap boards, I use core foam board for the foundation, wrap them with batting and then cover with muslin.

• I have also made a "mini-ironing board" which resides on my sewing table. It is a square of 1/2" plywood constructed in similar fashion to the lap boards, save for a thicker batting between the board and muslin wrapping. It is extremely useful and handy when pressing seams and individual blocks.

>>>>>>>>>>>>>>>>>>>>>>>>>>>>>>
Helen King
Horton, Kansas

• Color is SO deceptive. Most of you who work with quilts have discovered to your sorrow that white isn't necessarily WHITE! Watch the shades of other colors. We recently wanted RED. We found orangy red, red red, maroon red, and a red that went to the purple. In the store, before you buy, ask the clerk to take the bolt to the doorway, into daylight. That is the only way to know the true shade of the material. Fluorescent and incandescent bulbs come in various tones. What looks right under artificial light might be totally wrong when you get home. Save yourself some grief. ALWAYS check this.

• Another hazard is fabric content. Only by READING the END of the BOLT can you be sure. I can usually tell blends of wool and cotton, rayon and cotton, but I CANNOT detect some of the polyester blends.

• I believe I know why many quilt makers like applique better than patchwork. With patchwork, you are always working on the wrong side, the unlovely side of the material. Also, there is more creative opportunity with applique. I heard another reason why a person might prefer applique to patchwork. The gal said, "Patchwork is such an exact skill. With applique, if corners don't meet, I can slap on a leaf and people will say I'm creative!"

• Yes, you can make a quilt with drapery samples. Use the shape of the sample for your block. Stitch together, alternating light and dark pieces, but with no attempt to match colors. Go to a bedspread size, if you can. Whether you have this product machine quilted or hand tied (it would be almost impossible to hand quilt this) do not attempt to use a batt or filler. It just gets too heavy to handle, to wash, and the spread won't cuddle around the body in the bed. It just sits its weight on top and these drafts go up each side and feel awful. (Guess how I learned this!)

• Sometimes a little bit added with a bit more can cause a real trouble. I'm thinking of the WIDTH OF A PENCIL LEAD when you allow seams on a pattern. Then again you need to see around the pattern, so there's a bit more, now you're up to a 1/16th of an inch. The

Page 180, Hints for better quilting

pattern pieces may have 8 joinings. What have you got? You have added 8/16 of an inch, that's 1/2" wider and 1/2 inch longer than you expected! Frightening, isn't it?

•If for instance, you are working for 12 1/2" to finish at 12" in a sampler quilt, (each different), and your block turns out 13", you have a problem! If you are just repeating a pattern, say for 20 or 30 for a quilt top, this isn't so important. Still it is worth thinking about.

•A new item I've seen for crafted comfort. Make a "throw", patch-worked and quilted, about a yard square. Fold it into a matching square bag, with a soft handle, and Velcro fastener. Use it in the car as a little cushion. If the air conditioner causes a draft, whip out the square and use it as a draft deflector.

•So you've agreed to "finish up" a quilt for a friend. When figuring the costs of materials you have "on hand", remember - it's not what it cost you, but rather how much it will cost to REPLACE what you used, that must be figured. Fabric and thread are so expensive in today's market place. Use the above advice to figure on quilts you make for sale, also.

>>>>>>>>>>>>>>>>>>>>>>>>>>>>>
Gladys Shook
Hutchinson, Kansas

•If you should ever have to eradicate a seam, it is easier if you cut about every 5th thread on the top thread side of the stitch. Continue for the length you need to remove, then simply pull the bobbin thread, and your seam will come undone! This prevents any raveling that might occur on the edge.

•When hand sewing and finishing your seams - after you have made a knot, take another small stitch in the fabric and come out a short distance away from the knot. Clip the thread, then this will prevent an end on the knot.

•Two technical skills, which are the basis of quilting, are cutting a straight line and sewing a straight seam. Quiltmaking must be done with accurate measurements, precision cutting, and avoiding speed sewing. Always remember the 5 P's. **Prior Planning Produces Perfect Performance!** (A positive approach to the old adage prior planning prevents poor performance!)

•Cross cutting your strip pieced fabric when it needs to be made into a tube - turn fabric wrong side out and tape the sides with drafting tape. Write the width of your cut piece on the tape.

•Remember above everything else, to always autograph your quilt. Artists always sign paintings, and you should be no different. The time, work, expense and most of all, love, that has gone into your project deserves your thumb print. To prevent anyone from removing a label from the quilt, I always sew my information directly into the lining before quilting.

>>>>>>>>>>>>>>>>>>>>>>>>>>>>>
Joan Waldman
Platte Center, Nebraska

•Design your quilts to please yourself. Don't be afraid to break the rules. There really are no rules, only what you want to do. Use colors and fabrics that please you, and don't let anyone else's opinion bother you. These are YOUR quilts and YOUR opinion is really all that matters.

•When cutting strips for a quilt, put them over a plastic hanger. Hang the hanger from a long peg on a peg board or use a clothes rack. This keeps the strips from wrinkling and keeps them in order.

•Pin baste a quilt using a plastic serrated knife to close the pins.

•To keep an inventory of your *stash*, cut a small square of each fabric as you bring it home. Tape it in a notebook by color. Add the amount purchased and where you got it. When you need a certain color fabric, look in the notebook and you will know instantly if you have what you need, and also how much you have. If you use part of a yardage, subtract it from your notebook. If you use all the fabric, take the swatch out and cross out yardage.

•Explore garage sales and thrift shops. You will find yardages, patterns, books and even quilt tops and blocks. Also check out auctions.

>>>>>>>>>>>>>>>>>>>>>>>>>>>>>
Edith O. McGhee
Mercer, Pennsylvania

•I have made myself learn to use my sewing machine, almost to it's fullest potential. I do as much of the work on a quilt by machine, as possible. While I have done quite a bit of machine quilting, I still feel that nothing can replace the look of a hand quilted quilt.

Hints for better quilting, Page 181

Teresa Binder
Emporia, Kansas

• Always keep a project ready to work on. I try to have applique, piecing, quilting and thinking projects ready, so whatever I am in the mood for, there is something to do.
• Keep a tin or basket by the phone, in the car and by your favorite chair with handwork in it. A few minutes waiting or visiting with friends is prime sewing time.
• Let several items accumulate at the iron and sewing machine. When you turn either one on you can accomplish several things at one time.

Barbara Clukey
Carriere, Mississippi

• One favorite quiltmaking tip that I would like to share is this: Experience the joy of your own creativity and do not be bound by what other quilters might do or think. Express your own sense of color and design and you will love what you are creating.

Helen P. Johnston
Bowie, Maryland

• B.C. (before computer) I had so many great inspirations from my mountain of quilting magazines and books, that when I wanted to make a project I'd seen, it would take me forever to find it. A.D. (after database) I can easily look up any articles that interest me or projects I want to do.
• Examine each magazine or book. Decide how best to categorize it. For example: with Quilter's Newsletter, my database contains headings like _article, applique, pieced, series quilts, then & now, and possibilities_. It's easy to plug titles and page numbers in the appropriate columns. It takes time and my job is only half done, but as I began working on my Baltimore Album Quilt, it was very easy to locate articles and pictures published throughout the years.
• A flannel wall has also become indispensable. It has helped me on colors, and keep correct piecing order. My _wall_ is just a large section of flannel tacked up. Nothing fancy. I've seen patterns for some elaborate ones but mine seems to work fine.
• I have a traveling project bag that I can pick up on my way out the door to a soccer game or the pool. Everything I need for a hand piecing or applique project is in the bag. These are _back-burner_ projects. Some of them take years to complete, but I'm always doing something while riding in the car or sitting by the pool.

Marcene Gunter
Hillsboro, Kansas

• Cut out all the pieces for a quilt at the same time. Do as much sewing of the same kind or method, while you are in that part. Do not jump from one thing to another while you are sewing. Have everything ready. Wash fabric as soon as you bring it home so it is ready to use.

DeEtta Beebe
Waters, Michigan

• Find a spot all your own - no matter how small - organize it, and create when the moment arises, walk away and return without disrupting others or your need of daily living.
• Share your joy with other family members, teach them a new discovery - they, in turn, share in your hobby - this adds up to family life and does not take away.

Roxanne H. McElroy
Mililani, Hawaii

• Keep your needles and scissors sharp.
• Always use your thimble and persevere.
• By machine standards, I am slow. For a hand-quilter, I am speedy!

LaRue Nuest
South Hutchinson, Kansas

• When I am reading a quilting magazine and run across an article about some subject I'm particularly interested in and think I may want to refer to it later; or find a pattern or project that I may want to make at some time, instead of cutting out the article or tearing out a page in the magazine, I photocopy the article or pattern and place it in a file labeled with the subject. The largest file I have is labeled _Quilts I want to Make_. I also set up files labeled with the names of teachers I have taken workshops from, then when I

Page 182, Hints for better quilting

want to refer back to something that teacher taught, I just go to that file. Guess this probably comes from being a business teacher for so many years. A place for everything and everything in it's place!

• Many of the meals I prepare, I plan the whole meal to go in the oven so that I can spend more time quilting, instead of hovering over the stove while the meal is cooking. We also eat many casseroles that can be prepared ahead and put in the oven.

>>>>>>>>>>>>>>>>>>>>>>>>>>>>>>
Carole Flasch
Weslaco, Texas

• I'm learning to machine quilt and it's wonderful, gets the quilts finished so much faster. It takes as much practice as learning to hand quilt. This is a whole new learning experience for me and I'm getting better with each project I make.

>>>>>>>>>>>>>>>>>>>>>>>>>>>>>>
Betty J. Knack
Essexville, Michigan

• I love to quilt on an old-fashioned frame. Using a sharp new needle. Good scissors, rulers, lights, and the Good Lord be with you.

>>>>>>>>>>>>>>>>>>>>>>>>>>>>>>
Janet P. Wyckoff
Hopewell, New Jersey

• What I have to offer is experience in working with fancy fabrics on a muslin foundation. Buy clothing and men's ties at yard sales and rummage sales - bag day is great - and buy *good* quality satins and velvets when you shop at fabric stores.

>>>>>>>>>>>>>>>>>>>>>>>>>>>>>>
Judy Wolfrom
Southampton, New Jersey

• A requirement for my students to bring to class is new, fine sandpaper. I glue 2 pieces to the inside of calendar covers, this closes up and slips into a tote with ease. Also, fabric pieces for making a block can lay out inside this for traveling, without getting scrambled.

• On my quilting-hand fingers while quilting, I wear 2 things. On *tall man* goes my thimble with the ridge around the top as Sue Rodgers taught me; and on my *pointer* goes the 1 1/4 inch tip cut off a long, narrow balloon. This balloon helps grip the needle to pull it through the fabric layers.

• Most of the patterns I have made and/or used, are slipped into sheet protectors. These are see-through and act as a pocket for storage in 3-ring binders.

>>>>>>>>>>>>>>>>>>>>>>>>>>>>>>
Maria Lage
Cumberland, Rhode Island

• Applique is my favorite technique, but instead of hand basting the seam allowance the traditional way, I use the following method: Trace the applique design onto freezer paper and cut it out on the pencil line. Pin the freezer paper, shiny side up to the wrong side of the applique fabric. Cut the applique, adding 1/4" wide seam allowance around the outside of the freezer paper. Use the tip of the iron to press the applique seam allowance onto the shiny side of the freezer paper. Apply pressure to make the fabric adhere to the paper.

• Clip concave curves to within one to two threads of the paper. The more clips, the smoother the curves. After the applique is stitched in place, remove the freezer paper by cutting away the background fabric behind the applique, leaving a 1/4" side seam allowance or background fabric all around, inside the stitching.

• When machine piecing and quilting, I like to spray starch all the fabrics. They stitch better and make cutting and marking easier.

• I use fine silk pins for pinning. This is a long, thin sharp pin that leaves no hump and I can sew over it without difficulty.

• I like to use a copy machine for reducing and enlarging designs. I like to do my own patterns, and using a copier is a great time saver.

>>>>>>>>>>>>>>>>>>>>>>>>>>>>>>
Nancy H. Ehinger
West Branch, Michigan

• The rotary cutter has been the greatest time-saver invented. It makes light the job of cutting out a quilt.

>>>>>>>>>>>>>>>>>>>>>>>>>>>>>>
Patricia L. Carl
Rhinebeck, New York

• I take time every day to prepare fabrics for hand-piecing that evening. Amazing how quickly piecing goes when the mind is occupied with music, conversation or listening to TV.

Lassie Wittman
Rochester, Washington

(Continued from page 158)

• When I first learned about Seminole Patchwork in 1975, I was impressed with the speed and efficiency of the technique. Being a dress maker, this was right up my alley.

• I tear my strips (from selvage to selvage) when I am doing Seminole and using poly/cotton blends, the reasons for this are: it is fast, fabric is on grain, and Indians do it and I learned this work before all this wonderful cutting equipment was available. I am more a patchworker than a quilter.

Author's Note: I met Lassie at Paducah where she had a booth in the Kentucky Oaks Mall. We found we had a lot in common and became *friends from a distance*. I knew I had Lassie's *Wittman Shirt Pattern*, but was surprised after I got back home to discover that one of the earliest books I had purchased on quilting was Lassie's wonderful book on Seminole Patchwork. It's been much used!

Marilyn T. Guy
Delhi, New York

• I think I have learned when starting a quilt, to make one block and then do all the cutting. If I have pieces to cut, I can sew them together quickly. If I have to stop to cut more, it seems to take a lot longer and I hate doing it. I use no thimble on my left hand, but when my finger gets sore, I use black electrical tape. Aunt Becky's thimble works pretty good for me, too. I rarely baste anymore.

• When sandwiching a quilt, I do it at the church where our group meets. I tape the backing to the tables, then batting and top. Then I use MANY small safety pins. I leave them all open until I'm finished and close them all at once. I saw that on a TV show.

Lynn Graves
Albuquerque, New Mexico

• Invest in the best equipment, it makes your quilting life easier, and the finished product better.

Alba Lee Elliott
Asheville, North Carolina

• The things I enjoy working with most are: categories, animals, figures, flowers and color.

Ruth Powers
Carbondale, Kansas

• Take the time to do it right. Taking out mistakes or trying to match seams that are not accurate only takes up more time in the long run. Because my sewing machine is computerized, I use a seam guide that is made of a little strip of adhesive foam for padding shoes. It is easily removable when it's in the way, and is cheap to replace when necessary.

• When I do make a mistake, I don't waste time pondering what to do about it. I used to do that and always ended up taking it apart and fixing it anyway. So now, if I find a mistake, I just fix it right away. Saves time and worry.

Carolyn Koopman
Carnavillo, Iowa

• When doing intricate piecing, I find spray starching the fabric first, sure makes the piecing easier.

Emily Laubaugh
Gladstone, Oregon

• The only hint I can think of was given to our group by our senior member, Thelma Pierson (our Scrap Queen). She suggests that you use a deflated balloon to pull your needle thru if it gets stuck. Thelma has made some of the most beautiful quilts without even venturing into a fabric store. She is our jewel!

Norma Jean Rector
Center Point, Indiana

• I have a quilting lamp - one with an adjustable arm, that is a big help to me as I do a good bit of my quilting at night.

• I use a soap sliver (I like a piece of Ivory soap) to mark any quilting lines on dark material of my quilts.

• Our son, Kenny, who is a carpenter, made me a sewing

table, 32"x60", from a sheet of plywood with a laminated top. It is a drop leaf table, that can be dropped back against the wall when not is use. It has been so helpful in cutting, sewing, etc.

>>>>>>>>>>>>>>>>>>>>>>>>>>>>>>
Betty Verhoeven
East Jewett, New York

- For me, one of the most important things to have, is a cutting table that's the right height. It really saves strain on your back. Another back saver is a good sewing chair, one that's comfortable and gives good support.
- There are a lot of great new products for quilters. I love the rotary cutters and mats and rulers, what a time saver, and the cuts are so much more accurate. The marking pens and pencils that are available are terrific, too.
- My gripe however, is with the straight pins. Does anyone know of a good, long straight pin whose head won't pop off when you pull it from fabric?

>>>>>>>>>>>>>>>>>>>>>>>>>>>>>>
Suzanne K. Roy
Newkirk, Oklahoma

- One of my favorite tools is the rotary cutter. The first time I saw one, I couldn't imagine anyone even wanting one. Since that time, I've found myself using it for all kinds of sewing when making clothes.
- I substitute my rulers and cutter for square and rectangular clothing pattern pieces.
- They also make great substitutes for a paper cutter. I do use an old blade.

>>>>>>>>>>>>>>>>>>>>>>>>>>>>>>
Margaret Kooda
Idaho Falls, Idaho

- My solution to the time crunch is to not wait for an extended period of time to come along. I cut out a block or project one day, and then over the next week, when I have a half hour free, I am ready to sit down and sew.

>>>>>>>>>>>>>>>>>>>>>>>>>>>>>>
Betty J. Pribil
Portland, Oregon

- When I got a pair of Gingher scissors, I thought that was the ultimate. Then came the Olfa Cutter and Pad, and Fiskars Cutter and all the rulers. The serger has been a great time saver, particularly when sandwiching quilts the envelope way. You not only sew, but you trim at the same time.

>>>>>>>>>>>>>>>>>>>>>>>>>>>>>>
Alyce C. Kauffman
Gridley, California

- Have a peg board to hold rulers, glue gun, rotary cutter, extra blades, etc.
- Put items back in their place after each use.
- At first, I stacked fabrics by color only. Frustration caused me to re-organize. I now stack all fabric by:

1. Size: 1/4 yd, 1/2 yd, 1 yd, etc.
2. Color in applicable sizes.

Now, if I need a 1/2 yd of blue, I can instantly check to see if color needed is in my stash.
- Buy fabrics in at least 1/2 yard to 1 yd pieces, unless a lesser amount is required for a specific project.
- A most helpful hint is a water bottle for filling the steam iron. I use a *clean* liquid dish soap container and fill. The top pushes down to close tight. No chance of spilled water. It's also dust free, and very transportable for classes, workshops, etc.
- I also use a fabric material made especially for ironing to take to classes, so I can wrap my warm or hot iron in it, and know all is safe.
- I have made a tote bag using the fabric the size of my iron and can slide it inside. Be sure to put the pressing side of fabric to the inside.
- My projects in progress (PIP's) are stored in plastic (clean) shoe boxes with a 3x5" index card at the front listing the project in the container. A brief description, etc. can be listed on the backside of the card.
- To avoid going through Quilt magazines, I use a Xerox machine to copy the index and file in a binder with separations. Any quilt, wall hanging, etc. that tends to interest me, is highlighted before filing.
- Another long term time saver is to list all patterns (that are in quilt books) on 3x5" index cards. Include book title and page number. File by pattern name, such as Drunkard's Path, Better Homes and Garden, page 94. I also list block size, like: 8", 10", 12", etc.

>>>>>>>>>>>>>>>>>>>>>>>>>>>>>>
Julie Fox
Blackwell, Oklahoma

- Rotary Cutter and Mat.
- Having my own room for quilting.

Hints for better quilting, Page 185

Pamela T. Young
Minot Air Force Base, North Dakota

• Being organized is the key. I used to waste valuable time hunting for tools or just the right color thread. I have a thread rack hanging on the wall and all my tools are very accessible. My fabric is stored by color and all my other supplies have their own place. Rummaging through boxes is time consuming and it breaks up your creativity. I attended a lecture by Crystal Carter and she gave us many tips on how to train yourself to be creative. Being organized is one of them.

• Another important tip she gave us was to surround yourself with things that inspire you; pictures with color combinations you enjoy, batches of fat quarters, work in progress hanging on the wall, so that you can look at it and think about it.

• I also sew as many things as I can at once, eliminating needless trips to the ironing board after every seam. I call this *chain sewing*. I remember being in Home Economics class in Junior High School and going to the ironing board with a chain of pieces; a sleeve attached to the leg that was attached to the collar, etc. My teacher almost had a heart attack.

• My *specialty* is hand quilting. It is the part of the quilting process that I like the best.

• I teach hand quilting classes and the one thing women always complain about is the awkwardness of the thimble. Here is a tip for people who are uncomfortable with using a thimble; Try wearing your thimble on your finger all day. In the shower, while washing dishes, eating lunch, driving the car, by the end of the day it will feel like an extension of your finger and not like a foreign object.

Ella May Reusser
Blackwell, Oklahoma

• The rotary cutter and cutting board saves a lot of time. Strip piecing is also much faster.

Jean Ann Eitel
Marietta, Georgia

• I never use scissors when a rotary cutter will work.
• I have a child's ironing board and a small travel iron right next to my sewing machine so I can press each seam as I sew without getting up.
• I pre-cut log cabin strips (1 1/2" wide) and different geometric pieces (in 2" size increments, such as 2" and 4" squares, triangles, etc.) for quilt blocks and store them by size in plastic containers. When I am ready to make a scrap quilt the pieces are cut and ready to sew. This saves hours of time in unfolding fabric, cutting pieces, then refolding fabrics when I am hot to sew. I like to make scrap quilts the most to discover the play of one fabric against another when putting them together in traditional quilt blocks.

Etta Grace Edwards
Council Grove, Kansas

• The only thing that may be different I have done is: we had a large upright freezer and I didn't need it anymore for food, so I collected those clear plastic refrigerator drawers and stacked my material upright in them. Now, all I have to do is pull out a drawer and there is the material I need. The freezer is located near my sewing area. My notions and patterns are in the small shelves in the door.

• Happy quilting to you all, and may God enrich all your lives. Thank you, Joyce, for all your love and concern and here's to this book!

Janice A. Miller
Jaffrey, New Hampshire

• I find that marking the actual template on the back of the material and then stitching on the lines is the most accurate method of piecing.

• When appliquing, I do it one of two ways. I either draw on top of the material and then needle turn the narrow edges, or I apply freezer paper to the front of the material and then needle turn under the upper.

Pauline A. Cook
Idaho Falls, Idaho

• After gathering all my materials and templates for a quilt project, I put them in a Jumbo ziplock bag for wall hanging size or smaller, or in a clear plastic storage box for bed size quilt projects. It's easy to carry your project from cutting area to sewing area. I also use sticky labels to keep track of sizes of squares, triangles and strips.

Pat Campbell
Rigby, Idaho

• Having the right tool certainly makes each job easier. I try to purchase the tools I need for each job, as I do it. I don't have room to hang up my rulers, etc., so I have a shelf where I put them, they always go directly back to the shelf at the end of a project. That way, I *always* know where my tools are.

Sally Smith
Kodak, Tennessee

• A piece of tape and the end of fingers from a rubber glove are two of my best quilting helps. The tape (preferably masking) on my hand kept under the quilt keeps the pricks down, while the piece of rubber glove helps pull the needle through.

Christine Klinger
Fayetteville, Arkansas

• Quiltmaking began as a hobby and grew to become a significant interest in my life. I am not particularly concerned with making quilting quicker or easier, great things take time. Rather, I have learned from quiltmaking to slow down, appreciate life, and try to do things that you have a passion for. This philosophy in turn, has led me to resign from a stressful, unsatisfying job. Quiltmaking has taught me to take risks.

Mary Lou Kantz Evans
Flagstaff, Arizona

• Best tip I can give is to take classes and read a lot of books on quilting, so you can learn from others and not waste time and effort, re-inventing the wheel. There are lots of ways to do a technique, try them, learn them and decide what works for you.
• Get in the habit of ALWAYS closing your rotary cutter EACH time you put it down.
• I also cut a 4" square of each fabric from my collection and when I am putting together a project it is easier to get out my 4" square collection and make fabric choices, than to pull the yardage from my shelves and drawers.
• One technique that I do, that does not seem to be in common practice is: after I have sewn my strips together and pressed them, I like to lay them right side down to cut them. I find lining up my ruler with the stitch line gives me more accurate cuts.
• Try to keep an open mind about everything, not always easy but a rewarding goal to strive for.

Bonnie Kay Browning
Paducah, Kentucky

• I use freezer paper for lots of things in quiltmaking....for paper to draft my patterns, for templates to piece and applique blocks, and as tracing paper when I need to trace a design. When you are asked to make a single block for your guild, draw the design on freezer paper, cut it apart and press on the back side of your fabrics. Cut out adding a seam allowance. Now sew your block together using the edges of the freezer paper as the stitching line.

Sandra L. Hatch
Lincoln, Maine

• I learned to use my sewing machine for many quiltmaking tasks and when I need fast projects, I can whip them up. I still enjoy hand-piecing, hand-applique and hand-quilting as a relaxing form of entertainment. I feel like I am accomplishing something when I sit down to quilt.

Z.Z. Gilmore
Pocatello, Idaho

• Having my four-year-old granddaughter, Laura, thread my needles when she visits.
• When one loses a needle, turn off the lights and turn on a flashlight to spot it quickly.

Sue Hausmann
Lincolnshire, Illinois

• I do everything by machine. In fact, home dec and clothing items that will be unlined are pieced on my Huskylock Serger, fast! Most of my quilts are enveloped together and I do not cut the batting or backing to size - simply lay it out (put batting in dryer for a couple of minutes so it lays flat and seeks it's size) on a carpeted floor (doesn't slip around), and pin quilt top (cut to size). Sew around outside edge, leaving a hole to turn the quilt right side out. Because the backing and batting are somewhat bigger (hack off major excess), they do not skip under the top as you sew (you know, those little holes you have to go back and fix). At the hole - before turning, stay stitch over the hole area to prevent stretching and/or tearing (it's happened), *then* press the seam allowances to the wrong side in the staystitch line before turning.

• The new Viking/Husqvarna has Quilting Embroideries that actually stitch favorite quilting and quilt block motifs through all layers. I recently made doll quilts for my granddaugther's dolls, and a quilt bunting for a new grandson using these for quilting. I also love the new *hand look* quilting stitch that uses monofiliment thread on the top and regular thread in the bobbin, then stitches as if the needle sewed by hand with every other stitch invisible to the eye.

>>>>>>>>>>>>>>>>>>>>>>>>>>>>>

Jane Newhouse
Wedderburn, Oregon

• I find that open shelves, i.e. not cupboard or closet doors, is beneficial. I can *eye* the stash and contemplate - before dragging out everything.

• I do like clear plastic boxes with lids, so they stack. Some things I put in plastic baskets that also stack. Both of these are usually on sale once or twice a year.

• Of course, the rotary cutter, mats and rulers are the greatest help. That and strip piecing sold me on quilting. In the beginning, the thought of sewing all those little pieces together one at a time didn't interest me, so strip piecing got me started. Now I do find myself sewing *those little pieces* together and enjoying it.

>>>>>>>>>>>>>>>>>>>>>>>>>>>>>

Celeste Lipp
Idaho Falls, Idaho

• Once I learned to use the smaller quilting needles, I could quilt up a storm. I use off-white cotton quilting thread for everything, and I keep a supply on hand. I cut the thread at a sharp angle to speed up threading the needle, and I sharpen the needle often by passing it through an emery strawberry, such as the one on a *tomato* pin cushion. The emery also helps remove adhesive from my needle when I use 1/4" masking tape to mark my outline quilting.

• The item I couldn't do without is the Ziplock bag. I rely on them to keep my supplies together and most of all, to make quilter's travel kits. I do a lot of applique on the go. I'll only drive at night on trips, so I can sew in the car during daylight hours.

>>>>>>>>>>>>>>>>>>>>>>>>>>>>>

Barbara Shook Davis
Williams, Arizona

• Flannel for batting, it's flat, can be ironed, inexpensive, warm, full of body, can be hand or machine quilted easily.

>>>>>>>>>>>>>>>>>>>>>>>>>>>>>

Joanna Bessey
Rhinelander,
Wisconsin

Quicker quilting has not necessarily been a goal with me, as I enjoy the process of all of it - deciding on pattern and fabrics, cutting, piecing, applique, layering, stitching, etc. Easier quilting...Yes! I'm all for that!

• Join a quilt guild. Ideas shared with other quilters always *easy-up* a project. One of my quilt club members, Sarah, once demonstrated the making of ruched flowers. Because I sew my own day-dresses and gowns for our Civil War activities, I then used this technique. I added satin-like ruched flowers to my ballgown that I wore at the most recent military ball we attended downstate. At each of our monthly quilt guild meetings, we also have a *show and tell* time to share our completed projects. It is so neat to have other quilters appreciate your work, with sometimes even *ohh's and ah's*, and applause. Wow! Then one's long and pain-stitching work becomes easy! (Hey, get my pun - pain-stitching!!?) Last fall I brought a little-out-of-the-ordinary project to our meeting's *show and tell*. For the last year's Civil War skirmish season, our ladies' carbine-shooting team had decided we needed new shooters' outfits. Basic uniform in style and color, each gal (there are nine of us) used her own choice of printed cotton for her bodice (blouse). I asked for everyone's remnants and created a banner/flag for our unit - crazy - quilt pattern. I must say - we were unique!

• Make a point of taking a class periodically at your local Quilt Shop. There's always something new to learn and try, and the companionship of others working on a similiar project is such fun. Plus, you have that extra push to complete your project. Goodness knows, we all have enough of those UFO's to finish who-knows-when!

Why I am a Quilter!

Quilts are a comfort to all who wrap themselves up in one!

Quilts are a joy to all who make them for the pleasure of creating!

- I love to survey my stash, to see the colors lined up on my shelves, like the rainbow!

- I love the feel of fabric, as my fingers touch the cloth!

- I love to roll the rotary cutter carefully along the lines, creating clean even cuts.

- I love to select the pattern for my quilt, playing with fabrics and color!

- I love to spend hours mulling over my Quilt books and magazines!

- I love the decision making process! I am in control, it is all up to me!

- I love to sew all those tiny pieces of fabric together, creating a thing of beauty!

- I love to select the quilting pattern for quilting my quilt!

- I love the quilting process. By hand, or by machine, It's pure joy!

- I love the friends I meet through my quilting, friends who share my love of quilts.

- I love sharing my knowledge of quilting with those who are just beginning their quilting adventure!

- I love knowing my quilts will be around for generations, leaving evidence of my love!

I am a Quilter because I must Quilt!

Joyce Livingston

Quilters Share Their Advice On Quilting!

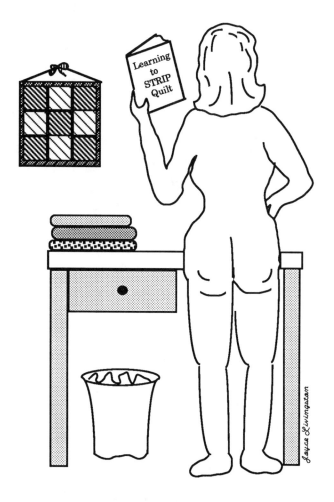

Page 190, Quilters offer advice

Joyce Livingston
Council Grove, Kansas

• When presenting a program to the Pride City Quilt Guild in Pueblo, Colorado I mentioned *cheater's cloth*. One of the members admonished me saying, "We no longer call it cheater's cloth, it's now *user-friendly fabric!*" I got to thinking about that...so in this day of high-tech, I decided to rename my stash. I now call it my *resource center!*
• I like to keep the little items I use frequently (fraycheck, chalk, rulers, rotary cutters and blades, small scissors, screw drivers, etc.) hung on hooks on a peg board on the wall right above my sewing area. Other smaller items go into small drawers in those wonderful storage units you find in the hardware sections of stores.
• If you have small children, spend time with them now. They'll be grown and gone from home all too soon! Enjoy them now. Build those memories while you can. Quilting will wait.
• Try finishing a project, before starting the next one. It's difficult to do, but sure gets rid of the guilt feelings! If you don't want to finish it, give it to someone who will.
• Thank God for each day, and live it to the fullest! Count your blessings, and don't forget to say "I love you!" to those whom you love.

++++++++++++++++++++++++++++

Thelma Tiefel
Clay City, Indiana

• I most always buy material when it is on sale.
• I made crib quilts for grandchildren as part of their gifts.
• I store my extra quilts in old pillow cases on the top shelf of a closet, not used for anything else.
• Some of my material I keep coordinating colors together.
• I have been using adhesive tape on my fingers to keep them from getting so sore.
• I haven't sold any of my quilts. They are too much a part of me to part with them, unless they stay in the family.

++++++++++++++++++++++++++++

Jan Jacobson
Tripoli, Wisconsin

• I organize my fabric stash in baskets - one color to a basket. I cut my scraps into varying widths and have baskets for each width. Then it's easy to find what I need, when I need a certain size strip.

++++++++++++++++++++++++++++

Nadine Dozier
North Augusta, South Carolina

• Try to make a space that is just for your quilting supplies.
• I store my scrap fabrics in old shaker boxes. These stack very well.
• One idea is to keep all of the same supplies together in one place, such as stencils and rulers.
• Keep books and magazines on a bookcase, along with your sewing basket. I also use a peg board and cork board in front of my machine.

++++++++++++++++++++++++++++

Betty Lou Cassidy
Linwood, New Jersey

• A few years ago I felt very out-of-touch with conversations about Best Sellers. Most of my leisure reading is taken up by quilting books and magazines. I read novels, but only at night in bed and by that time, my eyes are so tired that it can take over a month to finish. I buy paperbacks rather than borrowing from the library because two weeks is not enough time. Then I discovered "Books on Tape" at the local library. Now I *listen* to current novels while sewing. This way I feel I'm using my time twice as efficiently. I also know what my friends are talking about and can join in the discussion.

++++++++++++++++++++++++++++

Ruth Rhoades
Toccoa, Georgia

• Scraps too small to keep look pretty in a pint or quart jar in my sewing room. Reminders of your fabrics (and quilts) as well. Even snippets add up.

++++++++++++++++++++++++++++

Elizabeth A Akana
Kaneohe, Hawaii

• The first quilt you make, make for your child and then they will always understand when you are a busy quilter. "See this is just like when Mommy made yours."
• I always go to my fabric stash first.
• I make book marks for everyone with LOVE IS---, and their initials and a favorite button.

- I hang my quilts on large blanket hangers with cotton sheets over them.

Elaine Helen (Revier) Baker
Watertown, Minnesota

- Flexible bandages help hold onto big metal thimbles or keep your finger safe, when the leather thimble starts getting a little thin.

Barbara S. Moss
Locust Grove, Georgia

- Quilt like the older quilters, and let the children play house under your frame while you quilt.

Lynn Lewis Young
Houston, Texas

- I do store quilts and projects in the large transparent plastic containers mentioned in the Quilting Hints Section. Keeps them dust-free and you can see what's in the box without digging through it.

Josephine Hannah Jirva Burgwyn (Jo Jo)
Jackson, North Carolina

- I haven't found the secret to keeping my 3 year old busy!
- A friend of mine helped me organize my fabric by color, which I keep in a pie safe (antique, which my loving mother-in-law gave me!

Colleen Taylor
Indialantic, Florida

- I organize my fabric stash by sorting by color and keeping it on open shelves, away from sunlight. Got a file cabinet from a fabric store going out of business, to use for patterns and supplies.

Louise Murphy
Mammoth Lakes, California

- I keep enough 5 1/2 year old projects hidden in my sewing room, my granddaughter rarely gets bored. I remember my grandmothers sewing room (off limits to us) held many boxes and barrels full of mysterious treasures. My granddaughter is not only welcome into my sewing room, but feels perfectly at home while still respecting my requests not to touch certain things. Under my work table is a wonderful space for her and her dolls to have tea.
- I keep my fabric stash as organized as possible, stored on shelves in a chest away from damaging sun.
- I don't think it comes under the heading of *stash* any longer though. Somehow, *stash* seems like such a small word. I am partially color blind, purples and greens mostly, therefore, I must keep my collection pretty well organized. One of mother's jobs when she visits is to reorganize it by color and we tie it into neatly stacked bundles. However, there are also certain collections, i.e. "Red Wagon plaids and stripes, pastel plaids and stripes, and it goes on and on....
- Whenever I do have a visitor (usually another quilter), I flaunt my fabric. I love to give them free time in my sewing room to peek and poke in all the nooks and crannies. If they get a few minutes or so of enjoyment, then we have both been rewarded. To me, this is what quilting is all about. Sharing!
- My scraps, after careful thought, are collected in a large shopping bag and I love to give these to new quilters trying to build a collection of varied color and texture and design.
- Another way of sharing with another quilting friend is to buy a yard or 1/2 yard, and give half away. It's nice to keep little bundles all folded and tied neatly, just ready to give someone.
- By the way, Linda Ballard puts on a wonderful "Mystery Weekend" in Northern California which I am lucky enough to attend. Good place to hook up with my little sis and her entourage from Dunsmier, California. I have started a small informal quilt group here in Mammoth Lakes. We meet at a local Bed & Breakfast every other week, in the evenings. We have anywhere from 6 to 12 members. A very prolific group we are.

Mary Anne Keppler
St. Olaf, Iowa

- I have no real advice. Some things work well for some people and not for others. You just have to experiment to see what works for you.

Page 192, Quilters offer advice

Kathryn Rippeteau Greenwold
Niskayuna, New York

• My girls have a corner in my studio and they have access to my scrap basket. They also may choose 1/4 yard each time we go to the quilt shop. They make quilts, doll clothes, pillows and Christmas ornaments. My husband has just built them a table, and we revamped an old sewing machine for them. It's fun having them with me as I create. We share ideas, and their sewing skills have developed naturally.

Florence Edith Goggin
Eureka, California

• I keep my rotary cutter in an old firm eyeglass case.
• I use a thimble on both hands.
• Scraps, strips and small pieces are kept in clear plastic boxes and labeled.
• Patterns are placed in plastic sheet protectors and then placed in binders according to Piecing-Applique & etc.

Beverly J. Relph
Leavenworth, Kansas

• Entertaining little ones: A "hunk of cheese packed into the center of a hollow bone" for each Yorkie at 5 p.m. keeps Fred and Mildred occupied for an hour.
• Call a carpenter. To organize my stash, we built floor to ceiling cabinets with shelves and doors on two sides of my studio. One of the most tangible results of getting organized is that I ended up with a lot of scraps. All of my "Ragamuffin Jackets" are made entirely from these scraps.
• Gifts: My sisters, Judy and Kay, enjoy receiving my clothing creations as gifts.

Patricia (Pat) Jones
Oroville, California

• My sewing room is off limits to everyone except a fellow quilter or my grandchildren. Yes, my grandchildren love this room and treat it with great respect. When I am cutting, I let them cut. They have their own scissors that are kept in a scissors block with mine, and I have instructions never to use "their" scissors. Cutting and gluing bits of scraps to paper will keep them busy for hours! My project for this summer is to help 10 year old Zach make his first quilt!
• I also suggest that you try the new commercial machine quilting that is being offered today. I had many of my quilts done this way and with great success.
• My feeling about this is a practical one. If I tried to hand quilt them all, my grandchildren would be in college before they ever owned a quilt. After all, I'm not hanging them in the "Smithsonian Institute". The children don't care how they are stitched, they just want to roll up in them, or hide from the dog, or make a tent. After all, I have made this quilt with love and they can use it in any way they choose.
• The most recent quilt I made was a Christmas present for an exchange student living with my son and his family. Sanja, is a 17 year old girl from "Yugoslavia". She really is a darling, and I immediately set about the make her a quilt! It used all red, white and blue with stars and stripes and flags. I put a "story label" on the back, as I do on all my quilts, and the whole family signed it. I hope this helps her to remember her stay with all of us!
• I store my "stash" by color in see-thru containers. I always keep them in a cupboard away from light and dust. My Christmas fabrics are kept in a giant plastic tote. (I love Christmas fabric). I toss my scraps into a big wicker basket with Christmas scraps in their own basket.
• I hang my tools and gadgets on a peg board on the wall. This way, my cutters and templates, etc. are always at my fingertips. My scissors are kept in a scissor block on the cutting table (if the grandchildren haven't used all the slots).
• I store my quilts and quilt tops in pillowcases and sheets. They should never be stored in plastic of any kind, as plastic is a petroleum based product and eventually will destroy your quilts.
• I make lots of mini quilts and really am hooked on the new machine paper piecing method. These are great for using up scraps. How come my scrap pile isn't getting smaller?
• I have been doing craft fairs for about 20 years, and now that I am a quilter, I can make and sell wonderful things. Mini quilts, wall hangings, table cloths and runners are always good sellers. Decorated clothing is also very popular. How much to charge is always a problem, but you can get only what the "traffic" will allow. Remember, you never get paid for your time! However, never sell yourself "short".

Quilters offer advice, page 193

Chloe Rhodes
Clay City, Indiana

• I have made two 9-Patch tops using up some of my scraps. A great way to use them up.

Jill Marie Tanking
LIberal, Kansas

• Like I said before, I save my scraps in a large plastic bag for a lady who does miniatures. This year I made wall hangings for my Christmas gifts. A group of us got together at Hugoton and made the *White House Christmas Tree* for several people. We have one lady who we can not get to quilt, who does our *taking-out*. When I was making a *Sailboat Wall Hanging*: from the *Better Homes and Gardens Quilting Ideas*, the border of stars was a little short and had to be taken out to make the band between the stars a little longer. She helped. She was such a good *taker-outer*, that when I sent to see what was taking her so long, she was even taking my stars apart.

• My stash is slowly growing. I don't buy material just because I like it, since my quilting money comes from my job. But, my large scraps are sorted by color scheme. I got some plastic dividers from a store that are U-shaped, put the material inside of it and put another U-shaped divider slipped into the side of it. Then they are put in a cardboard box.

• When I buy for a particular project and don't know when I will get to it, they go into a plastic shoe box with a picture of the project.

Rebecca Kelly
Kingsburg, California

• Try to set a time limit on your sewing/quilting. About 20 minutes at a time is all I can do because of my small children.

• Have a basket of toys in your sewing room so that children can play. You can spend time together, while quilting. I also give my kids scraps to play with. They have come up with very imaginative play with them.

Mary Andrews
Grand Blanc, Michigan

• Since my 8 year old granddaughter has lived with me since she was born, I have had to think of ways to keep her entertained. When she was little, she loved to cut with scissors, and I would give her paper to cut. I keep a little lap desk in my room with her crayons, paper, coloring books, etc. there, and she does art projects while I sew. I ask her to sort or count my charm squares occasionally, or sort my buttons and beads. This past year I took her to sewing lessons, but most of the time she needs help from me for that.

• Quilts as gifts make a great opportunity to cash in on several holidays using one quilt. Last May I gave my daughter the quilt squares of an Ocean Waves with fish appliqued on them. For Christmas she got the top put together with the fish decorated. I keep reminding her that even at minimum wage, she is getting the most expensive gift considering my time. I just finished it, but photographed it to enter into Paducah, so she will get it to hang in her house for her birthday in May.

• I keep my projects in plastic see-thru boxes. I always have many projects in progress, or collecting things for future quilts. Each one has a separate box, and when I get around to making it, everything is in one place. My beads and sequins are in plastic boxes with dividers, and all my decorative threads and do-dads are in a tackle box, which can be carried around. My ironing board is to the right of my sewing machine, and all I have to do is turn my chair to press a seam. A table with my cutting board is to the left, but I do have to stand up to rotary cut.

• A hint for bad hands or carpel tunnel is to take vitamin B6 (a hint from another quilter) and at night wear wrist guards to bed. I got mine when I bought my Rollerblades. The kid who sold them to me said I needed them in case I fell, he probably looked at me and thought I would fall. I only used them once when Rollerblading, but found they worked great to wear at night for my hands (I don't fall when I'm Rollerblading!). They only cost $12.

• You're probably wondering how I can make so many quilts, work full-time and raise a family. I have learned to sew, if I only have 5 or 10 minutes at a time. I have many projects going, in all different stages, so I can work on anything, depending on how much time I have and where I am. I leave everything out all the time, so I can go into my room and sew a few seams, and then do something else. I try to get a little done in the morning, before I go to work, and at night I read Stefi stories before she

Page 194, Quilters offer advice

goes to bed, and many times I fall asleep before she does and sleep for an hour or so, and get up and sew a few more hours. I don't seem to require a lot of sleep, maybe my brain is too busy.

•I keep a pencil and paper by my bed and in the kitchen to write down ideas and notes to myself. I use my crock pot and pressure cooker a lot, and when I do cook, I make a lot and put some in the freezer to use another day. We eat a lot of spaghetti, rice and soup. They are good and easy to make. I have a bread machine, too, that takes 5 minutes to put in the ingredients for delicious homemade bread.

++++++++++++++++++++++++++
Minabess P. Randolph
Toms River,
New Jersey

•I don't like to waste time. My advice to any quilter who must spend time waiting, is to have portable projects. It keeps one from being bored or frustrated. I have quilted in doctor's offices, airports, back seats of vans, and on soccer fields. One time we sat 3 hours in the Newark Airport. While others fussed and fumed, I quilted!

•During the years my sons were on soccer teams I always carried my quilting stuff in a tackle box. One afternoon, my son Eric tore his soccer shorts. I said, "Well, I guess you'll have to play in your warm-up suit" and we headed back to the van. As we walked he looked at the tackle box and then up at me and asked, "Couldn't you just sew them?" That hadn't occurred to me and we both laughed. In the van, I sewed up the shorts and he ran back to the field, very happy to be in uniform like the other boys.

++++++++++++++++++++++++++
Mary Jane Cemer
Trenton, Nebraska

•As to entertaining children, hold their arms down, sit them on your lap and sew, they love it. I did that with all my kids and grandkids and now great-great grand-daughter, Jordan, loves it. I put their arms firmly under one elbow and my hands are free to sew. Keep up a constant descriptive chatter of what you're doing. They're very interested.

•Money-saving tip: Do not leave the house and under NO circumstances go into a...gasp!...Quilt Shop!

•Gifts: Everyone I know has a lap quilt to keep warm while watching TV.

•Storage? Ha, ha, ha, ha, ha, ha! Organize? Scraps? Everything has to be in front of my nose! I get along fine, until someone shames me into cleaning, and then I hate everyone because I can't find ANYTHING!

•Sew all the scraps and make a crazy quilt. Wish I could sell what I make, then I could buy MORE FABRIC!

++++++++++++++++++++++++++
Susan Hanna
Brownlee, Nebraska

•I have made two yo-yo coverlets and several pillows, decorative items, etc. Yo-yos are an excellent means of using scraps, and a stack of fabric circles. Needle, spool of thread and scissors are easy to carry in a ziplock bag in your purse, and can be pulled out to work on in waiting rooms, riding in the car or when just visiting.

•For a template for the circles for the coverlet, I use a full 1 quart can of paint. The weight holds several layers of fabric and keeps it from shifting, when tracing the circles. It will make a 4" circle and with sharp scissors you can cut about 4 layers at a time.

++++++++++++++++++++++++++
Tonya St. Berg
Woodinville,
Washington

• I utilize my extra scrap sack fabric by first adhering the fabric to the paper piece patterns and then sew them onto a card by using a decorative stitch. These cards are sold at the guilds boutique or go to help support the Woodinville Historical Society.

•Children can be entertained by making figure fragrances. This recipe calls for only two ingredients, a finely chopped spice (allspice, cinnamon, etc) and applesauce. 1 cup spice and 1 cup applesauce (or equal parts if you wish to make a larger batch). Mix together. Roll mixture out 1/4" or more. Cut with cookie cutters, or cut desired shapes. Cook for 2 hours at 200 degrees. Place them in your dresser, hang them in a room for aroma, glue a magnet on the back, or hang them on the tree at Christmas. They are wonderful!

Quilters offer advice, page 195

Barbara MacDonald
Oscoda, Michigan

- I manage to set aside at least 2 hours every evening for my hand quilting.
- I try to keep my fabrics organized by color. I'm lucky enough to have a sewing room with built-in shelves and drawers. The drawer is filled with binding, left over from different quilts I've made. I recently made 20 fabric stationary holders and I didn't need to make any binding, it was already done.
- The rubber finger cots are wonderful, pulling the needles through is a breeze.
- Protecting your under finger is hard for me, but udder cream is great!

Carole P. Kenny
Providence, Rhode Island

- The local libraries have many audio tapes of books, fiction and non-fiction, that make piecing and quilting time pass quickly.

Lassie Wittman
Rochester, Washington

- I have 3 six-foot high book shelves and have arranged all my poly/cotton solids like a rainbow. What a happy place to sew. No direct sunlight.
- My prints are stored in 4 plastic _see thru_ blanket boxes.
- Solid scraps are saved (each color in a separate plastic bag) for string projects.
- Print scraps are saved for foundation piecing.
- Apply clear finger nail polish to "under the quilt' healed finger - sure saves some pain.

Bonnie Swecker
Roanoke Rapids, North Carolina

- Children can be encouraged to be creative while you quilt. Give them (if old enough) safety scissors, construction paper and some simple patterns, and let them create paper quilts. Then you can use them as placemats for dinner. They'll be so proud!
- If your Guild does block drawings, you can make an extra one to keep in a "gifts to be made" collection. Almost anyone would like a hand-made pillow, small wall hanging or table runner made from those blocks.
- Once your children start leaving home, the dresser in their room makes an excellent place to store fabric or projects in the works.
- Many ladies in our guild use their scraps to make children's quilts for the Ronald McDonald house. One is given to each sick child when they leave the hospital. Each of us set a goal of at least two quilts per year, or approximately 50 quilts.

Jean Van Dusen
Kingsford, Michigan

- I store my stock in a closet that my husband took the rod out, and put in shelves from floor to ceiling. Now I can see at a glance, what I have.

Jean Eng Underhill
Flemington, New Jersey

- Quilt or hand stitch when you can. I always carry something to work on during the spring and fall - for soccer and swimming in the summer.
- As I am limited in space, I have 2 dressers where I store my fabrics, so my clothes and fabrics compete for space.
- With many of my scraps, I store them in the 2 1/2 pound pop corn tins. They are cut up into either charm squares, or saved and then donated to the primary schools. I've used many of the scraps to teach 2nd grade children about quilting, and then to produce quilts, which have been shown at the local quilt show - Courthouse Quilters.
- My girls are always using the scraps to make scrap quilts using a straight stitch. For my youngest, I use wonder-under with her scraps, so she can snip and design her squares.
- To keep the young children occupied when we quilt, we have a playgroup that's about 9 years old. During this time we exchange ideas, talk about fabrics and sew. The kids are busy, as we unwind and enjoy ourselves with our quilting.
- For the safe disposal of broken needles and/or pins, I use the plastic child safe cover capsule containers.
- My kids like to use my scrap fabrics to make catnip toys for Tiki's Christmas presents. For the mice, we add a braided yarn tail. This keeps Tiki happy until the next catnip crop is ready for harvest.

Page 196, Quilters offer advice

++++++++++++++++++++++++++
Joyce Nichols
Bethany, Missouri

• "New skin" has saved my finger! I'm so glad I found it!

++++++++++++++++++++++++++
Ann Littleton
Fairfax, Virginia

• I always did my cutting and machine sewing, while the children were napping or at preschool. I saved my handwork to do while they were playing nearby. That way they didn't feel too neglected.
• Money-saving tip: I'm not too disciplined in this area. The best tip for me to save money is to STAY OUT of fabric stores.
• Gift idea: "Quillos"!! These simple lap quilts that fold up into a pillow have been a hit for those on my gift list. They don't take long to make, and I've used up a lot of extra quilt blocks to make the pillow part. I try to put a personal message on the inside, so that the receiver will feel special when wrapped up in the quilt. My friend, Deb, shared this pattern with me.
• Organizational Ideas: I'm lacking in this area. (Ask Deb). However, I do have an organized pile of unfinished projects that I'm trying to finish, one a month, (That's my goal!), so I'll have some Christmas gifts ready by next December.

++++++++++++++++++++++++++
Eugenia A. Barnes
(Genie)
Marcellus, New York

• My 4 grand daughters are here (my daughter in school full-time), so at this writing, I have a 3 year old and 5 year old at home. I have a child's tape player and lots of Roffi, etc. - or art box with crayons and paper! Scissors and stickers - small flannel board and scrap bag for "quilt play". Books and clay!!
• Sarah, age 3, loves to make "board quilts" on flannel. I also tell her stories/rhymeS and she in turn, tells me stories. Great for imagination times.

++++++++++++++++++++++++++
Eleanor K. Hunnel
Johnstown, Nebraska

• There was a time after I had been fitted with bifocal glasses I thought I would have to give up machine sewing as I had to tilt my head back so far to see through the corrective part - until my husband suggested a higher chair - voila! It worked, and I've sewing in comfort since.
• Because I visit friends and family often, I had to give up the comfort and companionship of a pet. I do feed birds, but feel sorta guilty on that score, too, as when I am away 'what does the robin do then, poor thing! I do have a few hardy plants and 20 grandchildren.
• Sometimes youngsters can be entertained while you're sewing, with a box of band-aids, a roll of scotch tape, or a magnet. Children love making play houses of a quilt-draped card table or chairs.

++++++++++++++++++++++++++
Dotti Greto
Ocean City,
New Jersey

• A great gift idea for a quilt guild, with 20 members or more, to give another member for some occasion, is a basket lined with green florist paper and filled with rolled-up fat quarters in bright "flowery" colors, looks like a basket of flowers. You'll need a few green pieces for leaves, too.
• I keep my *traveling* quilt supplies in a clear-top fishing tackle box. It has sections that you change to fit your needs, and you can get boxes in many sizes.
• I have several thimbles and change while quilting, to relieve the pressure points.
• My quilt fingers just suffer. I can't quilt with anything on them. I put Hydrocortisone cream on them when I go to bed - feels better in the morning and I start again.
• I keep my fabric in a glass-front office cabinet in a darker corner of my sewing room, and my cutting table is an office conference table top resting on two 33-drawer file cabinets. As you can see, it helps to have a retired insurance man for a husband.
• I also love to make rag dolls and Christmas ornaments, so I save my scraps in clear shoe boxes for these things.

++++++++++++++++++++++++++
Jeanne K. Ferg
Asheville,
North Carolina

• I use Rubbermaid units to store fabric mostly.
• My fingers are just calloused.
• I send scraps to an elderly (93 years young) family relative in Arkansas.
• I stack and store by color mainly.

Quilters offer advice, page 197

Doris Holland
Winterset, Iowa

• My scraps are accumulating and I have hopes in making at least one scrap quilt sometime.
• I store my fabrics in plastic storage containers by colors. This works well for me.

Jean S. Branham
Halifax,
North Carolina

• I don't sell any of my work.

Helen Blankenship
Flint, Michigan

• I use all my quilts.
• I keep small pieces in one box for paper piecing and applique, a box for charm squares, and separate prints from solids - darks from lights.
• I have only a small "stash", as I mostly buy and use material for each quilt.

Edna R. Harbison
Ontonagon, Michigan

• Much of our income is from the quilted wall hangings I design and make.
• I work full-time, year round and to keep from being bored with the duplications of certain designs, I listen to talk shows on public radio (we don't have TV), or I think about the book I am writing, and jot notes.
• I take short 5 minute breaks often, and as soon as weather permits in Spring, I take my work outside to watch and listen and enjoy our beautiful clearing in the woods.
• To save time when I want to tan my pale skin a bit for swimsuit season and can't take time off from quilting, I sometimes cut out appliques while in the nude on the roof of our lumber shed. Thank goodness for privacy! I use a rock to hold my little pile of fabrics from blowing away, and I keep a sharp ear on the traffic out on the road.

Susan D. Fellin
Flemington,
New Jersey

• I just recently shopped at IKEA and bought 4 pieces of furniture to organize my room, with plenty of drawers and basket draws. I also have a copy machine at work and the boxes that paper comes in, they're great for storing items, and can be easily marked and stacked!

Lori Hauswirth
Iron River, Michigan

• I always try to have some completed projects on hand for unexpected wedding, showers, etc.
• Grab bag scrap exchange is a fun way to get rid of some old fabric, at the same time getting some new ones.
• The only way I know how to protect my finger (under my project) is to keep it calloused. Freshly pricked fingers are no fun - ouch!

Audrey Derscha
Flint, Michigan

• For organizing threads: fishing tackle box. I travel to workshops so I put threads in a 2-sided (Plano Brand) Tackle Box. It has see-through sides and looks like a suitcase.
• Check other than quilting supplies for needs, I found a multi-sized circle template in an office supply store.

Paula Kay Garrison
& Duncan Garrison
New Braunfels, Texas

• I use a rubber finger to pull needle through.
• I use a liquid bandage when my finger is bleeding.
• Take scraps, and when you have enough cut them in 3" squares, and make placemats or doll quilts with matching colors.

Paula Gore
Osmond, Nebraska

I don't organize my stash. After doing a program for my quilt guild, where I visited and filmed other quilter's sewing rooms, I thought I'd better re-arrange my fabric. I discovered that I like it in no apparent order. So, when I go looking for a piece, I get to rediscover why I bought all those pieces. I love the feel, the color, the variety. I enjoy looking at and refolding the beautiful pieces of rainbow sitting on my shelf. It revitalizes me and reminds me of all the projects that I want to do, that I have planned or started in my head.

It alleviated my guilt at a 'messy' collection of fabric.
• I have gotten my children involved with quilting, by involving them in something that means a lot to me, it makes them appreciate the time that I spend quiltmaking. Using a stencil and foundation piecing, the kids made their teachers (with a little help) a Santa quilt for Christmas. It taught them the joy of making a gift and involved them in quiltmaking and we all did it together, it was fun!!!

++++++++++++++++++++++++

Sherry Cook
Council Grove, Kansas

• When you see fabric on a good sale, but don't know how to use it in a quilt, think about the backing. Unusual fabrics make great backings.
• Store sewing thread in Plano Magum double sided tackle box. I store polyester thread on one side, and cotton thread on the other.

++++++++++++++++++++++++

Melissa Armstrong
Oshkosh, Nebraska

• I try to get my children involved. They (usually) know what they can touch or what they cannot. They are 2 and 6 and they can help sort colors, hand me pieces or even help sew some of the larger strips. If it isn't forbidden, pretty quick their attention will turn to something else, without inhibiting their budding love of quilting.

++++++++++++++++++++++++

Janet Kugler
Holdrege, Nebraska

• Let children play with scraps.
• The wire baskets in a framework works great to store each color of fabric. You can tell at a glance what you have.
• Scraps can be used for all the fusible projects or for English Piecing projects like: flower garden and dresden.

++++++++++++++++++++++++

Kathy Palmiter
Williams, Indiana

• I like to give quilted gifts to family and friends. Most times it's a miniature - "a little something" to remember the occasion. This is a great way to use up scraps, since they only require small snips and bits of fabric.
• I also like to give "Fabric Samplers". Again, these are miniatures, but they are made from the 2 and 4 inch fabric collections you can order. The nice thing about Fabric collections you can order is they have a uniform look, since the fabrics all come from one designer, and the investment for a wonder array of fabrics is only a few dollars.

++++++++++++++++++++++++

Mary Lou Sayers
Clarkson, Nebraska

• My small grandchildren love to take my quilting stencils and draw around them. Also, they love stacking and playing with charm squares and my basted appliques for my Sunbonnet Sue quilt, and my Pansy quilt.
• I sort my large pieces of fabrics: 1 yard or more, into color groups and store them in open metal shelves.
• Large covered boxes from the grocery store make good storage for scraps. Boxes from peaches or other fruit are especially good. I can the peaches and use the boxes for scraps!! Label on end, and stack for easy locating.
• I spread most of my spare quilts on our spare bed and cover with a clean sheet. It saves fold creases and is easy to locate a particular quilt, simply roll back quilts to the one you want.
• I have what I call "carry along" projects ready, usually applique in a tote bag. I include pieces to be basted, blocks with designs traced on them and a special clip board with emery board finish.
• Sewing supplies and scissors are all stored in tote ready to grab when going to doctor's appointments, etc. I meet so many interesting people when I'm waiting for appointments. They can't seem to resist asking what I'm working on.

++++++++++++++++++++++++

Edna E. Holdsworth
Johnston,
Rhode Island

• Scraps can often be used for baby quilts. We once made a string quilt, using all pastel scraps sewed diagonally on 6" paper backgrounds, removing the paper after the block was finished.
• I protect my finger under the quilt, when quilting, with a cheap plastic thimble. The needle just glances off it enough to know you have penetrated the quilt.
• I like to make small wall hangings or miniatures for shower or housewarming gifts.

Quilters offer advice, page 199

(They can be hung anywhere) Make sure you give them only to people who will love and cherish them, also.

++++++++++++++++++++++++++++

Susan Nicholson
Muskegon, Michigan

Oh, how I love to organize my stuff! Here are a few of my tricks:
- First, my husband, Bill, put shelves in two double closets with bi-fold doors.
- I then bought clear plastic storage boxes at the discount store. I put my fabric in them.
- I fold each piece and stand it on end, so I can see every piece of my fabric at a glance.
- Each box has a color in it, except for some pieces I want to leave together for a particular project.
- Each project is in a basket from start to finish, including fabric, thread, and pattern.
- The second shelved closet has my magazines (I never throw one away) and some of my books in it. The magazines are in those cardboard magazine holders.
- In my sewing room, my work table is an office desk top that is 36x72". My machine is at one end, as is my light box, at the other end is my cutting mat. I have a swivel office chair which is wonderful. It goes from the machine, to the ironing board, to the cutting mat, to the phone, to the resident computer, without me getting up.
- My cutting tools are all on Shaker pegs, including the rulers.
- All the large patterns I have, that I don't want to fold, I roll up and stand in a large crock.
- The last improvement I made was track lighting. Wow, what a difference, I can really see and besides, it keeps the room warmer.
- All my patterns are stored in files, according to subject matter.
- As I teach quilt making classes, all my handouts and notes are also in a file drawer. These are all in the basement, because my sewing room is full!
- My quilts are stored on quilt racks and clothes drying racks, covered over with upside down quilt tops for sun protection.
- Every available drawer is full of small projects and UFO's. I have many!

++++++++++++++++++++++++++++

PIONEER QUILTERS
Eugene, Oregon

- Shop the fabric sales.
- I'm still looking for an adequate market for what I make.
- Organize fabric by color and keep it where you can see it.
- Scraps get saved in clear plastic containers or ziplocs.
- Wear a thimble.
- Don't be afraid to say *no* to people wanting to use up your precious quilt time.
- We don't bring kids to our meeting.

++++++++++++++++++++++++++++

Florence L. Tyler
DeLancey, New York

- I am short on closet space so I store fabrics in suitcases, by color.
- Recycle a flannel backed table cover as a flannel board. Can be pinned to a sturdy backing, or folded for easy storage.

++++++++++++++++++++++++++++

Dawn Golden
Milford, New Jersey

My advice to other Quilters like me would be:
- Don't find other ways to entertain your small children, spend the time with them (visiting Quilt Shops, of course). Before you know it, they will want to go to their friends house, or to play ball, or to college, and you may find yourself with all the time you ever wanted - and more. That's why I observe and learn and listen as much as I can. Once a month I spend a few hours at a Guild meeting, but I try not to take too much time from my kids and my family. That doesn't mean I can't buy fabric!

++++++++++++++++++++++++++++

Teresa A. Walton
New Braunfels, Texas

- I believe the most important thing a quilter can do is take classes, learn the basics from an excellent teacher. I was very fortunate to have Charlotte Flesher, San Antonio, as my instructor. She gave us every trick in her book, the knowledge she passed on to us "quilters" was priceless. Continue to take classes, never believe you are too old to learn new techniques, experiment.
- Get involved in your community quilt guild. I joined my guild in 1991, held the treasurer position in 1992 thru 1994, and yes..."The President" '95.
- Support your quilt stores, New Braunfels does not have one (Hint), we have to drive 50 to 90 minutes to get inspired and touch the magic of cotton.

Page 200, Quilters offer advice

++++++++++++++++++++++++++
Darlene Brazil
Escalon, California

- Keep a very happy spirit!
- When you need to stop a project because of another's need (child, husband, dog), leave your project with good will. You can easily return to it and have peaceful moments.
- Don't let your project "stress you out". Strive for the "best you can do" - however, don't let it overwhelm you. Grandmothers quilts were not always perfect either. Quilting should be enjoyable and calming to the spirit.
- As far as scraps go, I keep larger scraps (i.e. fat quarter size), for my stash. Anything smaller, I give to my mother or an older friend who does not have the financial resources to buy her own fabrics for quilting. My mother uses the scraps to make lap quilts for needy children.

++++++++++++++++++++++++++
Roberta Schroeder
Deer Park, Washington

- I feel the best advice is to continue taking classes. The fellowship and community building at a class is wonderful. I learn far more than I expect, including tricks and tips I never would have known, such as:
- Threading the needle and know tying for invisible knots.
- I use all my scraps for applique or whatever.
- I love using Heat N' Bond for applique and scrap quilts.

++++++++++++++++++++++++++
Virginia L. Brown
Ogallala, Nebraska

- My best quilts are stored in pillowcases on a shelf in the closet. I take them out and refold periodically. Sewing supplies are kept mostly together in a large tackle box, with much of my embellishing laces, Brazilian and Silk Ribbon Embroidery in baskets.

++++++++++++++++++++++++++
Merrilyn Muir-Rennau
Vienna, Austria, Europe

- I always carry a small notebook or sketch pad with me and jot down ideas or patterns from a ceramic tile, stained glass windows, etc.
- When making placemats, I iron the batting to the backing fabric before cutting placemats, individually.
- Batting, which is bought in plastic bags, I take it out and roll in a cylinder bolt for storage.

++++++++++++++++++++++++++
Susan Southworth
Gulf Shores, Alabama

- When my sons flew the coop, I spent 10 minutes being sad, out of respect. Then I turned their old rooms into a studio and office. I installed 8 shelves to hold some of my fabric and covered one wall with insulation board, giving me an 8 foot by 8 foot designing wall. My fabric over-flow goes into 8 fifty-five gallon new trash cans in my garage. The lids snap down and they are on rollers, so when I need something I just roll one of them into my studio. I call my space my 'Quilting Queendom' and You-Know-Who doesn't darken the doorway, unless he is needed to lift heavy objects, or add another shelf.

++++++++++++++++++++++++++
Pamela Thompson
Clinton Twp, Kansas

- Sew like crazy while kids are napping. A lot of hand quilting with a hoop can be done while they are playing near by.
- I enjoy listening to TV while quilting.
- Cook a large meal on weekends, and eat leftovers for the rest of the week. I cook a turkey breast on Sunday, Turkey Divan on Monday, Turkey a la King later on, etc. Pork roast or ham turns into casseroles, linguine, fried rice, and ham bone turns into my famous split pea soup.

++++++++++++++++++++++++++
Cynthia England
Houston, Texas

- As far as keeping small children entertained, I set up a children's table for crafts and puzzles in my sewing room. They loved it.
- I also found friends that had children of the same age and we swapped kids one day a week. This way, the children had playmates and the moms got some quiet time to sew. I've even heard of one group of quilting moms that have their bee at McDonald's, so the kids can play while they do handwork. Where there's a will, there's a way!
- Because quilting has many different stages, I will do most of

my designing late at night when the children are asleep. Cutting and hand-quilting are usually done in the evening with the family. I carry small things to cut out while waiting in line picking up the children from school or waiting for doctor appointments. There are times, however, when I'm on a roll and I do not emerge from my sewing room for hours.

• A lot of quilters were crafters first. Here is a way I organized my spools of ribbon. I hung up two cup hooks in the top of my closet and used a dowel to "thread" my spools through. Then I took 2 pieces of ribbon and suspended the dowel from the cup hooks. Viola! The ribbon was accessible and out of the way at the same time.

++++++++++++++++++++++++++++

Lesley Ann Hill
Granville, Ohio

• I store my fabric in stacking wire baskets by color, so I can quickly find what I need.
• Fabrics and patterns that I'm given that I know I won't use, I store in an old, small laundry basket so when I'm asked to give something to a quilt auction or to donate items to some quilt cause, I have something on hand and it's not taking up room in my stash. (I am a contemporary quilter, so the items in the basket are traditional, not just junk.)

++++++++++++++++++++++++++++

Mary A. Sovran
Phoenix, Arizona

• Use good basic sewing techniques for accuracy, but don't follow any one's rules on quiltmaking. Do it the way that pleases you, it's your quilt and it should be done your way. Don't let anyone impose their restrictions on your creativity. If it pleases you, then it's exactly right. Enjoy!

++++++++++++++++++++++++++++

Judy Allen
Nevada, Iowa

• I would like to share with you my diary/calendar quilt. The inspiration for this quilt came from an article written by a member of our guild who was going to start a diary quilt because she would be having a significant birthday that ended in either 5 or 0. That year my birthday had both of those numbers. I thought I could do that...and since I was reading this on a New Years Day, I started right away.

She suggested using the Wave pattern from Georgia Bonesteel's book *New Ideas for Lap Quilting*. If you make the quilt 18x21 rows you will need 378 patches, which is one for every day, plus 13 extra. As I went along, I used one of the extra patches for the month and appliqued or fused a decoration representing the month....a flag for July and a birthday cake for August, etc. I made a patch and the first day of the month from the same fabric throughout the quilt and that provided a visual marker for the beginning of each month.

I cut several patches at a time, and then had fun matching the fabric to what happened on that day....a yellow one for the first day of sunshine after 14 cloudy days, snowy looking fabric for the snow storm, etc. To write on the patches I had the most success with a 03 Pigma Pen. The 01 pen was just too fine and was difficult to read. The fabric needs to be light and not real busy print. I did hand piece the quilt, but it could just as easily be pieced by machine. I did, however, machine quilt it, using the serpentine zig zag stitch.

I enjoyed doing that quilt so much, that I began a new quilt on Sept. 17th. That was the day I was installed as Co-President of our State Guild and this will be my record of my term of office. Who says the year begins on January 1???

Authors Note: I was lucky enough to get to see Judy's quilt when I presented a Program and Workshops to the Iowa Quilters Guild. Marvelous! I loved it! She had the cutest notations on the patches. I read every one. One day simply said "Nothing happened today!" On another one she told of the number of pairs of shoes she had bought on sale that day! I have started my own Diary/calendar Quilt (using the wave pattern from Georgia's Book), and plan to hang it on the wall, when completed. I hope I don't embarrass my husband or family, as I tend to get very personal in a diary! Try one yourself, could be great fun!

++++++++++++++++++++++++++++

Margo J. Clabo
Cleveland, Tennessee

READ! READ! READ! There is so much literature out there now, with an incredible amount of information. You can save yourself a lot of time and frustration and money, if you take advantage of other quilters' experience. THERE IS NO

Page 202, Quilters offer advice

REASON TO RE-INVENT THE WHEEL. Spend your valuable resources on the fun stuff!

++++++++++++++++++++++++++++

John Flynn
Billings, Montana

• I don't try to organize my quilting stuff. I have 2 homes and a 40'x100' shop building on 15 acres of land; I can keep pretty much all of my stuff inside the fence!

++++++++++++++++++++++++++++

Candra J. Sowder
Willliamsburg, Iowa

• Take as many classes as you can afford to, even for items you may not be totally interested in. You will learn something new from every class and be able to see many variations of the same theme, that you would never experience by looking at one picture of a pattern. Tips and techniques will help you on items you really do want to do. Other classmates can be just as informative as the teacher, at times.
• If you really want to learn about something, volunteer to teach it in your local club, community college, or just to friends around your dining table. It forces you to research, experiment, and really understand your topic. Many clubs are constantly seeking volunteers to speak or demonstrate techniques or patterns to their groups. You can even earn a little money to fund your projects!
• Scraps. Take up colorwash quilting or postage stamp quilting (1 1/2" squares) to use up scraps of fabric, or buy Granny Nanny mini-block papers to use up small pieces. Almost anything an inch square can be used to complete these projects, with little or no waste.
• Seam ripping. Cut every fourth thread on one side of the material with the seam ripper, then take both sides of the material and pull, it will pull apart with ease, or pull the unbroken string on the backside for an effect like opening a bag that has been sewn shut with a chain stitch. The second would be better for fabrics that ravel easily.
• Lame'. Lame' is beautiful used in clothing and other quilted items. Back it with a woven fusible interfacing, pressing slowly and checking for bubbles and wrinkles as you do, they are easily taken care of by simply pulling a little area apart and re-ironing. Lame' is best used as an accent fabric in small areas (narrow strips, centers of log cabins, etc.) and on items to be washed seldom, or hand treated.
• For richer looking quilts, use tone-on-tone fabric for backgrounds, as opposed to solids or muslin. This can really make a difference in the overall appearance of the quilt. It adds texture to the piece. Not much tone contrast is desired.
• If you do not belong to a quilt guild, join one. Try to get the club to invest in a library of resource materials for it's members. People can loan books to each other through the group's library.

Visit libraries of all kinds (the local university library has a large section on quilts and textiles). Go to your local library and see what they have to offer. Then let them know you want quilting books in the collection. They will more likely honor your request. Go with a list of books prepared that they can choose from. They will more likely want to purchase books with broad ranges of patterns, history, and techniques than single pattern booklets or single theme books.

Most libraries have an inter-library loan policy which will enable you to borrow books from libraries across your county or state. Many collections could use an infusion of quilting resources, using the newer techniques, and more modern designs. Libraries cater to their users, especially those who are willing to do the foot-work for them. This will make your budget stretch farther and offer quality titles to the general public, furthering their interest in quilting and design.

Author's note: Remember, Candra Sowder has a Master's Degree in Library Science, so she knows whereof she speaks!

++++++++++++++++++++++++++++

Marilyn Thomas
Harpster, Ohio

• When my grandson, David, and granddaughter, Chelsea Foreman, are here (they are 6 & 8 years old), they string buttons with needle and thread. Entertains very well.
• I have a cupboard my quilts are stored in, covered with fabric so they won't touch wood.
• For my sore fingers I use "Vicks Vapor Rub: at night. I have tried everything, that's the best for me.

Quilters offer advice, page 203

++++++++++++++++++++++++++++++
Diana Alfuth
Hudson, Wisconsin

•I have no children but I do have cats, which can be worse than children. Cats are drawn to quilts like magnets. They crawl into the middle of whatever I'm doing. I've found that if you wrap them up in another, already finished quilt, they often leave you alone!

++++++++++++++++++++++++++++++
Juanita Gibson Yeager
Louisville, Kentucky

•I keep all of my scraps in a covered bin under the table where I do most of my cutting. When the bin is full I call my sister-in-law, who makes scrap quilts, and tell her to expect a box in the next few days. If your scraps and UFOs are accumulating and making you feel guilty, find someone who does scrap quilts or adopt a quilter who is less skilled than you who is still exploring the art and will be happy to take off your hands all those scraps and UFOs you feel guilty for not working up into a quilt or completing.
•My fabric is folded and stacked in 28 stackable white plastic coated wire baskets. As my collection grew, I added more baskets which is less expensive than adding more shelving.
•My fabric is organized by color and those that defy categorization in that manner are grouped by type, e.i., Japanese, African, or Lame', Tropical, etc.
•I protect my underfinger with a double layered strip of electrical tape or 3M plastic repair tape.

++++++++++++++++++++++++++++++
Carol Thelen
Pearland, Texas

•My quilting "room" is about half of a 10x10' room with desk, computer and bookshelves in the other half. My fabric was stored in three boxes stacked in the corner. I couldn't find anything! I needed something that looked nice but would enable me to reach all my fabric. I love antiques and there are many antique markets and flea markets in my area. I found an antique maple wardrobe with a door in the center. It is about 6' high and 4' wide and 2' deep. The price was $65 compared to new wardrobes priced at $600 to $1000. My husband installed four wooden shelves stained to match the wardrobe. With the bottom of the wardrobe I have five levels to store my fabric. Each shelf holds about five stacks of fabric. I even have room for my books and magazines, notions, etc. On the side that faces the wall I placed a nail at the top, I looped one end of a ribbon over the nail and the other end I put through my hoops (3), then I looped the other end of the ribbon over the nail. The hoops hang on the side of the wardrobe out of sight, and easily accessible.

++++++++++++++++++++++++++++++
Jane Aruns
Franklin, Tennessee

•Never give your labor to someone who won't appreciate it! Cheater cloth pillows and wall hangings are fine for a homemade touch for the unenlightened.
•I cut scraps into 2" triangles, 2" squares or just stuff them on their own shelf. Some year I plan to make a scrap quilt (don't hold your breath).
•Much of my work is sold through show contracts and I have a list of collectors that I offer the work to first. I work slowly, so I never have too many things available.

++++++++++++++++++++++++++++++
Shirley Gardner
Evergreen, Colorado

•If I make a quilt to give away or to sell, I make it on the machine. If it is to hang on my living room wall, I make it by hand. Since I do programs and show the quilts to hundreds of people, I usually make them by hand. The machine is faster and I can create more designs with it so I am making more work these days by machine, but I shall always prefer beautiful hand work. Either method works. The important part is the design, color and fabric.

++++++++++++++++++++++++++++++
Carol Younce
Fairfax, Virginia

•I had my small children make many a button necklace out of a blunt needle, carpet or quilt thread, and they loved playing with and choosing the buttons.

++++++++++++++++++++++++++++++
Joyce Benitez
Omaha, Nebraska

•I usually don't sell what I make, I usually give away my items (I joke you have to get married or have a baby to get one), also if I am going to give them away, I usually will machine quilt those items. If it's going to "live" at my house and can be cared for like a baby, then I will spend time to hand quilt it.

++++++++++++++++++++++++++++

Debra J. Ruisard
Whitehouse Station, New Jersey

Having small children, I learned early on that if I don't let them in my sewing area, that is where they want to be. I throw small scraps and strips in a basket and leave out a portable design wall, so that anytime they want, they can arrange strips on the board to create their own quilts. I've even been known to sew together a few of their masterpieces.

• Spools of thread make wonderful toys and my oldest likes to write on fabric with my pigma pens. I have had little trouble with them playing with mommy's toys, although my 2 year old has rearranged my sewing machine on occasion.

• I have a large and varied fabric stash that sits on open shelves in my 'studio'. I don't hide it away in drawers, else I forget what I have. I often spend time looking through my fabric and find wonderful combinations. I buy fabric when I see something I like. I usually buy a yard, then put it away for that right project. I like to say my fabric gets put into the 'aging room' to age a bit! Fabric is more valuable the older it is, right? Inevitably, when working on a project, I still need to buy some more fabric, because what I have isn't exactly right.

• I order many of my supplies from discount mail-order companies and get most of my books from AQS through my Guild. I drive 2 hours to Lancaster, PA to buy cheap fabric. I find it hard to pay full price for anything except that which is unusual, that is what I go to quilt shows for - the vendors often carry the unusual fabrics, books and patterns.

• I like to make quilted tree skirts and stockings for weddings and births. I also enjoy making baby quilts. Of course, like the shoemaker's kids who have no shoes, my children do not have quilts. Each time I was pregnant, the thought of quilting made me nauseous! I couldn't quilt a bit! But I figure I will enjoy making my daughters their own quilts when they are old enough to help pick out fabric and patterns they like. In the meantime, all my nieces and nephews and friend's children have quilts made by me. I usually piece the top, give it as a gift and then take it back to finish in my own sweet time.

• As a quilter and a mother, I know how hard it is to find the time to quilt. I try to do something everyday, even it just for 10 minutes. I find that if a few days go by and I haven't gone in my quilting room, I get irritable and frustrated easily. It is my creative outlet - I need to do it. I am blessed with a husband who respects my needs and never asks how much I spend on fabric!

++++++++++++++++++++++++++++

Fran Soika
Novelty, Ohio

• The most important thing in quilting is to enjoy what you are doing, and know that your ideas are as good as anyone elses.

++++++++++++++++++++++++++++

Anne-Donia B. Hafskjold
Tiller, Norway

• Presently I don't have much space for all my quilting equipment, so a big closet with many baskets, one for each color of fabrics is a great help. The rest of my equipment is stored in a suitcase, and I fortunately have a very nice family who do not complain about my unfinished project lying around.

• During the years, I have collected many samples, and a great project is to make a big Charm Quilt. A one-of-a-kind quilt, and best of all, it is free!

• My best quilting friend is my thimble, I never leave home without it!

++++++++++++++++++++++++++++

Bonnie Swannack
Lamont, Washington

• I try to organize my fabrics by color but they rarely stay that way. I have fabric in boxes, on shelves, under the bed, anywhere there is a little room.

++++++++++++++++++++++++++++

Connie Sager
Nashville, Kansas

• Debbie's little Briana is the only one close enough to come visit often, she thoroughly loves to play with a few rolled up "fat quarters", plastic scissors (that can't cut the fabric), an old rotary mat and old ruler. She is only two and knows she is making great quilts. The others are out of state and when they come, we just go and do fun things for a few days.

Quilters offer advice, page 205

Lynda Milligan
Denver, Colorado

• I'm seriously considering moving my sewing room into my living room. The living room is hardly ever used since we have a great family room. The LR is over 2x the size, very light and convenient. My Sewing Room is a made-over library, where I could move the computer, a pull-out couch and the desk that are now in the LR. Of course, it will no longer be called my sewing room, it will be my STUDIO!

Nancy Smith
Denver, Colorado

• (To get my fabric into my sewing room.) I won't let fabric come in, until it has been washed. All new fabric goes directly to the laundry room and is washed and dried, and then I can take it on down. That way I know anything I pull out to work with is ready to sew.

Carole Collins
Norfolk, Nebraska

• As I said in the first section, our children are not living at home so I don't have to worry about keeping small children busy, while I quilt.
• I have two jelly cupboards and a carpenter's chest that I keep my "whole" fabric in. I sort it by color on different shelves. I have refinished old tool carriers, cutlery trays, and cheese boxes that I store fabric that is cut into strips or leftover squares and triangles.
• When I am cutting out a project and there are narrow strips left, I will cut them into a specific width. These are stored in baskets according to color, and used in log cabin quilts.
• I use a thimble on my quilting hand, but nothing on the hand in under the quilt. I do use bag balm after finishing quilting for the day.
• Teaching has really helped me to grow as a quilter, too. I am always trying a new ruler or method that will help me to be a better teacher. It is a real sense of accomplishment when I see the projects that my students have made; and it is very encouraging when a class is ending and they ask "What is our next class going to be?"

Betty E. Ives
Windsor Ontario, Canada

• When I machine applique, I use "deli" paper next to the feed dogs. A few pins hold it in place and it tears easily with no paper showing. You can purchase or beg it at the sliced meat or cheese counter, but I bought a "Kleenex" looking box from the Pfaff dealer booth in Paducah many, many years ago. I am still using it. It was $5 then.
• My stash is overflowing into clear plastic boxes on the floor. I must quit buying fabric! Love to feel and look at it!!!!

Constance T. Hall
Mannington, West Virginia

• It has been so long since I have had little ones around, I do not know what I would do with them! I suppose, like most people, put a videotape on the VCR for them to watch.
• I have saved a lot of money by visiting stores that sell pieces of fabric from garment factories. I have been able to buy 15 pounds for $3.00 at some of these places. I have lived on a farm for the 64 years of my married life and have had Feed Sacks to use. They make nice quilts and never wear out it seems. I have my fifty some quilts wrapped in feed sacks, and stored in a dry wardrobe.
• My scraps are sorted and placed in marked boxes, according to colors and designs.
• As for protecting your fingers from being stuck, I have learned to let the needle come through and just touch in between my first and second fingers underneath the quilt. That way my finger never gets stuck and sore like most quilters.
• As for selling my quilts, I have never sold any. I have given my six grandchildren each one, and also have completed six for the six great grandchildren. My daughter, Reita, has quilted them for me.
• I quilt with the West Augusta Historical Society Ladies each Thursday. I am Chairman of the quilting committee. We quilt for other people and also make some for the Society to sell. We hold a Quilt Show each June. We have had as many as 127 quilts at our Show. Come and see it sometime. It is always on Father's Day Weekend.

Zelda Lynch
San Augustine, Texas

- Being 79 and living alone, I have no problems with children.
- I sell quilts through magazines and going to craft shows. But now, I only go to 3 shows a year, and 2 days at a show (inside). I have mailed quilts to 34 states. I wish I could sell to all 50, but selling is slow. Too much trash coming in from China and Taiwan.

Kathy Munkelwitz
Isle, Maine

- All my fabric is sorted and in plain sight in a cupboard. I can see at a glance what I have. My cupboard is just like a bookshelf.
- We make tied quilts from scraps, or else give them to organizations that will make use of them.

Sandra A. Anderson
Lincoln, Nebraska

- When my children were smaller, I let them sort out pieces of material as to colors (helps small ones learn colors), they also liked to find the different designs, teddy bears, circles, cats, etc. They also enjoyed sorting through buttons, grouping them by colors and sizes and shapes. They made up games trying to find buttons that matched or were opposites (a round button and a square button).
- I use a lot of Rubbermaid see-through containers to hold projects, sorted materials, cut pieces, etc.
- I have found lots of ribbons and laces at garage sales. I gently wash these and use a warm curling iron to press them. Just run the ribbon around the rod and it looks just like new.
- One of the smartest things I did was hang a peg board next to my sewing machine where I have all my *tools* hanging on it. So whatever I need is right at hand and I don't have to hunt for it.
- Also I once "lost" the instruction book to my sewing machine and I was having some trouble with the tension and was very frustrated. When I found my instruction book, I punched a hole in the corner and hung it on a hook right next to my machine, so it is always there if I need it.

Joan Biasucci
CedarCreek, Nebraska

- Take frequent road trips with other quilters, and always adhere to the following *very important rule:*

Never tell anyone (meaning, a husband) what any member of the group purchased and/or ate on the trip. Always remember, and recite very carefully to anyone (meaning, a husband) who asks, the all-important phrase "I think it was some kind of salad...."

Sharon J. Mason
Coos Bay, Oregon

- My children all love to string buttons. Also my children, boys included, could sew the stem stitch by 5 years old and some muslin in a hoop is all they need for a good pass time. Mom can draw their favorite picture (keep it simple) with a water soluble marker. Just for them!

Doris Lott Aultman
Hattiesburg, Mississippi

- I feel that each quilter should work on quilts that make them happy, not try and copy someone else. Even though we strive to appeal to the judges, we should after all, make the quilts we enjoy, then if it should appeal to a judge, that is even better.
- I make swatch listings of all the fabrics that I have on hand and the amounts I have, and carry these with me. Then I can see the fabrics and know if the new prospective buy will match or work well with what I have on hand. This helps me.
- I love scraps, and have a real supply. I do separate them into color families and put them into labeled boxes. Then I can pull, blue & pink, or brown & green.

Wilma Dooley Muse
Fayetteville, Tennessee

- Washed fabrics of similar colors are stored together in see-thru plastic cases.

Jennifer J. Danly
Arlington, Massachusetts

- I keep my fabric "stash" in an old dresser. The drawers hold a lot, are easy to sort by color, and easy to browse through. Also, a dresser works well in almost any

room, any decor.
• Keeping my kids entertained is a challenge. They enjoy playing with scraps or coloring with my colored pencils.
• I do mostly handwork, and mostly small projects which are easy to pick up and put down, and carry from room to room.

++++++++++++++++++++++++++

Suzanne Peery Schutt
Clinton, Mississippi

• Storing: All my wall hangings, I stack them on a bed, then roll them together and place on shelf, no folds & they are ready to hang with no wrinkles.
• I keep small scraps in baskets under my quilt frame.
• Sell items through your local quilt shop.
• Do your own designs - don't do what "everyone else" is doing. Follow your own star!

++++++++++++++++++++++++++

Ellen Vollmer
Nickerson, Nebraska

• I don't have real young children, but I let my 11 year old take scraps of fabric that I don't use on quilts. He cuts with rotary cutter and can hand sew together. Keeps him busy and takes pride in his project.
• Most of my projects are given away. I have a large family and at Christmas time, we trade homemade gifts.
• I use plastic shoe boxes, they are marked 1", 1 1/2", 2", etc. for my strips of fabric and if I need a 2" square, cut 2" off.

++++++++++++++++++++++++++

Pauline Hess 'Ping' White
Seaboard, North Carolina

• I have stored my material in large plastic boxes (with lids removed so air can circulate through the material). I have separated the red, blues, greens, blacks, browns, yellows so that I can easily find what I want.
• I also put cut strips, 1", 1 1/2", 2", etc. into individual plastic boxes so they are convenient, when I need them.

++++++++++++++++++++++++++

Pat Milne Hitchcock
Sequim, Washington

• Take a photo of all your completed projects. I use these photos and prints of them to make greeting cards for about half the cost of a commercial one. You can buy matching paper and envelopes by the ounce at a stationary store - fold the paper, glue your picture with rubber cement. Your friends will love them, and you can even do up a small packet for a quick gift.
• Two of the best equipment purchases I have made, aside from the obvious, are a cheap package of small hair clips which I use to "pin baste" the final stage of attaching the binding - and the other is to purchase the absolute best quality half-hoop you can get. This will allow you to quilt to within a quarter inch from the edge of your item, and it certainly is a time saver, as well as alleviating a lot of frustration.
• Last of all, I would encourage each and everyone of you to put your work into shows - it is such a pleasure to enjoy the work of others, and even if you are a beginner and you feel your work is not up to the standard of others, I assure you, you will be inspiring others to give it a try. And, please, please, always sign your work with ALL of your name and date it; I surely do wish I could know who made the old quilts which give me such pleasure - these ordinary women who satisfied their creative needs by making extra-ordinarily beautiful and useful bed coverings for posterity.

++++++++++++++++++++++++++

Alice Furrey
Carter, South Dakota

• Fabric is stored by color. When I plan a quilt I lay out the fabrics I plan on using on one of the spare beds and play with it for several days. I substitute different fabrics in the same color or other colors until everything "feels" just right.
• This step should not be hurried.
• Having a good stash of fabric is essential in designing quilts to sell. It is just having the right tools to work with.
• A good sewing machine is also essential. My favorite feature is a needle positioner. It makes piecing and pivoting much easier.
• Understanding even-feed with your own sewing machine can make a big difference when strip piecing, sewing on multiple borders and putting on edging with a sewing machine.
• I receive a lot of quilts with rippling borders, especially those with many borders. (Remember, Alice is a professional at

finishing quilts...J.L.) Evidently this is a common problem as I have seen it referred to in judges comments in the quilting magazines. Most quilters do not understand why this happens. Most often it is due to the fact that most sewing machines do not have an even feed mechanism. Any time two long strips are sewn together that are the same size, one will end up being shorter. Borders are usually placed over the quilt top and sewn on the machine. It is best to pin the border to the top in several areas, about every 10", rather than just letting it feed in as you sew. It will be necessary to give the top piece a *gentle* tug as you sew to keep them even. If you don't do this each border will be larger, overall, than the previous one without there having to be a tuck.

• When sewing strips for strip quilting, this is also a problem. Have you ever sewn several strips together that curved like a rainbow? This can be eliminated by giving that top strip a gentle tug as you sew.

• This same problem with even fee also applies when sewing on the outside edging; which is usually done by sewing on either a bias or straight strip of fabric to the top, and hand finishing it on the back. In this case, it is beneficial to have the edge just a bit smaller than the actual quilt, because the very act of quilting has taken up inches across the quilt, and the edge will look ripply, if it is kept the same size as the edge. If a bias strip is used, a very gentle tug is necessary, if a straight grain is used, a more than gentle tug is necessary.

• Another solution to the problem can be to buy a walking foot for your machine. They are often expensive and I have found I cannot do as accurate of sewing with them. I do use them for sewing on bias edges, and can even machine sew on the second side on the curved edge with them quilt successfully.

++++++++++++++++++++++++++
Ilene L. Burdick
Coudersport, Pennsylvania

• My first experience of selling was by word of mouth of family members who work with people who expressed an interest in different items. Then I got involved with some community activities, which involved this type of craft and when people asked where to get handmade items, I was right there to reply.

++++++++++++++++++++++++++
Sarah M. Bruso
Rhinelander, Wisconsin

• I have made small, colorful quilt squares for the grandchildren to play with while I quilt, also I use an old tied quilt on the floor for them to play on. They seem perfectly happy as long as they can be by me.

• My stash is mostly organized by color, although I separate my plaids, Christmas fabric, and fancy Hoffmans, etc. My scraps are separated by color in high box plastic containers.

++++++++++++++++++++++++++
Merrilee Tieche
Ozark, Missouri

• Since I share my quiltmaking space with a washer and dryer, storage of all the necessary gear has been a challenge. A clear plastic shoe storage bag that hangs on the door solved the problem of what to do with many small items. I purchased mine through the Lillian Vernon catalogue. It has 28 compartments and holds pins, needles, rotary cutter, etc. right next to my sewing machine.

• Sarah and Emily, my 3 and 4 year old granddaughters, will play quietly for hours with Gramma's scrap bag, sorting by color, shape and size.

++++++++++++++++++++++++++
Dean Valentine
New Braunfels, Texas

• I believe all quilters should belong to a BEE, the membership in my Wednesday Bee ranges from ages of 30's to late 70's. The knowledge and experience you gain from the interaction, is priceless.

++++++++++++++++++++++++++
Marilyn A. Lewis
Glendale, Oregon

• I keep baby quilts made up for gift giving.

• I often trade scraps, I have traded with two English traders, really fun. (just scraps!)

• I also collect and trade feedsack fabric and have traded feedsack scraps.

• I buy second hand cotton garments anywhere I see them. Jr. dresses are good, as they are 100% cotton and not usually worn.

Christine Miller
Medway, Ohio

(I'm an organization freak!)
- I built a "cubby-hole" system with (same size) boxes covered with contact paper for my sewing room - wall length closet.
- Scraps are sorted by color in other plastic small boxes easily accessible to my sewing machine.
- My quilt books and magazines are stored in covered (soap box) units - all indexed by pattern - list is stored on my computer's hard drive, which I market under The Patchwork Puzzle name.

Laura Estes
Odessa, Washington

- Buy quality fabrics, a poor quality fabric can ruin the project.
- Learn when your local shops generally hold sales and try to stock up then.
- Shop with a friend and buy 1/2 yard pieces you both like, then split and you each have a fat quarter that's more suitable in many projects.
- Tell all your relatives and friends, who you exchange gifts with, that your favorite gift would be a gift certificate to your favorite shop or mail order house.
- I organize my fabrics by projects for the most part, though I have 4 large Rubbermaid keepers with fabrics by color, that are awaiting being assigned to a project.
- I keep the projects in large shoe boxes on a large shelf unit. I have over 50 quilts under construction. If it's a good year I will complete 8 to 10, a slow year 4 or 5.
- I don't sell too many quilts, most I keep or give away. I know this about selling, quality speaks, matched points and corners and neat quilting will bring higher prices. Sign your work and aim for quality.
- Florence Calla was my inspiration in needle arts. I just wish I would have payed more attention to her hints and suggestions, while she was still living.

Lois K. Ide
Bucyrus, Ohio

- A legend block is a MUST for each quilt. It should include the following:
    Name of quilt
    Date
    Name of Quiltmaker
    Size
    State
    How to clean and
        with what
    In Collection
        of_____
And any other pertinent information such as a very special story of quilt, if there is one. (Awards, etc.)
- About scraps: keep them all, as you may need that square inch sometime! Every time I do throw something out, I need it the very next week it seems.
- If you are not now wearing a thimble, learn to do so. I also wear a thimble on my left hand, either my index or middle finger. It certainly eliminates specks of blood on the back side of quilt! Both these habits are easy to form and if formed, save much time and pain.
- If you do not already know how to do beautiful shadow applique, learn! Very lovely and quick gifts can be made using this technique, and can be as simple or as elaborate as you choose, according to time allowed.
- Never handle things twice. When I get a bill, I pay it. When I'm finished with a fabric, I fold it and put it back where it belongs. When I pull a reference book I put it back where it belongs, as soon as I am finished with it. All this keeps a reasonable semblance of order on all work spaces and makes it easier to find things, because all are in their places and not simply not piling up.

Grace Moone
High Falls, New York

- I've found if I pick smaller projects, they are much more do-able in my schedule. Because I still want to "try" everything, so wall hangings pillows, and ornaments are my main projects.

Merry May
Tuckahoe, New Jersey

- The small swatch packs, which you can order from catalogs, are a great way to keep five year olds busy. With about 400 to 600 little pieces of fabric to play with, you'll be amazed at some of the results they'll come up with. You may even be inspired to create something based on their combinations.
- If someone asks you to make something for them and they tell you it's "no rush", either *make* them give you a deadline, or make one for yourself. Otherwise, as the old saying goes, "Tomorrow never comes!"

Quilters offer advice

++++++++++++++++++++++++++++

Jacque' J. Holmes
Big Bear Lake, California

• Storage: When my fabric stash wound up all over the floor after our big earthquake of *92*, I decided to devise a new way of stacking it. I bought 30 or more plastic storage crates, each 13"x15"x10" and as many 12" bungee cords as I could find. I sorted the fabrics by color and placed them in the crates as you would place books. Then I stretched the cords in a crisscross fashion in front of the fabric. The crates stack well on the shelves of my closet.

++++++++++++++++++++++++++++

Penny Hand
Woodbridge, Virginia

• I store my fabric in a 9-drawer dresser by color.

++++++++++++++++++++++++++++

Judith Clonan
Fitchburg, Massachusetts

• Time management and organizing my stash. Don't mention it to my husband. I had a shaker jelly cupboard made and now I need 2 more!'
• I try to shop sales and not feel guilty!
• Have given wall hangings as gifts, just completed King-sized Sampler and Christmas Full-sized quilts for myself. Other projects are in various stages of "incompletion".
• Quilting keeps me going!

++++++++++++++++++++++++++++

Virginia H. Flowers
Flushing, Michigan

• I do have a sewing room with a writing table, a 4x8' sheet of plywood on built-up saw horses for a cutting table, a desk with a Viking® 630 machine, a Simplicity® 4-thread serger and a lot of storage bins of material. I am strictly a home grown quilter.

++++++++++++++++++++++++++++

Martha A. De Turk
Kutztown, Pennsylvania

• I do drop everything to take time to sew, somehow other necessities get done.
• My grandchildren love to be included in the projects, 3 of the girls, Rebecca age 5, Laurabeth age 6, and Colleen age 8, have done some handquilting and pieced simple squares on the sewing machine (under supervision at machine). They love to use wonder-under to applique and the toddlers love playing with scraps. Great for learning shapes and colors.
• Many scraps I cut into 2x45" strips for strip piecing or Roman Strips to use for comforters at Women's Shelter.

++++++++++++++++++++++++++++

Kathleen Nyman
Oswego, Illinois

• The only advice I'd have is "stick with it!" It's hard to find time, money, energy, etc. for quilting, but it's worth it. Find 10-15 minutes a day to piece or quilt, so you can say you did it.
• A good friend always answers my "How should I do this - what's the right way.". "Try it and you'll find out.", or "It's whatever you like. The *correct* color combination is what pleases you.
• I keep several projects going, so I don't get bored.

++++++++++++++++++++++++++++

Betty M. Abel
Sheboygan, Wisconsin

• My stash is on book shelves according to color. Solids are separate. Novelty fabrics on another shelf. Quilt patterns I place in large manila envelopes along with templates, notes and samples. Tape the pattern picture on the outside of envelope. Then file in cabinets under wearables, holidays, wall hangings, etc.

++++++++++++++++++++++++++++

Doris Callaway,
Greensburg, Kansas

• Most of my gifts are homemade, using my quilting & sewing as the basis for gifts. I'd rather sew than eat! I go to a few craft fairs & sell my items, but give most away!

++++++++++++++++++++++++++++

Mary J. Ruda
Elida, Ohio

• I send my small scraps to my quilting friend in New Zealand. I also make AIDS baby quilts and quilts for the Crisis Center Children, children under 2 years of age.
• I buy most of my fabric on sale. That what I do to use my calico fabrics. For designer fabrics, I am making..squares, triangles and other shapes of scrap quilts.

Quilters offer advice, page 211

++++++++++++++++++++++++++
Ruth E. O'Connor
Burlington, Mass

• Try to color code material. Keep checks and plaids together, also solids.
• I love to make things out of the tiniest scraps like doll quilts. They sell good at Benefits for Historical Society.
• I can't use thimbles much...just bleed.

++++++++++++++++++++++++++
Georgina Doss
Milton, West Virginia

• I make mostly wearables and small pieces because my daughter has always wanted to do what I am doing. She once used scissors on a piece in my quilting frame. I have avoided large pieces since. When she was younger, I could do machine piecing by giving her a battery operated toy sewing machine (minus the needle) and pre-quilted and cheaters cloth to run under the foot. Now that she's older, she practices her quilting stitches on counted cross-stitch fabric, using bright colored floss and a plastic needle. I also save all my fabric scraps for her to arrange onto iron-on interfacing. She has progressed from crazy quilt squares to designing more geometric blocks.

++++++++++++++++++++++++++
Linda Boedigheimer
Perham, Minnesota

• I work on about 20-25 different quilting projects at a time, as I store each project in their own basket, case, box, bag, etc. That makes it easier to pick up any one, at any given time, to work on.

• I always have a hand-quilted pot holder done to use as a quick, personal gift.

++++++++++++++++++++++++++
Bernice Tessibel I
Inman Cashman
(Tessie)
Coal City, Indiana

• Buy fabric on sale, if at all possible.
• Subscribe to a good quilting magazine.
• Join a quilt guild to keep motivated and up to date.

++++++++++++++++++++++++++
Anna Eelman
North Plainfield,
New Jersey

• My best quilting time when the kids were little, was after they were in bed. When they were teenagers I often quilted and prayed, while waiting for them to return home on late nights.
• I save money by not succumbing to every new gadget for quilters.
• I use shoe boxes to store scraps. I cut them to shape before putting them away such as circles, strips, various sizes of squares and triangles, when I want to start a new project, many scraps are then ready to cut to size.

++++++++++++++++++++++++++
Nancy Wagner Graves,
Manhattan, Kansas

• I have two cabinets I keep my fabric in. The fabric gets washed before it gets put away. I arrange it by color. When I have small scraps, I put these in plastic bins stored in a closet. I also sort these by color.
• Whenever I find a really good deal on fabric ($1 or $2 a yard) I buy 10 yards of it and use it as backing in future quilts.

++++++++++++++++++++++++++
Dort Lee,
Leicester,
North Carolina

• For small children:
1. Let them play with embroidery thread or jars of buttons (age 3 and up) - sorting, teaching to count, learning colors. The embroidery thread will end up a tangled mess, but you only need small pieces at a time, and these will easily pull out!
2. Buy a decent set of blunt nosed children's cloth scissors (Fiskars makes some) and give the child lots of scraps of cloth, a piece of cardboard, and some "tacky" glue. They can make collage quilts. Make child clean up their own mess every time, so you don't resent him making a mess. You should not think of it as a *mess*, rather as "a learning experience."

++++++++++++++++++++++++++
Judi Robb
Manhattan, Kansas

• I save all scraps, put them in plastic storage boxes, and use them for applique.
• Buy lots of fabric-in all colors-not just your favorite. Remember to look for lights, as well as the beautiful medium and darks. Store fabric by color, where you can see it all the time, but not in direct sunlight.
• Take pictures of quilts you like at quilt shows, etc. - to use when you need ideas or inspiration.

Page 212, Quilters offer advice

Eleanor Burenheide
Emporia, Kansas

• Prepare the hand sewing needle for storage by threading the needle with a 5 inch piece of thread. Tie the two ends together in a knot. Easier to find the needle if dropped, or if worked into a pin cushion.
• Select stripe fabric for beginners to learn to sew. Make pot holders. Let them quilt it on the machine with the walking foot. Remember...cotton batting...and match the stripes with the correct thread. Teaches many things...How to: thread the machine, how to quilt and how to bind. Then, they have their Christmas presents ready.
• Use exposed x-ray film for templates.
• Place a few streaks of rubber cement on the "gripping" side of your rulers when you use the rotary cutter. PRESTO...no slipping. Cement can be removed by rolling it off with your thumb.
• Straight pin your *textile sandwich* to a 3/4" piece of styrofoam. Use the Quilt-tack to baste your project. You can do a twin sized quilt in 15 minutes.
• Save lots of money! Purchase 100% cotton thread cones in 6000 yard amounts. This is NOT serger thread. You may have to ask your quilt store to special order. White, off white, gray, and black are good basic colors to use on most projects.
• Difficult time pulling the needle thru your quilted project? Place a rubber finger stall on your index finger. They come in all sizes at the office supply store.
• Prairie points....made easily...from a continuous band of fabric. (See QNL-Sept. 89)

• Methodist Quilting. Actually, it is a tied procedure. Only the knots are inside the project, between the batting and the backing of the quilt. Simply lay the textile sandwich on the table. Pin only the center. Roll back the backing and tie as usual, only the knots are inside the Project.

When the center row is completed, fold the backing down for one row, lay it back and then tie the second row. Do this to the edge and turn the project around and do the same thing to the other side. A fun way to tie a comfort.
• Let children help make blocks by using color crayons. Especially nice to welcome a new baby into the family.

• STORING QUILT SUPPLIES: All you need is: a series of drawers for small items. A Peg board to hang bulky items. And, a large amount of shelves, for everything else. Use containers for different colors of fabrics, separate the plain from the printed fabrics. Sort by the color wheel. Attach pieces of cloth to the outside so children can see what's in the box. (They can help you put fabric away, and they love it) Use separate boxes for: blacks, browns, Christmas, juvenile prints, etc. When the pieces become scraps....they become fair game for the children to create. (Some projects are sewn, some become paste-ups.

Helen M. Ericson
Emporia, Kansas

• In the beginning I bought fabric for a specific quilt and kept them in packets; now I store the fabric in colors on shelves where it can be seen, felt, and used for any project.
• Each January make a list of what you want to do and what is unfinished; also take out fabric and restack it.
• Keep a bag of scraps to rummage through from time to time and share with new quiltmakers.
• Buy on sales, especially backing and battings that you use a lot.
• Accept the fact that your tastes may change and use outdated fabric for AIDS babies or for other worthy projects.
• Make quick projects for Guild auctions, wedding and baby showers gifts.
• Be happy to help a beginning quilter or young family member to be interested in our Art. Have joy in their progress, which may be more than your old fingers can do in the future.

Susan J. Spencer
Felton, California

• Now that my kids are older, I expected to have more time for quilting while they were in school. Instead, I was frittering time away here and there. Now I make a date with myself one day a week for a quilting workshop to work on those techniques I've come across in books or magazines and think "I'd like to try that someday." It really helps me to have a focus, and is an inexpensive way to

improve my skills.
- Speaking of focus, I've found that a project notebook is invaluable. Mine is a 9 1/2x6" 3-subject notebook from the drug store, and in it I keep track of what I'm working on now, as well as a section listing all those "to do someday" projects - and where to find the directions for them later! I keep an on-going goals list - to do this week, this month, to finish by a certain date, or by the end of the year.

Each year, around Jan. 1st, I try to map out what I hope to accomplish by the end of the year, and the short-term goals list helps keep me on track.
- I've found that trading blocks with other quilters has really helped me develop a better color sense. Because others will always have different tastes they may request colors that I'd normally avoid, and making blocks for them has made me stretch my creative muscles. (It's a good way to practice your piecing skills, if you're not currently working on a quilt of your own.)
- I have my fabric folded and stacked in color groups on shelves, so if I need a particular color for a project, I pull out the whole stack to find what I want. Anything smaller than a fat quarter goes into one of my scrap baskets - one for darks and one for lights. I've got usable sizes - 1 1/2", 2", 2 1/2" squares, 1 1/2", 1 3/4" strips and so on.

++++++++++++++++++++++++++++
Fanny Naught
Quincy, Illinois

- I don't have much of a problem storing quilts. I give them away almost as fast as I make them. With some exceptions, I do have a few of my mother's, and some wall hangings that I have made. These are kept in all cotton bags made from old sheets. I have my mother's cedar chest and it is full.
- Nothing outstanding about my stash, except it seems to grow all the time. I do keep it in drawers and in order of colors. I would like to use up the older fabrics faster, so I can buy more of the new and more beautiful ones on the market today.
- Happiness Arithmetic
+ The Joys that come to you
- Your cares away
x Your Blessings - and
+ Them while you may!

++++++++++++++++++++++++++++
Sheryl Mielke
McGregor, Iowa

- I started organizing my fabric stash by color, but I'm finding that I can't throw away smaller & smaller pieces. So I am accumulating boxes of smaller and smaller scraps.
- I so some hand-quilting for hire and use an old fashioned C-clamp frame. Because of sore fingers, I have developed a pre-quilting ritual. A plastic thumb goes on my right hand for quilting upwards or away from myself. A rubber secretarial finger is worn to help pull the needled loaded with stitches, and cheap bandage strips are worn on the finger tips on the left hand under the quilt.

++++++++++++++++++++++++++++
Bettie Rushin
Boulder Creek, California

- How to keep babies entertained....I always let my tiny babies lay on the quilt I was currently quilting, if that is too scary for you, put them on a blanket on your quilt.
- How to keep toddlers busy....throw all your scraps on the floor, include any scraps of paper, it's like confetti and little kids will play with the colors for hours.
- How to keep preschoolers busy...bring over a friend.
- How to keep school age kids busy....bribe them with their own first quilt (make it special and make it for them) they will be thrilled, and they will help you on your next project.
- I store my quilts and my supplies on wire shelves. The fabrics are sorted by color and by texture. My cutting supplies are in a drawer that can be secured. My old quilt patterns and blocks are organized in pizza boxes, because they don't need to be folded.
- Selling quilts can be difficult, because you must have a market in which you can sell. I started selling quilts by hand-quilting people's quilt tops, that is hard work, you can bring in some cash and you can build a name for yourself. When you have a supply of things to market, take them to local merchants for display, be sure you have a firm price, a business card and a huge dose of self-confidence, because there will be some rejection.

++++++++++++++++++++++++++++
Author's Note:
From the personal notes I received with the returned questionaires, it seems many people would like to sell products but find marketing difficult. The best advice I heard was "Keep trying, eventually it pays off!"

Page 214, Quilters offer advice

++++++++++++++++++++++++++++
Catherine Litwinow
Davenport, Iowa

• Son and husband opinions asked---not always followed.
• I keep my fabric in large Rubbermaid containers. Pull fabrics and put in plastic baskets, when there is a work in progress.

++++++++++++++++++++++++++++
Linda Ballard
Palo Cedro, California

• Mainly enjoy the time you have when quilting. Don't be hard on yourself if your points or seams are not as accurate as they should be, or could be. I tell my students, "I will rip 3 times and if I can't make it right by then, it was meant to be off!"

++++++++++++++++++++++++++++
Carol L. Robbins
Overland Park, Kansas

• I organize my stash by season and color. Scraps are used in miniature projects and crazy quilting projects.
• If you're short of time and want wonderful unique gifts, try stenciling with the new dry stenciling paints and then machine quilt around the designs---use whole cloth, not blocks! Whole cloth painting and quilting saves on more time!

++++++++++++++++++++++++++++
Beth Donaldson
Lansing, Michigan

• This is a tip for older children. I have an extensive fabric collection. After a few projects my fabric piles get very messy and it is hard to see what fabrics I have. I pay my daughters to straighten out my shelves and sort my fabrics ($1 for a small shelf, $2 for the larger ones). Often times they will sort it in such a way that I can see fabrics that I forgot I had or have been hidden for years. They also enjoy seeing all the colors and textures. This job is especially good during the summer or on school breaks. I make sure they only do one shelf at a time so they don't start too big, get tired of the job and then leave me with a bigger mess than I started with.
• How many of us have grand ideas for giving gifts? I think this is a beginner's phenomena. I also think it is a great idea. If you are a new quilter, make quilts for children. They are smaller and the recipient is easy to please. This way you can practice your skills and allow yourself the freedom from perfection. After all, if the quilt is not perfect, you will allow the child to drag it around and use it. Another great size is the lap quilt for the living room. You can experiment with colors and patterns and know the quilt will be loved and used, but the quilt doesn't have to be perfect, because it won't last forever, anyway. When you've made quilts for all your family members and kids on your list you'll be a much better quilter, and you'll be ready to tackle an "Heirloom" project. Keep this quilt for yourself, after all you've made them for everyone else already!
• Last, think of a quilt as "the gift that keeps on giving"! For the wedding, give them a quilt top with a lovely coupon for it to be quilted. Next, on the second to fifth anniversary, give the quilt, quilted with a coupon for it to be bound off. Last, give them the completed quilt. Since it takes time and dedication to produce a beautiful quilt, shouldn't it cover more than one gift?

++++++++++++++++++++++++++++
Marcia Knopp
Bay City, Michigan

• I don't know that I have any advice. I think quilting is an expensive, but satisfying hobby. I personally would never sell anything I made. I wish I had more time to get things done. My sewing room is a mess. I could use some advice on organizing things. Scraps are stored according to color or size.

++++++++++++++++++++++++++++
Shannon Royer
Otis, Kansas

• My daughter has had her own basket of fabric scraps for quite some time. I give her a pile that is hers alone, and she is less likely to want (or help herself to my quilt pieces. Now that she is older, I have given her a 12"x14" piece of foam board and a few pins (with supervision). She really enjoys arranging her pieces!
• I have recently followed suit and arranged my fabric by color in separate containers. Many times I have heard ladies say how nice this works, but after a while things get out of order, again. I have a container to put pieces in after I use them until I can "file" them away.

Quilters offer advice, page 215

++++++++++++++++++++++++++++
Netta Ranney
Overland Park, Kansas

•Give small children a scrap of loosely woven fabric and a blunt tapestry needle with double thread knotted at the end and a large button. They can sew with Mommy!
•Sewing cards can be made with colorful magazines glued to thin cardboard, then punched with a paper punch. Make a stiff point with scotch tape on the end of a piece of yarn. Thread back & forth through the holes.

++++++++++++++++++++++++++++
Karen Crosby
Ocala, Florida

•My best tip for saving time is to cook ahead. If you must cook, make extra and freeze it for another time when you are into a project that you just can't put down.
•The crock pot dinner is also great for throwing everything in, and by 6:00, it's ready to eat.

++++++++++++++++++++++++++++
Tedi Lambert
Los Banos, California

•To those who have small children underfoot, may I suggest locating another quilter who has small children and either exchange babysitting hours for quilting hours, or just meet together for quilting and have the children entertain each other. This works well for children of all ages.

•GIFTS: One of my favorite gifts to give is a small quilted box filled with candies. This is especially nice for teachers and principals or any last-minute gift you may need.
•STORING SUPPLIES: I store all my quilting thread in a clear, compartmentalized plastic box.
•To keep the dog from sleeping on my quilt-in-progress, I put it in the laundry basket. This works well for those who use a hoop instead of a frame.
•SCRAP STORAGE: I sort my scraps by color and store them in large boxes or tubs. That way when I need just a little bit of any color, I can go straight to it's container and find just what I need.
•FINGER PROTECTION: I don't have too much of a problem with my off hand, but I do have a problem with my thimble finger. Since I find leather thimbles too cumbersome to use, I prefer the English thimble. It is metal with a ridge around the top. Fit is usually the problem. Large is just a tad too large. Medium is way too small. Nail polish wears off and after many coats affects the size of the thimble.

Solution: Cut the fingers off a latex clear plastic glove (the kind the doctors and dentists wear) and use the finger portion on your finger. Gone is the discoloration from the metal. Gone is the poor fit. Gone is the cutting your finger due to needle drag (palm side where the eye of the needle drags across your finger). I once actually wore thru the skin on my finger, and that is how I discovered this solution.

++++++++++++++++++++++++++++
Julie L. Kimberlin
Anchorage, Alaska

•I organize my fabric collection by color. Some speciality fabrics (Batiks, Japanese, African) are kept together regardless of colors. Scraps are kept in a large wire mesh basket. Larger "scraps" (under 1/3 yard) are kept in a small wire mesh basket. (It's a 4-basket Elfa unit on casters.)

++++++++++++++++++++++++++++
Phyllis Hansen Giersch
Madera, California

Tips for keeping quilting alive in the future:

•Belonging to a local quilt guild is the best way to keep in touch with new techniques, books, patterns, and other quilters. I helped to organize our local quilt guild just 2 months after selling my store, from a list of interested customers that I had been collecting for about 6 months prior to the sale. We started with 18 and now have 70 members.
•Another opportunity opened up for me in 1991, in the form of a program called PACES. Each school in our district is given a list of artists that will come to the elementary schools and present programs for the students. I do quilting programs and have really enjoyed it. I spend a total of three hours in each classroom (90 minutes each day) and always do at least 2 different classes each day.
•I use fabric squares that are 50% poly and 50% cotton for the

design squares and we use fabric crayons, because I don't have to worry about ruining good school clothes with that medium. We design in the first class and do the quilting in the second class. I do not try sewing with kindergarten and first grade, we have other activities that we use for that age group, but they do get to make a square and when the crayon is ironed on to fabric, they get very excited! With the sixth grade classes we are arranging a new program where we will be exchanging quilt blocks with a sixth and seventh grade class in Poland, and also with an orphanage in Russia.

++++++++++++++++++++++++++++++

Gladys Shook
Hutchinson, Kansas

Helpful hints on making a sellable project:

- Use quality fabrics.
- Create a very durable product that will withstand much handling (and love!).
- Remember that your favorite colors may not be those of the general public.
- Keep current and be aware of what is in style.
- The price must be right. I often think about what I would pay for the product.
- Always make your delivery date as promised.

Helpful hints when working around children:

- Inventory your work area for small items (needles, buttons) that could easily be swallowed by small tykes.
- Watch not to place plastic sacks from fiberfill and the like where children can reach them and possibly suffocate.
- Rotary cutters and scissors can be very harmful, if not stored properly.
- Spend time with your children, and find a craft or project they can do while you are sewing. Children who are able to make projects are more apt to learn the proper use & safety of the tools you have.
- Just as you should make a point to keep your work area and room free from stray pins, etc. teach your children the benefit of this also.
- Today's technology has developed several products that could pose a hazard if swallowed by kids. Fabric stabilizers and stain removers, oil and other cleaning products should be kept out of reach of the smaller kids.

Other Philosophies for daily living:

- Always be willing to make an adjustment. When you thought it had to be Plan A, Plan B might be the best way.
- Make your own decisions. When the task has to be accomplished, someone else's decision might not be what you want.
- Priorities are essential. You aren't able to do everything in a day, so decide what is most important and get to work, other tasks can be postponed.
- Daily laughter - somedays it comes easy and often. If not, stimulate some good happy thoughts and maybe can recall something that has made you laugh.
- Don't worry! Worrying will eventually become a worry itself!
- Smile and the world smiles with you, cry and you cry alone. Quilters, when the day becomes gray, take out one of your pieced quilts and think of the story of it's making. You'll find love, warmth, comfort, fond memories and when you wrap it around yourself, you will have given yourself a big hug.

++++++++++++++++++++++++++++++

Teresa Binder
Emporia, Kansas

- Scraps. I use clear plastic stacking shoe boxes. This keeps all the colors together and visible.
- If you put a project in a box, for whatever reason, label the box. The same goes with patterns, fabrics, anything you put in a box. Why waste valuable time looking for anything?
- My children love to be read to. I record books on audio tapes for them to listen to at home, as well as on the road. If you use books you have at home, you can record then just as the expensive book/tape combinations you can buy. The kids love to be the "beep" that indicates it is time to turn the page. If you check a book out of the library that is well liked, recording it on tape is a great way to hear that favorite story, long after the book has been returned.
- In my sewing room I have a scrap box, just for the kids. Whatever bits and pieces of fabric, batting and trims I don't want, I put in the box for them. this along with safety scissors, glue, paper, markers and any other creative things your kids like, will keep them creating right along with you. A small table and storage area in one corner makes them feel special, and keeps the room a little neater and always ready to create.

Betty A. Lenz
Marshall, Missouri

• All quilter's must use baggies, I couldn't walk thru my quilt room without them. Every project has a baggie with patterns, applique templates, fabric swatches, layout sheet, notes & scratchings to myself, quilting design, anything pertaining to the project.
• I sort savable scraps into light-medium-dark, & brown paper bag them for later use.

Charlotte Fry
St. Charles, Missouri

• I store my small wall quilts rolled & wrapped in old pillowcases. My large quilts are on a quilt stand, and every 3 months or so, I refold them, trying not to get them folded in the same spots. If I had a spare bed, I would simply lay them on the bed.
• I try to keep my stash color coordinated, but that's almost impossible, especially if you use your fabrics. I've been buying see thru storage boxes for some color groups. I have a large box with Christmas, another with gingham, etc. That really helps keep it neat and clean and together.
• When my fingers get sore, I dip them in alcohol. It seems to heal and toughen.
• Try to set aside an hour a day to work on your projects. It's amazing what can be done in a short amount of time. I also am not a television watcher. So I get a lot done in the evening.

Barbara Clukey
Carriere, Mississippi

• My advice to other quilters has been learned by personal experience. Question yourself closely, before you sell your creation. It is an expression of yourself and your quilt may be valued by your loved ones as an heirloom to treasure.

Helen P. Johnston
Bowie, Maryland

• A lot of my projects involve hand piecing or applique. This fits in perfectly while caring for young children. Before I had children, I thought hand piecing was a waste of time. That's what sewing machines were for. After the birth of my son I realized that the time that's available for focusing on task completion, only comes in short increments. While piecing on the machine, I need long periods of uninterrupted time. Hand-piecing or applique is something I can pick up for even a few stitches, and then put down if I'm needed. I accomplish a lot sitting beside the sand box and the children enjoy going on a hunt for little pieces of fabric blown away by the wind.
• The children also enjoy sitting under my quilt hoop. I make sure I remove all the needles before allowing this as they usually trace the pattern shapes the light from above makes. I have a memory from when my son was little. I was quilting. My son and the dog were quiet under the hoop at my feet. All was right with the world. I realized they were too quiet.

I lifted a side of the quilt just in time to see my son pick a piece of batting off of the side of my quilt and feed it to the dog! Looking at the edge, it was apparent they had been enjoying this sport for a while. As a result, I now roll over and baste the excess backing - covering the tempting batting.
• Many usable scraps find homes with two of my out-of-state nieces, who derive a lot of pleasure playing with them. They are teaching themselves to sew. Last year I received a pillow one had made with two squares of fabric stuffed with scraps and sewn with large red basting stitches. They both want to sew like *Aunt Helen*.
• The best money saving tip I have learned is *buy quality materials!* My second quilt was made using bargain department store fabric. it now has several areas where the fabrics have completely rotted away. I made this quilt in 1978! The quilt only had a couple years of gentle use before this happened.

Edith O. McGhee
Mercer, Pennsylvania

• My daughter and I have put our quilting knowledge to use in entertaining groups of people - particularly church women's groups. We present a program which tells about the Bible. We have presented this program 19 times during the past year, and have met so many lovely people in doing so. One thing that constantly amazes us is the number of men quilters who somehow find their way into the audience.

Beulah T. Gilbert
Bellevue, Ohio

• I try to make something for children and grandchildren every year for Christmas. Some little thing, wallhanging, pillow, etc. They all seem to enjoy it. One year, I made some teddy bears from a quilt my mother gave me that was worn out. They all got a part of my mother's quilt.

Joan Waldman
Platte Center, Nebraska

• To keep little ones occupied, make a flannel board about 29x20". Then give them a bag of squares (1 1/2 to 2") and let them "design" a quilt. Occasionally stitch their "design" into a quilt for their doll or stuffed toy.
• Form a co-op with another Mom that has kids around your kids age. You take her kids one afternoon and she watches yours another. Keep this time for yourself. You earned it.
• Scraps! We all have lots of them. Use see through plastic stack boxes and put scraps in by color. Be sure scraps are sorted and pressed. Makes it easier to use them, if they are already pressed.

Marcene Gunter
Hillsboro, Kansas

• To save money I check out the auctions and garage sales for fabric. I have gotten a lot for very little money.
• I store my quilts in a pillowcase on shelves in the closet.
• In my quilting room I have a lot of shelves, so it is easier to see the fabric. I organize my fabric, first all of one quilt, together with the pattern. Then, by color. Small scraps go into a basket. Patterns are under categories in another basket. Backings are all together, and batts are together. I have a large peg board for tools, rulers, and plastic quilting patterns.
• Whenever I get a new fabric, or scraps from other people, the first thing I do is cut out a six inch square for a charm quilt or what ever. I use all my squares either in quilts, miniatures, or on clothing.

Michelle Hazelhoff
Mt. Evelyn, Vic Australia

• I have a scrap drawer in my studio and my three year old just loves playing in it. While I'm sewing, he sorts it, he rolls in it and it keeps him amused for hours. My older, school-aged children have their own basket of two-inch squares and when I'm sewing they'll often stitch a few together and we'll talk, it's really nice to have them there, sharing what I love.
• I also have a large button jar and they really enjoy sorting and making patterns with them, a lot of the buttons have been cut off their old clothing, and they'll often sit there and say "I remember the dress this button came from...".
• One of the best ways I've found to save money is to be practical, do we really need every quilting gadget known to man? There are several shops I frequent and a couple of mail order places I'm listed with and when they have a sale, I really take advantage of it.
• Recently my quilt group has made charity quilts, we raised a substantial sum of money and naturally bought fabric, thread and batting in bulk. It amazed me what a saving you can negotiate by buying this way, some items we saved up to a third, so if you have the funds and the storage space, I suggest you buy in bulk. You needn't buy a truck load either, on twenty six yards of polyester batting we saved $36, that's quite a difference.
• There are so many lovely gift ideas using quilting, besides the obvious-quilts, I've made some great cushions, pot holders, tea cozies, placemats, bags, clothes, toys, the list is endless. My Canadian quilting friend, Lorie, made me a fabulous armchair sewing caddy for Christmas. I received another wonderful gift not so long ago, my best friend, Laura, made me a miniature sailboat quilt for being her "taxi" all year, you see she doesn't drive, I think of her each time I look at it.
• Regarding the storage of all my quilting stuff, my husband, Steve, built me a huge bookcase, it's great, there's heaps of room for everything. I have a couple of folders with plastic sleeves, one holds quilting patterns, the other pieced and applique patterns, it makes it so much easier to find just the pattern I'm after.
• I like to see my fabric collection, so it too lines the shelves on my bookcase. If I'm keeping fabric for a certain project, I stack it all up together and put the plans or pattern I've decided for it on top, that way it doesn't get used by accident.
• I also sort my fabric into prints

and plains, it makes it easier to find what I'm looking for, I've tried to sort it by color, but I find I'm always in there mucking it up!

• Many of my friends have asked me how I manage to do as much quilting and craft work as I do. Firstly, I tell them I have a great supportive husband, who knows when I get one of my creative urges, it's best to leave me alone to get on with it. He'll go off and bath the kids or cook a meal, he's really good about that, he understands my drive. But really though, it's all about priorities, of course, your family comes first, but I think each of us really needs their own time as well. This is how I go about it, three or four days a week when my eldest children are in school, and I only have my little one at home, we spend the morning cleaning, shopping, paying bills, going to appointments, etc. and in the afternoons until I pick up the kids from school, I sew, my little boy knows it's quiet time and he'll have a nap, watch a video or read a book with me in my studio. Of course this doesn't happen every day, but I manage it often enough, it makes me feel good to do a little work most days, I think I'm a better mother and wife for it, too.

• Remember to take small projects with you, fifteen minutes in the doctor's waiting room, a half hour when you're under the dryer at the hair dresser, and the five or ten minutes while you're waiting for the kids to come out of the school gate, really add up.

• I have sold quite a number of quilts and quilt-related items I've made, by various methods. When I first began selling, I had business cards printed up and made up a price list of sorts, I let everyone know that I was selling my craft and, of course, people I knew and word-of-mouth were my first, and are still my best customers. I have sold at markets, exhibitions and party plan and they've all been good. In Australia quilting isn't as commonplace as it is in the US, but is really catching on and much in demand.

• I think the important things are to put in your best work, be prompt, and keep deadlines with your customers, use quality materials, ask a fair but not outlandish price, provide follow-up service, and above all...be honest!

• To date, I have no quilting credits to my name, and maybe in time I'll enter some of my "masterpiece" quilts in shows. However, so much of myself goes into each project, I'm not sure how I'd feel about having my work assessed and judged. I love what I do and each quilt tells a little of my life that I don't feel I need to validate the item as such. I must admit though, some of the prizes sure are tempting!

++++++++++++++++++++++++++++
Rebecca Dutcher
Culbertson, Nebraska

• When my sons were little and I had a quilt to put in the frame, my Mom would come over and help. We'd settle the little boys under the frame as a "tent" and they'd play, and Mom and I would sew for hours. I didn't realize how big the boys were getting until one day my youngest boy, Joshua, excited in play, bounced up and hit the underside of the quilt right where an open box of pins was sitting on top. Pins flew everywhere! After that, Mom and I always kept the pin box shut!

++++++++++++++++++++++++++++
Alta M. Edwards
Clay City, Indiana

• My goal is that my children and grandchildren each have a quilt. I have about reached this, but there's always one more I want to make.

• I have also made probably 20 *comforts* out of scrap knits. Each of the grandchildren have one, and they just love them. You know Grandma won't allow them to use the *quilts*. They are saved, until they get their own home.

++++++++++++++++++++++++++++
LaRue Nuest
South Hutchinson, Kansas

• In my workshop, my husband put up a 1"x1" board about six feet long, and he drove nails in it for me to hang my plastic rulers on. He spaced the nails so that the rulers would not overlap.

• Fabric is organized in three ways. If it's a part of a collection of designs, such as Judike Rothermel's Aunt Grace's Scrap Bag or Debbie Mumm designs, I store the collection all together. If I am collecting an assortment of fabrics for a particular project, all those are stored in a see-through plastic box. If the fabric is purchased just because I like it, I store it by color. If the color stash gets too large, I sub-divide that color into light, medium, and dark.

Carole Flasch
Weslaco, Texas

• Won a purple ribbon for my Baltimore Quilt at the Rio Grande Valley Show! Enter!

Betty J. Knack
Essexville, Michigan

• My youngest sister, Lois, arranged all my materials by color, because basically she could not stand the mess that I had - they look beautiful now.
• My tiny pieces of scrap, I sew together to make covers for needle cases for our quilt show.
• I never sell anything, (well, hardly ever!), just give it away most of the time.
• I've been quilting since I was 11 years old, (71 years old now) and my mother and grandmother used alcohol on our sore fingers. I can not quilt unless I feel the needle pricking my fingers.

Nancy H. Ehinger
West Branch, Michigan

• Give small children squares and triangles cut from construction paper along with a glue stick. Let them design a quilt while you are working on yours.
• If you know someone who works at a hospital, ask them to bring you some scissors, clamps, x-ray film, etc. that will be disposed of, so that you can use it for quilting. The clamps work well in pulling needles through. X-ray film makes great template material. The paper used on the examining tables at the doctor's office is great for tracing.
• A good ongoing gift throughout the year is to send a quilt block per month (anonymously) to a friend. She/he will have enough for a quilt at the end of the year.
• I use baskets to store a stash on shelves in my studio. Each basket holds a different color.

Janet P. Wyckoff
Hopewell, New Jersey

• Only this - Join a quilt group and talk about quilting every chance you get.
• Everywhere you look, see quilts in natural objects and events, architecture and art, even in piles of brick. Write down your ideas.

Diane Johnson
Rhinebeck, New York

• My tip is on organizing the leftover strips from your rotary cut projects. If they are sorted by size and you don't have to dig through a basket measuring every time you need one, you'll use them! Each time you finish a project, put like-sized strips in large ziplock bags. I put a piece of masking tape with size (1 7/8", 2") on the outside of the bags. Add new bags as you get new sizes. The bags can be stored in plastic shoe boxes or, for very prolific quilters, under bed boxes. As they multiply, you may also want to sort them by color, too. Then, for real fun, challenge yourself to make a quilt or wallhanging from just your scrap strips!

Judy Wolfrom
Southampton, New Jersey

• My advice to all people I talk to who would like to learn quilting, is to take classes and start with the basics. Learn the best techniques for hand piecing and quilting, FIRST. Anyone comfortable and accurate with a sewing machine will easily adapt their new skills to an old friend.

Maria Lage
Cumberland, Rhode Island

• Take as many classes and workshops as possible, whether through your Guild, Quilt Conferences or your local Quilt Shop. Taking classes not only teaches you new quilting techniques, but gives you confidence to explore new ideas and designs even further.
• Join at least one quilting guild. The support, encouragement and inspiration you will receive from other quilters is truly amazing.
• Don't limit yourself to just quilting books and magazines. Art books and magazines of all types offer great inspiration for color and design.
• For quilting designs without marking the quilt top, I use clear contact paper to make my own quilting design stencils. After tracing the design on the paper side of the contact paper, I use an x-acto knife to cut out the design. I peel off the paper backing and reposition the stencil on the quilt top until it loses it's stickiness, quilting along the edge of the stencil.

Unless you are quilting, don't leave the stencil on the quilt, it can leave a sticky residue.

• To protect the tip of my finger underneath the quilt from pricks while I quilt, I use a small piece of black electrical tap or first aid bandage tape wrapped around the finger tip.

• I store all of my quilting supplies in drawers underneath my large work table, which I acquired when the department store I work for was remodeling it's fabric department. I use vertical wood organizers to divide the drawers into compartments.

• All my thread is laid out flat by color, so at a glance I can pick up the color I need.

• I store fabric scraps in clear see-thru plastic boxes. These stack easily on shelves and permit easy viewing of the contents. I love doing miniature quilts, so no matter how small the piece, it usually finds a home. I store regular fabric yardage on shelves by color.

• Try to be as organized as you can. There's nothing more frustrating than wanting to start a project and not being able to find what you need right away. Countless hours are wasted.

++++++++++++++++++++++++++

Lynn G. Kough
Middletown, New Jersey

• Above all else, enjoy what you are doing. When quilting becomes another way to feel like you can't get everything done, stop doing it - get the other impediments taken care of, and then relax and enjoy. Why make it another chore?

++++++++++++++++++++++++++

Alba Lee Elliott
Asheville, North Carolina

• Children love colors and pictures.

• I save my birthday cards, Mother's Day and Father, and let them write on them, while they tell a story. Children can be very creative.

++++++++++++++++++++++++++

Roxanne H. McElroy
Mililani, Hawaii

• If you are a really serious quilter, you will figure out that organization is impossible, except that you really need to have a complete set of supplies and fabric selection in every single room. I have a thimble for every room, as well. That way I never feel isolated from my dreams.

++++++++++++++++++++++++++

Patricia L. Carl
Rhinebeck, New York

• Family gifts: I'm presently transferring old family photos to fabric, and creating nostalgic collages, pillows and wallhangings, using old-looking fabrics, antique linens and laces, old buttons, ribbons, etc.

++++++++++++++++++++++++++

Ruth Powers
Carbondale, Kansas

• Be organized--so much time is wasted simply because I can't find what I am looking for. Being organized is a never ending battle, but I hope if I keep at it, one day it'll happen.

• My sewing room is also my laundry room. New fabric goes directly into the laundry tub (dry) where it stays until I have time to prewash it to check for color fastness or shrinkage. Fabrics are getting better all the time, but I still find enough problem ones to make this step mandatory. After the fabric is washed, dried in the dryer and ironed, it is folded, and stored on shelves adjacent to my sewing machine.

• The fabric is sorted by color or project. There is separate storage for works in progress. Even small scraps are kept within their groups, if they are large enough to be usable; if they seem too small, they go into a special box for miniatures.

• Of course, a rotary cutter with a sharp blade is indispensable, actually you really need two...a large one, and a small one for curves. To go with it, a mat or two (a small one is nice for cutting small pieces that need to be turned) and at least one see-through ruler that has 1/8" markings.

• I much prefer hand quilting, it is my favorite part of the whole process, apart from designing, however for pattern samples, I find it necessary in the interest of time, to machine-quilt.

• I like to use a low-loft batting and hand baste my sandwich together, using a basting frame that my husband made me, unless it is to be machine quilted. Then, I use brass pins to hold the layers together. Brass pins are so much softer to open and close than silver ones are, and are much nicer for your fingers. I hand quilt everything in a Q-snap frame - the square lap quilting size. For borders, I use two long and two short sections to build a rectangular Q-snap. I might do some

marking before the basting is done, depending on the project, but since I mark with a silver pencil and it wears away during the quilting (which if why I like it), generally I mark as I go.
• I have a tendency to bend needles, so I only use Piecemakers, size 12. They don't bend for me, and seldom break.
• To protect my fingers, I use an inexpensive thimble with a ridge around the bottom that holds the needle well. My underneath finger is protected by a porcelain Needleglider.

Lenore Scott
Pittstown, New Jersey

• I have one tip for quilters. Whenever I purchase new fabric, I cut out a piece about 1 1/2" by 2 1/2" wide, and sew it to a piece of muslin strip. Thereafter, at a glance, I can tell what a fabric looks like, before searching through my "stash" for it. It's easier to carry the *strip of fabrics* to the fabric store, when you need to buy matching fabrics.

Norma Jean Rector
Center Point, Iowa

• I've found in selecting fabrics, if I choose the more predominant color (or print), it's easier to select coordinating fabrics.
• I store my fabrics together, by their color families, and keep a record of which colors are located in each of the drawers in my sewing room.
• Scraps can be worked up in simple or decorative designs in pot holders, place mats, toss pillows, or lap quilts for nursing home residents.

Betty Verhoeven
East Jewett, New York

• A fellow quilter, Micky, and I tried a new method of basting quilts together. We layered the top, batting, and backing together, smoothing on a bed, and pinned the edges. Then, we carried it to the basement and tacked the top edge to a beam. We inserted a dowel in the sleeve created by the bottom. The weight of the dowel acted as a weight, so the quilt hung smoothly. Then we basted, one of us working from the front, and the other pushing the needle back through from behind. We quickly had the entire quilt basted.
• Another way I like to baste, is to put the quilt in a regular frame, clamp it well, and set it on edge. Then you can work with a friend, as in the previous method, one from either side. The frame seems to keep the quilt nice and taut for basting. You don't have to roll the quilt, just turn the frame to another side when you can't reach any longer.
• There are a lot of good thimbles on the market to help protect your fingers, but in the event that you still have a finger that is sore and calloused and rough..."Bag Balm" is very good for soothing and smoothing the skin. It is available at farm supply stores, and works extremely well.
• When my children were young, they often were at my side (or under foot), while I sewed. One way I kept them occupied in the sewing room was to give them the button box. They would sort the buttons by color and size, etc., and when they tired of that, I would give them a darning needle and yarn, and let them string the buttons into necklaces. Also, you might try giving them some graph paper and crayons, and let them design your next quilt. You never know!

Emily Laubaugh
Gladstone, Oregon

• The best advice I could give would be to organize a quilt group in your own area, or join your local quilt guild. You can make lifelong friends and get some great ideas from some great people.

Ella May Reusser
Blackwell, Oklahoma

• Iodides Tinture, actually a white iodine. It does not protect the finger, but helps to heal them fast.
• Small children like to be with grown ups. Thread a larger needle, double the thread and make a knot, so the needle can't come unthreaded. Let them quilt with you. It's much fun for them. You may take the stitches out later.

Suzanne K. Roy
Newkirk, Oklahoma

• Fabric to wrap gifts is great for quilting friends. I've developed fabric ribbons out of fabric strips, as well as selvages, that quilters are always trimming off and throwing away, and don't know what to do with.
• Many of my scraps are recycled into scrap miniature quilts.

Margaret Kooda
Idaho Falls, Idaho

• I keep a child's easel next to my sewing machine. I covered the cork board with flannel and it is the perfect height when piecing blocks.
• The other side is a chalkboard. My toddler is happy drawing beautiful pictures, while I piece my blocks.
• I also keep all my scraps collected, by color, in baskets. When I'm not using the flannel board, my toddler makes fabric pictures with the scraps. It takes time to separate them, but we use it as a color lesson and I've had some uninterrupted time for my project.

Julie Fox
Blackwell, Oklahoma

• I can sew only when my daughter is sleeping. Right now, she takes all my time.

Betty J. Pribil
Portland, Oregon

• I store my large fabric stash in a floor to ceiling 16 foot wide cabinet, plus 12 letter size cardboard file drawers. These drawers are stacked 3 high, and on top I have two 4x4" plywood boards, which is my work table. This works great, as it is adjustable.
• When I have pieces left, I usually cut them into 1 1/2 or 2" strips and then use them to make toss up log cabins. (Darks in one box, lights in another. Pick out a color and sew).
• I mostly machine quilt, but when I hand quilt I use the Original Quilting Spoon, and quilt one stitch at a time.

Alyce C. Kauffman
Gridley, California

• To save money I use my rotary cutter blades until dull, then have them re-sharpened. After initial use of blades, I put a drop of oil on them and clean off lint frequently. This extends the life of the blade.
• When cutting anything but fabric, I keep an old blade marked *old*, to use for cutting paper or templates.
• To enable me to purchase name brand fabric, I take advantage of discount sales, as I'm on a limited budget.
• My scraps I cut into useable squares, triangles, rectangles, etc., and file in containers marked accordingly. If making a 9-Patch using 2" squares, I bring out my 2 1/2" square container. Eliminates odd size pieces of fabric pushed into bags or boxes. Great for small projects. Time consuming initially, to clean up scraps, but if I do this with leftover scraps after each future project, it's a simple task.
• To sell what you make, contact your local quilt or craft shops and check amount they request for handling merchandise. Shop around for the advantage. Rent a space, or participate in a co-op craft shop, or quilt show.

Pamela T. Young
Minot Air Force Base, North Dakota

• When my daughters decide that they want to *sew*, too, I pull out a plastic container that has construction paper, glue sticks, and fabric scraps in it. Then, they can glue a quilt of their own.
• The best money saving tip I can pass on to quilters is: Don't buy fabric on sale, unless you need it. Every time one of the fabric stores had a sale, I would wander down and buy 5 or 6 years of fabric, just because it was on sale. I didn't have any idea what I was going to use it for. "But, it was on sale" (so is cat food, but we don't have a cat); "it was a good price" (yes, but do you know what you are going to use it for?); and "you never know when they will have a sale like this again" (probably in a couple of months), I would think to myself to help justify my purchases. Pretty soon, I saved my budget right into the poor house. Then my husband, Scott, gave me the command, "Go right ahead and buy fabric at full price, but only if you need it for some project you're working on." Well, I didn't take my husband's entire directive to heart, but it did change my buying habits. I still buy fabric just to have in my *stash*, but instead of buying yards of fabric with no purpose "just because it's on sale", I save my money so that I can buy 1/4 yards of fabric I really find striking, to have for my stash. I have cut down on the amount of money I spend on fabric that just sits around.
• I keep my stash in several clear plastic containers, separated into warm solids, cool solids, neutral solids, Christmas prints, novelty prints, nature prints, all other prints and scraps. When I buy more than 2 yards of a particular fabric, after I wash and dry it, I roll it back onto a cardboard bolt. The bolts are then lined up across my cutting table. The fabric stores just

throw the cardboard forms away after the fabric is all gone, so just ask for them.

++++++++++++++++++++++++++++

Janice A. Miller
Jaffrey, New Hampshire

•After making a quilt, I always make a scrap quilt with the leftover pieces. I sell the quilts at the Inn, usually 40x60" in size. They are machine quilted, only because they are price valued and sell better. Everything is machine washed several times and quilted closely, so they can be washed after purchase.
•When I take a trip, I do quilting on the airplane to pass the hours. Most of these small quilts are made into Christmas presents.
•Stenciling and/or painting areas of a quilt is a very time saving technique, and very impressive when quilted around.

++++++++++++++++++++++++++++

Pauline A. Cook
Idaho Falls, Idaho

I keep my *stash* in cabinets with 5 shelves. I separate it into colors. I also take my new material to the washing machine, and pre-shrink and color test it, as soon as I bring it home. After it's dry, I fold it and put it in the correct color stack.
•If I have *leftover* squares or triangles, I put them in a zip lock bag separated by size, i.e. 2" squares, 2 1/2" triangles, etc. Then, when making a scrappy quilt, grab the correct size of *leftovers*.

++++++++++++++++++++++++++++

Barbara Shook Davis
Williams, Arizona

•I've learned to machine quilt the quilts that go on beds and backs of couches and chairs, and hand quilt the wall hangings, miniatures, etc. I've been known to spend two years hand quilting a queen size quilt that almost always shows signs of wear, within two years,

++++++++++++++++++++++++++++

Pat Campbell
Rigby, Idaho

•My advice to quilters is to keep an open mind - a closed mind represses creativity, don't ever say "I can't do this or that." Your own mind is what limits you.
•I organize my scraps down to 1 1/2" squares. All smaller leftover project scraps are cut into strips, squares, and triangles, as large as possible, then I work down toward the smallest squares and 2 1/2" triangles. These are placed in shoe boxes with others their size. It doesn't take long to have enough scraps for placemats, wall hangings, and I even made a full size strip quilt!

++++++++++++++++++++++++++++

Jean Ann Eitel
Marietta, Georgia

•I have installed closet maid shelving in a walk-in closet in my sewing room and arrange all my fabrics by color family on these shelves. I use plastic see through boxes to store my projects in progress until they are complete (I have about twenty in use at this time, each with a different project).
•I try to buy fabrics on sale as often as I can, but never resist buying a particular piece of fabric if it catches my eye.
•As for time management, I try to work on a task without interruption to complete as much of it as I can at one sitting.
•I also do assembly line type work in units on my quilts...all the cutting at once, sewing all the pieces, clipping the threads, pressing the seams and so on. Each time a quilter changes from one task to the other, time is lost. I see myself as a little solo quilt factory with the quilt cutter completing her job, the quilt stitcher running everything through the sewing machine, the thread clipper separating the pieces, the presser ironing all the seams, etc. Before I became editor I won many ribbons for the quilts that I made. Since becoming an editor and judging so many quilt shows, I show my quilts on an "exhibit only" basis to share what I am doing with others but not compete with them.

++++++++++++++++++++++++++++

Celeste Lipp
Idaho Falls, Idaho

•I store my fabrics in large plastic crates with lids. The plastic is clear and the crates are stackable.
•Dust and bugs are not allowed in!
•I keep separate crates just for my collection of *conversation or novelty* prints, and one crate holds only scraps. I intend to cut my scraps into strips, then use muslin to make four-patch units of the scraps for future scrap quilts or fast project borders.

•I protect my finger with a sterling silver thimble when I

quilt. I use a leather thimble (Nimble Thimble) when I applique.

My time management advice:

• When I'm on a roll and getting a lot done, I try to stay with it and do just a little more. It means ignoring the little voice that tells me I should be cleaning (or sleeping!).
• I always have several *unfinished objects* in progress. Periodically, I try to get three or four projects advanced, that is, get some of the rotary cutting done, get a stack of things ready for the sewing machine, or do some required ironing on projects for a stretch of time. When I keep busy with this sequence, finished items begin to roll off my *quilter's assembly line*.

++++++++++++++++++++++++++++
Christine Klinger
Fayetteville, Arkansas

• When I began quiltmaking, I used an antique china hutch to store my fabric. As my fabric collection grew, I did not want to limit my collecting because of space restrictions, so I've started to purchase clear storage containers. Eventually, I hope to add on to our home and take over my daughter's current bedroom.

++++++++++++++++++++++++++++
Mary Lou Kantz Evans
Flagstaff, Arizona

• My fabric is put into color groups and then placed on edge in drawers so all the choices are available to me as I open the drawer.
• The overwhelming job is to try to stay organized, I need such a vast collection of *stuff* to do the type of primitives I like that keeping things where I can actually find them is quite challenging, so I spend a fair amount of time organizing and re-organizing.

++++++++++++++++++++++++++++
Sandra L. Hatch
Lincoln, Maine

• I organize my fabrics in several ways. Because I sometimes get samples from manufacturers for use in publication, I have separate places to keep fabrics from different companies.
• The fabrics I purchase for myself are only sorted by whether they are solids or prints. I have solids in a huge old pattern cabinet and prints in an old jelly cupboard and floor-to-ceiling shelf. I have no idea how much fabric I have. All I know is when I want to make something I have to go out and buy because I can't bear to use some of the prints I have. There are some fabrics I will never cut because I just love looking at them the way they are. I never want to use them all up!
• I also have a cabinet similar to those in the store filled with thread of every color of one brand. I don't live near stores and want to be able to sew any time with threads to match.
• I collect shears and scissors. I don't have many antiques, but I have some lovely new ones. I must have more than thirty pairs and I love to look at them. I also collect gold thimbles, old sewing items and more. I also collect old quilts. I am not sure exactly how many I have, but I know it is over 30. They are all special.

I haven't revealed any secrets nor have I given anyone any good hints except the one about finding the right husband. I believe any success I have comes from the support of him and my children and a heritage of friends and family who appreciate needlework in all forms.

++++++++++++++++++++++++++++
Sue Hausmann
Lincolnshire, Illinois

• I organize fabrics (have I got fabric! Herb says he is going to build shelves along the outer walls so we can insulate!) by color in laundry baskets and notions and other sewing supplies in the plastic craft containers, however, I certainly could be more organized, especially books which are simply on shelves by category.

++++++++++++++++++++++++++++
Z.Z. Gilmore
Pocatello, Idaho

• My granddaughter, Laura Gilmore, chooses the blocks from stacks while I sew them together.
• I have such a large stash of fabrics that my daughter-in-law, Shellie, who attends the Houston Quilt Shows with me, thinks that I need counseling. I told her that counseling wouldn't help a *fabraholic*. There is no cure.
• I do sort my fabrics into colors and stack them in boxes so that I can see every piece in the box. It works great.

Jane Newhouse
Wedderburn, Oregon

• What to do with those *small* scraps? You just might need that bit in an applique. I keep a basket under my sewing machine and toss them in there. Every now and then when I just want to *sit*...I sort them by color and put the separate colors in ziplock bags. I punch a hole in one upper corner of the ziplock and put them on a large metal ring. Like the ones in loose-leaf notebooks - only a single ring about three inches in diameter. This makes the small scraps easy to go through and to get to.

Sally Smith
Kodak, Tennessee

• When my children were very young, I used their sleeping time to quilt. The housework, etc. was done while they were up. Snack time after naps allowed for a little more quilting by putting my daughter in her highchair for her snack and talking to her while I quilted. As the children got older, they received (and still do) their own quilting supplies which kept them entertained. Even now I always bring home a gift for each when I attend quilt shows, it keeps them a little more tangibly in touch with quilting.
• Since I am a graphic artist, some of the supplies I use for quilting (rulers, pencils, etc.), I purchase from art supply houses as they tend to be less expensive, but are top quality.
• Of all the advice I could give to quilters it would be enjoy...enjoy...enjoy! I set tentative deadlines for my work, but I refuse to go crazy if I don't make them. Life's too short and quilting's too much fun!

Joanna Bessey
Rhinelander, Wisconsin

• If I were asked for any words of advice on quilting, I would answer one word..SHARE! When I started quilting, I assumed this was more of a solitary kind of hobby, like *stitching alone by lamp-light!* Yes, it can be that, but also so much more. Little did my husband know that the book he gave me a year ago last Christmas (Machine Paper Piecing) would create such a strong bond between my daughter-in-law, Lara (Spyque, as Bill calls her!) and me. She picked it up, it caught her attention, she decided she could do that, and in less than a month, she had her own book and we started a project together. This has since led to many more fabric shop visits, leisurely wanderings thru all the wonderful supplies available, like books and patterns and stencils and of course, more fabrics - and, some weekend evenings into the *wee* hours as our sewing machines purr across from each other at the dining room table. By this Christmas, my daughter-in-law, Belinda (Bill calls her Indy!) visiting from Nebraska and already a much-talented crafts person, decided, "Hey, I can do that, too!" And, what a three-some we are. The day after Christmas we were at the fabric shop - of course, we had to use Belinda's gift certificate she'd received from Lara and Todd. And recently, Belinda has signed up for a 4-week session beginning quilting class back in Nebraska. I love it! Only wish we lived nearer each another. But, our bond is set!
• Sharing works with friends, too. Exchanging quilt blocks with Donna, Fran, and Nancy have now produced two wonderful sampler quilts for each of us. Each quilt block in all the quilts is signed, dated, and bears the block name. What treasures of memories. Do SHARE your love of quilting!

Author's Note: Good advice to end this section! Thanks, Joanna!

Strip and block yardage chart for 44" wide fabric

This chart will assist you in figuring how much yardage you will need for your projects by showing you the number of strips or patches obtained from the yardages show below.

Strips (cut across 44" fabric.. from selvage to selvage)			Squares		
Strip Size	1 yard	1/2 yard	Cut size	1/2 yard of fabric	1/4 yard of fabric
1 1/2"	23	11	2"	178	89
2"	17	8	2 1/2"	104	52
2 1/2"	13	7	3"	77	38
3"	11	5	3 1'2"	54	27
3 1/2"	10	5	4"	40	20
4"	8	4	4 1/2"	31	15
4 1/2"	7	3	5"	28	14
5"	7	3	5 1/2"	21	10
5 1/2"	6	3	6-6 1/2"	15	7
6"	5	2	7"	12	6
7"	5	2	7 1/2"-8"	10	5
8"	4	2	8 1/2"	8	4
			9-10 1/2"	6	3
			11"	4	2
			11 1/2 to 12 1/2"	3	2

- This chart can be extremely helpful in estimating the yardage for your quilts. If you piece by hand, cutting hundreds of pieces at a time, this chart is definitely for you!

- Many quilters now use quick cutting and piecing methods, like half-square triangles and strip piecing, this chart will assist by giving you an approximate idea of what you might need. You will find directions for quick methods of cutting in the back of this book, where it will be convenient for you to refer to them often.

Templates for Squares

The most frequenty-used sizes:

2 inch Square
(Add 1/4 seam allowance when cutting)

3 inch Square
(Add 1/4 seam allowance when cutting)

1 inch Square
Add 1/4" when cutting

4 inch Square
(Add 1/4 seam allowance when cutting)

Templates for Triangles & Circles

The most frequenty-used sizes:

2 inch Circle
(Add 1/4" seam allowance when cutting)

3 inch Circle
(Add 1/4" seam allowance when cutting)

2 inch Triangle
(Add 1/4" seam allowance when cutting)

4 inch Triangle
(Add 1/4" seam allowance when cutting)

3 inch Triangle
(Add 1/4" seam allowance when cutting)

Page 230, The Busy Quilter's Survival Guide

Nine Patch...

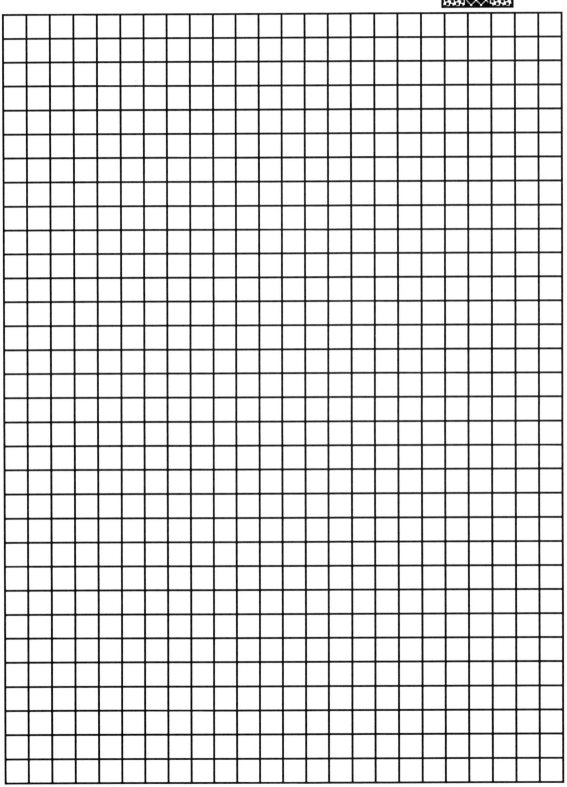

2-Patch Pinwheel

The Tumbler

Great for Charm Quilts using a different fabric for each piece.

The Busy Quilter's Survival Guide, Page 233

Flying Geese

See Page 239 for pieceing ideas

The Barbara Frietchie Star

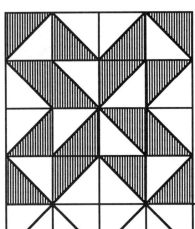

Patchwork Stars....
A great way to use up those scraps!

- To create the pattern placement shown to the left, rotate each of the four blocks a quarter-turn each time to create the star in the center of the four blocks.

- Join a number of these squares (made from those wonderful half-square triangles) to create a marvelous wallhanging or a bed-sized quilt!

- Sixteen half-squares make up a block.

- Four blocks make a square.

- This could be made as a Charm Quilt.....using a different fabric for each half square. Or you could use only three dominant colors .....by using shades of each, like red, white and blue. Or peach, white and green. Or burgandy, blue and white. The combinations are endless. Try it in your favorite combination. What ever colors you use, it's sure to be a hit!

Page 236, The Busy Quiter's Survival Guide

Spinning Stars

(Several other patterns an be created from this block)

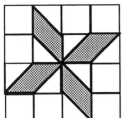

_____The Busy Quilter's Survival Guide, Page 237

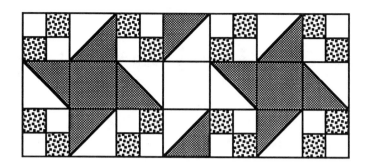

A Galaxy of Stars!

Half-square triangles, 4-patch and squares.

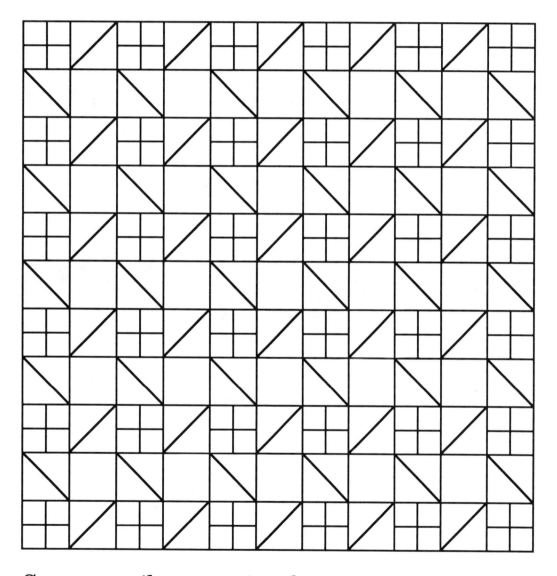

Scrappy quilts are uniquely yours,
   a reflection of your own personal stash!

Evening Star

FLYING GEESE..the Easy Way!

- For a flying geese unit 4x2", cut your base fabric 4 1/2" x 2 1/2". For the upper fabric, cut two 2 1/2" squares.

- Place on square on the right side, right sides together and draw lines as shown. Stitch on the DOTTED lines.

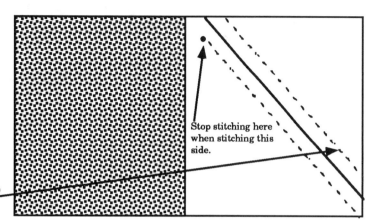

Stop stitching here when stitching this side.

Flip the little corner down, as shown in the diagram before sewing the next seam.

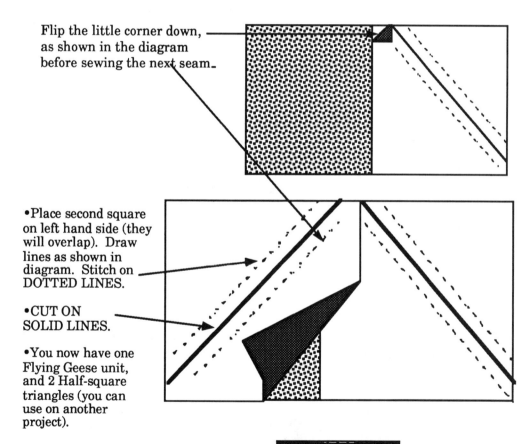

- Place second square on left hand side (they will overlap). Draw lines as shown in diagram. Stitch on DOTTED LINES.

- CUT ON SOLID LINES.

- You now have one Flying Geese unit, and 2 Half-square triangles (you can use on another project).

- Press open the Flying Geese Unit. Make as many units as necessary for your project.

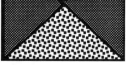

Half-Square Triangles
....using the Grid Method

Half-square triangles can be made to any finished size. Just remember, if you want a finished 2" square, draw your grid using 2 7/8" squares. Always add 7/8" to your finished size.

Step #1. Layer your two fabrics right sides together, with the lighter-colored one on top. Using a sharpened lead pencil and a ruler, draw your grid lines (see picture below) onto the top fabric. Then draw the diagonal lines, as shown. Draw the dotted stitching lines 1/4" from solid lines.

Step #2. Sew on the DOTTED lines only, after pinning fabric together securely.

Step #3. Cut apart on the solid lines, horizonally, vertically and diagonally.

Step #4. Press cut squares open, pressing seam allowances to the darker side.

Step #5. Trim off points that extend beyond the block.

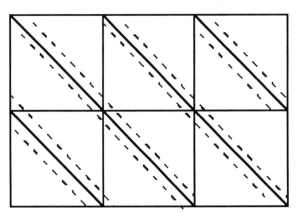

You will get 2 Half-square triangles from each square you have drawn on your grid. You may use another configuration, as shown below:

Begin stitching here:

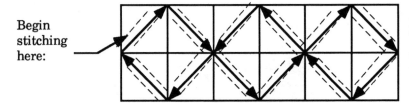

Follow arrows around to beginning, on <u>each</u> side of on the diagonal dotted lines. Cut apart on the solid lines.

Page 242, Main Dishes & Casseroles

AUTHOR'S NOTE:
When the idea for this book came into being, I had visions of hundreds of wonderful recipes contributed by quilters. Surely every quilter had recipes that were delicious, could be prepared quickly and inexpensively. Recipes that would simmer all day, yielding wonderful aromas throughout the house!

Well, it didn't take me long to realize, after reading the first few questionaires that were returned, that most quilters not only don't like to use their precious time cooking, many of them dislike cooking with a *purple passion*!

So....to those quilters who shared their recipes with us, I say a hardy "Thank you!" To those who didn't, I challenge, "Try the easy recipes you'll find in this book. You may find some that you can fix on days you really don't want to go out to a restaurant, or on days your husband (if he's the one that cooks) wants a break from the kitchen!"

Joyce Livingston
Council Grove, Kansas

SLOW COOKER BAR-B-CUE BEEF

3 pounds beef
    (stew or chuck roast)
3/4 cup brown sugar
2 green peppers, chopped
3 1/4 tsp chili powder
2 tsp Worcestershire® sauce
1 onion, chopped
1/4 cup vinegar
small can tomato paste
salt and pepper (optional)
squirt of prepared mustard
    (or could use 1 tsp
    dry mustard)

Combine all the ingredients in your crockpot and mix well. This will go in a 3 1/2 quart cooker, or you could use a 5 quart. Cover and cook on high for 8 hours. Stir twice during the cooking period. Separate meat with two forks until shredded. Serve on buns. This is good for a buffet, if you lower the temperature to *low*.

BAR-B-Q MEATBALLS FOR A CROWD

Combine well, and form into large meatballs, a little bigger than a golf ball:

6 cups ground meat
2 eggs
2 cups oatmeal
1 cup milk
2 medium onions, finely chopped
1/2 tsp (or more) garlic
salt and pepper to taste
1/2 to 3/4 tsp chili powder

Place meatballs in 9x13" pan. Next, make the sauce by combining in microwavable bowl:

1/2 cup chopped onion
2 cups catsup
1+ cup brown sugar
2 tsp liquid hickory smoke
1/4 tsp chili powder
Optional: 1/4 cup
    finely chopped onion

Microwave on high for 3 minutes, stirring once. Pour over meatballs, cover and bake for one hour in 350 degree oven. Uncover last 10 minutes.

Glenda Phipps
Whitman, Nebraska

ONE STEP LASAGNA

1 pound ground beef
3/4 cup water
1 tsp oregano
1 egg, beaten
3 cups shredded
    mozzarella cheese
1 (32 oz) jar spaghetti sauce
1 tsp basil
1(12oz) pkg creamed
    cottage cheese
9 pieces lasagna, uncooked
1/3 cup grated parmesan cheese

Heat oven to 350 degrees. In large skillet, brown ground beef, drain. Stir in spaghetti sauce, water, basil, and oregano. Simmer 5 minutes, stirring occasionally. In small bowl, combine cottage cheese and egg. In ungreased 9x13" pan, layer 1/3 of noodles, 1/3 of meat mixture, 1/3 of cottage cheese mixture, and 1/3 of mozzarella cheese. Repeat layers, ending with mozzarella on top. Sprinkle with parmesan cheese. Cover with foil, bake for 30 minutes. Remove foil, bake an additional 20-30 minutes. Let stand 10 minutes before serving. This is 8 servings.

Beverly J. Relph
Leavenworth, Kansas

POT LUCK

You get the biggest pot, fill it up with stuff, and cook it all day. Bill calls it his "Big Pot Supper", knowing he will eat it all week. When in doubt, Bill will eat anything with a salad or whipped cream.

TACO SOUP

1 pound ground beef
1 onion, chopped
1 pkg (1 1/4 oz) taco seasoning
water
1 (16 oz) can tomato juice
1 (16 oz) can kidney beans,
    or ranch style Jalapeno
    pinto beans (15 oz)
1 (17 oz) can whole kernel corn
    and its liquid
1 (8 oz) can tomato sauce
Sour cream, cheddar cheese and corn chips for garnish

Brown beef and onion. Add taco seasoning, following directions on the package for amount of water and simmering time. Add remaining ingredients and bring to a simmer. Serve piping hot with sour cream, cheese, and corn chips for garnish. Ground turkey can be substituted for ground beef.

Betty Lou Cassidy
Linwood, New Jersey

No matter who does the cooking, time can be saved during the week by using these ideas:

• *Cook Too Much/Planned Leftovers*: Make a meat entree' that may be used in several different ways over the next few days. For example, make a roast in the oven using carrots, onions, and red wine as seasoning. Bake potatoes at the same time in the oven. The first night, serve the beef sliced with baked potatoes, the cooked carrots and a salad. (optional)

The next night, re-cook the meat in Stir Fry with rice. (There are several excellent brands in the grocery store. These have everything to make an instant 15 minute meal).

• An oven-roaster chicken or turkey can become soup, or *A la King* on another night. Put pieces of chicken in two buttermilk biscuits which have been pressed together into a large circle on a baking sheet. Fold over the edges to make a small *pot pie*, and bake as per the biscuit directions. If you already have gravy from the last meal, heat that and ladle over the *pot pie*. Heat some veggies and you have another instant meal.

• Use the crockpot: You can brown beef cubes or make meatballs at night, cool and keep in the refrigerator until the morning. Then add cold sauce, meat, and seasonings, and cook on *Low* all day. When you get home, you just have to make spaghetti or noodles, for meatballs and spaghetti, or beef goulash. (As an extra touch, it takes only ten minutes for garlic bread). I make turkey cutlets and spaghetti the same way.

• Shop wisely: Buy no-fuss, one-step, boxed or frozen vegetables and rice side dishes - - the kind that requires only water, butter, the package ingredients, and can be done in the microwave. While the meat entree' is baking, you can stir up a side dish, set it in the microwave and program in the time, but DON'T push start. Train your husband to come home and push the button. Then fifteen minutes later you're eating dinner, and you've had 1

and 1/2 hours of guilt-free quilting time.

• Don't measure: Measuring ingredients takes extra time and clean up. I make baked breaded chicken or fancy Cordon Bleu without a recipe. Buy boneless, skinless chicken breasts, and rinse. Beat two eggs and a dash of pepper in a bowl. Heat vegetable oil in a pan (about 3 Tablespoons worth) over medium-low flame. (If you wish to make a lower fat dish, "fry" meat in chicken bouillon). Dip chicken in egg, then roll in seasoned bread crumbs. Fry about four minutes on each side. Place pre-cooked chicken in a covered oven-safe glass dish which has a splash of white wine in the bottom. Bake one hour at 350 degrees.

To make Cordon Bleu, just fold a slice of ham and two of swiss cheese in half, pin inside raw chicken breast with skewers, then dip in egg batter and continue as above.

Elizabeth A Akana
Kaneohe, Hawaii

KOREAN SHORT RIBS

1 1/2 to 2 pounds
    short ribs (beef)
1/2 cup soy sauce
4 Tbsp chopped green onion
1 tsp pepper
3 Tbsp sesame seed, toasted
3 Tbsp sesame oil
1 Tbsp sugar
1 Tbsp garlic, mashed

Marinate ribs for 2 hours in above sauce, turning often. Broil.

Kathryn Rippeteau
Greenwold
Niskayuna, New York

QUICK TAMALE PIE

Prepare one cornbread mix as directed, or prepare your favorite "scratch" recipe.

Combine one can of chili (with or without beans - whatever you please), and one can of corn (drained).

Put the cornbread batter in a greased 9x9" baking dish, and place the chili mixture in the center of the batter.

Bake it for about 10 minutes, longer than you would normally for the cornbread alone.

You can add corn chips stuck into the chili if you like. My kids like it that way. I like this because it is quick. I almost always have the ingredients on the shelf, and my kids will eat it! Add a salad and some sliced apples, and you've got a good dinner.

Jill Marie Tanking
Liberal, Kansas

FRIED CHICKEN

I could not fry chicken to suit the family. The lady who got the franchise *Colonel Sanders* in Liberal gave me this recipe several months ago and my family loved the chicken. (This in not the KFC recipe, it's a well-kept secret!)

Soak your chicken in salty water for several hours.

Fix your favorite dry dipping mixture: Flour, salt, pepper and what else you use for dry ingredients.

Fix your favorite wet dipping mixture: Milk, eggs and whatever else.

I dip wet, then dry, then wet, then dry. (When we had a cafeteria, as a kid, one of the cooks told me to always double dip. That was why she made the best onion rings.)

Next, put the chicken on a rack or two, and let dry 20 minutes. Fry in deep hot oil for 20 to 30 minutes. I have always used a cast iron skillet.

Then put the chicken on a good size wire rack or two, with a cookie sheet under it. Let bake at 350 degrees for 30 minutes. You will be amazed at the amount of grease that drips off the chicken.

PORTUGUESE SOPA

I got this recipe from Helen Lunceford, Atwater, California.

6-8 pound roast, brisket, or
    shank bone with meat
    (I use roast)
1/2 small head cabbage
5-6 ribs celery
3 small onions
1 bottle catsup, large
2 cans tomato paste (I use 3, the
    largest I can find)
1 cup dark red wine or vinegar
    (I used vinegar, it was
    not as good, remember
    that the alcohol cooks
    out and the flavor of the
    wine stays and this is
    used to tenderize the
    meat)
3-4 garlic cloves
dash of sugar
1 good hand full of mint, for later

The following should be put into a cheesecloth bag:

1 large handful of whole allspice
3-4 sticks cinnamon
1/2 handful of whole cloves
1 Tbsp cumin powder or more
    (or 1/2 tsp cumin seeds)

Brown meat. Cut cabbage, celery, garlic, onion into small pieces. After meat has browned, add water to cover, add all ingredients, and let cook slowly for 5-6 hours. Cool.

After cooled, take out meat, and add water to suit taste. Shred the meat, and put back into the juice.

To serve, put a thick slice of sourdough bread into the soup bowl. Pour juice over bread and add meat to the soup bowl. Where we ate it, they took out the vegetables, but they said you could try it with the vegetables. Sprinkle some mint over the juice. Good eating!

SWEET AND SOUR CHICKEN

1 (8 oz) bottle
    russian Salad Dressing
1 envelope dry onion soup mix
1 (10 oz) jar apricot preserves
4 whole chicken breasts
    (deskinned and deboned)
    or mix chicken parts

Combine all, but chicken parts. Place chicken in large, shallow baking dish, 9x13" works well. Pour sauce over chicken. Bake

Main Dishes & Casseroles, Page 245

at 350 degrees for 1 1/2 hours or less. I have put this in the crock pot.

This is delicious served over rice, with an orange Jello, hot bread and an apple dessert. I like wild rice best, but most people use white rice.

POTATO CASSEROLE

2 (1 pound) bags of frozen hash brown potatoes
1 (8 oz) carton sour cream
1/2 cup milk
1 stick oleo
1 can cream of celery soup
1 cup grated cheddar cheese
1 tsp salt
1 tsp coarse ground black pepper

Combine together, and bake at 350 degrees in 9x13" greased pan for 45-60 minutes.

MEXICAN CASSEROLE

Brown:

2 pounds hamburger
1 chopped onion

Add 1 can enchilada sauce, cook over medium heat. Salt and pepper.

In another pan, mix and heat:

2 cans mushroom soup
1 can water
2 small cans diced green chilies

Have 3/4 pound shredded cheddar cheese ready. Grease casserole dish. Line with broken corn chips. Layer meat mixture, shredded cheese, soup mixture, chips, and repeat. Top layer will be cheese. Let set in refrigerator for 2 hours. Bake at 350 degrees for 30 minutes.

I have always used this for carry-in meals. Could make it in two pans, so can freeze one or fix for family, if they aren't going to the carry-in meal.

Florence Edith Goggin
Eureka, California

BEEF CASSEROLE

Pat 1 and 1/2 pounds of ground beef into bottom of a 9x13" pan (not cooked). Sprinkle with minced onion.

Arrange 1 package frozen Tator Tots® in rows on meat mixture.

Cover with a mixture of:

1 can of celery soup
1 can cream of chicken soup
1 can of milk (that you have rinsed out the cans with)

Pour over the meat and potato mixture. Season with pepper, if you wish. Bake without a cover at 350 degrees for 1 hour. To reheat, put on a cover.

Kathy Palmiter
Williams, Indiana

GRINGO TACO

1 pound ground beef
3/4 cup chopped onion
3/4 cup chopped green pepper
1 (10 oz) can enchilada sauce
1 (8 oz) can tomato sauce
1 tsp salt
1 tsp chili powder
12 tortillas
1 cup shredded cheddar cheese
1 can Milnot® (canned milk)

Brown beef, onion and green pepper. Drain, add sauces, salt and chili powder. Simmer 5 minutes. In large cake pan, layer 1 cup meat sauce, tortillas and cheese. Pour Milnot® over the top, and bake at 350 degrees for 35 minutes.

CHICKEN AND RICE

1 cup long cook rice, uncooked
1 can each...cream of chicken,
    cream of celery and
    cream of mushroom
    soups, undiluted
1 chicken, cut-up and skinned
1/4 cup melted butter/margarine

Mix the rice and soups together in a 9x13" pan. Roll the chicken in the melted butter and lay on top of the rice mixture. Drizzle the remaining butter over the top. Bake uncovered for 2 hours at 300 degrees.

CHILI

Brown one onion in oil. Add 1 pound hamburger and brown. Add 1 can chopped tomatoes. Dissolve 1 cube beef bouillon in 1 cup hot water. Add to above mixture. Add 2 Tbsp sugar. Add salt, garlic powder and chili powder to taste. Add 1/2 can kidney beans and juice. To thicken, add 2 Tbsp flour mixed in 1/2 cup water. Simmer.

LIQUID PIZZA

1 pound lean ground beef
1 (5 1/2 oz) pkg
    scalloped potatoes
1 (16 oz) can tomatoes
1 (10 1/2 oz) can pizza sauce
1/2 cup water
1/2 tsp salt
1/2 tsp oregano leaves
1/4 tsp basil leaves

Page 246, Main dishes & Casseroles

1/8 tsp garlic powder
1 cup Mozzarella cheese, cubed
1/4 cup grated Parmesan cheese

Brown meat and drain. In crock pot, combine beef with dry sauce mix from potatoes, tomatoes, pizza sauce, water, potatoes, salt, oregano, basil and garlic. Cook on low 4-5 hours.

Turn crockpot on high, stir in mozzarella cubes, top with parmesan cheese. Cover and cook on high 10-15 minutes.

SHIPWRECK

Layer these ingredients:

sliced potatoes
sliced onions
salt and pepper
hamburger
kidney beans
tomato sauce
chili powder

Cover, and bake at 350 degrees for 2 hours.

∞∞∞∞∞∞∞∞∞∞∞∞∞∞∞∞∞∞∞

Colleen Taylor
Indianlantic, Florida

SALMON MACARONI PIE

4 beaten eggs (I use 2 or 3)
2 (15 oz) cans macaroni in cheese sauce (I used the deluxe pkg of dry macaroni and cheese mix)
1 (16 oz can) of salmon, drained, bones and skin removed and broken into chunks
1 1/2 cups soft bread crumbs (2 slices of bread)
1 cup shredded sharp American cheese (4 oz)
dash of salt

In large bowl, stir together eggs, macaroni and cheese, salmon, bread crumbs, shredded cheese and salt.

Turn mixture into a greased 10" baking dish. Bake, uncovered at 350 degrees until set in center, 40-45 minutes. Cut into wedges or squares. Makes 6-8 servings.

∞∞∞∞∞∞∞∞∞∞∞∞∞∞∞∞∞∞∞

Nadine Dozier
North Augusta,
South Carolina

My favorite recipes are anything that will fit into a crockpot!

∞∞∞∞∞∞∞∞∞∞∞∞∞∞∞∞∞∞∞

Lynn Lewis Young
Houston, Texas

ENCHILADA CASSEROLE

Brown 1 pound of lean ground beef with minced garlic clove, and drain off liquid.

Add:

1 pkg mushrooms
1 small onion, chopped
1 1/2 cup of Picante® sauce
1 (10 oz) pkg frozen chopped spinach, thawed and squeezed dry
1 (8 oz) can tomato sauce
2 or 3 chopped tomatoes, seeded
1 red pepper, chopped
1 Tbsp lime juice
dash salt

Arrange 6 tortillas in bottom and up sides of 9x13" baking dish. Top with the ground beef mixture. Arrange 6 more tortillas over the top. Spread with 1 cup commercial sour cream. Bake at 350 degrees for about 30 minutes, or until hot and bubbly. Remove from oven and sprinkle on:

1 cup each, shredded:
    monterey jack cheese
    cheddar cheese

Garnish with 1 cup shredded lettuce and ripe olives.

∞∞∞∞∞∞∞∞∞∞∞∞∞∞∞∞∞∞∞

Mary Anne Keppler
St. Olaf, Iowa

CHEATERS LASAGNA

1 large pkg wide noodles (NOT lasagna noodles)
1 pound hamburger
1 onion, chopped (optional)
1 green pepper, chopped
1 large jar spaghetti sauce
1 can cheddar cheese soup
mozzarella cheese, amount you prefer

Cook and drain noodles. Brown hamburger, onion, pepper. Drain, and add to noodles. Add sauce and soup. Put in casserole. This makes a large batch. Sprinkle with cheese. Bake. Enjoy. This freezes well.

∞∞∞∞∞∞∞∞∞∞∞∞∞∞∞∞∞∞∞

Deb Meneely
Seattle, Washington

WAIKIKI GROUND BEEF

1 pound ground beef
2 Tbsp cornstarch
1/2 cup brown sugar
1 (20 oz) can pineapple chunks
1 green pepper, diced
1/3 cup apple cider vinegar
1 Tbsp soy sauce
1 tsp fresh grated ginger root

Main Dishes & Casseroles, Page 247

Brown ground beef, draining fat, and set aside. Drain the pineapple chunks, reserving syrup and set aside. Combine pineapple syrup, vinegar and soy sauce in saucepan, and heat. Mix cornstarch and sugar and add to saucepan, stirring constantly. Bring to a boil over medium heat and boil for 1 minute, until thickened. Add beef, pineapple, green pepper, and ginger. Heat through, for about 3 minutes. Serve over rice.

Rebecca Kelly
Kingsburg, California

'GOULASH'

Brown 1 pound of hamburger

Add:

1 cup cooked macaroni
   (any type)
1 can stewed tomatoes
1 can corn
1 bottle of your
   favorite spaghetti sauce
Add anything else you like,
   zucchini, etc

Cook all ingredients together on medium heat for about 20 minutes. Serve with bread, or use as a "sloppy joe" mix.

Mary Andrews
Grand Blanc, Michigan

ITALIAN MEAT BALLS

This recipe is a combination of my mother-in-law's recipe, and one from an Italian that cooked for an Italian Church in Saginaw.

3 pounds of ground beef
1 pound of ground veal
6 eggs
9 slices of bread soaked
   in 18 oz of milk
1 1/2 cups grated
   parmesan cheese
3 tsp parsley
2 tsp garlic powder
salt and pepper

Mix all together in a large bowl, using your hands. Form into meat balls, and fry on the stove. This recipe makes a lot, so you can freeze them in a big plastic bag, and then take out a few at a time when you need them.

COMPANY CHICKEN

Spread chipped beef into the bottom of a baking pan, wrap boned chicken breasts in 1/2 slice of bacon, over all pour a sauce of one can cream of mushroom soup and 2 cups sour cream for each 8 pieces of chicken. Bake at 325 degrees for 3 hours, uncovered. Check after 2 hours to make sure it is not drying out.

BEEF BURGANDY

3 cans cream of chicken soup
3 cans cream of mushroom soup
3 cans cream of celery soup
1 envelope dry onion soup mix
1 cup burgandy wine
3-4 pounds of stew beef

Mix all together and place in a large baking pan or roasting pan, and bake uncovered at 350 degrees for 3 to 4 hours until meat is tender. Serve over rice or noodles. Left-overs taste good, too. This recipe is supposed to serve 15 people, so you can cut it down. It doesn't taste as good as fresh, if you freeze the leftovers.

Tonya St. Berg
Woodinville, Washington

BAR-BE-CUE PORK

(This recipe only takes 10 minutes to prepare and will get rave reviews from your family or guests!)

Mix:

1 can cream of mushroom soup
1 cup catsup
1 Tbsp Worcestershire® sauce
1/2 cup chopped onion

Pour over (4-6) porkchops and bake for 2 hours at 375 degrees.

Patricia (Pat) Jones
Oroville, California

BARBECUED RIBS

I think the best recipe for a quilter is one you can put in a crockpot. It uses very little electricity and takes all day to cook, leaving lots of time for quilting! My favorite is listed below:

I use slabs of back ribs, cut apart to fit in my large crockpot. Place ribs only, in the pot and cook on *low* for 6 hours. Remove ribs from crock pot, and brush with barbecue sauce. Place under broiler, or on outside barbecue, for 10 to 12 minutes, just long

Page 248, Main Dishes & Casseroles

enough to flavor the ribs and dry the sauce. Add a salad or two and dinner is ready. Enjoy!

Bonnie Swecker
Roanoke Rapids,
* North Carolina*

CROCKPOT DINNER

I love cooking meals that make themselves, so to speak, so you have some time before the final *putting it all together,* to quilt.

3 to 4 medium potatoes
1 small cabbage
2 to 3 carrots
kielbasi or smoked beef sausage
2 cups beef broth
    (made from bouillon)
salt and pepper

Peel and halve potatoes, and place in bottom of crock pot. Peel and halve carrots and add to pot. Quarter the cabbage and place in pot.

Sprinkle everything with salt and pepper, then add the sausage, cut into links. Pour the broth over all and cook on *low* 6 to 8 hours. Pots do vary in cooking speed, so check to see if your vegetables are tender. I serve this with fruit salad and bread.

Susan Hanna
Brownlee, Nebraska

MUSHROOM BURGERS

Use very lean ground beef and form into patties, 1/2 to 1/3 pound each. Place in pyrex baking dish. Sprinkle patties with garlic salt. Spoon undiluted cream of mushroom soup on top of patties. One can does about four patties. Cover with foil, and bake at 350 degrees for 1 hour. Uncover the last 15 minutes, spooning soup over patties.

Barbara MacDonald
Oscoda, Michigan

SPAGHETTI PIE

In large frying pan:

Fry 1 pound bulk sweet
        Italian sausage - drain

Add:

chopped onion
chopped green pepper
1 can mushrooms

Season with:

garlic powder
parsley
oregano

Add, and simmer:

2 small cans tomato paste
2 cans water

Meanwhile, cook and drain one pound of spaghetti.

Add 2 eggs.
Toss, and layer in casserole dish.

Top with sausage mixture. Top with sour cream (8 oz).

Bake 15 minutes at 300 degrees. Top with mozzarella cheese. Bake until melted, let set 15 minutes before cutting.

MEXICAN CASSEROLE

4 oz cheddar cheese
8 oz mozzarella cheese
1 box tostada shells
1 can refried beans
1 pound hamburger, browned,
    cooked and seasoned
    with chili powder, cumin,
    green onions, and
    green peppers
2 cans tomatoes with chilies

Layer:

broken tostada shells, beans, 1/2 the mozzarella, 1/2 the tomatoes, beef. Repeat layers.

Add:

rest of mozzarella, and all the cheddar cheese. Bake at 300 degrees, til bubbly.

COCKTAIL MEATBALLS

Mix together:

1 pound ground chuck
1/3 cup bread crumbs
1 egg

Form into small meatballs. Brown in oven.

In crockpot, mix 1 bottle chili sauce and 1 small jar grape jelly. Add browned meatballs. Simmer on low for 4-5 hours.

Carole P. Kenny
Providence,
*   Rhode Island*

QUICK DINNER

Put 1 pkg prepared biscuits in oven, while they are baking, combine 1 one pound pkg prepared salad mix (cabbage, lettuce, carrots) and one pound cooked shrimp (cut into chunks), and equal amounts of cocktail sauce and raspberry vinegrette dressing (low cal), about 1/2 cup each.

If you are feeling generous, and you have them in the refrigerator, toss in a tomato or two, some olives, cucumber, or even hard boiled egg. (Don't make any special trips to the store, it takes away from the quilting time).

By the time you have the salad made, the biscuits are ready to come out of the oven and dinner is ready to be served.

Total time: walking into the kitchen to service=10 minutes. Enjoy.

Jean Eng Underhill
Flemington,
New Jersey

TUNA SALAD SANDWICH

2 cans tuna
　　or 1 (15 oz) can salmon
1 small green pepper, chopped
1/2 cup salted peanuts
1/4 cup sliced green onions
1/3 cup chili sauce
1 tsp dry mustard
2 to 4 drops red pepper sauce
6 6" pita breads
3 cups shredded lettuce
alfalfa sprouts

Mix first 7 ingredients, divide pita in half. Fill each half of pita bread with about 1/4 cup tuna mixture. Add some lettuce. Top with sprouts. Serve with additional chili sauce.

HONEY SAUCE CHICKEN

1/2 cup soy sauce
2 Tbsp honey
2 Tbsp dry sherry
2 garlic cloves, minced
8 chicken thighs
steamed rice

Combine first 4 ingredients in large bowl. Add chicken and toss to coat. Cover and refrigerate overnight, turning occasionally. Transfer chicken and marinade to heavy large saucepan. Bring to boil over medium heat. Reduce heat and simmer till just cooked through, turning occasionally, about 20 minutes. Serve with steamed rice.

Jean Van Dusen
Kingsford, Michigan

BARBECUED CHICKEN WINGS

12 chicken wings
1/2 cup flour
1/2 tsp chili powder
1/3 cup cooking oil
1/2 cup barbecue sauce
1/2 tsp hot pepper sauce

Remove wing tips and cut wings in half. Dust in a mix of flour and chili powder. Fry in hot oil 8-10 minutes on each side, till golden brown. Drain on paper towels. Heat barbecue sauce and hot pepper sauce, add wings and simmer a few minutes.

HEARTY RICE CASSEROLE

1 can cream of mushroom soup
1 can creamy onion soup
1 can creamy chicken soup
1 pound ground meat, uncooked
1 pound pork sausage
　　or italian sausage
1 onion, chopped
1 green pepper, chopped
2 stalks celery, sliced
1 1/2 cups rice

Mix, and put into a 4 quart casserole. Bake at 350 degrees for 1 hour, covered.

Joyce Nichols
Bethany, Missouri

My favorite recipe is to start up the bread machine, putting on a pot with stew meat and stop by to drop in veggies as the morning goes by.

Eugenia A. Barnes
Marcellus, New York

As to food, soups and stews and casseroles, steaks and chops with fast baked potatoes and quick salads. Since we live in apple country, a good waldorf salad with walnuts and raisins is fast and easy, as well as the standard caesar or tossed....fast!

A real indulgence is a bread maker...they think you are so clever and they have fresh bread...hot, too...just toss in the ingredients and let the machine do the work! I do not use a sewing machine....although I am learning...but I do believe that machines make my life easier...a microwave and bread maker.

Ann Littleton
Fairfax, Virginia

QUILT CAMP TACO SALAD FOR A CROWD

Provide bowls of the following:

chopped onions
shredded cheddar cheese
sliced olives
chopped tomatoes
chopped cilantro
crushed tortilla chips
thousand island dressing

Prepare a large amount of chili ahead of time and warm amount needed, depending on number of guests. Guests fill their plates with chopped ingredients and top with a ladle of chile.

ITALIAN SANDWICH RING

Buy bread baked in a ring, or use Italian or French Bread. Slice bread in half, horizontally. Layer cold cuts, lettuce, tomato slices, and onion slices on bread. Sprinkle with Good Seasons Italian Dressing and crushed oregano. Top with provolone or mozzarella cheese, and top half of bread. Leave in ring shape, until you know how many pieces you will need to cut it into.

STUFFED SHELLS WITH GARDEN VEGETABLES SAUCE

Buy frozen prepared stuffed shells. Buy Prego® chunky style spaghetti sauce. Grease casserole dish. Place desired number of shells in casserole, on top of a thin layer of sauce. Coarsely chop zucchini and yellow squash, and layer over shells. Top with remaining sauce, and sprinkle with mozzarella cheese. Bake until hot and bubbly at 350 degrees.

Eleanor K. Hunnel
Johnstown, Nebraska

CASSEROLE

Cook 2 cups pasta per instructions. Drain, and pour into a casserole bowl. Add 1 cup spaghetti sauce or more to taste. Mix well. Top with 1 cup grated cheese. Microwave on high, until the cheese is melted.

Dotti Greto
Ocean City, New Jersey

A cook, I'm not! Mostly what I make for dinner, is reservations! My recipe book is a loose leaf notebook, with (again) those vinyl sheet protectors filled with all the local restaurant menus. When I do cook, I swear by any of the Ronzoni boxes. Fortunately, my husband loves to eat out.

Paula Gore
Esmond, Nebraska

Sorry, I'm uninspired!

Doris Holland
Winterset, Iowa

LASAGNA

8 oz Creamette®
    Lasagna noodles
1 pound ground beef
2 (15 oz) cans tomato sauce
1 tsp Italian seasoning
    (optional)
1/4 tsp pepper
1 pound dry cottage cheese
2 cups grated
    mozzarella cheese
1/2 cup parmesan cheese

Brown ground beef. Drain. Add tomato sauce and seasonings. Simmer slowly for 20 minutes.

Prepare Lasagna noodles, as directed on package. Drain. Arrange one layer of noodles in parallel strips in bottom of greased 9x13" baking pan. Top with layers of meat sauce, mozzarella and cottage cheese. Repeat layers, ending with cottage cheese. Top with parmesan. Bake in a 350 degree oven for 30 minutes. Let stand 10 minutes before cutting. Serves 6 to 8. I sometimes make it up ahead, and freeze it. It takes longer to bake, when frozen.

Janet Kugler
Holdrege, Nebraska

ENCHILADAS

Brown:
1 pound hamburger (for 4 to 6)

Grease 9x9", or 9x13" pan
    if using more than 5 shells

Main Dishes & Casseroles, Page 251

Lay out 4 or more flour tortillas. Add hamburger to each, dividing equally. Add chopped onion, and a sprinkling of shredded cheddar cheese. Roll up tortillas. Place in pan. Pour a can of enchilada sauce over top. Sprinkle with more cheese. Bake covered 20 to 25 minutes at 350 degrees.

HAM AND COLESLAW

1 bag (16 oz) coleslaw blend
12 oz ham, cut in thin strips
1 1/2 cups red, and/or
    green pepper strips
1/4 cup chopped cilantro,
    or chopped parsley
    (optional)
1/4 cup low-fat coleslaw
    bottled dressing.

Toss and serve.

Marilyn T. Guy
Delhi, New York

CHICKEN CHILI

Saute' in margarine or oil:

1 or 2 sliced onions
3 cloves garlic

Add, and simmer 2 or 3 minutes:

2/3 cup uncooked regular rice

Add:

1 quart canned tomatoes
1 Tbsp chili powder
salt and pepper to taste
1 tsp marjoram powder
1/4 tsp oregano

Place chicken pieces of your choice in large covered casserole (Thighs are good!). Add the onion/rice mixture. Cover and bake 1 to 1 and 1/2 hours in 350 degree oven.

Check after 45 minutes, if it seems dry you can add some tomato juice, more tomatoes, or chicken broth or white wine. You shouldn't need that much.

Mary Lou Sayers
Clarkson, Nebraska

Whenever I cook potatoes, pasta or various meats, I cook extra amounts. I use the potatoes, or pasta, and cubed leftover meat in a quick casserole, as follows:

Cube leftover meat (chicken, ham or roast beef or turkey).

Combine with 1 1/2 to 2 cups leftover boiled or baked potatoes in a casserole dish, along with a can of cream of mushroom (or celery or cheese) soup that has been mixed in with 1/2 can water. Drain a can of peas or corn, or mixed vegetables, and add to above mixture. Sprinkle buttered bread crumbs over top (or crushed crackers, or potato chips, or canned onion rings). Heat in a 350 degree oven for about 30-35 minutes, or until well heated through. A friend once called this Hobo Stew!!! You can add seasoning to taste.

If I make a roast, I generally make a complete oven meal. Putting potatoes, or sweet potatoes, carrots, etc. in with a roast and baking apples, all at the same time.

Susan Nicholson
Muskegon, Michigan

Cooking is NOT my thing!! I do make large batches of whatever I cook, and freeze for the future!

Dawn Golden
Milford, New Jersey

MARY'S CHICKEN

6 to 8 chicken thighs, with the
    skin removed
3 to 4 potatoes, peeled and cut
    into 1 1/4" (Ha, ha!) cubes
1 onion, sliced
12 (or so) mushrooms, sliced
3 to 4 cloves of garlic, minced
1/4 cup low salt soy sauce
pepper or season to taste

Place all items, in the order listed, in a 9x13" baking dish. Bake at 350 degrees for 60 to 75 minutes, turning chicken and potato mixture twice (when you get up to use the iron). I usually put an easy vegetable, like string beans, in an oven safe dish and pop it in the oven for the last 15 minutes to heat it up.

Teresa A. Walton
New Braunfels, Texas

My kitchen talents far exceed the demands of my husband. I grill outside several times a week, no stove or pans to clean. Fresh vegetables are steamed in my dishwasher safe steamer,. Since low fat is necessary, desserts are forbidden, so fresh fruit or low fat ice cream and cookies. And when I feel a little

Page 252, Main Dishes & Casseroles

guilty about not cooking, I throw ingredients in my bread machine and crockpot for that fresh, home cooked taste.

Roberta Schroeder
Deer Park,
Washington

CHICKEN & RICE CASSEROLE

2 frozen chicken breasts, cut into bite-sized pieces
1 cup Calrose® rice
1 can cream chicken soup
1 can cream mushroom soup
1 cup water
1 can mushrooms - stems and pieces, not drained
1 envelope onion soup mix

Stir all together, and pour in 9x13" baking pan. Cover and bake 325 degrees for 2 hours. Remove cover, and bake 20 minutes.

This is quick and easy.

IMPOSSIBLE MEXICAN PIE

1 pound ground beef
1 chopped onion
1 envelope taco mix
1 can whole green chilies
1 cup shredded jack cheese
1 1/4 cup milk
3 eggs
3/4 cup Bisquick®
1/8 tsp tabasco sauce

Heat oven to 400 degrees. Spray 10 inch pie pan with pan coating. Brown ground beef, add onion, and cook til transparent. Add taco mix. Spread in pie pan. Sprinkle with cheese and chiles. Blend remaining ingredients, and pour into pie pan. Bake 25 to 30 minutes. Garnish with more cheese, if desired.

TAPIOCA STEW

3 pounds stew meat
6 carrots, quartered
4 medium potatoes, quartered
4 stalks of celery, chopped
2 medium onions, chopped
1 Tbsp sugar
1 Tbsp salt
1 1/4 cup water
1/4 tsp pepper
1 can mushrooms
2 Tbsp tapioca
1/2 cup burgandy wine
1 (10 oz) can tomato soup

Combine all ingredients in a 4 quart casserole. Cover and bake 300 degrees for 4 hours, or til tender. Stir in mushrooms and burgandy, just before serving.

Merrilyn Muir-
Rennau
Vienna, Austria,
Europe

CHICKEN AND MUSHROOMS IN DILL SAUCE

1 frying chicken, about 3 1/2 pounds, cut in pieces and skinless
4 Tbsp butter
1 medium onion, minced
salt and pepper to taste
1 cup chicken broth
1 cup sour cream
1 cup sliced fresh mushrooms
1 tsp lemon juice
1 Tbsp flour
2 Tbsp fresh dill, chopped

Melt butter in a saucepan, saute' chicken pieces until light golden, add onion, and continue to cook until onion is soft. Add mushrooms, lemon juice, salt and pepper and chicken broth.

Cover, and cook gently until chicken is tender, about 30 to 40 minutes. Remove chicken, and keep warm. Blend sour cream, flour, and dill, stir into the sauce, and simmer for 5 minutes. Return chicken to pan, heat thoroughly, and serve.

Darlene Brazil
Escalon, California

GASPACHO SOUP

1 clove garlic
4 cups chopped tomatoes
2 to 3 large cucumbers, chopped
1 large green pepper, chopped
1 large onion, chopped
1 large can Snappy Tom®
3 Tbsp olive oil
2 T. vinegar
2 to 3 cups celery, chopped
Salt & pepper, & tabasco
    (all to taste)

Mix all together, chill and serve.

STIR FRY

2 cups chopped carrots
2 cups chopped celery
1 cup chopped onion
1/2 cup chopped green pepper
2 cups chopped broccoli
2 cups chopped zucchini
1 can water chestnuts
1 can bamboo shoots
1/4 cup Mallard® Ginger
    Stir Fry Sauce

Mix. Keep refrigerated in a big Tupperware® bowl. Stir fry about 2 to 3 cups of stir fry vegetables for approximately 5

Main Dishes & Casseroles, Page 253

minutes in 1 Tbsp of hot oil. Add Stir Fry Ginger Sauce, and cover for 1 minute. Serve over hot rice. Save remaining vegetables for another meal.

Jane Aruns
Franklin, Tennessee

TUNA NOODLE CASSEROLE

Cooked noodles
one can of mushroom soup
pkg of cooked frozen peas

Mix. Add tuna. Heat and serve. Add onions and/or mushrooms for variety. (Not elegant, but quick and it gets the job done!)

Susan Southworth
Gulf Shores, Alabama

GUY'S NIGHT
FROM GARY, MARC AND MICHAEL SOUTHWORTH

3 movies, one western, one
    comedy and one scary
3 Pepsis® (3 liter each)
3 bags Doritos®
3 bags Snicker® Snaks
3 bags popcorn
3 Alkaseltzer®

Lay 3 quilts on the floor in the family room in front of the large-screen TV. Add 6 to 9 pillows off all the beds in the house. Turn on movie after distributing the goodies to participants. Watch all movies, eating and drinking until daylight, or everyone falls asleep.

ALDO GALLEGO
(Green Spanish Soup)

Saute' 5 minutes:
1/4 cup olive oil
1/4 pound salt pork,
    cut very small pieces
1/4 pound diced ham

Add:

one (10 oz) pkg frozen chopped
    spinach (or 2 cups fresh)
one can canelli beans
    (or use great northern)
one (4 oz) can chorizo's (Spanish
    sausage), or use fresh
    chorizo, or use hard
    pepperoni, or summer
    sausage, diced into small
    pieces.
2 cups diced potatoes
4 cups chicken broth
sprinkle of comino

Bring to boil, simmer until potatoes are tender (20-25 minutes). Serve with large chunks of black bread, as a meal.

Pamela Thompson
Clinton Twp,
Michigan

SPLIT PEA SOUP

This is a crockpot/slow cooker meal, and an original recipe.

2 cups dry peas
1 ham bone or 2 smoked hams
2 bay leaves
1 tsp salt
pinch of cayenne pepper
2 Tbsp Worcestershire® sauce
1/4 tsp thyme
1 clove garlic, chopped fine
1 Tbsp sugar
1 medium potatoes, chopped
3 carrots, chopped
3 onions, chopped
1 stalk celery,
    chopped with leaves
1 quart water (if pot will hold it)

Rinse and pick over split peas, place in 5-quart crockpot with ham or ham hocks, bay leaves, salt, cayenne pepper, Worcestershire® sauce and spices. If you have a food processor, process potatoes, onions, carrots, garlic and celery, until they're small chunks. Add to crock pot. Add the quart of water, if the pot will hold it. Be careful not to overfill it. Cook on high heat setting for at least 5-7 hours. Stir occasionally, if you happen to be at home. Serves 6-8. Remove bay leaves before serving. You may have to adjust the salt seasoning.

This recipe fits a 5 quart crockpot, if yours is smaller, cut down the recipe a bit. I serve this with corn bread, muffins, or crusty bread for a hearty meal.

Lesley Ann Hill
Granville, Ohio

CHICKEN TAQUITOS

1 pound boneless
    skinless chicken breasts
1 cup water
1/2 minced green onion
1 tsp minced garlic
3 to 4 cups Crisco® oil
1 cup finely chopped tomatoes
6 Tbsp chicken broth
2 tsp flour
1/2 tsp each: cumin, oregano,
    and chili powder
1/2 tsp salt
1 dozen (6") corn tortillas
shredded lettuce, & guacamole

Simmer chicken in water in 10" skillet covered, 20 to 25 minutes. Remove from water and cool. Shred chicken with fork. Saute' onion and garlic in Tbsp Crisco oil 1 to 2 minutes. Stir in chicken, tomatoes, chicken broth, flour cumin, oregano, chili powder and salt. Simmer 3 to 5 minutes.

In a heavy 10" skillet, heat about 1" Crisco oil. Dip tortillas in oil quickly to soften; drain on paper towels (reserve oil). Spoon about 2 Tbsp of the chicken mixture down the center of each tortilla. Roll up tortillas tightly. Secure with wooden toothpicks. Fry rolled up tortillas at 375 degrees till golden brown. Drain on paper towels. Keep taquitos warm in a 300 degree oven. Remove toothpicks. Serve on shredded lettuce with guacamole. Makes 6 servings.

Mary A. Sovran
Phoenix, Arizona

MINESTRONE

3 slices bacon, cut in pieces
1/2 cup chopped onion
1 clove garlic, minced
1 carrot, chopped
2 stalks celery, chopped
salt and pepper to taste
1/2 cup pieces of zucchini
4 cups water
1 cup marinara sauce, either homemade or from a jar
1 can (10 1/2oz) pinto beans, drained
1/2 cup pasta - shell macaroni or vermicelli, broken into 1 inch pieces

In a large soup pot, fry bacon until crisp. Drain all but 1 Tbsp of fat from pot. Saute' onion, garlic, carrot and celery in fat, until crisp and tender. Add water and the rest of ingredients, except pasta and zucchini. Simmer about 30 minutes. A few minutes before serving, add pasta and zucchini, cooking just until tender. Serve with hot rolls, and parmesan cheese sprinkled on top.

PORK CHOP AND PILAF BAKE

4 to 8 lean pork chops
1 box Rice-a-roni®
garlic salt
Rosemary leaves

In a large frying pan, brown chops just until seared and a little brown on both sides. Place chops in a large casserole. Sprinkle with garlic and rosemary leaves. Remove all fat from pan, except 1 Tbsp. In the same pan, with half as much butter as called for on the box of Rice-a-roni®, prepare the rice as directed. After combining all ingredients, pour over the chops. Seal casserole tightly, and place in a pre-heated 350 degree oven, until most of the liquid is absorbed and the rice is tender. This takes about 30 to 40 minutes, depending on the oven. This is a no fail recipe that is great for company, it needs no fussing over.

Marilyn Thomas
Harpster, Ohio

HAMBURGER CASSEROLE

2 pounds ground beef
2 onions
1 can cream of celery soup

Fry onions and beef til done. Drain. Pour into mixture of the soups. In a 9x13" pan, crumble 1/2 loaf of bread, put a little butter on top, put in oven for a while. Then pour hamburger mixture on top. Bake 350 degrees 30 minutes (or you can make dressing in place of bread).

Candra J. Sowder
Williamsburg, Iowa

CHICKEN PAPRIKA

3 to 5 chicken breasts
    or 3 to 4 pounds of chicken, cut up
3 Tbsp oil
1 small onion, chopped
1 Tbsp paprika
2 cups water
1 Tbsp flour
1/2 pint sour cream

Brown onions in oil. Cut chicken and add to onions (or to cut cooking time in half, use chicken breasts, cutting in half thickness...the major meat portion and the slightly meaty breast bone section to make chicken thinner).

Brown chicken under tight lid for a few minutes. Add salt, paprika and water. Cover, and cook 1 hour (or 1/2 hour, if meat is thinner and deboned). When thoroughly cooked, stir flour into sour cream and add to chicken mix. Cook 5 minutes. Serve chicken, and spoon sauce over mashed potatoes or noodles.

Diana Alfuth
Hudson, Wisconsin

TORTELLINI WITH BROCCOLI AND PEPPERS

1 frozen cheese tortellini
1 red or yellow bell pepper, sliced
1 cup chopped broccoli,
    fresh or frozen
1 cup white or blush wine
2 cloves garlic, minced or
    pressed olive oil
fresh grated parmesan cheese

Cook the tortellini according to package directions; set aside.

Meanwhile, saute' garlic in about 2 Tbsp of olive oil; add sliced pepper and broccoli, and stir about 2 minutes, being careful not to burn. Add wine, and cook until reduced to about half. Toss vegetable mixture and tortellini, and serve. Pass fresh grated parmesan to top it all off.

This meal takes less than 20 minutes to prepare and everyone loves it. Serve with crackers or rolls.

Juanita Gibson Yeager
Louisville, Kentucky

With only my husband (who is not known for his love of eating, he weighs the same as he did at age 17) at home to cook for, the days are few and far between, when I break out the pots and pans in earnest. Since the kids left home, my idea of preparing a meal consists of stopping by the closest market, and there select my favorite veggies already sliced from the salad bar. I make a low fat pasta dish, or toss a potato into the microwave. I've been known to zap a few stalks of frozen broccoli until they are warm and slightly limp, or on the potato I pile cubes of cucumbers, sometimes chunks of chicken, or diced ham (also from the salad bar). The gourmet sliced, baked turkey from the deli is great, too. I top the potato with non-fat cottage cheese and salsa. I am watching my fat grams...doing quite well, thank you. Have lost 50 pounds to boot, without exercising (there is a God). For the hubby who isn't watching his weight or fat grams, I toss on shredded cheddar cheese and sour cream. BUT, when an occasion comes and I can't avoid cooking, I generally make a Sausage Casserole which I find is easy to do. The dish is versatile. I have served it for breakfast and/or brunch with eggs, with either from scratch or canned biscuits and peach preserves and with hot brandied peaches topping with spiced whipped cream. For dinner, I have served it with a variety of steamed vegetables (broccoli, squash, cabbage, etc.) or a cabbage salad, baked apples and hot rolls.

SAUSAGE CASSEROLE

1 box of Uncle Ben's® Long
    Grain Wild Rice
1 pound of very lean ground beef
1 pound of breakfast sausage
    (mild or hot)
1 pound of mushrooms
1/4 cup of slivered almonds
2 to 4 Tbsp of soy sauce
2 Tbsp peanut oil, or
    other oil of your choice

Cook rice, as instructed. In a large skillet, brown sausage and ground beef. Drain well. Brown almonds in peanut oil. Remove and drain on a paper towel. Add sliced mushroom to skillet, saute' until tender. Combine all cooked ingredients in a large mixer bowl. Stir to mix. Add soy sauce to taste, depending on the number of people being served. This recipe can make as many as four meals. Divide into casserole dish(s). Freeze, or refrigerate. Reheat before serving. Taste best, if prepared at least 12 hours before serving.

Donna Olson
Rogersville, Missouri

BARBECUE BRISKET

3 to 5 pound beef brisket

Rub liquid smoke, garlic, onion, pepper, celery salt, and worcestershire® sauce on both sides of beef. Put in a roaster, and let sit overnight (or day) before.

Bake at 250 degrees for 5 hours. Before the last hour, take out and cut off fat. Return brisket to oven for last hour. Cool, before cutting. Mix the juice in pan with a bottle of barbecue sauce (my favorite is KC Choice) and serve with meat.

Shirley Gardner
Evergreen, Colorado

I like to use the Colorado Cash Cookbook. I also have a bread machine. It's quick, good and makes the house smell nice.

Page 256, Main Dishes & Casseroles

Joyce Benitez
Omaha, Nebraska

1. Let your friends know you accept leftovers.

2. If you cook a roast, turkey or ham, take time to put at least 2 cups in ziplock bag for freezer. It can be added to Ramen Noodles with frozen mixed vegetables, and in 3-5 minutes, you have a meal.

Or...add it to cream of mushroom or cream of chicken soup, add extra water and mixed peas or carrots, put in instant rice and 5-10 minutes, you can have a meal. Or, Beef Stew can be made with beef, broth, and cream soup, and vegetables over instant rice. Meal in 10 minutes!

Your family will think you have slaved, and you can sew right up til they walk in the door.

PIZZA BURGERS

On the table, lay out an assortment such as: a jar of spaghetti sauce, hamburger buns, pepperoni, onions, olives, cheese, etc. Let each member make individual sandwiches.

I use 1/4 slice of American cheese in center of each, and the kids love to cook them by themselves, and make their own Pizza burgers. Pop them into 400 degree oven to warm them up enough to melt the cheese, 3 to 5 minutes. Serve with salad and ice cream. No cooking. Fast meal! Only a cookie sheet to wash. Quick! Get back to your quilting!

Virginia L. Brown
Ogallala, Nebraska

SKILLET STEW

Dredge in flour, 1 to 1 1/2 pounds cubed lean meat, and brown in 1 to 2 Tbsp shortening in an electric skillet. Salt and pepper to taste. Add about 1 quart water, and put control on *high simmer*, and add 2 or 3 carrots, 4 or 5 potatoes, and 1 medium onion, cut in chunks. Mushrooms and peas can also be added. Simmer covered, about 1 and 1/2 hours. Stir occasionally, adding more water, if needed.

Margo J. Clabo
Cleveland, Tennessee

EASY VEGETABLE BEEF SOUP

Cooking is not my forte', but this is easy enough that even my college age boys will cook it!

In a 6-quart pot, brown and drain 1 to 1 1/2 pounds of ground beef and a large chopped onion.

Add:
1 (28 oz) can crushed tomatoes (concentrated)
2 (15 oz) cans Veg-All Original® (with liquid)
2 (15 oz) cans whole kernel corn (with liquid)
1 (48 oz) can V-8® Juice®

Simmer several hours, stirring occasionally. Serve with salad and bread. (We think it tastes even better the next day.) This makes about 4 quarts.

Debra J. Ruisard
Whitehouse Station, New Jersey

COUNTRY CALICO BEANS

1/2 pound bacon
1 pound lean ground beef
1 cup chopped onion
3/4 cup brown sugar
1 tsp salt
1 tsp dry mustard
1 Tbsp vinegar
1/2 cup ketchup
1 (15 oz) can butter beans (partially drained)
1 (15 oz) can kidney beans (partially drained)
2 (16 oz) can pork and beans

Preheat oven to 350. Fry bacon until crisp. Crumble. Saute onions and ground beef. Drain. Combine bacon bits, onion and ground beef with remaining ingredients in 3 quart casserole and bake, uncovered, for 40 minutes.

PIZZA CASSEROLE

1 pound ground beef
1 medium onion, minced
1 tsp salt
1 tsp pepper
2 large cans pizza sauce
1/4 tsp garlic salt
1 (7 oz) pkg elbow macaroni, cooked
1 cup milk
1 egg
1 cup mozzarella, shredded

Brown meat and onion. Drain. Add pizza sauce and seasonings. Drain cooked macaroni. Beat egg and milk, and add to macaroni. Spread macaroni mixture in shallow dish. Cover

with meat mixture, and sprinkle with shredded cheese. Bake 30 to 40 minutes at 350 degrees.

Anne-Donia B. Hafskjold
Tiller, Norway

MAIN DISH

4-6 slices of bacon,
    cut in thin strips
1 pound of minced meat
1/2 tsp salt
1/2 tsp ground ginger
1/2 tsp pepper
1/2 of an onion, chopped
1 egg
1 boiled potato, mashed
strips of red & green pepper

Quickly fry the bacon. Mix all ingredients, except peppers. When bacon is slightly brown, pour the thick mix into the pan, shape it into a big cake. Fry at medium heat 8 to 10 minutes. Turn the "cake" carefully, sprinkle with pepper, and continue to fry, medium heat, for about 8 minutes. Serve with rice.

Bonnie Swannack
Lamont, Washington

HAMBURGER CASSEROLE

In about 3/4 cup milk, soak 4 slices of bread, cubed. Add seasonings (onion, salt & pepper) to taste, and mix with about 2 pounds of hamburger. Form into patties, and brown over medium heat in fry pan. Place in 9x13" pan, and cover with cream of mushroom soup (2 cans). Bake at 350 degrees about 45 minutes to one hour.

Lynda Milligan and Nancy Smith
Denver, Colorado

SCRAP SOUP

1 pound boned chicken breast
7 to 8 cups chicken broth
1 onion, chopped
8 oz Patchwork Pasta® (or what ever pasta you prefer, cooked, drained and added 10 minutes before serving time)
1 (7oz) can mild green chilies, chopped
"scraps" of your favorite "veggies"
1 bay leaf
1/4 tsp black pepper
1/2 tsp celery seed
salt to taste

This simmering "Scrap Soup" provides several hours of stitching time! This can also be simmered in a crock pot.

Connie Sager
Nashville, Kansas

BROCCOLI RICE CASSEROLE
(My favorite casserole)

2 cups Minute Rice®®, prepared
1 (10 oz) pkg cooked broccoli
1 can cream of celery soup

Stir together with 1 1/2 cups shredded cheddar cheese. Bake 350 degrees 25 to 30 minutes.

Carol Collins
Norfolk, Nebraska

EASY SWiSS STEAK

1 large round steak
1 can golden mushroom soup
1 can stewed tomatoes
    (with onion, celery, green pepper)

Cut steak into serving size pieces; brown well on both sides in large, heavy skillet. Remove any fat or liquid from pan. Add tomatoes, soup, and one can of water. Cover, and simmer for several hours until tender. Stir occasionally, and turn meat to keep from sticking to pan. Add water, as needed. Serve with rice and a vegetable. This freezes very well.

Susan Southworth
Gulf Shores, Alabama

'CHIC 'CHICKEN

Lean Cuisine®
    (any chicken entree')

Follow directions on the box, put the food on plates, making sure to throw out the boxes and plastic. so your loved ones don't know the difference.

Serve with a nice bottle of wine, use only candlelight to eat by because your family may get suspicious if they can see that silly grin on your face, as they enjoy your hard work.

Betty E. Ives
Windsor Ontario, Canada

Food is secondary....I'd rather create!

Constance T. Hall
Mannington, West Virginia

MOCK HAM LOAF

1 pound ground beef or venison
1 cup crushed saltine crackers
1/2 pound hot dogs, ground
1/2 tsp salt
1/2 tsp pepper
1 egg

Glaze:

3/4 cup brown sugar
1/2 cup water
1 Tbsp vinegar
1/2 Tbsp dry mustard

Mix ingredients together. Add half of the glaze mix. Put in pan, and cover with remaining glaze. Bake at 350 degrees for 1 hour.

For moister loaf, double the amount of glaze mix.

ZUCCHINI CASSEROLE

4 cups grated zucchini
1 1/2 cups cheddar cheese, grated
1 1/2 cups Bisquick®
1/2 cup oil
3 eggs, well beaten
1 tsp salt
1/2 tsp pepper
1 tsp oregano

Mix all, except oil and eggs. Add them last. Mix well. Bake at 350 degrees for 1 hour, or until done. I have used cucumber instead of zucchini for this, and 1/4 cup onion, instead of oregano.

Kathy Munkelwitz
Isle, Maine

TV Dinners!

Sandra A. Anderson
Lincoln, Nebraska

TUNA CASSEROLE

Prepare this recipe the night before.

2 cans cream of mushroom soup
2 soup cans milk
2 cups uncooked macaroni
1 small onion, diced
4 hard boiled eggs, diced
2 cans tuna - packed
   in water, drained
1/2 pound grated or
   cubed Velveeta® cheese

Mix all together in 9x13" pan, let set in refrigerator over night, or at least 8 hours. Bake at 350 degrees for 1 hour.

Joan Biasucci
Cedar Creek, Nebraska

1. Dial 402-234-ANNA, Anna's Restaurant, Cedar Creek and make reservations for dinner.

2. If hunger strikes at a time other than ANNA'S normal hours of operation, journey to the restaurant anyway, go inside, and approach the walk-in cooler while carrying the door key. Unlock the door, open it, step inside, survey the shelves and remove whatever seems like a good idea at the time. Keep in mind that a "balanced meal" is obtained by removing two desserts of equal weight and size from the cooler at the same time. PLEASE NOTE: During the winter months, I travel my in motor vehicle to Anna's, otherwise I walk. Which is why it is called a walk-in cooler.

3. Store-bought, frozen "cardboard pizzas" are a last resort alternative. I'm married to an Italian, who has learned to do wonders with them....as a matter of survival.

4. Actually, I have done some cooking. Some of my more memorable dishes include tomato aspic, homemade yogurt (fondly referred to by my son as *tasteless slither*, and peanut butter-and-bacon-bits-on-white-bread. Broiled. However, I think my personal best was a pan of Rice Krispie Bars. Made with real rice. Uncooked. Which is probably why we have ANNA'S.

Doris Lott Aultman
Hattiesburg, Mississippi

MEXICAN PIE

Bake one pie shell
   for 10 minutes

Brown: 1 pound hamburger
   meat with 1 onion

Mix 1/2 jar Old ElPaso® Hot Sauce and 1 can refried beans with 4 oz cheddar cheese.

Layer meat, beans, and remaining cheese in pie shell, and bake 30 minutes at 400 degrees.

Wilma Dooley Muse
Fayetteville, Tennessee

CHICKEN CASSEROLE

1 fryer, cooked and chopped
1 can cream of celery soup
1 small carton of sour cream
black pepper to taste
1 stack of saltine
      crackers, crushed
1 stick of oleo

Mix chopped chicken, soup, sour cream, and pepper. Pour into greased casserole. Melt oleo and add cracker crumbs. Pour crumb mixture over chicken. Bake at 350 degrees for 30 minutes, or until it bubbles. Serves 6 to 8. Instead of cream of celery, any 'cream of...' soup can be used.

Jennifer J. Danly
Arlington,
Massachusetts

Cooking is not one of my favorite pursuits. Alas, we all have to eat. We don't eat meat often, but when we do, pork is our favorite. Here's a really quick recipe to prepare:

PORK CHOPS WITH
HONEY AND HERBS

one pork chop per person,
   boneless or bone-in
   (or more if you wish)
honey
marjoram, dried or fresh
thyme, dried or fresh
pepper

Directions:

Drizzle or brush honey over pork chops on both sides. Sprinkle generously with marjoram, thyme, and fresh ground pepper to taste. Broil for 10 minutes per side, or until pork is thoroughly cooked. Serve with rice or potatoes and a vegetable. See my Acorn Squash recipe in the Vegetable section.

Ellen Vollmer
Nickerson, Nebraska

AFRICAN CHOW MEIN

1 cup uncooked rice, not instant
1 pound ground beef
2 cups celery, diced
1 medium onion, diced
1/4 cup soy sauce
2 cups boiling water
1 can cream of mushroom soup

Brown beef, add onion and celery, and saute'. Add soup, soy sauce, rice, and boiling water. Put into greased 3 1/2 quart covered baking dish. Bake at 350 degrees for 1 hour. Stir at least once, during baking.

*To shorten your time, precook rice, saute' beef, onion and celery. Put into Corningware® dish with rest of ingredients, and microwave until hot. This dish freezes well.

CHICKEN CASSEROLE

8 slices (or heels) of bread
2 cups diced, cooked chicken
1 small onion (chopped)
1/2 cup chopped celery
1/2 cup mayonnaise
1/2 tsp salt
1/8 tsp pepper
2 eggs
1 1/2 cups milk
1 can condensed cream of
   chicken soup
1/4 pound american cheese,
   shredded (1 cup)

Cube 2 slices of bread, place in greased 11x17" baking dish. Combine chicken, onion, celery, mayonnaise, salt & pepper in medium bowl, spoon over cubed bread. Cover, refrigerate 4 hours or overnight. Spoon soup evenly over bread. Sprinkle with cheese, cover. Bake in 325 degree oven for 1 hour. Let stand, covered, for 5 minutes before serving.

Suzanne Peery Schutt
Clinton, Mississippi

TUNA ROCKEFELLER

6 bacon strips, crisply
   fried and crumbled
1 pkg chopped frozen spinach
   (thaw and drain and
   squeeze out all water)
1 (8 oz) carton of sour cream
1/4 tsp lemon juice
2 (6 1/2 oz) cans white tuna,
   packed in oil
parmesan cheese
salt and pepper

Mix all and place in casserole. Fluff with fork. Sprinkle additional parmesan cheese on top. Cook at 350 degrees for 20 minutes. Delicious, and easy.

Pat Milne Hitchcock
Sequim, Washington

I give credit to others for my recipes, I have never cheerfully cooked a meal in my life! This recipe is from a Scottish quilter friend, Carol Lenagan, acquired while on a home exchange in Edinburgh, Scotland.

COCKY-LEEKY SOUP

1 whole chicken
    (skinned and fat-trimmed)
1 large leek, sliced
1 or 2 small garlic cloves,
    chopped or pressed
2 peppercorns
1 grated carrot for color

Boil until chicken falls off bones. You may add rice or noodles toward the end.

Sarah Bruso
Rhinelander,
Wisconsin

POPPY SEED CHICKEN

1 Tbsp butter
8 oz sliced fresh mushrooms
5 cups cubed cooked chicken
1 can cream mushroom or
    cream of chicken soup
1 jar sour cream
1 jar (2 oz) pimento,
    drained & diced

Topping for chicken:

1/2 cup butter
1 1/3 cups finely crushed
    butter flavored crackers
2 tsp poppy seeds

In a skillet, melt butter. Saute' mushrooms, until tender. Stir in chicken, soup, sour cream and pimento; mix well. Spoon mixture into a greased 2 quart casserole. In a small bowl, combine all topping ingredients. Sprinkle over the chicken, bake at 350 degrees for 20 minutes.

Merrilee Tieche
Ozark, Missouri

60 MINUTE REUBEN LOAF

This is great for an easy supper or picnic lunch. Use your imagination and vary the filling ingredients to make a pizza loaf or taco loaf or......?????

3 1/4 cups flour
1 Tbsp sugar
1 tsp salt
1 pkg rapid rising yeast
1 cup hot water
    (105 degrees to 115 degrees)
1 Tbsp softened margarine
1/4 cup thousand
    island dressing
6 oz sliced corned beef
1/4 pound sliced swiss cheese
8 oz drained sauerkraut
1 egg white (beaten)
caraway seeds

Set aside 1 cup flour. In a large bowl mix remaining flour, sugar, salt, and yeast. Stir in hot water and margarine. Mix in only enough reserved flour to make soft dough. On floured surface, knead dough four minutes. On greased baking sheet, roll dough to 14x10: rectangle. Spread dressing down center one third of the dough. Top with layers of corned beef, cheese and sauerkraut. Cut 1" wide strips horizontally from center filling to the outside edges of dough. Braid alternate sides of dough strips across filling. Cover loaf with clean dish towel. Place covered baking sheet over large pan half filled with boiling water for 15 minutes. Brush loaf with egg white and sprinkle with caraway seed. Bake 400 degrees for 25 minutes. Slice to serve.

KALUA PIG IN THE OVEN

I was given this recipe by the Captain of the CHEERS, a charter boat out of Kailua-Kona, Hawaii. I didn't get my Marlin, but have enjoyed this succulent dish many times since.

4 to 5 pounds Pork Roast
2 Tbsp Hawaiian salt,
    Kosher Salt or lots of
    regular salt
1/4 cups soy sauce
1 1" piece of Ginger root,
    grated or crushed
1 Tbsp liquid smoke
1 Tbsp Worcestershire® sauce
Ti or banana leaves

Mix salt, soy sauce, worcestershire®, garlic, ginger and liquid smoke. Place Pork on several Ti or Banana leaves. Rub Pork with seasoning marinade and let stand one hour. Fold leaves over pork, and double-wrap in aluminum foil. Place in a shallow pan and bake at 325 degrees for 4 to 6 hours. Unwrap and shred.

If you're not lucky enough to live in Hawaii or some other tropical clime where Ti or bananas grow outside your window, check with your local florist; they often have Ti leaves for use in arrangements or can order some for you. If you can't find them anywhere, don't worry; it tastes almost as good wrapped in aluminum foil alone.

Dean Valentine
New Braunfels, Texas

SPICEY CABBAGE CASSEROLE

1 pound ground turkey
2 cups V-8® juice
1 can rotel tomatoes
1 medium chopped onion
1 medium chopped green pepper
1 cup rice
1 small head of cabbage
salt and pepper to taste

Brown the turkey, onion and green peppers, add 2 cups of V-8® juice, tomatoes, rice and bring to a boil.

Take a casserole dish, spray with PAM, slice cabbage, put in baking dish. Pour turkey mixture over top, cover tightly with foil. Bake 1 hour at 350 degrees.

Serve with Caraway Seed Bread and tossed green salad. This is a low fat meal and your family thinks you cooked all day!

Christine Miller
Medway, Ohio

I have TOO many recipes to choose from! Sorry!

Marilyn A. Lewis
Glendale, Oregon

MEALTIME MINESTRONE

3 pounds turkey
      thighs or drumsticks
2 zucchini, sliced
3 celery ribs
2 onions, coarsely chopped
2 tsp basil
1 tsp oregano
4 tsp, or cubes, chicken bouillon
2 (10 oz) cans kidney beans,
      rinsed, and drained
2 garlic cloves (or 2 tsp dry
      minced garlic)
1 (28 oz) can tomatoes
14 cups water
2 cups pasta (shells, elbow
      macaroni or use rice)

Combine everything, but beans, pasta & zucchini. Simmer 1 1/2 hours. Take turkey from broth, and debone and cut in small pieces, and return to soup. Add remaining ingredients and simmer 15-20 minutes, or until pasta is tender. Can be halved for smaller family.

NO-PEEK TURKEY VEGETABLE STEW

3 turkey thighs, or drumsticks
1 (10 oz) can chicken broth
2 cups sliced onions
2 cups sliced carrots
2 cups sliced potatoes
1 tsp salt, 1/4 tsp pepper
1/2 tsp thyme
1 1/2 Tbsp cornstarch
2 Tbsp cold water

Put turkey in stew pan, add broth, and sprinkle with 1/2 of the seasonings. Arrange vegetables over the turkey and sprinkle with more seasonings. Cover tightly. Place in 300 degree oven, and bake for 3 hours.

Take out turkey and veggies. Mix cornstarch and water, add to liquid. Simmer, stirring constantly until liquid boils and thickens. Return turkey and veggies.

P.S. Take skin off turkey and slice before putting back into the stew liquid.

Laura Estes
Odessa, Washington

AUNT FLORENCE'S CASSEROLE

2 to 2 1/2 pounds hamburger
2 onions, chopped
4 cans kernel corn, drained
      (or 4 pkgs frozen
      corn, thawed)
4 cans tomato soup
2 cans mushrooms
1/2 tsp pepper
Optional: (1 can sliced olives
      1 cup grated cheese)

Use your microwave to thaw anything not thawed.

Brown hamburger and onion together. Drain off fat. Stir in corn, soup, and mushrooms and pepper.

Line one dish with a plastic bag. Spoon 1/2 the mixture into that dish, seal bag and freeze.

Pour remaining mixture into other dish. You can stir in the olives if you desire, this will make it different from the one in the freezer. Bake at 350 degrees 30-45 minutes.

Page 262, Main Dishes & Casseroles

When the other one is frozen, remove it from the dish, double bag, and return it to the freezer. On the day you want to use it, take it out early and put in refrigerator to thaw. If you forget, thaw it in the microwave. Top with cheese if you like, and bake as directed, or if you're pressed for time, 10 minutes on *high* in the microwave, putting the cheese on after cooking.

Judith Clonan
Fitchburg, Massachusetts

No favorite recipes, takes time from quilting. I'm very protective of my quilting time!

Lois K. Ide
Bucyrus, Ohio

1-2-3 OVEN EASY CHICKEN

In paper sack, combine:

3/4 cup flour
2 tsp salt
1/8 tsp pepper
1 Tbsp paprika.

Shake pieces of chicken, (use a 2 1/2 to 3 pound chicken or just thighs, or just drumsticks) to coat well.

Melt 1 stick (1/4 pound) butter in shallow baking pan. Arrange chicken pieces, skin side down, in single layer in pan. Cover with aluminum foil for first 30 minutes. Turn, and continue to bake without foil, until crispy brown. Bake in hot oven (400 degrees) for 45 minutes to one hour until tender.

Merry May
Tuckahoe, New Jersey

CRANBERRY CHICKEN

1/2 cup all-purpose flour
1/2 tsp salt
1/4 tsp pepper
6 boneless skinless
    chicken breast halves
1/4 cup butter or margarine
1 cup fresh or frozen cranberries
1 cup water
1/2 cup packed brown sugar
dash of ground nutmeg
1 Tbsp red wine
    vinegar, optional
cooked rice

In a shallow dish, combine flour, salt and pepper; dredge chicken. In a skillet, melt butter over medium heat. Brown the chicken on both sides. Remove and keep warm. In the same skillet, add cranberries, water, brown sugar, nutmeg and vinegar, if desired. Cook and stir until the cranberries burst, about 5 minutes. Return chicken to the skillet. Cover, and simmer for 20-30 minutes, or until chicken is tender, basting occasionally with the sauce. Serve over rice. Yield: 4-6 servings.

Penny Hand
Woodbridge, Virginia

HAM BISCUITS & MUSTARD SAUCE

4 Tbsp mustard
2 sticks butter
3 Tbsp chopped onion
3 cans 1869® biscuits
3 pounds shaved ham
2 pkgs provolone, mozzarella,
    or swiss cheese slices

Bake biscuits. Slice in half. Layer with ham and 1/4 piece of cheese. Mix mustard, onion, and butter (and poppy seed, optional) over heat. Spoon over assembled biscuits, and store overnight in refrigerator. Bake at 350 degrees til cheese melts, and serve hot.

Martha De Turk
Kutztown, Pennsylvania

CHICK DELIGHT

chicken parts
1 can mushroom soup
1 envelope onion soup mix
3 cups water
1 cup raw rice

Mix, and put in 9x13" pan. Lay chicken parts of your choice on top, and dot with butter. Quilt while chicken is cooking!

Bake 350 degrees for 1 1/2 hours.

Betty M. Abel
Sheboygan, Michigan

My hint for Quick and Easy Cooking? Get car keys. Drive to local grocery store, visit the Deli Section!

Main Dishes & Casseroles, Page 263

Virginia H. Flowers
Flushing, Michigan

EASY HAMBURGER CASSEROLE

1 pound lean ground beef
1 (10 oz) package,
　　frozen peas, thawed
2 cups diagonally sliced celery
1 (10 3/4oz) can of
　　mushroom soup
3 Tbsp milk or dry sherry
3 scallions, chopped
3 Tbsp chopped pimento
1/2 tsp salt
1/2 tsp pepper
1 cup crushed potato chips

1. Preheat oven to 375 degrees. In a deep 9" ovenproof, or a 1 1/2 quart flameproof casserole, cook beef on top of stove over medium heat, stirring often, until browned and crumbly, about 5 minutes. Drain off excess fat. Spread meat evenly in skillet. Arrange peas evenly over beef, then sprinkle celery over all.

2. In a medium bowl, mix together undiluted soup, milk, scallions, pimento, salt and pepper; pour evenly over celery. Sprinkle potato chips on top.

3. Bake 30 minutes or until hot and bubbly. I deleted the crushed potato chips, and added a single layer of Tater Tots.

Preparation time: 10 minutes, Serves 6.

VEGETABLE CHOWDER

1/3 cup half-inch cubes salt pork
1/2 cup carrot, chopped
1 onion, finely chopped
1/2 cup white turnip, chopped
1 1/2 cups half-inch potato cubes
1 quart boiling water
1 cup half-inch parsnips cubes
3 cups hot milk
2 tsp salt
1/4 tsp pepper
1/4 cup dried bread crumbs
1 tsp chopped parsley

Cook pork and onion 5 minutes, add vegetables and water, and cook about 20 minutes, or until veggies are tender. Add milk, seasonings, crumbs and parsley.

Anna Eelman
North Plainfield, New Jersey

CHILIES RELLENOS CASSEROLE

2 cans (4 oz each) whole
　　green chilies, seeded
1 pound monterey jack cheese,
　　shredded or cut in thin strips
2 large eggs
1 container (16 oz) frozen
　　pancake batter, thawed
4 oz shredded sharp
　　cheddar cheese
salsa or taco sauce
　　at room temperature

Heat oven to 375 degrees. Grease a shallow 1 1/2 quart baking dish. Stuff chilies with Jack cheese (don't worry if chilies tear or come apart). Arrange side by side in prepared dish. Beat eggs with electric mixer until pale and fluffy. Fold pancake batter into eggs; pour over chilies. Sprinkle cheddar over top. Bake 30 minutes or until puffed, firm, and lightly browned around edges. Spoon on salsa; serve immediately. Makes 6 servings. (541 calories per serving. 33 g. fat)

Ruth E. O'Connor
Burlington, Mass

BROCCOLI CASSEROLE

1 pkg frozen, chopped broccoli,
　　thawed and drained well

Add:

1 can cream of celery soup
1/2 can milk
1/2 cup bread crumbs
1 tsp grated cheese
dash of pepper and garlic
3 slices process cheese

Mix all together. Top with process cheese slices and bread crumbs. Bake about 35 minutes at 325 degrees. This is also good with Italian cheese and seasoning.

Georgina Doss
Milton, West Virginia

SESAME CHICKEN

1 cup fine bread crumbs
1/2 cup grated Parmesan cheese
1/2 cup sesame seed
2 tsp grated lemon rind
1/2 tsp salt (optional)
1 tsp paprika
1/2 tsp basil
1 tsp oregano
1/8 tsp pepper
16 skinless, boneless chicken breasts, washed, but not dried.

Combine all ingredients, except chicken. Wash chicken breasts and immediately roll in coating mixture, without drying first. Roll each breast jelly-roll fashion in a shallow, foil-lined baking dish. Bake at 375 degrees for

35-45 minutes. Test for doneness with a fork. If juices run clear, the chicken is done. Do not turn during baking. May be served hot or cold, and freezes well.

Doris Callaway
Greensburg, Kansas

HAM CASSEROLE

2 cups ground ham
1 cup cheese cut small or ground
1 can mushroom soup
    with 1 can water
1 (10 oz) package noodles, cooked

Mix well. Bake 350 degrees, 50 minutes.

Sheryl Mielke
McGregor, Iowa

CROCK POT DRESSING

1 cup butter or margarine
2 cups chopped onions
2 cups chopped celery
1/4 c. dehydrated parsley flakes
2 (8 oz) cans mushrooms,
    drained and diced
12 to 13 cups dry bread crumbs
1 tsp poultry seasoning
1 1/2 tsp salt
1 1/2 tsp sage
1 tsp dried thyme
1/2 tsp pepper
1/2 tsp marjoram (optional)
3 1/2 to 4 1/2 cups chicken broth
2 well beaten eggs

Melt butter in skillet, and saute' onion, celery, parsley and mushrooms. Pour over bread cubes in large mixing bowl. Add all seasonings, and toss. Pour in enough broth to moisten, add beaten eggs, and mix well. Pack lightly into slow cooker. Cover, and set on *high* for 45 minutes, then reduce to *low* for 4 to 8 hours.
•Note: If using seasoned stuffing mix - omit the herbs and salt.

Bernice Tessibel
Inman Cashman
(Tessie)
Coal City, Indiania

BARBECUED CHICKEN BREASTS

Mix together:

1 can cranberry sauce
1 pkg Lipton® Dry
    Onion Soup Mix
1 bottle Kraft® Creamy
    French Dressing

Bake chicken breasts using a small amount of oil, if necessary. Pour sauce mixture over chicken the last 15 or 20 minutes of cooking time.

Linda Boedigheimer
Perham, Minnesota

(I'm the Crock Pot Queen, so I'll share a couple Crock Pot Recipes)

CROCK POT CONTINENTAL CHICKEN

Skin and debone
    2 to 6 chicken breasts

Roll and wrap each
    with 1 bacon slice

Lay on a bed of dried beef on
    bottom of large crock pot

Cover with sauce (1 can golden mushroom soup and 8 oz. commercial sour cream, mixed) Set crock pot on low and forget for about 8 hours. Serve over rice or with mashed potatoes and vegetables.

PORK CHOPS AND SAUERKRAUT

Use a large crockpot and medium jar of kraut.

Spoon a little sauerkraut on the bottom.

Place 3 loin chops on kraut (or 4 boneless).

Peel and dice one apple and place it on chops.

Cover all with remaining sauerkraut. Sprinkle 1 tsp caraway seed on top.

Turn Crockpot on *low* and bake all day. Serve with peach and cottage cheese salad, baked potato and brown bread.

Nancy Wagner Graves
Manhattan, Kansas

CHICKEN SPAGHETTI

1 chicken
1 stick of butter
1 medium onion, chopped
1 green pepper, chopped
1 can rotel tomatoes
1 (12 oz) vermicelli
1 pound Velveeta® cheese, cubed
salt and pepper to taste

Cook and debone chicken, save broth. Saute' onion and green pepper in l stick of butter.

Cook vermicelli in chicken broth, don't drain! Add Velveeta® to spaghetti. Stir, until melted.

Main Dishes & Casseroles, Page 265

Add other ingredients and mix well. Salt and pepper to taste. Spray 9x13 pan with Pam. Pour mixture into pan, bake 350 degrees until heated through. Approximately 30 minutes.

•*Nancy Wagner Graves*
Manhattan, Kansas
•*Judi Robb*
Manhattan, Kansas
•*Eleanor Burenheide,*
Emporia, Kansas

WEST VIRGINIA SOUP

1 pound ground beef, browned & drained
1 (46 oz) can V-8® juice
1 cup finely shredded carrots
1 onion chopped
1 can cream of celery soup
small amount of sugar & basil
1/4 cup raw rice

Combine all ingredients in sauce pan, and simmer until rice and carrots are done.

***Eleanor Burenheide says in her recipe to place all ingredients in the crock pot and cook on *high* for 4 hours, or 6-8 hours on *low*. Yummie!

Dort Lee
Leicester,
North Carolina

PASTA DELIGHT
(fast & easy)

Put pasta on to boil. While it's cooking, drain one small can of tuna. Put it in a casserole dish, and mix in 1 large spoonful of mayonnaise, 4 large spoonfuls of low-fat plain yogurt, and 1 glug of Italian Dressing. Add cooked pasta, salt & pepper. Stir. Serve immediately. Leftovers make a good salad base for the next days lunch.

Susan J. Spencer
Felton, California

CHICKEN ITALIANO

2-3 lbs. chicken thighs, skinned
1 (26 1/2 oz) can spaghetti sauce (Del Monte® w/onion is good)
1/2 cup red wine
parmesan cheese

Put chicken in greased 2 1/2 quart casserole. Sprinkle with parmesan. Combine wine and spaghetti sauce, and pour over chicken. Cover casserole, and bake at 375 degrees about 1 and 1/4 hours, until chicken is no longer pink at bone. Serve over rice or noodles. (Note: If I'm feeling really ambitious, I'll add sliced mushrooms and/or zucchini to the casserole.)

Judi Robb
Manhattan, Kansas

CHICKEN WINGS

1/2 cup Worcestershire® sauce
1/2 cup soy sauce
1 stick butter
1 1/2 cups brown sugar
1 tsp garlic salt
1 tsp onion salt
6 pounds chicken wings

Combine soy and Worcestershire® sauce, butter, garlic and onion salts in saucepan. Bring to gentle boil.

Cut tips off wings and separate wing pieces at main joint. Spread pieces in a shallow cookie pan, and pour sauce mix over wings.

Cook uncovered in 325 degrees oven, till done. Turn at least once. Bake 1 hour.

Helen M. Ericson
Emporia, Kansas

CROCKPOT CHILI

In the evening, wash 3 cups pinto beans and put in crockpot covered with water. Set crockpot on *low* heat. Leave over night.

In the morning after breakfast: Turn the crockpot heat to high and add 1 pound lean ground beef - RAW. Chop up one or two onions. Add green peppers, parsley, celery, whatever.

Add a can of home-canned tomatoes or sauce. Add some salt & pepper. Cook all morning lightly covered, stirring frequently. Add chopped Chilies or powdered Chile to taste. Just before serving, stir in several pinches of yellow cornmeal to thicken juice.

I always say that Chili isn't hot enough unless it takes the skin off your face when you open the lid to stir!!

This is good today, and will keep in the refrigerator in a glass casserole for several days. Can

M. Jeanne Poore
Overland Park, Kansas

JAMBALAYA

1 pound smoked sausage
2 medium onions, chopped
4 cloves garlic-chopped
1 large green pepper, chopped
1 pound boneless chicken
    thighs/breasts, chopped
1 large can tomatoes
1 can chicken broth
1 cup white wine
1 cup chopped celery
1 tsp thyme
2 Tbsp soy sauce
2 Tbsp hot sauce
1/2 tsp cayenne pepper
1 tsp white pepper
1 Tbsp black pepper
1 pound shrimp
1 cup converted rice

Cut sausage into bite size pieces. Brown in large pot. Add onions, green pepper and garlic. Cook until onions are translucent. Add the next 11 ingredients, and bring to boil. Reduce heat, simmer uncovered for 1/2 hour to 45 minutes. Season to taste. Return to a boil. Add shrimp and rice, reduce heat to very low, and cover tightly. Simmer 25 minutes. Check rice for doneness. This is spicy.

LEFT-OVER TURKEY POT PIE

turkey pieces cleaned
        from bones
celery, chopped
carrots, chopped
potatoes, diced
onion, chopped
garlic, chopped
canned milk
canned biscuits
1 can peas
turkey broth (or chicken)
bouillon cubes
salt/pepper to taste
1 tsp turmeric
cornstarch

Chop turkey pieces into cubes, place in a large pot with enough water to cover the vegetables. Cook until vegetables are tender, add bouillon cubes, seasoning to taste. Add 1/2 cup of canned milk, thicken with cornstarch. Put in casserole dish. Split canned biscuits in half, place on top of hot pot pie filling, bake until biscuits are done. You can make up the filling, put in bakeware, and freeze. Take them out of the freezer, thaw, and heat them in the microwave or conventional oven, put biscuits on top to complete baking.

Doris Haggard
Topeka, Kansas

We enjoy a nice pot roast fixed in the crockpot. No recipe included. "Happy Quilting, wherever you are."

Bettie Rushin
Boulder Creek, California

WHITE STUFF

1 pound browned hamburger
1/2 pound of sliced mushrooms
2 cans of cream of
        mushroom soup
6 cups of cooked white rice
1 (8 oz) tub of sour cream
salt and pepper to taste

Brown the hamburger in a frying pan, add sliced mushrooms, cook combined ingredients until mushrooms are still slightly firm, add mushroom soup, cook until warm, thoroughly mix in rice and sour cream. When it's all warm, (it should be the texture of oatmeal) serve. This takes about 15 minutes and the kids love it. Serve with a salad, dinner rolls.

Carol L. Robbins
Overland Park, Kansas

SOUR CREAM ENCHILADAS

24 corn tortillas
1 can cream of chicken soup
1 can cream of celery soup
1 small can diced chilies
1(8 to 12 oz) carton sour cream
1 1/2 pounds shredded cheddar
        cheese (I use 1 pound.
        mild cheddar and 1/2
        pound sharp cheddar)

Mix all ingredients in large bowl, except tortillas. Soften each tortilla for a couple of seconds in boiling water in small skillet. Put one heaping tablespoon filling in center of each softened tortilla, roll up and put in cake pan. Continue until two cake pans are full of enchiladas. Spread remainder of filling on top of enchiladas. Bake in 300 degree oven for 30 minutes. Take out of oven and let set for several minutes before serving.

I serve this dish with refried beans, shredded lettuce and

diced tomatoes. Don't forget picante sauce! This is my family's favorite meal.

Shannon Royer
Otis, Kansas

SWEET AND SOUR CHICKEN

1 (8 oz) bottle russian dressing
broth from chicken
1 cup chunky pineapple
4 skinless chicken breasts
1 (8 oz) jar apricot preserves
1 pkg dry onion soup
1 cup green pepper (optional)

Cut chicken breasts into bite size cubes, place in glass baking dish and microwave on high for 5-8 minutes, or until meat is white and firm. In a separate bowl, combine dressing, preserves, soup mix, and chicken broth. Pour over chicken pieces and bake 1 hour at 375 degrees, covered. Uncover, add pineapple and green pepper, bake 30 minutes. Remove from oven, ladle off sauce, and thicken on stove top with 2 tablespoons corn starch mixed with cold water. Serve over rice. 15 to 20 minutes preparation.

TUNA WITH A TWIST CASSEROLE.

1 can cheddar cheese soup
1 can cream of mushroom soup
1 small carton sour cream
1 small can tuna (double if you
    really like tuna)
1 pkg (box) egg noodles

Prepare noodles to package directions, do not over cook. In a large bowl, mix the soups, sour cream, and flaked tuna. Add drained noodles, spread in a 9x13" baking dish and bake 30 to 40 minutes, or until hot and bubbly, at 400 degrees. This takes 15 to 20 minutes preparation.

Karen Crosby
Ocala, Florida

MICROWAVE CHICKEN COR-DO-BLEAU

Cut chicken breasts in half, and pound until flat. Place a thin slice of ham and 1 slice of swiss cheese on top, and roll up and secure with toothpicks. Roll in melted butter, and then in crushed corn flakes. Cook for about 10-12 minutes, depending on your microwave and how many breasts you are cooking.

Tedi Lambert
Los Banos, California

11 YEAR-OLD SPAGHETTI

Ingredients:

One 11 year old child
Spaghetti noodles and sauce

Con one 11-year old male child into cooking spaghetti noodles and sauce. Serve warm. If you're really adept at conning the male child, maybe you'll get sewing room service!

Julie L. Kimberlin
Anchorage, Alaska

CHICKEN-TORTILLA

This recipe is from my husband's aunt. It gets used so much, it never gets filed! It sits right in front in my recipe box!

1 pkg corn tortillas
4 chicken breasts, split and
    boned, after cooking
1 can cream of chicken soup
1 can cream of mushroom soup
1 can Ortega® green
    chili salsa (chopped)
1 cup milk
2 cups sharp cheddar
    cheese (grated)

Butter (cooking spray works fine) 9x13" pyrex dish, and line with tortillas, quartered. Layer chicken, picked off bones. Mix two soups and milk. Pour half of this over chicken. Then put half of salsa over all and 1 cup grated cheese. Repeat layers, topping with rest of cheese. Bake 35-45 minutes in 325 degree oven. Serves 6 to 8.

Pat Reep
Bakersfield, California

ZUCCHINI CASSEROLE

2 cups grated zucchini
5 Tbsp Bisquick®
2 beaten eggs
1 Tbsp chopped green onion
1 Tbsp chopped green pepper
1/2 cup parmesan cheese

Bake at 350 degrees for 1/2 hour in greased casserole.

Phyllis Hansen Giersch
Madera, California

QUILTER'S SPECIAL STEW

Since our three children and their families all live here in Madera, we do lots of entertaining, (we have five grand children and one foster grandson). Also, because of my husband's involvement with Rotary International, civic groups, church and etc., we seem to have lots of opportunities to use our home for parties. My mother was the world's best Swedish cook, at least we thought so, and I like to cook, but also try to keep us all healthy and slim. In about one month for the time that I am writing this "dissertation", we are moving into a larger home that backs up to our local country club golf course. The new house is a two story cape cod, and we are not used to stairs since leaving Kansas, some 32 years ago. Therefore, I may get out some of my old recipes for Christmas that use butter and all that good stuff, because moving just before Christmas is going to be some feat of endurance!

2 pounds of stew meat
    (or sirloin tips)
1 can of cream of celery soup
1/2 cup red wine
1 can cream of mushroom soup
1 pkg dry onion soup mix
    or beef and mushroom soup mix

Combine all of the above ingredients, and put into a slow cooking crock pot. Start the stew on *high* for about one hour and then turn to *low* temperature, and cook for 5 to 6 hours. Serve over noodles, rice or potatoes.

Teresa Binder
Emporia, Kansas

TAMALE PIE
Preheat oven to 375 degrees

1 (16 oz) can creamed corn
1 (15 oz) can chili with beans
1 (14 1/2 oz) can tamales, chopped

Combine in a 2 quart casserole. Bake 20 minutes. Stir.

Sprinkle on:

3/4 cup crushed tortilla chips
1 cup shredded cheese...
over the tamale mixture.

Return to oven, and bake 10 minutes more. Garnish with shredded lettuce and ripe olives.

Betty A. Lenz
Marshall, Missouri

SAUSAGE SOUP

1 pound country style sausage
2 cups celery, sliced
2 pounds zucchini, sliced
1 tsp oregano
1/4 tsp garlic powder
1 cup chopped onion
2 green peppers, cut in strips
2 (28 oz) cans tomatoes
1 tsp Italian seasoning
1 Tbsp basil

Cook sausage, and drain well. Combine all other ingredients and simmer on low heat for several hours, or until vegetables are tender.

Charlotte Fry
St. Charles, Missouri

CHICKEN CASSEROLE
(Turkey works well, too.)

1 1/2 cups cooked chicken
    or more....diced
1 can cream of mushroom, cream
    of celery or cream of
    chicken soup
1 cup diced celery
1/2 cups nuts-almond slivers or
    water chestnuts, diced
1 small onion, chopped
1 Tbsp lemon juice
1/2 cup salad dressing or mayo
    (can use light)

Mix well, pour into casserole sprayed with cooking spray, top with crushed potato chips or croutons. Bake 400 degrees about 20 minutes, or browned lightly.

Marcene Gunter
Hillsboro, Kansas

EGG AND SAUSAGE CASSEROLE

1 pound ground sausage or beef
6 eggs, beaten
1 1/2 to 2 cups diced
    american cheese
1 tsp dry mustard
2 cups milk
1/2 tsp salt

Main Dishes & Casseroles

Brown the meat, drain. Mix with all other ingredients, put into a 1 quart greased casserole, or 8x8" pan. Keep in refrigerator for 12 hours. Stir. Bake 350 degrees for 45 to 55 minutes.

OVEN-BAKED STEW

2 pounds beef stew meat, cut into bite-size pieces
6 carrots, angle cut in 1" pieces
8 stalks of celery, cut in 1" pieces
6 medium potatoes, cut in quarters
1 large onion, sliced thin
2 tsp salt
3 Tbsp minute tapioca
1 can (16 oz) vegetable juice

Put all ingredients in 9x13" pan. Cover tightly with foil. Bake at 300 degrees for 4 hours. Serves eight.

MICROWAVE TIPS!

Always under cook and check. It takes 20% of the time of other cooking. Hamburger takes less time than other meats. Cook 6 minutes per pound. Cut back on 1/4 to 1/3 of liquid. 1/4 of the regular cooking time. Salt at end. Cook vegetables on high 5 minutes, then reduce power. Potatoes 6 minutes per pound.

Joan Waldman
Platte Center,
Nebraska

HASH BROWN QUICHE

Thaw, drain and press into bottom of 9" pan 3 cups hash browns.

Drizzle 1/3 cup melted margarine over top of potatoes.

Bake at 425 degrees for 25 minutes.

Cook, drain, and crumble: 1/2 pound bacon.

Grate 1 cup cheddar cheese and toss with bacon.

Mix:

2 eggs
1/2 cup milk
salt and pepper

When hash browns come out of the oven, lower heat to 350 degrees. Sprinkle bacon/cheese mixture on hash browns. Then pour on egg mixture. Return to oven and bake an additional 25 to 30 minutes, or until a knife inserted in center comes out clean. Cool 10 minutes, and cut into wedges and serve.

REUBEN CASSEROLE

Place: 2 cups sauerkraut (rinsed and drained) in bottom of 9x13" glass pan.

Mix: 1 cup sour cream (low fat), 1/2 tsp garlic powder and 1/2 tsp onion powder. Spread on top of kraut.

Chop: 1 pkg corned beef, spread on top of sour cream mix.

Slice: 1 pkg swiss cheese (10 to 12 oz size) Put slices on top of corned beef.

Cube: 6-8 slices dark rye bread, put on top of cheese.

Melt: 1 stick margarine and drizzle over the crumbs.

Bake: 350 degrees 35 minutes.

Edith O. McGhee
Mercer, Pennsylvania

• I don't like to cook, and really hate to bake!

Michelle Hazelhoff
Mt. Evelyn,
Vic Australia

I'm no cook! My husband's a chef!

Richard F. Zimmerman
New Milford,
New Jersey

In addition to quilting, I like to cook/bake. You might describe me as a creative cook, because whenever I prepare food for the family I rarely follow a recipe, but proceed with whatever is at hand, mixing spices and flavors as seems best. So far nothing has proven *uneatable*.

Betty J. Knack
Essexville, Michigan

JOAN'S BAKED BEANS

2 cans (16 to18 oz) store brand or cheapest brand of beans you can buy, juice and all
4-6 slices bacon, cooked but limp
2 Tbsp onions, chopped and sauted, can use more
1/4 cup catsup
1 tsp dry mustard
1/4 to 1/2 cup brown sugar
1/3 cup crushed ginger snaps

Page 270, Main Dishes & Casseroles

Mix everything. Pour into a casserole. Bake 325 degrees for 1 and 1/2 hours, uncovered. Or...microwave for 10 minutes, but add 3/4 cup ginger snaps.

Note: The ginger snap can be spicy, use as you want, they are also used as a thickener or flavoring. Looks as if the beans have baked for hours.

Janet P. Wyckoff
Hopewell, New Jersey

SEAFOOD ROSEMARY
(after my friend Rosie)

Saute' in butter:
1/2 pound bay scallops
2 green onions, chopped

Add:
1/2 pound shrimp,
    cooked and peeled
1/2 to 3/4 pound imitation crab,
    broken up
1 pound tri-color pasta, cooked
2 cans cream of shrimp soup
1 cup half & half or
    evaporated milk
sherry

Mix together, put into a greased casserole. Top with bread crumbs, Parmesan cheese and melted butter. Bake at 350 degrees, till heated through.

Judy Wolfrom
Southampton,
New Jersey

KARTOFFELS

4 large baking potatoes
1 pound loose sausage
1 small onion, finely diced
8 oz fresh mushrooms, sliced
dash black pepper
1 Tbsp chopped chives
dash salt
8 oz (8 slices) jarlsberg cheese

Heat oven to 400 degrees. Bake potatoes until tender; cool them slightly on counter. Cut in half lengthwise and spoon out meat, reserving skins. Set aside. Saute' sausage: as it cooks, break up clumps. Add onion and mushrooms, and continue to cook until vegetables are tender; drain excess fat, season with pepper and chives; add salt to taste.

Add potato meat, and toss gently for one minute. Place mixture in skins. Top each with slice of Jarlsberg cheese. Bake 10 minutes.

HEARTHSIDE SANDWICHES

2 cups finely cubed cooked ham
1 cup shredded
    sharp cheddar cheese
2 Tbsp mayonnaise
2 Tbsp pickle relish, drained
1 Tbsp grated onion
2 tsp prepared mustard
8 picnic (hot dog) buns

Heat oven to 350 degrees. In mixing bowl, combine all ingredients, except buns. Fill split buns with mixture. Wrap sandwiches individually in foil. Heat for 20 minutes, or over hot coals in a charcoal grill for 10 minutes.

Maria Lage
Cumberland,
Rhode Island

OVEN-FRIED CHICKEN

3 pounds chicken pieces
3 Tbsp flour
3/4 tsp paprika
1/8 tsp pepper
3/4 tsp salt
1/4 cup margarine

Preheat oven to 425. Wash and dry chicken pieces. Combine flour, paprika, salt and pepper. Coat chicken with flour mixture.

In shallow pan in oven, melt margarine. Remove from oven and place chicken in pan, single layer, skin side down. Bake uncovered, 30 minutes. With tongs, turn chicken pieces, and bake 15 minutes longer, or until brown.

Nancy H. Ehinger
West Branch,
Michigan

ROSEMARY PORK CHOPS

1 pork chop per person
4 Tbsp margarine
1 medium onion
1 garlic bud
potatoes
chicken broth (1 cup)
1/4 tsp rosemary

Brown chops in 2 Tbsp margarine in pan large enough to hold chops and potatoes. While chops are browning, peel enough potatoes to serve the number of people who will be eating dinner. Slice thinly.

Main Dishes & Casseroles, Page 271

Remove chops to plate. Scrape bottom of pan: add additional 2 Tbsp of margarine. Saute' onions and garlic until tender.

Arrange potatoes on top of onions and garlic. Pour chicken broth over top. Arrange chops on top, and sprinkle rosemary over all. Turn stove to *low* and simmer for 1/2 hour. Lamb chops may also be used in this recipe. Fast and delicious.

Patricia L. Carl
Rhinebeck, New York

EASY OVEN STEW

2 pounds cut-up beef for stew
2 Tbsp flour
1 tsp salt
pepper & paprika
2 Tbsp Wesson® Oil
4 onions
4 potatoes
4 carrots
1 cup sliced celery
salt and pepper to taste
1 (15 oz) can tomato sauce
1 can water

Sprinkle beef with flour and seasonings. Toss in Wesson Oil® in a 3 quart casserole.

Bake, uncovered, at 400 degrees for 30 minutes. Stir once or twice. Add vegetables (cut in half, if large). Salt and pepper. Pour tomato sauce and water over all. Cover and bake at 350 degrees for 1 3/4 hours. Four servings.

Alba Lee Elliott
Asheville,
North Carolina

"WHAT IS IN THE POT?"

1/2 pound black eyed peas
2 Italian sausages
1/2 onion
3 garlic cloves
1/2 tsp cumino and oregano
1/2 green pepper
1/2 cup Pace® medium sauce

In a deep casserole, boil enough water to cover the peas. Brown the sausage. In a food processor, mince onion, peppers and garlic. Add to peas, along with sausages, cumino, oregano, and Pace sauce. Cook, keeping the water level over the peas until peas are soft. Serve over rice.

Carolyn Koopman
Carnavillo, Iowa

AUNT CLARA'S CHICKEN STRATA

In a greased 9x13" pan, place 9 slices of bread.

Layer:
2 cups cooked chicken
1 can drained mushrooms
1 can water chestnuts

Beat together, and
            pour over top:
4 eggs
2 cups milt
salt and pepper

Cover with slices of cheese.

Mix, and pour over the top:

1 can cream of mushroom soup
1 can cream of celery soup

Cover, and refrigerate overnight. Cover with buttered bread crumbs. Bake at 350 degrees, 1 hour and 10 minutes. Serves 12.

LaRue Nuest
South Hutchinson,
Kansas

OVEN STEW

2 pounds cubed beef
3 potatoes
1 stalk of celery
1 onion
bay leaf
1 tsp salt
1 tsp chili powder
1 cup carrots
1 can tomato soup
1 *soup can* full of water

Mix all ingredients well. Bake at 275 degrees for 5 hours.

Roxanne H. McElroy
Mililani, Hawaii

HOT SHREDDED BEEF FROM KING'S TSIN RESTAURANT

(If you want the recipe, ask them!)

Norma Jean Rector
Center Point, Indiana

SKILLET HASH

In the bottom of an ungreased skillet, slice 3 carrots, then slice 4 potatoes over carrots. Salt and pepper to taste. Slice one onion over potatoes. Pour 1/2 cup water over all. Cover vegetables with 1 1/2 pounds ground beef, spreading meat to edge of skillet to "seal" in the vegetables. Cook over medium heat for 30 minutes. All ingredients can be increased or decreased, according to how well you like each. Serves four. If some of the kids come by unexpectedly, I like to double this, and fix it in my electric skillet.

Betty J. Pribil
Portland, Oregon

I like to make large dishes of meat loaf, lasagna, stuffed green peppers, etc. and freeze into serving pieces. This saves a lot of time.

Alyce C. Kauffman
Gridley, California

LASAGNE

1/4 cup minced celery
1 medium onion, minced
1 clove garlic, minced
2 Tbsp shortening or oil
1 pound ground beef
2 1/2 to 3 1/2 cups
      canned tomatoes
1 (6 oz) can tomato paste
1 1/2 tsp salt
1 tsp sugar
1/4 tsp cayenne pepper
1 bay leaf
1/2 pound corkscrew noodles
3/4 pound mozzarella cheese
1/2 pound cottage cheese
grated parmesan cheese

Cook celery, onions and garlic in oil until tender. Add ground beef, and cook over medium heat until crumbly, and no longer red. Add tomato and paste. Add spices (except bay leaf). Lay bay leaf on top of mixture. Simmer uncovered, for 20 minutes. Remove bay leaf.

Meanwhile, cook noodles according to directions. Cut mozzarella cheese into thin slices. Arrange a layer of noodles in a 3 quart container or 12x18x2" baking pan. Spoon on half of meat mixture, half of the cottage cheese, and a layer of mozzarella cheese. Repeat. Finish with grated Parmesan cheese on top. Bake in 350 degree oven for 30 minutes. Freezes well.

It's time consuming, but makes a large quantity, which is divided into smaller portions after cooking, and provides quick meals for several days.

Pamela T. Young
Minot Air Force Base,
North Dakota

The following recipe is easy, but time consuming. Once you have made a batch, you can eat it for days! It tastes better the longer it sits. Just add a little water and pop it into the microwave, to reheat.

MINESTRONE SOUP

1 pound Hot Italian Sausage
1 (16 oz) can plum tomatoes
3 cloves of garlic
1 (16 oz) can kidney beans
1 zucchini
1/4 cup chopped parsley
1 tsp fennel seed
1 tsp red pepper flakes
1 cup Ditalini®
    or other small macaroni
1/2 cup grated parmesan cheese
1 quart beef stock
1 green pepper
salt and pepper
1 onion
1 large potato
1 tsp basil
1 tsp oil
2 tsp oregano

Cut sausage into pieces. Chop onion, potato, pepper, tomatoes - keep juice. Mince garlic. Cut zucchini in quarters lengthwise, then slice. Heat oil in soup kettle over medium heat.

Cook sausage until brown, drain on paper towel, save 1 Tbsp fat. Add onion, garlic, potato, pepper, and cook 5 minutes. Add tomatoes with liquid, herbs, spices, pepper flakes, salt and pepper.

Bring to a boil, then reduce to low heat. Cover, and simmer until potatoes are tender. Add kidney beans with their liquid, zucchini and pasta. Simmer until pasta is tender (20 minutes). Taste for seasoning, add salt and pepper, if needed. Serve cheese with the soup and let guests help themselves.

Janice A. Miller
Jaffrey,
    New Hampshire

HONEY DIJON CHICKEN WINGS

1/2 tsp hot sauce
1/4 cup dijon mustard
1/3 cup honey or maple syrup

Main Dishes & Casseroles, Page 273

Bake wings in 425 degree oven for one hour. Drain. Pour the sauce that has been mixed well, over the wings, and serve.

Bonnie Kay Browning
Paducah, Kentucky

EASY BAKED CHICKEN BREASTS

8 chicken breast halves
    (skinned and boned)
8 (4x4") slices swiss cheese
1 (10 oz) can cream of chicken
    (or mushroom) soup
1/4 cup dry white wine
    (or water)
1 cup herb seasoned
    stuffing mix, crushed
2 to 3 Tbs butter or margarine
Parsley

Arrange chicken in a lightly greased (12 x 8") baking dish. Top with cheese slices. Combine soup and wine (or water). Stir well. Spoon *soup* sauce over chicken, sprinkle with stuffing mix. Drizzle butter over crumbs. Bake at 350 degrees for 45 minutes.

Sandra L. Hatch
Lincoln, Maine

My quickest and easiest recipes all involve meals that can be made in less than half an hour. I like to buy frozen soups and chowders. All you do is open the container and add water and heat. They taste so good! I love chop suey with macaroni, canned tomatoes (which I can myself!), tomato soup, mushrooms, and onions and ground beef. We have that at least once every two weeks. It is still my favorite meal after all these years. It takes me about 20 minutes to get it on the table. I use freeze-dried onions and you can't tell the difference.

Sue Hausmann
Lincolnville, Illinois

I love church cookbooks because every recipe is the donor's favorite. The following casserole was in a church cookbook given to me in thanks for giving a sewing class in Shreveport, Louisiana about 10 years ago. Soon after, my new daughter-in-law, Nan, a vegetarian was coming for dinner and this Spinach Noodle Casserole has been a family favorite ever since.

SPINACH NOODLE CASSEROLE

1 (4 oz) pkg cooked, drained,
    spaghetti (I use the
    nests -very fine noodles)
1 pkg frozen chopped spinach
    (cooked and drained,
    you can use 2 pkgs)
8 oz monterrey jack cheese,
    grated, can use more)
1 egg
2 Tbsp Parmesan cheese and
    some to sprinkle on top
1/2 cup sour cream
1/4 cup milk

Beat the eggs, mix with grated cheese, parmesan cheese, sour cream, milk and salt. Fold in cooked spaghetti and spinach. Pour into casserole dish. Sprinkle with parmesan cheese. Bake at 350 degrees for 1/2 hour or until warm through. Cover the first 15 minutes - uncover the last 15 minutes.

Jane Newhouse
Wedderburn, Oregon

BEEF-MACARONI SKILLET

In a large skillet (with cover) brown:

1 pound ground beef
1 medium onion

Add:

2 cups tomato juice
    or stewed tomatoes
1 Tbsp Worcestershire® sauce
1 Tbsp vinegar
1 tsp salt
pepper
1 tsp dry mustard
1 cup uncooked macaroni

Cook uncovered until macaroni is done, about 20 minutes, stirring occasionally.

Sally Smith
Kodak, Tennessee

EASY CREAMED HAM

1 (16 oz) pkg
    deli ham lunchmeat
2 Tbsp margarine
2 Tbsp all-purpose flour
1 cup milk
1/2 tsp Worcestershire® Sauce
Toast, per serving

Cut up ham and saute' until slightly brown. Remove from skillet. Add margarine to pan, when melted, add flour. Mix well, then add milk all at once. Cook, stirring constantly until thick and bubbly. Add Worcestershire® and a dash of salt and pepper. Cook until thickened. If mixture becomes too thick, simply add a little more milk. Add ham back to the sauce and serve all over toast points. This is a 15-minute one!

CHICKEN STUFFING CASSEROLE
My daughter's favorite!

1 can cream of chicken soup
1 can cream of celery soup
1 box cornbread stuffing (chicken flavor)
chicken (canned, or cooked and boned)
2 cups chicken broth

Combine seasoned packet from stuffing mix with chicken broth, warmed. Combine chicken with soups and put into casserole dish. Spread stuffing on top of chicken mixture. Pour chicken broth mixture over all and bake at 350 degrees for 30 minutes or until bubbly. Lowfat soups can be used for weight conscious folks!

Joanna Bessey
Rhinelander,
Wisconsin

GOLDEN LEMON CHICKEN

4 boneless skinless chicken breasts (about 1 pound)
1 egg
flour
3 Tbsp butter or margarine
1 envelope Lipton's® Secrets' *Golden Herb with Lemon* Recipe Soup Mix
1 cup water
4 lemon slices (optional)

Cook rice. (I use a blend of wild, brown and white)

Dip chicken in egg, then flour. In skillet, melt butter and brown chicken over medium heat 4 minutes, turning once. Stir in the herb with lemon soup mix blended with water; arrange lemon slices on chicken. Bring to a boil and simmer covered about 10 minutes or until chicken is done and sauce is slightly thickened. Arrange chicken and lemon on rice and spoon sauce over all. Serves four.

"Better is an dinner of herbs where love is, than a stalled ox and hatred therein!"
Proverbs 15:17

This has got to be one of my favorite scriptures. How many times have we counted our blessings and found we had so much to be thankful for? Things money can't buy! A tiny hand clutching our finger. A *sticky* kiss. A burst of pride as a wee one goes off to kindergarten. The quietness that settles over the house after babies are tucked into bed, all pink and warm beneath the quilts. The delicious aromas that drift thru the home as cookies are baking. An unexpected rose. The sight of the entire family lined up side-by-side in the pew on Sunday morning. The warmth, shelter, and security of home. So many pleasures and blessings we take for granted.

No matter how spacious or grand a home is, without *love* it is no home at all. The cupboards may be bulging, the freezers laden with the finest food the world has to offer, but if there is hatred and strife in the home, it is nothing. It is more desirable to have hot dogs and potato chips served (and eaten) with *love*. And, God's love, too!

Joyce Livingston

QUILTERS SHARE THEIR FAVORITE SALAD RECIPES!

Joyce Livingston
Council Grove, Kansas

FANTASTIC CRANBERRY SALAD

2 pkgs raw cranberries, ground
1 1/2 cups sugar (or more)
1 cup pecans, coarsely chopped
1 cup mini-marshmallows
3/4 cup of halved red grapes

Stir sugar into cranberries, add rest of ingredients and refrigerate overnight. Make up 2 packets of Dream Whip®, as instructed on package. Sweeten with 1/2 cup of powdered sugar. Fold into cranberry mixture. Chill and serve.

My family loves this salad! I make it year around, using frozen cranberries we purchased in season and froze. Rarely does a Thanksgiving pass, that I don't get a call from someone wanting this recipe.

RED HOT JELLO®

Dissolve 1 medium pkg of red hots (about 1/2 cup) in 2 cups boiling water. Add 1 large pkg lemon Jello® and stir until dissolved. Add 1 cup cold water. Stir in 1 can of applesauce. Let set, stirring occasionally.

Just before serving, combine a few drops of milk and one small pkg cream cheese, using a hand mixer. Frost top of Red Hot Jello® with cheese mixture.

EASY COTTAGE CHEESE

Combine 1 carton cottage cheese, chopped green pepper, chopped radishes, and chopped celery. Serve on lettuce leaf.

Elizabeth A. Akana
Kaneohe, Hawaii

O-GO (SEAWEED SALAD)

Combine sauce and stir well:

1/2 cup shoyu
6 Tbsp vinegar
2 Tbsp sugar (to taste)
1/4 cup oil
1 tsp salt
dash pepper
small piece of ginger root
    (chopped fine)
1/4 tsp garlic puree or powder
small red chili pepper
    (chopped fine)

Boil water and throw in 2 packages O-GO. It turns green-- take out immediately and put under cold water to crisp. Let drain. Later, cut O-GO into 1/2" slivers.

1 can Abalone or Abalone-like or
    2 cans chopped clams,
    cut into small pieces.
1 big, or 2 small tomatoes, cut
    into small pieces
1 white onion, slivered
2 stalks celery,
    cut into small pieces

Put 1/2 of O-GO, 1/2 abalone and 1/2 sauce into bowl. Stir. Repeat, stir. Stir every hour. Make 6 hours early and chill.

Alice Furrey
Carter, South Dakota

MEAL IN ONE PASTA SALAD
(Original Low-fat Recipe)

Cook about 3 cups spiral or other pasta and drain.

While cooking, stir together:

one cup recipe Mrs. Dash® garlic and herb salad dressing mix (or dressing of your choice)

(In place of the 1/2 cup oil, use 1/2 cup corn syrup or part corn syrup and water, or water and sweetener, as desired.) Pour about half of the dressing over the warm pasta to absorb flavors.

Chop and add:

3 stalks celery
1/2 green or red pepper
1/2 onion
1 cup or more diced chicken,
    white turkey or tuna
1 cup or more seedless
    grapes, halved
rest of dressing

Jean Van Dusen
Kingsford, Michigan

BOK CHOY SALAD

8 oz sliced almonds
2 pkgs Ramen® noodles,
    without seasoning
1/2 cup sunflower seeds
    or sesame seed
1/2 cup margarine

Brown above in frying pan - set aside. Cut up 1 head bok choy and one pack green onions. Mix all. Twenty minutes before serving, top with dressing.

Dressing for above:

3/4 sugar
1/2 to 1 cup of vegetable oil
1/2 cup vinegar
2 Tbsp soy sauce

Sandra A. Anderson
Lincoln, Nebraska

CHERRY COLA SALAD

1 (16 oz) can bing cherries,
    packed in water
1 (16 oz) can crushed pineapple,
    packed in it's own juice
1 (6 oz) box sugar-free
    cherry Jello®
1 (12 oz) can diet cola

Drain cherries and pineapple, add water to make 2 cups liquid. Heat to boiling. Pour over Jello® to dissolve. Add cola, chill till semi-fluid. Add cherries and pineapple. Mix. Chill.

Suzanne Peery Schutt
Clinton, Mississippi

HOLIDAY SALAD

2 pkgs (3 oz each) cherry gelatin
2 cups hot water
1 pint sour cream
1 (one pound) can whole
    cranberry sauce
1/2 cup chopped pecans

Dissolve gelatin in hot water. Chill until slightly thickened. Add cranberry sauce; mix well and chill. When nearly set, fold in sour cream and pecans. Return to refrigerator until ready to serve. Serves 8.

Ellen Vollmer
Nickerson, Nebraska

CAULIFLOWER
& BROCCOLI SALAD

1 head cauliflower
1 bunch broccoli
1 red onion
1 green pepper

Break cauliflower and broccoli into bite size pieces. Cut onion and pepper into small pieces. Mix.

Dressing: (Mix and blend well)

1 cup mayonnaise
1/2 cup oil
1/2 cup vinegar
1/2 cup sugar
1 tsp dry mustard

Add dressing to salad. Stir until mixed well, and let stand at least 4 hours in your refrigerator.

Jill Marie Tanking
Liberal, Kansas

WILD TABOULI SALAD

2 1/2 cups water
1 Tbsp butter
1 box (6 oz) long grain wild rice
1 large tomato, diced
1/2 cup green pepper
1/2 cup cucumber,
    peeled and diced
1/2 cup sliced black olives
1/2 cup minced parsley
1/3 cup olive or vegetable oil
    (I use olive)
1/3 cup lemon juice
3 Tbsp fresh mint,
    or 1 Tbsp dried

Combine water, butter, rice and seasoning packet from the rice box in a medium saucepan. Bring to a boil. Cover tightly and cook over a low heat until all water is absorbed, about 25 minutes. Place rice in medium bowl and cool to room temperature. Add remaining ingredients. Chill.

TOMATO-CANTALOUPE
SALAD

This is a super easy salad to fix first thing in the morning. It makes it's own dressing. People usually say EEK! but when they try it, they like it.

Cut up tomatoes and cantaloupe into bite-size pieces, first thing in the morning. Put in a glass bowl and into the refrigerator. Serve salad that evening.

Got this recipe from a show called "Dinah's Place" years ago. Dinah Shore was the host.

Kathy Palmiter
Willliams, Indiana

FRESH VEGETABLE
MARINADE

Break blossoms of broccoli
    into small pieces
Break cauliflower in small pieces
Chop fresh green onions
Slice pieces of carrots
Cut celery into bite size pieces

Pour Italian garlic dressing over all ingredients. Marinate at least one day. Stir occasionally.

SEVEN LAYER SALAD

Layer:
1 head of lettuce
1/2 head cauliflower
1/2 cup onion
1/2 pound bacon, drained
    and crumbled

Mix together 1/2 cup mayonnaise and 1/4 cup sugar. Pour over salad ingredients. Sprinkle parmesan cheese on top. Refrigerate at least 2 hours. Mix before eating.

Salads, page 278

Elaine Helen (Revier) Baker
Watertown, Minnesota

PUCKER-UP POTATO SALAD

8 peeled potatoes
1 medium white onion
1/2 stalk celery, chopped
8 pickles, chopped
1/2 cup pickle juice
1 cup yellow mustard
2 1/2 cups Miracle Whip®
2 tsp garlic powder
salt and pepper to taste
6-8 eggs, boiled, peeled
     and chopped small

Cut potatoes into 1 inch cubes, boil until soft. Place potatoes in bowl, mash. Add all other ingredients, mix and chill covered for 3 hours. Should feed at least five people. (My husband really likes it)

Author's note: That's right, 1 cup yellow mustard! That's what Elaine's recipe called for! I checked it out with her.

Florence Edith Goggin
Eureka, California

TOP RAMEN® CHICKEN COLESLAW

1 pkg Top Ramen® (Chicken)
2 Tbsp Sesame seeds
1 pkg slivered almonds

Toast these lightly for 3-4 minutes in a 350 degree oven.

Dressing for above:

Add the pkg of flavor from pkg of Top Ramen® noodles to 1/2 cup oil. Add: 2 tsp sugar, 1 tsp salt, 1/4 tsp pepper and 3 tsp vinegar. Add to coleslaw (amount you desire) 1/2 hour before serving.

Mary Andrews
Grand Blanc, Michigan

SPINACH SALAD

2 bags of washed spinach
3 cans mandarin oranges
1 pkg of peanuts, ground
1 cup cooked bacon, crumbled

Toss with dressing, just before serving.

Dressing:
     (make the day before)

Boil 1 cup of vinegar with 3/4 cup sugar for 2 minutes. Then add:

1 tsp celery seed
1 tsp dry mustard
1 tsp salt
1 Tbsp paprika
1 tsp onion salt
2 cloves of garlic, remove before
     serving or use
     garlic powder
1 cup of tomato soup
1 cup salad oil

Shake all together in a jar and refrigerate over night.

Tonya St. Berg
Woodinville, Washington

SPAGHETTI SALAD

Cook one (12oz) package thin (Angel Hair) spaghetti. While spaghetti is cooking, cut up the following vegetables:

1 cucumber
2 tomatoes
1 red onion
1 green pepper
1 regular size italian dressing
     (not zesty)
1 bottle salad elegance
     (seasoning mix)
1/4 cup red wine vinegar

Drain the spaghetti after it is cooked. Mix everything together and let set over night.

Bonnie Swecker
Roanoke Rapids, North Carolina

ANYTIME FRUIT SALAD

Some fruits are always in season and make an excellent salad.

1 apple, 1 pear, 1 banana, grapes
     and raisins

Cut up all the fruit and gently mix together (save the banana until ready to serve). Sprinkle with 1 Tbsp sugar and 2 Tbsp orange juice. Stir to coat.

Ann Littleton
Fairfax, Virginia

GREEK SALAD

Tear up lettuce, add sliced cucumber, sliced red onion rings, crumbled feta cheese, and Greek olives into bowl. Add Good Season's® Italian Dressing mix, made with Balsamic vinegar and olive oil. Toss and serve.

Salads, page 279

Eleanor Hunnel
Johnstown, Nebraska

SALAD

1 pkg pre-cut cabbage & carrots

Make dressing of:

1 tsp sugar
dash salt
1/4 cup cider vinegar
1 Tbsp canola oil

Toss above dressing with cabbage and carrots.

Stir in:

contents from one pkg of
    Oriental Ramen® Noodles
up to 1/2 cup sunflower seeds
    or chopped almonds

Just before serving, stir in the crushed Ramen® Noodles.

Doris Holland
Winterset, Iowa

2 CUP SALAD

2 cups coconut, shredded
2 cups miniature marshmallows
    (I use colored ones)
2 cups crushed
    drained pineapple
2 cans mandarin
    oranges, drained

Mix together with small-sized container of Cool Whip®. Chill and serve.

FROZEN FRUIT CUP

Combine, but do NOT drain:

6 mashed bananas
3 cups crushed pineapple
2 cups mandarin oranges
1 (6 oz) can frozen orange juice
1 (30 oz) bottle 7-Up®

Mix all together and freeze, stirring once before frozen solid. Top with maraschino cherries to serve. (Freeze in short plastic glasses, makes 12.)

Lori Hauswirth
Iron River, Michigan

CHICKEN PASTA SALAD

Cooked pasta (I use rotini)
1 can black olives, sliced
4 oz pkg slivered almonds
green grapes, halved
    (as many as you like)
1 can white chicken (or leftovers)
ranch or buttermilk dressing
    (as much as you like,
    could use fat-free)

Mix all ingredients and chill. I mix a day ahead and save time. This is a great pot luck dish, or even as a main dish with some bread.

Paula Kay Garrison
& Duncan Garrison
New Braunfels, Texas

PASTA TWIRL SALAD

Boil colored twirls as indicated on pkg. Put pkg of frozen peas and pkg frozen chopped broccoli into the colander you are going to use as drainer. Add 1 can of black olives. After pasta has cooled, put it and pasta mixture into bowl, and add 1 bottle of Kraft® Italian Dressing. Also, if you like, add chopped celery, dill pickles and onion.

Sherry Cook
Council Grove, Kansas

COTTAGE CHEESE SALAD

1 small box Jello®, any flavor
1 1/2 cups cottage cheese
1 cup crushed pineapple
1/2 cup mayonnaise

Mix Jello® with 1 cup boiling water, till dissolved. Add 1 cup ice cubes and stir until cubes are melted. Add remaining ingredients, and chill until set.

Janet Kugler
Holdrege, Nebraska

SURPRISE SALAD

1 cup chopped apple
1 container Cool Whip®
1 Snicker® bar, chopped

Mix and chill. Can add grapes, peach, banana, strawberries or any fruit.

Marilyn T. Guy
Delhi, New York

MOROCCAN ORANGE WALNUT SALAD

Peel and section 6 large oranges. Drizzle with 1 Tbsp honey and sprinkle with cinnamon. Cover bowl and let stand at room temperature at least 1 hour.

Clean:

1 pound of fresh greens
    (or 1/2 head of lettuce)
1/2 cup thinly sliced red onion
1 cup thinly sliced radishes

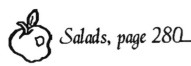 Salads, page 280

Combine in large bowl with 1 cup toasted walnut pieces. Toss well. Drizzle 3 Tbsp olive oil over salad, season with salt and pepper. Just before serving, add oranges and all liquid. Mix well. Very good!

••••••••••••••••••••••

Edna E. Holdsworth
Johnston,
Rhode Island

HAWAIIAN SUNRISE SALAD

1 large can sliced pineapple
1 small pkg lime flavor Jello®
lemon flavor yogurt or sour
    cream for garnish

Open can of pineapple, drain off juice and save. Leave the pineapple in the can. Mix jello® with boiling water and use the pineapple juice for part of the cold water. Pour Jello® into the can over the pineapple, and refrigerate until set. (You will have some Jello® left over.) When ready to serve, remove the bottom of the pineapple can and slide the Jello® and pineapple out onto the plate. Arrange lettuce leaves on serving plates. Cut between the pineapple slices. Put a slice on each plate, topping it with a dollop of yogurt or sour cream. A nice cool salad for lunch, or goes well with a heavy meal as appetizer.

••••••••••••••••••••••

Chris Miller
Medway, Ohio

WALDORF SALAD

4 cups 1/2" pieces of apple
2 cups 1/4" pieces of celery
2 Tbsp lemon juice
1 cup chopped walnuts
1 cup mayo
1/2 cup heavy cream

Combine apples with lemon juice. Stir in celery and walnuts. Mix mayo with cream. Combine all, and serve on lettuce.

••••••••••••••••••••••

PIONEER QUILTERS
Eugene, Oregon

GLORIA ZEAL'S TOMATO ASPIC

3 1/2 cups tomato juice
2 (3 oz) pkg lemon Jello®
2 Tbsp chopped onion
4 Tbsp vinegar
4 Tbsp sugar
1/2 tsp ground cloves
1/4 tsp black pepper
1 can shrimp
3/4 cup walnuts

Heat 1 cup tomato juice with vinegar, sugar, spices, onion. Add to Jello® and dissolve. Pour cold juice into the mixture. Cool. Add other ingredients. Pour into 5-6 cup ring mold. Serves 8.

••••••••••••••••••••••

Barbara MacDonald
Oscoda, Michigan

BROCCOLI SALAD

1 large bunch broccoli
8 to 10 slices bacon
    (cooked and crumbled)
3/4 cup shredded mozzarella
6 green onions, chopped

For Dressing, mix together:

1 cup Helmans® light mayo
1/2 cup sugar
1/4 cup red wine vinegar

Pour dressing over broccoli mixture before serving.

••••••••••••••••••••••

Roberta Schroeder
Deer Park,
Washington

BROCCOLI SALAD
(a little different from Barbara MacDonald's salad)

Salad:

2 bunches broccoli, in small
    bite size pieces
3 or 4 onions, chopped
3 or 4 slices bacon, cooked
    and crumbled
1 cup raisins
1 cup salted peanuts

Dressing:

1 cup Miracle Whip®
1/4 cup sugar
1/4 cup vinegar

Mix salad ingredients. Mix dressing ingredients, and add just before serving.

SIMPLE SALAD

5-6 bananas, sliced
2 small cans mandarin oranges
1 can chopped pineapple

Combine and sprinkle with powdered sugar. Serve.

••••••••••••••••••••••

Florence L. Tyler
DeLancey, New York

GARDEN RELISH

Make syrup by combining:

1 quart vinegar
2 Tbsp celery seed

2 Tbsp mustard seed
6 cups sugar

Boil above, then cool.

Grind or chop, using coarse blade, and put in large bowl:

12 medium onions
8 carrots
4 red peppers
4 green peppers
1 medium head cabbage

To vegetables, add:

1/2 cup salt, cover with ice water and let stand 2 1/2 hours. Drain in colander, with hands squeeze as dry as possible.

Pour syrup over vegetables. Mix well. Put in jars - seal. Store in cold place. Will keep several months. I use peanut butter jars with plastic lids.

••••••••••••••••••••••

Lesley Ann Hill
Granville, Ohio

GRANDMOTHER'S ORANGE SALAD

1 can mandarin oranges
1 (8oz) can crushed pineapple
1 pkg (6oz) orange Jello®
1 pint orange sherbet, softened
2 bananas

Drain oranges & pineapple, reserving juices. Set oranges and pineapple aside. Add water to juice to measure 2 cups. Place in saucepan and bring to boil. Pour over gelatin in large bowl. Stir until gelatin is dissolved. Stir in sherbet, until smooth. Chill until partially set (watch carefully). Fold in pineapple, oranges and bananas. Pour into oiled 6 cup mold. Chill til firm.

••••••••••••••••••••••

Donna Olson
Rogersville, Missouri

STRAWBERRY-BANANA SALAD

Dissolve 1 small box strawberry or raspberry Jello® in 1 cup hot water.

Add:

1 small box frozen strawberries
1 small can grated pineapple
2 mashed bananas

The juices from the fruit are sufficient to make up the second cup of liquid needed for Jello®. Chill till set.

••••••••••••••••••••••

Mary A. Sovran
Phoenix, Arizona

APPLE CRUNCH SALAD

2 pkgs (3 oz each) strawberry flavor Jello®
2 cups boiling water
1 1/2 cups cold apple juice
1/4 tsp cinnamon (optional)
1 cup diced, peeled apple
1/2 cup diced celery
1/4 cup chopped nuts

Dissolve gelatin in boiling water. Add cold juice and cinnamon, and chill until thickened. Fold in apple, celery, and nuts. Spoon into 6 cup mold or bowl. Chill until firm, about 4 hours. Makes 5 cups or 10 servings. Serve with Fluffy Dressing.

Fluffy dressing for apple salad:

1 cup dairy sour cream
1/2 cup salad dressing or mayo
1 1/2 cups mini-marshmallows

Combine sour cream and salad dressing, mix well. Fold in marshmallows.

OUR FAVORITE BROCCOLI SALAD

1 bunch of broccoli, cleaned and trimmed and cut into serving size pieces. Cook broccoli until tender crisp, using your favorite method of cooking. Drain off water, if any.

While broccoli is still hot, sprinkle with oil (preferably olive), vinegar, and salt and pepper. Toss to coat. Allow to come to room temperature, tossing occasionally. Serve.

••••••••••••••••••••••

Susan Southworth
Gulf Shores, Alabama

ANTIPASTO TRAY

Salami
Pepperoni rounds wrapped around ripe olive, held with toothpick
Artichoke hearts
Anchovies
Circle of Provolone Cheese
Chick Peas
Italian Peppers

Arrange attractively on a tray. You may like to sprinkle some oil and vinegar over the top before serving.

••••••••••••••••••••••

Ilene L. Burdick
Coudersport,
Pennsylvania

SALAD

1 Tbsp gelatin
2 Tbsp cold water
1/2 cup hot water

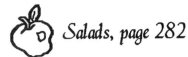

Salads, page 282

1/8 cup vinegar
1 tsp salt
1/8 tsp pepper
2 Tbsp sugar
1 cup chicken
1/2 cup celery
1 Tbsp pimento
1/2 cup mayonnaise

Dissolve the gelatin and stir in the remainder of the ingredients. Pour into salad mold or large bowl. Put in refrigerator to cool. I sometimes add a cup of cooked macaroni.

•••••••••••••••••••••••

Kathy Munkelwitz
Isle, Maine

Chop up lettuce and use bottled dressing!

•••••••••••••••••••••••

Jane Aruns
Franklin, Tennessee

SALAD

I'm not big on salads, but I will grow cucumbers in the summer. Pick, peel, slice and add Italian dressing. Nothing is better.

I grow pickling cukes because they are good as a salad, or made into pickles. (I do Bread & Butter and Polish Dills.)

•••••••••••••••••••••••

Marilyn Thomas
Harpster, Ohio

BANANA SALAD

Sauce:

1 cup cold water
1 egg yolk
1 cup brown sugar
1 Tbsp cornstarch

2 Tbsp oleo
1 tsp vinegar

Mix all ingredients and cook. Pour over bananas.

•••••••••••••••••••••••

Virginia L. Brown
Ogallala, Nebraska

JELLO® SALAD

I serve Jello® salad made with lime or lemon Jello® with chopped celery, apple and a few nuts added. 1/2 cup mayonnaise may be added. Let set overnight.

•••••••••••••••••••••••

Debra J. Ruisard
Whitehouse Station,
New Jersey

FRUIT SALAD

1 large can of peaches
　　(save juice)
1 large can of pineapple chunks
　　(save juice)
2 small cans of
　　mandarin oranges
　　(save juice)
2 pkgs of French Vanilla
　　Instant Pudding
9 oz carton of Cool Whip®

Pour dry pudding over fruit juice (about 2 cups of juice). Beat. Add Cool Whip® and other fruit. Refrigerate. Add sliced bananas on top just before serving. May also add strawberries & grapes.

•••••••••••••••••••••••

Connie Sager
Nashville, Kansas

SALAD

1 head of cauliflower, chopped

broccoli, several flowerettes
1 small can pitted black olives
1 small jar of ranch dressing (or as much as needed to cover)

•••••••••••••••••••••••

Anne-Donia B.
Hafskjold
Tiller, Norway

CUCUMBER SALAD

1 cucumber, thinly sliced

Mix, and pour over the cucumber:

1/2 cup vinegar
1/2 cup water
3 Tbsp sugar
white pepper
chives/parsley

Hint! If you have a cheese-slicer, it is great for slicing the cucumber. The slicer is an old Norwegian invention.

•••••••••••••••••••••••

Bonnie Swannack
Lamont, Washington

COLE SLAW

1 head cabbage, chopped
1 pkg Top Ramen®
　　Chicken Noodles
Sunflower seeds
Almond slivers

Dressing:

1/2 cup oil
1 Tbsp sugar
1 tsp salt
1/2 tsp pepper
3 Tbsp vinegar
1 tsp Accent

Add half of seasoning from the noodles. Add noodles just before serving.

Grace Moone
High Falls, New York

SHRIMP SALAD
(Main dish or side, depending on your menu)

3 cups cooked rice
    (I use a rice steamer)
8 oz crab meat (frozen is okay)
16 oz small shrimp, no tails
16 oz peas (frozen is okay)
8 oz Italian dressing
1 small jar pimento, drained
salt and pepper to taste
fresh herbs (Basil, parsley,
    sage optional)
tomato, cut up (optional)

Mix everything in a bowl, let marinate and thaw, serve cold. Serves 4-8.

Carole Collins
Norfolk, Nebraska

SEVEN LAYER SALAD

1 head lettuce, shredded and dry
1/2 cup chopped green pepper
1/2 cup chopped green onion
1/2 cup chopped celery
1/2 pkg frozen peas
4 to 6 ounces shredded
    cheddar cheese
real bacon bits
tomato wedges
hard boiled egg slices
2 cups Miracle Whip® with:
    2 Tbsp sugar
    1/2 tsp salt

Fill bottom of *glass* dish with lettuce, add vegetables by layers. Spread Miracle Whip® over entire contents, then sprinkle with cheese. Cover with plastic wrap. Refrigerate for eight hours or overnight. Before serving, garnish with bacon bits, tomato, and egg slices.

Karen Crosby
Ocala, Florida

PINEAPPLE JELLO® SALAD

2 small pkgs lime Jello® dissolved in 2 cups of boiling water. Add 2 cups ice water and 1 can drained crushed pineapple. Add 1 (3 oz) pkg cream cheese and 1 heaping spoon of mayonnaise. Blend, and refrigerate until set.

Doris Lott Aultman
Hattiesburg, Mississippi

MEXICAN CORN SALAD

2 cans mexican corn, drained
2 Tbsp bell pepper, chopped
1/2 cup mayo
1 onion, chopped
1 small tomato, chopped

Mix all ingredients and let stand overnight.

Sarah Bruso
Rhinelander, Wisconsin

FRUIT SALAD

2 eggs
3 Tbsp sugar
1 heaping tsp flour
juice of 1 lemon
1/2 cup pineapple juice
1 cup whipping cream
1 can pineapple tidbits,
    drained, reserve juice
1 can white grapes
1 (4 oz) can mandarin oranges
1 banana, sliced
1 apple, chopped
1 bag miniature marshmallows

Dressing:

Beat eggs, add sugar, salt, flour, lemon & pineapple juice. Put in top of double boiler, boil until thick. Cool.

Beat cream until half whipped, put in dressing, beat until stiff. Add marshmallows and canned fruit. Refrigerate. Add fresh banana and apple just before serving.

Constance T. Hall
Mannington, West Virginia

If I am in a hurry, I use a tossed salad or cole slaw for a quick salad.

Tedi Lambert
Los Banos, California

TACO BELL'S ®TACO SALAD

Ingredients:
    one teen-age driver
    money

Con one teen-age driver into driving over to the local Taco Bell® and purchasing said salad.

Salads, page 284

Laura Estes
Odessa, Washington

SALADS

Buy the stuff in the bag and some fresh dressing from the produce case. Truly gourmet! If you really want to be extravagant, add some tomato wedges or the sliced olives you forgot to put in the casserole!

Anna Eelman
North Plainfield, New Jersey

SEAFOOD SALAD

1 cup cooked crab meat
1 cup cooked lobster meat
1/2 pound cooked shrimp
1 cup cooked white fish
2 sliced tomatoes
6 ripe olives, halved
mixed greens
salad dressing

Arrange meat and tomatoes on a bed of mixed greens. Garnish with olives. To serve, toss with French dressing. Serves 6.

Martha De Turk
Kutztown, Pennsylvania

VEGETABLE PIZZA
(Salad for finger snacking)

Pat 2 pkgs crescent dinner rolls flat onto cookie sheet:

Bake until brown at 350 degrees.

Mix:
1 (8oz) cream cheese
1 (3oz) cream cheese
1/3 cup mayonnaise
1 Tbsp ranch dressing
   (dry powder mix)

Spread on baked crescent rolls. Finely chop the following vegetables and put on top: tomatoes, carrots, celery, cauliflower, broccoli and onion. Top with freshly grated cheddar or mozzarella cheese. Serve.

Virginia H. Flowers
Flushing, Michigan

CORN SALAD

2 cups fresh or frozen sweet corn
3/4 cup chopped tomato
1/2 cup chopped green pepper
1/2 cup chopped celery
1/4 cup chopped onion
1/4 cup prepared
       ranch salad dressing

In a large salad bowl, combine vegetables; stir in dressing. Cover and refrigerate until serving. Yield: 8 servings

Bernice Tessibel
Inman Cashman
(Tessie)
Coal City,
Indiana

STRAWBERRY-SPINACH SALAD

2 bunches fresh spinach or
      lettuce combination
2 pints fresh strawberries,
      hulled and halved
1/2 cup sugar
1 1/2 tsp minced onion
1/4 tsp worcestershire
1/4 tsp paprika
1/2 cup olive oil
1/4 cup vinegar

Arrange strawberries and spinach in a bowl. Mix, blend, or shake the remaining ingredients together, until thick. Do not pour over salad until ready to serve.

FIVE-CUP SALAD

1 cup commercial sour cream
1 cup miniature marshmallows
1 cup shredded coconut
1 cup mandarin orange sections
1 cup cubed pineapple
1 large pkg lime Jello®
2 cups boiling water
1 pint lime sherbet

Combine first five ingredients; set in refrigerator overnight. Dissolve Jello® in boiling water, stir and cool to lukewarm. Add lime sherbet and stir. Set in refrigerator. Cut the Jello® into squares and spoon fruit mixture over the top to serve. Serves 6 to 8 persons.

Nancy Wagner Graves
Manhattan, Kansas

CABBAGE SALAD

1 cup safflower oil
6 Tbsp red vinegar
2 pkg Ramen® noodles
1 1/2 tsp salt
4 Tbsp sugar
1 tsp pepper
1/4 cup sunflower seeds
1 cup slivered almonds
1 head cabbage
8 green onions

DRESSING:

Combine oil, vinegar, sugar, packets of flavor in noodles, salt and pepper. Make dressing night before, and refrigerate.

Mix noodles (broken up), seeds & almonds in baggie. Shred cabbage and onions. In large bowl, mix everything together prior to serving.

••••••••••••••••••••

*Doris Haggard
Topeka, Kansas*

ORANGE BLENDER SALAD

1 (8 oz) pkg cream cheese
1 large pkg orange Jello®
2 cups boiling water
15 large marshmallows

Blend the above 4 ingredients in large blender. Add 1 small can crushed pineapple and 1/2 cup real mayonnaise. Blend more. Pour in mold. Chill.

••••••••••••••••••••

*Merrilee Tieche
Ozark, Missouri*

SPINACH SALAD IN A WOK

1 bunch spinach (washed,
           stemmed, and dried well)
1/2 pound bean sprouts
1 can mandarin oranges, drained
   (or 2 oranges, peeled and sliced)
1/4 cup soy sauce
2 Tbsp sugar
2 Tbsp toasted sesame seeds

Mix dressing in a bowl. Remove stems from spinach. Rinse well and pat dry with paper towels. Cut large leaves in half. Sort bean sprouts, rinse and pat dry. Peel oranges and slice in rings or wedges. Heat half of dressing in Wok or large skillet. Add spinach, and toss quickly until leaves are just partially wilted. Serve immediately with remaining dressing.

••••••••••••••••••••

*Shannon Royer
Otis, Kansas*

CANDY BAR SALAD

5 medium red apples
1 small tub whipped topping
3 Snickers® candy bars
1 Butterfinger® candy bar

Chop apples into small (almost diced) pieces. Cut Snicker® bars into small pieces equal to apples (helps to refrigerate 10 minutes). Crush Butterfinger® bar into fine crumbs. Mix apples and candy together with whipped topping. Refrigerate at least 30 minutes before serving. This sounds peculiar, but tastes terrific!

••••••••••••••••••••

*Bettie Rushin
Boulder Creek,
      California*

QUICK CAESAR SALAD

one head of romaine lettuce
parmesan Cheese
croutons
caesar salad dressing
   (I like Paul Newmans®)

Break lettuce into bite-size pieces, add croutons (check deli section at the grocery store for some gourmet croutons. They make a better salad and will impress your dinner companion). Add Parmesan cheese and salad dressing to coat the lettuce. Done in 5 minutes.

••••••••••••••••••••

*Carol L. Robbins
Overland Park,
      Kansas*

SALAD

I put together a big salad in a Tupperware® container that lasts for 3 or 4 days. I use lettuce, shredded carrots, sliced cucumber, celery, green onion...sometimes spinach leaves, sliced mushrooms, cut up broccoli, diced green pepper...anything in season at reasonable prices!

For a quick lunch...try heating up a pita round in the microwave for 20 seconds, tear off small pieces to open up the pita, then stuff it with salad that has the dressing on it. (I use my homemade ranch dressing)

••••••••••••••••••••

*Betty Lou Cassidy
Linwood, New Jersey*

AUNT STELL'S
    POTATO SALAD

While I was growing up, my grandparents (in Northeast Pennsylvania) hosted huge family picnics. My Great Aunt Stell always brought a potato salad that was the hit of the summer meal. It is her legacy and is filed in my recipe box under "A" for "Aunt Stell's Potato Salad". The original recipe is written to serve 20 people, and I usually make it as is. My husband and I are big eaters, but there is a limit.

One day, early in our marriage, Charles looked at the recipe and said, "I really love this salad, but

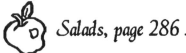

couldn't you just cut the portion in half and make it for ten people, instead of twenty?" That made sense to me, so I did, and it tastes just as good. Since it has mayonnaise and sour cream in it, the flavor seems to change by the third day anyway, so plan accordingly.

Aunt Stell's Potato Salad was written before our concern about excess fats, so feel free to substitute low fat ingredients for high ones. I hope you enjoy this recipe, and pass it on *with* the name.

1/2 cup sugar
1 tsp salt
1/3 cup cider vinegar
1/3 cup water
1 1/3 Tbsp flour
1 tsp mustard
2 eggs
2 Tbsp butter
1 cup mayonnaise
2 cups sour cream

Mix and cook the first seven ingredients over medium heat. Stir until creamy and thick. Take off stove. Add last three ingredients. Whip with whisk, until creamy.

Pour over pre-cooked potatoes. (At least 5 pounds). Add chopped onions and celery to taste. Mix, chill and serve.

••••••••••••••••••••••
Sheryl Mielke
McGregor, Iowa

PISTACHIO-COCONUT SALAD

1 pint dairy sour cream
1 pkg (4 oz) instant pistachio pudding
1 1/3 cups flake coconut
1 can (3 1/4 oz) crushed pineapple

Combine sour cream and pudding mix. Add coconut and pineapple, and stir until blended. Refrigerate.

Note: If you wish, add a sliced banana and 2/3 cup miniature marshmallows.

••••••••••••••••••••••
Georgina Doss
Milton, West Virginia

CUCUMBER SALAD

3 cucumbers
1/2 cup sugar
2 Tbsp vinegar
1/2 to 1 cup minced onion
dash pepper and salt

Slice cucumbers thinly. Salt down and drain in colander for 20 minutes. Squeeze out all of water. Add sugar, vinegar, onion and pepper. Marinate 24 hours.

••••••••••••••••••••••
Julie L. Kimberlin
Anchorage, Alaska

CAESAR SALAD

Garlic olive oil
3 medium heads Romaine, torn
    into bite-size pieces
3 Tbsp wine vinegar
1 lemon, halved
2 eggs
dash of worcestershire
salt & pepper to taste (optional)
1 3/4 cup grated
    parmesan cheese
croutons

First: Coddle eggs. Place eggs in shell in saucepan of boiling water. Remove from heat and let stand for 45 minutes. Remove eggs, and let cool slightly.

At serving time: place torn romaine in a chilled serving bowl. Drizzle with about 1/3 cup of garlic olive oil and the vinegar. Squeeze lemon over. Break cooled eggs over romaine. Add worcestershire, sprinkle with salt and pepper, and sprinkle parmesan cheese. Toss lightly until dressing is well-coated over romaine. Sprinkle on croutons. (Husband fixes simple green salads, Caesar is always good!)

••••••••••••••••••••••
Phyllis Hansen
Giersch
Madera, California
&
Charlotte Fry
St. Louis, Missouri
&
Marilyn T. Guy
Delhi, New York

FRESH BROCCOLI SALAD

1 large bunch broccoli, cut up
1 small red onion, chopped
1 pound bacon,
    cooked and crumbled
1 cup raisins
1 cup sunflower seeds

Dressing:

Combine 1 cup mayonnaise and 1/2 cup sugar.

Mix salad ingredients together.

Mix dressing ingredients, and toss with salad just before serving.

Author's Note: Marilyn Guy added that this recipe is fast, easy, everyone likes it...except maybe President Bush!

Salads, page 287

Helen King
Horton, Kansas

HELEN'S BEANS AND CORN SALAD

Make the sauce by mixing with rotary beater, 1/2 cup vinegar, 1/2 cup salad oil, 3/4 cup sugar, 1 tsp salt and pepper.

Drain, and add 1 can cut green beans and 1 can whole grain corn. Add 1 can red kidney beans (not drained), 1/2 cup chopped green pepper, and 1/2 cup chopped onion. Stir well. Cover, refrigerate over night. Stir once or twice to meld flavors. Recipe says to drain before serving, but I like the sauce!

Helen's note: Don't you wonder how many "new" recipes were developed just because someone successfully substituted an ingredient?

Pat Reep
Bakersfield, California

BASQUE COTTAGE CHEESE SALAD

1 carton of cottage cheese
2 sliced green onions (or more)
2 Tbsp mayonnaise
black pepper to taste

Mix altogether and let chill in refrigerator for at least 2 hours, for the flavors to blend. This is a nice light side dish for luncheon or dinner.

Barbara Clukey
Carriere, Mississippi

QUILTER'S LONG-LASTING CABBAGE SALAD

Keep this delicious cabbage salad covered and refrigerated, and it will keep indefinitely.

In a large container, arrange the following ingredients in layers:

1 large head cabbage, shredded
1 green pepper, sliced paper-thin
2 medium onions, thin sliced
    (separate the rings)
1 medium jar of
    pimento, drained
DO NOT STIR!

For the dressing, mix together the following ingredients, and boil for 2 minutes:

1 cup of salad oil
1 cup of sugar
3/4 cup of white vinegar
1 1/2 tsp salt
1 tsp celery seed

Pour the hot dressing over the vegetables, cover tightly, and refrigerate at least 4 hours before serving. Makes about 15 servings.

Helen P. Johnston
Bowie, Maryland

PRETZEL SALAD

I make this recipe twice a year for our quilt group dinners. The one time I made something different, everyone was upset and let me know it! (Lovingly, of course!) It tastes a lot better than it sounds. The pretzels taste like walnuts.

1 (6 oz) box strawberry gelatin
2 cups heated pineapple juice
2 (one pound) cartons frozen strawberries, in juice and thawed.

Dissolve gelatin in pineapple juice. Add strawberries. Chill till partically set..

Mix:

2 cups crushed pretzels
1/2 cup sugar
3/4 cup melted butter

Spread in 9x13" pan. Bake at 350 degrees for 10 minutes. Cool.

Mix, and spread over pretzels:

1 (8 oz) pkg cream cheese
1 cup sugar
1 (8 oz) tub of frozen
    whipped topping

Take partially set gelatin mixture, and spread on top of cream cheese mixture. Chill for at least 2 hours.

Joan Waldman
Platte Center, Nebraska

HOT TACO SALAD

For meat mixture:

Brown 1 pound hamburger,
    drain fat

Add:

1 pkg taco seasoning
    mix (I use Ortega®)
1 (8 oz) can tomato sauce
1 (8 oz) water
2 cans kidney beans
    (drained and rinsed)

Salads, page 288

Simmer over low heat for about 25 minutes. Cool, and put in closed container in refrigerator.

To make salads:

Layer chopped lettuce in bowls
Add chopped tomatoes
Add crushed Doritos® corn chips
Add grated cheese
    (I use cheddar or colby)

For each salad, heat 3/4 cup of meat mixture to bubbly. Pour over cheese. Top with additional cheese, if desired. Makes a quick evening meal.

••••••••••••••••••••••

Betty J. Knack
Essexville, Michigan

SAUERKRAUT SALAD

1 large can sauerkraut,
    rinsed and drained
1 cup diced celery
1 medium onion, chopped
1 cup grated carrots, or
    shredded (optional)
pimento, diced (I use a small jar)
3/4 to 1 cup sugar
1/2 cup oil
1/4 cup vinegar
salt and pepper to taste

Mix all together. Let stand overnight in refrigerator. Will keep a long time.

••••••••••••••••••••••

Marcene Gunter
Hillsboro, Kansas

SAUERKRAUT SALAD

Mix and chill:

1 large can sauerkraut, drained
1 cup sugar
1 carrot, chopped or grated
1/4 cup celery

1 green mango pepper

••••••••••••••••••••••

Betty Lenz
Marshall, Missouri

ORANGE DELIGHT SALAD

1 pkg orange Jello®
1 pkg instant vanilla pudding
1 1/4 cups hot water
1 small can crushed pineapple
1 can mandarin oranges, drained
1 small tub Cool Whip®

Mix Jello®, pudding mix and hot water. Stir well, and let cool till nearly set. Add pineapple, oranges, and fold in Cool Whip®. Chill & serve.

••••••••••••••••••••••

LaRue Nuest
South Hutchinson,
    Kansas

FROZEN SALAD

1 (9 oz) carton of Cool Whip®
1 can crushed pineapple
1 can Eagle Brand® Milk
1 can cherry pie filling
1/2 cup coconut
1 cup pecans

Mix together and freeze. Cut in squares to serve.

••••••••••••••••••••••

Nancy H. Ehinger
West Branch,
    Michigan

CUCUMBER SALAD

In the summer when cucumbers are plentiful, prepare this and store in the freezer. When winter comes, you will have a few more minutes to quilt, because your salad will already be made.

2 quarts sliced,
    unpared cucumbers
1 quart onion slices
2 Tbsp salt

Mix above, and let set for 2 hours.

In another bowl, combine:

1 1/2 cups sugar
1/2 cup white vinegar

Squeeze moisture from cucumbers. Add sugar and vinegar mixture. Put in bags or containers, and freeze. VERY CRISP--LIKE FRESH CUKES!

••••••••••••••••••••••

Patricia L. Carl
Rhinebeck, New York

AMBROSIA FRUIT SALAD

1 (11 oz) can mandarin
    oranges, drained
1 (13 oz) can pineapple
    chunks, drained
1 cup flaked coconut
1/2 cup of heavy cream, whipped
    (or 1 container lite
    Cool Whip®)
Optional...1 cup miniature
    marshmallows

Mix all ingredients, chill.

••••••••••••••••••••••

Judy Wolfrom
Southampton,
    New Jersey

SEAFOOD SALAD

1 loaf French Bread, cubed
1 onion, chopped fine
6 (or more) hard cooked eggs

Salads, page 289

celery
1 can crab meat
2 cans shrimp
mayonnaise

Mix all ingredients, except mayonnaise, and refrigerate overnight. Mix together with mayonnaise before serving.

Amazing flavor! I have also used pretend-crab, as the meat.

••••••••••••••••••••••
Roxanne H. McElroy
Mililani, Hawaii

CHICKEN SALAD FROM MCDONALDs®

(If you want the recipe, ask them!)

••••••••••••••••••••••
Lenore Scott
Pittstown, New Jersey

TOMATO-ONION SALAD

Marinate:

4 Tbsp olive oil
1/2 tsp oregano
1 Tbsp lemon juice
salt and pepper to taste
1 tsp parmesan cheese (topping)

Prepare:

10-12 fresh basil leaves (or more)
2 ripe tomatoes, sliced thinly
1 medium red onion,
  sliced thinly

Method:

1. Arrange the tomato, basil leaves and onion slices.

2. Pour marinade over it. Sprinkle with cheese.

3. Let rest in refrigerator at least 1/2 hour. Serve.

••••••••••••••••••••••
Norma Jean Rector
Center Point, Indiana

ORANGE PINEAPPLE SALAD

1 (3oz) pkg orange Jello®
1 (16 oz) carton cottage cheese
1 (8 oz) can crushed,
  drained pineapple
1 (8 oz) carton Cool Whip®

Sprinkle dry Jello® over cottage cheese, and mix together. Then, mix in drained pineapple and the Cool Whip®. You may garnish the top with a slice of pineapple, 3 or 4 orange segments, or miniature marshmallows. Keep refrigerated. Serves 6-8.

••••••••••••••••••••••
Teresa Binder
Emporia, Kansas

BOB'S PINEAPPLE SALAD
(from Mom Binder)

Dissolve:

2 small pkgs lemon Jello® and 1/4 cup sugar in 2 cups of hot water. Add 2 cups of cold water and stir.

Add:

1 #2 can crushed pineapple
  (drain, save juice)
3-4 bananas, sliced

Pour into 9x13" pan and chill till set. Cook until thick, the pineapple juice and 1/2 cup sugar, 2 Tbsp flour, 1 Tbsp vinegar, salt, and 1 beaten egg. Cool, fold in Dream Whip®, and spread on top of Jello®.

••••••••••••••••••••••
Ella May Reusser
Blackwell, Oklahoma

POTATO SALAD

6 to 8 potatoes, medium sized,
  boiled with peeling on
3 hard boiled eggs

Cool, and peel both potatoes and eggs.

Make a dressing with:

1/2 cup salad dressing
1 tsp salad
onion powder
celery salt
1 tsp vinegar
garlic powder
salt and pepper to taste
some chopped dill pickle
2 tsp prepared mustard
seasoned salt
2 Tbsp Milnot® (evaporated
  milk) or cream

Mix dressing, and pour over potatoes and eggs. Mix together.

••••••••••••••••••••••
Maria Lage
Cumberland,
Rhode Island

SPAGHETTI SALAD

1 pound spaghetti
2 green peppers, diced
2 tomatoes, diced
1 cucumber, diced
1 red onion, diced
8 oz italian salad dressing
4 Tbsp Salad
  Supreme® seasoning

Cook spaghetti, and drain. Mix remaining ingredients, add to spaghetti, and refrigerate.

Barbara Shook Davis
Williams, Arizona

Caesar Salad....from a jar!

Pat Campbell
Rigby, Idaho

MARINATED BEAN SALAD

Drain one (one pound) can of cut green beans, cut wax beans and kidney beans.

Combine 1/2 cup chopped or sliced onions with the bean mixture. You may add 1/2 cup chopped or sliced green peppers.

Combine 3/4 cup sugar, 2/3 cup vinegar, and 1/3 cup salad oil, and pour over mixture of beans and onions.

Add 1 tsp each of salt and pepper, and toss. Chill overnight. Before serving, toss to coat beans, and drain.

Other things you can add if you wish, are garganzo beans, black olives and small carrot sticks (cut thin). When you double the amount of ingredients, you will need to add more sugar, vinegar and salad oil.

I put the whole thing in a large sealable bowl and when it is in the refrigerator, I turn it over every time I get into the fridge. That way, the marinade is constantly covering the ingredients. Lasts several days in the fridge, or feeds a large party.

Christine Klinger
Fayetteville, Arkansas

SUNSHINE DELIGHT

1 (6 oz) pkg orange Jello®
2 cups boiling water
1 (11 oz) can mandarin oranges, drained and chopped
1 (18 3/4 oz) can fruit cocktail drained
1/2 cup chopped pecans
1 medium banana, sliced
1 (3 oz) pkg cream cheese, softened
1/4 cup commercial sour cream
Lettuce leaves

Dissolve gelatin in boiling water, add oranges, fruit cocktail, pecans, and banana, stirring gently. Pour half of gelatin mixture into a lightly oiled 9" square dish, chill until firm.

Combine cream cheese and sour cream in a small mixing bowl; beat at medium speed until smooth. Spread evenly over gelatin layer; chill slightly. Pour remaining half of gelatin mixture on top. Chill until firm. Cut into squares, and serve on lettuce leaves.

Mary Lou Kantz
Evans
Flagstaff, Arizona

BJ'S SHRIMP SALAD
(from my friend, Linda Carruthers)

2 cans of canned baby shrimp
2 boxes (10 oz) frozen baby peas
1 cup diced celery
1 minced onion
3/4 cup mayonnaise
1 Tbsp lemon juice
1/8 tsp curry powder
1 Tbsp soy sauce
1/8 tsp garlic salt
chopped candy ginger

Mix all of the above and refrigerate overnight or all day.

Just before serving add: chopped roasted almonds and 1 can of chow mein noodles.

Z.Z. Gilmore
Pocatello, Idaho

THREE LAYER SALAD

3 (3 oz) pkgs raspberry Jello®
1 envelope Knox ®gelatin
1/2 cup cold water
1 cup sugar
1 cup canned milk
1 (8 oz) pkg cream cheese
1 tsp vanilla
1/2 cups nuts, chopped fine
1 (15 oz) can blueberries

First layer: 2 pkgs Jello®, 3 1/2 cups hot water. Pour into 9x13" pan and chill until firm.

Second layer:
Soften Knox® gelatin in 1/2 cup cold water, add milk which is scalding hot. Add sugar, cream cheese, vanilla, and nuts. Beat together, mixing well. Chill. Pour over first layer.

Third layer: Dissolve remaining Jello® in 1 cup hot water. Add blueberries, juice and all. Chill and pour over second layer. Chill. Enjoy!

Jane Newhouse
Wedderburn, Oregon

SPINACH SALAD

2 large oranges
2/3 cup oil
3 Tbsp white vinegar
1 tap salt
1 tsp dry mustard
4 tsp sugar
1 bunch fresh spinach,
    romaine, or butter lettuce
1 small cucumber, cut in slices
3 green onions, chopped

Wash spinach or lettuce and set aside. Grate 1 Tbsp of orange peel and save. Peel oranges, hold over bowl and cut into sections between membrane. In glass measuring cup combine oil, vinegar, salt, mustard, sugar, dash of white pepper and orange peel. Tear greens, combine with green onions, cucumber and orange pieces. Toss with dressing.

Sally Smith
Kodak, Tennessee

EASY SPINACH SALAD
(a little different from Jane Newhouse's Spinach Salad)

fresh spinach leaves (I use the
    packaged kind already
    cut and washed)
2 small cans mandarin oranges
1 small pkg sliced almonds
your favorite dressing (we use
    honey mustard)

Combine spinach, oranges and almonds. Add your favorite dressing and...Voila!

GOURMET POTATO SALAD
(This recipe has a lot of ingredients but is quick to make, because you cook the eggs with the potatoes and the potatoes are not peeled. It also is a large recipe and can be halved.)

4 1/2 pounds potatoes,
    quartered (or smaller),
    cooked, not peeled
2 bunches green onions
1 (8 oz) jar sweet pickle relish
1 medium purple onion
9 hard boiled eggs
    (save one for garnish)
1 quart mayonnaise
    (not Miracle Whip®)
1 envelope Hidden Valley®
    Ranch Buttermilk Ranch
    Dressing, used dry
2 Tbsp mustard
1 capful white wine vinegar
2 Tbsp dry parsley

Combine all ingredients well, and enjoy! Great for quilt guild gatherings!

Joanna Bessey
Rhinelander, Wisconsin

RASPBERRY/CRANBERRY SALAD (OR DESSERT)

Dissolve one small package each of raspberry and lemon Jello® in 2 cups hot water. Add 1 pkg frozen raspberries and one (14 oz) cranberry-orange relish. Cool until almost set. Add 1 (7 oz) Sprite. Chill until set. For a refreshing dessert, simply put into a flour/shortening crust in a flat pan.

Page 292, The Busy Quilter's Survival Guide

Sewing machine needle sizes:

Fabric Weights	Fabric types	American	European
Delicate	Silk, silky fabrics, voile	7	60
Lightweight	Lightweight polyester	9	70
Medium weight	Cotton, cotton blends	12	80
Medium to heavy weight	Wool, corduroy	14	90
Heavy weight	Denim	16	100
Super heavy weight	Upholstery type	18	110

Did you know?

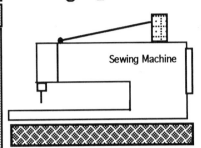
Sewing Machine

In **Sewing machine needles**..larger numbers mean larger needle diameters.
- Universal point sewing machine needles are available in both American and European.
- The points on denim needles are extra sharp to pierce the heaving threads.
- Topstitching neeldes have an oversized eye to accomodate thread without fraying it.
- Double needles will fit any zigzag machine that threads from front to back, be sure your machine has a wide enough hole in the throatplate to accomadate the extra width of the double needle. Double needles are available in sizes 1.6 to 4.0 mm. The size is the measured distance between the two needles.
- A new needle should be inserted when you begin each new project. Your needle may look fine, but tiny burs develop as the needle is used, and it may snag your fabric.

In **Hand Sewing needles**, the size is just the opposite as machine needles, the thickness of the needles decreases as the number increases. Size 12 needles are sliver thin.
- Needles for hand sewing come packages in all one size, or assorted sizes and styles.
- Platinum and gold needles are said to glide through fabric more easily.
- For ease in threading when hand quilting, thread a number of needles onto your spool of thread, and pull of the length of thread you desire, and only one needle at a time.

Threads for machine and hand Sewing come in a variety of sizes.
- The larger the number, the finer the thread. For instance, size 80 embroidery thread is very fine, size 40 quilt thread is much heavier, and consequently stonger, which is necessary when quilting layers of fabric together.

Thimbles come in a variety of sizes, styles and finishes.
- Sizes are not always true, so it is best to try several on your finger before making a decision.
- The style you choose wll also make a difference in the fit and comfortableness of your thimble.
- If you experience discomfort or irratibility around your cuticle, try a sterling or silver thimble. Sometimes the metals used can irritate your skin.

Rotary cutters are made by several manufacturers and with different styles, sizes and features. Some are especially designed for ease in cutting, with shaped handles and other features. Several blades are availble including straight cut, pinking, and wave. A cutting mat must always be used with a rotary cutter. Close blade when not in use.

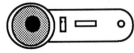

QUILTERS SHARE THEIR FAVORITE VEGETABLE RECIPES!

Vegetables, page 294

Author's Note:
Many Quilters, who responded to my questionaire, said they do not like to cook....apparently *vegetable* cooking is their least favorite of all! But, we all know, "we should eat our veggies!"

I've decided to supplement those that Quilters sent with several of my own. You'll find them at the end of this section.

Joyce Livingston
Council Grove, Kansas

QUILTING DAY CROCKPOT SPUDS

8 medium potatoes, sliced thinly
1 medium onion, sliced thinly
1/2 tsp cream of tartar
3 Tbsp flour
salt and pepper
1 can of cream of
    mushroom soup
2 or 3 slices of cheese

Slice potatoes into bowl of water with cream of tartar. Drain.

Layer 1/2 potatoes and onion into greased crockpot. Sprinkle on half of flour. Repeat. Spoon soup over the top. Place lid on crockpot. Cook on *low* 6-8 hours, or *high* for 2 hours. 15 minutes before serving, layer cheese on top. Delicious!

MAKE-AHEAD POTATOES

12 to 14 medium potatoes,
    boiled and cooled
1 pint heavy cream (evaporated
    canned milk can be
    substituted for cream)
minced dehydrated onion
cheddar cheese

Peel 1/3 of the potatoes and shred them in the bottom of a greased 9x12" pan. Salt and pepper. Sprinkle dry dehydrated chopped onions over the top. Shred cheese evenly over onions. Repeat potatoes and cheese layers until you have 3 layers of each.

Pour heavy cream (or evaporated milk) over all, cover with foil, and bake at 350 degrees for 45 minutes. Uncover, and bake for 15 minutes more, until bubbly and browned.

This can be made ahead and kept in refrigerator overnight, or for several days. Just don't add cream or milk, until just before baking.

VEGETABLE CORNBREAD CASSEROLE

1 pkg cornbread stuffing
2 cups frozen mixed vegetables,
    slightly thawed. (You
    can even use the
    Chinese-type)
1 1/2 cups cooked
    left-over meat, cubed
    (can use ham, turkey,
    chicken, etc)
3 slightly beaten eggs
salt and pepper to taste
2 cups milk

In 12x18x2" ovenproof casserole dish, place one 8oz package cornbread stuffing mix. Pour above mixture over stuffing mix. Cover with plastic wrap and refrigerate overnight, or for at least 6 hours. Remove plastic wrap, and bake in 350 degree oven for 40 minutes, or until a knife inserted in center comes out clean. Sprinkle with 1/2 cup of your favorite cheese, shredded. Bake 5 more minutes.

Thelma Tiefel
Clay City, Indiana

ONION ROASTED POTATOES

Preheat oven to 400 degrees. In large plastic bag, shake all ingredients until thoroughly coated:

one envelope Lipton® Recipe
    Secrets Onion or
    Mushroom Soup Mix
2 pounds all purpose potatoes,
    cut into large chunks
1/3 cup vegetable oil

Empty potatoes into shallow baking dish or pan. Discard bag. Bake, stirring occasionally, 40 minutes or until potatoes are tender and golden brown.

Kathy Palmiter
Williams, Indiana

COLD PIZZA

1 tube crescent rolls
1(8oz) Philadelphia®
    cream cheese
2 Tbsp mayonnaise
1 Tbsp finely chopped onions

Topping suggestions: Finely cut chipped beef or ham, chopped vegetables, olives (black or green), mushrooms, carrots, radishes, celery, green pepper.

Place pieces of dough on pizza pan and press edges together, filling pan with dough. Bake at 375 degrees for 10 minutes. Cool. Mix cheese, mayonnaise and onion. Spread on pizza crust. Arrange toppings of choice, as desired. Eat cold.

Vegetables, page 295

Karen Crosby
Ocala, Florida

SCALLOPED CORN

1 can creamed corn
1 egg
1/2 cup milk
saltine crackers - enough to thicken (about 1/2 pack of singles)

Mix together and dot with 2 Tbsp butter. Bake in microwave about 10 to 12 minutes.

Mary Andrews
Grand Blanc, Michigan

BAKED TOMATOES

Peel and cut up tomatoes, enough to fill the bottom of a medium sized baking dish. On top sprinkle:

salt and pepper
oregano
garlic, minced or powder
romano cheese
large bread cubes
small amount of oil sprinkled on top of bread cubes

Bake at 350 degrees for 30 minutes.

PASTA AND BROCCOLI

Cook your favorite kind of pasta (the flavored ones work best) and 1 minute before the pasta is to be done, dump cut-up broccoli into the water. Drain and serve with heated olive oil. To make the heated olive oil, put some olive oil into a small pan and generously sprinkle white pepper and garlic powder (or minced garlic if you have it) and warm it up, just until the garlic turns golden. Toss the pasta with this oil, and then sprinkle with Italian bread crumbs and parmesan cheese.

PIONEER QUILTERS
Eugene, Oregon

BAKED SLICED POTATOES

4 large baking potatoes
1/4 cup butter or margarine, melted
1/4 cup salad oil
2 garlic cloves, minced or pressed
1/2 to 1 tsp salt
1/2 tsp dried thyme leaves

Cut unpared potatoes into 1/4" thick slices. Place overlapping slices in buttered oven-to-table 13x9" baking pan.

Mix butter and oil. Brush slices with mixture. Pour remaining over potatoes. Sprinkle with garlic, salt and thyme.

Bake at 400 degrees for 25 to 30 minutes, or until potatoes are done and browned at the edges. Serve immediately. Good served with steaks or hamburgers, tossed green salad, crusty bread.

Karen Crollick
St. George, Australia, QLD

POTATO CASSEROLE

500 g potatoes
1 Tbsp butter
1 egg
1/2 cup thickened cream
1/2 cup grated cheese
salt & pepper

Peel and cube potatoes. Cook until tender. Drain, add butter and mash. Spread mashed potatoes into a small buttered baking dish. Beat remaining ingredients together, and pour over potatoes. Bake in an electric oven 350 degrees for 30 minutes, or until set and golden.

Author's note: I didn't take time to find a conversion table. So, if you don't know what 500g of potatoes is, maybe you'll just have to use 8 or 10 potatoes, and hope that's right.

BROCCOLI FRITTATA

2 cups broccoli florets
4 eggs
1 cup milk
1 packet thick vegetable soup
1/3 cup grated tasty cheese

Place broccoli into greased ceramic quiche dish. Beat eggs with milk and soup mix, pour over broccoli. Sprinkle cheese on top. Bake at 350 degrees for 40-45 minutes. Serves 4.

Susan Hanna
Brownlee, Nebraska

CRISS CROSS POTATOES

Scrub baking potatoes and pat dry. Cut in half, lengthwise. With sharp paring knife, cut criss crosses to form diamond shapes, a scant 1/2" deep on one side of potatoes. Pat dry. Sprinkle with garlic salt and put cut side down in oven proof pan, in which you have melted margarine (about 2 Tbsp per potato). Bake 15 minutes. Turn cut side up. Spoon melted margarine over potatoes and continue baking until brown. 30-45 minutes. Before serving, spoon margarine over potatoes.

Jean Eng Underhill
Flemington, New Jersey

ASPARAGUS TIPS ORIENTAL

2 pounds asparagus, trimmed
2 Tbsp sesame oil
1 Tbsp soy sauce
1 Tbsp sesame seeds, toasted
1 scallion, thinly sliced

Cut off top 2 inches of asparagus and other sections, too. Heat sesame oil in frying pan/wok, until quite hot. Add asparagus and cook over medium heat, tossing frequently for 3 minutes. Add soy sauce and sesame seeds. Cook over medium flame for another 2 minutes. Serve immediately.

Eleanor K. Hunnel
Johnstown, Nebraska

VEGGIES

Cut a carrot into 1/4" circles
Cut a stalk of broccoli into bite-
 sized pieces, stem and all
Cut 1/4 head cauliflower into
 bite-sized pieces

Place in a steamer insert in pan with lid. Add 1/2 cup water and steam until barely cooked, still crunchy. Remove to heated bowl. Top with 1/2 cup shredded cheese. Cover with pan lid to allow cheese to melt.

Kathy Munkelwitz
Isle, Maine

For a vegetable dish, open a can of green beans!

For bread, buy a loaf!

Sherry Cook
Council Grove, Kansas

CREAM CHEESE CORN

Combine in sauce pan, and cook over low heat, stirring constantly, until cheese melts and is blended:

1/4 cup milk
1 (3 oz) pkg cream cheese
1 Tbsp butter
salt and pepper

Add 2 (12 oz) cans whole kernel corn, drained. Heat and serve.

Jean S. Branham
Halifax, North Carolina

SWEET POTATO PIE

1 cup sugar
1/2 tsp salt
1 tsp cinnamon
1 tsp nutmeg
1/2 tsp ginger
2 cups drained, steamed
 sweet potatoes
1 cup milk
2 eggs, slightly beaten
unbaked pie crust (I use 2)

Combine all dry ingredients, add to sweet potatoes, mix in milk, and eggs. Line pie pan with pastry, pour in filling. Bake 450 degrees for about 10 minutes, reduce heat to 350 degrees. Bake 35 minutes more.

SQUASH PUDDING

2 quarts squash
2 sticks margarine
salt
2 Tbsp flour
2 Tbsp lemon flavoring
3 eggs
1 1/2 cup sugar

Cook squash, drain, mash. Add all other ingredients. Pour into a greased casserole, and bake at 350 degrees until brown.

Chris Miller
Medway, Ohio

BROCCOLI CASSEROLE

3 (10 oz) pkgs frozen broccoli,
 cooked crisp

Mix together, and pour over
 cooked broccoli:
8 Tbsp melted butter
1 cup mayo
1 small can mushroom soup
2 Tbsp chopped onion
2 eggs, well beaten

Lay 3 slices American cheese over the top. Sprinkle 3/4 cup cracker crumbs over all.

Bake at 350 degrees for 30-45 minutes.

Vegetables, page 297

Wilma Dooley Muse
Fayetteville, Tennessee

MARINATED ASPARAGUS

2 cans asparagus spears, drained
1/3 cup vinegar
3 whole cloves
1 stick cinnamon
1/2 tsp salt
1/4 cup sugar
1/4 cup water
1/2 tsp celery seed

Mix all ingredients except asparagus spears. Bring to a boil and pour over asparagus. Marinate at least overnight, but will keep for several days. Serves 6-8.

Roberta Schroeder
Deer Park, Washington

QUICK BROCCOLI SOUP

In medium saucepan, melt 1 cube margarine.

Add:
1 box frozen chopped broccoli
1 can cream mushroom soup
1 1/2 can milk
1 to 2 cups Velveeta® cheese
1/2 tsp garlic granules
1/4 cup chopped onion flakes (if desired)

Beverly J. Relph
Leavenworth, Kansas

Vegetables? No comment!

Ann Littleton
Fairfax, Virginia

POTATOES AUGRATIN

1 (2 pound bag) frozen hash brown potatoes
1 1/2 cups grated sharp cheddar cheese
1 can cream of chicken soup
1 1/2 cups chopped onion
1/4 cup melted butter
1/2 cup melted butter mixed with 2 cups dry bread crumbs for topping

Mix first 5 ingredients and place into a greased casserole. Top with crumbs and bake at 350 degrees for 45 minutes or until hot and bubbly. This may be made ahead and frozen. Thaw and bake, as directed above.

Cynthia England
Houston, Texas

CORN PUDDING

1 can cream style corn
1 can drained whole corn
2 eggs
1 1/2 Tbsp evaporated milk
2 Tbsp sugar
2 Tbsp butter
salt and pepper

Beat the eggs with the milk and sugar, empty the corn into a casserole dish, add the beaten egg mixture, salt and pepper, mix well. Dot with butter, bake at 350 degrees for 30-45 minutes.

This is Ingrid's (my mother-in-law) recipe. It's fool-proof. Even I can't mess it up.

Mary A. Sovran
Phoenix, Arizona

ROASTED POTATOES WITH GARLIC AND ROSEMARY

1 Tbsp olive oil
2 pounds potatoes, peeled and cut into chunks
3 garlic cloves, silvered
2 tsp rosemary, crumbled
salt and pepper

Coat a jelly-roll pan with oil, put slivered garlic in oil to marinate, while you prepare the potatoes. Preheat the oven to 450 degrees. Add potatoes and remaining ingredients. Toss to coat well. Bake 30 minutes, or until potatoes are tender and crisp, stirring and turning over once during cooking time. Makes 4 servings.

Virginia Flowers
Flushing, Michigan

SWEET AND SOUR CABBAGE

1 egg
1/4 cup sugar
1/4 cup vinegar
salt and pepper
cabbage

Cut cabbage, cook in boiling water until tender. Drain. Beat egg, add vinegar, sugar, add to cabbage with seasoning. Serve hot. If red cabbage is used, cook longer.

SCALLOPED TOMATOES

1 can tomatoes
few drops onion juice
salt & pepper

little sugar
buttered bread crumbs

Drain off some of the liquid, cover bottom of buttered baking dish with bread crumbs. Add seasoning to tomatoes. Cover with buttered crumbs, bake in 375 degree oven, 45-50 minutes.

MEXICAN CORN

2 cans whole kernel
   corn, drained
1/4 cup chopped green pepper
1/4 cup chopped red pepper
1/2 cup diced onion
2 Tbsp reduced-calorie
   margarine
1 tsp salt
1/4 tsp oregano
1/4 tsp allspice
1 cup peeled and
   diced fresh tomato

Combine all ingredients, except tomato, in large nonstick skillet. Cover; cook over medium heat 7 minutes, add tomato and heat thoroughly.

VEGETABLE SOUP

1 beef bouillon cube
1 cup boiling water
1 1/2 cups potatoes, diced
1/2 cup carrots, diced
1/2 cup celery, diced
1/2 onion, sliced
2 cups water
2 cups canned tomatoes
1 cup canned green peas
dash of pepper

Dissolve bouillon cube in boiling water. Add potatoes, carrots, celery, onion, and 2 cups water. Cook until vegetables are tender. Add tomatoes, peas, and pepper. Simmer 10 minutes, and serve.

Joyce Benitez
Omaha, Nebraska
and
Margo J. Clabo
Cleveland, Tennessee

VEGETABLE PIZZA

Press 2 pkgs refrigerator crescent rolls into 10x15" pan, bake as directed. Cool.

Cream together, and
   spread on crust:
1 (8oz) pkg cream cheese
1/3 cup mayonnaise
1/2 pkg Hidden Valley®
   Ranch Dressing

Top with: crumbled bacon, onions, chopped tomatoes, broccoli, cauliflower, green peppers, mushrooms, cheeses.

Joyce Benitz commented:
If all else fails, call Pizza Hut®! It's not cheaper, but it is faster!

Ellen Vollmer
Nickerson, Nebraska

SCALLOPED CORN

1 can of creamed corn
1 can whole kernel corn
1 cup *thin* spaghetti -
   broken into 1" pieces
onion (as much as you like)
1/4 cup oleo
1 cup shredded cheddar cheese

Stir all together. Bake at 350 degrees for 20 min. Stir again, and continue baking for 50 minutes.

I have done baking in microwave for 10 minutes, then let rest. Stir, then bake 10 more minutes and rest again. Repeat until the spaghetti is done.

BAKED CORN PUDDING

2 eggs, slightly beaten
1 (8 1/2oz) pkg corn muffin mix
1/2 cup margarine, melted
1 (8 oz) can cream style corn
1 (8 oz) can whole kernel
   corn, drained
1 (8 oz) carton sour cream
1 cup shredded swiss cheese

Mix eggs, muffin mix, margarine, corn and sour cream. Spread into 7x11" baking dish. Bake at 350 degrees for 30 minutes, sprinkle with cheese. Bake 5 to 10 minutes longer. Makes 8 servings.

Jennifer J. Danly
Arlington,
   Massachusetts

ACORN SQUASH
WITH MAPLE

1/2 acorn squash per person
real maple syrup
toasted pecans (or walnuts,
   chopped) optional

If maple syrup is unavailable in your area, substitute brown sugar and butter.

Cut squashes in half, remove seeds. Place in oven-proof casserole dish, with cut sides up. Fill center of each squash, half with maple syrup and a sprinkling of nuts, or brown sugar, a "pat" of butter and nuts (optional). Add water to pan to depth of about 1/2". Cover with microwave proof plastic wrap or wax paper, microwave on high for about 10 minutes, or until squash is soft. (Or cover with foil and bake in the oven at 350 degrees for about an hour, or until soft.) Remove from pan carefully to avoid spilling the melted syrup or sugar mixture.

Lois K. Ide
Bucyrus, Ohio

GREEN BEAN CASSEROLE

2 cans french cut green beans, well drained
1 Tbsp dried onion flakes
2 cans sliced water chestnuts
1 can mushroom soup
bread crumbs and butter

Mix first 4 ingredients, and pour into buttered casserole dish. Cover with bread crumbs, or crushed potato chips, with dots of butter.

Bake in preheated 350 degree oven, uncovered for 15 minutes. Then cover and bake for 30 minutes. I always make this for Thanksgiving and any family gathering.

CORN BAKE

1 can whole kernel corn
1 can creamed corn
3/4 melted butter or margarine
1 pkg Jiffy® corn bread muffin mix
1 Tbsp sugar
1 cup sour cream
2 eggs, well beaten

Mix together and pour into 9x13" pan. Bake in 350 degrees for 45 to 50 minutes.

Merry May
Tuckahoe, New Jersey

MRS. FISHER'S BAKED BEANS

3 or 4 slices bacon
8 oz pkg of mini-sausages (brown and serve type), cut into 1/2 inch slices
2 (20 oz) cans of pork & beans
1/2 can of apple pie filling
1/4 to 1/3 cup of A-1® sauce
2 to 3 Tbsp molasses

Brown the bacon in a deep, 2 quart pan or Dutch oven over medium heat. Remove bacon and drain on paper towels, but leave the drippings in the pan. Lower heat to medium-low, add the sliced sausages to the pan and brown them. Add remaining ingredients. Crumble the bacon, and add it to the pan as well. Simmer over low heat for an hour, stirring occasionally, or bake at 375 degrees for about 1 to 1 1/2 hours. (This is always a big hit at barbecues or potluck suppers!)

Penny Hand
Woodbridge, Virginia

SWEET POTATO PUDDING

Cook, peel and mash 6 medium sweet potatoes. Add 1 cup sugar and blend well.

In separate bowl, mix 2 beaten eggs, 2 Tbsp milk, 1 tsp vanilla, dash of cinnamon and nutmeg.

Add this to potatoes and mix well. Stir in about 1/2 pkg of mini-marshmallows. Pour all into greased (or sprayed) casserole. Cover with rest of marshmallows.

Bake covered at 350 degrees for 40 minutes, uncovering last 12 to 15 minutes to allow marshmallows to brown.

Martha DeTurk
Kutztown, Pennsylvania

CARROT CASSEROLE

4 cups sliced cooked carrots

Stir next 3 ingredients into carrots:

1 onion, chopped and browned
1 can cream celery or mushroom soup
1/2 cup grated cheddar cheese

Melt 1 stick butter and mix with 3 cups Pepperidge Farm stuffing (dry cubes). Layer 2 mixtures starting with carrots and ending with bread cubes. Bake 350 degrees for 45 minutes.

Now....sew! Great for covered dish suppers.

Anna Eelman
North Plainfield, New Jersey

ASPARAGUS PUFF-PASTRY PIZZA

1/2 package (1 sheet) frozen puff pastry
1 3/4 pounds asparagus
3 Tbsp butter

2 oz swiss Cheese
   (about 1/2 cup grated)
1 onion
salt and pepper

Heat oven to 425 degrees. Thaw pastry. Snap off end of asparagus where stalks break easily, and peel stalks, if desired (canned asparagus may be used instead). Cut off tips. Cut stalks into thin slices. Chop onion. Melt butter in fry pan, add onion and cook until soft, about 5 minutes.

Add all the asparagus, 1 tsp salt and 1/4 tsp pepper and cook until tender, stirring often. Roll out pastry on floured surface to 10"x12" rectangle. Put on greased baking sheet, prick with fork every 1/2". Bake until golden, 8 to 10 minutes. Grate cheese. Top pastry with asparagus and cheese. Return to oven and bake until cheese melts, 5 to 10 minutes. Serve immediately.

∞∞∞∞∞∞∞∞∞∞∞∞∞∞∞∞∞∞∞∞

Carol L. Robbins
Overland Park,
Kansas

ZUCCHINI AND
SOUR CREAM

2 medium zucchini, sliced
1/4 to 1/2 cup onion, chopped
Sour cream (I use non-fat)
Parmesan

Saute' zucchini and onion in a little oil, until tender. Turn off hea,t and immediately add sour cream and parmesan cheese, and blend well. Serve immediately. Use however much sour cream and cheese you like. I like at least 1/2 cup sour cream and about 1/4 to 1/3 cup cheese.

• I love to make a lot of different new recipes, especially since I am now a vegetarian. I substitute a lot with old recipes (tofu for hamburger in lasagna, etc.). My family is getting to where they like to eat the way I eat, but splurge on McDonald's once in awhile!! Anyway, as you can tell, I don't always have specific measurements, since everyone is different on how much they want of certain ingredients...plus, my Mom always cooked with a handful of this, a pinch of that, etc. and I picked up on that. It gets difficult trying to explain exactly how much to others who want any of our recipes!

∞∞∞∞∞∞∞∞∞∞∞∞∞∞∞∞∞∞∞∞

Tedi Lambert
Los Banos, California

TEEN-AGE CHINESE
TAKE-OUT

See salad recipe for Taco Bell® Taco Salad and make the appropriate changes!

∞∞∞∞∞∞∞∞∞∞∞∞∞∞∞∞∞∞∞∞

Marcia Knopp
Bay City, Michigan

BROCCOLI CASSEROLE
SUPREME
This is a favorite holiday recipe for our family.

4 cups cooked broccoli stems and
   buds cut in one inch pieces
   (Do not overcook)
1 (10 1/2 oz) can cream of
   mushroom soup
1 (2 oz) jar of sliced pimentos
3/4 cup dairy sour cream
1 cup sliced celery
1 cup sliced mushrooms
salt and pepper
1/2 cup grated cheddar cheese

Cook celery and mushrooms slightly. In large mixing bowl combine all ingredients, except the cheese. Place in pyrex casserole, cover with cheese. Bake in 350 degree oven for 20 to 25 minutes.

∞∞∞∞∞∞∞∞∞∞∞∞∞∞∞∞∞∞∞∞

Barbara Clukey
Carriere, Mississippi

MARINATED
FRESH VEGETABLES

2 to 3 cups of bite size
   broccoli fleurettes
2 to 3 cups of bite size
   cauliflower fleurettes
about 4 carrots, cut into
   2 inch shoe strings
about 1 pint of fresh
   mushrooms, sliced
   into bite size pieces

Drizzle over this, 1/2 pint of Wishbone Italian Dressing. Cover tightly, and marinate about 4 hours before serving. Stir the vegetables occasionally, to distribute the dressing. This will last several days.

∞∞∞∞∞∞∞∞∞∞∞∞∞∞∞∞∞∞∞∞

Lenore Scott
Pittstown, New Jersey

MARINATED CARROTS

1 pound carrots, peeled and cut
   on the diagonal
2 Tbsp freshly chopped parsley
2 Tbsp chopped scallion
salt and pepper

2 Tbsp olive oil
2 Tbsp red wine vinegar

Method:

1. Steam carrots, until cooked.
2. In a large bowl, mix warm carrots with rest of ingredients.
3. Let marinate at room temperature for 15 minutes. Serve.

Carolyn Koopman
Carnavillo, Iowa

IOWA HARVEST POTATOES

1 (32 oz) pkg frozen
    hash brown potatoes
2 cups shredded cheddar cheese
1 medium onion, finely cut and
    browned in butter
1 can cream of chicken soup
1 1/2 tsp salt
1 cup sour cream

Top with:
2 cups crushed cornflakes
1/4 cup butter

Grease 9x13" pan. Mix first 6 ingredients in dish. Top with cornflakes. Bake at 350 degrees for 45 minutes.

Norma Jean Rector
Center Point, Indiana

GOURMET POTATOES

1 (2 pound) pkg frozen hash
    brown potatoes, thawed
1 small onion, chopped
1 can cream of chicken
    soup, undiluted
salt and pepper
1 (8 oz) jar Cheese Whiz®

1/2 cup melted margarine
2 cups cornflakes

Mix potatoes with onion, soup, salt, pepper, sour cream, and Cheese Whiz. Put into lightly greased 9x13" pan. Combine corn flakes and melted oleo. Sprinkle on top of potatoes. Bake at 350 degrees for 1 hour. Can be prepared ahead and refrigerated over night before baking. Serves 12.

Alyce C. Kauffman
Gridley, California

BROCCOLI CASSEROLE

2 large bunches of broccoli
1 can of mushroom soup
1 can creamy chicken soup
1 large jar (16 oz) Cheeze Whiz®
1 1/2 cups Minute Rice®
    (uncooked)

Clean and steam-cook the brocccoli. Put in greased casserole. In a pan, combine soups and Cheeze Whiz®. Cook on low heat, until it is all melted. (Can be microwaved instead.)

When melted, add uncooked rice and mix well. Don't cook! Pour immediately over broccoli. Cover and bake at 350 degrees for 30 to 40 minutes (until bubbly). Uncover for the last few minutes, if a browned top is desired.

Author's Note:

Here are my vegetable recipes I mentioned at the beginning of this section.

SAUERKRAUT RELISH

1 large can kraut, drained
1 small can pimentos, drained
    and cut up
1 cup diced celery
1 small onion, chopped
1 green pepper, chopped
3/4 cup sugar

Combine and store, covered, in refrigerator overnight or several hours. Will keep in refrigerator for several weeks. This has good flavor and is a good addition to any meal!

COMPANY HARVARD BEETS

1 (one pound) can beets
1/2 cup brown sugar
2 Tbsp cornstarch
1/3 cup vinegar
1/4 tsp salt
1/2 cup water
1/2 cup raisins
1 cup crushed pineapple
2 Tbsp butter

Combine the sugar, cornstarch, and salt. Add the vinegar, water and juice from beets. Cook till thick and clear. Add the raisins and simmer for 5 minutes, add butter, pineapple and beets and simmer a few minutes more. Your kitchen smells wonderful, and the beets taste scrumptious!

ESCALLOPED CABBAGE
CASSEROLE

1 medium head of cabbage
1 cream of chicken soup
1/2 soup can milk
2 cups grated cheese of choice
1 1/2 cups butter bread crumbs

Shred cabbage. Cook in water in the microwave till tender. Drain. Combine soup and milk.

Alternate cabbage with soup mixture, then cheese in 9x13" greased pan, ending with cheese. Top with buttered bread crumbs. Bake at 350 degrees 30 to 40 minutes.

COPPER COINS (CARROTS)

Cook and drain 2 (one pound) bags of carrots, cut into 1" pieces.

Add:
1 can tomato soup
1/2 cup chopped onion
1/2 cup chopped green pepper

Mix:
1/2 cup sugar
1/2 cup vinegar
1/4 cup oil

Combine all, and refrigerate until chilled. Keeps well.

BAKED CARROTS

Peel and slice 2 (one-pound) bags of sliced carrots into baking pan. Salt, pepper and dot with butter or margarine. Pour 1/2 cup water over all. Bake for nearly an hour at 350 degrees.

HEARTY LIMA BEAN SOUP

Immediately after breakfast, sort and wash as many beans as necessary to provide several meals for your family. Put them in a big pot. (I use the largest Visions Cookware glass pot) and add enough water to cover them, plus several inches more! If you like garlic or bay leaves, now is the time to add them. Bring to a boil, lower the heat and let simmer ALL day, stirring to the bottom of the pan every hour or so, to keep from sticking. If necessary, more water may be added. Cook till beans are soft, tender.

Serve piping hot in nice big bowls with grated (or finely chopped) onion, and catsup. Better each time it is reheated!

If lima beans aren't your favorite (my husband prefers navy or pinto beans), cook other beans with this same method. To thicken them, use a potato masher to mash beans slightly.

STUFFED PEPPERS

Precook rice, by putting 1/2 cup rice in a microwavable glass bowl with 1 1/4 cups water. Cover, and place in microwave on high for 5 minutes. Lower to medium setting and cook 22 minutes longer.

Brown one pound hamburger with 1 small chopped onion. Drain. Stir in 1 can tomato sauce. Salt and pepper. Add cooked rice, and combine well.

Parboil 4 large green peppers, with the centers and seeds removed. When cooked, but still firm, fill them with the hamburger mixture, and place in baking dish. Cover, and bake 45 minutes to one hour at 350 degrees. Top with cheese.

UNUSUAL BAKED POTATOES

Wash as many large potatoes as necessary for your family. Using a sharp knife, make slits crosswise in potatoes, not quite cutting all the way through, about 1/4" apart. Make a foil boat for each potato. (foil folded into the shape of a boat to fit closely around each potato, leaving the entire top exposed). Melt butter or margarine, in glass measuring cup with pouring spout, in the microwave. Pour butter over each potato, trying to pour a small amount into each *cut* of each potato. Place foil boats closely together in baking pan and bake in your oven at 400 degrees until done (about 45 minutes to 1 hour). Delicious! Be prepared to be asked for a repeat performance!

SWEET POTATO CASSEROLE

Peel sweet potatoes, and cut into small pieces. Boil, until tender. Mash with potato masher.

Add to potatoes,
    and combine well:
brown sugar (1/4 cup per potato)
2 Tbsp butter or margarine
    per each potato
salt and pepper

Place in baking dish and bake in microwave until HOT clear through. Remove from microwave and place marshmallows over the top. Place under broiler in oven and brown tops of marshmallows. Be careful.....it doesn't take long, and they'll burn easily. Serve.

CIRCLES AND CHUNKS

1 can pineapple chunks, drained,
    but save the juice
2 cups cooked carrot slices,
    save 1/2 cup water you
    have cooked carrots in
1 Tbsp cornstarch
dash salt and pepper
1 Tbsp butter or margarine

Combine juice and carrot liquid

Vegetables, page 303

with cornstarch, butter, salt and pepper and cook until thick. Add carrots and pineapple. Bring to boiling, and serve hot.

BROCCOLI AND CORN CASSEROLE

1 can cream style corn
1 pkg frozen chopped broccoli, cooked and drained
1 beaten egg
1/2 cup saltine cracker crumbs
1 Tbsp minced dry or fresh onion
2 Tbsp butter or margarine, melted
salt and pepper

Combine corn, broccoli, egg, cracker crumbs, onion, melted butter, salt and pepper in a one quart casserole.

Crush 6 or 7 saltine crackers, combine with 1 Tbsp melted butter, and sprinkle over corn and broccoli mixture. Bake 35-40 minutes in 350 degree oven.

ESCALLOPED CORN

Beat together:
2 eggs
2 cups milk
1/2 cup sugar

Add 2 cans cream style corn. Salt and pepper to taste. Pour into greased baking dish. Crumble saltine crackers over top. Bake 45 minutes in 350 degree oven.

BAKED SWISS CAULIFLOWER

Boil till tender, 10 cups cauliflower cut into flowerettes, about 2 to 2 1/2" long. Put in shallow baking dish.

Sprinkle 2 cups shredded Swiss cheese over cauliflower.

Mix, and pour over all:

1 cup half and half
    (or canned milk)
salt and pepper
dash of cayenne pepper
2 egg yolks, beaten (or 1 egg)
1/4 tsp nutmeg
1/4 cup melted margarine

Sprinkle buttered bread crumbs over all, and bake 15 to 20 minutes at 350 degrees.

GREEN BEANS & BACON

That's it! Just bacon fried and drained, and broken into small pieces. Heat 2 or more cans of either regular cut or french-style green beans in microwave. When HOT, stir in bacon pieces and 2 Tbsp bacon grease and reheat. Serve hot!

ESCALLOPED HASH BROWNS

2 pounds frozen hash browns
1/2 cup melted margarine
dash salt and pepper
1 can cream of chicken soup, undiluted
2 cups cheddar cheese, grated
1/2 cup dry onion flakes, or fresh
2 cups sour cream
2 cups corn flakes, crushed and mixed with 1/4 cup melted butter

Thaw potatoes. Combine them with all ingredients, except corn flake mixture, and place in baking dish. Sprinkle cornflake mixture on top. Bake for 45 minutes.

You could divide this and bake one half today, and freeze the rest for next week.

SPINACH BAKE

1 pkg frozen chopped spinach, cooked and drained
1 cup cooked rice
1 cup shredded Velveeta® cheese
2 eggs beaten slightly
2 Tbsp softened butter
1/3 cup milk
2 Tbsp minced onion
1/2 tsp Worcestershire sauce®
dash salt and pepper

Mix all ingredients. Pour into large baking dish, and bake 20 to 25 minutes at 350 degrees.

BAKED BEANS

In large microwavable glass bowl, place 8 strips of bacon (which have been cut into 1" pieces) and 1 small chopped onion. Cook on high, until bacon is done and browned. Drain.

Add to bacon/onion mixture and stir together well:

2 cans Van Camp®
    Pork & Beans
1 cup brown sugar
1/2 to 3/4 cup catsup
salt and pepper
2 Tbsp flour

Microwave on high for 10-12 minutes, stirring once. Let set a few minutes before serving, to thicken.

POTATO CASSEROLE

10 medium potatoes, peeled and diced
1 can cream of celery soup
1 can cream of mushroom soup
1 cup grated cheese (your choice)
salt and pepper

Spread potatoes in baking dish. Combine soups and pour over potatoes. Salt and pepper. Cover and bake 45 minutes at 350 degrees. Uncover, and bake 15 minutes more.

CALICO BEANS

Brown 1/2 pound ground beef with one chopped onion. Add:

1/2 pound bacon, fried and cut
       into small pieces,

Combine below ingredients, and add to meat mixture:

4 Tbsp sugar
1/2 cup brown sugar
1/3 cup catsup
1 tsp liquid smoke
a squirt of yellow
       (or dry) mustard
salt and pepper to taste

In a large casserole dish or baking pan, combine:

1 (16 oz) can pork & beans
1 (16 oz) can red beans, drained
1 (16 oz) can butter beans,
       drained
1 (16 oz) can garbanzo beans,
       drained

Stir meat mixture into bean mixture. Bake at least one hour at 350 degrees.

This can be made in a large crockpot.

QUILTERS SHARE THEIR FAVORITE DESSERTS!

Desserts, page 306

Joyce Livingston,
Council Grove, Kansas

<u>WONDERFUL
   WONDER CAKE</u>

1 box German Choc. Cake Mix
1 can of Eagle Brand® Milk
1 carton of Cool Whip®
2 frozen Heath® Candy Bars

Prepare and bake cake in 9x13" pan, as instructed on box. When baked, poke holes all thru hot cake with an ice pick. Pour entire can of Eagle Brand® over top of cake. You'll think it's too much, but it soaks into the cake and gives it a wonderful flavor. Cool. When cool, spread Cool Whip® on top. Before opening Heath® bars, use hammer to break up frozen bar. Sprinkle broken candy over top of Cool Whip®. Delicious!
<u>Variation</u>: Use lemon cake mix and crushed lemon drop candy on top. Equally delicious!

ΣΣΣΣΣΣΣΣΣΣΣΣΣΣΣΣΣΣΣΣΣΣ
Thelma Tiefel
Clay City, Indiana

<u>PEACH AND NUT CRUMBLE</u>

3 pounds fresh or canned peaches. If fresh peaches are used, use Fruit Fresh in enough water to cover. Pour water off, when ready to use peaches.

1 cup unsifted flour
1 1/2 cup sugar
1/2 cup chopped nuts
dash salt
1 tsp cinnamon
1 egg, well beaten
1/2 cup melted butter

Dip fresh peaches into boiling water 30 seconds. Cool and remove the skins. Pour water off peaches. In bowl, mix flour, 1 cup sugar, nuts, salt, cinnamon, and egg until mixture is crumbly. Mix peaches with remaining sugar. Place in 8x12" baking pan. Sprinkle crumbs evenly over peaches. Drizzle melted butter over crumbs. Bake 375 degrees for 30 to 35 minutes or until top is brown.

ΣΣΣΣΣΣΣΣΣΣΣΣΣΣΣΣΣΣΣΣΣΣ
Eleanor K. Hunnel
Johnstown, Nebraska

<u>DESSERT</u>

Peel and section fresh fruits. Place in a lettuce leaf in individual plates. Garnish with a dollup of plain yogurt.

ΣΣΣΣΣΣΣΣΣΣΣΣΣΣΣΣΣΣΣΣΣΣ
Beverly J. Relph
Leavenworth, Kansas

<u>BLACK WALNUT
    SPICE CAKE</u>

1/2 cup shortening
3/4 cup brown sugar
3/4 cup sugar
2 eggs
2 cups sifted cake flour,
   or 1 3/4 cup all-purpose flour
1 tsp soda
1/3 tsp salt
1/3 tsp allspice
1 cup buttermilk
2/3 cup black walnuts

Grease and flour two 8" round cake pans. Cream the shortening, brown sugar and white sugar together thoroughly until fluffy, beat in eggs, set aside. Sift together the flour, baking soda, allspice, and salt. Alternately stir in buttermilk and the flour mixture. Lastly, fold in the black walnuts. Pour into pans, bake at 350 degrees for 40 minutes, or until done. Frost with cream frosting.

ΣΣΣΣΣΣΣΣΣΣΣΣΣΣΣΣΣΣΣΣΣΣ
Elizabeth A. Akana
Kaneohe, Hawaii

<u>CORN CAKE</u>

3 cups Bisquick®
1 cup sugar
2 1/2 tsp baking powder
1/4 cup corn meal

Combine:

3 eggs
1 1/4 cup milk
1 cup margarine, melted

Beat eggs lightly with milk. Stir this mixture and melted margarine into dry ingredients. Pour into 9x13" greased pan. Bake at 350 degrees for 30-35 minutes.

ΣΣΣΣΣΣΣΣΣΣΣΣΣΣΣΣΣΣΣΣΣΣ
Florence <u>Edith</u> Goggin
Eureka, California

<u>LEMON JELLO® CAKE</u>

Blend for one minute:

1 pkg yellow cake mix
1 pkg lemon or orange Jello®
4 eggs
3/4 cup water

Add 3/4 cup oil and beat for 1 minute more. Bake at 350 degrees for 40-45 minutes in a 9x13x2" greased and floured pan.

Icing for Lemon Jello® cake:

Mix together:

2 cups powdered sugar
juice & rind of 2 lemons

When the cake comes out of the oven, poke holes in it with a fork about 1/2" deep and 1/2" apart. Pour topping over cake, while it is still hot.

ΣΣΣΣΣΣΣΣΣΣΣΣΣΣΣΣΣΣΣΣΣ
Chloe Rhodes
Clay City, Indiana

CUSTARD PIE

4 eggs
2/3 cup sugar
1/2 tsp salt
1/4 tsp nutmeg
2 2/3 cup hot milk (do not boil)
vanilla

Beat the eggs. Add sugar, salt, vanilla and nutmeg with hot milk. Bake in heated oven, 400 degrees for 10 minutes. Reduce the heat to 350 degrees. Bake until inserted knife or toothpick comes out clean.

ΣΣΣΣΣΣΣΣΣΣΣΣΣΣΣΣΣΣΣΣΣ
Ann Littleton
Fairfax, Virginia

FRUIT SLUSH

1 large can apricot nectar
1 can crushed pineapple and juice
1 large frozen sweetened pkg strawberries, or 2-3 cups sliced fresh strawberries
1 can frozen raspberries
24 oz prepared orange juice
6 ripe bananas in pieces

Mix, and put in 2 cup freezer containers. Freeze. When ready to serve, thaw in microwave until it is the consistency of a soft sorbet. This recipe is from my friend, Lois.

ΣΣΣΣΣΣΣΣΣΣΣΣΣΣΣΣΣΣΣΣΣ
Glenda Phipps
Whitman, Nebraska

EASY CHERRY DESSERT

Pour one can cherry OR apple pie filling into an 8x8" pan. In small bowl, combine 1 cup biscuit mix, 1/2 cup sugar, and 1/4 cup melted butter. Sprinkle over cherries in pan. Bake at 350 degrees for 30 minutes. Can be topped with whipped topping or ice cream.

ΣΣΣΣΣΣΣΣΣΣΣΣΣΣΣΣΣΣΣΣΣ
Connie Sager
Nashville, Kansas

CHOCOLATE BUTTERMILK SHEET CAKE

2 sticks oleo
1 cup water
2 cups sugar
2 cups flour
1/4 cup cocoa
2 eggs
1/2 cup buttermilk
1 1/2 tsp soda
1 tsp vanilla

Bring to a boil, oleo and water. Mix sugar, flour, cocoa. Pour hot mixture over dry mixture and mix. Add eggs, soda, vanilla and buttermilk. Bake in prepared pan, 350 degrees for 20 minutes.

While cake is baking, mix the following for frosting:

Melt 1 stick oleo and 2/3 cup buttermilk. Add 1/4 cup cocoa, 1 cup nuts and 1 Tbsp vanilla. Add enough powdered sugar to mixture to make the right spreading consistency. Beat very well. Frosting should be very fluffy, it melts some when spread on hot cake. Frost cake as soon as the cake is pulled from the oven.

ΣΣΣΣΣΣΣΣΣΣΣΣΣΣΣΣΣΣΣΣΣ
Susan Hanna
Brownlee, Nebraska

FANTASTIC FUDGE CAKE

In a 9" square pan, combine:

1/2 cup +1 tsp salad oil
6 Tbsp cocoa
1 egg
1 cup sugar
1 1/4 cups flour
1/2 tsp soda
1/2 tsp salt
1/2 tsp vanilla
3/4 cup water.

Beat above with fork until smooth, about 2 minutes. Scrape sides and bottom with rubber spatula after one minute. When all ingredients are blended, pour into greased pan or baking dish and sprinkle batter with 1 cup real chocolate chips. Bake at 350 degrees approximately 30 minutes or when cake springs back when touched in center. Serve warm.

ΣΣΣΣΣΣΣΣΣΣΣΣΣΣΣΣΣΣΣΣΣ
Lynn Lewis Young
Houston, Texas

CHOCOLATE APPLESAUCE CAKE

1 1/2 cup sugar
1/2 cup solid shortening
2 eggs
2 tsp vanilla
2 cups flour

Desserts, page 308

dash of salt
1 tsp cinnamon
1 1/2 tsp cocoa
1 can applesauce
1 cup or more, chocolate chips
3/4 cup nuts

Grease and flour a 9x13" pan. In large bowl, combine sugar and shortening, add eggs and vanilla. Mix well.

In separate bowl, combine dry ingredients, add to shortening mixture, then stir in applesauce.

Pour into pan and smooth the top. Sprinkle on the chocolate chips and nuts. Bake in 350 degree oven for 35 to 40 minutes.

TUNNEL OF FUDGE CAKE

In large bowl cream until light:

1 3/4 cups sugar
1 3/4 cups margarine or butter

Add 6 eggs, one at a time, beating well after each.

Gradually, add 2 cups powdered sugar, and blend well.

By hand, stir in until well blended:

2 1/4 cups flour
2 cups chopped pecans
3/4 cup cocoa

Grease and flour 12 cup bundt cake pan, generously. Spoon batter into pan. Bake 55 to 65 minutes in preheated 350 degree oven. Cool, and turn out onto plate.

In small bowl, combine and blend the following, until it can be drizzled over cake, allowing some to run down sides:

3/4 cup powdered sugar
1/4 cup cocoa
small amount of milk

HOUSTON'S FINEST APPLE CAKE

2 cups flour
3 teaspoons baking powder
3/4 cup sugar
dash of salt
2 tsp cinnamon
1 beaten egg
3/4 cup milk
1/3 cup melted solid shortening
1 1/2 cups peeled chopped apples

Sift flour, baking powder, sugar, salt and cinnamon. Set aside.

Combine beaten egg and milk. Add shortening. Add egg mixture all at once to dry ingredients. Fold in apples, and mix thoroughly. Turn into greased 8" square pan. Prepare topping *before* baking.

Topping for above cake:

Combine all, and sprinkle over cake batter before baking:

1/2 cup sugar
3 Tbsp flour
2 Tbsp softened butter
1/2 tsp cinnamon

Bake at 400 degrees for 25 to 30 minutes.

MARVELOUS PUMPKIN CAKE WITH CREAM CHEESE FROSTING

In large bowl, mix:

2 cups flour
2 cups sugar
2 tsp soda
1 tsp baking powder
1 1/4 tsp cinnamon
dash of nutmeg

Gradually add, and blend:

4 eggs
3/4 cup oil
2 cans canned pumpkin

Pour into greased and floured 9x13" pan, and bake for 35 to 40 minutes at 350 degrees. Cool.

Cream Cheese Frosting for Pumpkin Cake:

Cream until smooth:

1 stick butter, or margarine
1 (8 oz) pkg cream cheese, softened

Add gradually:

1 (one pound) box powdered sugar

Add 1 tsp vanilla, and frost cake. Store any leftover cake in the refrigerator.

ΣΣΣΣΣΣΣΣΣΣΣΣΣΣΣΣΣΣΣΣ
Suzanne Peery Schutt
Clinton, Mississippi

APRICOT CAKE

1 pkg yellow cake mix
1 pkg orange Jello®
3/4 cup apricot nectar
1 tsp lemon extract
4 egg yolks - save whites

Mix together, adding egg yolks one at a time, beating into mixture. Beat 4 egg whites until stiff. Fold in. Bake in 2 greased loaf pans. Cook at 325 degrees for 40 minutes. Cool for 10 minutes, then turn out on racks.

Louise Murphy
Mammoth Lakes,
California

BETTER THAN SEX CAKE

Bake a German Chocolate cake mix according to directions, in a 9x13" pan. Let cool 10 minutes, poke holes with a fork over entire cake. Pour onto warm cake, 1 jar of Butterscotch or Caramel ice cream topping. Let soak in. Before serving, place generous dollop of Cool Whip® on top, and sprinkle on crushed Heath® bars. Something could be done with chocolate cake mix, instead of butterscotch use Hershey® chocolate, or favorite fudge topping. Mix a scant amount of Creme de menthe in Cool Whip®.

Mary Anne Keppler
St. Olaf, Iowa

BERRY BARS

1/2 cup softened butter
2 cups quick oatmeal
1 cup flour
1 cup nuts, optional
1 cup packed brown sugar
1 1/2 tsp baking powder

Mix together, and put half in pan. Spread with any flavor pie filling. Put other half of crumbs on top. Bake at 350 degrees in 9x13" pan. Enjoy.

CHOCOLATE CHIP COOKIES

Cream together:

4 cups shortening, not butter!
4 cups brown sugar
1 cup white sugar

8 eggs
4 Tbsp soda - dissolved
  in 1/2 cup hot water

Add:

9 cups flour
1 large bag chocolate chips

Bake 350 degrees, 9 to 10 minutes. These freeze well.

Kelly Lum Newgarde
Phillipsburg,
New Jersey

CARROT OR PUMPKIN BARS

Beat together:

4 eggs
2 cups sugar

Add, and mix well:

1 cup oil
3 small jars of baby food carrots,
  or 1 cup canned pumpkin

Add to above:
2 cups flour
2 tsp soda
1/2 tsp cinnamon

Beat well, and pour into greased and floured cookie sheet (with sides). Bake at 350 degrees for 30 minutes.

Frosting for above bars:

Beat together, frost cooled cake.

4 Tbsp margarine
1 1/2 cups powdered sugar
1 tsp vanilla
1 (3 oz) package cream cheese

Desserts, page 309

Deb Meneely
Seattle, Washington

MICROWAVE DOUBLE CHOCOLATE FUDGE

1 (14 oz) can sweetened
  condensed milk
2 cups semi-sweet
  chocolate chips
1 oz unsweetened
  baking chocolate
1 tsp vanilla

Butter an 8x8" glass baking dish. Stir milk and chips into 2 quart glass casserole dish. Microwave uncovered on high for 1 minute. Stir. Microwave for an additional 2 minutes, until mixture can be stirred smooth. Stir in vanilla. Spread in buttered glass baking dish. Refrigerate, and cut into 1" squares.

Kathryn Rippeteau
Greenwold
Niskayuna, New York

CHOCOLATE OATMEAL COOKIES

1 cup brown sugar
2 cups white sugar
1 stick butter or margarine
1/2 cup milk
1 cup chocolate chips
2 cups quick oats
3/4 cup chopped pecans

Bring the sugars, butter and milk to a boil, stirring constantly. Boil for 2 minutes. Add the chocolate chips, and stir to melt them. Remove from the heat. Add the oatmeal and nuts. Beat to blend until it begins to thicken. Drop by small

Desserts, page 310

teaspoons onto aluminum foil. Allow to harden, and store in a tin. These are very rich, delicious cookies that take less than 30 minutes to prepare.

**The recipe makes 50 to 60 cookies. You may use any kind of chips...butterscotch, choc/rasp, choc/mint, etc. to vary the taste with good results. A teaspoon of cinnamon added to chocolate will give them a mexican chocolate taste. The kids love to help with these cookies, and it always makes enough!

ΣΣΣΣΣΣΣΣΣΣΣΣΣΣΣΣΣΣΣΣΣΣ
Jill Marie Tanking
Liberal, Kansas

JILL'S CAKE

This cake has been one where everyone changes the name of the cake to the maker's name. When I got the cake, it was called Shirley's Cake.

1 cup sugar
1/2 cup shortening
1 egg
1 1/2 cups flour
1/2 tsp salt
dash of cinnamon
1/2 cup cool coffee
1 tsp soda
1 tsp vanilla
brown sugar
1 cup black walnuts or pecans

Add all (but the brown sugar and the nuts), plus 2 cups of diced apples with peelings on. Mix together, pour into glass pan, then sprinkle generously with brown sugar and nuts.

Bake at 350 degrees about 30 minutes, or until cake springs back from side of pan.

Good served with whipped cream dabbed on top.

ΣΣΣΣΣΣΣΣΣΣΣΣΣΣΣΣΣΣΣΣΣΣ
Mary Andrews
Grand Blanc,
Michigan

APPLE CAKE

Cream:

3/4 cup margarine
1 cup white sugar
1 cup brown sugar
2 eggs

Stir in:

1 cup buttermilk
1 tsp soda
1 tsp cinnamon
2 1/2 cups flour

Fold in 2 cups diced apples. Make the topping, and put on cake *before* baking.

Topping for apple cake:

1/2 cup nuts
1/2 tsp cinnamon
1/2 cup brown sugar

Bake in a 9x13" pan at 350 degrees, for 45-60 minutes.

CHOCOLATE CHIP APPLESAUCE CAKE

Cream:
1 1/2 cups sugar
1/2 cup margarine
2 eggs

Add:
1 can (#303) or
    2 cups applesauce
1 tsp vanilla

Sift together and add in fourths:

2 cups flour
1 1/2 tsp soda
3 Tbsp unsweetened cocoa

Pour into 9x13" pan and sprinkle on top one small pkg chocolate chips, and then sprinkle on about 2 Tbsp granulated sugar. You can put chopped nuts on, too, if you like them. Bake at 350 degrees for about 35 minutes.

GREAT PUMPKIN COOKIES

2 cups flour
1 cup quick or old-fashioned oats
1 tsp baking soda
1 tsp cinnamon
1 cup butter or margarine
1 cup firmly packed brown sugar
1 cup granulated sugar
1 egg, slightly beaten
1 tsp vanilla
1 cup canned pumpkin
1 cup chocolate chips

Preheat oven to 350 degrees. Combine flour, oats, baking soda, cinnamon and salt; set aside. Cream butter, gradually add sugars, beating until light and fluffy. Add egg and vanilla; mix. Alternate additions of dry ingredients and pumpkin, mixing well after each addition. Stir in chocolate chips. Drop onto cookie sheet, and bake for about 15 minutes.

ΣΣΣΣΣΣΣΣΣΣΣΣΣΣΣΣΣΣΣΣΣΣ
Tonya St. Berg
Woodinville,
Washington

BLUEBERRY CRISP

1 1/2 to 2 quarts fresh
    blueberries or 2-3 pkgs
    frozen berries
    (10 oz each)

1 Tbsp lemon juice
generous sprinkling of cinnamon and nutmeg
2 cups flour
2 cups sugar (you can get by with less)
1 cup butter

Place washed berries in ungreased 3 quart casserole. Add lemon juice. Sprinkle with cinnamon and nutmeg. In separate bowl, put sugar and flour. Cut in butter until crumbly. Spread evenly over blueberries. Bake at 375 degrees for 40-45 minutes, or until top is browned and berries are bubbling. Let cool 1/2 hour. Serve warm with whipped cream, Cool Whip® or ice cream.

PEANUT BUTTER LOGS

1/2 cup peanut butter
2 Tbsp honey (optional)
2 1/2 cups powdered milk
1/2 cup raisins

Blend peanut butter and honey, work in as much powdered milk as needed, to make mixture easy to pick up and knead in raisins, distributing them evenly. Roll out 10" long to form log, and wrap in waxed paper. Store in freezer. The family can cut off an inch or so, when they want a snack. A 1" slice provides 7 percent of the daily protein allowance or 3 grams of protein.

ΣΣΣΣΣΣΣΣΣΣΣΣΣΣΣΣΣΣΣΣΣ
Barbara MacDonald
Oscoda, Michigan

PUPPY CHOW

1 bag chocolate chips
1/2 to 1 cup peanut butter
1/2 to 1 stick butter
9 cups rice chexs cereal
powdered sugar

Melt chocolate chips, peanut butter and butter. Pour over cereal, mix well. Cover with powdered sugar to coat. Store in a plastic bag.

CHERRY CHEESECAKE

1 stick butter
2 cups graham cracker crumbs
1 (8 oz) pkg Phildelphia® cheese
1/2 cup sugar
1 pkg Dream Whip® (prepared)
2 (21 oz) cans baking cherries

Melt butter, mix with crumbs, fill bottom of oblong pan. Blend cheese, sugar and Dream Whip® til creamy. Pour over crumbs evenly, let set in refrigerator for one hour. Top with cherries - keep refrigerated.

7-UP® CAKE

1 box yellow cake mix
1 box instant vanilla pudding
4 eggs
3/4 cup oil
1 (10 oz) 7-Up®

Mix first 4 ingredients. Beat until smooth. Add 7-Up. Stir. Bake at 350 degrees for 40 minutes.

Frosting for above cake:

2 eggs beaten
1 1/2 cup sugar
1 Tbsp flour
1 stick margarine
1 cup crushed pineapple (undrained)

Cook until thick. Add 1 can coconut. Spread on warm cake.

ΣΣΣΣΣΣΣΣΣΣΣΣΣΣΣΣΣΣΣΣΣΣΣ
Bonnie Swecker
Roanoke Rapids, North Carolina

DUMP COBBLER

1 can pie filling (any flavor you like)
Jiffy one-layer cake mix, white or lemon
1/2 stick margarine, melted

Dump the pie filling into an 8x8" pan, that's been sprayed with Pam®. Sprinkle the cake mix on top, breaking up big lumps, but don't stir. Drizzle the melted margarine over the cake mix. Bake at 350 degrees for 30-40 minutes, or until brown and bubbly.

ΣΣΣΣΣΣΣΣΣΣΣΣΣΣΣΣΣΣΣΣ
Jean Van Dusen
Kingsford, Michigan

CREAM CHEESE TORTE

1 cup flour
1/2 cup oleo
2 Tbsp sugar

Combine above, and add 1/2 cup chopped nuts - press into 9x13" pan. Bake 10 minutes in 425 degree oven. Cool.

Combine:

8 oz cream cheese and 1 cup powdered sugar with mixer. Fold in 1 cup Cool Whip®. Spread on crust. Refrigerate at least 1 hour.

Mix two (4 1/2oz) packages of instant chocolate pudding mix and 3 cups of milk. Pour over cheese layer. Top with remaining Cool Whip®. Top

Desserts, page 312

with toasted coconut. Refrigerate. Variation: Try butterscotch or vanilla pudding.

ΣΣΣΣΣΣΣΣΣΣΣΣΣΣΣΣΣΣΣΣΣΣΣ

Jean Eng Underhill
Flemington,
New Jersey

QUICK AND EASY CREAM PUFFS

1 cup Cool Whip®
1 (3 oz) cream cheese (optional)
1 (8 oz) pineapple, crushed
1 pkg Stella Doro Anginetti® Cookies (5oz)

Cut the cookies horizontally in half. Blend the first three ingredients. Stuff this mixture onto the Anginetti cookie bottom and cover with the top half.

ΣΣΣΣΣΣΣΣΣΣΣΣΣΣΣΣΣΣΣΣΣΣΣ

Martha G. Wilson
Roanoke Rapids,
North Carolina

NORWEGIAN DUMP CAKE

Dump 1 can cherry pie filling into a 9x13" cake pan, then dump 1 can crushed pineapple over the pie filling, and spread evenly over pan. Dump one white or yellow cake mix straight from the box, without mixing. Chop up 1/2 cup nuts and sprinkle over top. Take 2 cubes of butter and cut into pats. Cover the top of cake with butter, and bake at 350 degrees, until nice and brown. Approximately 1 hour.

ΣΣΣΣΣΣΣΣΣΣΣΣΣΣΣΣΣΣΣΣΣΣΣ

Jean S. Branham
Halifax,
North Carolina

COCONUT PIE

1 cup sugar
2 Tbsp flour
1 can coconut
1 cup milk
2 eggs
1 tsp vanilla
2 Tbsp butter
1 unbaked pie crust

Combine sugar and flour in one bowl. In another bowl, combine milk, coconut and eggs. Mix with sugar and flour. Add vanilla and melted butter. Pour into unbaked pie crust, and bake 45-60 minutes or until brown in a 350 degree oven.

PAT'S PIE

large cream cheese
small box Dream Whip® (2 pkgs)
1 box powdered sugar

Mix cream cheese. Prepare Dream Whip® (follow directions). Beat all together. Pour into graham cracker crust. Top with fruit pie filling (your choice).

ΣΣΣΣΣΣΣΣΣΣΣΣΣΣΣΣΣΣΣΣΣΣΣ

Susan D. Fellin
Flemington,
New Jersey

QUICK & EASY CARROT CAKE

1 pkg yellow cake mix
1/3 cup packed brown sugar
2 tsp cinnamon
1/2 cup water
1/3 cup vegetable oil
3 eggs
2 cups finely shredded carrots
1/2 cup raisins
1/2 cup chopped walnuts

Combine first 6 ingredients. Beat 2 minutes at full speed. Add carrots, raisins and walnuts. Spoon batter into a greased and floured 10" tube pan. Bake at 350 degrees 45 to 50 minutes. Cool.

Icing for Carrot Cake:

Mix and spread on cake:

3/4 cup powdered sugar
1/2 Tbsp lemon juice
1 (3 oz) pkg cream cheese

PEACH PIE

1 All Ready® Pie Crust
4 cups quartered peeled peaches
1/2 cup sugaR
1/2 tsp nutmeg
1 egg
2 Tbsp cream or milk
1/4 cup brown sugar
1/2 cup all purpose flour
1/2 cup softened butter

Preheat oven to 350 degrees. Arrange cut peaches in pie crust. In bowl, mix together egg and cream, then pour over peaches and sugar. Mix the remaining ingredients until crumbly. Sprinkle crumb mixture over fruit in pie pan. Bake 35 to 45 minutes, or until browned. Serve slightly warmed. For an elegant garnish, pass a bowl of whipped cream or ice cream.

GERMAN SWEET CHOCOLATE CAKE

4 oz semi-sweet morsels
1/2 cup boiling water
1 cup butter or oleo
2 cups sugar
4 egg yolks

Desserts, page 313

1 tsp vanilla
2 1/4 cups sifted flour
1 tsp baking soda
1/2 tsp salt
1 cup buttermilk
4 egg whites, stiffly beaten

Melt chocolate in boiling water. Cream butter and sugar, until fluffy. Add yolks, one at a time, beating well after each. Blend in vanilla and chocolate. Sift flour with soda and salt; add alternately with buttermilk to chocolate mixture, beating after each addition until smooth. Fold in beaten whites. Pour into three 9-inch layer pans, lined on bottoms with paper. Bake at 350 degrees for 30 to 35 minutes. Cool. Frost tops only.

Coconut Pecan Frosting for German Sweet Chocolate Cake:

Combine 1 cup evaporated milk, 1 cup sugar, 3 slightly beaten egg yolks, 1/2 cup butter or margarine, and 1 tsp. vanilla. Cook and stir over medium heat until thickened, about 12 minutes. Add 1 1/3 cups flaked coconut and 1 cup chopped pecans. Cool until thick enough to spread, beating occasionally. Makes 2 1/2 cups.

SOUR CREAM WALNUT COFFEE CAKE

3 cups all-purpose flour
1 1/2 tsp baking powder
1 1/2 tsp baking soda
1/2 tsp salt
3/4 cup butter
1 1/2 cups sugar
3 eggs
2 tsp vanilla
2 cups sour cream

Nut mixture:

3/4 cup light brown sugar
2 tsp cinnamon
1 cup chopped walnuts

Mix first 4 ingredients together, and set aside. Cream butter until soft and gradually add sugar, beat well. Add eggs, one at a time, and beat after each. Add vanilla. Then add dry ingredients (flour mixture) to batter, alternately with sour cream. Mix until smooth. Mix the next 3 ingredients.

Pour 1/3 (1/6 for 2 pans) batter in 10" tube pan or (2 loaf pans) that has been greased and floured. Sprinkle with 1/3 nut mixture. Repeat until batter and nut mixture are used (3 layers each). Bake at 350 degrees for 1 hour - tube pan (50 minutes for loaf pans). Let cakes stand for 5 minutes. Then turn out of pan. While they are still warm, spread with frosting allowing it to run down sides.

Confectioner's Frosting for Coffee Cake:

Mix 1 1/2 cups powdered sugar with 1/2 tsp vanilla, and enough water to mix. It should be thick.

CHOCOLATE ZUCCHINI CAKE

1/2 cup butter or oleo
2 cups sugar
3 eggs
2 tsp vanilla
2 tsp grated orange peel
1/2 cup milk
3 squares (1oz each) unsweetened chocolate, melted
2 cups grated zucchini
2 1/2 cups flour
2 1/2 tsp baking powder
1 1/2 tsp baking soda
1 tsp salt
1 tsp ground cinnamon

Preheat oven to 350 degrees. Spray a 10" tube or bundt pan with non-stick cooking spray. Set aside. In large bowl, with electric mixer at high, cream butter and sugar. Add eggs, one at a time, beating well after each addition. Stir in chocolate, vanilla, orange peel and milk; fold in zucchini. In medium bowl, combine next 5 ingredients: add to zucchini mixture. Pour batter into prepared pan. Bake at 350 degrees for about 1 hour, until wooden pick inserted near center comes out clean. Cool in pan 10 minutes, then remove to wire rack to cool completely.

Chocolate frosting for Zucchini Chocolate Cake:

6 Tbsp unsweetened cocoa
6 Tbsp butter
1/4 cup milk
1 (16 oz) pkg powdered sugar

In large bowl, with electric mixer on high, beat together butter, cocoa and milk until smooth. Gradually beat in powdered sugar, until fluffy.

ΣΣΣΣΣΣΣΣΣΣΣΣΣΣΣΣΣΣΣΣΣ
Lesley Ann Hill
Granville, Ohio

REECE CUPS

2 cups peanut butter
1 cup soft butter
4 cups powdered sugar
1 cup brown sugar
1 Tbsp vanilla
1 (13 oz) bag chocolate chips

Mix all ingredients together, except chips. Spread ingredients

Desserts, page 314

into 9x13" dish. Melt choc chips in microwave or double boiler, pour over batter. Cool half hour, and cut in squares.

Paula Kay Garrison & Duncan Garrison
New Braunfels, Texas

THE GREEN THING
(This is Duncan's favorite dessert)

1 (one pound) can of crushed pineapple
1 pistachio pudding mix
1/2 cup chopped nuts
1/2 pkg small marshmallows
1 regular Cool Whip

Mix together pineapple and pistachio pudding. Add Cool Whip, marshmallows and nuts.

Janet Kugler
Holdrege, Nebraska

LITTLE CHEESE CAKES

Beat until fluffy:

2 (8 oz) pkgs cream cheese
3/4 cup sugar
1 T. lemon juice
2 eggs

Fill muffin tin with foil baking cups. Place vanilla wafer in bottom of each cup. Pour in cream mixture about half full. Bake at 350 degrees 10-12 minutes.

Marilyn T. Guy
Delhi, New York

CHOCOLATE CINNAMON BARS

Mix:

2 cups flour
1 tsp baking powder
1 cup sugar
2 tsp cinnamon

Add:

1/2 cup softened margarine
1/2 cup shortening
1 egg + 1 yolk (save the white)

Spread mixture into 9x13" greased pan. Whip egg white, and spread over top.

Mix, and sprinkle over top:

1 cup chocolate chips
1/2 cup chopped walnuts
1/3 cup sugar
1 tsp cinnamon

Bake 30 to 35 minutes at 350 degrees. Cut in squares.

PUMPKIN UPSIDE DOWN CAKE

Filling:

3 large eggs
2 cans pumpkin (1 pound each)
1 1/4 cup sugar
1 can evaporated milk (12 or 13 oz)
2 tsp cinnamon
1 tsp nutmeg
1/2 tsp ginger

Preheat oven to 350 degrees. In large bowl, beat eggs. Add remaining filling ingredients. Stir until well combined. Pour into ungreased 9x13" baking pan.

Topping:

1 full-sized box of yellow cake mix
3/4 cup melted butter or margarine

Sprinkle dry cake mix evenly over the filling in pan. Drizzle melted butter evenly over cake mix. Bake for 30 minutes. Remove from oven. Sprinkle chopped nuts over top, and return to oven. Bake for 25 minutes longer. Cool. Serve with whipping cream.

GRAHAM CRACKER PUDDING SQUARES

2 packs graham crackers
2 pkgs French Vanilla Instant Pudding
2 1/2 cups milk
1 (12 oz) carton Cool Whip, thawed

Layer graham crackers in 9x13" pan. Mix pudding and milk, fold in Cool Whip. Spread 1/2 mixture on crackers. Add layer of crackers, spread rest of pudding over top. Add the last layer of crackers.

(I haven't had any luck with this chocolate frosting, but it's the one that came with the recipe. You might want to try one of your own.)

For Frosting, bring to a boil:

1 cup sugar
1/3 cocoa
1/4 cup milk

Add: 1 stick margarine, and boil 1 minute. Add 1 tsp vanilla.

Desserts, page 315

Beat until spreadable. Make the night before, or chill 6 hours before serving.

Sherry Cook
Council Grove, Kansas

FRUIT DESSERT

Place 1 Pillsbury All Ready pie crust in pan

Add 1 can pie filling, cherry, apple or peach

Mix:

1/2 cup butter, 1 cup quick cooking oats
1/2 cup flour
1/2 cup packed brown sugar

Spread over pie filling. Press pie crust up around filling and topping.

Roberta Schroeder
Deer Park, Washington

MICROWAVE CARROT CAKE

3 eggs
1 1/2 cups sugar
1 cup oil
1 tsp vanilla
1 1/2 cups flour
1 1/4 tsp baking soda
2 1/2 tsp cinnamon
1 1/4 tsp cloves
2 1/2 cups grated carrots
3/4 tsp salt

In large mixing bowl, combine eggs, sugar, oil and vanilla. Blend in flour, salt, baking soda, cinnamon, and cloves. Fold in carrots and nuts. Pour into 12 cup glass bundt pan. Microwave on high 12 to 14 minutes, rotating 1/4 turn every 4 minutes. Rest 10 minutes. Invert on serving plate, frost with cream cheese frosting.

Cream Cheese Frosting:

1 (4 oz) pkg softened cream cheese
3 Tbsp softened butter
1/2 pound powdered sugar
1 tsp vanilla

Beat together until light and fluffy. Frost.

Mary Lou Sayers
Clarkson, Nebraska

I don't make many fancy desserts anymore. My husband, Alvin, is diabetic, so we keep fresh fruit on hand and carrots, celery and other veggies for dipping. Good for everyone!

Dawn Golden
Milford, New Jersey

HOT CHOCOLATE CHIP COOKIES

I use the standard 'Butter Flavored Vegetable Shortening' recipe - on the back of the tub. Mix it up and keep in the refrigerator for a week or more, and you get a dozen 'hot from the oven' cookies each night, in minutes.

Florence L. Tyler
DeLancey, New York

MOON BALLS

Nutritious, delicious, and easy unbaked cookies, perfect for children to make, eat and give.

1 cup non-fat dry milk
1/2 cup honey
1/2 cup peanut butter
1/2 cup granola-type cereal, crushed

Mix dry milk, honey, peanut butter together until well blended. Chill. Form into balls the size of marbles and roll in cereal. Makes 3 dozen.

MAINE HONEY PEANUT BUTTER BALLS

1 cup powdered milk
1/2 cup peanut butter
1 tsp vanilla
1/2 cup honey
1/2 cup graham cracker crumbs

Mix all together, and roll in powdered sugar. This is the way I make them, and take them to quilt doings. I'm often asked for the recipe.

HONEY PEANUT-BUTTER SQUARES

In mixing bowl combine:

1 cup honey
1 cup crunchy peanut butter

Place bowl over hot water and stir until mixture is "soupy".

Add 2 cups powdered milk and mix. Add 1/2 to 1 cup crispies-type cereal and continue to mix.

Desserts, page 316

Add more milk, 1/2 cup at a time, until spoonful will make a ball.

Lay plastic wrap in a 7x11" or similar size pan. Sprinkle with crisp rice cereal. Using spatula or spoon, slice or scoop mixture from bowl, place on rice cereal in pan, as evenly as possible. Press to fill in the gaps. Sprinkle choc chips on top. Let stand 5 minutes. The warm mixture will soften the chips. Spread softened chips over top. Cool one hour. Cut into squares. Chill longer until chocolate is no longer soft.

ΣΣΣΣΣΣΣΣΣΣΣΣΣΣΣΣΣΣΣΣΣ
Chris Miller
Medway, Ohio

HERSHEY'S® COCOA CHOCOLATE CAKE

1 3/4 cup unsifted
　　　all purpose flour
1 1/2 cup sugar
1/2 cup vegetable shortening
1/2 cup + 1 Tbsp hot water
1 cup sour milk (1 Tbsp vinegar
　　　added to milk to
　　　make it sour)
1 tsp baking powder
1 tsp vanilla
2 eggs
1 tsp baking soda
2/3 cup Hershey's® Cocoa

Grease bottoms and sides of cake pans (9 x 1 1/2" layer pans). Combine flour, salt, baking soda and baking powder. Beat sugar, eggs and vanilla in large bowl, until light and fluffy. Blend cocoa into hot water - make a smooth paste. Gradually add to creamed mixture. Add flour and milk. Bake at 350 degrees for 30 minutes, or until tops spring back when lightly pressed.

Bakery Frosting for Chocolate Cake:

3/4 cup shortening
1 egg white
1/4 tsp salt
3 1/2 Tbsp water
1/2 tsp vanilla
4 cups confectioner's sugar

Cream shortening, vanilla and salt. Add sugar, water.....repeat, till blended. Beat smooth. Add egg white, and beat until blended. Makes 3 cups.

ΣΣΣΣΣΣΣΣΣΣΣΣΣΣΣΣΣΣΣΣΣ
PIONEER QUILTERS
Eugene, Oregon

COCONUT-CREAM CHEESE BROWNIES

Coconut Cream Cheese Batter:

1 (8 oz) pkg cream cheese
1 Tbsp all-purpose flour
3 Tbsp sugar
1 large egg
1 cup sweetened coconut

Fudgy Brownie Batter:

4 oz unsweetened
　　　chocolate, melted
1/2 cup unsalted butter, melted
1 cup sugar
1/3 cup light brown sugar
3 large eggs
1 tsp vanilla
1/4 cup unsifted flour
1/4 tsp salt
1/2 cup chopped toasted almonds

Preheat oven to 350 degrees. With cooking spray, grease 13x9x2" baking pan.

Make Cream-cheese batter:

In bowl of electric mixer, at medium speed, beat cream cheese, flour, sugar and egg until smooth. Stir in coconut.

Make Fudgy Brownie Batter:

In another bowl, mix chocolate, butter, and sugars. Stir in eggs one at a time, until blended. Stir in flour and salt. Stir in almonds; reserve one cup batter. Spread remainder in prepared pan.

Spoon Cream cheese batter over brownie batter, spread to cover. Top with dollops of reserved brownie batter. With a chop stick (or handle of a teaspoon), swirl batters, but do not blend. Rap pan on counter. Bake 26-28 minutes or until wooden pick inserted in center comes out with moist crumbs attached. Cool completely in pan on wire rack before cutting. Makes 24 brownies.

CARAMEL BARS

Mix one German Chocolate Cake with 3/4 cup melted oleo and 1/2 cup evaporated milk. Spread half the batter in greased 9x13" pan. Bake 5 minutes in 350 degree oven. Cool.

Melt one bag Kraft® Caramels in double boiler, with 1/3 cup evaporated milk. Drizzle over baked batter. Sprinkle 1 cup of chopped pecans or walnuts and 1 cup chocolate chips over caramel sauce. Drop remaining batter by teaspoons over chips. Bake 18-20 minutes, or until done by testing with a tooth pick. Cut into bars when cool.

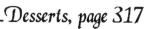

Desserts, page 317

ΣΣΣΣΣΣΣΣΣΣΣΣΣΣΣΣΣΣΣΣΣ
Joyce Benitez
Omaha, Nebraska

Rice Krispie® Bars are always a favorite and, like the TV commercial says, "they'll think you slaved for hours!"

ΣΣΣΣΣΣΣΣΣΣΣΣΣΣΣΣΣΣΣΣΣ
Jane Aruns
Franklin, Tennessee

CHOCOLATE REFRIGERATOR PIE

1 chocolate crumb pie crust
   (purchased, pre-made)
1/3 cup skim milk
4 oz semi-sweet baking chocolate
1 (4 oz) Neufeschal®
   (or cream) cheese
2 Tbsp sugar
1 (8 oz) thawed
   Whipped Topping
   (any brand, lite is OK)

Microwave chocolate and 2 Tbsp milk in microwavable bowl 1 1/2 to 2 minutes, or until chocolate is almost melted, stir halfway through. Then stir until chocolate is melted. Watch carefully.

Beat in cheese, sugar and remaining milk. Cool for 10 minutes. Beat in thawed topping. Pour into crust. Freeze until firm. Let stand at room temp or in the refrigerator, until pie can be cut (about 1/2 hour at room temp or 1 hour in the refrigerator).

ΣΣΣΣΣΣΣΣΣΣΣΣΣΣΣΣΣΣΣΣΣ
Merrilyn Muir Rennau
Vienna, Austria,
Europe

AUSTRIAN STRUDEL

To make the strudel dough is rather laborious and difficult undertaking, and it takes long experience to master the art.

There are, however, easier ways to make and enjoy homemade strudel. Many supermarkets and specialty stores, especially areas with a population of Austro-Hungarian or Greek origin, carry factory made and packaged sheets of dough of extreme thinness. They are sold as Strudel Dough, or Phyllo Dough.

The pastry of the two is nearly identical, though the size of packaged dough sheets is larger than Phyllo dough sheets. Both can be stored in the freezer for long periods. Defrosting should be done slowly in the refrigerator. Keep unused dough moist in a rolled moist cotton towel, while preparing the strudel. For Phyllo sheets, use several at a time, spread with butter and repeat with 3 layers.

Filling for Apple Strudel:

2 pounds apples, peeled and
   chopped, or thin slices
1 cup raisins
1/2 cup white sugar
3/4 cup brown sugar
1 cup finely chopped walnuts
cinnamon, nutmeg,
   ground cloves
1/2 cup small bread crumbs
1/2 cup melted butter
1 tsp lemon juice for each layer

To prepare and fill strudel:

Put one sheet of strudel dough or five Phyllo sheets of dough on a slightly dampened dish towel, brush with butter. Sprinkle with white sugar, brown sugar, cinnamon, ground cloves, finely chopped walnuts and bread crumbs. Add raisins and apple, sprinkle apple with juice. Repeat layers, always butter dough. Roll dough, with help of towel and butter dough as it is turned. Roll flat, instead of cylinder form, or fold over using Strudel dough.

Or using Phyllo, leave flat and place towel and Strudel on baking sheet, then holding towel left and right sides, pull towel towards you underneath strudel. Pull slowly. Spread top of strudel with lots of butter, sprinkle brown sugar and cinnamon on top. Pinch end together before baking. Bake at 325 degrees for 30 to 45 minutes.

Serve warm or room temperature, and sprinkle with powdered sugar.

ΣΣΣΣΣΣΣΣΣΣΣΣΣΣΣΣΣΣΣΣΣ
Cynthia England
Houston, Texas

ORANGE SLICE CAKE

This is from the kitchen of Aunt Nina.

2 sticks butter
2 cups sugar
4 eggs
3 1/2 cups flour
2 cups chopped pecans
2 cups (11 1/2 oz bag) diced
   orange slices (candy)
(Use knife dipped in hot water, roll pieces in flour to keep from

Desserts, page 318

sticking together)
1 tsp baking soda
4 1/2 oz coconut
1/2 cup buttermilk
2 tsp grated orange rind
1 tsp almond extract

Cream butter, sugar, beat in eggs, one at a time, dissolve soda in buttermilk and add to cream mixture. Put flour in little at a time, few orange slices, alternate, and continue mixing. Add a little more buttermilk, if needed. Spray Pam® in 8x4x2" pan. Pour mixture in. (Or fill bundt pan 2/3 full) Bake at 300 degrees.

This cake is my substitution for the dreaded fruit cake. It is really wonderful!

ΣΣΣΣΣΣΣΣΣΣΣΣΣΣΣΣΣΣΣΣΣ
Susan Southworth
Gulf Shores, Alabama

"SUNDAE ON MONDAY"

TCBY® Sugar Free/Fat
    Free Vanilla Ice Cream
TCBY® Sugar Free/Fat
    Free Hot Fudge

Put one cup of the ice cream in a dish. Pour one cup of the hot fudge on top. Top with whipped cream and nuts, if desired.

Make sure you serve this in a large wine glass to make it fancy. Serve very cold.

Author's Note: Oh! That Susan!

ALMOST FAT-FREE POUND CAKE

1 cup Promise Ultra®
    fat-free margarine
2 1/2 cups sugar
4 egg beaters (1 cup)
4 Tbsp vanilla
3 cups self-rising flour
1 cup skim milk
2 egg whites

Blend together with hand mixer; butter, sugar, egg beaters & vanilla. Alternate, adding a little flour and then a little milk. Keep alternating until you have added all the flour and milk, beat egg whites until stiff. Fold egg whites into cake mixture. Bake at 325 degrees for 50-55 minutes, in a bundt pan sprayed with non-fat cooking spray.

Make a glaze with almond extract and confectioner's sugar and spread on thin layer.

BEST EVER RUM CAKE

1 tsp sugar
1 cup dried fruit
1 tsp soda
2 bottles rum
brown sugar
1 cup butter
lemon juice
nuts
baking powder
2 eggs

Before starting, sample the rum to check quality. Good, isn't it? Now, proceed. Select large mixing bowl, measuring cups, etc. Check the rum again. It has to be just right. To be sure rum is of proper quality, pour 1 level cup of rum into a glass and drink it as fast as you can. Repeat with a larger glass.

With an electric mixer, beat one cup of butter in a large fluffy bowl. Add one teaspoon of thugar and beat again. Meanshile, make sure rum is still good. Drink another glass. Open second quart if necessary. Add eggs, 2 cups fried druit, and beat til high. If druit gets stuck in beaters, pry loose with a drewscriber. Sample rum again, checking for tonscistricity. Next, sift 3 cups pepper or salt (really doesn't matter). It's time toshrample the rum again. Sift 1/2 pint lemon juice, fold in chopped butter, and strained nuts. Add one babblespoon of brown gredience. Pour badder into boven and hake. Check rum again and bo to ged. G'night. sleep tight.

Author's note: The above was NOT the result of my typo's. Just Susan's creative imagination!

ΣΣΣΣΣΣΣΣΣΣΣΣΣΣΣΣΣΣΣΣΣ
Mary A. Sovran
Phoenix, Arizona

PHILLY POUND CAKE

1 (8 oz) pkg cream cheese
3/4 cup margarine
1 1/2 cups sugar
1 1/2 tsp vanilla
4 eggs
2 cups sifted cake flour
1 1/2 tsp baking powder

Combine cream cheese, margarine, sugar and vanilla, mix well. Add eggs; mix at low speed of mixer until blended. Gradually add flour sifted with baking powder, blend. Pour into greased and floured 9x5" pan. Bake at 325 degrees, 1 hour and 20 minutes. Cool 5 minutes. Remove from pan. Sprinkle with powdered sugar.

Men love this cake, it's a great neglected husband pleaser.

ΣΣΣΣΣΣΣΣΣΣΣΣΣΣΣΣΣΣΣΣ
Marilyn Thomas
Harpster, Ohio

GRANDMA ROSE CHILD'S APPLE DUMPLINGS

Sift:

1 cup flour
2 tsp baking powder
1/4 tsp salt

Add to flour:

1 Tbsp sugar
1 1/2 Tbsp oleo
1/3 cup milk

Mix well. Roll out 1/2" thick. Then spread 2-3 apples on dough. Roll up and slice 1" pieces. Put in baking dish. Make syrup.

Syrup:

Heat till boiling, and pour over dough:

1 1/4 cup water
1/2 tsp cinnamon
1 Tbsp butter

Bake at 350 degrees for 35 to 45 minutes.

ΣΣΣΣΣΣΣΣΣΣΣΣΣΣΣΣΣΣΣΣ
Sandra A. Anderson
Lincoln, Nebraska

SURPRISE CUPCAKES

Cheese Mixture:

Combine, and beat:
(Don't mix in plastic bowl)

1 (8 oz) cream cheese
1/3 cup sugar
1/2 tsp salt
1 egg
1 (6 oz) package of choc chipc

Batter:

3 cups flour
2 cups sugar
2/3 cup salad oil
2 tsp vanilla
2 tsp soda
2 tsp salt
1/2 cup cocoa
2 cups water
2 Tbsp vinegar

Mix, and fill cupcake cups 2/3 full of batter. Add 1 large teaspoon of cheese mixture on top. Bake at 350 degrees for 25 minutes. Frost with favorite topping or icing.

ΣΣΣΣΣΣΣΣΣΣΣΣΣΣΣΣΣΣΣΣ
Anne-Donia B. Hafskjold
Tiller, Norway

DESSERT

Half a canned pear per person
Thin mint chocolate per person
(After Eight®)

Place the pears in a dish you can use in the microwave, the round side up. Pour on the juice from the can. Place one chocolate on each pear. Heat in microwave until the chocolate *just* melts. It takes only a few minutes. Serve with ice cream or whipped cream. M-m-m!

QUICK CAKE

Beat until very stiff:

3 eggs
1 2/3 cups sugar

Mix in carefully, but quickly

1/2 cup butter or
    margarine, melted
1 2/3 cup flour
2 tsp baking powder

Pour in prepared pan. Sprinkle 1/4 cup sliced almonds on top.

Bake at 350 degrees for about 30 minutes. Very quick, very easy, very tasty.

ΣΣΣΣΣΣΣΣΣΣΣΣΣΣΣΣΣΣΣΣ
Virginia L. Brown
Ogallala, Nebraska

CHERRY CHEESE CAKE

Crush 1 pkg (11 or 12 double
    graham crackers)
Mix with 1/3 cup melted oleo.

Press most of mixture into bottom of 8" square pan, reserving a few crumbs for topping.

Melt: 1 (20oz) pkg marshmallows in 1/2 cup milk. Cool until just starts to gel.

Whip: 1 pkg Dream Whip® according to directions on package, then whip in marshmallow mixture, and add 1 (8 oz) pkg softened cream cheese. Pour half of mixture on crust. Gently add a can of cherry pie filling, then rest of marshmallow mix. Top with reserved crumbs. Refrigerate.

ΣΣΣΣΣΣΣΣΣΣΣΣΣΣΣΣΣΣΣΣ
Candra J. Sowder
Williamsburg, Iowa

EASY LEMON CHEESECAKE

1 small lemon pudding
1 (8 oz) cream cheese
1 graham cracker crust

Cream the cream cheese until soft and *slowly* add milk required by pudding recipe, to make a smooth batter. Add the pudding mix and mix until blended. Pour into crust and refrigerate until set (about 10 minutes). Delicious and *too* easy!

ΣΣΣΣΣΣΣΣΣΣΣΣΣΣΣΣΣΣΣΣ
Carole Collins
Norfolk, Nebraska

ICE CREAM CAKE

Crust:
1 cup crushed saltine crackers
1 cup crushed graham crackers
1 stick melted oleo

Mix the above, and put into 9x13" pan. Do not bake.

With mixer, combine:

2 cups milk
2 pkgs vanilla instant pudding
2 pints butter pecan ice cream

Pour over crust. Before serving, add a carton of Cool Whip®. (If you really feel like splurging on calories, add bits of crushed Heath® Bars.)

ΣΣΣΣΣΣΣΣΣΣΣΣΣΣΣΣΣΣΣΣ
Debra J. Ruisard
Whitehouse Station,
New Jersey

CRANBERRY APPLE CRISP

Preheat oven to 375 degrees.

5 medium Granny Smith apples
    (peeled and sliced thin)
1 can (16 oz) whole berry
    cranberry sauce
3/4 cup sugar
2 Tbsp flour

Combine above ingredients, and put in a 9x13 pan.

Topping:

1/4 cup chopped walnuts
1 cup rolled oats
1/2 cup firmly packed
    brown sugar
1/3 cup flour
1 tsp cinnamon
1/4 cup butter or
    margarine, melted

Combine all topping ingredients. Sprinkle evenly over fruit. Bake for 30-40 minutes, or until top is golden brown and fruit is tender.

ΣΣΣΣΣΣΣΣΣΣΣΣΣΣΣΣΣΣΣΣ
Bonnie Swannack
Lamont, Washington

CHOCOLATE LUSH

Layer one:

Melt 1 1/2 cubes margarine and stir in 1 1/2 cups flour. Pat in bottom of 9x13" pan and bake at 325 degrees for 25 minutes. Cool.

Layer two:

Beat together 1 (8 oz) pkg of cream cheese, 1 cup powdered sugar, and half of a (12 oz) carton of Cool Whip®. Spread over crust.

Layer three:

1 large pkg of instant chocolate pudding mixed with 2 1/2 cups milk. Pour over layer two.

Layer four:
Spread remaining Cool Whip® over pudding layer. May sprinkle with grated chocolate.

ΣΣΣΣΣΣΣΣΣΣΣΣΣΣΣΣΣΣΣΣ
Ellen Vollmer
Nickerson, Nebraska

SPONGE ROLL NUT BARS

4 eggs
1 cup cold water
2 tsp baking powder
2 cups sugar
2 cups flour
1/2 tsp salt
2 tsp vanilla

Beat eggs and sugar 10 minutes. Add water, flour, baking powder, salt and vanilla. Pour into greased jelly roll pan. Bake at 350 degrees for 20 minutes. Cool and frost.

Frosting:

1/2 cup soft margarine
1 beaten egg
3 cups powdered sugar.

Combine and spread over bars. Top with chopped peanuts (skinless).

ΣΣΣΣΣΣΣΣΣΣΣΣΣΣΣΣΣΣΣΣ
Constance T. Hall
Mannington,
*   West Virginia*

CHERRY CRUNCH

1 (9 oz) pkg yellow cake mix
1/4 cup nuts, chopped
2 Tbsp brown sugar
2 tsp cinnamon
1 (21 oz) can cherry pie filling
1/2 cup butter or
    margarine, melted

In bowl, combine dry cake mix, nuts, brown sugar and cinnamon. In a glass baking dish, spoon cherry pie filling into bottom. Sprinkle cake mixture evenly over pie filling. Drizzle

Desserts, page 321

melted butter over top. Cook on High in the microwave 12 to 14 minutes or until topping is no longer doughy. Rotate dish during cooking, if cake does not appear to be rising. Let stand 5 minutes. Serve warm, or cold with whipped cream or vanilla ice cream. Makes 6-8 servings. You may also use blueberry pie filling.

COTTAGE CHEESE DESSERT

1 large carton cottage cheese
1 large package Jello® (any flavor)
1 large can pineapple (crushed and drained)

Mix all three together and refrigerate over night. Just before serving, add a carton of Cool Whip®, and mix well. You may add Cool Whip® when you add all the other ingredients, and let set for a few hours if in a hurry for a quick dessert.

ΣΣΣΣΣΣΣΣΣΣΣΣΣΣΣΣΣΣΣΣΣΣ
Marilyn A. Lewis
Glendale, Oregon

EASY CHERRY NUT CAKE

1 can (21 oz) cherry pie
    filling (prepared)
2 cups flour
1 1/2 tsp. soda
1 tsp salt
1 cup sugar
2 eggs, beaten
2/3 cup vegetable oil
1 tsp vanilla
3/4 cup chopped walnuts

Spread pie filling over the greased bottom of 9x13" pan. Combine dry ingredients in small bowl. Sprinkle over filling in pan. Mix together all remaining ingredients, including nuts and pour over ingredients in pan. Stir with fork, until blended. Bake at 350 degrees, 40 to 50 minutes. P.S. Good served with Cool Whip®.

ΣΣΣΣΣΣΣΣΣΣΣΣΣΣΣΣΣΣΣΣΣΣ
Doris Lott Aultman
Hattiesburg,
Mississippi

WALNUT PIE

1/3 stick margarine
    (left out to soften)
1/3 cup sugar
3 eggs
1 cup dark Karo® syrup
pinch salt
1 cup whole or sliced walnuts

Mix, and bake in unbaked crust at 325 degrees, or until center moves only slightly.

ΣΣΣΣΣΣΣΣΣΣΣΣΣΣΣΣΣΣΣΣΣΣ
Wilma Dooley Muse
Fayetteville, Tennessee

CARAMEL NUT PIE

2 graham cracker crusts
1 can Eagle Brand® Milk
1 (8 oz) block of softened
    cream cheese
1 (12 oz) carton of Cool Whip®
2 cups coconut
1/2 stick oleo
1 cup pecan pieces

1 bottle of Caramel
    ice cream topping

Prepare mixtures below:

Mixture #1..Mix together Eagle Brand® milk, cream cheese and Cool Whip®.

Mixture #2...Melt oleo in skillet, brown coconut and pecans.

Mixture #3...Caramel topping.

Layer in crusts in order mixed. Refrigerate, or freeze. Makes 3 pies.

ΣΣΣΣΣΣΣΣΣΣΣΣΣΣΣΣΣΣΣΣΣΣ
Jennifer J. Danly
Arlington,
Massachusetts

BROWNIES WITH ICE CREAM

Make brownies from any packaged mix, following directions on the box. Cool, cut. Serve pieces topped with a scoop of vanilla ice cream, and chocolate syrup, if desired. This is always popular with kids and grownups.

ΣΣΣΣΣΣΣΣΣΣΣΣΣΣΣΣΣΣΣΣΣΣ
Pat Milne Hitchcock
Sequim, Washington

This recipe is from a music teacher and friend, Ruth DeWitt Peters, whom I met in an alumni group. She also was my daughter's piano teacher for 11 years.

GRAHAM CRACKER COOKIES

Break apart and cover bottom of cookie pan with graham crackers (Pan must have sides)

Boil, EXACTLY 3 minutes:
1 cube butter and 1 cube margarine with 3/4 cup packed brown sugar.

Pour over crackers, spread and sprinkle with slivered or shaved almonds.

Desserts, page 322

Bake, EXACTLY 7 minutes at 400 degrees. Break apart when cool (You may wish to drizzle melted chocolate over tops) Divine!

ΣΣΣΣΣΣΣΣΣΣΣΣΣΣΣΣΣΣΣΣΣΣΣΣ
Alice Furrey
Carter, South Dakota

CAN'T BELIEVE IT BROWNIES
(Original Low-fat Recipe)

Beat until soft peaks form:

3 egg whites
1/4 tsp cream of tartar.

Add:

1 1/4 cups sugar and continue beating till stiff.

Mix:

1/2 to 3/4 cup dry instant coffee
1/2 cup + 2 Tbsp flour, unsifted
1/3 cup dry milk powder

With mixer on low speed or by hand, fold this dry mixture into the egg white mixture along with 1/4 cup applesauce and 2 tsp. vanilla. Pour into 9" square non-stick pan that has been sprayed. Bake at 350 degrees for 22 to 25 minutes. Do not overbake.

Total calories=1550
Fat grams=8.5%

Cut into 9 pieces, each piece has 161 calories, less than 1 gram of fat. May be frosted with powdered sugar, cocoa, corn syrup and coffee.

ΣΣΣΣΣΣΣΣΣΣΣΣΣΣΣΣΣΣΣΣΣΣΣΣ
Ilene L. Burdick
Coudersport,
*   Pennsylvania*

DESSERT

Use instant lemon pudding and substitute water for the milk. Drain canned chunk pineapple and put in bowl. Pour pudding mixture over the pineapple. Chill and serve. It is best to use just a little bit less water than called for.

ΣΣΣΣΣΣΣΣΣΣΣΣΣΣΣΣΣΣΣΣΣΣΣΣ
Sarah Bruso
Rhinelander,
*   Wisconsin*

CHOCOLATE MINT DESSERT

Cake Layer:

1 cup flour
1 cup sugar
1/2 cup butter or oleo, softened
4 eggs
1 1/2 cup (16 oz can)
   Hershey's® Syrup

Heat oven to 350 degrees. Grease 13x9" pan. In large bowl combine flour, sugar, butter, eggs and syrup until smooth. Pour into prepared pan. Bake 25 to 30 minutes. Cool completely in pan.

Mint Cream Center:

2 cups powdered sugar
1/2 cup soft butter
1 Tbsp water
1/2 to 3/4 tsp mint extract
3 drops green food coloring

Mint Cream Center on cake, and chill.

Chocolate Topping:

6 Tbsp butter
1 cup Hershey's®
   Semi-sweet chips

In saucepan over low heat, melt butter and chips. Remove from heat. Stir until smooth. Cool slightly. Pour Chocolate Topping over chilled dessert, cover and chill at least 1 hour before serving.

ΣΣΣΣΣΣΣΣΣΣΣΣΣΣΣΣΣΣΣΣΣΣΣΣ
Ruth E. O'Connor
Burlington,
*   Massachusetts*

BLUEBERRY TART

Wash and drain
   1 quart of blueberries.
Mix:

1 cup sugar
2 Tbsp corn starch
1/8 tsp salt
1 cup water
1 cup of the blueberries

Cook and stir over low heat, till thick. Add rest of blueberries and 1 Tbsp butter. Cool. Fill tart shell, and serve with ice cream or any cream topping.

ΣΣΣΣΣΣΣΣΣΣΣΣΣΣΣΣΣΣΣΣΣΣΣΣ
Merrilee Tieche
Ozark, Missouri

CARAMEL APPLE CAKE

This recipe won "Best of Show" at the 1991 Christian County Fair.

3 eggs
2 cups sugar
1 cup Canola Oil
2 cups flour

2 tsp cinnamon
1 tsp baking soda
1/2 tsp salt
1 tsp vanilla
1 cup chopped walnuts
4 cups thinly sliced tart apples, pared (5 medium apples)
1/2 jar caramel ice cream topping

In large bowl, beat eggs with a mixer until thick and light. Combine sugar and oil; pour into eggs, with mixer set on medium speed. Stir together flour, cinnamon, soda and salt; add to egg mixture with vanilla; beat to mix. Stir in walnuts. Mix in apples and caramel ice cream topping and spread in buttered 13x9x2" pan and bake for 1 hour at 350 degrees. Remove from oven and cool on wire rack. Spread with Cream Cheese Icing.

Cream Cheese Icing:

Soften 2 (3 oz) packages cream cheese. Beat until fluffy. Beat in 1/4 cup melted butter, then beat in 2 cups powdered sugar and 1 tsp lemon juice. Spread over cooled cake. Refrigerate. Makes 12 to 15 servings.

ΣΣΣΣΣΣΣΣΣΣΣΣΣΣΣΣΣΣΣΣ
*Doris Callaway,
Greensburg, Kansas*

LEMON DESSERT

1 lemon cake mix, prepared following box directions

1 can frozen lemonade

After cake is baked, pour undiluted lemonade over warm cake. Serve with Cool Whip® topping.

ΣΣΣΣΣΣΣΣΣΣΣΣΣΣΣΣΣΣΣΣ
*Merry May
Tuckahoe, New Jersey*

Hershey's®
CHOCOLATE MOUSSE

1 tsp unflavored gelatin
1 Tbsp cold water
2 Tbsp boiling water
1/2 cup sugar
1/4 cup Hershey's® cocoa
1 tsp vanilla
1 cup heavy cream, very cold

Sprinkle gelatin over cold water in a small bowl; stir and let stand 1 minute to soften. Add boiling water; stir until gelatin is completely dissolved (mixture must be clear). Stir together sugar and cocoa in small cold mixer bowl; add heavy cream and vanilla. Beat at a medium speed until stiff peaks form; pour in gelatin mixture and beat until well blended. Spoon into serving dishes. Chill about 1/2 hour. Makes four one-half cup servings.

Note: To double this recipe, use 1 envelope unflavored gelatin; double remaining ingredients.

ΣΣΣΣΣΣΣΣΣΣΣΣΣΣΣΣΣΣΣΣ
*Penny Hand
Woodbridge, Virginia*

ROASTED PECAN CHOCOLATE CAKE

Mix together:

2 cups flour
2 cups sugar

Mix the following, until it foams and add to flour mixture:

1/2 cup buttermilk
2 eggs
1 tsp soda
1 tsp vanilla

Mix the following, and add to above mixture:

2 sticks margarine
1 cup water
2 Tbsp cocoa
1/8 tsp salt

Pour into greased jelly roll pan. Bake at 350 degrees for 20-30 minutes.

Chocolate Icing for above recipe:

Bring to a boil:

3 Tbsp cocoa and 1/3 cup sweet milk. Add 1 stick margarine. Pour this over 1 box powdered sugar with 1 tsp vanilla, and 1 cup toasted pecans, added last. Mix and spread over cake, while hot.

(To toast pecans, spread chopped nuts on baking sheet and bake for 15 to 20 minutes at 300 degrees, stirring occasionally, do not let them burn. Taste at 15 minutes for doneness.)

CHOCOLATE PIE FILLING

1 cup sugar
3 Tbsp flour
3 Tbsp cocoa
1/2 tsp salt
2 1/4 cups milk
3 egg yolks
2 1/2 Tbsp butter
1 tsp vanilla

Mix all dry ingredients together. Then add milk a little at a time, while stirring. Cook until it becomes thick. Mix yolks and butter in cup, then add to

Desserts, page 324

thickened mixture, and cook a little longer. Take off of heat and add vanilla. Set aside and let cool before putting into baked cooled shell. Enough for 9" pie. Top with meringue.

ΣΣΣΣΣΣΣΣΣΣΣΣΣΣΣΣΣΣΣΣΣΣ
Virginia H. Flowers
Flushing, Michigan

LAYERED COOKIE PUDDING

4 cookies, coarsely crumbled
1 cup thawed Cool Whip®
2 cups cold milk
1 pkg (4 serving size) Jell-O Instant Pudding and Pie Filling any flavor

Gently fold cookies into whipped topping. Pour cold milk into bowl. Add pudding mix. With electric mixer at low speed, beat until well blended, 1 to 2 minutes. Pour half of the pudding into individual dessert glasses. Spoon 3 to 4 Tbsp of the whipped topping mixture over pudding in glasses. Spoon remaining pudding over whipped topping mixture. Garnish with halved cookies.

ΣΣΣΣΣΣΣΣΣΣΣΣΣΣΣΣΣΣΣΣΣΣ
Anna Eelman
North Plainfield,
New Jersey

VIENNESE PLUM CAKE

1/2 cup butter
2 eggs
1 tsp salt
10 plums, pitted and halved
2 tsp cinnamon for top
1/2 cup sugar
1 cup flour
1 tsp baking powder
1/2 cup additional sugar

Work butter until soft; add sugar and mix well. Add 1 egg, beat well, then add second egg and beat until very light. Sift flour, baking powder and salt; add to first mixture.

Spread in well buttered deep pie plate or baking dish. Place halved plums skin down on top and press well into batter. Mix sugar and cinnamon and sprinkle over top. Bake at 350 degrees for 30 minutes.

ΣΣΣΣΣΣΣΣΣΣΣΣΣΣΣΣΣΣΣΣΣΣ
Doris Haggard
Topeka, Kansas

Since there are only two of us, 1 dog, and several out-door cats, we don't cook like we did when the children were home. One of our favorite pies is graham cracker crust with lemon filling. I like to use the MT Fine lemon pudding that comes in a box and you add your own ingredients, and cook it.

ΣΣΣΣΣΣΣΣΣΣΣΣΣΣΣΣΣΣΣΣΣΣ
Mary J. Ruda
Elida, Ohio

GRANDMA'S SUGAR COOKIES

Sift together:

2 cups sifted flour
1/2 tsp soda
1/4 tsp salt
1/4 tsp nutmeg

Cream 1/2 cup butter. Gradually add 3/4 cup sugar, creaming well.
Blend in 1/2 cup sour cream (thick or commercial). Add dry ingredients. Blend well. Chill. Roll out on floured surface, half at a time, to 1/8" thickness. Cut into desired shapes. Place on ungreased cookie sheets.

Bake at 350 degrees for 8 to 10 minutes.

ΣΣΣΣΣΣΣΣΣΣΣΣΣΣΣΣΣΣΣΣΣΣ
Georgina Doss
Milton, West Virginia

APPLE JOHN

Place sliced apples in a well-buttered, deep baking dish (9" square pan is one recipe, 9x13" is a double recipe.)

Cover with:

1 cup sugar
cinnamon
nutmeg
a squirt of lemon
several dots of butter.

In a separate bowl, combine:

1 cup flour
1 tsp baking powder
1/2 tsp salt
1 Tbsp sugar
4 Tbsp shortening

Add evaporated milk, enough to make a batter easy to spread over apples. Bake at 350 degrees for 1 to 1 1/2 hours until golden brown.

ΣΣΣΣΣΣΣΣΣΣΣΣΣΣΣΣΣΣΣΣΣΣ
Martha De Turk
Kutztown,
Pennsylvania

DELICIOUS ROLL-OUT COOKIES

4 cups sugar
1 pound butter

1 tsp baking soda
1 tsp cream of tartar
6 eggs
9 cups flour

Cream butter and sugar. Alternate eggs and dry ingredients. Roll and cut rather thin. Brush with beaten egg and sprinkle with colored sugar.

Bake at 350 degrees. These store well. Taste more buttery after a few days. Great Christmas cookies. This recipe makes lots.

ΣΣΣΣΣΣΣΣΣΣΣΣΣΣΣΣΣΣΣΣΣΣΣ
Karen Crosby
Ocala, Florida

FAST APPLE CRISP

Place 2 cans apple pie filling into 9x13" cake pan, top with 1 box yellow cake mix and dot with 1 stick of butter. Bake at 350 degrees for 1 hour.

ΣΣΣΣΣΣΣΣΣΣΣΣΣΣΣΣΣΣΣΣΣΣΣ
Fanny Naught
Quincy, Illinois

HEATH® BAR COFFEE CAKE

1 cup brown sugar
1 cup granulated sugar
1 stick margarine
1 tsp vanilla
2 cups flour
pinch of salt

Mix all ingredients together, as for pie crust. Set aside 1/2 cup of the mixture. To the remainder add:

1 egg
1 cup buttermilk
1 tsp baking soda

Pour mixture into a 13x9" pan. Prepare topping by combining 1/2 cup of reserved mixture, 4 Heath® bars crushed and 1/2 cup pecans. Bake at 350 degrees for 30 minutes. Yummy!!!

ΣΣΣΣΣΣΣΣΣΣΣΣΣΣΣΣΣΣΣΣΣΣΣ
Dort Lee
Leicester,
North Carolina

GREAT AUNT LULA'S FRUIT COBBLER
(Good enough for company)

Great Aunt Lula was such a good cook that the daily train from South Georgia to Atlanta would stop dead on the tracks everyday at lunch time, across from her house. The train crew would all go over and eat there. (When passengers learned what was happening, they started going, too!) After they had eaten, they'd all board the train and go on.

1. Fill baking dish with fruit (cut up apples or blueberries, or pitted cherries, or cut up peaches, etc.)

2. Add 1/4 cup water. Then sprinkle on some flour and sugar, about 1/4 cup of each. Stir. (I use wholewheat flour for extra nutrition and I melt the butter and mix with flour and sugar 'til crumbly. Then spread on top of fruit.)

3. Dot with butter.

4. Bake at 350 degrees 'til fruit is soft and juicy and top is nicely browned, about 1 1/2 hours.

ΣΣΣΣΣΣΣΣΣΣΣΣΣΣΣΣΣΣΣΣΣΣΣ
Judi Robb
Manhattan, Kansas

HERSHEY'S® BROWNIES

Mix:

1/4 pound (1 stick) oleo
1 cup sugar

Add:

1 cup flour
4 eggs
1 large can Hershey's® syrup
1 tsp vanilla
1 cup nuts

Bake at 350 degrees, 40 minutes in 9x13" pan. Sprinkle with powdered sugar.

ΣΣΣΣΣΣΣΣΣΣΣΣΣΣΣΣΣΣΣΣΣΣΣ
M. Jeanne Poore
Overland Park,
Kansas

WACKY CAKE

Sift into greased cake pan:

3 cups flour
1/2 cup cocoa
1 level teaspoon salt
2 cups sugar
2 level teaspoons soda

Spread evenly over pan. Make 3 holes in mixture, in one put 2 teaspoons vanilla, in one put 2 Tbsp vinegar, and in the last put 1 cup oil. Over all pour 2 cups cold water. Mix well with fork. Bake in 350 degree oven for 25-30 minutes. Frost or not, as desired. Easy, quick, one pan.

Desserts, page 326

LEMON JELLO® CAKE

1 lemon cake mix
1/2 cup oil
4 eggs
1 small box lemon Jello®
1 1/4 cup water

Follow directions on cake box using large pan.

Icing:

1/4 cup lemon juice added to 2 cups powdered sugar. Poke holes in cake while it is still hot with a large fork, pour icing over cake. It will soak into cake.

CRUMB PIE CRUST

1 1/2 cups fine graham cracker crumbs
1/4 cup white sugar
1/2 cup butter melted

Mix crumbs and sugar together, stir in butter, line pie pan with mixture by pressing it firmly into place. Chill 20 minutes or bake in moderate oven 350 degrees for 10 minutes. Cool. Makes one 9" pie shell. I usually bake mine.

ΣΣΣΣΣΣΣΣΣΣΣΣΣΣΣΣΣΣΣΣΣΣΣ
Sheryl Mielke
McGregor, Iowa

RHUBARB BARS

1 cup flour
5 Tbsp powdered sugar
1 stick margarine

Cut together like pie crust and press into 9x9" pan. Bake 15 minutes at 350 degrees.

Mix:

1 1/2 cups sugar
1/2 to 3/4 cup of flour
2 beaten eggs
1/2 tsp salt

Add:

2 cups diced rhubarb

Pour over crust and bake 35 to 40 minutes at 350 degrees.

ΣΣΣΣΣΣΣΣΣΣΣΣΣΣΣΣΣΣΣΣΣΣΣ
Bettie Rushin
Boulder City,
California

ROOTBEER FLOATS

Impress the kids and your spouse with Rootbeer Floats. Purchase one gallon vanilla ice cream and one pack of A&W Rootbeer. Put two scoops of ice cream in a glass and cover with Rootbeer. Takes five minutes.

ΣΣΣΣΣΣΣΣΣΣΣΣΣΣΣΣΣΣΣΣΣΣΣ
Carol L. Robbins
Overland Park,
Kansas

FAST & EASY CHEESECAKE

For a fast, easy dessert, fix "Cheesecake" pie or pudding.

Filling:

1 small pkg. Jello® Instant French Vanilla Pudding (or flavor of your choice)
1 (8 oz) pkg cream cheese
2 cups milk

Put milk in blender, add cream cheese, cut up; cover and start blender. Immediately add pudding mix and blend 20 to 30 seconds. Pour filling into prepared graham cracker crust, or pour into four parfait glasses. Serve with chilled canned cherry pie filling and/or Cool Whip®.

**Note: Buy prepared crust or follow easy instructions on graham cracker box. I like to layer graham cracker crumbs and pudding mix in the glasses, ending up with crumbs. Can be eaten immediately. BUT, refrigerate pie for at least 4 hours to firm up for slicing. Also, for less calories and fat, try substituting Neufchatel® Cheese for the cream cheese, and skim milk instead of regular milk.

ΣΣΣΣΣΣΣΣΣΣΣΣΣΣΣΣΣΣΣΣΣΣΣ
Marcia Knopp
Bay City, Michigan

FUDGE NUT BARS

1 cup butter
2 cups brown sugar
2 tsp vanilla
2 eggs
2 1/2 cups flour
1 tsp soda
1 tsp salt
3 cups quick oats

Cream together butter and sugar. Mix in eggs and vanilla. Sift flour, cocoa and salt. Stir in oatmeal. Add dry ingredients to creamed mixture. Set aside.

Mix fudge nut filling:

1 (12 oz) pkg of choc chips
1 cup Eagle Brand® milk
2 Tbsp butter
1/2 tsp salt
1 cup chopped nuts
2 tsp vanilla

In saucepan over boiling water, mix choc chips, Eagle Brand®

Desserts, page 327

milk, butter and salt. Stir until smooth. Add nuts and vanilla.

Spread about 2/3 oatmeal mix in bottom of greased 15 1/2" x 10 1/2" x 1" jelly roll pan. Cover with chocolate mixture. Dot with remaining oatmeal mixture and swirl over choc filling. Bake at 350 degrees 25 to 30 minutes, until lightly browned.

ΣΣΣΣΣΣΣΣΣΣΣΣΣΣΣΣΣΣΣΣ
Netta Ranney
Overland Park,
Kansas

I leave the cookie baking to those who enjoy it, and appreciate them always.

ΣΣΣΣΣΣΣΣΣΣΣΣΣΣΣΣΣΣΣΣ
Tedi Lambert
Los Banos, California

DESSERT

Never mind the recipe, just head for the local bakery!

ΣΣΣΣΣΣΣΣΣΣΣΣΣΣΣΣΣΣΣΣ
Pat Reep
Bakersfield, California

CHOCOLATE MOUSSE PIE

1 (8 oz) carton Cool Whip®
1 cup milk
1 pkg instant chocolate
          pudding mix

Mix all ingredients, and put in a pie shell. Refrigerate and garnish with whipped cream.

ΣΣΣΣΣΣΣΣΣΣΣΣΣΣΣΣΣΣΣΣ
Phyllis Hansen
Giersch
Madera, California

PECAN PIE

(My oldest son's dessert. He's a civil engineer like his dad, but is presently flying for the Air National Guard. Graduated from the Air Force Academy and flew for 5 years in the Air Force and flying gets in your blood.)

1/4 cup butter or margarine
1 cup of honey
1/4 tsp salt
1 tsp real vanilla
3 eggs
1 cup of pecans
one 9" unbaked pie shell

Cream butter to soften, add honey gradually, and cream till fluffy. Add eggs one at a time, beating well after each. Stir in pecans. Pour into unbaked shell and bake at 350 degrees for 50 minutes. Cool.

ΣΣΣΣΣΣΣΣΣΣΣΣΣΣΣΣΣΣΣΣ
Teresa Binder
Emporia, Kansas

CHERRY CHOCOLATE CAKE

1 box chocolate cake mix
1/4 tsp baking soda
1 can cherry pie filling
2 eggs
1/3 cup boiling water.

Mix all ingredients and beat 2 minutes. Grease and flour 9x13" pan (I use a bundt pan). Bake at 350 degrees for 35 minutes. Frost and refrigerate. May be kept in refrigerator 5 days.

ΣΣΣΣΣΣΣΣΣΣΣΣΣΣΣΣΣΣΣΣ
Betty A. Lenz
Marshall, Missouri

ALMOND CHEESECAKE
(My favorite cheesecake,
used for many years)

Crust:

1 1/2 cups graham
          cracker crumbs
1/4 cup melted butter
2 Tbsp sugar
1 tsp flour

Mix all ingredients and press into springform pan, bake at 350 degrees for only 5 minutes.

Filling:

4 (8 oz) pkgs cream cheese
          (room temperature)
1 cup sugar
2 lightly beaten eggs
1 tsp vanilla
1 tsp almond extract

Beat until smooth,-pour into crust and bake another 30 minutes at 350 degrees.

Mix:

2 cups sour cream
3/4 cup sugar
3/4 tsp almond
1/2 tsp fresh lemon juice

Spread over above filling. Return to oven and bake for 8 minutes. Cool at least 2 hours, and refrigerate 8 hours or overnight. Any fruit filling is delicious on top, serves up to 16 servings.

Desserts, page 328

ΣΣΣΣΣΣΣΣΣΣΣΣΣΣΣΣΣΣΣΣΣΣ
*Charlotte Fry
St. Charles, Missouri*

<u>ANGEL BARS</u>

1 pkg one-step angel food mix
1 can pie filling--your choice

Spray jelly roll pan, preheat oven to 350 degrees. Mix dry cake mix with pie filling until well blended. Pour & spread onto pan. Bake 25 to 30 minutes at 350 degrees. Either ice with powdered sugar icing or dust with powdered sugar. I've used Apricot & Blueberry pie filling and both worked well. Also, no fats or cholesterol.

ΣΣΣΣΣΣΣΣΣΣΣΣΣΣΣΣΣΣΣΣΣΣ
*Marcene Gunter
Hillsboro, Kansas*

<u>LEMONADE PIE</u>

Graham cracker crust

1 (8 oz) pkg cream cheese
1 can sweetened condensed
     Eagle Brand® milk
1 can frozen pink lemonade
1 (9 oz) carton frozen
          whipped topping

Combine all ingredients and mix well. Pour into crust and chill.

ΣΣΣΣΣΣΣΣΣΣΣΣΣΣΣΣΣΣΣΣΣΣ
*Joan Waldman
Platte Center,
         Nebraska*

<u>HAWAIIAN CAKE</u>

Prepare yellow cake mix as directed on box and bake in jelly roll pan. Cool.

1 pkg instant vanilla pudding
1 cup milk
1 (8 oz) pkg cream cheese

Beat above until smooth and then add by hand, add 1 large carton whipped topping. Smooth over cooled cake.

Drain well: 1 (16 oz) can
                crushed pineapple

Add:
1/2 cup shredded coconut
1/2 cup chopped pecans

Sprinkle over topping. Cut into squares to serve. Keep refrigerated.

<u>CEREAL SNACK BARS</u>

Bring to boil:

1 cup light corn syrup
1/2 cup white sugar
1/2 cup brown sugar

Stir in:

1 cup peanut butter
6 cups corn flakes
1 cup chopped nuts

Press into 9x13" buttered pan.

Topping:

Melt together: 1 small Hershey® bar and 1/2 cup semi-sweet chocolate chips. Spread over cereal. Cool, cut in squares.

<u>QUICK PEACH COBBLER</u>

9" cake pan
Pour #2 can of sliced peaches
          and juice into pan
Top with 1 Jiffy® cake mix (put
          on dry, do not mix)
Cut 1 stick margarine in squares
          and dot on top
          of dry mix.

Bake at 350 degrees for 50 minutes. DO NOT OPEN OVEN DOOR! Turn oven off and leave cake in oven for another hour. Take out and serve with whipped topping or ice cream.

<u>PECAN CARROT CAKE</u>

Mix:

2 cups sugar
1 1/4 cups oil

Add:

4 eggs
2 tsp vanilla
3 cups flour
2 tsp baking soda
2 tsp cinnamon
1 tsp baking powder
1/2 tsp salt

Mix. Then add:

2 cups finely shredded carrots
1 1/2 cups shredded coconut
1 cup crushed
      pineapple (drained)
1 cup pecans (chopped)

Put in greased and floured 9x13" pan. Bake 350 degrees 35 to 40 minutes or till toothpick comes out clean. Cool.

Frosting:

Soften 1 (8 oz) pkg cream cheese. Add 1/2 cup butter and 1 tsp vanilla and blend well. Beat in 1 pound of powdered sugar (add a little milk if necessary to make a good spreading consistency.)

Toast 1 cup shredded coconut, and sprinkle on top of frosting. Press into frosting.

CARAMEL BARS

Mix:

1 cup flour
1 cup oatmeal (quick)
3/4 cup brown sugar
1/2 tsp baking soda
1/4 tsp salt
3/4 cup melted margarine

Reserve 1/2 cup of this mixture. Press the remaining mixture in 9x13" pan. Bake at 350 degrees for 10 minutes.

Melt 32 light caramels in 5 Tbsp evaporated milk. When crust comes from oven, sprinkle on 1 cup chocolate chips and 1 cup nuts, then caramel mixture. Sprinkle reserved crust on top. Return to oven and bake for another 20 minutes.

ΣΣΣΣΣΣΣΣΣΣΣΣΣΣΣΣΣΣΣΣΣ
DeEtta Beebe
Waters, Michigan

IN A HURRY ONE-STEP "PINEAPPLE CAKE"

1 large can crushed pineapple
2 cups sugar
2 eggs
dash salt
1 tsp vanilla
1 tsp baking soda
1 cup crushed nuts
2 cups WONDRA® flour

Put all ingredients in large mixing bowl. Mix until well blended.

Bake in greased 9x3" pan. Bake at 350 degrees, 40 minutes.

ΣΣΣΣΣΣΣΣΣΣΣΣΣΣΣΣΣΣΣΣΣ
Richard F. Zimmerman
New Milford, New Jersey

What I really enjoy is baking. A number of years ago, we bagan collecting stoneware cookie molds. These are similar to the old Dutch and German cookie molds which were carved out of wood, except they are made from a very hard and durable ceramic material. The cookie dough is quite stiff, especially after it has been chilled for several hours. A portion of the dough is pressed into the clay mold, leveled off with a sharp knife, knocked out of the mold and placed on a cookie sheet to bake. When I first began making these molded cookies, I could only make three or four in an hours time. Now with experience, I can make them at the rate of one every five minutes. They are still a time consuming pursuit, but they are SO beautiful and delicious that it is worth the time and effort.

On the more practical side, a very simple cookie, especially if you have an electric iron is the Pizzelles. This is my modification from one found in a recipe book.

PIZZELLES

In a large mixing bowl, put:

3 1/2 cups all-purpose flour
1 1/2 cups sugar
1 cup melted
    butter or margarine
2 Tbsp vanilla or anise extract
6 eggs

With mixer at low speed, beat all ingredients until well blended, occasionally scraping bowl with rubber spatula. The dough will be quite stiff and sticky. Our Pizzelle iron makes 5" cookies at a time, so I use a heaping teaspoon of dough for each, since they take only about 30 seconds to bake, I can make about 70 cookies from this recipe in less than an hour.

Now for my variation: Using only 1 Tbsp of vanilla instead of 2, I then add 1/3 cup baking chocolate powder for a really special Chocolate Pizzelle. They are light, delicate and go down like potato chips.

Another standby for the family, company, a Church supper or a treat at work is:

SHAKER APPLE CAKE

1/3 cup butter
3/4 cup sugar
1 egg
1 1/3 cups flour
1/4 tsp salt
2 tsp baking powder
1/2 cup milk
1 tsp vanilla
3 apples, peeled and chopped
1/4 cup currants or raisins
powdered sugar
ground cinnamon

Cream butter, and add half the sugar gradually, beating well. Beat egg with remaining sugar, add to first mixture. Sift in flour, and baking powder, alternately with the milk. Flavor with vanilla. Add apples and currants, or raisins. Beat well to mix, and turn into well-buttered 9" cake tin, square or round. Sprinkle with powdered sugar and cinnamon, and bake in moderate 350 degree oven for 30 minutes. Makes one cake.

My variation on this recipe is to shred the unpeeled apples, using a hand-held course or medium grater. The apple skin gives the cake a nice texture and a little added color.

ΣΣΣΣΣΣΣΣΣΣΣΣΣΣΣΣΣΣΣΣΣΣ
LaRue Nuest
South Hutchinson, Kansas

STRAWBERRY DESSERT

1 pkg red gelatin
1 cup boiling water
1/2 pkg strawberries
1 pint ice cream

Pour water over gelatin, and let set a while. Add strawberries and ice cream. Pour over crumbled vanilla wafers. Top with crushed vanilla wafers.

ΣΣΣΣΣΣΣΣΣΣΣΣΣΣΣΣΣΣΣΣΣΣ
Ella May Reusser
Blackwell, Oklahoma

WONDER DESSERT

1 cup sugar
1 cup flour
1 tsp soda
1 tsp vanilla
1/2 tsp salt
1 egg
1 (#303) can fruit cocktail

Mix together above ingredients, and pour into 9x9" greased square pan.

Spread on mixture of 1/2 cup brown sugar and 1/2 cup chopped nuts. Bake at 350 degrees for 30 to 35 minutes. Serve with whipped cream. Or ice cream.

ΣΣΣΣΣΣΣΣΣΣΣΣΣΣΣΣΣΣΣΣΣΣ
Betty J. Knack
Essexville, Michigan

PINEAPPLE COTTAGE CHEESE DESSERT

2 cups whipped cream
    or Cool Whip®®
1 (one pound) carton of small
    curd cottage cheese,
1 small pkg Jello® (lemon, lime,
    cherry, orange, etc)
1 can crushed pineapple,
    well drained

Mix cottage cheese and dry Jello®. Fold in Cool Whip®® and pineapple. Cool in refrigerator, plump up before serving.

MARY MAXIM'S STRAWBERRY PIE

Combine:

1 heaping quart of firm
    strawberries, washed
    and hulled in large bowl
2/3 to 1 cup sugar

Let mixture set overnight. The next morning, drain the juice and scrape down the excess sugar. Add water to juice to make 1 cup of liquid. (Optional: Add 3 drops red food coloring)

Combine juice/water mixture with:

1 1/2 Tbsp cornstarch, and cook until clear. Cool.

Add Berries, stir gently and pour into baked pie shell. Chill. Top with whipped cream or Cool Whip®

ΣΣΣΣΣΣΣΣΣΣΣΣΣΣΣΣΣΣΣΣΣΣ
Nancy H. Ehinger
West Branch, Michigan

NO-BAKE CARAMEL COOKIES

In a large pan, combine:

2 cups sugar
3/4 cup margarine
2/3 cup evaporated milk

Bring to a rollling boil, stirring often. Remove from heat and add 1 (4 oz) pkg of instant butterscotch pudding, and mix in 3 1/2 cups quick oatmeal. Mix well. Cool ten minutes. Drop onto wax paper with teaspoons. Allow to cool completely.

ΣΣΣΣΣΣΣΣΣΣΣΣΣΣΣΣΣΣΣΣΣΣ
Janet P. Wyckoff
Hopewell, New Jersey

CHOCOLATE CHEESECAKE

Crust:

1/3 cup chocolate wafer crumbs

Spray bottom and sides of 9" springform pan with PAM®. Coat with crumbs. Leave excess, spread in bottom of pan.

Cake:

1 1/2 cups semi-sweet
    chocolate bits
2 Tbsp butter
1/4 cup water
1 tsp instant coffee
    (or substitute 1/4 cup
    Kahlua for water
    and coffee)

Heat slowly in a measuring cup in a pan of water, stirring until melted and smooth. Cool slightly.

1 pound cream cheese, softened
2 large eggs
1/4 tsp salt
1 cup sour cream

Beat above, until smooth. Slowly beat in chocolate mixture. Pour into pan. Bake 40 minutes, until filling is barely set in center.

Top with sour cream, or creme fraiche and mocha sauce. (Optional, we like it plain.)

Combine over low heat until smooth and drizzle on top.:

6 oz chocolate chips
1/3 cup Kahlua
1/3 cup light corn syrup

ΣΣΣΣΣΣΣΣΣΣΣΣΣΣΣΣΣΣΣΣΣΣ
Maria Lage
Cumberland,
Rhode Island

CHERRY SWIRL COFFEECAKE

4 cups Bisquick® baking mix
1/2 cup sugar
1/4 cup butter or
      margarine, melted
1/2 cup milk
1 tsp vanilla extract
3 large eggs
1 tsp almond extract, optional
1 (21 oz can) cherry or blueberry
      pie filling
Glaze (recipe follows)

Place all ingredients, except pie filling and glaze, in bowl. Beat with mixer at medium speed for 30 seconds. Evenly spread about 2/3 of batter in greased 15 /2" by 10 1/2" jelly roll pan. Spread pie filling evenly over batter. Drop remaining batter by tablespoons onto filling, at random. Filling will not be completely covered. Bake at 350 degrees until lightly browned, 20-25 minutes. Cool a bit, then drizzle with glaze. Serve warm or cool.

Glaze for Coffee Cake:

Beat 1 cup confectioners sugar and 1 to 2 Tbsp milk until smooth.

ΣΣΣΣΣΣΣΣΣΣΣΣΣΣΣΣΣΣΣΣΣΣ
Emily Laubaugh
Gladstone, Oregon

CHOCOLATE CHIP COOKIES

1/2 cup packed brown sugar
1/2 cups chopped walnuts
1 cup semi-sweet
      chocolate mini-pieces
3 cups cake flour
1 3/4 cup sugar
1 1/4 cups milk
1/2 cup shortening
1 1/2 tsp baking powder
1 tsp salt
1 1/2 tsp vanilla extract
2 eggs

Prepare topping:

In small bowl, mix brown sugar, walnuts, and 1/2 cup semi-sweet chocolate pieces. Set aside. Preheat oven to 350 degrees. Grease and flour 13x9" baking pan.

Into large bowl, measure flour and remaining ingredients, except remaining chocolate pieces. With mixer at low speed, beat until mixed, constantly scraping bowl. Increase speed to high, beat 2 minutes. Stir in reserved mini-chocolate pieces; pour into pan.

Spread topping over batter. Bake 40 to 45 minutes, until toothpick inserted in center of cake, comes out clean. Cool in pan on rack.

ΣΣΣΣΣΣΣΣΣΣΣΣΣΣΣΣΣΣΣΣΣΣ
Roxanne H. McElroy
Mililani, Hawaii

MARIE CALLENDER'S ® BLACK BOTTOM PIE

(If you want the recipe, ask them!)

ΣΣΣΣΣΣΣΣΣΣΣΣΣΣΣΣΣΣΣΣΣΣ
Norma Jean Rector
Center Point, Indiana

APPLE PUDDING

Mix together:

2 cups raw, sliced apple
1 cup sugar
1 egg

Sift together:

1 cup flour
1 tsp soda
1 1/2 tsp cinnamon

Add dry ingredients to apple mixture, along with 1/4 cup sliced almonds or 1/2 cup nuts. Spread in greased 9x9" baking dish. Bake in preheated 350 degree oven. While cake is baking, cook the topping.

Topping for apple pudding:

Combine, cook until thick, and pour over hot pudding (cake):

1/2 cup sugar
1/2 cup brown sugar
2 Tbsp flour
1/4 cup margarine
1 cup water

Desserts, page 332

1 tsp vanilla

When cool, serve with Cool Whip® Serves 8 or 9.

SIMPLE DESSERT

For a very simple dessert, and a favorite of my grandsons, prepare a box of chocolate cake mix, as directed on package. Bake in whatever size pans you choose. Set out a quart of vanilla ice cream to soften. After cake has cooled, spread ice cream over top (as a frosting). Either drizzle chocolate and carmel ice cream topping around over ice cream, or crumble a few Oreo cookies over top.

ΣΣΣΣΣΣΣΣΣΣΣΣΣΣΣΣΣΣΣΣΣΣ
*Janice A. Miller
Jaffrey,
   New Hampshire*

CRISPY-COATED FRIED ICE CREAM

1 tsp margarine or butter
1 Tbsp brown sugar
1/4 tsp cinnamon
1/3 cup bran flakes cereal,
   (without raisins) crushed
   to about 1/4 cup
1 1/3 cups vanilla ice cream

Melt margarine in small saucepan; remove from heat. Stir in brown sugar and cinnamon; blend well. Stir in cereal. Form ice cream into 4 balls. Roll in cereal mixture to coat. Cover; freeze. Let stand at room temperature a few minutes before serving.

In this low-fat version of fried ice cream, a crispy coating is achieved without frying.

ΣΣΣΣΣΣΣΣΣΣΣΣΣΣΣΣΣΣΣΣΣΣ
*Margaret Kooda
Idaho Falls, Idaho*

GRANDMA CRAIG'S GINGER SNAPS

3/4 cup shortening
1 cup sugar
1/4 cup molasses
1 egg
2 cups all-purpose flour
2 tsp baking soda
1 tsp cinnamon
1/2 tsp cloves
1/2 tsp ginger
1/2 tsp salt

Combine shortening, sugar, molasses, egg, and beat well. Sift flour, soda, spices, salt. Add to shortening mixture, and mix well. Form 1 inch balls, and dip in granulated sugar. Bake 8 minutes at 375 degrees.

ΣΣΣΣΣΣΣΣΣΣΣΣΣΣΣΣΣΣΣΣΣΣ
*Betty Verhoeven
East Jewett, New York*

CHOCOLATE CHIP PEACH COBBLER

5 cups sliced peaches
1/2 cup brown sugar
1/2 cup sugar
4 Tbsp tapioca
1 tsp almond extract
2 Tbsp butter or margarine
1 (20 oz) pkg refrigerated
   chocolate chip
      cookie dough

Grease a 9x13" baking pan. Preheat oven to 350 degrees. Mix peaches with sugars, tapioca and almond flavoring. Spread into prepared pan, Dot with butter. Slice well chilled cookie dough into 1/4" slices, and arrange over peaches in baking dish. Bake for about 20 minutes. Enjoy it warm (with ice cream, ooohh!).

ΣΣΣΣΣΣΣΣΣΣΣΣΣΣΣΣΣΣΣΣΣΣ
*Alyce C. Kauffman
Gridley, California*

LEMON PIE

One ready-made graham
   cracker crust
1 carton of Cool Whip®
1 small can frozen lemonade
   concentrate (you can use
      other juices)

Blend lemonade into Cool Whip®, until it is evenly distributed. Pour into pie shell. Freeze for at least 4 hours. Let thaw slightly before serving.

BUTTERMILK FUDGE CAKE

Mix, and set aside:

2 cups flour
2 cups sugar

Melt together, and stir:

1 cube margarine
1/2 cup shortening
1 cup water
4 Tbsp cocoa

Bring to a boil, and pour into flour and sugar. Stir and add:

2 slightly beaten eggs
1/2 cup buttermilk
1 tsp cinnamon
1 tsp soda
1 tsp vanilla

Mix above combined mixtures, and pour into greased and floured cookie sheets with one inch (or more) sides on them.

Bake at 350 degrees for 20 minutes. Five minutes before cake is done, start icing.

Icing for Buttermilk Fudge Cake:

1 cube margarine
4 Tbsp cocoa
1/3 cup buttermilk
1 pound pkg powdered sugar
1 tsp vanilla
1 cup nuts, chopped coarsely

Melt margarine with buttermilk and cocoa. Bring to a boil, and add sugar, vanilla, and nuts. Mix and spread over hot cake.

ΣΣΣΣΣΣΣΣΣΣΣΣΣΣΣΣΣΣΣΣΣ
Lenore Scott
Pittstown, New Jersey

WACKY CAKE

1/4 cup oil
1 tsp vanilla extract
1 Tbsp cider vinegar
1 cup cold water
1 1/2 cups flour
1 cup sugar
4 Tbsp cocoa powder
1 tsp baking soda

Preheat oven to 350 degrees. In a large bowl, mix oil, vinegar, vanilla and water.

Add slowly, sugar, cocoa, baking soda, and flour. Mix well. Pour in cupcake holders, and bake for 10 minutes. Turn off oven, and bake for 5 minutes more.

Remove, and cool on wire racks. Makes 14 cupcakes. Or, you can bake in a greased, floured pan.

ΣΣΣΣΣΣΣΣΣΣΣΣΣΣΣΣΣΣΣΣΣ
Pat Campbell
Rigby, Idaho

BOILED RAISIN CAKE

2 cups sugar
2 cups hot water
1 cup shortening
pinch of salt
1 tsp cinnamon
1/2 tsp cloves
2 cups raisins

Boil the above ingredients for 1 minute and add 2 tsp baking soda. Let cool. Add 3 1/2 cups flour. Stir the mixture together. Pour into greased/floured baking pan, and bake for 1 hour at 350 degrees.

ΣΣΣΣΣΣΣΣΣΣΣΣΣΣΣΣΣΣΣΣΣ
Christine Klinger
Fayetteville, Arkansas

PUMPKIN CAKE WITH
CREAM CHEESE ICING

2 cups sugar
4 eggs
1 cup salad oil
2 cups pumpkin
2 cups all-purpose flour
2 tsp cinnamon
2 tsp baking soda
1/2 tsp salt

Combine all ingredients in large bowl. Turn into a large 13x9" pan, greased and floured. Bake at 350 degrees, 30 minutes or more.

Icing for Pumpkin Cake:

1 stick butter
1 box powdered sugar
1 (8 oz) pkg softened
    cream cheese
2 tsp vanilla
1 cup chopped nuts

Blend all ingredients with mixer and spread on top of cooled cake. Sprinkle nuts on top.

ΣΣΣΣΣΣΣΣΣΣΣΣΣΣΣΣΣΣΣΣΣ
Mary Lou Kantz
Evans
Flagstaff, Arizona

ORANGE DELIGHT

Crust:

1 cup flour
1/2 cup Crisco®
2 Tbsp butter
1 egg
1/4 tsp salt

Mix well and pat into 9x13" pan, bake at 350 degrees, 15 minutes.

Topping:

2 (11 oz) cans mandarin oranges
1 (8 oz) carton Cool Whip®
1 (16 oz) pkg softened
    cream cheese
3/4 cup Tang®
3/4 cup sugar
3 eggs

Soften cream cheese, combine with sugar and Tang® until creamy, add 1 egg at a time, beat until creamy, fold in Cool Whip® and oranges and pour into crust. Refrigerate or freeze.

ΣΣΣΣΣΣΣΣΣΣΣΣΣΣΣΣΣΣΣΣΣ
Bonnie Kay Browning
Paducah, Kentucky

WHITE CHOCOLATE FUDGE
(a family favorite!)

2 cups sugar
1 cup evaporated milk
1/2 cup butter or margarine

Desserts, page 334

.8 oz white almond bark
1 cup tiny marshmallows
1/2 cup flaked coconut
1/2 cp chopped pecans

Butter sides of heavy 3 quart saucepan. Add the sugar, evaporated milk and butter. Cook over medium heat to soft ball stage (234 degrees), stirring frequently. Remove from heat. Add almond bark and marshmallows; beat until melted. Quickly stir in coconut, pecans and vanilla. Pour into buttered 10 x 6" dish. Cut when cool.

ΣΣΣΣΣΣΣΣΣΣΣΣΣΣΣΣΣΣΣΣΣΣ
Sandra L. Hatch
Lincoln, Maine

DUMP RHUBARB DESSERT

As for dessert--my dump-rhubarb dessert is the easiest I know. 4 cups cut-up rhubarb in a butter-greased pan (9x13") covered with 1 cup sugar, 1 package strawberry Jello®, 2 cups cake mix, 1 cup water and 5 Tbsp melted margarine--all dumped in that order. Bake at 375 degrees for 50 minutes and serve warm with ice cream or whipped cream. You can vary that and create any other kind using different fruits. No mess and everyone loves it.

ΣΣΣΣΣΣΣΣΣΣΣΣΣΣΣΣΣΣΣΣΣΣ
Sue Hausmann
Lincolnshire, Illinois

Several years ago, while attending the Martha Pullen School of Art Fashion in Huntsville, the entire student body was invited to Martha's home (a tradition of the school). Part of the buffet was a large selection of pies for dessert. I selected a custard type pie that was delicious. They called it Chess Pie. The following year at the school, I looked for the same dessert but was told the baker had passed away that year.

I never forgot the pie and last year the *Ash Anne and Dan column* in my local newspaper featured the following recipe from S.M.R. Aurora, Illinois. My 80 year old father was visiting, and shares my sweet tooth as he quickly made a pie. I love it as is, but Daddy and my dear husband, Herb, perfer it *laced* with pecans. It is the best pecan pie base I've ever tasted!

CHESS PIE (also known as Brown Sugar Pie - you'll see why!)

1 box (16 oz) light brown sugar
4 eggs, large
1/4 cup milk
1 1/2 tsp vanilla
1/2 tsp salt
1/2 cup butter or
    margarine, melted

Preheat oven to 350 degrees. Blend together brown sugar, eggs, milk, vanilla and salt. Mix in butter, a little at a time. Pour filling into unbaked pie shell and bake about 1 hour, until fluffy and golden. Cool pie to room temperature.

ΣΣΣΣΣΣΣΣΣΣΣΣΣΣΣΣΣΣΣΣΣΣ
Jane Newhouse
Wedderburn, Oregon

CARROT CAKE

2 eggs
1 cup sugar
3/4 cup oil
1/2 tsp salt
1 tsp cinnamon
1 cup grated carrots
1/2 cup nuts
1 tsp soda
1 1/2 cups flour

Mix all ingredients together. Bake in a loaf pan for 1 hour at 350 degrees.

ΣΣΣΣΣΣΣΣΣΣΣΣΣΣΣΣΣΣΣΣΣΣ
Sally Smith
Kodak, Tennessee

QUICK NUT FUDGE

1 pound confectioners sugar
1/2 cup cocoa
1/4 tsp salt
6 Tbsp margarine
4 Tbsp milk
1 Tbsp vanilla
1 cup nuts (optional)

Combine all ingrendients except nuts in top of double boiler. Place ever over hot water and stir until smooth. Add nuts and mix. Spread candy in buttered dish. Cool and cut into squares. No fail and fast!

GLAZED GRAHAM CRACKERS

1/3 box graham crackers,
    separated at perforations
1 cup chopped pecans
1 stick margarine
1/2 cup sugar

Lightly grease bottom of 11x15" cookie sheet. Place graham crackers side by side and sprinkle pecans over the top. Melt butter and sugar together and boil for 2 minutes. Pour sugar mixture over crackers and bake for 10 minutes at 350 degrees. Remove immediately from pan and enjoy.

ΣΣΣΣΣΣΣΣΣΣΣΣΣΣΣΣΣΣΣΣΣΣ

QUILTERS SHARE THEIR FAVORITE MISCELLANEOUS RECIPES

Joyce Livingston

Page 336, Miscellaneous recipes

Joyce Livingston, Council Grove, Kansas

CHEESE BALL

3 (8oz) pkgs cream cheese, softened
1 carton sour cream
1 pkg of Hidden Valley® dressing (added dry)
2 or 3 Tbsp Pace® Picante Sauce
3/4 cup of grated cheese of your choice

Mix all ingredients together. Form a ball, and chill overnight in the refrigerator.

This can also be used as a cheese spread for sandwiches.

>>>>>>>>>>>>>>>>>>>>>>>>>>>>>>

Beverly J. Relph, Leavenworth, Kansas

Bread? Miscellaneous? No comment!

>>>>>>>>>>>>>>>>>>>>>>>>>>>>>>

Elaine Helen (Revier) Baker, Watertown, Minnesota

KEEP THEM BUSY PLAY DOUGH

3/4 cup flour
3 Tbsp corn starch
1/3 cup salt
1 tsp alum
1/2 cup HOT tap water
1 tsp cooking oil
Optional: Glitter, sequins, food coloring

Mix all dry ingredients in a bowl. Glitter and/or sequins to your liking. Mix several drops of food coloring in hot water. Add to dry ingredients, knead until smooth. If too wet, add some flour, if too dry, add a little water. Let dough cool before using it. Store in a sealed container to keep it soft. This keeps my kids happy for hours while I quilt!!!

>>>>>>>>>>>>>>>>>>>>>>>>>>>>>>

Betty Lou Cassidy, Linwood, New Jersey

LOW FAT PUMPKIN BREAD

3 1/2 cups flour
2 tsp baking soda
2 tsp cinnamon
1 tsp nutmeg
4 eggs (or 8 egg whites)
2 cups pumpkin
1 1/2 cups white sugar
1 1/2 cups brown sugar (packed)
1 cup applesauce
2/3 cup water

Mix dry ingredients together in large bowl. Mix pumpkin, water, applesauce, and eggs together. Pour into dry mixture, mix well.

Pour into two "greased" medium loaf pans. Bake at 350 degrees for 1 to 1 1/4 hours. Cool before removing from pans. This bread freezes very well.

>>>>>>>>>>>>>>>>>>>>>>>>>>>>>>

Karen Crollick, St. George, Australia, QLD

QUICKIE QUICHE

3 eggs
1 1/2 cups milk
salt & pepper
1 chopped onion
1/2 cup self rising flour
1/4 cup melted butter
1 cup grated cheese
1/2 to 1 cup meat, etc.

Beat eggs and add remaining ingredients. Pour into a pie plate and cook in a slow oven until brown.

>>>>>>>>>>>>>>>>>>>>>>>>>>>>>>

Kathy Palmiter, Williams, Indiana

BAR-B-Q MEAT BALLS

2 pounds lean hamburger
1 medium onion, chopped fine
1 tsp worcestershire® sauce
1 tsp garlic powder
1 tsp chili powder
2 beaten eggs
2 cups quick oats
salt and pepper
1 cup milk

Mix ingredients and make into bite size balls. Place in a 9x13" pan. Cover with sauce (below) and bake uncovered for 45 minutes to one hour at 350 degrees.

Sauce for above:

1 1/3 cup brown sugar
2 cups catsup
1 tsp chili powder
1 tsp mustard
1 tsp Worcestershire® sauce

>>>>>>>>>>>>>>>>>>>>>>>>>>>>>>

Colleen Taylor, Indialantic, Florida

JUMBO CINNAMON ROLLS

1/2 cup warm water
2 pkgs (or 2 Tbsp) dry yeast
2 Tbsp sugar
3 oz pkg of instant vanilla pudding mix
2 cups whole milk
1/2 cup salad oil
2 eggs
8 cups flour

1 tsp salt
3 Tbsp cinnamon
1 cup brown sugar

Mix water, yeast and sugar. Let stand until the yeast foams up. Mix pudding mix, milk and oil. Beat eggs, and stir into milk mixture.

Sift flour and salt together. Add all the wet ingredients. Mix well and knead. Let rise for 1 hour.

Punch down and divide dough in half. Roll each half out into a long rectangle. Mix cinnamon and brown sugar together. Sprinkle half of sugar mixture onto each rectangle of dough. Roll up long sides of dough. Cut into 1 inch slices and put in large, greased baking pan. Let rise for 30-45 minutes. Bake at 350 degrees for 15 minutes.

Glaze with a mixture of 2 Tbsp softened butter, 2 or 3 Tbsp of milk and confectioners sugar to make a thin icing. Use this to glaze the top of warm rolls.

>>>>>>>>>>>>>>>>>>>>>>>>>>>>>>>

Mary Anne Keppler
St. Olaf, Iowa

BANANA BREAD

Cream together:

6 ripe bananas
1 cup vegetable oil
4 eggs
1 cup sugar

Add:
3 cups flour
2 tsp soda
1/2 cup nuts, optional

This makes 4 large loaves and freezes well.

PIE MIX COFFEE CAKE

Cream together:
1 cup margarine
1 3/4 cup sugar
4 eggs
1 tsp vanilla

Add:
2 1/2 cups flour
1/2 tsp baking powder

Mix well. Save 1/2 to 1 cup batter. Spread remaining in a jelly roll pan. Pour any flavor pie filling on batter. Drop remaining batter on top. Spread with fork. Bake at 350 degrees, 25 minutes.

>>>>>>>>>>>>>>>>>>>>>>>>>>>>>>>

Kathryn Rippeteau Greenwold
Niskayuna, New York

CRANBERRY NUT YEAST BREAD

This makes a hearty bread that is especially good toasted. My husband loves this bread!! It's very good for chicken sandwiches, too.

This is a bread machine recipe, but if you make bread by hand, you can easily convert it for your use. Remember all the ingredients should be at room temperature.

2 1/2 tsp (or one pkg) dry yeast
2 1/2 cups white flour
1/2 cup whole wheat flour
3 Tbsp dry milk powder
1 Tbsp sugar
1 tsp salt (could be omitted)
1 Tbsp butter or margarine
1 cup + 2 Tbsp lukewarm water

Place ingredients in your machine in the order they are listed and turn on. I often also add a couple of Tablespoons full of wheat bran, but it's not necessary. When the machine begins its second kneading (or when it beeps to indicate it's time for additions) add in:

1/2 cup dried cranberries
1/2 cup shelled sunflower seeds
(salted or unsalted)

Then, bake in the machine or remove it and bake in the oven. I have used dried cherries which were also *delicious*.

>>>>>>>>>>>>>>>>>>>>>>>>>>>>>>>

Barb Bennett
Washington, D.C.

BLENDER PANCAKES

1 cup cold milk
1 egg
2 Tbsp cooking oil
1 cup flour
2 Tbsp baking powder
2 Tbsp sugar

Blend in blender. Bake on griddle with bacon drippings.

>>>>>>>>>>>>>>>>>>>>>>>>>>>>>>>

Jill Marie Tanking
Liberal, Kansas

CHUTNEY CHEESE BALL

Shannon Hunting Farms had a Quilters Retreat for a couple of years and have served this cheese ball.

Mix:

1 (8oz) cream cheese, softened
2 Tbsp sour cream
2 tsp curry powder
1/2 cup chopped green onion
1/2 cup raisins
1/2 cup coarsely chopped
    dry roasted peanuts

Mix all ingredients. Roll into a ball. Can be made 4 days ahead, but flavors will intensify.

To serve, pour 1 cup chutney over the cream cheese ball and serve with crackers.

Variation: Roll ball in coconut before pouring chutney. Garnish with kumquats and onion brushes.

QUICK MONKEY BREAD

1/2 cup chopped pecans
1/2 cup sugar
1 tsp cinnamon
3 (10oz) cans
    buttermilk biscuits
1 cup firmly packed brown sugar
1/2 cup butter, melted

Sprinkle pecans evenly in the bottom of a well-greased bundt pan. I reserve some to add as I put in the biscuits. Set aside.

Combine sugar and cinnamon. Cut biscuits into quarters, and roll each piece in sugar mixture and layer in pan.

Combine the brown sugar and butter. Pour over dough. Bake at 350 degrees for 30 to 40 minutes. Cool bread for 10 minutes. Invert on serving plate.

>>>>>>>>>>>>>>>>>>>>>>>>>>>>>

Mary Andrews
Grand Blanc,
Michigan

APPLE PANCAKES

1 1/2 cups flour
2 Tbsp sugar
1 Tbsp baking powder
dash of nutmeg

Mix the ingredients together, make a well in the middle and add:

2 eggs beaten, or
    1 whole egg and 2 whites
3/4 cup skim milk
2 Tbsp melted butter
1 cup applesauce

Stir until moistened, and cook on hot griddle. I usually double the recipe and put each one in a plastic sandwich bag, and then in a big plastic bag and put them in the freezer. They can be taken out one by one and warmed in the microwave. The sandwich bag can be wiped dry and used again.

PEA SOUP

1 pkg split peas,
    either green or yellow
1 small onion, chopped or
    use onion salt if there
    are no onions
    in the house.
1 stalk of celery or use celery
    salt if there is no celery
    in the refrigerator
6 carrots sliced
    (there is no substitute)
2 1/2 quarts of water
6 chicken bouillon cubes
1 tsp white pepper
1 tsp cumin
2 Tbsp lemon juice

Put all ingredients into a crock pot and cook on *high* all day. If you are home, stir it occasionally.

BEEF BARLEY SOUP

Chunk of left over roast, some stew meat, short ribs or if you don't have any meat you can use 6 beef bouillon cubes.
1 quart of canned tomatoes or
    1 purchased large can
1 stalk of celery including leaves
    or 1 tsp celery salt
1 small onion, chopped or
    onion salt
1 Tbsp parsley
2 quarts of water
1/2 cup barley
    (not the instant kind)
6 carrots sliced
white pepper

You can add some fresh green beans or peas, or not, if you don't have them. Put all this in the crock pot, cook on *high* all day.

APPLE BREAD

1/2 cup butter
3/4 cup brown sugar
2 eggs
1 cup coarsely grated apples
1/4 cup sour cream
2 cups flour
1 tsp baking powder
1/2 tsp baking soda
1 tsp cinnamon
1/2 tsp nutmeg

Mix in order given, and bake 55-60 minutes at 350 degrees

>>>>>>>>>>>>>>>>>>>>>>>>>>>>>

Joanna Bessey
Rhinelander,
Wisconsin

PISTACHIO BREAD

1 small pkg pistachio
    pudding mix
1 large white or yellow cake mix
4 eggs, slightly beaten
1 cup sour cream
1/4 cup water
1/4 cup oil

Mix all of the above together and put 1/4 of batter in each of two greased and floured bread pans. Sprinkle of half of the topping. (Topping is mixture of 4 Tbsp sugar, 2-4 tsp cinnamon, and 1/2 cup nuts. Add rest of batter, then remaining topping. Bake 1 hour at 350 degrees. This is especially good at Christmas - add a few drops of green food coloring to delight the kids!

>>>>>>>>>>>>>>>>>>>>>>>>>>>>>>
Jan Jacobson
Tripoli, Wisconsin

JAN'S BREAD RECIPE

1/2 cup honey
1/2 cup light or dark molasses
2 1/2 cups dry milk
1/2 cup oil
3 scant Tbsp salt
2 cups rolled oats
2 quarts water
1/4 cup dry yeast
8 eggs
12 cups whole wheat flour
10 cups unbleached white flour

In large bowl, combine the first six ingredients. Then stir in 1 quart boiling water, followed by 1 quart of cold water. When the mixture has cooled to wrist warmth, blend in the yeast and allow it to bubble. Break in the eggs, beat the batter vigorously.

Add the whole wheat flour, two cups at a time, and stir the dough until it pulls away from the sides of the bowl in elastic strands. Next, work in the bleached flour, kneading in the last of it before you turn the dough out onto a lightly floured board, and knead it smooth. Oil a clean bowl, put the dough in, and let it rise in a warm spot, to twice its original size (approx. 50 minutes.). Then punch it down and let it rise again.

After it has risen twice, turn the dough out and cut it into eight to ten lumps. Shape each into a loaf, and put into greased bread pans. Let rise once more, and bake in 375 degree oven for 30-40 minutes or until well browned and sound hollow when tapped.

>>>>>>>>>>>>>>>>>>>>>>>>>>>>>>
Janet Kugler
Holdrege, Nebraska

MY MOM'S DRESSING

1 loaf white bread, torn in pieces
3 eggs, slightly beaten
1/2 cup melted oleo
1/4 cup chopped onion, or more
1/4 cup chopped celery
1/2 tsp sage
1/2 tsp salt
1/2 tsp pepper

Add broth or milk to make moist. Mix everything together. Put in greased 9x13" pan. Cover. Bake 30 minutes.

>>>>>>>>>>>>>>>>>>>>>>>>>>>>>>
Tonya St. Berg
Woodinville, Washington

BRAN LOAF

Stir, soak 30 minutes or overnight:

1 cup all bran cereal
1 cup sugar
1 cup raisins
1 cup milk

Add: 1 cup self-rising flour and stir together. Bake one hour at 350 degrees in a one pound (7 3/4 x 4x 2 1/2") bread pan.

COTTAGE CHEESE BREAD

(This is a bread machine recipe for a medium size loaf of bread. Set for a light colored loaf.)

2 1/2 Tbsp water
2/3 cup cottage cheese
1 1/4 pounds of margarine
1 2/3 eggs
2 tsp sugar
1/8 tsp baking soda
2/3 tsp salt
2 cups bread flour
1 1/2 tsp yeast
2 tsp dill
1 Tbsp dehydrated onion.

>>>>>>>>>>>>>>>>>>>>>>>>>>>>>>
Barbara MacDonald
Oscoda, Michigan

BEER BREAD

1 (12 oz) can beer
3 cups self-rising flour
3 Tbsp sugar

Mix together, pour in a greased loaf pan. Bake at 350 degrees approximately 45 minutes.

ZUCCHINI BREAD

3 eggs
1 cup oil
2 cups brown sugar
1 Tbsp vanilla
3 cups flour
1 Tbsp cinnamon
2 tsp baking soda
1 tsp salt
1 tsp nutmeg
2 tsp allspice
1 tsp cloves
1/2 tsp baking soda
1 cup zucchini, shredded
1 1/2 cup chopped nuts
1 1/2 cups raisins

Combine eggs, oil, sugar and vanilla. Beat until blended. Blend dry ingredients, add to creamed mixture. Stir in remaining ingredients. Makes 3 foil pans. Bake 1 hr. 325 degrees.

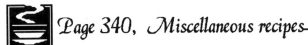

Miscellaneous recipes

>>>>>>>>>>>>>>>>>>>>>>>>>>>>>

Ann Littleton
Fairfax, Virginia

BEER MUFFINS

4 cups Bisquick® baking mix
2 Tbsp sugar
1 (12 oz) beer

Mix, and bake in 24 greased muffin cups, at 400 degrees for 15 minutes. Serve warm. This recipe is from my friend, Reese.

>>>>>>>>>>>>>>>>>>>>>>>>>>>>>

Eleanor Hunnel
Johnstown, Nebraska

TEA RING

1/4 cup warm water
    (110-115 degrees)
1 pkg active dry yeast
3/4 cup lukewarm milk, scalded
1/4 cup sugar
1 tsp salt
2 eggs
1/4 cup soft shortening
4 cups unbleached flour

In bowl, dissolve yeast in water. Measure flour by dip and level method. Add milk, sugar, salt, eggs, shortening and half of flour to yeast. Mix with spoon until smooth. Add enough remaining flour to handle easily. It may take more than 4 cups. Turn onto lightly floured board; knead until smooth (5 minutes). Round up in greased bowl, bring greased side up. Cover with cloth and place in sink of warm water until double, about 1 1/2 hours.

Punch down; let rise again, until almost double. Pat dough into a rectangle about 14x10. Spread with butter, cinnamon, sugar and raisins. Join into a circle on a cookie sheet. With scissors cut almost through the roll - alternately place the slices to the right and to the left. Allow to rise until about double, bake in 375 degree oven for 15 minutes, or until golden brown. Frost with thin powdered sugar - maple and vanilla flavored - frosting.

>>>>>>>>>>>>>>>>>>>>>>>>>>>>>

Jean S. Branham
Halifax,
North Carolina

(I wrote to Jean asking if there was an error in the recipe, since the name of it is Cornbread Cake and there was no corn meal in the ingredients. She called and said the recipe is correct, and she has no idea why it is called Corn Bread Cake.)

CORN BREAD CAKE

4 eggs
1 cup sugar
1 cup brown sugar
1 1/2 cup self-rising flour
1 cup oil
1 cup pecans
vanilla flavoring

Mix. Bake 350 degrees 35-40 minutes.

>>>>>>>>>>>>>>>>>>>>>>>>>>>>>

Doris Holland
Winterset, Iowa

SWEET POPPY SEED BREAD

3 cups flour
1 1/2 tsp salt
1 1/2 tsp baking powder
3 eggs
2 1/4 cups sugar
1 1/2 cups vegetable oil
1 1/2 cups milk
1 1/2 Tbsp poppy seeds
1 1/2 tsp almond flavoring
1 1/2 tsp butter flavoring

Preheat oven to 350 degrees. Mix all ingredients together. Pour into lightly greased loaf pans. Bake 1 hour. While still warm, pour this glaze over loaves.

Glaze for the above:

1/4 cup orange juice
3/4 cup sugar
1/2 tsp vanilla
1/2 tsp butter flavoring
1/2 tsp almond flavoring

>>>>>>>>>>>>>>>>>>>>>>>>>>>>>

Susan D. Fellin
Flemington,
New Jersey

**BROCCOLI-CHEESE
    APPETIZER SPREAD**

1 (10 oz) pkg frozen
    chopped broccoli,
    thawed and drained
1 cup mayonnaise or dressing
2/3 cup grated parmesan cheese
1/2 cup chopped fresh
    or frozen chives
1/2 cup chopped fresh parsley
1 Tbsp dried basil
1 Tbsp lemon juice
1/2 tsp chili powder

Combine all ingredients in a lightly greased, 1-quart baking dish. Bake at 350 degrees for 20 minutes, or until thoroughly heated. Spoon into a serving bowl, if desired, and serve with crackers and turnips, or other vegetable sticks. Yield: 2 1/2 cups.

BLUEBERRY MUFFINS

1/2 cup butter
2 eggs

2 cups flour
1/2 tsp salt
1/2 cup milk
1 cup+2 tsp sugar
2 tsp vanilla
2 tsp baking powder
2 cups fresh
   or frozen blueberries

On low speed of an electric mixer, cream the butter and one cup of the sugar, until fluffy. Add the eggs, one at a time, and mix until blended. Sift the flour, baking powder, and salt together. Mix the dry ingredients with the butter mixture, alternately with the milk. Add blueberries and vanilla.

Grease a muffin tin, including the top of the tin, or you can use paper-cup cake liners. Pile the batter high in tins, and sprinkle with the remaining 2 Tbsp of sugar. Bake at 375 degrees for 30 minutes.

BUTTERMILK CHOCOLATE BREAD

1 cup sugar
1/2 cup margarine, softened
2 eggs
1 cup buttermilk
1 3/4 cup flour
1/2 cup cocoa
1/2 tsp baking powder
1/2 tsp salt
1/2 tsp soda
1/3 cup chopped nuts
6 oz chocolate chips

Heat oven to 350 degrees. Grease bottom of loaf pans. In large bowl, combine sugar and margarine. Blend thoroughly. Add eggs; mix well. Stir in buttermilk. Lightly spoon flour into measuring cup, level off. Add flour, cocoa, baking powder, salt and soda. Stir just until dry particles are moistened. Stir in nuts. Pour into greased pans. Bake for 55-60 minutes, or until toothpick comes out clean. Cool for 15 minutes in pan. Remove from pan and cool completely, before slicing.

>>>>>>>>>>>>>>>>>>>>>>>>>>>>>>

Donna Olson
Rogersville, Missouri

GRAMMY'S COFFEE CAKE

3 cups flour, unsifted
2 cups sugar
1 cup shortening
1 rounded tsp cinnamon
1 rounded tsp nutmeg
3/4 tsp ground cloves
2 tsp soda
1 slight tsp salt
2 cups buttermilk
1 cup softened raisins
1 cup softened apricots

Mix first 8 ingredients together. Take out 1/3 cup for topping. Mix remaining ingredients into dry mix. Place batter into a 9x13" pan, pat reserve topping on top. Bake about 55 minutes at 350 degrees or until toothpick comes out dry, but don't over bake.

>>>>>>>>>>>>>>>>>>>>>>>>>>>>>>

Paula Kay Garrison
& Duncan Garrison
New Braunfels, Texas

CHEESE BROCCOLI SOUP

1 Kraft® roll garlic cheese
1 pkg frozen chopped broccoli
2 cans Healthy Choice® Cream
   of Mushroom soup
2 cans milk and 1/4 can water

Microwave broccoli and water for 5 minutes. Add garlic cheese and microwave 3 minutes. Add soup and milk, and microwave 5 more minutes. Delicious!

CHILI CON QUESO DIP

1 pound Velvetta® cheese
1 can rotel tomatoes

Unlike all other queso recipes, you DO NOT heat this one. Put rotel in blender, cut up Velvetta® and add a little at a time, and blend. You can refrigerate and it never gets hard and always stays smooth.

>>>>>>>>>>>>>>>>>>>>>>>>>>>>>>

Marilyn T. Guy
Delhi, New York

BROCCOLI SOUP

3 cups or 2 (14-1/2oz) cans
   chicken broth
1 large bunch broccoli, chopped
1 1/2 cups chopped onion
3 bay leaves
6 Tbsp butter or margarine
7 Tbsp flour
3 cups milk
salt and pepper to taste

In a saucepan, bring the chicken broth to a boil. Add broccoli, onion and bay leaves. Reduce heat and simmer until broccoli is tender; remove bay leaves. Meanwhile, in another saucepan, melt butter. Stir in flour to make a smooth paste. Gradually stir in milk. Cook over medium heat until mixture is hot and thickened, stirring occasionally. Add 1 cup broccoli stock to milk mixture; stir until well blended. Gradually add remaining broccoli stock to milk mixture. Heat and stir until well-blended. Salt and pepper.

Page 342, Miscellaneous recipes

BARBECUED HAMBURGER

Brown:

2 pounds ground chuck or sirloin
2 chopped onions

Add:

1 cup catsup
1/2 cup water
4 Tbsp lemon juice
2 Tbsp vinegar
2 Tbsp brown sugar
3 Tbsp Worcestershire®
2 Tbsp mustard

Cover and simmer. Serve on open toasted hamburger rolls. Sauce is good for other barbecue recipes like pork tenderloin, or ribs, or chicken.

>>>>>>>>>>>>>>>>>>>>>>>>>>
Florence L. Tyler
DeLancey, New York

BARBECUE RELISH

Put in grinder, using coarse blade:

40 green tomatoes
30 onions
12 red peppers
12 green peppers

Pour boiling water over them and let stand 5 minutes. Then drain well. Cover again with boiling water. Let stand 10 minutes. Drain well.

In a large kettle, bring to a boil:

8 cups sugar
8 cups vinegar
4 Tbsp salt
1 tsp turmeric
1 tsp celery seed

Add vegetable mixture. Boil 10 minutes, can, seal. Process 10 minutes in boiling water bath.

CUCUMBER RELISH

Chop or grind together:

12 large cucumbers
8-10 green peppers
3 red peppers
8 medium onions

Add 2 Tbsp salt. Let stand for 3 hours. Drain well.

Combine, and heat to dissolve sugar:

1 quart vinegar
3 pounds sugar
4 Tbsp mustard seed
2 Tbsp celery seed

Add vegetables. Boil 20 minutes. Can and seal jars. Process in boiling water bath 10 minutes.

>>>>>>>>>>>>>>>>>>>>>>>>>>
Chris Miller
Medway, Ohio

JEAN'S PUMPKIN BREAD

Cream together:
1 cup oil
3 cups sugar

Add and combine:
4 eggs
2 cups pumpkin
2/3 cup water

Add and combine:
3 1/3 cups flour
2 tsp soda

Add and combine:
1 1/2 tsp salt
1 tsp cinnamon
1 tsp cloves
1/2 tsp ginger
1 cup nuts
Bake at 350 degrees for 1 hour. Makes 2 loaves or 8 mini-loaves.

>>>>>>>>>>>>>>>>>>>>>>>>>>
Darlene Brazil
Escalon, California

VEGETABLE STEW

5-6 potatoes, chopped
5-6 carrots, chopped
5-6 stalks of celery, chopped
1 can green beans, drained
1 large onion, chopped
2 cans tomatoes
2 cans tomato sauce
water to cover
2 pkg brown gravy mix

Simmer until done. Other vegetables or meat can be added as preferred.

>>>>>>>>>>>>>>>>>>>>>>>>>>
Roberta Schroeder
Deer Park,
Washington

LEMON BREAD

1 box lemon cake mix
1 box *instant* lemon pudding mix
1 cup water
2 Tbsp poppy seeds
4 eggs
1/2 cup oil

Beat together 4 minutes. Makes 2 loaves bread. Bake at 350 degrees about one hour.

>>>>>>>>>>>>>>>>>>>>>>>>>>
Helen King
Horton, Kansas

PUMPKIN MUFFINS

1 cup flour
1/2 cup brown sugar

2 tsp baking powder
1 tsp pie spice
1/2 tsp soda
3/4 cup pumpkin
1 egg slightly beaten
1/4 cup milk
1/4 cup oil
1 cup oatmeal
1/2 cup raisins

Mix above ingredients and fill prepared muffin tins.

Mix and sprinkle on top before baking:
1/3 cup brown sugar
1 Tbsp melted oleo
1 Tbsp flour
1/4 tsp pie spice

Bake at 400-425 degrees for 18-20 minutes.

>>>>>>>>>>>>>>>>>>>>>>>>>>>>
Merrilyn Muir-Rennau
Vienna, Austria, Europe

HORSERADISH CREAM SAUCE

1/3 cup grated fresh horseradish
1/2 cup boiling water
2 Tbsp butter
2 Tbsp flour
1/2 cup chicken broth
1/3 cup light cream
1/2 tsp sugar
salt and white pepper to taste
1 Tbsp lemon juice
1/3 cup sour cream

Pour boiling water over horseradish, let stand for a minute, drain well. Heat butter in a small skillet. Add flour and saute' for 2 minutes. Do not let brown. Stir in broth and light cream. Blend well and simmer until smooth and thickened. Add salt, pepper, and sugar. Simmer 2 minutes longer. Blend in horseradish and lemon juice, simmer gently for 15 minutes. Stir occasionally. Do not let boil. Just before serving, take off fire and whisk in sour cream.

VEGETABLE, MUSHROOM POTATO SOUP WITH BEEF
(This is my recipe)

10 slices crisp bacon, crumbled
1 pkg mushrooms, sliced
1 pound of fat-free
    stew beef, cubed
1 bunch celery, chopped
1 large onion, chopped
6 potatoes, steamed and diced
1 small can green beans
1 small can Italian
    skinless tomatoes
1 small garlic clove,
    finely chopped
1 Tbsp chopped parsley
1 Tbsp oregano
1/2 Tbsp celery salt
    for rubbing meat
1 tsp rubbed sage
4 medium carrot, shredded
1 small pinch thyme
1 bay leaf
2 cups beef broth
freshly grated horseradish
    cream sauce on the side.

Steam potatoes. Fry bacon until crisp, and remove from skillet. Rub meat with sage and celery salt, set aside. Saute' onions, mushrooms, garlic until tender, remove from skillet. Then cover and simmer for 20 minutes, and then set aside. Add oregano, bay leaf, broth, celery, potatoes, green beans, thyme, mushroom and onions and simmer 10 minutes. Add tomatoes, carrots, parsley, salt and pepper to taste. Crumble bacon on top. Serve with horseradish, or horseradish cream sauce. Serve meat on a dish, with toothpick to dip in sauce while eating stew, or add meat directly to stew. A small amount of horseradish cream sauce can be added on soup top.

>>>>>>>>>>>>>>>>>>>>>>>>>>>>
Susan Southworth
Gulf Shores, Alabama

HOLIDAY SAUSAGE AND CHEESE ROLL

3 loaves frozen bread dough
1 pound mild sausage
    (Jimmy Dean's®)
1 pound hot sausage (J.D.'s®)
1 pound mozzarella cheese
1 pkg monterrey jack
    cheese with jalapenos

Thaw bread, according to directions on the pkg Brown sausage, drain most of grease out. Roll out one loaf of bread at a time. Sprinkle 1/3 sausage, 1/3 grated cheeses on each rolled out dough. Roll up the dough, seal edges with water on your fingers. Brush tops with beaten egg wash (1 egg beaten up with a little water in it). Bake at 350 degrees until brown. Check pkg for recommended time of baking.

I've made this amount of filling, and put it inside only 2 loaves. It was wonderful, a bit messy, but worth it.

>>>>>>>>>>>>>>>>>>>>>>>>>>>>
Pamela Thompson
Clinton Twp, Michigan

RICH WHITE BREAD

3 cups all-purpose flour
2 Tbsp sugar
1 pkg Fleischmann's
    Rapidrise® Yeast
1 1/4 tsp salt
3 Tbsp margarine, cut in pieces
1 egg

3/4 cup water 105-115 degrees

Insert metal blade in food processor bowl. Add flour, sugar, undissolved yeast, and salt; process 5-10 minutes to combine. Add butter and egg. Begin processing, then slowly pour warm water through feed tube just until dough forms a ball, about 10-15 seconds to knead dough. Carefully remove dough from processor bowl to lightly floured surface. Cover, let rest on floured surface 10 minutes.

Roll dough into 12x7" rectangle, at short end, roll up tightly as for jelly roll. Pinch seam and ends to seal. Place, seam side down, in greased 8 1/2x 4 1/2" loaf pan. Cover, let rise in warm, draft-free place until doubled in size, about 30-45 minutes.

Bake at 375 degrees for 35 minutes, or until done. Remove from pan; let cool on wire rack.

Variation: Substitute 1/3 cup whole wheat flour for a light wheat bread.

FOOD PROCESSOR PIZZA DOUGH

3 cups all-purpose flour
1 pkg Rapid-rise® Yeast
3/4 tsp salt
2 Tbsp vegetable or olive oil
3/4 to one cup water (105-115 degrees)

Insert metal blade in food processor bowl. Add flour, undissolved yeast, and salt; process 5 to 10 seconds to combine. Add oil, begin processing. Then slowly add water through feed tube until ball forms, about 10 to 15 seconds (all water may not be used). Continue processing 60 seconds to knead dough.

Carefully remove dough and blade from processor bowl. Shape dough into ball. Cover, let rest on floured surface 10 minutes. Shape, top, and bake for 20 minutes at 450 degrees, or until crust is golden. Bake on 14" round pizza pan. Makes one pizza. Bake on lower shelf of oven.

>>>>>>>>>>>>>>>>>>>>>>>>>>>>>>

Connie Sager
Nashville, Kansas

MONKEY BREAD

1 can biscuits, cut each in half
1 stick of margarine, melted.

Dip each piece in margarine, and roll in mixture of cinnamon, sugar and chopped nuts. Place in loaf pan and bake until done. This is great for breakfast.

Or, substitute sugar, cinnamon and nuts by using a mixture of: parmesan cheese, garlic, onion powder, dill weed. Great for evening meal of soup and salad.

>>>>>>>>>>>>>>>>>>>>>>>>>>>>>>

Carole Collins
Norfolk, Nebraska

BUNSTEADS

1/4 pound cubed
    American cheese
3 hard cooked eggs, chopped
1 (7 oz) can tuna, drained
2 Tbsp sweet pickle relish (opt.)
1/2 cup Miracle Whip®
6 hamburger or hot dog buns

Combine all ingredients except buns, and mix lightly. Split buns and fill. Wrap each one individually in foil. Bake in 350 degree oven for 20 minutes.

May be made several hours ahead, refrigerate until ready to bake..

>>>>>>>>>>>>>>>>>>>>>>>>>>>>>>

Lesley Ann Hill
Granville, Ohio

MORNING GLORY MUFFINS

2 cups flour
1 cup sugar
2 tsp baking soda
1 tsp ground cinnamon
1/2 tsp salt
2 cups finely grated carrots
1/2 cup raisins
1/2 cup chopped
    pecans or walnuts
1/2 cup shredded coconut
1 apple, peeled and
    cut into little pieces
3 eggs
1 cup vegetable oil
2 tsp vanilla

In a bowl, sift together flour, sugar, baking soda, cinnamon and salt. Stir in carrots, raisins, pecans, coconut and apple.

In a bowl, beat eggs with oil and vanilla. Stir egg mixture into flour mixture, until batter is just combined. Spoon batter into well-greased muffin pan cups, filling them to the top. Bake at 350 degrees for 35 minutes, or until they are springy to the touch. Let muffins cool in the tins on a wire rack 5 minutes, then turn out onto rack and let cool completely. Makes about 15 minutes.

Miscellaneous recipes, *Page 345*

>>>>>>>>>>>>>>>>>>>>>>>>>>>>>
John Flynn
Billings, Montana

HOT PEPPER CHEESE LOGS

Blend together 8 oz cream cheese and 8 oz hot pepper cheese. Spread on dried beef and roll up into logs. Chill.

A great non-sweet snack for quilters......no greasy fingers!!

>>>>>>>>>>>>>>>>>>>>>>>>>>>>>
Candra J. Sowder
Williamsburg, Iowa

BREAD MACHINE

Use your bread machine to knead every kind of dough from cinnamon rolls to pizza. It saves on dirty hands and countertops and makes short work of breads and rolls that used to require hours of effort and mess. Dough only needs to be shaped before it is baked.

>>>>>>>>>>>>>>>>>>>>>>>>>>>>>
Marilyn Thomas
Harpster, Ohio

CORNMEAL ROLLS
(VERY GOOD)

Cook until thick - then
         cool until warm:
1/2 cups corn meal
1/2 cup sugar
2 cups milk
1 tsp salt
1/2 cup Crisco®

Combine and dissolve:
1 pkg yeast
1/2 cup warm water

Add to cornmeal mixture.

Then add:

2 beaten eggs
4 cups flour

Knead well. Grease bowl and let rise 1 hour. Punch down and divide into rolls in a 9x13" pan. Grease top with butter. Bake at 350 degrees 35-40 minutes. (Dough will be soft until you knead extra flour)

>>>>>>>>>>>>>>>>>>>>>>>>>>>>>
Jane Aruns
Franklin, Tennessee

SUGAR CREEK FARM BREAD

Mix:

2 cups sugar
3 eggs

Stir together and set aside:

1 1/2 tsp baking soda
1/8 tsp salt
1 cup whole wheat flour
3 cups non-bleached bread flour

Add these to sugar/egg mixture:
1 cup non-fat sour cream
1/2 cup concentrated frozen
      orange juice, thawed,
      not diluted

Mix in the flour mixture. Beat until well blended.

Stir in:

1 cup finely chopped pecans
1/2 cup finely grated carrots.

Pour into two 8x4" greased bread pans. Bake at 350 degrees for 1 hour.

>>>>>>>>>>>>>>>>>>>>>>>>>>>>>
Juanita Gibson Yeager
Louisville, Kentucky

COMPANY'S COMING
CREAMED EGGS

2 large eggs per person being
    served, plus one extra
    for skillet

For every two eggs you'll need:

2 Tbsp cream cheese, cubed
1 1/2 to 2 Tbsp half & half or
    whole milk
salt and white pepper to taste
butter or margarine to oil skillet

In mixing bowl, beat eggs and half and half with a wire whisk until frothy. In a warm skillet, melt butter or margarine. Over medium heat, cook eggs in skillet, stirring and scraping from the bottom of the skillet the egg mixture until almost set. Stir in small cubes of cream cheese, stirring until cream cheese is melted and incorporated into the scrambled eggs. Garnish with parsley sprigs and serve immediately.

>>>>>>>>>>>>>>>>>>>>>>>>>>>>>
Bonnie Swannack
Lamont, Washington

ANGEL FLAKE BISCUITS

5 cups flour
3 Tbsp sugar
1 tsp soda
1 tsp baking powder
1 tsp salt
3/4 cup shortening
1 pkg yeast
1/2 cup warm water
2 cups buttermilk

Sift together dry ingredients and work in shortening. Dissolve yeast in warm water and add buttermilk. Stir well. Store in a tightly covered container in the refrigerator. Will keep several days. Roll out and cut for biscuits. Bake at 450 degrees for 10 minutes.

>>>>>>>>>>>>>>>>>>>>>>>>>>>

Pauline Hess 'Ping' White
Seaboard, North Carolina

PEANUT BUTTER FUDGE

Put in saucepan, bring to a boil, cook to soft ball stage;

1 cup sugar
1 cup water

Immediately, take off stove and add:

1 Tbsp butter
2 heaping Tbsp crunchy peanut butter
1 tsp vanilla

Beat until thick, spread into 9x9x2" pan that has been sprayed with PAM®. Let set until hard enough to cut into pieces.

>>>>>>>>>>>>>>>>>>>>>>>>>>>

Joyce Benitez
Omaha, Nebraska

When kids are hungry and you aren't ready to stop sewing, microwaved popcorn will fill them until you get those last few seams done!

CARAMEL ROLLS (Fast!)

2 loaves of Frozen Bread dough, thawed. Tear apart one loaf into pieces. Roll pieces in a mixture of cinnamon and sugar. Place in 9x13" buttered pan.

Melt 1/2 cup margarine over low heat, add and beat the following until smooth:

1/2 cup margarine
2 Tbsp milk
2 tsp cinnamon
1 cup brown sugar
1 large or 2 small pkgs vanilla or butterscotch pudding (not instant)

Pour over bread, add nuts or raisins, let rise 2-3 hours. Bake 375 degrees, 30 minutes. (Smells heavenly.) Cool 15 minutes, turn pan over. These are a great dessert or Sunday AM starters.

>>>>>>>>>>>>>>>>>>>>>>>>>>>

Virginia L. Brown
Ogallala, Nebraska

FRENCH VIENNA BREAD

1st step:

Mix well, and let rise 1 hour or until double in bulk. Then proceed with the second step.

1 1/2 pkg yeast
1 cup warm water
1 Tbsp sugar
2 cups flour

2nd step:

Scald:
1 cup milk
2 Tbsp sugar
1 1/2 tsp salt
2 Tbsp shortening.

Cool to lukewarm, then add to 1st mixture, and beat well. Stir in about 3 1/2 cups flour to make a stiff dough. Knead until elastic. Let rise until double. Punch down, and let rise again.

Cut in half, and roll each out, then roll up as jelly roll. Seal, and place seam side down on greased cookie sheet. Slash 2 or 3 times across loaf. Let rise until double, then brush with beaten egg white, and bake in a 350 degree oven about 40 minutes. Makes 2 large loaves.

>>>>>>>>>>>>>>>>>>>>>>>>>>>

Debra J. Ruisard
Whitehouse Station, New Jersey

CHEESY BACON BITES

1 pkg (3 oz) cream cheese, softened
1/4 cup bacon bits
2 Tbsp chopped onion
1/8 tsp pepper
1 pkg (8 oz) refrigerator crescent rolls

Preheat oven to 350 degrees. Combine cream cheese, bacon, onion, and pepper in bowl. Separate crescent rolls into 2 rectangles. Pinch seams together. Spread cheese mixture on each rectangle. Roll up, starting at longest side and seal. Cut each roll into 16 slices. Place slices cut side down, on baking sheet. Bake for 15 minutes or until golden brown.

FRUIT PIZZA

Pillsbury sugar cookie dough coated in 2 Tbsp of flour. Spread on cookie sheet. Bake according to package.

Miscellaneous recipes, Page 347

Mix:

8 oz cream cheese (room temp)
8 oz Cool Whip®
2 Tbsp powdered sugar.

Spread on cooled dough. Arrange fruit (peaches, bananas, kiwis, grapes, strawberries, mandarin oranges, etc.).

Glaze:

1/2 cup sugar
1/4 cup water
dash of salt
1/2 cup orange juice
1 Tbsp cornstarch
2 Tbsp lemon juice

Heat together, until thickened. cool to room temp, and drizzle over fruit. Refrigerate.

TACO DIP

16 oz of sour cream
8 oz pkg of cream cheese
1 pkg dry taco mix

Mix above ingredients together until well blended. Place in 8x8" dish or pan.

On top sprinkle: grated cheese, chopped tomatoes, shredded lettuce. Refrigerate. Serve with tortilla chips.

POPPY SEED LEMON BREAD

Bread:

2 1/2 cup flour
1 1/2 cup sugar
3/4 cup milk
1 cup margarine, softened
3 eggs
2 Tbsp poppy seed
1 1/2 tsp baking powder
1 tsp salt
1 Tbsp grated lemon peel

Heat oven to 350 degrees. Grease bottom only of loaf pan. Combine all bread ingredients. Beat at medium speed, until well mixed (2-3 minutes). Pour into pans. Bake for 60-70 minutes.

Glaze:

1/3 cup sugar
3 Tbsp margarine, melted
1 1/2 Tbsp lemon juice

In small bowl, combine all glaze ingredients. Pour over warm bread. Cool 10 minutes, loosen edges with knife, and remove from pan.

>>>>>>>>>>>>>>>>>>>>>>>>>>>>>
Lynda Milligan
Denver, Colorado

MAJA TOFFEE

2 cups butter (not oleo)
1 cup sugar
1 Tbsp Karo® syrup
1 Tbsp warm water
pinch salt
1 cup diced, toasted almonds
6 large Hershey® bars
1/4 cup ground almonds

Put first 5 ingredients in a heavy pot on high heat. Stir with a wooden spoon, until a rolling boil. Stir about 5-7 minutes until a little bit darker than brown sugar. Stir in nuts. Pour onto greased cookie tin. Place Hershey bars on top of candy. Let melt. Spread around and top with ground almonds. Cool, chill, and break with a sharp knife.

>>>>>>>>>>>>>>>>>>>>>>>>>>>>>
Sandra A. Anderson
Lincoln, Nebraska

FRENCH BREAD LOAF

1 loaf french or vienna bread
1 pound ground beef,
         browned and drained
1/2 can cream of mushroom soup
1/2 cup sour cream
shredded cheese...
        mozzarella or swiss
garlic powder to taste

Cut bread along top of loaf and form a valley. Mix meat, soup, sour cream, garlic powder and cheese. Mix well. (If this is too thick, add a little milk) Fill bread shell and wrap in foil. Bake at 350 degrees 45 minutes or till hot. Take out of oven, let set 10 minutes before slicing.

>>>>>>>>>>>>>>>>>>>>>>>>>>>>>
Ellen Vollmer
Nickerson, Nebraska

YUMMY CINNAMON ROLLS

1 Pillsbury Plus®
     yellow cake mix
2 pkg dry yeast mixed
     in 2 1/2 cups warm water
5 cups flour

Mix everything together and let rise for 2 hours. Roll out and spread with butter, sugar, brown sugar and cinnamon. In sauce pan, put:

1 stick oleo
1/2 bag light brown sugar
3 Tbsp milk

Boil until it bubbles. Pour into two 9x13" pans. Sprinkle with nuts. Put rolls on top and let rise for 20 minutes. Bake 20 minutes at 375 degrees.

QUICK CINNAMON ROLLS

1 bag Rhodes Frozen Dinner Rolls

Place 20 rolls in 9x13" pan. Sprinkle 1 box dry pkg butterscotch pudding (NOT instant). Sprinkle a little cinnamon.

Boil:

1/2 cup brown sugar
1 stick oleo
1/3 cup water

Pour over rolls. Let set overnight, or 8 hours at room temperature. Bake at 350 degrees 25-30 minutes. Turn over onto foil to cool. Serve warm.

>>>>>>>>>>>>>>>>>>>>>>>>>>>>>>>

Pat Milne Hitchcock
Sequim, Washington

The most moist and tasty stuffing ever! Acquired from my "resident mother", Helen Bogaard, whom I met the day my oldest child died in 1965. She was new in the neighborhood and came to stay with our daughter who was a baby, while we went through the early part of that ordeal. She is now 82 years old, this is her mother's recipe.

POULTRY STUFFING

1 large loaf of dry bread (you can substitute a 1# pkg of something like Pepperidge Farm® mix)
2 1/2 cups milk
    (less if using fresh bread)
1 cup finely chopped ham
1 1/2 cup diced celery
1 1/2 cup chopped onion
    (about 2 medium)
2 Tbsp parsley
4 tsp poultry seasoning
1 tsp each: sage,
    marjoram, thyme
1/4 tsp pepper
1 tsp salt
8 eggs, beaten

2 cubes butter, melt, and use to toss fry above ingredients, which have been mixed together. Add to the bread, and toss together.

The above quantity is sufficient to stuff a large turkey. I have never made any other stuffing in about 25 years - this is just the very best!

INDIAN FRY BREAD
It's not a Crow Indian gathering without it!

Flatten a piece of risen bread dough in your hands before frying in hot grease. Drain, sprinkle with sugar, or a cinnamon/sugar mixture.

>>>>>>>>>>>>>>>>>>>>>>>>>>>>>>>

Alice Furrey
Carter, South Dakota

GOLDEN HARVEST MUFFINS

1 1/2 cups all-purpose flour
1 cup whole wheat flour
3/4 cup sugar, white or brown
1/2 tsp cinnamon, or allspice
2 1/2 tsp baking powder
1/4 tsp salt

In food processor, finely chop and measure:

1 apple with seeds removed
1 cup carrots (about 2 large)

Beat together: (very important)

1 cup non-fat milk
    (made from dry)
3 egg whites
2 tsp vanilla

Optional ingredients - 1/2 cup raisins and a few nuts.

Mix all ingredients together with a spoon. Do not use a mixer. Spray muffin tins with non-stick spray, and bake 18-20 minutes at 375 degrees. May require longer. Makes about 15. Wrap in plastic bag while still warm.

>>>>>>>>>>>>>>>>>>>>>>>>>>>>>>>

Jacque' J. Holmes
Big Bear Lake, California

BANANA NUT BREAD-CAKE

A favorite recipe that involves using those too ripe bananas.

1 1/2 cups sugar
3 eggs, separated
1 cup walnuts, chopped
1 tsp baking powder
1/4 cup sour milk, or buttermilk
1 1/2 cup pastry flour
1 tsp soda
1/2 cup butter or margarine
1 cup banana pulp
1/2 tsp salt

Heat oven to 350 degrees. Cream butter or oleo, add sugar, and blend thoroughly. Add yolks of eggs, beaten slightly, next banana pulp, nuts, sour milk, flour sifted with baking powder and salt. Add the whites of eggs, beaten stiff, and lastly add soda dissolved in warm water. Bake in 3 round tins for 20-30 minutes.

Icing:

Combine 2 cups powdered sugar, 1 Tbsp butter, 1 Tbsp cream and 1 tsp flavoring. (vanilla, almond,

Miscellaneous recipes, Page 349

your choice) Note: This cake keeps for days and is so good.....!

>>>>>>>>>>>>>>>>>>>>>>>>>>>>>
Lois K. Ide
Bucyrus, Ohio

CHICKEN SANDWICH FILLING

1 can shredded chicken
1 cup bread crumbs
1 can celery soup

Stir well, and if not thick enough, add more crumbs. Heat and put in buns. Can be frozen.

CRAZY CORN

2 1/2 quarts popcorn
 (measure, and remove all unpopped kernels)
1 1/3 cups whole pecans
2/3 cup almond slivers

Mix the above together in large roasting pan.

1/2 cup clear Karo® syrup
1 1/2 cups granulated sugar
1 cup margarine
1 tsp vanilla

Combine sugar, margarine and syrup in 1 1/2 quart sauce pan. Bring to a boil, stirring constantly. Boil, stirring occasionally for 10-15 minutes, until mixture turns light caramel color, or reaches 240 degrees on candy thermometer. Remove from heat, and stir in vanilla. Pour over popcorn and nuts. Mix to coat well, and spread on teflon cookie sheet to dry.

Very effective packed loosely in tins for mailing. Excellent as small 1 inch balls, as candy. Has been a family favorite for years.

CHEESE SPREAD

1 pound sharp cheddar cheese
1 jar red pimento
scant cup mayonnaise

Blend pimento and mayonnaise together in blender. Gradually, add cheese. Blend until creamy. Cool in refrigerator. Very good cracker spread.

>>>>>>>>>>>>>>>>>>>>>>>>>>>>>>
Arla Schaap
Holland, Michigan

BANANA BREAD

For as long as my husband has carried his lunch to work, I have had to include 4 slices of banana bread each day. If I make it in the little loaf tins, he wants 6 slices. I have sometimes substituted carrot, apple, or pumpkin, but he really prefers banana. If I run out, or forget, (heaven forbid!) I can expect a call by 9:15 a.m. asking "Where's my banana bread?" This is not my original recipe, but it is tried and true. Would anyone like to calculate how many tons of banana bread I've baked in 30 years?

1 overripe mashed banana
1 stick oleo
1 cup sugar (scant)
1egg, plus milk to equal 1 cup
 (beat egg with fork; add milk)
1 1/2 cups flour
1 tsp soda
1/2 tsp salt
1 tsp vanilla
chopped walnuts

Bake at 300 degrees for 1/2 hour; increase to 350 degrees for another 1/2 hour.

>>>>>>>>>>>>>>>>>>>>>>>>>>>>>>
Georgina Doss
Milton, West Virginia

MAC'S CARAMEL CORN

Pop 3 quarts popcorn (about 1/2 cup of unpopped corn)

Combine:

1 cup brown sugar
1 stick butter
1/4 cup corn syrup
1/2 tsp soda

Microwave 2 minutes. Stir. Microwave 1 minute more, add 1/2 tsp soda and stir.

Pour over popped corn in a brown paper bag. Roll down bag and microwave 45 seconds. Shake hard and pour out on foil to cool.

>>>>>>>>>>>>>>>>>>>>>>>>>>>>>>
Bernice Tessibel
 Inman Cashman
 (Tessie)
Coal City, Indiana

APPLE MUFFINS

2 cups flour
1/2 cup sugar
3 tsp baking powder
1 cup coarsely chopped,
 pared apples
1 egg, slightly beaten
1 cup milk
1/4 cup butter, melted

Topping:
1/3 cup each:
 brown sugar, pecans
1/2 tsp cinnamon

Sift dry ingredients, and add apples. Combine liquid ingredients and add to flour mixture. Spoon a small amount of batter into greased muffin tins. Add a small amount of topping mixture, and then fill with the rest of the batter. Sprinkle remaining topping mix on top of the muffins. Bake at 400 degrees 20 minutes or until done.

>>>>>>>>>>>>>>>>>>>>>>>>>>>>>>
Doris Callaway
Greensburg, Kansas

BANANA BREAD

3 crushed bananas
2 cups sifted flour
2 1/8 tsps. baking powder
1 tsp salt
1 cup sugar
1/2 cup oleo (softened)
2 eggs
1 tsp lemon juice
1 cup nuts

Mix all the above till moistened, about 2 minutes. Bake at 350 degrees for 1 hour and 15 minutes. Don't overmix.

For variation: add a package of diced dates (dried) to Banana Bread recipe for delicious surprise.

>>>>>>>>>>>>>>>>>>>>>>>>>>>>>>
Nancy Wagner Graves
Manhattan, Kansas

BAR-B-Q BEEF SANDWICHES

Brown 1 1/2 lbs. hamburger meat with one onion, chopped Simmer, drain, then add:

14 oz ketsup
1 Tbsp mustard
1 Tbsp vinegar
4 Tbsp sugar
1/2 cup water
1 tsp salt
1 1/4 tsp pepper
1/4 tsp paprika

Serve hot on buns.

>>>>>>>>>>>>>>>>>>>>>>>>>>>>>>
Susan J. Spencer
Felton, California

SEASHELL SOUP

1 (one pound) can chili beans
1 (10 1/2 oz can) tomato soup, plus 1 soup can of water
1/2 cup red wine
2 Tbsp grated Parmesan
1/8 tsp each: basil, oregano, rosemary
1 Tbsp parsley
1 cup small seashell macaroni, cooked according to package directions

Combine all ingredients, except macaroni, in large saucepan and bring to boil. Reduce heat; simmer 15 minutes. Add cooked macaroni and heat through. Serve with more grated Parmesan, and garlic bread or quick Foccacia:

QUICK FOCCACIA

3 cups buttermilk baking mix
2 tsp oregano
 (or italian seasonings)
1 cup milk
olive oil
garlic salt

Combine biscuit mix and oregano; stir in milk to form soft dough. Pour about 2 Tbsp olive oil in bottom of 9x13" baking dish, coat pan evenly. Pat dough into pan, brush with additional oil. Sprinkle with garlic salt. Bake at 400 degrees for 25 minutes, until browned. Cut into squares to serve.

>>>>>>>>>>>>>>>>>>>>>>>>>>>>>>
Helen M. Ericson
Emporia, Kansas

CUCUMBER, ONION AND CARROT RELISH

This uses all of the end-of-season cucumbers, and the carrots add color and crunch.

Grind with coarse knife:
    6 cups cucumbers

Grind with #2 knife:
    3 cups carrots
    2 cups of onions

Put in large mixing bowl and add 4 Tbsp coarse or pickling salt. Cover with an inverted plate and put in refrigerator overnite.

The next morning, heat to boiling in a large cooking pan:

5 cups sugar
3 cups vinegar
3 tsp. celery seed
3 tsp. mustard seed

Drain all juice from the ground mixture, by pressing in a sieve. Discard juice. Add to vinegar mixture, and simmer uncovered, for 20 minutes. Stir frequently, to prevent scorching on bottom.

This makes at least 6 pints of relish, that is great with all kinds of meat, especially hamburgers or hot dogs.

>>>>>>>>>>>>>>>>>>>>>>>>>>>>>>
Julie L. Kimberlin
Anchorage, Alaska

Store-bought croissants...yum!

Miscellaneous recipes, Page 351

M. Jeanne Poore
Overland Park, Kansas

MICROWAVE FUDGE

1/2 cup margarine
5 oz evaporated milk
7 to 10 oz jar of
    marshmallow cream
1 cup nuts--optional
2 cups sugar
12 oz semi-sweet morsels
1 tsp vanilla

Place butter in 9x9" dish. Cook at full power until melted. Blend sugar and milk into melted margarine, mix well. Cook 15 to 17 minutes, until soft ball stage. Stir frequently. Mix in semi-sweet morsels, marshmallow cream, vanilla and nuts. Stir until smooth. Pour into buttered shallow pan/dish.

Charlotte Fry
St. Charles, Missouri

BUNDT BREAD

Melt 1 stick margarine in bundt pan. Put 3 cans flaky biscuits on their sides all around pan. Bake 400 degrees 15-20 minutes, until golden. Invert onto serving plate. Good with soups.

Sheryl Mielke
McGregor, Iowa

HOT CHEESE DIP

1 (2 pound) box Velvetta®
2 Tbsp chopped onion
1 can rotel tomatoes
1 pkg taco seasonings
1 1/2 lb hamburger, browned

Mix, and heat in a slow cooker. Great dip for party chips.

Teresa Binder
Emporia, Kansas

CHEDDAR MUFFINS

Heat oven to 400 degrees and grease muffin pans.

In large bowl combine:

2 cups unsifted flour
1 Tbsp baking powder
1 tsp sugar
1/2 tsp salt

In small bowl combine:

1 cup milk
1/4 cup (1/2 stick) butter, melted
1 large egg

Stir milk mixture into flour mixture, just until flour is moistened. Batter will be lumpy.

Fold in 1 cup coarsely chopped cheddar cheese (and chives). Using small spoon, divide batter. Bake 10-12, minutes or until centers spring back when lightly pressed with fingertips. Cool in pan on wire rack 5 minutes. Serve warm.

Beth Donaldson
Lansing, Michigan

KATY'S SOFT PRETZELS

This is my 13 year old daughter Katy's recipe for soft pretzels. She loves the ones you get in the mall, and tried these out one day. Since I no longer take cooking as seriously as I used to, my children are starting to cook more (especially their after school snacks). That is really a time saver for me! Now, she makes them all the time, either as a snack or as a nice addition to our dinner.

one loaf frozen bread dough (she
    likes white, I like wheat
    or both work great!)
one egg, beaten
Kosher salt

Thaw out the bread dough. Divide into eight to ten pieces. Roll the dough in your hands to form long tubes. Twist the tubes into pretzel shapes, and place on a greased cookie sheet. Brush the pretzels with the beaten egg, and sprinkle Kosher salt on top. Bake until golden brown at 350 degrees (about 15 minutes). Serve warm, with mustard, for a snack or butter at dinner.

Phyllis Hansen
Giersch
Madera, California

PEDROS

My youngest son's favorite snack. He's a youth pastor at a local Madera church, and a loyal Viking football fan! He helped to coach the freshman high school team this fall.

1 lb of ground chuck
one large jar Cheese Whiz®
4 steak sandwich style rolls or
    sub-sandwich type french rolls
1 can tomato sauce
1 1/2 Tbsp oregano flakes
dash of tabasco sauce
1/4 cup diced onion

Brown the chuck in a skillet, and break up into small pieces with a fork. Add the diced onion and oregano to the meat, as it is cooking. Cut the rolls in half lengthwise, and spread each half with Cheez Whiz®.

Place rolls on a baking sheet, and spread each one with the cooked meat (on top of the Cheez Whiz®). Add desired amount of tabasco sauce to the tomato sauce, and spoon sauce on top of the ground meat mixture. Bake in 350 degree oven for 20 minutes. (These can be frozen and saved for future meals. To heat, use a microwave and heat on high for about 3 minutes).

>>>>>>>>>>>>>>>>>>>>>>>>>>>>>

Marcene Gunter
Hillsboro, Kansas

QUICK HOMEMADE BREAD

2 1/2 cups water
1 tsp salt
1/2 cup butter or shortening
1/3 cup sugar
6 cups all-purpose flour
    or bread flour
3 Tbsp instant potato flakes
2 pkgs (1/4 oz each) quick-rise
    yeast or 3 Tbsp dry yeast

In saucepan or microwave, heat water and butter to 125-130 degrees. In large mixing bowl combine sugar, potato flakes, yeast, salt and flour. Add water/butter mixture, and beat to make a stiff batter. Place in a large oiled bowl; oil top of dough.

Cover, and let rise in warm place until doubled, 30 to 45 minutes. Punch down on a lightly floured surface, knead dough until smooth and elastic, 4-6 minutes. Divide dough into 2 portions. Shape into loaves, and place in oiled standard loaf pans; oil tops of loaves. Cover lightly and let rise until doubled, about 30 minutes. Bake in preheated 350 degree oven, until bread sounds hollow when tapped, 30-35 minutes. Remove from pans, lightly butter tops and cool on wire racks. Makes 2 loaves.

>>>>>>>>>>>>>>>>>>>>>>>>>>>>>

Gladys Shook
Hutchinson, Kansas

MICROWAVE APPLE BUTTER FROM THE KITCHEN OF GLADYS SHOOK

Core, and peel 8 apples. Add 1 cup cider apple juice. Microwave for 10 minutes. Blend, and add 1 cup sugar, 1 tsp cinnamon, 1/2 tsp pumpkin spice and 1/4 tsp cloves. Mix, and microwave until thick. (Approximately 15 minutes)

QUICK ROLLS

Soften 3 packages of yeast in 1 7/8 cup water. Add 3/8 cup butter, 1 1/2 tsp salt and 1 pkg custard pudding, until dissolved. Add approximately 6 cups flour, and knead. Shape, and let rise until dough is about double (1/2 to 1 hour). Bake at 400 degrees for 10-12 minutes.

>>>>>>>>>>>>>>>>>>>>>>>>>>>>>

Betty A. Lenz
Marshall, Missouri

ZUCCHINI GEMS
(A GREAT MUFFIN!)

1 1/2 cups flour
1/2 tsp baking soda
1/2 tsp baking powder
1/2 tsp salt
1/2 tsp cinnamon
2 eggs
1 cup sugar
1/2 cup salad oil
2 cups grated zucchini
1 cup raisins and nuts, combined

Mix dry ingredients together, beat eggs, sugar and oil together separately, then add to dry mixture, blend *lightly*. Add zucchini and raisin/nut mixture. Stir gently, and fill greased muffin cups 2/3 full. Bake at 350 degrees for approximately 25 minutes.

>>>>>>>>>>>>>>>>>>>>>>>>>>>>>

Joan Waldman
Platte Center, Nebraska

CORN MUFFINS

1 cup yellow corn meal
1 cup flour
2 Tbsp sugar
4 tsp baking powder
1/2 tsp salt
1/4 cup shortening, melted
1 cup milk
1 egg

Mix until cornmeal, and flour are just moistened. Spoon into paper muffin cups. Bake 425 degrees for 15 minutes.

>>>>>>>>>>>>>>>>>>>>>>>>>>>>>

DeEtta Beebe
Waters, Michigan

DILLY CASSEROLE BREAD

This recipe was given to me from another quilter who shared a loaf with me. You may exchange herbs for your own special tastes. (Thanks to Jane Ide)

1 pkg active dry yeast
1/4 cup warm water
    (110-115 degrees)

Miscellaneous recipes, Page 353

1 cup large curd cottage cheese
2 Tbsp sugar
1 Tbsp instant minced onion
1 Tbsp dill seeds (may be
 exchanged with dill
 weed, rye, etc)
1/4 tsp baking soda
1 egg
2 1/4 to 2/12 cup
 sifted all-purpose flour

Sprinkle yeast over warm water, stir until dissolved.

Heat cottage cheese until lukewarm, combine in bowl with sugar, onion, butter, dill seeds, salt, baking soda, egg and yeast. Add flour a little at a time to make sure mixed well. Cover, and let rise in warm place until doubled, 50-60 minutes.

Stir down with 25 vigorous strokes. Turn into well-greased 1 1/2 quart round 8" casserole. cover, and let rise in warm place 30-40 minutes. Cover with foil last 15 minutes to prevent excessive browning. Makes 1 loaf.

*Batter bread - beat, don't knead. You have beaten enough, when it leaves the side of bowl.

>>>>>>>>>>>>>>>>>>>>>>>>>>>>>
LaRue Nuest
South Hutchinson,
Kansas

HOME MADE BREAD

Empty contents of bread mix into your bread machine and set timer. Remove when machine beeps.

>>>>>>>>>>>>>>>>>>>>>>>>>>>>>
Nancy H. Ehlinger
West Branch,
Michigan

EARTH BREAD

Pour two cups boiling water over one cup dry rolled oats. Let mixture stand for one half hour (until oats are thoroughly soft). Then soak two packets of yeast in 1/3 cup lukewarm water. Add one Tbsp salt, 1/2 cup honey, and 2 Tbsp melted butter to the oats...then stir in the yeast. Gradually add enough flour to make the dough kneadable (between four and five cups...the flour does not have to be sifted). Knead five to ten minutes, adding flour as necessary, until the dough is smooth and elastic.

Put the dough in a big bowl, oil its surface, cover with plastic wrap and place in a warm place to rise...(on a heating pad turned to low if you do not have a warm place). When the dough has doubled in bulk, punch it down,, divide it in two, shape into two loaves, and put each in an 8x4" bread pan. Warm your oven to 325 degrees while you mix a few drops of water into an egg yolk and use the mixture to coat the tops of the loaves. Sprinkle lots of poppy seed on the bread and bake for about 50 minutes.

>>>>>>>>>>>>>>>>>>>>>>>>>>>>>
Janet P. Wyckoff
Hopewell, New Jersey

LIPTAUERE CHEESE

8 oz cream cheese, softened
4 Tbsp butter, softened
3 minced anchovies, or
 squirts of anchovy paste
2 Tbsp grated onion
2 tsp capers
3/4 tsp caraway seed
1 tsp paprika
3 drops of Worcestershire®

Mix together. Chill. Spread on pumpernickle slices.

Sounds awful, doesn't it? Try it!

>>>>>>>>>>>>>>>>>>>>>>>>>>>>>
Maria Lage
Cumberland,
Rhode Island

PINEAPPLE BREAD

1/4 pound butter
1 cup sugar
2 eggs
2 cups flour
1 tsp baking powder
pinch salt
1 cup crushed
 and drained pineapple
1/2 to 3/4 cup chopped nuts

Cream the sugar and butter. Beat eggs in one at a time. Sift flour, baking powder, and salt. Alternate adding flour mixture and pineapple to egg mixture. Add nuts. Pour into greased and floured loaf pan. Bake at 350 degrees for 45-60 minutes.

>>>>>>>>>>>>>>>>>>>>>>>>>>>>>
Patricia L. Carl
Rhinebeck, New York

SPICED CIDER

2 quarts apple cider
1 tsp whole cloves
1 tsp allspice
3 sticks cinnamon
1/2 unpeeled lemon, thinly sliced
1/4 to 1/2 cups sugar

Combine and simmer. Remove spices. Serve hot. Can be reheated.

>>>>>>>>>>>>>>>>>>>>>>>>>>>>>
Roxanne H. McElroy
Mililani, Hawaii

DOES PIZZA HUT® COUNT?

>>>>>>>>>>>>>>>>>>>>>>>>>>>>>
Emily Laubaugh
Gladstone, Oregon

CINNAMON BUTTERFLY ROLLS

1/2 cup sugar
1 tsp salt
1 pkg active dry yeast
4 1/3 cups all-purpose flour
1 cup milk
butter or margarine
2 tsp vanilla
2 eggs
1/2 cup packed brown sugar
1/2 cup chopped pecans
1/2 cup dark seedless raisins
1 tsp ground cinnamon

In large bowl, combine sugar, salt, yeast and 1 cup flour. In 1-quart saucepan over low heat, heat milk and 1/2 cup butter or margarine (1 stick) until very warm (120 to 130 degrees). Butter or margarine does not need to melt.

With mixer at low speed, gradually beat liquid into dry ingredients just until blended. Increase speed to medium; beat 2 minutes. Beat in vanilla, 1 egg, and 1 cup flour to make a thick batter; continue beating 2 minutes. With wooden spoon, stir in 2 cups flour to make a soft dough.

Turn out onto floured surface and knead until smooth and elastic, about 10 minutes, working in more flour (about 1/3 cup). Shape into ball; place in greased large bowl, turn to grease top. Cover. Let rise in warm place (80 to 85 minutes) until doubled.

Punch down dough. Turn dough onto lightly floured surface; cut dough in half; cover and let rest 15 minutes. Grease 2 large cookie sheets. In small bowl, mix brown sugar, pecans, raisins, and cinnamon. In small saucepan over low heat, melt 4 Tbsp butter or margarine (1/2 stick).

With floured rolling pin, roll half of dough into 17 12/" by 12" rectangle. Brush with half of melted butter; sprinkle with half of brown sugar mixture. From 17 12/" edge, roll dough jelly roll fashion; pinch seam to seal. Cut roll into 9 wedges, 2 1/2 inches at wide side, 1" at short side.

Turn wedges short side up. Press handle of wooden spoon across each. Repeat with other half of dough.

Place rolls 2 inches apart on cookie sheets. Cover, let rise in warm place until doubled, about 1 hour.

Preheat oven to 350 degrees. In cup, beat remaining egg; with pastry brush, brush rolls. Bake rolls 20 minutes or until golden. Remove rolls from cookie sheets, cool on wire racks.

>>>>>>>>>>>>>>>>>>>>>>>>>>>>>
Leonore Scott
Pittstown, New Jersey

NAVY BEAN SOUP

1 pound dried navy beans,
    soaked in water
    (to cover) overnight.
1 medium onion, chopped
2 medium carrots, cubed
1 ham bone, or cubed ham
2 (13oz) cans stewed tomatoes
2 to 2 1/2 tsp marjoram
1 to 2 cups of water, as needed

Method:

1. Add all ingredients to a crock pot.

2. Cook approximately 6-8 hours, or until beans are tender.

3. Serve hot with sliced bread.

>>>>>>>>>>>>>>>>>>>>>>>>>>>>>
Betty Verhoeven
East Jewett, New York

GRANDMA'S QUICK SOUP

5 medium tomatoes, diced
1 large onion, chopped
1 pound carrots, diced
water
1 cup egg noodles
2 Tbsp cornstarch
1 cup milk
beef bouillon (to taste)
1 Tbsp chopped parsley
1 Tbsp sugar
leftover, cubed meat
    (beef, chicken, pork)

In a large pot, place tomatoes, onion and carrots. Cover with water and boil until tender. Transfer this mixture to a food processor or blender, and blend until smooth. Put it back in the pot, and bring to a boil. Add bouillon, noodles, sugar, and parsley, and any leftover meat. Simmer for about 10 minutes. Mix cornstarch into milk and pour slowly into soup, while stirring. Simmer a bit longer, and serve.

Miscellaneous recipes, Page 355

BEER BREAD

3 cups buttermilk baking mix
2 Tbsp sugar
12 oz beer
1/2 cup shredded cheese

Mix all ingredients together, and pour into a greased loaf pan. Bake at 350 degrees for 45 minutes.

>>>>>>>>>>>>>>>>>>>>>>>>>>>>>
*Ella May Reusser
Blackwell, Oklahoma*

BISCUIT MIX

Makes about 12 cups.

9 cups flour
1/3 cup baking powder
1/4 cup sugar
2 cups shortening
2 tsp cream of tartar
1 Tbsp salt

Mix, and store in covered container till ready to use.

TO MAKE BISCUITS:

2 1/4 cups mix
2/3 cup milk

Mix and bake for 450 degrees at 20 minutes.

FOR MUFFINS:

2 cups mix
2 Tbsp sugar
1 egg
1 cup milk

Bake 20 minutes at 425 degrees in greased muffin tins. Serves 6.

FOR CORNBREAD:

1 1/2 cup mix
3/4 cup corn meal
1/2 tsp salt
2 Tbsp sugar
3/4 cup milk
1 egg

Bake at 400 degrees for 30 minutes in 10x10" pan.

FOR PANCAKES:

1 cup mix
1 egg
1/3 cup milk

Mix all ingredients and bake on hot griddle. Makes 8 pancakes.

FOR YELLOW CAKE:

3 cups mix
1 1/4 cups sugar
1 tsp vanilla
1 cup milk
2 eggs

Stir sugar into mix. Beat in eggs, milk and vanilla. Bake in 375 degree oven for 25 minutes.

>>>>>>>>>>>>>>>>>>>>>>>>>>>>>
*Suzanne K. Roy
Newkirk, Oklahoma*

BLUEBERRY CORN MUFFINS

1 1/2 cup corn meal
3/4 cup all-purpose flour
1/2 cup whole wheat flour
1/4 cup sugar
1 Tbsp baking powder
1/4 tsp salt
2 tsp grated lemon rind
    or 1 Tbsp lemon juice
1 1/2 cup blueberries
1 egg, slightly beaten
1 1/4 cup skim milk
1/3 cup oil, or melted margarine

Combine first 6 ingredients. Mix well with lemon and berries. Stir only to coat berries. Combine eggs, milk and oil (or melted margarine). Make a well in dry ingredients. Pour liquids in and stir just enough to moisten dry ingredients. Fill greased muffin pans 2/3 full. Bake at 400 degrees for 25 minutes. Yield: 16 muffins.

Author's Note: Sue added a note to my letter she'd sent, saying, "Try it! This recipe was not only good....it was good for you!"

>>>>>>>>>>>>>>>>>>>>>>>>>>>>>
*Janice A. Miller
Jaffrey,
    New Hampshire*

CARAMEL WALNUT COFFEE CAKE

1 1/2 cups brown sugar
1 cup chopped nuts
10 Tbsp butter
1/4 cup water
4 cans Pillsbury®
    Refrigerated Biscuits
    (10 biscuits per can)

Heat oven to 350 degrees. Generously grease a 12 cup bundt pan. Combine sugar, butter, and water and heat until butter melts. Add nuts. Cut each biscuit into quarters. Place in a large bowl; pour sugar mixture over biscuits and mix well. Spoon into bundt pan and bake 40 minutes. Let stand in pan 10 minutes before removing. Invert on serving platter.

>>>>>>>>>>>>>>>>>>>>>>>>>>>>>
*Mary Lou Kantz
    Evans
Flagstaff, Arizona*

TORTILLA STACK

1 1/2 cup sour cream
1 1/2 cup cottage cheese

or ricotta cheese
2 cups mozzarella cheese, shredded
3/4 cup parmesan cheese
1 can green chilie, chopped

Mix together, using 1/3 mixture at a time, layer 1 tortilla, mixture, tortilla, etc. Bake 20 minutes at 350 until cheese bubbles up, then sprinkle on another cup of mozzarella cheese and put back to melt.

When it comes out of the oven, sprinkle on chopped green onion, tomatoes, and sliced black olives. Cut into wedges and serve.

OVEN BAKED CRAB DIP

2 (8 oz) pkg cream cheese softened
1/3 cup mayonnaise
1 Tbsp powdered sugar
1 Tbsp white wine
1/2 tsp onion juice
1/2 tsp mustard
1/4 tsp garlic salt
1/4 tsp salt
1 (6 oz) can crab, drained and flaked
chopped fresh parsley

Combine first 6 ingredients. Mix well. Gently mix in crab. Spoon into a lightly greased 1 quart baking dish. Top with parsley. Bake 15 minutes at 375 degrees. Serve warm with crackers.

>>>>>>>>>>>>>>>>>>>>>>>>>>>>

Z.Z. Gilmore
Pocatello, Idaho

FRIED RICE

1 cup bacon, leftover roast, ham, shrimp, or any cooked meat
1 to 2 cups cooked rice
1 to 2 eggs
1 bunch green onions, chopped using greens (optional)
1/4 tsp garlic salt
3 Tbsp soy sauce (or more)
1/2 pkg frozen pea pods
1/2 can mushroom stems and pieces, drained
1/2 can bean sprouts, canned or one cup fresh
3/4 cup diced celery

You can vary all these ingredients to your taste. Heat wok (or frying pan) and add 2 Tbsp cooking oil. Shake garlic salt into oil with chopped green onion and dry onion flakes (if desired), and let brown. Dip the browned garlic and onion out of the oil and throw away. Add egg to the oil and cook stirring frequently. Then add cooked rice and mix it into the egg. Add all the other ingredients and stir fry until hot. Serve. I use Minute Rice® and cook 1/2 cup per each person.

BUTTERHORNS

1 pkg active dry or 1 cake compressed yeast
1/4 cup water
3/4 cup milk, scalded (I use canned milk diluted with one-half warm water)
1/2 cup shortening
1/2 cup sugar
1 tsp salt
3 beaten eggs
4 1/2 cups sifted enriched flour

Soften the dry yeast in warm water (110 degrees), or the compressed yeast in lukewarm water (85 degrees). Combine milk, shortening, sugar, and salt; cool to lukewarm. Add yeast mixture and mix well. Add eggs, then flour; mix to smooth, soft dough.

Knead lightly on floured surface. Place dough in greased bowl, turning once to grease surface; cover and let rise till double in bulk. Divide dough in thirds; roll each third on lightly floured surface to 9" circle. Brush with melted fat. Cut each circle in 12 to 16 wedge-shaped pieces. Roll each wedge, starting with wide end and rolling to point.

Arrange rolls in a greased baking pan; brush with melted fat or oil. Cover and let rise till very light. Bake in hot oven 400 degrees, 15 minutes.

For crescent rolls, shape in curve on baking pan. Makes 3 frozen rolls. These freeze beautifully and can be zapped in the microwave for 1 minute for great rolls.

>>>>>>>>>>>>>>>>>>>>>>>>>>>>

Sally Smith
Kodak, Tennessee

ALMOST YEAST ROLLS

2 1/2 cups self-rising flour
2 Tbsp sugar
1 pkg yeast
1/4 cup warm water
3/4 cup milk
1/2 stick margarine

Combine sugar and yeast in warm water until dissolved. Add to flour in mixing bowl. Add milk. Mix well and turn out on floured surface. Put margarine (cut into tablespoons) on baking sheet and place in oven to melt. Roll out dough after a *little* kneading. Cut dough with pizza cutter in odd squares and place over melted butter on cookie sheet. Bake at 400 degrees 12-15 minutes. These are great the next day, split and toasted, for breakfast.

>>>>>>>>>>>>>>>>>>>>>>>>>>>>

Index:

A
Abel, Betty M. 60, 111, 142, 170, 210, 262
Akana, Elizabeth A. 16, 88, 129, 152, 190, 243, 276, 306
Alfuth, Diana 44, 102, 136, 164, 203, 255
Allen, Judy 33, 164, 201
Anderson, Sandra 48, 105, 137, 168, 206, 258, 277, 319, 347
Andrews, Mary 24, 91, 131, 155, 193, 249, 278, 295, 310, 338
Armstrong, Melissa 38, 96, 132, 160, 198
Aruns, Jane 44, 102, 137, 165, 203, 253, 282, 317, 345
Aultman, Doris 51, 106, 140, 169, 206, 258, 283, 321

B
Baker, Elaine 21, 89, 129, 153, 191, 278, 336
Ballard, Linda 63, 115, 144, 177, 214
Barbieri, Phyllis K. 8
Barnes, Eugenia 30, 94, 133, 158, 249
Beebe, DeEtta 73, 119, 147, 181, 329, 352
Benitez, Joyce 45, 102, 166, 203, 256, 298, 317, 346
Bennett, Barb 32, 147, 168, 337
Bessey, Joanna 28, 125, 150, 187, 226, 274, 291, 338
Biasucci, Joan 49, 105, 139, 168, 206, 258
Binder, Teresa 70, 117, 146, 181, 216, 268, 289, 327, 351
Blankenship, Helen 31, 96, 134, 157, 197
Boedigheimer, Linda 61, 111, 143, 173, 211, 264
Bonesteel, Georgia 7
Branham, Jean 19, 96, 150, 197, 296, 311, 340
Brazil, Darlene 39, 99, 135, 162, 200, 252, 342
Brown, Virginia 45, 103, 166, 200, 256, 282, 319, 346
Browning, Bonnie 13, 128, 186, 273, 333
Brusco, Sarah 54, 108, 141, 171, 208, 260, 283, 322
Burdick, Ilene L. 53, 108, 139, 208, 281, 322
Burenheide, Eleanor 57, 114, 131, 174, 212, 265
Burgwyn, Josephine 23, 90, 130, 153, 191

C
Callaway, Doris 54, 112, 134, 176, 210, 264, 323, 350
Campbell, Pat 81, 123, 149, 186, 224, 290, 333
Canning, Mary R. 58, 111
Carl, Patricia 75, 182, 221, 271, 288, 353
Cashman, Bernice 58, 112, 143, 174, 211, 264, 284, 349
Cassidy, Betty Lou 17, 86, 128, 152, 190, 243, 285, 336
Cemer, Mary Jane 26, 92, 131, 156, 194
Centeno, Patti 25, 92, 132, 157
Clabo, Margo 42, 101, 136, 164, 201, 256
Clonan, Judith 47, 109, 142, 172, 210, 262
Clukey, Barbara 71, 117, 146, 181, 217, 287, 300
Collins, Carole 48, 104, 139, 167, 205, 257, 283, 320, 344
Cook, Patricia 56, 122, 149, 185, 224
Cook, Sherry 35, 98, 132, 161, 198, 280, 296, 350
Crollick, Karen 19, 88, 129, 152, 295, 336
Crosby, Karen 68, 116, 145, 179, 215, 267, 283, 295, 325

D
Danly, Jennifer 38, 106, 140, 169, 206, 259, 298, 321
Davis, Barbara 81, 123, 149, 187, 224, 290
De Turk, Martha 57, 110, 142, 172, 210, 262, 284, 299, 324
Derscha, Audrey 35, 98, 134, 161, 197
Donaldson, Beth 64, 114, 144, 178, 214, 351
Doss, Georgina 60, 111, 143, 211, 263, 286, 324, 349
Dozier, Nadine 21, 89, 128, 153, 190
Dutcher, Rebecca 73, 119, 219

E
Edwards, Alta 74, 120, 219
Edwards, Grace 82, 123, 147, 185
Eelman, Anna 60, 110, 143, 173, 211, 263, 284, 299, 324
Ehinger, Nancy 74, 121, 147, 182, 220, 270, 288, 330, 353
Eitel, Jean Ann 11, 82, 149, 185, 224
Elliott, Alba Lee 76, 121, 139, 183, 221, 271
England, Cynthia 41, 100, 136, 163, 200, 297, 317
Ericson, Helen 66, 113, 130, 177, 212, 265, 350
Estes, Laura 54, 108, 141, 171, 209, 261, 284
Evans, Mary Lou 82, 124, 149, 186, 225, 290, 333, 355

F
Fellin, Susan 33, 97, 134, 160, 197, 312, 340
Ferg, Jeanne 33, 97, 132, 159, 196
Flasch, Carole 74, 121, 138, 182, 220
Flowers, Virginia 58, 111, 142, 193, 210, 263, 284, 297, 324
Flynn, John 42, 101, 136, 164, 202, 345
Fox, Julie 76, 148, 184, 223
Fry, Charlotte 71, 117, 146, 177, 217, 268, 328, 351
Furrey, Alice 53, 107, 140, 170. 207, 296, 322, 348

G
Gardner, Shirley 44, 102, 137, 165, 203, 255
Garner, Zelda Ziegler 82
Garrison, Paula & Duncan 34, 97, 134, 156, 197, 280, 314, 341
Gierach, Phyllis 69, 116, 146, 176, 215, 268, 286, 327, 351
Gilbert, Beulah 72, 118, 145, 171, 186, 218
Gilmore, Zelma Ziegler 82, 290, 356
Goggin, Florence 24, 90, 130, 154, 192, 245, 298, 306
Golden, Dawn 39, 92, 135, 162, 197, 251, 315
Gore, Paula 34, 97, 132, 160, 197, 150
Graves, Lynn 75, 121, 148, 183
Graves, Nancy 63, 112, 143, 174, 211, 264, 284, 350
Greenwold, Kathryn 23, 90, 130, 153, 192, 244, 309, 337
Greto, Dotti 32, 96, 13, 159, 196, 250
Gunwall, Peggy 29, 96, 157
Gunter, Marcene 72, 118, 146, 181, 218, 268, 288, 328, 352
Guy, Marilyn 35, 98, 161, 183, 251, 280, 314, 341

H
Hafskjold, Anne-Donia 47, 103, 138, 166, 204, 257, 282, 319
Haggard, Doris 62, 115, 135, 177, 266, 285, 324
Hall, Constance 49, 104, 168, 205, 258, 283, 320
Hand, Penny 57, 109, 142, 172, 210, 262, 299, 323
Hanna, Susan 28, 92, 132, 157, 194, 248, 295, 307
Harbison, Edna 31, 96, 134, 160, 197
Hatch, Sandra 9, 81, 124, 150, 186, 225, 273, 334
Hausmann, Sue 12, 84, 124, 150, 186, 225, 273, 334
Hauswirth, Lori 33, 97, 134, 160, 197, 280
Hazelhoff, Michelle 33, 120, 147, 178, 218, 269
Hill, Lesley Ann 41, 101, 136, 164, 201, 253, 281, 313, 344
Hitchcock, Pat 52, 107, 140, 170, 207, 260, 321, 348
Holdsworth, Edna 37, 99, 134, 162, 198, 279
Holland, Doris 34, 96, 134, 162, 198, 250, 280, 340
Holmes, Jacque 56, 142, 172, 210, 348
Hunnel, Eleanor 31, 95, 133, 159, 196, 250, 280, 296, 306, 340

I
Ide, Lois 55, 109, 138, 172, 209, 262, 299, 349
Ives, Betty 48, 139, 167, 205, 258

J
Jacobson, Jan 28, 92, 156, 190, 339
Johnson, Diane 75, 98, 147, 220
Johnston, Helen 71, 117, 145, 181, 217, 287
Jones, Patricia 24, 91, 131, 156, 192, 247

K
Kauffman, Alyce 80, 148, 184, 223, 272, 301, 332
Keppler, Mary Anne 23, 90, 130, 153, 191, 246, 309, 337
Kelly, Rebecca 24, 91, 130, 154, 193, 247
Kenny, Carole 32, 93, 132, 156, 195, 248
Kimberlin, Julie 68, 116, 145, 177, 215, 267, 286, 350
King, Helen 69, 179, 287, 342
Klinger, Christine 82, 124, 149, 186, 225, 290, 333
Knack, Betty 74, 121, 147, 182, 220, 269, 288, 330
Knopp, Marcia 62, 114, 145, 173, 214, 300, 326
Kooda, Margaret 80, 136, 184, 223, 332
Koopman, Carolyn 77, 121, 148, 183, 271, 301
Kough, Lynn 75, 98, 148, 221
Kugler, Janet 34, 98, 129, 162, 198, 250, 280, 314, 339

L
Lage, Maria 75, 101, 148, 182, 220, 270, 289, 331, 353
Lambert, Tedi 68, 116, 145, 178, 215, 267, 283, 300, 327
Laubauch, Emily 77, 148, 182, 222, 331, 354
Lee, Dort 64, 112, 144, 211, 265, 325
Lenz, Betty 64, 117, 145, 178, 217, 268, 288, 327, 352
Lewis, Marilyn 54, 108, 141, 171, 208, 261, 321
Lipp, Celeste 82, 123, 149, 187, 224
Littleton, Ann 31, 94, 133, 159, 196, 250, 278, 297, 307, 340
Litwinow, Catherine 66, 115, 144, 174, 214
Livingston, Joyce 16, 86, 128, 152, 190, 242, 276, 294, 301, 306, 336
Lynch, Zelda 48, 105, 139, 168, 206

M
McElroy, Roxanne 76, 121, 148, 181, 221, 271, 289, 331, 354
McGhee, Edith 72, 121, 148, 181, 221, 269
MacDonald, Barbara 28, 93, 132, 155, 195, 248, 279, 311, 339
Mason, Sharon 50, 106, 139, 166, 206
May, Merry 56, 109, 142, 169, 209, 262, 299, 323
Meneely, Deb 23, 90, 130, 154, 161, 246, 309

Mielke, Sheryl 61, 112, 177, 213, 264, 286, 326, 351
Miller, Chris 55, 108, 141, 171, 209, 261, 279, 206, 316, 342
Miller, Janice 81, 149, 185, 224, 272, 332, 355
Milligan, Lynda 50, 104, 138, 167, 205, 257, 347
Moone, Grace 56, 109, 172, 209, 283
Moss, Barbara 22, 89, 129, 191
Muir-Rennau, Merrilyn 40, 160, 135, 162, 200, 252, 317, 343
Munkelwitz, Kathy 47, 105, 138, 168, 206, 258, 282, 296
Murphy, Louise 18, 89, 130, 153, 191, 309
Muse, Wilma 51, 106, 140, 169, 206, 259, 297, 321

N
Naught, Fanny 63, 112, 144, 174, 213, 325
Newgarde, Kelly 23, 90, 154, 309
Newhouse, Jane 21, 125, 128, 187, 226, 273, 290, 334
Nichols, Joyce 30, 157, 196, 249
Nicholson, Susan 34, 98, 135, 162, 199, 251
Nuest, LaRue 73, 120, 147, 181, 219, 271, 288, 330, 353
Nyman, Kathleen 58, 111, 142, 173, 210

O
O'Connor, Ruth 60, 111, 143, 211, 263, 322
Olson, Donna 44, 102, 137, 165, 255, 281, 341

P
Palmiter, Kathy 36, 98, 134, 161, 198, 245, 277, 294, 336
Phipps, Glenda 20, 88, 129, 242, 307
Pietila, Barbara 60, 111, 143, 173
Pioneer Quilters 38, 100, 135, 163, 199, 277, 295, 351
Poore, M. Jeanne 65, 113, 144, 175, 266, 325, 351
Powers, Ruth 76, 121, 148, 183, 221
Pribil, Betty 80, 148, 184, 223, 272

R
Randolph, Minabess 26, 92, 131, 156, 194
Ranney, Netta 67, 116, 145, 178, 215, 327
Rector, Norma Jean 77, 122, 139, 183, 222, 271, 289, 301
Reep, Pat 66, 116, 146, 179, 267, 287, 327
Relph, Beverly 19, 86, 129, 154, 92, 242, 297, 336
Reusser, Ella Mae 77, 148, 185, 222, 289, 330, 355
Rhoades, Chloe 23, 90, 130, 154, 193, 307

Rhoades, Ruth 18, 87, 129, 153, 190
Robb, Judi 63, 112, 144, 174, 211, 265, 325
Robbins, Carol 67, 115, 142, 178, 214, 266, 285, 300, 326
Roy, Suzanne 22, 148, 184, 222, 355
Royer, Shannon 67, 115, 138, 178, 214, 267, 285
Ruda, Mary 60, 111, 143, 173, 210, 324
Ruisard, Debra 46, 103, 137, 167, 204, 256, 282, 320, 346
Rushin, Bettie 64, 115, 142, 175, 213, 266, 285, 326

S
Sager, Connie 41, 104, 140, 167, 204, 257, 282, 307, 315, 344
Sayers, Mary Lou 36, 98, 134, 162, 198, 251
Schaap, Audrey 57, 109, 142, 349
Scott, Lenore 76, 222, 289, 300, 332, 354
Schroeder, Roberta 39, 199, 135, 162, 200, 252, 279, 297, 315, 342
Schutt, Suzanne 51, 106, 133, 169, 207, 259, 277, 308
Shook, Gladys 70, 117, 133, 180, 216, 352
Smith, Nancy 48, 104, 140, 167, 205, 257
Smith, Sally 84, 125, 150, 186, 226, 273, 291, 334, 356
Soika, Fran 46, 103, 138, 204
Southworth, Susan 41, 100, 135, 163, 200, 253, 257, 281, 318, 343
Sovran, Mary 40, 101, 136, 164, 201, 254, 281, 297, 318
Sowder, Candra 43, 101, 137, 164, 202, 254, 319, 345
Spencer, Sue 62, 112, 144, 173, 212, 256, 350
Stapel, Jane Clark 40, 137, 165
Swannack, Bonnie 47, 138, 167, 209, 257, 282, 320, 345
Swecker, Bonnie 29, 93, 133, 154, 195, 248, 278, 311
St. Berg, Tonya 28, 92, 156, 194, 249, 278, 310, 339

T
Tanking, Jill 20, 88, 129, 157, 193, 244, 277, 310, 337
Taylor, Colleen 22, 90, 139, 153, 191, 246, 336
Thelen, Carol 41, 165, 203
Thomas, Marilyn 43, 100, 164, 202, 254, 282, 319, 345
Thompson, Pamela 40, 100, 135, 163, 200, 253, 343
Tieche, Merrilee 43, 108, 141, 171, 208, 260, 285, 322
Tiefel, Thelma 19, 87, 128, 152, 190, 294, 306
Tyler, Florence 37, 99, 135, 160, 191, 279, 315, 342

U
Underhill, Jean Eng 29, 93, 133, 158, 195, 249, 296, 312

V
Valentine, Dean 54, 108, 141, 171, 208, 261
VanDusen, Jean 30, 89, 133, 158, 195, 249, 276, 311
Verhoeven, Betty 78, 122, 139, 184, 222, 332, 354
Vollmer, Ellen 51, 106, 140, 169, 207, 259, 277, 298, 320, 347

W
Waldman, Joan 72, 119, 14, 180, 218, 269, 287, 328, 352
Walton, Teresa 39, 99, 160, 199, 251
White, Pauline 52, 107, 140, 169, 207, 346
Wilson, Martha 26, 96, 134, 312
Wittman, Lassie 29, 133, 158, 183, 195
Wood, Kaye 10
Wolfrom, Judy 74, 93, 147, 182, 220, 270, 288
Wyckoff, Janet 74, 121, 147, 182, 220, 270, 330, 353

Y
Yeager, Juanita 44, 102, 136, 164, 203, 255, 345
Younce, Carol 45, 137, 160, 203
Young, Pamela 80, 148, 185, 223, 272
Young, Lynn Lewis 22, 90, 130, 153, 191, 246, 307

Z
Zimmerman, Richard 26, 119, 146, 269, 329

RECIPES

Main Dish & Casseroles

Bar-B-Cue Beef	242
Meatballs	
Lasagna	
Pot Luck	
Taco Soup	243
Korean Short Ribs	
Quick Tamale Pie	244
Fried Chicken	
Portuguese Soup	
Sweet & Sour Chicken	
Potato Casserole	245
Mexican Casserole	
Beef Casserole	
Gringo Taco	
Chicken and Rice	
Chili	
Liquid Pizza	
Shipwreck	246
Salmon Macaroni Pie	
Enchilada Casserole	
Cheaters Lasagna	
Waikiki Ground Beef	
Goulash	247
Italian Meatballs	
Company Chicken	
Beef Burgandy	
Bar-Be-cue Pork	
Barbecued Ribs	
Crockpot Dinner	248
Mushroom Burgers	
Spaghetti Pie	
Mexican Casserole	
Cocktail Meatballs	
Quick Dinner	
Tuna Salad Sandwich	249
Honey Sauce Chicken	
Bar-b-cued Wings	
Hearty Rice Casserole	
Taco Salad for a Crow	250
Italian Sandwich Ring	
Stuffed Shells	
Casserole	
Lasagna	
Enchiladas	
Ham and Coleslaw	251
Chicken Chili	
Mary's Chicken	
Chicken and Rice	252
Impossible Mexican Rice	
Tapioca Stew	
Chicken and Mushrooms	
Gaspacho Soup	
Stir Fry	
Tuna Noodle Casserole	253
Guy's Night	
Aldo Gallego	
Split Pea Soup	
Chicken Taquitos	
Minestroni	254
Pork Chop and Pilaf	
Hamburger Casserole	
Chicken Paprika	
Tortellini Broccoli	255
Sausage Casserole	
Barbecue Brisket	
Pizza Burgers	256
Skillet Stew	
Vegetable Beef Soup	
Country Calico Beans	
Pizza Casserole	
Main Dish	257
Hamburger Casserole	
Scrap Soup	
Broccoli Rice Casserole	
Easy Swiss Steak	
Chic Chicken	
Mock Ham Loaf	258
Zucchini Casserole	
Tuna Casserole	
Mexican Pie	
Chicken Casserole	259
Pork Chops with Honey	
African Chow Mein	
Chicken Casserole	
Tuna Rockefeller	
Cocky-Leeky Soup	260
Poppy Seed Chicken	
Rueben Loaf	
Kalua Pig	
Spicey Cabbage	261
Mealtime Minestrone	
Turkey Veg Stew	
Aunt Florence	
1-2-3 Easy Chicken	262
Cranberry Chicken	
Ham Biscuits	
Chick Delight	

Page 259

Hamburger Casserole 263	Salad 279	**Vegetables**	Easy Cherry Dessert 307
Vegetable Chowder	2 Cup Salad		Chocolate Sheet Cake
Chilies Rellenos	Frozen Fruit Cup	Crockpot Spuds 294	Fantastic Fudge Cake
Broccoli Casserole	Chicken Pasta	Make-ahead Potatoes	Choc/Applesauce Cake
Sesame Chicken	Pasta Twirl	Vegetable Casserole	Tunnel of Fudge Cake 308
Ham Casserole 264	Cottage Cheese Salad	Onion Roasted Potatoes	Houston's Apple Cake
Crock Pot Dressing	Surprise Salad	Cold Pizza	Pumpkin Cake
Chicken Breasts	Moroccan Orange Nut	Scalloped Corn 295	Apricot Cake
Crockpot Chicken	Hawaiian Sunrise 280	Baked Tomatoes	Better than Sex Cake 309
Pork Chops/Sauerkraut	Waldorf Salad	Pasta and Broccoli	Berry Bars
Chicken Spaghetti	Tomato Aspic	Baked/sliced Potatoes	Choc/Chip Cookies
West Virginia Soup 265	Broccoli Salad	Potato Casserole	Carrot Bars
Pasta Delight	Broccoli Salad	Broccoli Frittata	Double Chocolate Fudge
Chicken Italiano	Simple Salad	Criss Cross Potatoes	Choc/Oatmeal Cookies
Chicken Wings	Garden Relish	Asparagus Oriental 296	Jill's Cake 310
Crockpot Chili	Orange Salad 281	Veggies	Apple Cake
Jambalaya 266	Strawberry Banana	Cream Cheese Corn	Applesauce Cake
Turkey Pot Pie	Apple Crunch	Sweet Potato Pie	Pumpkin Cookies
White Stuff	Broccoli Salad	Squash Pudding	Blueberry Crisp
Sour Cream Enchiladas	Antipasto Tray	Broccoli Casserole	Peanut Butter Logs 311
Sweet & Sour Chicken 267	Salad	Marinated Asparagus 297	Puppy Chow
Tuna with a Twist	Banana Salad 282	Quick Broccoli Soup	Cherry Cheese Cake
Cor-Do-Bleau	Jello Salad	Potatoes AuGratin	7-Up Cake
11 year old Spaghetti	Fruit Salad	Corn Pudding	Dump Cobbler
Chicken Tortilla	Salad	Roasted Potatoes	Cream Cheese Torte
Zucchini Casserole	Cucumber Salad	Sweet & Sour Cabbage	Cream Puffs 312
Quilter's Stew 268	Cole Slaw	Scalloped Tomatoes	Dump Cake
Tamale Pie	Shrimp Salad 283	Mexican Corn 298	Coconut Pie
Sausage Soup	Seven Layer Salad	Vegetable Soup	Pat's Pie
Chicken Casserole	Pineapple Jello	Vegetable Pizza	Carrot Cake
Egg & Sausage	Mexican Corn Salad	Scalloped Corn	Peach Pie
Oven-baked Stew 269	Fruit Salad 284	Baked Corn Pudding	German/Choc Cake
Hash Brown Quiche	Seafood Salad	Acorn Squash	Walnut Coffee Cake 313
Reuben Casserole	Vegetable Pizza	Green Bean Casserole 299	Zucchini Cake
Joan's Baked Beans	Corn Salad	Corn Bake	Reece Cups
Seafood Rosemary 270	Strawberry/Spinach	Baked Beans	The Green Thing 314
Kartoffels	Five Cup Salad	Sweet Potato Pudding	Little Cheese Cakes
Hearthside Sandwiches	Cabbage Salad	Carrot Casserole	Choc/Cinnamon Bars
Oven Fried Chicken	Orange Blender Salad 285	Asparagus Pizza	Pumpkin Cake
Rosemary Porkchops	Spinach Salad in Wok	Zucchini 300	Pudding Squares
Easy Oven Stew 271	Candy Bar Salad	Broccoli Casserole	Fruit Dessert 315
What is in the Pot?	Quick Caesar Salad	Marinated Vegetables	Carrot Cake
Chicken Strata	Salad	Marinated Carrots	Choc/Chip Cookies
Oven Stew	Aunt Stell's Salad	Harvest Potatoes 301	Moon Balls
Skillet Hash	Pistachio/Coconut 286	Gourmet Potatoes	Peanut Butter Balls
Lasagna 272	Cucumber Salad	Broccoli Casserole	Peanut Butter Squares
Minestrone Soup	Caesar Salad	Sauerkraut Relish	Hershey's Choc Cake 316
Chicken Wings	Fresh Broccoli Salad	Harvard Beets	Cream Cheese Brownies
Baked Chicken 273	Helen's Beans & Corn 287	Cabbage Casserole	Caramel Bars
Spinach Casserole	Basque Salad	Copper Coins 302	Choc Refrigerator Pie 317
Beef Macaroni	Quilter's Cabbage	Baked Carrots	Austrian Strudel
Creamed Ham	Pretzel Salad	Lima Bean Soup	Orange Slice Cake
Chicken Stuffing	Hot Taco Salad	Stuffed Peppers	Sundae on Monday 318
Lemon Chicken	Sauerkraut Salads 288	Baked Potatoes	Pound Cake
	Orange Delight	Sweet Potatoes	Best Ever Rum Cake
Salads	Frozen Salad	Circles and Chunks	Philly Pound Cake
	Cucumber Salad	Broccoli and Corn 303	Apple Dumplings 319
Cranberry Salad 276	Ambrosia Fruit	Escalloped Corn	Surprise Cupcakes
Red Hot Jello	Seafood Salad	Baked Cauliflower	Dessert
Easy Cottage Cheese	Tomato/Onion 289	Green Beans/Bacon	Quick Cake
Seaweed Salad	Orange/Pineapple	Escalloped Hash Browns	Cherry Cheese Cake
Pasta Salad	Bob's Pineapple	Spinach Bake	Lemon Cheese Cake
Bok Choy Salad	Potato Salad	Baked Beans	Ice Cream Cake 320
Cherry Cola Salad 277	Spaghetti Salad	Potato Casserole	Cranberry Apple Crisp
Holiday Salad	Marinate Bean 290		Chocolate Lush
Cauliflower/Broccoli	Sunshine Delight	**Desserts**	Sponge Roll Bars
Tabouli Salad	BJ's Shrimp Salad		Cherry Crunch
Vegetable Marinate	Three Layer Salad	Wonder Cake 306	Cottage Cheese 321
Seven Layer Salad	Spinach Salad	Peach/Nut Crumble	Easy Cherry Nut Cake
Potato Salad 278	Easy Spinach Salad 291	Dessert	Walnut Pie
Chicken Coleslaw	Gourmet Potato Salad	Black Walnut Cake	Caramel Nut Pie
Spinach Salad	Raspberry/Cranberry	Corn Cake	Brownies with Ice Cream
Spaghetti Salad		Lemon Jello Cake	Graham Cracker Cookies
Fruit Salad		Custard Pie	Brownies
Greek Salad		Fruit Slush 307	Dessert 322

Page 360

Chocolate Mint	322	Choc Chip Cookies	331	Beer Bread	339	Poultry Stuffing	348
Blueberry Tart		Apple Pudding		Zucchini Bread		Harvest Muffins	
Caramel Apple Cake		Simple Dessert	332	Beer Muffins	340	Banana/Nut Cake	
Lemon Dessert	323	Fried Ice Cream		Tea Ring		Chicken Sandwich	349
Chocolate Mousse		Ginger Snaps		Corn Bread Cake		Crazy Corn	
Pecan Chocolate Cake		Peach Cobbler		Poppy Seed Bread		Cheese Spread	
Chocolate Pie Filling		Lemon Pie		Broccoli/Cheese Spread		Banana Bread	
Cookie Pudding	324	Buttermilk Fudge Cake		Blueberry Muffins	341	Caramel Corn	
Plum Cake		Wacky Cake		Chocolate Bread		Apple Muffins	
Sugar Cookies		Boiled Raisin Cake	333	Grammy's Coffee Cake		Banana Bread	350
Apple John		Pumpkin Cake		Cheese Broccoli Soup		Bar-B-Q Beef	
Roll-Out Cookies		Orange Delight		Chili Con Queso Dip		Seashell Soup	
Fast Apple Crisp	325	White Choc Fudge		Broccoli Soup		Quick Foccacia	
Heath Bar Coffee Cake		Dump Rhubarb	334	Barbecued Hamburger	342	Vegetable Relish	
Fruit Cobbler		Chess Pie		Barbecue Relish		Microwave Fudge	351
Hershey Brownies		Carrot Cake		Cucumber Relish		Bundt Bread	
Wacky Cake		Quick Nut Fudge		Pumpkin Bread		Hot Cheese Dip	
Lemon Jello Cake	326	Glazed Graham		Vegetable Stew		Cheddar Muffins	
Crumb Pie Crust				Lemon Bread		Soft Pretzels	
Rhubarb Bars		**Miscellaneous**		Pumpkin Muffins		Pedros	
Rootbeer Floats				Horseradish Sauce	343	Homemade Bread	352
Fast & Easy Cheesecake		Cheese Ball	336	Potato Soup/Beef		Apple Butter	
Fudge Nut Bars		Play Dough		Sausage/Cheese Roll		Quick Rolls	
Chocolate Mousse Pie	327	Pumpkin Bread		White Bread		Zucchini Gems	
Pecan Pie		Quickie Quiche'		Processor Pizza Dough	344	Corn Muffins	
Cherry Chocolate Cake		Bar B Q Meatballs		Monkey Bread		Dilly Bread	
Almond Cheese Cake		Cinnamon Rolls	337	Bunsteads		Earth Bread	353
Angel Bars	328	Banana Bread		Morning Glory Muffins		Liptauere Cheese	
Lemonade Pie		Pie Mix Coffee Cake		Cheese Logs	345	Pineapple Bread	
Hawaiian Cake		Cranberry Nut Bread		Cornmeal Rolls		Spiced Cider	
Cereal Snack Bars		Beer Muffins		Sugar Creek Bread		Butterfly Rolls	354
Peach Cobbler		Chutney Cheese Ball		Creamed Eggs		Navy Bean Soup	
Pecan Carrot Cake		Monkey Bread	338	Angel Flake Biscuits		Quick Soup	
Caramel Bars	329	Apple Pancakes		Peanut Butter Fudge	346	Beer Bread	355
Pineapple Cake		Pea Soup		Caramel Rolls		Biscuit Mix	
Pizzelles		Beef Barley Soup		French Vienna Bread		Blueberry Muffins	
Shaker Apple Cake		7-Bean Soup		Bacon Bites		Caramel Walnut Cake	
Strawberry Dessert	330	Apple Bread		Fruit Pizza		Tortilla Stack	
Wonder Dessert		Pistachio Bread		Taco Dip	347	Crab Dip	356
Pineapple Dessert		Jan's Bread	339	Poppy Seed Bread		Fried Rice4	
Strawberry Pie		Mom's Dressing		Maja Toffee		Butterhorns	
Caramel Cookies		Bran Loaf		French Bread		Almost Yeast Rolls	
Chocolate Cheesecake		Cottage Cheese Bread	339	Cinnamon Rolls			
Cherry Swirl Cake	331			Quick Rolls	348		

ORDER BLANK or send on sheet of paper

The Busy Quilter's Survival Guide

- **1 book** $24.95, plus $4 shipping and handling
- **2 to 5 books**, $22.95 each, plus $8 total shipping and handling
- **6 or more books**, $19.95 each, plus $10 total shipping and handling

Number of books ordered ☐

Total cost of books _____

Total Shipping and handling cost _____

(Kansas Residents, add $1.70 per book for State Sales Tax) _____

Ode to a Quilter Poem (as shown on page 14)

Size: 8 1/2" x 11" printed on a beautiful rainbow colored background, suitable for framing.

$3.00 each, plus $2.00 shipping and handling (only one S & H charge for any number of poems)

Number of poems ordered ☐

Total cost of poems _____

Total Shipping and handling cost __2.00__

(Kansas Residents, add $.21 per Poem for State Sales Tax) _____

Send check, money order, or charge to your Visa or MC. Make checks payable to: **Good Life Treasures**

Total ☐

Name _____

Address _____

City _____

Sign here, if you are charging your order _____

Phone _____

Fill in your numbers ☐☐☐☐ ☐☐☐☐ ☐☐☐☐ ☐☐☐☐

Expiration date: ☐☐☐☐

VISA ☐   MasterCard ☐

Mail order to: Good Life Treasures, Rt. 1, Box 271A, Council Grove, KS 66846 or phone order to 316-767-6875